1952 The Canadian Broadcasting Corporation begins television broadcasts.

1957 The USSR launches Sputnik, the first satellite.

1989 High definition television is invented.

1958 A new Broadcasting Act removes the responsibility for broadcast regulation from the CBC and establishes the Board of Broadcast Governors.

1993 The Canadian Telecommunications Act is legislated, affirming that 'telecommunications performs an essential role in the maintenance of Canada's identity and sovereignty'.

1951 Marshall McLuhan's *The Mechanical Bride* is published.

1961 CTV, Canada's first private television network, is established, along with the first Canadian-content regulations for television.

1995 The Canadian government comes on-line.

1927 The first Canadian national radio broadcast occurs on 1 July.

1964 Marshall McLuhan declares in *Understanding Media* that 'the medium is the message'.

1996 A United States patent is issued for MP3.

1932 The Canadian Radio Broadcasting Commission (CRBC) is founded as a national public radio service.

1969 ARPANET is commissioned by the US Department of Defense for research into computer networking.

1997 Larry Page and Sergey Brin register Google.com as a domain.

1998 The Canadian government amalgamates several funding bodies to create the Canadian Television Fund (CTF).

1970 VCRs (video cassette recorders) enter the market.

1950 Harold Innis's *Empire and Communications* is published.

1971 The CRTC introduces Canadian content requirements in radio broadcasting.

1999 Kitchener–Waterloo, Ontario, company Research In Motion introduces its first BlackBerry.

2000

1951 The Royal Commission on National Development in the Arts, Letters, and Sciences (the Massey-Lévesque Commission) delivers the first federal report on Canadian culture.

1967 The Canadian government creates the Canadian Film Development Corporation to help spur the development of Canadian feature film.

1979 The first commercial cellular telephone system begins operation in Tokyo.

2000 Napster popularizes free down-loading/Internet piracy.

2006 Twitter is founded.

2010 The Canadian government creates the Canadian Media Fund.

1973 The first call is made on a portable cell phone.

1993 Smartphones enter the market.

1939 The National Film Board (NFB) is established.

1972 The first computer-to-computer chat takes place in California, at UCLA.

1936 The Canadian Broadcasting Corporation is founded to replace the CRBC.

1971 The first email messages are sent.

1991 CERN (European Organization for Nuclear Research) releases the World Wide Web (www).

2011 Facebook reaches over 750 million active users worldwide.

1929 The Aird Commission on public broadcasting recommends the creation of a national radio broadcast network.

1969 The Canadian government creates Telesat Canada to oversee the development of a Canadian satellite system.

2011 Canada officially switches from analog to digital television.

1927 Philo Farnsworth patents the image dissector, the first complete electronic television system, and transmits the first all-electronic television image.

1957 The Canada Council for the Arts is created.

1968 A new Canadian Broadcasting Act replaces the 1958 Act and brings cable under the jurisdiction of legislation, puts the social and cultural goals of broadcasting in legislation, and creates the Canadian Radio-Television Commission (now the Canadian Radio-television and Telecommunications Commission).

2004 Facebook is launched from a Harvard dorm room.

2001 Satellite-based digital radio is available.

Seventh Edition

Mass Communication in Canada

Mike Gasher
David Skinner
Rowland Lorimer

OXFORD
UNIVERSITY PRESS

OXFORD
UNIVERSITY PRESS

Oxford University Press is a department of the University of Oxford.
It furthers the University's objective of excellence in research, scholarship,
and education by publishing worldwide. Oxford is a registered trade mark of Oxford University Press
in the UK and in certain other countries.

Published in Canada by
Oxford University Press
8 Sampson Mews, Suite 204,
Don Mills, Ontario M3C 0H5 Canada

www.oupcanada.com

Library and Archives Canada Cataloguing in Publication

Lorimer, Rowland, 1944-
Mass communication in Canada / Rowland Lorimer, Mike Gasher, David Skinner. – 7th ed.

Includes bibliographical references.
ISBN 978–0–19–543383–8

1. Mass media—Canada—Textbooks. 2. Mass media—Textbooks.
I. Gasher, Mike, 1954- II. Skinner, David, 1956- III. Title.

P92.C3L67 2012   302.23   C2011-908060-5

Cover image: Ian McKinnell/Photographer's Choice/Getty

Part- and chapter-opening photo credits: p. 1: © iStockphoto.com/Calin Vasile Ilea; p. 2: © Alenmax/dreamstime.com; p. 31: © Sergeibach/
dreamstime.com; p. 58: © istockphoto.com/Aydın Mutlu; p. 87: THE CANADIAN PRESS/Darryl Dyck; p. 88: © istockphoto.com/
Anthony Brown; p. 119: © istockphoto.com/David H. Lewis; p. 154: © Instinia/dreamstime.com; p. 184: ©Tsian/dreamstime.com; p. 211:
© Katatonia82/dreamstime.com; p. 212: © istockphoto.com/Kathy Dewar; p. 243: © istockphoto.com/Günay Mutlu; p. 273: © Miluxian/
dreamstime.com; p. 305: © Vladru/dreamstime.com; p. 306: © istockphoto.com/Joel Carillet; p. 336: © istockphoto.com/Jen Grantham

Contents

PART I   THE SOCIO-CULTURAL CONTEXT

CHAPTER 1

CHAPTER 2

CHAPTER 3

PART II THEORETICAL PERSPECTIVES

CHAPTER 4

Theoretical Perspectives on Media Content

CHAPTER 5

Theoretical Perspectives on Audiences

CHAPTER 6

Communication Technology and Society: Theory and Practice

CHAPTER 7

PART III   THE COMMUNICA-
TIONS ENVIRONMENT

CHAPTER 8

CHAPTER 9

CHAPTER 10

PART IV   AN EVOLVING COMMUNICATIONS WORLD

CHAPTER 11

Globalization   306

CHAPTER 12

Communication in a Digital Age   336

List of Boxes

Preface

For most of its life, this textbook has been known as the 'Lorimer book' in reference to Rowland Lorimer, the professor of communication at Simon Fraser University who was the lead author of the first six editions of *Mass Communication in Canada*. With this edition, however, Rowly has decided to scale back his involvement.

Rowly and colleague Jean McNulty conceived of this book a quarter-century ago when they began teaching an introductory mass communication class to undergraduate students at Simon Fraser University. There was no Canadian textbook at the time. Rowly and Jean began gathering and developing teaching materials with encouragement from Simon Fraser's Centre for Distance Education and a grant from the Secretary of State's Canadian Studies Program. McClelland & Stewart published the first edition in 1987. A second edition was published by McClelland & Stewart in 1991. Oxford University Press took over McClelland & Stewart's textbook line and published subsequent editions in 1996, 2001, 2004, and 2008.

When Jean decided to step down after co-authoring the first three editions, Rowly invited Mike Gasher to become a co-author in 1999, the year Mike completed his Ph.D. in communication studies at Concordia University in Montreal and took up his new faculty position in Concordia's Department of Journalism. Mike had first met Rowly in the late 1980s, when Mike was an undergraduate student and Rowly was director of the Centre for Canadian Studies at Simon Fraser. Rowly later supervised Mike's M.A. thesis in communication.

After co-authoring the fourth and fifth editions, Rowly and Mike invited David Skinner to join the team for the preparation of the sixth edition in 2006. David had been an undergraduate student in the mass communication course taught by Rowly and Jean in 1983, and used *Mass Communication in Canada* as a core text in 1989 when he taught mass communication as a graduate student at Concordia University. David, presently the chair of the Department of Communication Studies at York University, has now taught versions of this introductory communications text at six universities across Canada.

Thanks particularly to Rowly, *Mass Communication in Canada* has served as an introduction to the field for several generations of college and university students, and not only for those in communication and media studies programs, but also those studying sociology, political science, and journalism. Building on his legacy, Mike and David hope to continue this tradition. But Rowly's imprint is plainly evident on this, the seventh edition. It remains a Canadian book, as it was envisaged from the outset, and it retains its structural approach, situating the theories and practices of mass communication within the particular circumstances of Canada's socio-economic context, its geography, its institutions, and its policy framework. And the book continues to be a comprehensive and current survey of an increasingly dynamic subject area. This is an especially exciting time in communications history, a period of great transition and one that we are pleased to be able to help document and analyze through the pages of this book.

Each time Oxford asks us to revise and update this text we underestimate the work involved. As students and instructors have discovered over the years, the book covers a tremendous amount of ground and seeks to be up-to-date, not only in terms of the factual material but also with respect to the research that informs our theoretical understandings of this broad field. We are always surprised at how many changes there have been in the three or four years between editions. As daunting as it is to keep up with all the changes—new media, new media forms, shifting ownership structures, changing government policy priorities—the real challenge for us as authors is determining which changes to the contemporary mediascape are fundamental, and which are merely new twists on old and enduring themes. But then, this dynamism is what makes the field of mass communication so interesting. Social media, for example, were in their infancy when we were preparing the previous edition. And we suspect that some websites, communications devices, and software applications that are popular as we prepare this edition will quickly fade into insignificance. Others, as yet unknown, will certainly emerge.

While we have maintained the same overall structure of the book in this edition, each of the chapters has been substantially revised and a number have been completely rewritten. The biggest single change is the extent to which digitization and new media now permeate discussion in the book, from how we define mass communication to how convergence has broken down previously clear distinctions between media platforms and industries, between communications policy domains, even between media consumers and content producers. How far convergence will extend, and what it will mean for all actors in communications, will be well worth monitoring in the coming years.

Part I of the book, 'The Socio-Cultural Context', situates media and mass communication within a socio-cultural context. Chapter 1 provides a broad introduction to the themes and ideas presented in this textbook, defining mass communication and considering the ways in which communications systems are central to contemporary society, orienting us within the world. Chapter 2 addresses the relationships between communication, society, and culture, and discusses the social roles of media and mass communication. Following the Canadian communication scholars Harold Innis and Marshall McLuhan, Chapter 2 asserts the idea that how people communicate plays a role in shaping the society and culture to which they belong. Chapter 3 adopts a historical perspective, tracing the evolution of modern mass media back to the mid-fifteenth century and Gutenberg's development of printing by means of movable type. In so doing, this chapter underlines the close relationship between communication forms and economic and political systems.

Part II, 'Theoretical Perspectives', surveys prominent theories pertaining to content, audiences, and technology. Chapter 4 provides an overall introduction to communication theory and reviews some of the main approaches to studying media content, particularly as they pertain to the creation of meaning and interpretation. Chapter 5 furthers the theoretical discussion by considering the very active interaction between media and audiences in the production of meaning, noting that communication scholars and industry researchers perceive audiences very differently. Chapter 6 surveys a range of perspectives on technology in general, and communications technology in particular, exploring some of the recent technological developments in the mass communications field. Chapter 7 examines the historical and theoretical background of communications policy development in Canada, with an emphasis on how technology and theory shaped the evolving policy field. It also provides a picture of society's communicative priorities and a sense of how those priorities can change.

Our discussion of technology and of the historical development of policy provides a nice bridge to Part III, 'The Communications Environment', which examines the structured environment within which mass communication in Canada takes place today. Chapter 8 surveys the contemporary policy framework sector by sector, from telecommunications and broadcasting to recorded music, cinema, new media, publishing, and the postal service. Chapter 9 addresses media ownership and the economics of mass communication, situating the mass media within the economy, outlining the distinctions between public and private ownership, and discussing the role of advertising. Chapter 10 brings together a number of themes in the book by providing a concrete discussion of journalism as a particular form of content production. Journalists, that is, practise in a media environment characterized by specific ideals, laws, settings, storytelling conventions, and economic imperatives.

Finally, Part IV, 'An Evolving Communications World', considers Canadian circumstances in the global context. Chapter 11 situates Canada's communication networks and practices within their larger global environment, underscoring the point that the activities and institutions we have described are not, and have never been, exclusively Canadian. Chapter 12 provides a concise summary of the ideas and perspectives covered in the book and points the way to future study and directions of growth and development in the mass communications field.

Acknowledgements

We would like to thank Dianne Arbuckle, Jennefer Laidley, Stephany Tlalka and our anonymous readers for their comments and contributions to this edition. We would also like to thank the editorial, management, and sales teams at Oxford University Press Canada for their work and continued support of this book.

From the Publisher

Today, messages come to us from countless different directions from all over the world. To make sense of these messages and their social implications, we need to ask several important questions: Who creates them? Who distributes them? How they are distributed? Who receives them? It is the responsibility of students and teachers to make sense of these questions and try to answer them by investigating historical and current trends in the field of mass communication.

Despite an obvious interest in the subject, designing an academic course on the many forms and sources communication is not an easy task. Instructors and authors must find a balance, presenting vast amounts of scholarship, but avoiding oversimplification. The book, and the course in which it is used, must fit within an academic term and be designed in a way that facilitates teaching and learning.

The seventh edition of *Mass Communication in Canada* builds on the successful approach used in the previous editions that has served instructors and students well. It gives first-time students a comprehensive, engaging, and clear introduction to the study of mass communication, ensuring that they understand mass communication in sociological, psychological, technological, and economic terms.

This edition retains many of the features that will be familiar to long-time users:

- An accessible writing style based on the belief that even complicated ideas can be presented in a straightforward way.

- Balanced coverage of historic and contemporary material to give students the perfect mix of classic perspective and cutting-edge information.

- A class-tested approach that has proven effective in presenting a unified and integrated account of mass communication in a Canadian context.

The coverage of the topics also retains the best features of the previous edition while adding new information on current trends and changes in mass media:

- An examination of the increasing presence of electronic surveillance in many Western societies (Chapter 1)

- An in-depth discussion of the significance of oral, literate, and electronic societies on our ability to communicate (Chapter 2)

- An examination of audience responses to different modes of communication and relevant scholarship in audience research (Chapter 5)

- A discussion about the role new technology such as cellphones and the social media has played in political movements, including the recent events in Egypt and Tunisia. (Chapter 6)

- Information on the future of broadcasting regulation in relation to a growing number of web-based services such as Netflix and GoogleTV (Chapter 8)

- A discussion of the Canadian media and the legal parameters that govern journalism in Canada (Chapter 9)

- An analysis of the role of the media in globalization (Chapter 11)

This new edition successfully mixes popular culture, substantive theory, and highlighted vignettes, helping students to grasp topics such as historical and social contexts, content, audiences, production processes, and technologies. Discussions of policy, law, and economics are invaluable to Canadian students of mass communication.

In addition to the features carried over from the sixth edition, this edition contains several improvements that reflect both progress in the field and refinements that help make the material clearer and more useful to students. Some notable changes include:

New chapter-opening questions and learning objectives at the start of every chapter draw students into the material.

New text boxes appear throughout the book and profile topics such as media and advertising, satellite communication, and net neutrality.

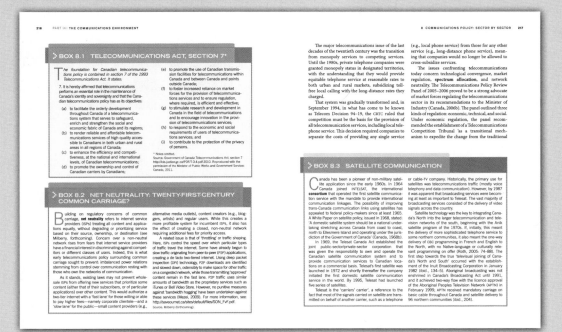

Contemporary design reflects the increasingly digital, quickly changing world of communication in which we live. We have striven for a look that is contemporary yet clean, a design that reflects the vibrancy and excitement of mass communication today without sacrificing content or authoritativeness. The use of colour and novel design elements is a necessary acknowledgement to the changes wrought by new media and how readers expect information to be packaged and presented. At the same time we remain well aware that this is indeed a printed book, with both the limitation and the very real and enduring strengths that are a product of the print's long history as the preeminent method of codifying and transmitting knowledge.

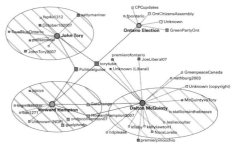

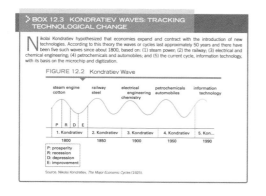

Aids to student learning

A textbook must fulfill a double duty: while meeting instructors' expectations for accuracy, currency, and comprehensiveness, it must also speak to the needs and interests of today's students, providing them with an accessible introduction to a body of knowledge. To that end, numerous features to promote student learning are incorporated throughout the book. They include the following:

- **Pre-reading Questions** help students focus their reading by asking the questions that each chapter will answer.

- **Learning Objectives** at the start of each chapter provide a concise overview of the key concepts to be covered.

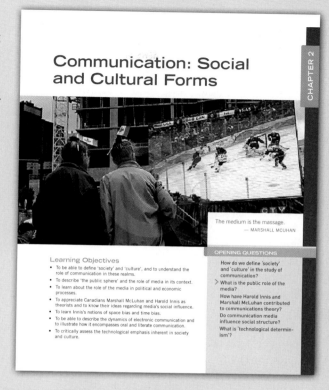

CHAPTER 2

Communication: Social and Cultural Forms

The medium is the massage.
— MARSHALL MCLUHAN

Learning Objectives

- To be able to define 'society' and 'culture', and to understand the role of communication in these realms.
- To describe 'the public sphere' and the role of media in its context.
- To learn about the role of the media in political and economic processes.
- To appreciate Canadians Marshall McLuhan and Harold Innis as theorists and to know their ideas regarding media's social influence.
- To learn Innis's notions of space bias and time bias.
- To be able to describe the dynamics of electronic communication and to illustrate how it encompasses oral and literate communication.
- To critically assess the technological emphasis inherent in society and culture.

OPENING QUESTIONS

How do we define 'society' and 'culture' in the study of communication?
> What is the public role of the media?
How have Harold Innis and Marshall McLuhan contributed to communications theory?
Do communication media influence social structure?
What is 'technological determinism'?

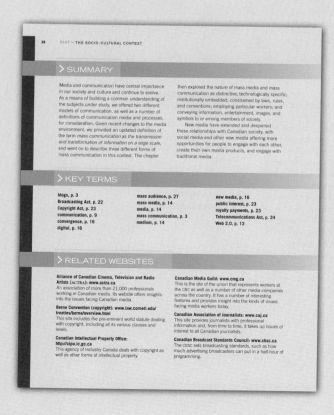

28 PART I: THE SOCIO-CULTURAL CONTEXT

SUMMARY

Media and communication have central importance in our society and culture and continue to evolve. As a means of building a common understanding of the subjects under study, we offered two different models of communication, as well as a number of definitions of communication media and processes, for consideration. Given recent changes to the media environment, we provided an updated definition of the term *mass communication as the transmission and transformation of information on a large scale*, and went on to describe three different forms of mass communication in this context. The chapter

then explored the nature of mass media and mass communication as distinctive; technologically specific; institutionally embedded; constrained by laws, rules, and conventions; employing particular workers; and conveying information, entertainment, images, and symbols to or among members of society.

New media have extended and deepened these relationships with Canadian society, with social media and other new media offering more opportunities for people to engage with each other, create their own media products, and engage with traditional media.

KEY TERMS

blogs, p. 3
Broadcasting Act, p. 22
Copyright Act, p. 23
communication, p. 9
convergence, p. 16
digital, p. 16

mass audience, p. 27
mass media, p. 14
media, p. 14
mass communication, p. 3
medium, p. 14

new media, p. 16
public interest, p. 23
royalty payments, p. 23
Telecommunications Act, p. 24
Web 2.0, p. 13

RELATED WEBSITES

Alliance of Canadian Cinema, Television and Radio Artists (ACTRA): www.actra.ca
An association of more than 21,000 professionals working in Canadian media. Its website offers insights into the issues facing Canadian media.

Berne Convention (copyright): www.law.cornell.edu/treaties/berne/overview.html
This site includes the pre-eminent world statute dealing with copyright, including all its various clauses and levels.

Canadian Intellectual Property Office: http://cipo.ic.gc.ca
This agency of Industry Canada deals with copyright as well as other forms of intellectual property.

Canadian Media Guild: www.cmg.ca
This is the site of the union that represents workers at the CBC as well as a number of other media companies across the country. It has a number of interesting features and provides insight into the kinds of issues facing media workers today.

Canadian Association of Journalists: www.caj.ca
This site provides journalists with professional information and, from time to time, it takes up issues of interest to all Canadian journalists.

Canadian Broadcast Standards Council: www.cbsc.ca
The CBSC sets broadcasting standards, such as how much advertising broadcasters can put in a half-hour of programming.

- **Lists of Key Terms,** at the end of each chapter, highlight the important words that students might want to explore further.

- **Related Websites and Further Readings** offer more resources for students who seek to expand their knowledge of mass communications.

- **Study Questions** at the end of each chapter are a great tool for study and review.

- **A Glossary** located at the end of the book defines important terms, which have been highlighted in bold throughout the book.

Instructor and Student Supplements Accompanying the Text

Today's textbook is no longer a volume that stands on its own—it is but the central element of a complete learning and teaching package. *Mass Communication in Canada* is no exception. The book is supported by an outstanding array of ancillary materials for both students and instructors, all available on the companion website: **www.oup canada.com/Lorimer7e**

For the Instructor

An Instructor's Manual includes numerous pedagogical elements such as overviews of each chapter, sample lecture outlines, outlines of key concepts, lists of online resources, and suggestions for student assignments.

A Test Bank offers a comprehensive set of multiple choice, true/false, short-answer, and discussion questions, with suggested answers, for every chapter.

PowerPoint® Slides summarizing key points from each chapter and incorporating figures and tables from the textbook, are available to adopters of the text.

Instructors should contact their Oxford University Press sales representative for details on these supplements and for login and password information.

For the Student

The Student Study Guide offers chapter summaries, self-testing questions, lists of related websites, and much more.

Media Awareness Resources provide students with respected resources for news on the web, print, and on television, as well as resources for commentary on media specifically.

To access these features, go to **www.oupcanada. com/Lorimer7e** and follow the links!

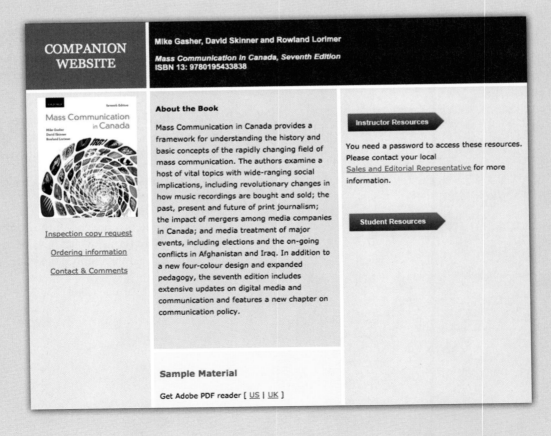

COMPANION WEBSITE

Mike Gasher, David Skinner and Rowland Lorimer

Mass Communication in Canada, Seventh Edition
ISBN 13: 9780195433838

Inspection copy request

Ordering information

Contact & Comments

About the Book

Mass Communication in Canada provides a framework for understanding the history and basic concepts of the rapidly changing field of mass communication. The authors examine a host of vital topics with wide-ranging social implications, including revolutionary changes in how music recordings are bought and sold; the past, present and future of print journalism; the impact of mergers among media companies in Canada; and media treatment of major events, including elections and the on-going conflicts in Afghanistan and Iraq. In addition to a new four-colour design and expanded pedagogy, the seventh edition includes extensive updates on digital media and communication and features a new chapter on communication policy.

Instructor Resources

You need a password to access these resources. Please contact your local Sales and Editorial Representative for more information.

Student Resources

Sample Material

Get Adobe PDF reader [US | UK]

PART I

The Socio-Cultural Context

CHAPTER 1

Media and Society

Without communication, what is there?

— ANONYMOUS

- How important are media to our knowledge and understanding of the world?
- How have shifts in communication media contributed to changing our understanding of the world?
- How do new technologies in media change our understandings of those media?
- What role do media play in different dimensions of our lives?

Learning Objectives

- To appreciate the centrality of media to our knowledge and understanding of the world.
- To be able to describe the ongoing, shifting character of media in 'shrinking space through time'.
- To understand the transportation and social models of communication.
- To comprehend both traditional and new media as forms of mass communication.
- To know the key social elements of mass communications.
- To appreciate the many roles of individuals producing media.

Introduction: Defining the Field

This chapter provides a broad introduction to the themes and ideas contained in this textbook. It illustrates the shifting nature of communication technology, considers how media and communication systems are central to the functioning and operation of our society, and examines the ways in which they orient our understanding of the world and our actions within it. Traditional media, new media, and social media are all illustrated as forms of **mass communication** and definitions are given for terms such as *communication, mass communication,* and *convergence.* Rigorous and comprehensive definitions are important as they provide the basis of building a common understanding of the subjects under study. In preparation for developing broader theoretical perspectives on media as social and cultural forms, the chapter goes on to outline and examine some of the key elements or dimensions of mass media and mass communication.

Media in an Ever-Changing Communications Universe

Media lie at the heart of our contemporary world. From cellphones to Facebook, television to **blogs**, newspapers to satellites, Twitter to Google, media and communication systems are central to our understanding of the world and how we co-ordinate our actions within it. Today, media are involved in almost all dimensions of our lives—deciding on a career, getting an education, thinking about politics and government, finding the music we listen to, getting a job, finding clothes, making a date, deciding what to eat and where to buy it, paying bills, and finding a place to live. Media help us decide what we need and want, why we care, and even who we are.

Statistics indicate how pervasive media are in our lives. According to polls, in 2009 Canadians spent approximately 38 hours per week either watching television or online. We also spent 8.9 hours per week listening to the radio, 2.9 hours reading newspapers, and 1.4 hours reading magazines. This yields an average total of about 50 hours per week of media consumption. More recently, Canada rose to first place in internet use; according to research firm comScore (2010; also El Akkad, 2011), the average Canadian spends 43.5 hours a month on the web, almost twice the worldwide average of 23.1 hours (Box 1.1).

But not only are communication media key to our individual lives, they are also central to the larger organization and functioning of our society. Media are the major means through which governments—federal, provincial, and municipal—communicate with residents and citizens. (It may surprise you to know that government is the largest single advertiser!) They provide us with regular portrayals of our world and who we are as a people. Media are the primary way that businesses develop and communicate with customers. They are also key agents in globalization. On one hand, they are the central vehicle for controlling the world economy and the movement of goods and services around the world, such as co-ordinating centres of production in China

Has the internet replaced traditional media sources or become another avenue for the delivery of content?

with markets in Canada. On the other hand, media introduce people to cultures around the world and keep immigrants in touch with the culture of countries from which they moved. Media also work to generate a global cultural consciousness through celebratory media events, such as the Olympics and the World Cup, as well as through informing us of disasters such as the earthquakes in Haiti and Japan and the Gulf of Mexico oil spill, and tragedies such as the attacks on New York and Mumbai and bombings in London and Madrid. At the same time, media also help raise our consciousness about our roles in impending environmental disasters—such as global warming—and political and economic events—such as elections and the G-8 and G-20 meetings. In this heavily mediated world where the implications of one person's or country's actions can span the globe, 'Think globally, act locally' has become the new universal mantra, and media are the vehicles through which such actions are co-ordinated.

While less than 20 years ago the internet was the purview of scientists and researchers, today it is a major industry, along with the more traditional media such as broadcasting, film, newspaper and book publishing, and sound recording (music). However, the internet isn't so much replacing these traditional media industries as it is incorporating them and serving as another vehicle for their distribution. Indeed, much of the content accessed and exchanged online is content generated by these industries. Music, film and video, news, and even books form a large part of internet traffic. However, the internet offers much more. By joining computing power with transmission capacity, many traditional businesses and services have been able to extend their reach 'virtually'. In department stores and boutiques, banking and investing, medical diagnosis, telecommuting and distance education and government services, the internet has become a medium for shopping, working, and delivering services. Similarly, social media such as Twitter, Facebook, YouTube, and Wikipedia have extended personal relationships and social networks, enabling once-passive consumers of media to become media content producers (see Box 1.2).

⬡ BOX 1.1   CANADIANS USE THE INTERNET MORE THAN ANYONE ELSE ON THE PLANET

According to a 2011 report, we spend more time on the internet than anyone else on earth. Canadians each spend an average of 42.2 hours online per month. This is almost twice the world average of 23.1 hours. People over 55 were the fastest growing group of internet users and use was spread equally between men and women. Not surprisingly, with the largest population, Ontario had the highest percentage of internet users in the country, followed by Quebec. As Box 11.7 in Chapter 11 illustrates, however, what this average masks is the differences in both use of the internet and access to it between people with different levels of income and living in rural and urban areas. The chart here illustrates average internet usage in other countries.

Average Hours Online per Person per Month

COUNTRY	HOURS
Canada	42.2
South Korea	35.6
United States	33.3
United Kingdom	31.3
France	28.1
Brazil	27.0
Germany	22.0
Japan	20.0
Russia	16.5
China	15.6
India	12.1
World Average	23.1

Source: *comScore* (2010).

➤ BOX 1.2 SOCIAL MEDIA SITES

As of August 2011, there were more than 750 million users on Facebook; in addition, numerous website chat lines and other social media, such as YouTube, MySpace, Twitter, LinkedIn, and Skype, have changed the way many people interact. How many of these do you use? Have social media changed the way you engage with your network of personal relationships? What have you gained? What have you lost?

But while these new media forms are challenging and changing the ways traditional media operate, they are not replacing them. A few years ago, downloading music from sites such as Napster and Pirate Bay was thought to spell the death of the music industry; but that industry adapted and the popularity and revenues of new sites like I-tunes indicate the industry is still very much

Queen's University is among a number of Canadian universities that offer distance education programs. This ad specifically targets the local Vancouver market.

FIGURE 1.1   The Shrinking Globe

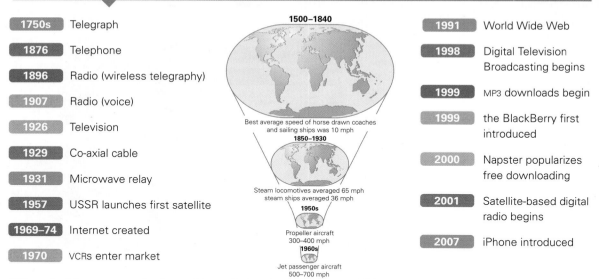

1750s Telegraph	**1991** World Wide Web
1876 Telephone	**1998** Digital Television Broadcasting begins
1896 Radio (wireless telegraphy)	**1999** MP3 downloads begin
1907 Radio (voice)	**1999** the BlackBerry first introduced
1926 Television	**2000** Napster popularizes free downloading
1929 Co-axial cable	**2001** Satellite-based digital radio begins
1931 Microwave relay	**2007** iPhone introduced
1957 USSR launches first satellite	
1969–74 Internet created	
1970 VCRs enter market	

1500–1840
Best average speed of horse drawn coaches and sailing ships was 10 mph
1850–1930
Steam locomotives averaged 65 mph steam ships averaged 36 mph
1950s
Propeller aircraft 300–400 mph
1960s
Jet passenger aircraft 500–700 mph

With each of these new media, the world seemingly gets smaller as our abilities to shrink space through reducing the time it takes to co-ordinate action across space is reduced.
Source: Harvey, David (1989). *The Condition of Postmodernity*, Wiley Blackwell, p.241, plate 3.1.

alive. Similarly, while blogging and citizen journalism were once seen as displacing newspapers and traditional news sources, today most of the news available on the web comes from traditional news sources, and bloggers develop much of the material they publish from those sources. Similarly, television, apparently becoming displaced by internet material, is finding a new means of distribution on the web.

Caught up in the wave of new media and its propensity for expanding the reach and speed of communication, it is easy to forget the internet is only one of many major electronic media innovations introduced in the last 200 years. These media, too, ushered in various forms of social change and, in some instances, made older media obsolete.

As the first electronic communication medium, the telegraph was one of the most 'revolutionary' of communications media. As James Carey (1989: 201) argues: 'Perhaps the most important fact about the telegraph is [that it] permitted for the first time the effective separation of communication from transportation.' No longer did letters and other

forms of communication need to be transported physically by horse and rider, carrier pigeon, or ship. Instead, messages could be transported 'at the speed of light'—the speed at which electricity travels—across vast distances. This innovation spurred other changes, such as standard time and modern markets.

To be sure, the telegraph was a key technology in 'shrinking space through time', that is, reducing the time it took to accomplish particular tasks in space (see Figure 1.1). For instance, with the telegraph, companies could co-ordinate the sale of their products across vast distances much more quickly. A short telegraphic message between Vancouver and Toronto could confirm the need for raw materials such as wood or iron ore to be shipped from the industrial periphery to factories at the centre of the country; a telegraph between Montreal and Halifax could send finished products such as stoves or furniture back out to the distant margins. With the telegraph, transactions that might in the past have taken weeks or even months to accomplish could be completed in a few minutes. Telegraphic technology was also helpful in controlling space. Uprisings and social discontent in distant colonies could be instantly communicated to political capitals, and troops dispatched to quell such disturbances expeditiously. Just as the internet and social networking sites seem to shrink the distance between friends, the telegraph shortened the time to accomplish or co-ordinate action at a distance, making the world seem smaller.

But the telegraph was not invented in a vacuum. From semaphore towers to smoke signals it had many predecessors, although due to their vulnerability to bad weather and other natural hazards none were as efficient. Neither the invention of the telegraph nor its adoption as a major medium of communication happened overnight. Principles behind the technology were developed in the early 1700s and by the mid-1700s proposals for telegraph systems were being written. While a number of attempts to establish telegraph lines began in 1800, it wasn't until the 1830s that the first successful telegraphs were established and not until the 1850s that they became relatively common.

The development and adoption of telephone and radio technology followed similar tracks. While specific individuals filed patents on specific forms of these technologies, these inventions leaned heavily on others that came before them and it was several decades before the specific techniques of transmitting voice messages by wire or over the air were adapted for widespread use and commercial exploitation. Both technologies were seen as shrinking space. The telephone initially was marketed as a business tool, and radio, in particular, was seen as creating common perspectives and understanding, or a common consciousness between people. For instance, speaking of the first Canadian national radio broadcast on 1 July 1927, Canada's sixtieth birthday, Prime Minister Mackenzie King said:

On the morning, afternoon and evening of July 1, all Canada became, for the time being, a single assemblage, swayed by common emotion, within the sound of a single voice…. Hitherto to most Canadians, Ottawa seemed far off, a mere name to hundreds of thousands of our people, but henceforth all Canadians will stand within the sound of the carillon and within the speakers of Parliament Hill. May we not predict that as a result of this carrying of the living voice throughout the length and breadth of the Dominion, here will be aroused more general interest in public affairs, and an increased devotion of the individual citizen to the common weal. (Quoted in Weir, 1965: 38)

Following in the tracks of the telegraph and radio, television, too, extended and deepened social ties. In 1969 television literally crossed space to yield images of humans' first footsteps on the moon. But while television was first demonstrated in the mid-1920s, it wasn't until the 1950s that it began to elbow radio off centre stage in living rooms across Canada. At the time, radio was seen by some as becoming obsolete and without any real future. However, moving from foreground to background, radio quickly took on a new life as a purveyor of popular music and is firmly entrenched in the pantheon of electronic media today.

Co-axial cable television technology first found application in US cities in the late 1940s and early 1950s. Co-axial cables carry much more information than regular copper wire and were used to bring multiple television channels to places where over-the-air signals were blocked by buildings or natural barriers. By the late 1960s, its carriage capacity heralded the 'wired city' and a wide range of new information services and interactive media similar to those available over the internet today. Experiments in building the wired city took place in countries such as Canada, the United States, Japan, France, Germany, and Britain, but it wasn't until the 1990s and the widespread use of computers, digitized information, and the internet that the vision of the wired city materialized.

From this brief history, we can see that media development and change are ongoing processes, and each advance in electronic communications technology is built upon previous technologies to continue to shrink space through time and extend in space and enhance the relationships established by the telegraph. As media have changed they have become more pervasive in our lives, helping to shape how we see, understand, and act within the world. Nevertheless, the roles media play in these respects is the subject of considerable debate.

Promoters of new media and communication technologies present a particularly *utopian* view of media development. They claim that communication technology increasingly delivers more choice in information and entertainment. From news to entertainment programs, whether via film, music, video games, or websites like Hulu, Netflix, and iTunes, media offer ever-increasing consumer choice and—as mobile technologies gain customers—increasingly from any location. Google Books is working to make all of the books ever published available electronically for free. Digital communication systems also offer an increasingly available and convenient range of consumer products. From this perspective, all of one's needs and desires can be met with a few strokes on a keyboard: one can purchase food, clothes, shelter, pets, and even sex online. Access to education and government services is said to be better. But wait, there's even more! New media are portrayed as ushering in truly participatory democracy on a global scale. With all the information available online, people are said to be able to inform themselves of the issues that affect their lives as never before. They can talk back to the institutions and people that hold power by telling governments and corporations what they think about issues and products. They can produce and circulate information that represents their point of view. The technology provides opportunities to vote on myriad issues. Supposedly, it offers true democracy where everybody knows and understands the issues that affect them, and has the ability to make their views known.

Others are not so sanguine in their assessment of new media technology. They contend that communication systems designed on the basis of market principles primarily serve owners and investors, not citizens. For instance, because new (and old) commercial communications enterprises seek revenue from advertisers, they first serve the needs of those adver-

tisers. Consequently only those media products that generate profits for advertisers are available. Owners of private media companies—radio or television stations, newspaper publishers, or internet service providers—are in business to make money for themselves and their shareholders, not to perform public service. If they can perform some pubic service or provide some public good, all the better, but this is not their primary purpose. As Raymond Williams, a British media scholar, once noted, within such a media system people are free to say anything they want as long as they can say it profitably. Ideas and perspectives that fail to meet the logic of increasing profits—such as those calling attention to the drawbacks of consumer lifestyles or issues affecting the poor and cultural and ethnic minorities—are sidelined or left out altogether. Media owners also want to attract the large audiences for the least amount of money. Consequently, because American programming is sold to Canadian broadcasters at a fraction of its cost of production, and a fraction of the cost to purchase Canadian programming, Canadian media are full of American shows—not because Canadians want or prefer such media fare, but because media companies make much more money carrying American programming than Canadian programs. Privacy is another key issue. In such a heavily mediated world, the information that people post about themselves on social networking sites or blogs is being accessed by advertisers, parents, schools, insurance companies and even police departments. As a result, some are finding themselves inundated with commercial spam, kicked out of school, denied medical insurance, and even charged with crimes. Access is yet another problem. There is little doubt that media are becoming the lifeblood of our society and that access to media is important not only for satisfying individual needs and desires but also for educational purposes and to exercise one's rights as a citizen. But access to media systems is not available to everyone. In our cities, large numbers of families and individuals cannot afford access to up-to-date computers and the internet. In some small towns and rural areas across the country, even dial-up internet service is not available, let alone high-speed. And in many developing countries around the world, even phone service is a luxury that many cannot afford. This digital divide is one of the key issues facing media policy-makers today.

So, do media serve public purposes or are they mere profit centres for investors? Is technology going to help in creating a better, more equitable world, or is it going to increase the gap between the rich and the poor—the digital divide? Ultimately, what are the implications of the current monumental changes in communications? Are we collapsing into a totally commercialized society that cannot differentiate between the worthwhile and the trivial, or are we evolving into a more equitable, free, informed, and just society? There are no easy answers to these questions.

In this book we approach the study of media and communications from a *critical* perspective. 'Critical' does not refer to the many complaints that can be levelled at the media—too much violence or being too commercial. Taking a *critical perspective* means that we look analytically at the ways media are implicated in our knowledge and understanding of the world. What role do they play in the construction of identity and the development of our tastes and desires? How do they inform our understanding of the places we live and work? What role do they have in political processes? Are television sitcoms, shows promoting celebrities, and other seemingly innocuous programs simply 'entertainment', or do they play other roles in our lives? Does it matter who owns the media? How does advertising influence what we see in the media? What role do the media play in the economy? In globalization? In other words, whose or what interests do media serve and what role do they play in creating and maintaining social relationships, particularly in relations of wealth and power? These are the kinds of questions that inform this book as it explores the centrality of media and communication to society and to our lives. But to understand the way media and communication systems are implicated in our lives we must first understand what it is we are investigating.

Communication: Two Models

Communication is the act of making something common between two or more people. Communication is something people actually do. It is a form of 'social' action in that it implies the involvement of two or more people in a process of creating or sending and receiving or interpreting a message or idea. This process has been conceived in several different ways.

One of the first models for thinking about the process of communication was proposed in 1949 by Claude Shannon and Warren Weaver, communication engineers working for Bell Laboratories in the United States. Shannon and Weaver's so-called mathematical or transmission model of communication makes reference to the basic technical characteristics of the process of sending and receiving messages. In this model, seen in Figure 1.2, a person, the encoder or 'source', formulates a message, for example, by putting an idea into words. (For instance: 'What are you doing?'). The message is then sent through a particular channel or medium, such as email, voice, or text message. On the receiving end, the decoder receives and interprets the signals and, on the basis of the symbols sent, formulates meaningful content.

The decoder may then give the encoder 'feedback' by letting the encoder know that she or he has received the message. By sending a message back the decoder becomes an encoder, for instance, by replying 'Studying!' Any interference in the transmission of the intended message (signified by the lightning bolts in the diagram) is referred to as 'noise'. Noise may be loud background noise that makes it difficult to hear; a heavy, unfamiliar accent; static on the telephone line; or a typographical error in an email or text message. A similar model based on verbal communication was proposed around the same time by Harold Lasswell: '*Who* says *what* to *whom* in what *channel* with what *effect*?' This model's strength is its simplicity. It breaks the process of communication into a few very basic elements. In this way, it works well for engineers and technicians who speak in terms of the fidelity of messages and transmission technologies like telephones and fax machines. But because it simplifies the process of communication so much, it works less well for researchers, social scientists, and others concerned with the social nature of communication, as we are here. In fact, except in terms of noise, it provides no consideration of the larger social context of communication.

FIGURE 1.2   Shannon and Weaver's Mathematical Model of Communication (1949)

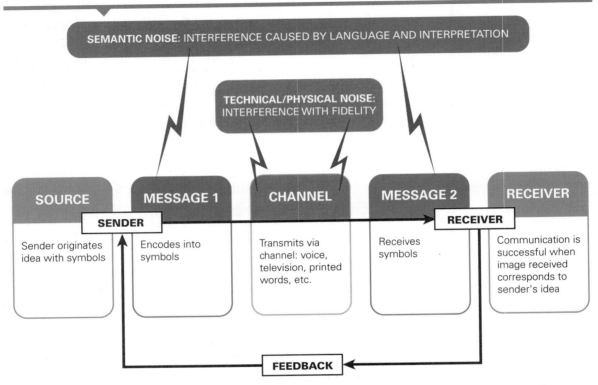

'The Communicative Process', adapted from Claude Shannon and Warren Weaver. *The Mathematical Theory of Communication.*
Source: Copyright 1949, 1998, by the Board of Trustees of the University of Illinois. Used with permission of the University of Illinois Press

The simplicity of this model has also been its major cause for criticism. Critics argue that while it helps to identify the elements of the complex process of communication, it is much too simplistic. Communication is a social process and the ideas, symbols, and techniques that we draw on to construct messages are drawn from our larger social experience. Language, culture, media forms—the social context within which messages are constructed and interpreted—all work to frame and determine not only the meaning we make of them but also the kinds of messages that we create. For instance, no two languages approach the world the same way. Each positions the speaker in sometimes subtly different ways to thinking about or being in the world. Similarly, there are differences in the way one's age, education, gender, race, and/or ethnicity nuance one's experience and understanding

of the world. Not only can these kinds of social variables influence the way communication takes place, but they can also determine whether or not it takes place at all.

The social nature of communication can be seen in Figure 1.3. This model emphasizes social and media-related variables that inform the process of communication. The larger social environment or milieu within which message formulation takes place is termed the 'encoding context'. At the other end, the 'decoding context' represents the ideas and understandings that the decoder brings to deciphering the encoded message. The nature of these larger frames of reference is the subject of theories of meaning-generation and communicative interaction that we will explore in Chapters 4 and 5. From this perspective, successful communication is always contingent on the sender

FIGURE 1.3   A Social Model of Communication

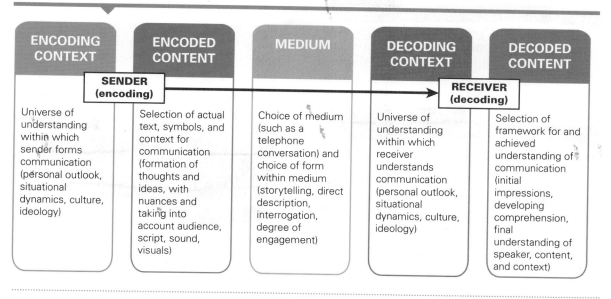

and receiver sharing some common idea or notion of the process and/or subject of communication, particularly in terms of language or experience. As John Durham Peters (1999: 14) points out, 'if meanings inhere not in words but in minds or references to objects, nothing can guarantee successful transit across the distance between two minds.' For instance, if provided with the letters a-p-p-l-e, you would probably conjure the image of a juicy red (or green) fruit. However, the letters p-o-m-a would probably not have the same effect, unless you speak Catalan. So here we can see that sharing a common language is an important condition for effective communication. But even speaking the same language is no guarantee of common understanding. For instance, words such as 'love' and 'happiness' can have very different meanings for different people.

From this perspective, not only is the process of communication structured by the social contexts of the sender and the receiver, it is nuanced by the medium of communication. For instance, to put an idea into words is not the same as painting a picture in an attempt to communicate the same idea. Nor is a news story on television the same as a newspaper write-up of the same story. Each provides different kinds of information about the subject of the story.

Similarly, a novel differs from its movie adaptation. The medium transforms the message by encouraging a certain structure in the encoding process, and further transforms it by making certain elements predominant for decoding. Television emphasizes the visual image. Writing emphasizes linearity and logic. Oral speech emphasizes social context, body language, and inflection—the individual instance rather than the general case.

The social model sees communication as both structured by and contingent on some shared social element or space. Communication is a cultural form, a social practice intimately woven into a larger set of ideas, values, and understandings of the world. Exactly how dependent communication is on the larger social context within which it takes place is an issue we take up in every chapter. For now, we will define *communication* as *the action of making a message common to one or more people.*

Of 'Mass' and 'Mass Communication'

In reference to communication, dictionary definitions of the modifier 'mass' tend to emphasize the meaning 'large in scale', as in **mass audience**, mass action, or mass murder. Thus, 'mass communication' means 'communication on a large scale'. The term can mean forms of communication addressed to large numbers of people or, perhaps, a large number of different messages being sent and received. However, 'mass communication' carries other meanings. We will see in Chapters 3 and 4 that the sense of 'mass' sometimes is based on the perceived character of *audiences* for media as they emerged in the context of industrial society. As a consequence of industrialization in the eighteenth and nineteenth centuries, many people in Europe and, to some extent, in North America, were uprooted from traditional, rural ways of life and moved to live in towns and cities where factories were located. This new way of life was fraught with problems. Cut free from the context of a traditional, essentially feudal, agricultural way of life and the social values, customs, and bonds that gave that way of life form and function, people were viewed by some analysts in their new industrial context as a collection 'of atomized, isolated individuals without traditional bonds of locality or kinship' (O'Sullivan et al., 1983: 131). According to these early social theorists, within this mass society the supposed lack of commonly held traditional social values left these individuals particularly vulnerable to '(i) totalitarian ideologies and propaganda; and (ii) influence by the mass media (largely comprising, in this period, newspapers and the emergent cinema and radio)' (ibid.). Until the early twentieth century, this perspective on 'the masses' had a strong impact on the development of communication theory. Hence, the term 'mass communication' sometimes carries with it the idea that audiences for forms of large-scale communication are unsophisticated and vulnerable to manipulation. While, as O'Sullivan et al. go on to point out, 'mass society theory has been refuted by historical evidence', vestiges of this evaluation of the nature of audiences survive in the literature on communication studies.

John Thompson (1995: 24) points out that the notion of 'mass' as 'large-scale' also is problematic:

It conjures up the image of a vast audience comprising many thousands, even millions of individuals. This may be an accurate image in the case of some media products, such as the most popular modern day newspapers, films, and television programs; but it is hardly an accurate representation of the circumstance of most media products, past or present… The important point about mass communication is not that a given number of individuals (or a specific portion of the population) receives the products, but rather products are available in principle to a plurality of recipients.

With literally hundreds of television channels available to the average household, as well as the myriad other forms of information and entertainment available over the internet, mass audiences numbering in the tens of millions for any particular scheduled program are becoming rare. Despite the fact that there still are mass audiences for some media events and programs, such as the Olympics, the World Cup, and *Canadian* or *American Idol*, media fare is catered to smaller audiences, today, such as programs on specialty channels devoted to golf, cooking, documentaries, or movies.

It is important to keep in mind, however, that just because the audiences viewing some media products may be small, that does not mean those programs won't be seen by much larger aggregate mass audiences over a particular time interval. For instance, audiences might see a film many different ways: at a theatre, through video rental, on a video-on-demand cable channel, downloaded from a website, on a smartphone or other mobile device, on a 'specialty' channel, or on a regular television channel. Although each of these audiences may be relatively small, in the aggregate they form a large or 'mass' audience. Similarly, although television programs or films are downloaded from the internet individually, in the aggregate audiences for such media fare may be huge.

Traditionally, the term *mass communication* has been used to describe the communication that happens by means of large traditional corporate media such as movies, large daily newspapers, and broadcasting. O'Sullivan and his colleagues captured that meaning of 'mass communication':

> Mass communication is the practice and product of providing leisure entertainment and information to an unknown audience by means of corporately financed, industrially produced, state regulated, high-technology, privately consumed commodities in the modern print, screen, audio, and broadcast media. (O'Sullivan et al., 1983: 131)

This definition was written prior to the development of the internet, smartphones, MP3 players, Google, Facebook, and blogs and, therefore, does not include them. Times and technology have changed.

Beginning about the mid-1990s, when the internet began to be publicly embraced, the possibilities for person-to-person communication on a mass scale expanded dramatically. Suddenly, it was possible to post an email to an address anywhere in the world where there was an email system. Transmission was instantaneous and generally free, obviating all the steps and costs in postal services, telegraph messages, and facsimile transmission. For instance, gone were the constraints and pitfalls of traditional person-to-person mailings: no writing paper, envelope, postage stamp, mailbox, mail pickup, imperfect sorting and handling, travel by air, land, or sea, re-sorting, and delivery. Instead, dashing out a few lines on a keyboard and pressing 'send' did the trick.

In quick succession, a number of technologies were added to early internet text-exchange protocols so that by 2000, digital files of any type—text, sound, or image—could be exchanged between computers. By 2000 it had also become possible for any person, with a bit of effort and little more expense than a computer, some software, and internet access, to create a website that was accessible from around the world. By 2005, blogs multiplied into the millions and wikis became common. By 2006, the term **Web 2.0** was being promoted to

describe the invention of such interactive online applications.

In short, while the internet started off as a means for person-to-person communication, with the success of the World Wide Web and digital technology and its increasing use by the business community and other organizations, it has become both a mass person-to-person communication system and a mass (decentralized) broadcast or distribution system. It has quickly evolved into a large-scale interactive communication system that allows people in Canada, or in many other countries, to create content for next to nothing and make it available to the world facilitated, now, by ubiquitous search engines. These many and continuing developments have fundamentally changed the nature of mass communication.

Thus, from our current perspective, the traditional definition of 'mass communication' focused on traditional media is incomplete. Today, *mass communication* is better understood simply as *the transmission and transformation of information on a large scale* no matter what specific media may be involved. Such a definition involves three dimensions or forms of organization (Lorimer, 2002):

1. *Mass communication is the production and dissemination of mass information and entertainment*—the traditional definition. This form of communication involves the corporately financed industrial production of entertainment and information to large, unknown audiences by means of print, screen, audio, broadcast, audiovisual, and internet technologies or public performance for both private and public consumption. In certain instances (e.g., broadcasting and, less often, print) it is state-regulated. Some examples are: radio, television, newspapers, film, magazines, books, recorded and performed music, and advertising.

2. The second form allows for greater participation by many members of society as part of either their work or leisure. *Mass communication is the decentralized production and wide*

accessibility of information and entertainment. Such communication is sometimes corporately financed, sometimes industrially produced, and often intended for small or niche audiences. It is rarely state-regulated and is undertaken by many individuals, organizations, and institutions. It includes websites, podcasts, blogs, print, film, audio, broadcast, and public performances.

3. The third form of mass communication accents interactivity as its defining attribute. *Mass communication is the interactive exchange of information (or messages or intelligence) to a number of recipients.* Such interactivity encompasses the exchange of information that takes place among individuals and groups by means of public access to communication media and media outlets. This form of mass communication encompasses the interactivity inherent in Web 2.0 and includes applications such as *Facebook.* This exchange of information might take place by phone, mail, email, pagers, two-way radio, and fax. It is an increasingly robust, decentralized, two-way exchange of information and creative expression. It encompasses such technologies as computer-facilitated phone technology (e.g., Skype, VOIP (Voice Over Internet Protocol), cellphones that encompass GPS (Global Positioning System) functionality and MP3-facilitated music recording and playback), email downloads and file exchanges, and enhanced security and electronic signature functions. A particularly interesting extension of interactivity is the collaborative creation of software that frees users from having to purchase commercial software at a relatively high cost. As traditional media adapt more interactive relationships and features, differences between these types of media are breaking down.

Such a three-part definition of mass communication—within the overall definition: the transmission and transformation of meaning on a large scale—repositions traditional media as one form of mass communication rather than its being the central and dominant form. By including decentral-ized and interactive media technologies, this three-part definition reflects a major change in the nature of mass communication. No longer are people merely provided with information and entertainment and hence positioned as audience members who may (or may not) actively interpret and engage with media products. Rather, two-way flows of information are of considerable significance.

'Media', 'Mass Media', and 'New Media'

A **medium** is *any vehicle that conveys information.* For instance, language is a medium, as are pictures, photographs, and musical instruments. Any vehicle or object that imparts meaning or information can be considered a communication medium. **Media** is the plural of *medium.*

We are particularly concerned with media involved in mass communication or **mass media**; thus, mass media *are the vehicles through which mass communication takes place.* O'Sullivan et al. (1983: 130) define mass media by providing a list: 'Usually understood as newspapers, magazines, cinema, television, radio and advertising; sometimes including book publishing (especially popular fiction) and music (the pop industry)'. Here the focus is on the large institutions and organizations that comprise traditional media. However, in the context of technological change and our three-part definition of mass communication, the media of mass communication have become larger in scope and now comprise the internet, websites, etc.

One form of mass communication can involve a range of different types of media. For instance, if we watch a video on YouTube of someone singing a song, the media at play are the language in which the song is written; the person's voice; musical instruments, if used; the video itself; and the internet.

From this perspective, mass media can be seen as *any kind* of vehicle that conveys information on a large scale and therefore includes such things as buildings, statues, coins, banners, and stained glass windows—any communication vehicle that comes in contact with a large number of people.

⁘ BOX 1.3   THE VARIOUS WAYS WE COMMUNICATE

A church stained-glass window

Source: © Jruffa/Dreamstime.com

The World Trade Center in New York City

Source: © iStockphoto.com/Markus Seidel

Toronto's CN Tower

Source: © Bcbounders/Dreamstime.com

Architecture, graffiti, memorial sculptures, public art, even clothing can be perceived as media of communication, even if their language isn't always accessible and their message isn't always clear. In some cases, these media evoke memories. The names of city streets—Papineau in Montreal, Granville in Vancouver, Yonge in Toronto—recall historical and political figures. Every town in Canada has some sort of war memorial serving as a symbol of personal remembrance and as a reminder to passersby of the sacrifice the town's citizens have made to Canada's past war efforts.

Building styles, too, can act as media or vehicles for communication of ideas and values. For instance, the number, size, and structural splendor of Montreal's churches speak to the power and influence the Roman Catholic Church once wielded in Quebec. Christian churches are often built in the shape of the cross, and the stained glass windows that adorn them usually relate stories from the Bible; as a result both act as communication media.

In New York, the twin towers of the World Trade Center soared over surrounding buildings providing a powerful symbol of the United States' power and primacy in the world economy, which is one of the reasons why al Qaeda targeted them on 11 September 2001.

The CN Tower pictured above is a clear reminder that Toronto is the country's communications centre because it is a telecommunications tower serving 16 Canadian television and radio stations, as well as representing a major rail, air, and road transportation hub.

If these media draw much of their authority from being sanctioned, permanent community symbols, graffiti draw their communicative efficacy from their ephemeral and rebellious qualities. Often dismissed simply as vandalism, graffiti nonetheless speaks to people. Sometimes the message is a straightforward 'I was here', as in the 'tags' or signatures we see on city buildings, or in the names of people spray-painted on rock faces at various spots along the Canadian highways. Or the message—often profane—may be one of protest or dissent. Whatever the case, graffiti serves very much as a 'voice of the voiceless' (see photo, below).

Source: © iStockphoto.com/Monica Armstrong

These forms of mass media involve institutions communicating with many members of society. But while there are many such media of communication, we tend not talk about them as media because their communicative role is secondary to housing people, commemorating history, serving as a medium of exchange, and so on (Box 1.3).

'New media' came into prominence in the mid-1990s. New media differ from the traditional mass media in that they do not focus on centralized institutional production and mass dissemination. Rather, they decentralize opportunities to create and distribute media information. They are decentralized in that any number of people, equipped with the right software applications, skills, and access to the internet, can produce new media content. But even though they are decentralized, these media still encourage wider participation and in some cases facilitate ongoing participation in the production and exchange of information. In other words, **new media** are *technologies, practices, and institutions designed to facilitate broad participation—or interactivity—in information production and exchange (i.e., communication) on a mass scale.* Email, file-sharing, text messaging, blogs, wikis, websites, social media—all these and more comprise new media.

But while new media bring fresh capabilities to media production and exchange, they also encompass and extend traditional mass media. For instance, websites and online delivery are becoming more important for newspapers. Books more often are sold and distributed in electronic form online and read via computers, Kindles, and iPads. And, music increasingly is marketed and distributed online in the form of MP3 technology as opposed to CD's, tape, or, vinyl records. Some traditional media are incorporating new media into their operations, by having audience members contribute news and other media content. This bringing together, or *convergence*, of media forms is a characteristic feature of today's media environment.

Convergence

Over the last several decades, the mediascape has been very rapidly transformed, a product of technological innovation, fundamental policy shifts, and massive corporate mergers. The term **convergence**—the buzzword of the last decade—was initially coined to describe the merging, or bringing together, of a wide range of previously separate and distinct communication technologies. For instance, in the past, photographs were taken on film and circulated in hard copy. Video was recorded magnetically on tape. Music was distributed on tape or vinyl records. But in a few short decades, electronic **digital** technology has changed those technologies. What was recorded previously on distinct media forms now can be turned into the binary language of 1s and 0s and manipulated, transmitted, and read via the internet on computers.

As discussed in Parts III and IV of this book, this *technological*

Source: *Communications Research Centre Canada, 1976.* Reproduced with the permission of the Minister of Public Works and Government Services Canada, 2011.

Telidon, from the Greek 'tele' meaning 'distant' and 'idon' meaning 'I see', was an early precursor to the home computer developed by the Canadian Communications Research Centre in the late 1970s. A number of countries, including Britain and France, developed similar teletext systems. However, unlike today's personal computers, these systems had very little computing power and stored very little information, depending instead on external, usually distant, databases. Pictured here is a Telidon trial conducted in 1976.

convergence of voice, video, data, and other communication media has precipitated change across a number of dimensions of communicative practice. For instance, changing media technology has been accompanied by changes in both government regulation and the structure of media industries, as companies that once operated in industries and fields held separate by technological and regulatory divides have restructured in an effort to gain competitive advantages in this shifting environment. This *corporate convergence* has led to the growth of increasingly large media companies with investments in a range of different kinds of media. Whereas not so long ago television, radio, cable systems, and newspapers were seen as quite different businesses, today companies like Rogers Communications have interests in a range of media such as radio and television stations, magazines, cable systems, and wireless telephone and broadband companies. Similarly, Quebecor owns newspapers, TV stations, cable systems, magazines, cable and wireless phone service, and music-video-book retail stores.

Convergence is also shifting the ways we understand and participate in media and media events. As Henry Jenkins (2006: 3) argues, new media are creating a 'participatory culture' that is replacing more traditional 'passive media spectatorship'. *Interactive media* enable audiences to participate directly in the outcomes of programs such as *Canadian Idol.* On another front, with shows such as *Survivor*, new media enable fans to track down and expose the outcome of programs before they run their course on network television, thereby spoiling the outcomes for the series producers. And for some fans of film series such as *Star Wars* and *Harry Potter*, co-opting the characters and settings of these films to write their own stories has landed such 'grassroots artists . . . in conflict with commercial media producers who want to exert greater control over their intellectual property' (ibid., 21). Copyright critic Lawrence Lessig (2008: 29–33) argues that digital technologies have produced what he calls a more participatory 'RW culture' in which people have the ability to create their own art or music or film, whether it is completely original or based on an artifact of popular culture. Consum-

ers of media become producers as well, or what are sometimes called 'prosumers'.

On a number of different fronts, then, convergence is a key feature of today's media environment.

The Dimensions of Mass Media

Equipped with our definitions, we can now more closely consider some of the larger dimensions and characteristics of mass media and mass communication. As we will consider in later chapters, mass media are an integral part of our culture—our ways of life—and images, ideas, and values gleaned from the media are deeply woven into the ways in which we understand and embrace the world. For now, however, we want to focus on some of the specific individuals, organizations, and institutions involved with mass media. Building on an early model of mass communication developed by British media researcher Denis McQuail, one can understand mass and new media as being comprised of the following dimensions or elements:

1. *a distinct set of activities*;
2. involving *particular technological configurations*;
3. associated, to some degree, with *formally constituted institutions*;
4. acting within *certain laws, rules, and understandings*;
5. carried out by *persons occupying certain roles*;
6. which, together, convey *information, entertainment, images*, and *words*;
7. to or among members of society.

We will examine each of these dimensions in turn.

A Distinct Set of Activities

From a technical perspective, such as Shannon and Weaver's mathematical model of communication (Figure 1.2), mass media are indeed a distinct set of activities in terms of their communicative form and function. Take a news broadcast for example: a news organization uses a device, such as a microphone, to turn a journalist's voice into a signal. The signal, travelling either as light in glass fibre or as an electrical impulse in a wire or coaxial cable, is connected to a carrier company, such as an internet service provider, telephone company, or cable company that distributes a signal out into the world. On the receiving end, a device such as a computer, television, or radio decodes the signal and reconstitutes it as the announcer's voice. New media may involve a broader range of hardware and software in this process, but this transmission of content is, by and large, an activity that is distinct from other social activities.

The social model of communication, with its focus on social context, takes this idea of 'a distinct set of activities' a few steps further. It stresses that the transmission function (moving meaning from one place or one person to another) accented by Shannon and Weaver is also integrated into a larger set of social ideas, values and actions; and that the communicators themselves are active in creating messages that provide particular perspectives on, and understandings of, the world. For instance, news programs not only inform us of particular events, they also tell us which of them are perceived as the most important events of the day. In focusing on accidents, celebrities, and violence associated with social protest, news programs can draw our attention

away from other important issues that shape our lives. For instance, in highlighting the vandalism and violence sometimes associated with social protests, they distract us from the reasons people were protesting in the first place. New media, too, operate in this manner, as the creators of media messages choose not only what to write about but also how, in terms of spin or angle, they will write about it. From this perspective, the social model stresses the role of both media and audiences as active, meaning-generating agents and the media as contributing to how we see and understand the world. This role media play in shaping our perceptions of the world is indeed a 'distinct set of activities'.

Photography provides another example of how media shape our perceptions. A photograph is simply a direct image of what was before the camera at a specific place and time. However, this reading of the image undervalues the role of the photographer in constructing that image. Focusing on one person, place, or event draws our attention to that particular thing or event over the larger set of circumstances within which it is situated. For example, pictures of a single, black-hooded individual breaking a store window draws attention away from the larger message that thousands of other peaceful protestors are trying to convey. And by concentrating on the action of a handful of individuals at the protest, rather than the tens of thousands of other people who were there, the concerns of the many are overshadowed and lost (see Van Ginneken, 1998: 166–89).

On a smaller scale, as Stephen Osborne says, even when we say 'smile for the camera' we are engaging in the construction of the visual object, a shaping of reality for a viewer of the picture. Two early media theorists, Peter Berger and Thomas Luckmann (1966), described the way media work to create meaning in this

Source: © iStockphoto.com/Jen Grantham

This image of an individual spray-painting graffiti on a police car draws attention away from the larger message that thousands of other, peaceful protestors are trying to convey.

⟩ BOX 1.4   TURNING THE WATCHERS INTO THE WATCHED

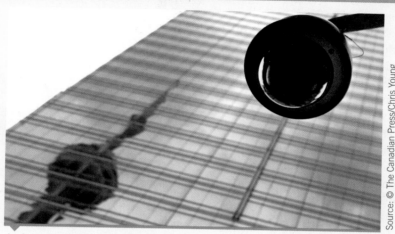

Source: © The Canadian Press/Chris Young

In George Orwell's *Nineteen Eighty-Four* the constant video surveillance of the dictator further permeates the consciousness of the citizens in the propaganda phrase, 'Big Brother is watching you'. Who is watching you today, and why?

While television was originally designed for broadcasting signals from a single point of origin to many receivers/audience members, over the years it has been adapted to a range of other uses. In recent incarnations, closed-circuit television has been adapted to respond to increasing demand for surveillance and social control and is now used on a large scale to monitor activities on downtown city streets. For instance, during the 2010 meetings of the G-20 in Toronto, police installed surveillance cameras on nearly every downtown corner of the city to keep an eye on protestors.

Source: © BBC/Corbis

In a famous April Fool's Day joke, in 1957 the British Broadcasting Company aired a report of a Swiss family harvesting spaghetti from a tree. Hundreds of people called in, some asking how they might get their own such trees. In this case, of course, as is sometimes the case with media reports, what the media presented as 'real', and some people thought was real, was not.

regard. Through representing objects, events, and ideas in certain ways, the mass media 'construct' images and encourage certain perceptions of reality.

In summary, the mass media are distinct sets of activities because they are the primary tools societies use to make or manufacture meaning and to signify or construct reality. The mass media are major contributors to our knowledge and understanding of the world because of the information they carry (transmission) and the interpretation they place on that information (transformation).

Particular Technological Configurations

Media are found in particular technological configurations. For instance, telephones are part of larger telephone systems, newspapers are produced by large newspaper companies that include large printing presses as well as online technologies, and internet service is configured within a system comprised of computers, modems, servers, and transmission systems. Moreover, such systems are constantly being restructured or reconfigured. As Raymond Williams (1974) has pointed out, such technologies are not invented outside of social context. For example, television emerged from the interests and conceptions of technical investigators and industrial entrepreneurs who foresaw an electronic medium of sound and visual communication for use in the nuclear family home. Similarly, inventors such as Marconi, Edison, and Bell were driven by the idea of inventing products that would have specific applications in the developing industrial and consumer-based societies. But just as the inventions of new technology are shaped by societal forces, how they are used is also shaped by society. The typewriter originally was built as a toy. Radio originated as an interactive, two-way medium.

Technologies develop form and function in the context of a larger set of social interests exerting pressure and direction on their development. Television serves the interests of owners, advertisers, technicians, actors, and many others. It allows the creation and production of content to be delivered almost free, subsidized as it is by the price we pay for advertised products. TV also allows large, established companies that manufacture brand-name goods to keep their products at the forefront of people's minds. It provides jobs in the entertainment sector. It also serves the interests of audiences by allowing diversion, entertainment, and a bit of education for people during their leisure time. In this configuration it is well entrenched in society, but it took decades to develop its role and it may be modified or replaced. Indeed, increasing uses to which television screens are being put, such as gaming or surfing the web, indicate this is already happening. Caught in shifting social currents, the technology may be adapted to altogether new uses, such as closed circuit television (CCTV), which in the context of increasing concerns for surveillance and social control is becoming more common, and quickly turning the watchers into the watched.

Source: © iStockphoto.com/Lachlan Currie, © Snr/Dreamstime

Significant improvements have been made in cellphone technology since the 1970s. Today, cellphones are smaller, have greater range, and have many more features and capabilities than their predecessors.

A more recent modern mass medium is the increasingly ubiquitous cellphone. In 1990 a cellphone had the weight necessary to double as a club and was only capable of telephone conversations. Today, however, smartphones are lightweight, and allow users to not only carry on conversations but take photographs, surf the internet, play music, exchange text messages, map their locations, and a host of other possibilities. Here we can see that in a short time the development of the cellphone has responded to a wide range of needs and desires on the part of pri-vate business and the public in general.

In summary, the modern mass and new media are a set of technological configurations that bring us information and entertainment in a variety of forms. But many different technologies and configurations make up different media. In the print medium alone there are broadsheet and tabloid newspapers, magazines, journals, and books—mass paperbacks, quality paperbacks, hardcovers, textbooks, school books, limited editions, coffee-table books, talking books, large-print books, children's literature. In television, we have public, community, educational, and commercial television, and radio is delivered by broadcast, cable, the internet, and satellite by a diverse array of stations. In addition, there are both feature films and non-theatrical films. Sound recordings are available on vinyl, audio cassettes, CDs, MP3s, and DVDs as well as, in their promotional version, video cassettes. And with the ongoing digitization of information and different forms of media convergence, current technological configurations are in a state of flux.

Formally Constituted Institutions and Organizations: Private Profit vs Mandate-Driven

Mass media are often characterized as formally constituted organizations and institutions that are focused on the production, processing, carriage, and marketing of content. Traditional media industries were based around particular technologies—such as newspapers, television, and radio—associated with media production. With convergence, the technological form and shape of these institutions is changing. But the technology deployed by media organizations is only one of the formative elements of institutions. Others might be found in the different organizations that give form to media practice, or in the way jobs are organized inside organizations. Some of the different kinds of organizations and jobs found in the larger media industries are discussed on page 24, in the section 'Persons Occupying Certain Roles'. Here, we will discuss another of the defining elements of institutional and organizational form: ownership (see also Chapter 9).

Because we live in a capitalist society—a society based on private property and economic relations mediated through markets—most media organizations are privately owned. As such, their primary purpose is to generate profits or income for their owners or shareholders, not to produce media content. First and foremost, if they are not profitable, eventually they go out of business.

Some privately owned new media, such as Facebook and YouTube, have been struggling to turn what they do into profitable enterprise, that is, find a business model that can both pay for the operation of the company and return a profit to its owners. Finding ways to make money from media is an old and familiar problem, however. In its early days, radio presented such a problem. As radio broadcasting began in the early 1920s, companies sent messages out over the air, without knowing who, if anybody, was listening. The only way to pay for the programs and other content they broadcast was with profits from the sale of radio receivers. Once those receivers left the store, getting money from their owners to pay for producing radio programs presented a difficult problem. In the beginning, one way of solving this problem was to charge people a radio licence fee and then use the money collected from the fee to pay for programming. While this model is still in operation in some countries (e.g., the UK), Canada and the US adopted the telephone companies' business model, charging people and organizations for broadcast time, that is, charging them to send broadcast messages. This system proved quite popular with large corporations, which began creating radio programming to attract audiences to whom they could pitch their products and services. Over time, this system of 'toll broadcasting' developed into the system of advertising-financed media programming that dominates radio and television today.

This system is not without its problems. For instance, it means that despite the fact we look to our media systems for news, information, and entertainment, by and large their primary purpose is to sell us goods and services. Programming and other forms of content are designed to attract only certain kinds of audiences—those with the interest and money to purchase the goods and services advertised with that content. Ideas and programs that don't meet this commercial imperative are weeded out. At the same time, producers are encouraged to spend as little money as possible on creating programs and content as this expense impacts the bottom line. Canadian television is dominated by American television programs not because Canadians necessarily prefer American programs over Canadian ones, but because it is much cheaper to buy American programs that attract large audiences than it is to produce Canadian programs that will attract large audiences. Having recovered much of their cost of production in the US market, American television producers sell their shows to Canadian television networks at a fraction of their cost of production; often 10 per cent or less. That means that a Canadian network can buy a show like *The Simpsons* or *CSI* that may have cost several million dollars to produce for several hundred thousand dollars or less. Obviously, it's very hard for Canadian producers to compete with this calibre of production.

Generally, privately owned traditional media, such as newspapers, magazines, and radio and cable systems, all are subject to the same profit imperative and their content is shaped by this same concern. However, this is not to say that privately owned media do not strive to serve some larger public interest, or that everything they do is driven solely by self-interest. Indeed, as discussed on the next page, in Canada private radio and television stations are licensed by the Canadian Radio-television and Telecommunications Commission (CRTC) and are specifically assigned public duties as a condition of licence. Similarly, many newspapers and other publications take their roles as important vehicles for public information very seriously and strive to provide timely and accurate information important to public decision-making and debate. However, many media institutions are formulated to create private profits and that directly impacts the character of the products they offer. How the business models adopted by profit-oriented new media will shape their content in the future remains to be seen.

Not-for-profit media are mandate-driven, rather than profit-driven. That doesn't mean that they don't have to make money or generate revenue to survive, simply that their primary purpose is something other than profit. Perhaps the best-known not-for-profit media corporation in Canada is the Canadian Broadcasting Corporation (CBC).

The CBC's mandate is laid out in Section 3.1(m) of the 1991 Broadcasting Act and charges the Corporation with a number of distinct responsibilities such as 'being predominantly and distinctively Canadian' and contributing to a 'shared national consciousness and identity'. Because of the difficulties that broadcasting systems based on private ownership have had in generating a wide range of

programming, many countries in the world have a government-owned broadcaster like the CBC. Such organizations are said to be publicly owned in that, through the government, they are owned by the citizens of the country. Such organizations generally operate at 'arms length' from government and are often protected through legislation from day-to-day government interference.

Other not-for-profit media include provincial broadcasters, community radio, the Aboriginal Peoples Television Network (APTN), Wikipedia, and Craigslist. As we shall see, generating the money necessary to meet their mandates is not always easy for such organizations.

Certain Laws, Rules, and Understandings

Besides being subject to the general national and international laws and regulations, there are a number of laws directly related to media in Canada. Formal laws include several important federal statutes or acts that govern the structure and operation of the media, particularly in the fields of broadcasting and telecommunications. In the case of newspaper and magazine publishing, most industrialized countries, including Canada, exercise little direct control. No licenses are required and media content is not restricted, except by broad laws directed at libel, sedition, hate, and pornography. However, there are various indirect supports and controls, such as taxation, subsidies, business policies, and distribution subsidies. For instance, in Canada there are a number of federal production funds devoted to promoting the development of the broadcasting, film, music, and magazine industries, as well as new media.

In Canada, the **Broadcasting Act** (1991) is the pre-eminent statute controlling broadcasting (see Chapter 6). There are no equivalent statutes for Canadian print or recorded music, although Section 19 of the Income Act encourages Canadian ownership of newspapers and magazines (see Chapter 7). Broadcasting has received particular attention because there has been a long-standing concern that broadcasting is important to nation-building, particularly in the face of the dominance of American media in Canada. In addition to other formalities, such as defining broadcast undertakings, who can own outlets, and technical matters, the Broadcasting Act outlines what broadcasting should do for society. In other words, it provides a framework for policy. The Act addresses the tacitly accepted values and ideals of Canadian society and the means by which broadcasting can contribute to their achievement.

The Broadcasting Act also provides for the existence of an agency to develop and administer regulations arising from the legislation. This organization, the Ottawa-based Canadian Radio-television and Telecommunications Commission (CRTC), administers the policies and provisions enunciated in the Broadcasting Act and in the Telecommunications Act. The CRTC translates the principles of the Act into rules for industry players and other stakeholder groups. It mediates between the ideals and values outlined in the Act and the practical realities of running broadcasting undertakings. This mediation has led to the development of many issues of concern, some short-lived and others recurring. The recurring issues are valuable indicators of critical points of tension in Canada's broadcasting system.

A second key legal statute in the field of communications is the **Copyright Act**. Copyright law transforms the expression of one's intellectual efforts, for example a poem, script, movie, story, newspaper or magazine article, or book into a piece of property that can be owned. It is designed to help ensure that writers and artists are paid for their work and that their work is not used without their permission. These days, however, when technology makes it so easy to copy and/or change media products, how control over them should be exercised is a matter of great public debate (Chapter 6).

Other laws influence how the media operate, but the Copyright and Broadcasting Acts are of primary importance. Radio, for instance, provides a good example of the effects of the Copyright Act and the Broadcasting Act on musicians and the music industry in general. Under the terms of the Copyright Act, radio stations must pay musicians for the right to play their songs. To this end, each radio station contributes 3.2 per cent of its gross advertising revenue to the Society of Composers, Authors, and Music Publishers of Canada (SOCAN). This money forms the basis for **royalty payments** to the artists. To administer the royalty system for the performing rights of musical compositions, SOCAN surveys each radio station five to six times a year. Based on the relative number of times a song has been played, SOCAN distributes the money to the song's creators, music composer, lyricist, performer, and publishing company (http://socan.ca/jsp/en/pub/about_socan/index.jsp).

Through the authority provided to it through the Broadcasting Act, the CRTC determines content rules which, in turn, promote the development of the Canadian music industry. For example, the CRTC requires AM and FM radio stations that specialize in popular music to devote at least 35 per cent of their play time to Canadian selections. Prior to the enactment of radio content regulations, less than 5 per cent of the music played on radio stations in Canada was by Canadian artists. As illustrated in Chapter 8, the reasons for this were rooted in the structure of the industry itself, not because Canadians could not make decent music. This regulation has encouraged the development of a thriving Canadian music industry and fuelled the careers of several generations of popular music artists such as Drake, K'Naan, Arcade Fire, Diana Krall, Michael Buble, the Tragically Hip, the Guess Who, Anne Murray, Céline Dion, and Gordon Lightfoot.

The laws and rules that govern the mass media have developed from a larger consideration of the social and economic value of media. Nevertheless, considerable debate remains over the public role media should play and the responsibilities they should shoulder. Some media spokespersons claim that if people are watching television (since they have the freedom not to watch), the television station is making an appropriate contribution to the enjoyment of their leisure time. Others claim that the media should set much more ambitious goals for themselves—to provide, for example, enlightening rather than escapist entertainment. This debate is over what constitutes the **public interest** in the media realm.

BOX 1.5 INTERPRETING THE BROADCASTING ACT

As time passes societies change. Less frequently do statutes change; and so it is important to write statutes in such a way that they can be interpreted within the context of the time. For example, Section 3d(iii) of the Broadcasting Act declares that 'the Canadian broadcasting system should through its programming and the employment opportunities arising out of its operations, serve the needs and interests and reflect the circumstances and aspirations, of Canadian men, women and children, including equal rights, the linguistic duality and multicultural and multiracial nature of Canadian society and the special place of aboriginal people within that society.' And Section 3i(i) notes that 'the programming provided by the Canadian broadcasting system should be varied and comprehensive, providing a balance of information, enlightenment and entertainment for men, women and children of all ages, interests and tastes'.

These two clauses address directly two basic differences in society, race and gender, and less directly a third: class. All three are often associated with inequality. The Act provides the framework and the impetus for the media strive to address the changing norms and ideals of society with respect to race, class, and gender.

Another important communications statute is the **Telecommunications Act**. This legislation generally focuses on the infrastructure underlying the transmission of messages. The importance of telecommunications service becomes apparent when we consider the new mass media and the interactive media. Who owns and controls service provision, what kinds of services are offered, to whom they are sold, and on what terms, all have an impact over the long term. In the past, telecommunications regulation was much more comprehensive and rigorous that it is today. There were strict rules governing the prices charged and the territories carrier companies could serve. However, since the 1980s, regulations have been relaxed considerably and competition between different companies has been substituted for direct regulation as means of controlling corporate behaviour. Moreover, for a number of reasons, the CRTC has decided not to regulate the internet in the same way that it does broadcasting or telecommunications. Consequently there are no specific laws addressed to the content, structure, or operation of the internet in Canada. This has been the source of some controversy as public interest groups have accused the large corporations that control the internet of operating in their own interest, rather than serving the broader public interest.

Persons Occupying Certain Roles: Organizational Dimensions of the Media

The number of people involved in the mass media and the number of roles people play are vast. Media have always been integrated into the larger society, but with new media the line between them has become even more blurred.

At one level, there are people both directly and indirectly employed by media organizations. These include journalists, on-air announcers, editors, printers, studio technicians, technical support personnel, camera operators, designers, producers, directors, advertising sales staff, security, and cleaning crews. Media companies also engage a huge number of part-time and contract employees, as well independent producers. Employers find part-time and contract employees attractive for several reasons. First, they generally don't have to pay them as much as full-time employees in terms of wages or benefits. Second, they offer employers flexibility, in that they can hire people with particular skills for particular jobs and then let them go without worrying about having to keep on paying them until their skills are needed again. Much of the content in the magazine and television industries is created under contract by independent producers, and other media industries are trying to integrate this model.

Also employed by media companies, but generally not directly by individual corporations, are industry organizations and lobby groups, such as the Canadian Newspaper Association. These organizations represent the collective interests of the owners of media companies and are generally involved with lobbying government and conducting other public relations campaigns, as well as collecting statistics and other information about the industry.

Playing a similar role, but for the employees of such organizations rather than their owners, are media unions and professional associations. Media unions in Canada, such as the Canadian Media Guild (CMG) and the Communication, Energy and Paperworkers (CEP) Union play strong roles not only in representing their members' interests to employers, but also forwarding those interests to local and national governments, as well as to national and international regulatory fora. The interests of media owners and media employees are not always the same, particularly in Canada, where it is often much cheaper to import foreign media products than produce them here. Performers in Canada also have their own professional organizations—in Anglophone Canada it is the 21,000-member Alliance of Canadian Cinema, Television and Radio Artists (ACTRA)—as do film and television producers—the Canadian Media Production Association (CMPA). These organizations represent the interests of their members with employers as well as conduct studies and keep statistics on the structure and health of their industries, and represent their interests in government studies and enquiries.

On the production side, also, are wire services that provide media content, particularly news (Chapter 9). Canadian Press (CP) is perhaps the best known of these organizations. Until 2010, the company was run as a not-for-profit news co-operative that supplied both print and broadcast news to its newspaper, radio, and television members. Since then, CP has been privatized and sold to its three largest member companies: Torstar (which publishes the *Toronto Star*), Gesca (*La Presse*), and CTVglobemedia (*The Globe and Mail*) (Iype, 2010). Founded in 1917, Canadian Press was an indispensable news service, providing local, regional, and national news coverage in English and French to hundreds of Canadian news organizations, coverage that the smaller newspapers and stations in particular would not otherwise be able to provide. With the escalating concentration of media ownership, media chains like Canwest (now Postmedia) and Quebecor established their own news services, sharing stories among their own properties, rendering membership in CP redundant and leading to the demise of its co-operative structure.

CNW Group (formerly known as Canada NewsWire) also provides content to media outlets. But it operates as a public relations service rather than a news company per se. CNW content primarily is press releases from companies advertising new products and services or event announcements. Rather than charge media outlets for using that content, they charge the organizations originating it. As media content is expensive to produce, the 'free' content offered by this organization is quite popular. CNW also specializes in posting and circulating client information on social media.

Another media level is the advertising industry (Chapter 5). Many newspapers, radio and television stations, and new media outlets such as large websites with heavy traffic employ their own advertising people who sell and design ads. Similarly, many large companies have their own advertising departments. Additionally, a go-between for big business and the media is a sizable Canadian advertising industry. The industry is comprised of both Canadian and foreign companies and has both large anglophone and francophone components. Advertising agencies generally operate on a fee-for-service basis and receive a percentage of the fee their clients pay media outlets to run their ads. Public relations companies are similar to advertising agencies—sometimes companies offer both kinds of services—only rather than market-specific products or services, they promote specific events and brands or manage the larger public image of the company.

Media relations people also are employed by government, private corporations, not-for-profit companies, charitable organizations, industry lobby groups, and more. Many organizations employ communications people who specialize in engaging with media, as well as performing other communication functions. These people actively engage with media to try to ensure that the interests of their organizations are well represented in news stories and other media content, as well as the promotion of events they sponsor.

BOX 1.6 GOVERNMENT INFORMATION

In an attempt to increase access to information that governments want citizens to have, all federal government departments have created their own websites. A good example is that of the Department of Canadian Heritage (for English: http://pch.gc.ca/eng /1266037002102/1265993639778). An interesting exercise in examining the impact of government information, and especially press releases, is to go to the section labelled 'Newsroom', find one or two press releases, and then try to find stories built from those releases on radio and television or in the newspapers. For newspapers, in addition to purchasing a copy, you can go to the websites of *The Globe and Mail* (www. the globeandmail.com) or the *National Post* (www.nationalpost.com) and try to find resulting articles. You will see how little some information is followed up, the angle or perspective taken by the newspapers, and the degree to which they rely on the supplied government information.

Government regulators and policy people play an important role in the operation of the media. In Canada, media largely come under federal jurisdiction; the departments of Heritage and Industry, as well as the CRTC, have considerable power and resources in developing and administering media regulations. Heritage Canada, for example, oversees a wide range of polices affecting books and magazines, film and video, broadcasting and interactive media and music.

Still another set of organizations that actively engage and influence media coverage are think-tanks and research institutes. Generally, the purpose of these not-for-profit organizations is to promote particular perspectives and understandings on issues of public importance and, where possible, influence the development of public policy in ways that promote their mandate or interest. Among these, the Alberta-based Pembina Institute promotes sustainable energy solutions; the Canadian Centre for Policy Alternatives undertakes research and campaigns to promote social, economic, and environmental justice; and the C.D. Howe Institute works on economic and social policy

issues. Arguably, over the last 20 years, conservative think tanks have been particularly successful in helping shift public policy in the direction of more market-oriented and individualist values.

Information, Entertainment, Images, and Words

The central role of the media is, of course to convey content: traditionally thought of in terms of information and entertainment, but delivered as images and words. Theoretical ways of thinking about and analyzing content are discussed in Chapters 4 and 5. For now we simply wish to highlight the ways in which both classifying media content and trying to specify the meaning it contains can be somewhat slippery and arbitrary.

For instance, distinctions are often drawn between different types of programming, including information programs such as news, documentaries, editorials, etc., and entertainment programs such as films, situation comedies, comedy specials, etc. However, we must bear in mind that entertainment is taken to be informative, just as information can be entertaining.

Meaning in media messages is not always clear or predetermined: images and words (and other media content) have at least two possible types or levels of meaning. The first is *denotative*, which is the obvious, literal, or readily apparent meaning. The second is *connotative*, which is the secondary, figurative meaning, or meanings that might be associated with the image or word. The word 'apple' might be read as having a denotative meaning as a kind of fruit and, connotatively, as representing knowledge or the Biblical story of Adam and Eve; or, perhaps, a particular computer company. Problems sometimes arise, however, in trying to develop agreement on exactly what are the denotative or connotative meanings associated with particular images or content. Take, for example, Japanese game shows, such as *Takeshi's Castle*, otherwise known as MXC or Most Extreme Elimination Challenge. In Japan, many of the colourfully dressed characters would be immediately recognized as specific cultural or folkloric characters—they would have immediate and specific denotative meaning.

However, to Canadian audiences such meaning is indecipherable. Similar problems arise in language use between generations. Words, like 'dude', 'dope', or 'boss' have quite different denotative meanings depending on who is asked. The point here is that meaning is never predetermined. Just as media producers often go to great lengths to 'encode' or put meaning into media content, so too audience members must bring their own understandings of those words and images to 'decode' that content.

Members of Society: The Mass Audience?

A **mass audience** is not to be thought of as a mob or as an unthinking mass of individuals vulnerable to the intentional or unintentional manipulations of media practitioners. Rather, it is a convenient shorthand term for the great number of people who consume mass entertainment and information. Rather than homogeneous, vulnerable, and passive, the mass audience is better conceived as consisting of individuals who, from their diverse backgrounds, bring varying degrees of engagement and a variety of readings or interpretations to media content—readings that are derived from their own specific histories, that is, their psychological, social, economic, political, cultural, and spiritual roots, as well as their age, race, ethnicity, and gender.

Despite the increasing number of media options, mass audiences persist. They form around events and international spectacles like the Olympics or the soccer World Cup, around popular books and films such as *Harry Potter* and *Star Wars*, around other sporting events such as the Grey Cup or Super Bowl, and around election coverage or news coverage of disaster. Similarly, new media also attract mass audiences. In 2010, YouTube was getting over a billion hits a day, while videos such as Lady Gaga's 'Bad Romance' received hundreds of millions of views.

However, the ongoing growth of new media has changed traditional notions of audience. Today, audience members are themselves often media producers. To be sure there is still a divide, and often a very big one, between professional and amateur media creators. Still, bloggers and citizen journalists are playing an expanding role in news

Mash-ups and remixes are a big part of new media culture. The *Grey Album* (2004) by Danger Mouse (aka Brian Burton, pictured here) was one of the first remixes to raise a major copyright controversy.

Source:© AP Photo/Peter Kramer

production, and traditional media outlets often turn to these sources for both content and ideas for stories and editorials. The huge number of reality TV programs blurs the line between the audience and performers, as audience members and regular people become TV stars. Social media sites, such as YouTube, are attracting both amateur producers and viewers by the millions. As well, audience members for traditional media products are often no longer content to play the role of passive consumer but instead want to take part in acting out characters and developing story lines for popular films and television programs. Indeed, media are an integral part of our culture—our ways of life—and images, ideas, and values gleaned from the media are deeply woven into the ways in which we understand and embrace the world.

❯ SUMMARY

Media and communication have central importance in our society and culture and continue to evolve. As a means of building a common understanding of the subjects under study, we offered two different models of communication, as well as a number of definitions of communication media and processes, for consideration. Given recent changes to the media environment, we provided an updated definition of the term *mass communication* as *the transmission and transformation of information on a large scale*, and went on to describe three different forms of mass communication in this context. The chapter then explored the nature of mass media and mass communication as distinctive; technologically specific; institutionally embedded; constrained by laws, rules, and conventions; employing particular workers; and conveying information, entertainment, images, and symbols to or among members of society.

New media have extended and deepened these relationships with Canadian society, with social media and other new media offering more opportunities for people to engage with each other, create their own media products, and engage with traditional media.

❯ KEY TERMS

blogs, p. 3
Broadcasting Act, p. 22
Copyright Act, p. 23
communication, p. 9
convergence, p. 16
digital, p. 16

mass audience, p. 27
mass media, p. 14
media, p. 14
mass communication, p. 3
medium, p. 14

new media, p. 16
public interest, p. 23
royalty payments, p. 23
Telecommunications Act, p. 24
Web 2.0, p. 13

❯ RELATED WEBSITES

Alliance of Canadian Cinema, Television and Radio Artists (ACTRA): www.actra.ca
An association of more than 21,000 professionals working in Canadian media. Its website offers insights into the issues facing Canadian media.

Berne Convention (copyright): www.law.cornell.edu/ treaties/berne/overview.html
This site includes the pre-eminent world statute dealing with copyright, including all its various clauses and levels.

Canadian Intellectual Property Office: http://cipo.ic.gc.ca
This agency of Industry Canada deals with copyright as well as other forms of intellectual property.

Canadian Media Guild: www.cmg.ca
This is the site of the union that represents workers at the CBC as well as a number of other media companies across the country. It has a number of interesting features and provides insight into the kinds of issues facing media workers today.

Canadian Association of Journalists: www.caj.ca
This site provides journalists with professional information and, from time to time, it takes up issues of interest to all Canadian journalists.

Canadian Broadcast Standards Council: www.cbsc.ca
The CBSC sets broadcasting standards, such as how much advertising broadcasters can put in a half-hour of programming.

Canadian Radio-television and Telecommunications Commission (CRTC): www.crtc.gc.ca
The CRTC provides everything you might want to know about its activities regulating Canada's media.

CBC: www.cbc.ca
The CBC site highlights CBC programs and issues dealt with on the CBC. The site changes continuously.

CBC Journalistic Standards and Practices: www.cbc. radio-canada.ca/docs/policies/journalistic/socio.shtml
This code of conduct is not only a guide to journalists but also an indication to the public that CBC journalists work within a set of standards.

CBC media policy: www.cbc.radio-canada.ca/htmen/ policies
The policy framework within which the CBC operates is found here.

CBC's The National: www.cbc.ca/thenational
This site provides headlines of the day's news as it is carried on the program, features, further elaboration on certain stories, and even a subscription service.

Canadian Centre for Policy Alternatives: www.policyalternatives.ca
A progressive think tank that works on issues of social and economic justice.

Facebook: www.facebook.com
You know what this is.

Flickr: www.flickr.com
A popular social media site for sharing photographs. It has more than 4 billion pictures archived.

Google Books: http://books.google.com
An extraordinarily ambitious effort to offer as many books as possible online. It has been hailed as a giant step towards the democratization of knowledge as well as criticized for undermining copyright.

Public Library of Science (PLoS): www.plos.org
Non-profit organization that through its website is making the world's medical and scientific literature available and free to everyone.

Society of Composers, Authors, and Music Publishers of Canada (SOCAN): www.socan.ca
The SOCAN site presents information for musicians, users of music, and the general public.

SourceForge: http://sourceforge.net
SourceForge is the world's largest open-source software development website and manages projects, issues, communications, and code.

Wikipedia: www.wikipedia.org
Wikipedia is a credible source of information about the media, and a whole lot else.

***Wired* magazine: www.wired.com**
Wired is an influential source of opinion on new media. It touts Marshall McLuhan as its patron saint.

YouTube: www.youtube.com
As the site says, 'Broadcast yourself'.

FURTHER READINGS

Burkell, Jacquelyn. 2010. 'What is "new media," anyway', in Leslie Regan Shade, ed., *Mediascapes: New Patterns in Canadian Communication*, 3rd edn. Toronto: Nelson, 312–25.

Hamilton, Sheryl N. 2010. 'Considering critical communication studies in Canada', in Leslie Regan Shade, ed., *Mediascapes: New Patterns in Canadian Communication*, 3rd edn. Toronto: Nelson, 27–40.

Martin, Michel. 2004. 'Communication and social forms: The development of the telephone, 1876–1920', in Daniel J. Robinson, ed., *Communication History in Canada*. Toronto: Oxford University Press, 66–76.

Winseck, Dwayne. 2004. 'Back to the future: Telecommunications, online information services, and convergence from 1840–1910', in Daniel J. Robinson, ed., *Communication History in Canada*. Toronto: Oxford University Press, 53–65.

❯ STUDY QUESTIONS

1. How does communication technology 'shrink space through time'?

2. What were some of the predecessors to the internet? What characteristics made them predecessors?

3. Define 'communication' and 'mass' as used in this chapter.

4. Explain 'mass communication' and its three parts.

5. What is the fundamental difference between the transportation and social models of communication?

6. Detail several ways media shape our perceptions of the world or construct reality.

7. How do not-for-profit broadcast institutions differ in their basic purpose and mission from private, profit-driven institutions?

8. What is convergence? What are some of its different forms?

CHAPTER 2

Communication: Social and Cultural Forms

The medium is the massage.
— MARSHALL MCLUHAN

Learning Objectives

- To be able to define 'society' and 'culture', and to understand the role of communication in these realms.
- To describe 'the public sphere' and the role of media in its context.
- To learn about the role of the media in political and economic processes.
- To appreciate Canadians Marshall McLuhan and Harold Innis as theorists and to know their ideas regarding media's social influence.
- To learn Innis's notions of space bias and time bias.
- To be able to describe the dynamics of electronic communication and to illustrate how it encompasses oral and literate communication.

OPENING QUESTIONS

- ❯ How do we define 'society' and 'culture' in the study of communication?
- ❯ What is the public role of the media?
- ❯ How have Harold Innis and Marshall McLuhan contributed to communications theory?
- ❯ Do communication media influence social structure?
- ❯ What is 'technological determinism'?

Introduction

This chapter considers the nature of the relationships between communication, society, and culture. After defining key terms, it considers the ways in which communication and communication media are integral elements of the social and cultural fabric, as well as key dimensions of politics, economics, and processes of identity formation. The chapter goes on to consider the idea that the ways in which people communicate shape the society and culture of which they are a part, and how the work of Harold Innis and Marshall McLuhan bears on this behaviour. Oral, written, and electronic media are discussed in this light. The structures of different forms of media are also examined, including prose and poetry literary forms, and broadcast, point-to-point, and network forms of electronic communication.

Society, Culture, and Media

Set at the intersection between people and different social groups, organizations, and institutions, the media are vital elements of both **society** and **culture**. While these terms are often used in the context of media and communication studies, what exactly do they mean? And what is their relationship to media and communication? Spending a little time thinking about this now will ease discussion later in the book. 'Society' is used in two main senses: (1) as a 'general term for the body of institutions and relationships within which a relatively large group of people live' and (2) as an 'abstract term for the conditions in which such relationships are formed' (Williams, 1976: 291). From this perspective, Canadian society is comprised of particular cities and neighbourhoods; municipal, provincial, and federal levels of government; the legal system; educational institutions; transportation systems; the health care system; businesses and corporations; sports teams, not-for-profit and voluntary organizations; religious organizations; and, of course, media. The institutions and organizations that we share connect and bind us together. Within the larger geographic dimensions of the country— and beyond—a complex overlapping weaving of

The Canadian flag and the national anthem provide symbols of Canadian society.

relationships and dependencies provides common bonds. These are the foundations of Canadian society.

'Culture', on the other hand, 'is one of the two or three most complicated words in the English language' (ibid., 87). One study found over 160 definitions circulating in the academic literature. We will do our best to sidestep this quagmire, limiting ourselves to three somewhat overlapping senses of the term.

An early English variant of 'culture' was drawn from an agricultural usage, where it meant 'the tending of something, basically crops or animals' (ibid., 87). This notion of tending or growing or developing was transferred to people so that 'culture' became thought of as developing one's mind; in particular, 'a general process of intellectual, spiritual, and aesthetic development' (ibid., 90). That's the first sense.

The second sense centres on the works and practices that are the focus of this process of development: intellectual and artistic works, such as music, painting, sculpture, and dramatic arts. Traditionally, however, this definition has been limited to classical or fine art forms, such as symphonies, ballet, classic literature, and Shakespeare's plays. These *high* cultural forms are sometimes contrasted against more everyday, and generally popular, forms of music, painting, writing, television programs, etc., which are termed *popular* culture (see Chapter 7). *Folk* culture represents yet another kind or dimension of culture and generally refers to traditional or ethnic practices and arts, such as storytelling, singing, carving, weaving, dance, and traditional costumes. As discussed in Chapters 3 and 4, one of the problems with this classification is that it sometimes carries elitist connotations whereby high culture is seen as superior, more intellectual, and more 'refined' than popular or folk culture.

The third definition has its roots in anthropology and is generally used to indicate a 'particular way of life, whether of a people, a group, or

A television show such as *Degrassi: The Next Generation* is an example of popular culture.

Source: George Pimentel/Getty

humanity in general'. From this perspective culture includes 'knowledge, belief, art, morals, law, custom, and any other capabilities acquired by man as a member of society' (Tylor in Thompson, 1990: 128). Canadian culture is multi-layered. We have a broad set of shared ideas and values regarding what it means to be 'Canadian' such as shared 'official' languages, customs, songs, holidays, laws, etc. We also have regional differences in culture and perspective, such as the distinctive uses of language, customs, songs, etc., in Alberta, Quebec, Newfoundland, and other regions or provinces. Further, we have the elements of cultures that various immigrant groups have brought to this country that make Canada multicultural. This third definition—culture as a way or ways of life—is the one we use in this book.

Media are central to how we come to understand and share in our culture and society. In a large industrial nation such as Canada, the media are woven into the complex social and cultural fabric. For instance sitcoms, like *The Simpsons*, are written to play off our knowledge and understanding of the world. They employ social institutions we recognize and understand, such as the nuclear family, schools, and corporations. The characters represent a range of familiar social stereotypes and cultural values—mischievous kids, dislike for school, greedy and cold-hearted boss. And the humour is created by playing off our knowledge of these ideas. Similarly,

Source: © Baytchev/Dreamstime.com

Ballet is an example of high culture.

Source: Paul Horsley/Getty

The world's largest pysanka in Vegreville, Alberta, is an example of folk culture.

sports, and hockey in particular, are a key element in our culture, and much media content is devoted to them, promoting values familiar to Canadians.

At the same time, because it is largely through media that we come to know our society and culture, concerns about the content of media drive a wide range of policies and support programs for broadcasting, film, newspapers, magazines, music recording, and new media in Canada. The threat is twofold. First is the concern that foreign media will simply eclipse local or national media. Such is the case with Canadian film and television products. As we will see in later chapters, the reasons for this state of affairs have very little to do with 'consumer choice'. Rather, because there is generally more money to be made from screening US films in Canadian theatres, less than 5 per cent of screen time in those theatres is devoted to Canadian film. Similarly, because US sitcoms and television dramas can be purchased from the US for a fraction of their cost of production, the vast majority of this

kind of programming on Canadian television—particularly the private networks—is American, not Canadian.

A second concern is that by consuming foreign media products people come to know more about foreign societies and cultures than about their own. For instance, polls often find that despite the fact most people in our country are proud to be Canadians and think of themselves as quite distinct from Americans, Canadians know more about American history than about Canadian history and more about how the American government and police system work than about their own (Box 2.1). While it is difficult to link this phenomenon entirely to media consumption, it does raise questions about the effects of having Canadian media so heavily dominated by US programs. As key elements of both society and culture, media play a number of other important social roles.

Some Social Roles of Media

A Political Role

Most media theory sees the media as playing a central role in **politics** (see Chapters 3 and 4). And we know media and journalists are vital to Canadian political life (see Chapter 7 and 8). Here, we will consider some of the more general aspects of media political roles.

While politics is sometimes thought of as simply the 'affairs of state', such as voting or specific debates over policy, a broader, more inclusive way of thinking about the term is as 'the process through which people make collective decisions'. This definition includes formal processes of government; but it also includes a much wider range of activities that frame and animate formal government policies and activities, as well as informal discussions of social norms and values. Wide-ranging public discussion often precedes government decisions to regulate in a particular area and can bring pressure on governments to take (or not take) regulatory action. For instance, over the last decade, public discussion and lobbying has resulted in different governments taking quite different positions on gay marriage. Similarly, in 2008, efforts by the Conservative

⠾ BOX 2.1   CANADA: OUR HOME AND NAÏVE LAND

Ipsos Reid/Dominion Institute History Quiz Reveals Canadians Know More about American History than They Do about Canadian History

It appears that Canadians know more about the history and politics of their neighbours to the south than they do about their own country. According to a new poll conducted in the format of a twenty-question quiz by Ipsos Reid on behalf of the Dominion Institute, Canadians have a higher average percentage of correct scores on questions about America (47 per cent) than they do on questions about Canada (42 per cent). The quiz featured ten questions about each country, asking questions ranging from questions about the founding of our two respective nations to the decade that woman's suffrage was granted in both countries. Questions about Canada were paired with similar questions about American history, so that knowledge about the two countries could be compared. The

largest discrepancy in knowledge had to do with heads of state. While three in four Canadians (75 per cent) know that George W. Bush, the president, is the American head of state, only two in ten (21 per cent) know that the Canadian head of state is Queen Elizabeth II. On the other hand, Canadians are much more likely to know the first line of their own national anthem (53 per cent) than the first line of the American anthem (25 per cent). The best-answered Canadian questions dealt with John A. Macdonald being the first prime minister of Canada (61 per cent correct answers) and the year of Confederation being 1867 (61 per cent). Canadians averaged 4.2 correct answers overall on the Canadian questions, and 4.7 correct answers overall on the American questions.

See the poll: www.dominion.ca/CanadaDay.Survey.DominionInstitute.1July08.pdf.
Source: www.dominion.ca/polling.htm.

government to introduce changes to copyright gave rise to more than 92,000 people signing a Facebook page against the move and delaying the legislation. From this perspective, politics is a key element of many aspects of social life. Whenever we are discussing or otherwise are engaged with issues of collective concern with other members of society, be it in a large or small group, or simply with just one other person, we are engaging in politics.

Political activity takes place in the **public sphere** (Habermas, 1989), an abstract place where people are able to discuss and consider matters of common concern and interest. We say 'abstract' because the public sphere is more of an idea than a specific place. In fact, any place where such discussion might take place can be considered part of the larger public sphere—whether coffee shops, auditoriums, public rallies and demonstrations, parks, or via media.

Some media, such as the comment sections of news websites and the editorial pages of newspapers, provide virtual or actual places to debate and discuss political ideas and concerns. For example, at any given time, a number of videos might be found on YouTube that provide different

perspectives on issues of common concern. These are greatly varied and might range from issues concerning the environment, to gender issues such as gay marriage, to media policy and social benefit regulations. Facebook provides a similar, although more interactive, venue for such discussions, and it is common practice for social activists and others to create Facebook pages addressing political issues. And, although controlled by the editors and owners, the editorial pages of newspapers provide a more traditional forum for discussing ideas and concerns about political issues of the day.

Secondly, and perhaps most importantly, media are key elements of the public sphere because of the information they provide about public life. As we have discussed, media are the key vehicle through which we come to know and understand the world. They are the central vehicle for the production and distribution of information about events taking place at different levels of government, of information about world events like wars, oil spills and other environmental disasters, natural disasters, visits of foreign dignitaries, and elections. Indeed, our knowledge of almost all events of public

The website openmedia.ca also maintains a Facebook page. Although it is privately owned, Facebook provides a public venue for the discussion of a wide range of political issues.

concern is, in some way or another, drawn from media sources. Hence, any decisions that we make regarding our larger collective interest are, to some degree, related to media.

In Canada, media owners have a long history of using their products to influence political discussion and action. An early English-Canadian example of communication famously used as a political instrument is William Lyon Mackenzie politicizing Upper Canadians through his newspaper, the *Colonial Advocate*, and eventually leading some of them into rebellion in 1837. Pierre Bédard similarly spread his political ideas in *Le Canadien*, the newspaper he helped to establish.

As the leader of the Parti Canadien (later the Parti Patriote), Bédard used *Le Canadien* as a nationalist party organ to oppose the Château Clique, the ruling elite group of Lower Canada. Even earlier, in 1778, through *La Gazette littéraire* (precursor to *La Gazette de Montréal* [1785]), Fleury Mesplet, a colleague of Benjamin Franklin, spread the ideals of the American Revolution in French Canada. Many contemporary media owners have admitted to controlling the range of perspectives available in their newspapers and other publications. When questioned about this, they have defended their actions by arguing that control of editorial perspective is a privilege of ownership.

⁑ BOX 2.2   THE 'TWO-STEP FLOW' OF COMMUNICATION

In a classic study in the 1950s, Elihi Katz and Paul Lazarsfield argued that the information from the mass media is transmitted or channelled to the larger population by 'opinon leaders'—that is, people with better access to the media and greater understanding of the news and topics covered there than most people have. Such people are then seen to be central in the larger diffusion or spread of ideas found in the media.

Two-step flow model

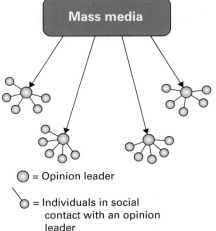

◯ = Opinion leader

◯ = Individuals in social
contact with an opinion
leader

Katz and Lazarsfeld's two-step flow theory of mass communication.
Source: Katz & Lazarsfeld, 1955

Governments, too, strive to control media coverage and thereby public opinion. For instance, government officials commonly refuse interviews and try to withhold information on controversial topics. Stephen Harper's Conservative government is well known for trying to control public opinion in this manner. When governments become dissatisfied with normal media coverage, they create media events to orchestrate the release of significant information, or they advertise in order to speak directly to the public. As well, in Quebec, *Le Devoir* is a staunch supporter of Quebec independence whereas the Desmarais family's *La Presse* supports the federalist option and the federal Liberal Party, in particular.

In general, the political role of communication is constrained on one side by a concern with **freedom of information** and on the other by a concern for **privacy**. Governments collect vast amounts of information through surveys, censuses, satellites, and mandatory reporting mechanisms such as income tax statements. Public access to some of that information, such as census data, is important because it is used by a great many organizations to plan and advocate for everything from social services to recreational programs to transit. Still, despite large public outcry, in 2010 Stephen Harper's Conservative government cut the long-form element of the Canadian census—some say to make it more difficult to gauge the impact of changing government policies. Such information is the lifeblood of informed public discussion. Similarly, access to government information is important for journalists and others working to monitor government actions. Other parties, such as businesses trying to sell products, also wish to have access; debates arise over exactly who should have access to such information.

Post-9/11, the US government, with very little resistance from its freedom-loving citizens, has put in place vast schemes, led by The Patriot Act, for the invasion of privacy of both US citizens and those who have any dealings with the US. Critics warn that such unbridled government access to information could lead to unwarranted charges of wrongdoing and the suspension of civil rights on the part of government and its agencies. On the other hand, websites like Wikileaks.com provide a controversial vehicle for government or industry insiders to leak or to release secret information to the press. Such information might expose government or industry wrongdoing or reveal activities or information that is kept secret for reasons of national security. Whether or not such information should be kept secret, particularly if it is information held by government, is a source of intense controversy.

In short, media are central to the political landscape and vital to the public sphere.

An Economic Role

Media play an important economic role in our society and culture. Not only are they important industries in their own right, they are also key elements of our consumer culture, a growing information economy, and, according to some, an information society.

Traditional media such as radio and television stations, newspapers, and related telecommunications companies are big business. For instance, there are over 750 community newspapers and 100 daily newspapers in this country, and daily newspapers posted $3.5 billion in revenue in 2009. There are over 1100 radio stations in Canada and 505 television channels. The Canadian broadcasting industry alone posted $14 billion in revenues in 2008. Combined, the telecommunications and broadcasting industries reported $54.3 billion. If one adds new media, such as computer, software, satellite, and video game companies, together these media and media-related organizations employ hundreds of thousands of Canadians.

Media are also central to the larger economy in a number of ways. As the major purveyor of advertising, they are the primary way that people are acquainted and connected with the myriad products they purchase. They are the central vehicles through which our consumer lifestyle is symbolically negotiated. Media are also central means for businesses to find employees and, through business radio and television programs, business-related articles in newspapers, magazines, websites, and other publications, they are one of the key vehicles through which people can contemplate and monitor their investments in companies. Companies also conduct public information and public relations campaigns through media, raising their profile and attempting to promote positive public images.

Media generally also promote the larger interests of consumer culture. Many programs and articles are addressed directly to consumers, comparing or trumpeting the benefits of particular products. Similarly, much of the news is related to consumer issues, such as the price of gas and other commodities, or the effects of particular events on the economy. Other programs also valorize or aggrandize the benefits of consumer culture, illustrating the lavish lifestyles of the rich and famous and teasing the general public with luxuries to aspire to.

Perhaps most importantly, media and communication industries are one of the fastest growing sectors of the economy. For many the recent rapid growth in information and communication technology (ICT) has signalled the rise of an **information society**, where the production, distribution, and consumption of information is the main driver of the economy. This development goes hand in hand with **globalization** and the de-industrialization of the traditional industrialized countries of the northern hemisphere, such as the United States, Canada, England, and the countries of Western Europe. From this perspective, media and information industries have not only been pivotal for facilitating the transfer of manufacturing industries to places such as China, India, and a number of other countries, but they are also essential to creating new economic activity in the old industrialized countries. Over the last 15–20 years, various federal governments and their agencies have invested considerable time and resources in attempting to better understand the role of ICTs in the economy and to develop policies that ensure Canada doesn't get left behind or become disadvantaged in this shifting information environment. Recent efforts in this direction include strengthening copyright legislation, establishing a fund to promote the development of new media content, and developing a policy to promote the growth of digital and broadband communication applications, products, and infrastructure—in short, the basis of an expanded Canadian information economy.

For all these reasons, media and ICTs are sometimes referred to as the shock troops of global **capitalism** (Box 2.3). Both directly and indirectly, they spread, advertise, and promote the benefits of capitalist society in newly industrializing countries in terms that seem to promise steady jobs and income, an endless supply and wide array of products, and the opportunity to live a rich and comfortable life.

⫶ BOX 2.3   WHAT IS CAPITALISM?

Capitalism is an economic system, that is, a system for the production, distribution, and consumption of goods and services. As Jim Stanford (2008: 34–5) points out in his book *Economics for Everyone*, 'two key features...make an economy capitalist':

1. Most production of goods and services is undertaken by privately owned companies, which produce and sell their output in the hopes of making a profit. This is called PRODUCTION FOR PROFIT.
2. Most work in the economy is performed by people who do not own their company or their output, but are hired by someone else to work in turn for a money wage or salary. This is called WAGE LABOUR....

Any economy driven by these two features—production for profit and wage labour—tends to replicate the following patterns, over and over again:

- Fierce competition between private companies over markets and profit.
- *Innovation*, as companies constantly experiment with new technologies, new products, and new forms of organization—in order to succeed in that competition.
- An inherent tendency to *growth*, resulting from the desire of each individual company to make more profit.
- Deep *inequality* (especially) between those who own successful companies and the rest of society who do not own companies.
- A general *conflict* of interest between those who work for wages, and the employers who hire them.
- Economic cycles or 'roller coasters', with periods of strong growth followed by periods of stagnation or depression; sometimes these cycles even produce dramatic economic and social crises.

Some of these patterns and outcomes are positive and help to explain why capitalism has been so successful. But some of these patterns and outcomes are negative, and explain why capitalism tends to be economically—and sometimes politically—unstable. In part, capitalism has its origins in the enclosure movement in rural England in the sixteenth century, when peasants lost their direct access to the land—the means of production—and instead had to exchange their labour for wages (Wood, 2002). Capitalism subsequently spread throughout Europe in the seventeenth and eighteenth centuries. In pre-capitalist societies, most people worked for themselves, one way or another, and had direct access to the means of production (e.g., farmland). Where people worked for someone else, that relationship was based on something other than monetary payment (e.g., a sense of obligation or the power of brute force). And most production occurred to meet some direct need or desire (for an individual, a community, or a government), not to generate a money profit.

One of the key effects of private ownership of media is that profit is the primary goal of such organizations. Without a profit, the company will go out of business. Hence, much of the organization and its products are oriented towards this goal. As we shall see, this has powerful effects on the range and kinds of information found in the media, as well as how that information is presented.

An Individual Role: Media and Identity

Understanding one's place in society—who one is, along with likes, dislikes, desires, fears, loyalties—can be thought of as aspects of identity. Identity may be innate and genetic, wrapped up in the physical features of our being; but in other ways it is a learned process, the product of our personal history, experience, and interactions with other people and institutions in the world. One might say that most (some would say all) of our identities are constructed through these social interactions, as we learn about the world and work to fit ourselves into it. In other words, much of our identity is socially constructed, as we negotiate and interact with social and cultural processes and institutions. Elements in this process include religion, family, work, social class, education, gender, race, and ethnicity.

Socially, people have particular roles—as adults, children, fathers, mothers, etc. Culturally, we see ourselves as having particular traits in terms of race, ethnicity, habits, and customs. Politically, we are citizens and members of the public. Economically, we are workers and consumers. As one of the principal vehicles through which we come to know and understand the world, media—particularly mass media—play a large role in identity formation. As audience members, we are exposed to ideas, perspectives, and ways of thinking about and understanding the world. Via news, films, music, cartoons, nature programs, and many other forms, media provide an environment in which to explore the world and our relationships to it. Through media, we enlarge our understanding of our place in the world. We can take political positions; develop a sense of national pride and patriotism; explore gender issues; develop ideas and interests around sexuality; take a position on the environment. Any number of our understandings of the world and our place(s) within it may be negotiated and/or enhanced through the media.

Consumer culture underwent a dramatic expansion through the twentieth century (Chapter 3). Media were in the forefront of spreading and developing that culture. Today it seems almost natural to satisfy our needs, wants, and desires through the market. As Leiss et al. (2005: 4–5) argue: 'material objects produced for consumption in the marketplace not only satisfy needs, but also serve as markers and communicators for interpersonal distinctions and self expression.' Media generally encourage that view of the world, reflecting consumer culture back to us in myriad ways. Advertising in particular strives to link specific products to how we feed, clothe, entertain ourselves, and make ourselves sexually and socially attractive. It encourages us to literally purchase who we are, or who we want to be. As some writers argue, not only is this an accelerating trend, but it is leading to spiralling psychological crises and increasing social inequality and is accelerating the destruction of the planet (Coulter, 2010; Jhally, 1997). Consequently, understanding the ways in which media encourage us to understand ourselves is an important element in the study of mass media and mass communication.

Media and Social Form

So far, our discussion has generally built on the social mode of communication outlined in Chapter 1 and focused on how media and communications processes and technologies are embedded in a larger social or cultural context. However, there are other ways of thinking about the relationship between forms of communication and society. For instance, two Canadians, Harold Innis and Marshall McLuhan, were the first scholars to bring serious attention to the idea that the ways in which people communicate might actually shape a society and its culture.

Innis (1950) was the first to articulate this perspective. He claimed that oral communication tends to maintain cultural practices through time, while written communication favours the establishment and maintenance of social relations through space, such as empires and power blocs spread over large geographic areas and across many different cultures. He used the Roman Empire as his example. To conquer and then co-ordinate, administer, and police such a vast empire required a written system for recording and communicating messages on a portable medium that could be transported across vast distances. Laws were created, written down accurately, and then transported to the far reaches of the Empire where they were applied. In this way, Roman society spread 'through space'. (As well, this communication system required an educated elite to maintain it and thus led to the emergence of a kind of class-based society.)

Innis argued that each communication medium had a particular bias and, thereby, a particular influence on social structure and culture. Oral communication and early hieroglyphic writing on clay emphasized a rather close-knit society and the preservation of outlooks, values, and understanding over long periods of time. In Innis's phrase, they have a **time bias**. Later, written communication using the phonetic alphabet on papyrus and paper emphasized basic social control (the rule of Roman law) across space (the entirety of the Empire). This latter medium displays what Innis calls a **space bias**. Such biases of the dominant media a society uses shape the characteristics of that society. As he states (Innis, 1951: 33):

A medium of communication has an important influence on the dissemination of knowledge over space and over time and it becomes necessary to study its characteristics in order to appraise its influence in its cultural setting. According to its characteristics it may be better suited to the dissemination of knowledge over time than over space, particularly if the medium is heavy and durable and not suited to transportation, or to the dissemination of knowledge over space than over time, particularly if the medium is light and easily transported. The relative emphasis on time or space will imply a bias of significance to the culture in which it is imbedded.

McLuhan, a scholar of English literature, took up Innis's ideas and extended them to the modern period. McLuhan first studied the impact of printing, capturing its influence on society by coining the term 'typographical man', which referred to humanity after the invention of printing with movable type (in the West) by Johann Gutenberg in 1454. The printed book was a tremendously powerful means of communicating ideas and knowledge in early modern Europe, and McLuhan and others have argued that the printed book transformed Western societies so that working with this technology encouraged particular ways of thinking, namely, logical, linear thought, as well as individualism, conceptuality, science, and monotheism (McLuhan, 1962). Interestingly, David Ze (1995) and others have argued that printing with movable type had no parallel effect in Korea and China, where it had been invented several hundred years earlier than in Europe.

Next, McLuhan turned to an analysis of electronic society—characterized by inventors such as Guglielmo Marconi (radio transmission) and Canadians Reginald Fessenden (radio transmission) and Alexander Graham Bell (telephone)—and revealed its dynamics to a skeptical world. He was the first analyst of the impact of the new media of communication (radio, TV, photography, film) on what we think of as modern societies, although certain British modernists, such as Wyndham Lewis, preceded him and had a paral-

lel concern (Tiessen, 1993). McLuhan expressed his ideas in a distinctive, aphoristic way, referring to them as **probes.** And while many scholars dismissed them, his ideas had a great impact in the 1960s in North America and Europe, spreading to politics, the advertising world, even the media. McLuhan's observations made the media and their influence an important issue. In somewhat the way that Sigmund Freud identified the subconscious as an unknown force affecting our behaviour and that Albert Einstein posited interactions at the level of atoms that were awesomely powerful, so McLuhan told us that the media were transforming society before our very eyes though we couldn't observe it—until his theory revealed it. As the quintessentially sophisticated US journalist of the period, Tom Wolfe, wondered, 'What if he's right?'

McLuhan argued that the electronic media created, for the very first time in history, the possibility of instant communication between any two points on the globe: he referred to this reality as the **global village.** He referred to electronic communication as an 'outered nervous system,' and saw such media as extending our senses of sight, touch, vision, and hearing. Although now—in the age of the internet, the World Wide Web, remote sensing, and virtual reality—we can understand the significance of instant worldwide communication in these terms, in the 1960s, when hardly a single computer existed and not a single non-military communications satellite flew above us, McLuhan's writing was greeted skeptically, although it has proven to be somewhat prescient.

Like print, electronic media are claimed to have powerful transforming effects on our understanding of the character of time and space. While 100 years ago most people only had vague ideas of distant places and events, today it is increasingly difficult not to have some knowledge of what is happening elsewhere in the world. Global television, a global telephone and telecommunications network, and the internet bring far places on the globe to us. When hundreds of millions of people scattered all over the world have simultaneous access to an event or when some television series are watched in dozens of different countries, it is clear that electronic media contribute to the formation of a global culture, underpinned by global capitalism. Similarly, when a handful people around the world who share a common interest or expertise can be in daily email contact, or when people can access a website with no thought whatsoever of location, a new globalism can emerge.

Both Innis (1950) and McLuhan (1962), as well as the **Toronto School** that followed in their wake (De Kerkhove, 1995; Ong, 1982; Goody, 1977), placed their emphasis on the ways in which particular forms of media influenced the structure and development of societies. To better understand these ideas, it is useful to explore the dynamics of oral, literate, and electronic societies in some detail.

Oral Society

Innis claims that the means of communication set the basic parameters for the functioning of any society. In an oral society, knowledge is invested in the community and preserved by certain members of society—rather than in books, libraries, and other institutions such as schools and universities. For instance, knowledge regarding medical treatment, how to build houses, where to fish, when to grow food, and how to do other activities for the maintenance and well-being of the community is held by particular individuals or family groupings. Similarly, the group's history and knowledge of the past—such as how they came to be in a particular place, patterns in weather, flooding, and other natural rhythms—as well as any other particularities of the time and space the community occupies, are held and shared by members of the community. As a result, the community is heavily dependent on each of its members for its well-being. Creating and storing knowledge in this way necessarily creates close-knit, interdependent communities—communities that must stick together through time to ensure their continued existence and prosperity. In other words, dependence on an oral tradition or oral culture has a time bias that predisposes the community to stay together and maintain communication throughout time. Interruptions

to close-knit ties can mean a loss of important knowledge for the community and can threaten its long-term existence.

In classical Greece, knowledge was maintained and transmitted through epic poems and what Innis (1951) called epic technique. Epic technique involved creating poems in rhythmic, six-beat lines—hexameters—that had certain rigidities and elasticities. The rigidities were the memorized parts. The elasticities were parts that permitted adaptation of certain elements according to time and place. Structural forms, words, stock expressions, and phrases acted as aids to memory, while the local language and situation provided the basis for ornamental gloss. The development of such techniques ensured that epic poetry would be undertaken by persons with excellent memories and poetic and linguistic abilities. The techniques for memorizing and reciting epics were often passed on within families of professional storytellers and minstrels. According to Innis, such families probably built up a system of 'mnemonic' or memory aids that were private and carefully guarded. Catholic priest and linguist Walter Ong (1982: 34) describes the oral process, thus:

> You have to do your thinking in mnemonic patterns, shaped for ready oral recurrence. Your thought must come into being in heavily rhythmic balanced patterns, in repetitions or antitheses, in alliterations and assonances, in epithetic and other formulary expression, in standard thematic settings, in proverbs, or in other mnemonic form. Mnemonic needs determine even syntax.

The epics permitted constant adaptation, as required by the oral tradition, and also allowed for the emergence of completely new content to describe conditions of social change. What was socially relevant was remembered, what was not was forgotten. As well, flexibility permitted the incorporation of sacred myths from other civilizations, with transformation and humanization conferred as they were turned into the epic poem. The Greeks could thereby foster the development of an inclusive ideology as they expanded their empire, and this ideology served colonizing efforts extremely well.

Oral history has been shown to be quite accurate. For instance, according to Maori oral history, New Zealand was settled by their Polynesian ancestors about 800 years ago, when eight to ten canoes of settlers set out one December from Eastern Polynesia to establish themselves in New Zealand. Recent genetic research confirms the oral history. Tracing changes in mitochondrial DNA, a genetic researcher has found that, in all likelihood, New Zealand indeed was settled by about 70 women (mitochondrial DNA is passed from mother to daughter) and their men approximately 800 years ago. Since the large canoes of the Polynesians carried about 20 people and there would have been approximately 150 settlers (not counting children) it appears they would have needed about eight to ten canoes (see *The Globe and Mail*, 5 Sept. 1998) for their voyage.

The dynamics of the oral tradition in a contemporary Canadian context are illustrated in the Delgamuukw decision, a landmark ruling of the Supreme Court of Canada in which Aboriginal oral history has been accepted as a legally valid foundation for pursuing land claims. While such a decision may seem only right and proper, it has taken centuries for our literate culture to accept the veracity and authority of oral culture. In part, that acceptance has come about because of our relatively recent understanding of oral communication and oral culture (e.g., *The Globe and Mail*, 15 Dec. 1997, A23).

The near destruction of the oral tradition among First Nations peoples in Canada was one of the tragedies of the residential schools. Through the early part of the twentieth century, the federal government and religious organizations worked together, particularly in the western provinces, to remove First Nations children from their families and place them in boarding schools for their education. The effect of this move was to severely undermine the social structure of these cultures, which, to a large extent, depended on oral communication for passing on traditional knowledge and cultural

understandings from one generation to the next. Removing the children from these communities broke the chain of learning and, as a result, knowledge of traditional languages and other cultural elements was severely weakened.

Providing a sense of the difference between oral and literate societies, anthropologist A.B. Lord explored the dynamics of a modern oral tradition in rural Yugoslavia, 1937–59, in *The Singer of Tales* (1964). Lord notes that, for the oral bard, the recording of the words of a song is a totally foreign experience. It preserves a particular performance at a particular time in a particular setting, in a dead, utterly useless form. It does not represent the correct or best version because there is no correct or best version. Rather like The Grateful Dead and Phish concerts, each performance is unique in itself. The antithesis of the oral, adaptive tradition is exemplified in the Canadian pianist Glenn Gould's 'literate' perspective. He believed a perfect performance, especially of the work of a composer such as Bach, could be created in the recording studio by splicing the best bits from many different performances (Payzant, 1984). He considered the concert stage as interfering with musical perfection. Communications theorist Simon Frith (1988) carries the literate perspective one step further. He notes that whereas the record used to be a reminder of a performance, today the live performance—complete with taped inputs and pre-programmed amplifier settings—is a simulacrum of the record.

The capacity of the oral tradition to preserve the past, to transform that past as necessary, to base law in custom, and to explain all events within a natural cosmology points to the stability of oral societies and their tendency to preserve, extend, and adapt culture. Rather than being concerned with the continued existence of specific formal structures and institutions, oral societies are most successful at extending the dynamics of interpersonal relations. Consequently, change in such societies often induces an adaptation that preserves ways of acting, but in new circumstances.

The ways in which oral societies preserve knowledge and cultural integrity are fundamentally different from those of literate society.

⁖ BOX 2.4   TIME BIAS

Societies have both history and geography—or, as Harold Innis would say, societies occupy both time and space. One way societies occupy time and space is through their communications media, which, Innis argued, have characteristic biases that make some media more conducive to carrying messages through time—e.g., heavy, durable materials like clay or the brick walls of buildings—and some media are more conducive to carrying messages through space—e.g., light, easily transportable materials like parchment or paper. Time-biased media are time-binding media, in that they connect us to the past through their enduring images and messages. Think of the stained-glass windows in churches that relate Biblical tales, war memorials that ask us to remember fallen ancestors, or buildings that carry the names of their founders etched in stone or concrete. Historical murals, such as those in Chemainus, British Columbia, or Vankleek Hill, Ontario (see photo), offer residents and visitors a sense of the town's past.

Source: Photograph by Mike Gasher. Reprinted with permission from artists, Elisabeth Skelly and Odile Têtu.

Historical murals, such as this one in Vankleek Hill, Ontario, offer residents and visitors a sense of the town's past.

Where literate cultures emphasize the written 'letter of the law', oral cultures emphasize the meaning underlying the law. In an oral society, the organizing and originating of myths justifies present-day reality rather than reliance on a chronology of historical events.

Today, every community has its oral processes. Music often plays an especially strong catalytic role in the creation of communities. In some countries, forms of music that give voice to the excesses of youth culture, particularly with regard to sex and violence, are banned. In Western countries restrictions against such anti-social music are less formal. Nevertheless, rock-music stations and television broadcast channels do not play certain songs and videos that are expressions of youth culture, although these may be available through record and video stores. Similarly some stores, such as Wal-Mart, refuse to carry CDS with explicitly sexual material or material that they feel undermines 'family' values.

Literate Society

Greece, for Innis, represented an oral society, whereas Rome represented a literate society. It was not that Greece was unaffected by writing. On the contrary, a number of authors, notably Eric Havelock (1976), claim that the basis of the enormous contribution Greek civilization made to modern civilization is to be found in its invention of the phonetic alphabet. Greek history provides a record of the transition from an oral to a literate society, however, and therefore Innis cites Greek sources from the period when writing emerged that express the significance of the change from oral to written modes. For example, in Plato's *Phaedrus,* Socrates reports a conversation between the Egyptian god Thoth, the inventor of letters, and the god Amon. Amon says:

> This discovery of yours will create forget-fulness in the learners' souls, because they will not use their memories; they will trust to the external written characters and not remember of themselves. The specific you have discovered is an aid not to memory, but to reminiscence, and you give your disciples not truth but only the semblance of truth; they will be bearers of many things and will have learned nothing; they will appear to be omniscient and will gener-ally know nothing; they will be tiresome company, having the show of wisdom with-out the reality.

After relaying the conversation, Socrates states:

> I cannot help feeling, Phaedrus, that writ-ing is unfortunately like painting; for the creations of the painter have the attitude of life, and yet if you ask them a question, they preserve a solemn silence, and the same may be said of speeches. You would imagine that they had intelligence, but if you want to know anything and put a question to one of them, the speaker always gives one unvary-ing answer. (Plato, 1973: 84)

This conversation resembles discussions of television, especially those that focus on its numb-ing effect on the mind. This is not surprising, for the transformation from an oral to a literate soci-ety was as major a change as that from a literate to an electronic society. It marked a distinctive shift in the ways in which knowledge was developed, stored, and passed on. The passage also points out the degree to which knowledge and wisdom were negotiated in oral discourse—the product of two or more people grappling with and applying concepts in a particular context—rather than derived from a singular, 'silent', written perspective. One cannot question and reason with a written text in the way one can with a living person.

Rome and the Roman Empire represent the origin of literate society because the operating concepts and processes of Rome were derived from the written rather than the spoken word. In legal proceedings, for example, the influence of writing can be seen in trained lawyers who were responsible for defining the exact nature of a dispute within written laws (a literate function). Nonetheless, once the dispute was defined, the case was handed to laymen (a jury) to determine a settlement among the claimants—an oral community function. The development of contract law illustrates the Romans' ability to supplant oral practices with written ones. A contract changes an oral pact into a legal obliga-tion and permits a much more complex and contin-gent agreement. It is a precise written record of an agreed obligation between persons or other legal entities. Such literate inventions allowed for an orderly and vast expansion of the Roman Empire. As Innis (1950, 1951) points out, writing and the

FIGURE 2.2 The Roman Empire at its Greatest Extent in the Third Century, AD

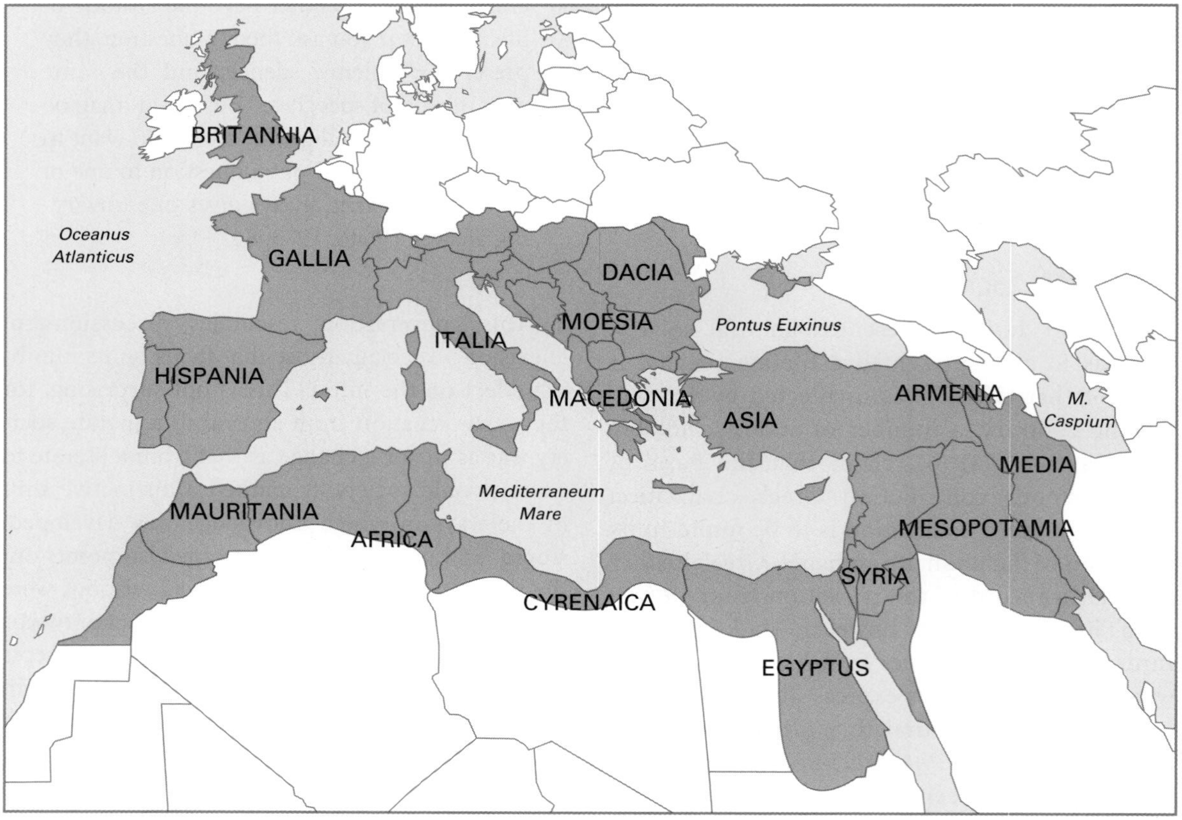

portability of written media gave the Roman Empire a space bias, that is, a tendency to extend itself over a larger and larger territory. At the greatest extent of the Empire, in the third century AD, the Romans maintained control of the lands and people around the entire perimeter of the Mediterranean, from Southern and Central Europe to the Middle East, North Africa, and the Iberian Peninsula, and on to the north and west through present-day France and Great Britain (Figure 2.1). Crucial to the exercise of administrative power in the Roman Empire was the formation of abstract laws to apply uniformly in particular situations, which were then written down on a portable medium, such as parchment, so they could be consulted in any location.

The development of literate society in Western civilization reflected an attempt to replace spoken, poetic, emotive language with clear, ordered, unambiguous, logical, written prose. This, in turn, led to the emergence of new ideas and concepts. For instance, in their writings, Cicero (106–43 BC) and other Stoic philosophers explained ideas that are now fundamental to modern thought, including the notions of a world state, natural law and justice, and universal citizenship, as did libraries, which were scattered throughout the Roman Empire. At the time of the Renaissance in Europe, these ideas became gradually more characteristic of literate societies. Such ideas and institutions were nurtured by writing—a technology for the static representation of ideas, which allows the eye to juxtapose and compare two ideas, and to view many individual instances from which to abstract the general case.

But while print was important in the formation and administration of the Roman Empire, as that empire began to dissolve, print spurred the emergence of the nation states of Europe. The **lingua franca** or primary language of the Roman Empire was Latin but places within the empire had their own languages and vernaculars. As the influence of Rome declined, these languages developed their own written forms and took on an important role in organizing the geography. In his book *Imagined Communities*, Benedict Anderson considers the development of nation states in regard to their languages. He argues that, in conjunction with the development of capitalism and a number of other factors, the creation of 'print languages'—that is, commonly understood

written languages—was essential to the process of developing independent countries because they provided a common medium within which people could develop an 'imagined community'. As Anderson states:

These print languages…created unified fields of exchange and communication below Latin and above the spoken vernaculars. Speakers of the huge variety of Frenches, Englishes, or Spanishes, who might find it difficult or even impossible to understand one another in conversation, became capable of comprehending one another via print and paper. In the process, they gradually became aware of the hundreds of thousands,

BOX 2.5 TV AS CULTURAL ANIMATEUR

The following historical anecdotes, based on a set of columns by John Doyle, *The Globe and Mail* newspaper's television critic, are meant to underline that just like newspapers and books, television is an important medium that signals key events and brings valuable information and perspectives to members of society. Some of those events were:

May 1939: RCA broadcasts the first live sports event, a baseball game. The broadcast laid the foundation of sports television and the new sports economy.

Fall 1951: *I Love Lucy* establishes a whole new pop culture comedy genre.

March 1954: Television cameras capture the bullying of Sen. Joseph McCarthy with contemptuous narration by Edward R. Murrow, thereby hastening an end to the Senator's witch-hunting career.

Fall 1960: Television watchers are convinced that John F. Kennedy wins his television debate against Richard Nixon. Radio listeners are of the opposite opinion. The television image assumes a key position in political campaigning.

May 1961: In the US, the chairman of the Federal Communications Commission—similar to Canada's CRTC—declares television a 'vast wasteland'.

Fall 1966: *W-Five* is launched by CTV as a detective-style public affairs show exposing corruption in politics and business.

July 1969: First person walks on the moon and the event is linked to earth by live broadcast.

November 1969: *Sesame Street* is created and is enormously popular for its role in helping children to learn.

September 1972: Paul Henderson scores the TV-captured winning goal in the Canada–Russia Summit Series of hockey.

June 1985: The rock concert Live Aid links two concerts in London and Philadelphia and raises millions for famine relief in Africa.

Fall 1996: CBC airs *The Newsroom*, created by Winnipegger Ken Finkleman, which satirizes the network. Finkleman becomes a television auteur.

11 September 2001: The destruction of the twin towers of the World Trade Center in New York on television marks a radical shift in how social freedoms are perceived.

December 2004: Television coverage of the Indian Ocean tsunami helped generate an unprecedented outpouring of $7 billion in humanitarian aid from individuals.

Summer 2010: World Cup Television coverage in over 200 countries generated a global cultural event.

even millions, of people in their particular language-field…. These fellow-readers, to whom they were connected through print, formed, in their secular, particular, visible invisibility, the embryo of the nationally imagined community.

Most other writings about literate societies focus on modern societies. While they discuss the influence of writing they do so within a context of an evolved technology and developed social, political, and legal institutions (e.g., McLuhan, 1962; Goody, 1977; Olson, 1980).

The basic claim of these authors is that writing has favoured the development of a particular way of understanding the world, a logical, linear, sequential, and conceptual thinking. Written discourse is logical because it is presented in such a way that anyone can understand the meaning of a written passage without the benefit of knowing the context within which the passage was written and without the possibility of further reference to the author.

⠸ BOX 2.6   SPACE BIAS

The notion of space bias does not come easily to some, perhaps because the word 'bias' most commonly has negative connotations. Innis used the word to mean tendency or emphasis. The following footprint diagram illustrates the space bias of satellite technology. By beaming down a signal to a particular area of the earth's surface, a satellite creates, at least to some degree, a community—a community of all those receiving the same signal. Of course, people choose whether to watch and which channel to watch, and different **satellite footprints** can carry the same content. However, the broadcast of a news program from a particular city to widespread geographic areas creates an artificial spatial extension of that city. For instance, in some ways CNN and the BBC are extensions of Atlanta, Georgia, and London, England, just as the print medium *The Globe and Mail* is an extension of Toronto. These are all instances of space bias.

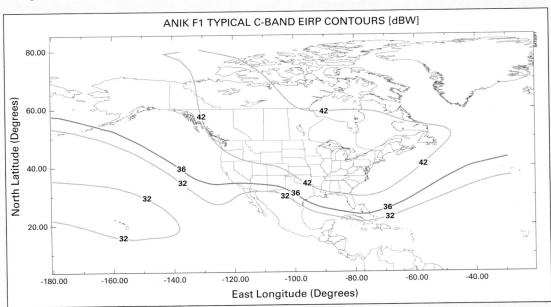

Telesat Canada's Anik F1 satellite creates a primary spatial community encompassing virtually all of Canada and much of the US. As the map shows, weather signals extend that community to the rest of Canada and the US.
Source: Footprint courtesy of Telesat Canada

It can stand by itself as a statement that is consistent both internally and with reference to other common knowledge. Literate thought is conceptual because it encourages the abstraction of salient variables within a framework of analysis and can present both the specific and general. Literate thought is linear and sequential because only one idea can be presented at a time, followed by another, and then another, each building on its predecessor. This restriction of writing contrasts with what can be done with some electronic media, such as television, where a picture can provide context while a spoken text presents other aspects of meaning in a message. Written media also contrast with the resources available to a speaker, who can communicate, through facial expression, demeanour, gesture, and appearance, certain aspects of a message while communicating other aspects of thought in words.

Electronic Society

While electronic communication is now heavily entrenched in our daily lives, in the early 1960s, when Marshall McLuhan introduced his notion of electronic society, it seemed both audacious and trivial to claim that somehow television, telephones, radio, and telex (the technologies that predominated in this period) were going to be as influential as writing, print, and literacy had been. In trying to understand the early impacts of electronic communication on society, McLuhan introduced the idea of the global village. By that he meant that electronic society has vast information-gathering and transmission capacities sufficient to make us intimately (perhaps too intimately) aware to some extent of the goings-on of people around the world. Though our electronic or virtual linkages with the whole world are always incomplete in the physical sense, they are becoming steadily more inclusive as technology and communications organizations and professionals extend their reach into our lives, thereby transforming our local and global environments. Various writers posit that such transformations are taking place at a number of different social and cultural levels.

A considerable literature argues that electronic forms of communication are bringing about the 'end of geography'. Until a short time ago, place and space were inseparable, but communications technologies, such as the telephone, email, and the internet, now allow two people in distant physical places to share the same communicative space and create a social linkage. Mosco (1998) summarizes this point of view:

> In the nineteenth century, spatial barriers meant that news took weeks by packet boat to get from New York to New Orleans. Now, distance is by and large insignificant and, particularly with the arrival of global mobile satellite systems, which will permit seamless wireless communication between any points on the globe, soon to be completely irrelevant.

The truth of what Mosco suggests is brought home by the fact that the most noted American victory of the War of 1812 occurred after the conflict was 'over'. The Battle of New Orleans, on 8 January 1815, when American troops led by Andrew Jackson routed the British, with several hundred men killed and over a thousand wounded, took place more than two weeks after the Treaty of Ghent ending the war had been signed—but the combatants had not yet heard the news! Of course, as Mosco goes on to point out, while many contemporary writers and analysts are keen to trumpet this 'triumph of technology over place', the reach of the virtual world extends only so far.

From the publication of McLuhan's *Understanding Media* (1964) to the 1990s, discussions of the relationships between electronic media and society were focused on television because television was the dominant new medium of the period. Joshua Meyrowitz (1985), for instance, has argued that electronic media, above all TV, weakened the once strong divisions between children and adults, as well as eroded gender differences. Drawing heavily on the perspectives of McLuhan and Canadian sociologist Erving Goffman (1959), he claims that by exposing the 'secrets' of the different social worlds inhabited by children and adults, or men and women, television affects the character of social relationships and breaks down the barriers between them. For instance, television undermines the innocence of childhood through allowing children a broader picture of goings on in the world, as well as blurs the differences between them and adults by giving them access to information about adult issues. In terms of gender, television programs offer everyone insight into what were separate male and female cultures. From this perspective, electronic media's influence on social roles is not simply confined to industrial societies. For instance, in India the social organization of domestic space in the household tended to keep men, women, and children apart for much of the time, thereby maintaining their distinct and traditional social roles and identities. But the arrival of TVs in the households of rural India has considerably disturbed traditional relations between the sexes and between young and old by breaking segregation barriers in the family (Malik, 1989).

Some analysts observe that television has shifted everyone into particular social modes of interaction and presentation. For instance, British theatre critic Martin Eslin (1980) has argued that, with the advent of television, dramatization has become the predominant form of argumentation and presentation of 'facts'. The drama of spectacle has replaced reasoned analysis. Information is not collected, pondered, and transformed into televised information; rather, events may or may not be staged outside the ken of the viewer, and TV crews select short clips that they

perceive as conforming to the 'logic' of the medium, which is essentially dramatic. Televisually, the idea of newsworthiness shifts away from what may be logically or politically interesting to the visually fascinating or dramatically arresting. Indeed, this transformation was evidently the case in the Iraq War of 2003, where television reporters who were 'embedded' with American and British troops were constrained from having much communication with the people affected by the invasion and thus often presented only a narrow, highly selective view of a broad and politically complex crisis.

In such an atmosphere, those who can create good television are those who become newsworthy. Greenpeace (Dale, 1996), for instance, became very good at playing the logic of television through the 1980s and 1990s so that now they usually are able to secure good media coverage for the issues they embrace. As Pagé (2004: 13) points out:

The objective is to obtain as much coverage as possible through the media in order to mobilize public opinion on certain issues. Greenpeace has mastered the art of using images, as for example in 2001 when two activists climbed the CN Tower in Toronto and unrolled a giant banner proclaiming: Canada and Bush, Climate Killers. Greenpeace

⠿ BOX 2.7   TV AS RELIGION?

In the 1980s Moses Znaimer, one of the founders of City TV and MuchMusic, created this list of what he saw as the ten central principles or features of television technology.

Moses Znaimer's Ten Commandments of television are:

1. Television is the triumph of the image over the printed word.
2. Print created illiteracy. TV is democratic. Everybody gets it.
3. The true nature of television is flow, not show; process, not conclusion.
4. As worldwide television expands, the demand for local programming increases.
5. The best TV tells me what happened to me, today.
6. TV is as much about the people bringing you the story as the story itself.
7. In the past, TV's chief operating skill was political. In the future it will be, it will have to be, mastery of the craft itself.
8. TV creates immediate consensus, subject to immediate change.
9. There was never a mass audience, except by compulsion.
10. Television is not a problem to be managed, but an instrument to be played.

Source: Anderson et al. (1996: 14).

used such high profile actions during the Bonn meeting on climate change when the US decided not to participate in the Kyoto protocol and at a time when the organization thought Canada would follow suit. Without a Greenpeace action, the media would probably not have pointed out that the United States and Canada were the two main forces working against co-operation. The action forced the Canadian government to take a public position.

Large corporations and politicians pay particular attention to this televisual logic, carefully staging public announcements and other media events whenever possible.

A similar feature of television that has affected our electronic society can be captured in the following, recast phrase: *the camera never tells the whole truth*. We never know what is going on outside the frame. We rarely know what happened the instant before the camera was turned on or the instant after it was turned off. We rarely know if what was filmed is typical or atypical of a larger picture. And while we do not usually know what has been omitted in any other means of communication, either, we are much more apt to feel with visual communication that we can 'trust our own eyes'. In short, the camera never presents the temporal or spatial frame, but tends to leave us convinced (Box 2.8).

Trust in the visual image has been further undermined with the development of digital technology that allows anyone with a computer and the right software to alter, or even create, images in any number of ways. Thus, the old aphorism 'seeing is believing' is quickly becoming obsolete.

With the development of, and widespread access to, personal computers and the internet, everyone, from communications scholars to government planners and members of the general public, has begun to realize just how profound are the social changes being brought about by electronic communications. The nature of education, commerce, the dynamics of cultures, political systems, and markets are being changed radically by electronic communications. For some, electronic communication is shifting both

BOX 2.8 THE CAMERA NEVER TELLS THE WHOLE TRUTH

In a famous incident from the Gulf War, the media reported on a large crowd toppling a statue of Saddam Hussein as troops moved into Baghdad, spontaneously expressing their joy at being 'liberated' by US forces. Later it was revealed that it was a staged event. American soldiers had orchestrated it and there were only a few dozen people in the square. The video footage was tightly shot, making it look like there were many more people there than actually were.

Source: AP Photo/APTN

One of the photos distributed by mainstream media outlets, this image is closely cropped, making the size of the crowd difficult to determine. To see the long-shot image go to: www.informationclearinghouse.info/article2838.htm.

the dimensions of human perception and the structure of society. Henry Jenkins (2006: 4) argues that electronic media are enabling a new 'collective intelligence'. 'None of us knows everything; each of us knows something; and we can put the pieces together if we pool our resources and combine our skills.' Commonly offered examples of such 'collective intelligence' include Google and Wikipedia. As MIT's Institute for Collective Intelligence puts it, Google 'uses the knowledge millions of people have stored in the World Wide Web to provide remarkably useful answers to users' questions', while Wikipedia 'motivates thousands of volunteers around the world to create the world's largest encyclopedia.' Thus, the research question for the Institute is: 'How can people and computers be connected so that collectively they act more intelligently than any individuals, groups, or computers have ever done before?'

Electronic communication networks are more often considered fundamental elements of social organization these days. For instance, in his influential book *Network Society*, Manuel Castells argues that electronic information networks are shifting the basic structure of society and driving globalization. For Castells, such networks are the new locus of social power, replacing geographic centres such as cities and countries in this regard. On a smaller scale, electronic communication networks are also seen as shifting the ways in which interest groups and social movements operate. Electronic networks allow much more flexibility in the ways such groups are formed and, as writers such as Nick Dyer-Witheford (1999) and Richard Day (2005) argue, a more effective means for social dissent and effecting progressive social change.

The increasing mobility of electronic forms of communication adds yet another dimension to the shifting influence of media technology. According to the CRTC (2009a: 236), while wireless services only reach 20 per cent of Canada, they are within reach of 99 per cent of Canadians. Although penetration rates are low in Canada by international standards, approximately 75 per cent of Canadians subscribe to such services. In the summer of 2010, the fourth generation (4G) of cellphones hit the Canadian market. Only a fraction of the size of the original brick-sized 'portable phones' of the 1970s and '80s, their capabilities go well beyond phone calls. 4G promises real-time voice, data, and high-quality multi-media capabilities any time and anywhere service is available, and 4G devices are cameras, word processors, music and video players, global positioning systems, gaming consoles, and admit myriad other creative applications. New forms of content are being developed that are tailored directly to the mobile nature of these devices, including short films and videos, 'smart' ads that that can hone in on specific demographics and locations, and tracking technologies that can tell you exactly where your friends and loved ones

are. Not only does this technology open up new kinds of things people can accomplish while away from home, it also raises new privacy concerns, particularly issues of surveillance as corporations and governments use it to locate and track what they perceive to be potential customers or criminals. At the same time, it can also work to create and empower what Rheingold (2008, 2003) calls 'smart mobs' involved in social protests or political actions, and citizen journalists reporting on and documenting breaking news.

Today, communication is instantaneous. Therefore, location and distance decrease in importance: space and time have shrunk. Electronic communication can encompass images, sound, text and, perhaps, **virtual reality** technology (Box 2.9). Consequently, the communication device is less restricting in its modes of expression. Because access to electronic media also is generally less restricted, electronic communication is as powerful as, if not more powerful than, traditional print forms of communication. Thus, determining who controls communication is of increased importance. Many are determined to preserve the internet as a place for public discourse, not just as a medium for business, because keeping the channels of communication open and accessible to all people provides more input and control over our public as well as our private lives.

Some Characteristics of Media

Marshall McLuhan used his famous aphorism 'The media is the message' (and later, the play on that aphorism 'The media is the massage') to draw attention to the idea that media themselves, and the effects they have on the human sensorium and, therefore, on the way we understand the world are important subjects of study. Following in the spirit of this dictum, this section provides a brief overview of some of the general characteristics of oral, literate, and electronic forms of communication.

As anthropologist E.T. Hall (1980) has so vividly explained, oral communication incorporates lived cultural patterns—how close we stand to one

⫶ BOX 2.9 OTHER WORLDS

Virtual reality or simulated environments or experience can be traced back to at least the mid-nineteenth century and various forms of photographic display. Electronic media, however, are taking such experience to a new level. From virtual reality games to other worlds of interactions such as Secondlife, virtual experiences and communities are being created in cyberspace. Some of the most recent developments focus on haptic technology, which provides virtual encounters with the sense of touch.

A child plays a virtual reality video game. What type of virtual reality activities do you enjoy?

Source: © istockphoto.com/Leah-Anne Thompson

accomplish anything, from entirely preserving the achieved social relations to disrupting them completely. Investigations in a variety of disciplines, including anthropology (Goody, 1977), communications (McLuhan, 1962, 1964; Innis, 1950, 1951; Ong, 1982), and classics (Havelock, 1976), have also shown that when people engage in conversation, they focus on the intent of the person with whom they are speaking. Oral communication also favours the formation of groups of like-minded people.

Oral chants are the conservative side of oral communication. By means of exact repetition they help affirm the fundamental shared understandings of a community, just as a national anthem does. They utilize voice and body, often adding adornments to the voice—rhythm, music, tone of voice—and adornments to the person, such as items of symbolic significance—masks, stoles, head-coverings, speaking sticks, incense, bells, etc. Such adornments heighten sight, smell, touch, and hearing, as well as the overall perception and conception of the chant. Oral chants encourage affirmation of the group through an emergent sense of the whole being greater than the sum of its parts. The orientation is one of consolidation, of affirming the whole community, and of its constituent members playing out their various established roles.

Literate communication is divided into two forms, the prosaic and the poetic. The prose style used for most writing must have internal consistency and comprehensiveness. It must stand apart from its author as a meaningful statement. Its framework of analysis is rational and linear—moving from one logical point to the next. It cannot be situationally contextualized, for example, by body language and tone of voice, as is a play or other theatrical production. Contextualization must be inherent through modifying words or images. Prosaic literate communication leads to the development of general and specific explanatory concepts. These explanatory concepts have a hierarchical relation to one another and, over the course of time, form an explanatory framework. Such a framework may be, for instance, a scientific theory, as when the behaviour of objects relative

another, how much inflection we put into our words through facial expression and body gesture, how we direct our gaze, and so forth. The radical side of oral communication is conversation: anyone may say anything in any manner and thereby

⸎ BOX 2.10   TWO EXPERIMENTS IN ORAL COMMUNICATION

You can test one of the variables surrounding oral communication. E.T. Hall called it social distance. Pick out a place near to where you are having your conversation and see if you can move the person with whom you are speaking to that spot. You can use one of two methods. One is to stand closer than usual to your fellow conversationalist. The other is to stand slightly further away. Either way, you can usually push or pull them to that spot as long as they are not conscious of your intent.

Ethnomethodologists such as Garfinkel (1984) were intent on demonstrating that conversation—at least in certain social settings—has implicit rules. They would take a behaviour from one social setting and insert it into another, for example, by getting up in the middle of a dinner and warmly greeting the hostess of the dinner as if one were first arriving at a dinner party. The surprised reactions of the other dinner guests confirmed, for Garfinkel, that rules are implicit in such social situations. Notwithstanding such rules, conversation is a form of communication with radical potential. You can try such an ethnomethodological experiment, but to elicit surprise you must not insert a behaviour that others might think justifiably spontaneous. The Quebec-produced, no-dialogue TV program, *Just for Laughs*, is a marvellous documentation of such experiments.

to other objects was defined by several laws until Newton conceived the notion of gravity to explain all such behaviour. Later, after Einstein proposed his general theory of relativity, Newton's notions of gravity were recast as specific instances within Einstein's more encompassing framework.

Written poetry diverges from written prose in the analytical framework it employs. Rather than emphasizing overtly logical and hierarchical language structures, poets create images to evoke emotional and thoughtful responses in the reader and, through those images, provide unusual insight into the real and/or the imaginary. The social philosophy consistent with the poetic mode of writing depends on the images created by the poet. Some poetry encourages elitism through arcane or obscure references and metaphors that resonate with a scholarly or otherwise restricted audience. Other poetry encourages plurality through a multiplicity of images and references that resonate with a wider public. How poets are viewed by their society—as agents of the court, as voices for the people, as noble, as obscure, as inspiring, or as corrupt—constrains their role and the power of their imagistic writing to alter that society.

Electronic modes of communication build on the characteristics of both oral and written forms of communication. These modes are complex and need to be distinguished to be understood.

Electronic communication has three submodes, *broadcast, point-to-point*, and *network* systems. Radio typifies the broadcast mode, telephone typifies point-to-point, and the internet typifies network communication. Broadcast proceeds from one to many, and generally flows one way. Point-to-point is one-to-one and generally flows two-way or interactively. Network can encompass one-to-one, one-to-many, or many-to-many and the flow usually is interactive. These basic characteristics influence the ways in which they can be integrated into social relations and in the types of relationships they can foster.

In general, electronic communication is not closely confined by space but can be confined by time. Sound and images sent over the air can reach many people, depending on the power of the signal and which part of the radio spectrum is used—short-wave signals bounce off the upper atmosphere and can travel more than halfway around the world, especially at night. Television signals travel only 'line-of-sight', which means an uninterrupted line must run between the originating antennae and the receiver. Telecommunication systems, comprised of satellites, microwave relays, wire and fiber optic lines, and various mobile technologies can reach around the world. Unless the signals they carry are recorded, archived, or exist as electronic data, books, or web pages, electronic messages are fleeting, heard or seen in the moment and then lost in the ether.

The cost of producing high-quality televisual products marks the major difference between amateur and professional productions. High production values have imbued media products and celebrities with an aura of legitimacy. Today, however, with the plunging cost of do-it-yourself (DIY) media technologies such as video cameras and the popularity of social network sites like YouTube, the line between professional and amateur media is blurring and traditionally 'amateur' production values—such as grainy pictures and jiggly, hand-held shots—are becoming more mainstream and acceptable to audiences.

A Note on Technological Determinism

Though Innis and McLuhan were among the first to theorize the transformative effects of communication media, one concern with this perspective is that it tends towards **technological determinism**. In other words, it tends to frame technology as the fundamental shaping social variable and society as a mere expression of the dynamics of technology (a phenomenon explored in greater detail in Chapter 6). Neither author was an avowed technological determinist. McLuhan once noted, 'We shape our tools; thereafter our tools shape us.' Thus, McLuhan begins his analysis with **human agency**, not technology. But McLuhan had very little to say about the 'we' in that statement, the nature of human agency. Certainly McLuhan inspired others, notably Elizabeth Eisenstein (1983), to place technology at the centre of explanatory frameworks. They, too, deny that they are technological determinists.

But rather than emphasizing human agency and social interaction, which shape both technology and the uses made of it, such analysts slide into technologically derived descriptions of the social process. They neglect to portray technology as a tool employed by those with power to advance their own interests. However, this critique does not mean that these analyses are not useful or that they don't tell us important things about the ways media and communications impact social action and organization. Rather, it alerts us to the complexities of the social world and reminds us that understanding entails several theoretical and methodological perspectives.

Other viewpoints, such as the social model of communication described in Chapter 1, take a more nuanced approach. (See also Chapters 4 and 5.) Raymond Williams (1974), for example, notes that communications technologies arise from the organization of society and reflect that organization. Working along these lines, David Ze (1995) challenges Elizabeth Eisenstein's (1983) thesis in her book, *The Printing Press as an Agent of Change*. As discussed earlier, he argues that even though the Chinese invented movable type before it was invented in Europe, printing was an agent of social stability rather than of change. His argument is that printing was controlled by Chinese emperors; it was used to transmit official versions of a limited number of texts; printers had everything to lose and nothing to gain in printing original material; and wood blocks were the most efficient means of reproducing texts as demand emerged. He concludes that, by itself, the existence of a technology does not necessarily affect society significantly. However, under the right social conditions, technology can speed and consolidate the evolution of a new social organization.

❯ SUMMARY

This chapter has conveyed the complex relationship between communication, society, and culture and has considered some of the social impacts of media and mass communication. We discovered how two Canadians, Harold Innis and Marshall McLuhan, were the first scholars to draw serious attention to the ways people communicate that might actually shape a society and its culture. In this context, we examined how oral, literate, and the various modes of electronic communication can affect social development, processes, and structures.

The relationships between communication media and social form are the focus of communication studies. Human affairs cannot be divorced from the communication system used to represent or discuss them and the design of our communication systems impinges on every element of our present and future lives. How new forms of electronic communication will work together with larger political, economic, and cultural forces—particularly contemporary capitalism—to reconfigure our society remains to be seen.

❯ KEY TERMS

capitalism, p. 38
culture, p. 32
freedom of information, p. 37
globalization, p. 38
global village, p. 41
human agency, p. 55

information society, p. 38
politics, p. 34
privacy, p. 37
probes, p. 41
public sphere, p. 35
satellite footprint, p. 48

society, p. 32
space bias, p. 40
technological determinism, p. 55
time bias, p. 40
Toronto School, p. 42
virtual reality p. 52

❯ RELATED WEBSITES

Canadian Journal of Communication: www.cjc-online.ca
The Canadian Journal of Communication is Canada's principal communication journal. Students can make good use of it by accessing the site and searching for essay topics. The CJC is a leading proponent of online journal publishing and makes its back issues accessible on the internet.

MIT Center for Collective Intelligence: cci.mit.edu
A centre at the Massachussetts Institute of Technology dedicated to considering how people across the planet might use ICTs to work together in new ways.

Council of Canadians: www.canadians.org
The Council of Canadians involves itself in a wide range of issues where it feels that Canadians have a distinct set of interests.

Harold Innis Research Foundation: www.utoronto.ca/hirf
The Harold Innis Research Foundation at the University of Toronto fosters research and other activities, including a research bulletin that focuses on the theories of Harold Innis. In his honour the University of Toronto named one of its colleges Innis College.

McLuhan Research Centre: www.marshallmcluhanmedia.org
The McLuhan Centre has quite a dynamic website. It runs courses and a web log along with many other McLuhanesque and McLuhan-oriented activities.

Secondlife: secondlife.com
A free 3-D virtual world.

Wikileaks: wikileaks.org
A controversial website that specializes in exposing government secrets.

❯ FURTHER READINGS

Castells, Manuel. 1996. *The Rise of the Network Society*. New York: Blackwell. The first in Castell's trilogy outlining his influential theory of network society.

Coulter, Natalie. 2010. 'Selling youth: Youth media and the marketplace', in Leslie Regan Shade, ed., *Mediascapes*. Toronto: Nelson, 149–64. A pithy discussion of the expansion of mass marketing to 'tweens' in the 1980s.

Eisenstein, Elizabeth. 1983. *The Printing Revolution in Early Modern Europe*. Cambridge: Cambridge University Press. Eisenstein examines the role of the printing press and movable type.

Innis, Harold. 2009. 'From empire and communications', in Daniel Robinson, ed., *Communication in Canadian History*. Toronto: Oxford University Press, 35–9.

McLuhan, Marshall. 1962. *The Gutenberg Galaxy: The Making of Typographic Man*. Toronto: University of Toronto Press. This was the first of McLuhan's two major works. It outlines orality and literacy and their historical development. Its key thesis is that typography created the world as we know it.

———. 1964. *Understanding Media: The Extensions of Man*. Toronto: McGraw-Hill. In this book McLuhan focuses on the influence of the media on the modern world. The various essays that make up the text explore the implications of (largely) electronic information systems. The book is interesting both for its insight and for its foresight.

❯ STUDY QUESTIONS

1. Define 'society' and 'culture' and describe the roles communication plays in the constitution of each of these realms.

2. What is the 'public sphere'? What is the role of media in it?

3. What did Innis mean when he described societies dependent on oral forms of communication as having a 'time bias' and those dependent on written forms as having a 'space bias'?

4. What does Marshall McLuhan mean by the aphorism 'The medium is the message'? Why did he let the misprint 'The medium is the massage' stand in the magazine incorporating his ideas?

5. Explain the reasons for this statement about audiovisual devices: In some sense, electronic audiovisual communication is the re-creation of face-to-face communication in a fully visualized context conceived by the literate mind.

6. How are new electronic media influencing the structure of our society?

7. What is 'technological determinism'? Why is it a concern when we are analyzing the possible social effects of communications technology?

CHAPTER 3

Media: History, Culture, and Politics

> The greatest power of the media
> is the power to ignore.
>
> — SAM SMITH

OPENING QUESTIONS

- What are the contributions to modernity of the Renaissance and the Enlightenment and how do they bear on modern notions of citizenship and democracy?
- How did media originate in our society?
  What are the larger social, political, and economic factors that influence the form and structure of the media?
- How might forms of media ownership impact their content?
- What is the history of media development in Canada?

Learning Objectives

- To understand the political and historical roots of the mass media and the connections between communication and education, citizenship, and democracy.
- To be aware of some of the ideas of the Renaissance and the Enlightenment, to compare differences in those world views, and to describe how they relate to modern concepts of democracy and communication.
- To identify the forms taken by the media in the context of industrial society.
- To recognize who owns and controls the media and to be able to relate some of the possible problems associated with having certain sectors of society participate as media owners.
- To know the history and structure of the Canadian media in relation to Canadian culture and politics.

Introduction

As we have seen, the mass media are far more than sources of information and entertainment. They are considered essential social and cultural institutions. This chapter delves deeper into their roles, examining the historical and current roles of communication and information in Western societies. It considers the developmental context of mass media and several perspectives for examining the roles they play in political life. The distinctive characteristics of the development of the Canadian media, as well as how they reflect and nurture Canadian culture and political values, are studied. The chapter ends with a comment on Canadian cultural concerns in an international context.

Much of Renaissance architecture and design (re-naissance: meaning born again) was taken from Greek and Roman designs.

The European Roots of Media and Western Society

While paper-making and movable type were first developed in Asia, it might be said that the modern mass media began to emerge in mid-fifteenth-century Europe with Johann Gutenberg's development of the printing press in Mainz, Germany, in 1454. This advance in technology is often used to designate the end of the Middle Ages and the beginning of the Renaissance—a transition from a social order where people were subservient to the powerful Church and monarch to a social order more sympathetic to the freedom of individuals and ideas. The **Renaissance** and the movements and conceptual developments that followed it—humanism, the Reformation, the Counter-Reformation, the **Enlightenment**, and finally, the **Industrial Revolution**—paved the way for liberal democratic industrial societies and modern forms of mass media.

A major aspect of the Renaissance was the rediscovery and revival of literature and learning from antiquity, especially the Greek and Roman empires, which had been lost and suppressed during the Middle Ages. This recovered knowledge helped to re-orient social perspectives concerning the place of humankind and nature in the cosmic order. Led by Italian thinkers and artists, the Renaissance was the beginning of a reassertion of

reason and the senses that had characterized classical Greece. Emerging from the Renaissance was humanism, a broad philosophy that celebrated human achievement and capacity. Although often couched in religious contexts, in art, sculpture, and architecture, humanism celebrated the human form and encouraged an empirical understanding of the world. The great works of art and architecture that characterize the period were grounded in human knowledge of mathematics, mechanics, and geometry, an awareness of perspective, and a theory of light and colour. In the practice of this empirical knowledge, humanism emphasized people's abilities to know and understand the world beyond what had been the teachings of the Church.

At this point in European history, the dominant **ideology** (Chapter 4) held that the world was ordered by a Divine hand and that true knowledge of the world came from God or through his emissaries on earth: the Pope and the priests of the Church. Religious and feudal traditions were the principal elements structuring the society. In the feudal system of production, social position and responsibilities were inherited by birth, and royalty and aristocrats held their stations and governed according to a doctrine of Divine Right. By demonstrating the abilities of individuals to understand and shape the world, humanism sowed the seeds of a secularized society within this traditional order.

Source: © Sarah Affleck

FIGURE 3.1 Feudal Society

The Feudal System

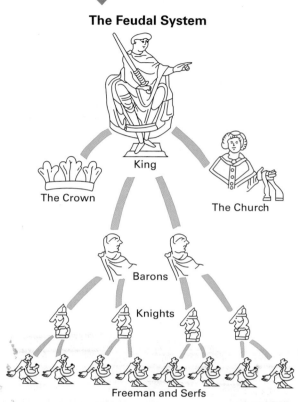

King

The Crown

The Church

Barons

Knights

Freeman and Serfs

Feudal society had a well-defined class structure and social position and responsibilities were inherited by birth.

The dissemination of humanist ideas was facilitated by the technologies of writing and printing, which allowed individuals to develop and record their ideas and communicate them in a manner understandable by many. Printing presses were established throughout Europe over the next centuries and encouraged the spread of literacy. As literacy spread, so, too, did the thirst for ideas. With printing, ideas rejected by the ruling elite in one regime could be exported into others, leading to a destabilization in these states. As American historian Robert Darnton (1982) has demonstrated, a regular business of printing books in Switzerland and smuggling them into France was an important precursor to the French Revolution.

The following passage from the writings of Italian printer Aldus Manutius (1450–1515) gives a

sense of the times and of the significance of early printers in their societies.

Aldus Manutius Basianas Romanus
gives his most devoted greetings to all students

Ever since I started this enterprise seven years ago, I have not had a single quiet hour, this I can swear. Everyone without exception says our discovery is most useful & beautiful, & it is widely praised & admired. To me, however, this striving for perfection & the eagerness to be of service to you, to supply you with the best books, has developed into an instrument of torture. I tell my friends, when they come to see me, two Greek proverbs which most aptly describe my situation. The first is: 'The thrush drops its own misfortune', or, more elegantly, as Plautus expresses it: 'The bird is father to its own death.' For it is said that bird lime (for trapping birds) is produced entirely from bird droppings, especially those of pigeons & thrushes.... The second proverb is: 'We draw ills upon ourselves like Caecias the clouds.' Aristotle tells us that Caecias, the wind, blows in such a way that the clouds are not driven away, as they are in other winds, but rather that he draws & summons them toward himself. This is exactly what happened to me: I have

Gutenberg, the inventor of the movable type printing press, inspects a page produced by his printing press in this nineteenth-century drawing.

begot my own misfortune. I have provided myself with trouble & over burdened myself with great labours. My only consolation is the assurance that my labours are helpful to all, & that the fame & the use of my books increase from day to day, so even the 'book-buriers' are now bringing their books out of their cellars and offering them for sale.

The transposition of Renaissance ideas from Italy to Germany led to a quite different manifestation of the search for knowledge, affirmation of the human spirit, and exploration of ideas. To capture the matter in a few words, the Italian Renaissance overcame what had been an avenging Church (which for centuries had taken vengeance against individuals for actions deemed not in keeping with the Church's preferred rules of living) and established a freedom of intelligence that led to a vibrant culture. The German Reformation followed with a freedom of conscience from institutionalization (the Roman Catholic Church)—arguing that each individual could come to know God directly—and attempted to redefine religion and morality on a more individual basis. The Reformation began in earnest with Martin Luther's nailing of his 95 theses to the castle church door in 1517 in Wittenberg to protest against the selling of indulgences—remissions, granted by the Pope, from temporal punishment for sins confessed and forgiven. Luther's theses, written in Latin, were quickly translated into German, printed, and circulated throughout Germany. Luther also translated the Bible into German. As Elizabeth Eisenstein (1983: 273–4) points out in *The Printing Revolution in Early Modern Europe,*

Intellectual and spiritual life...were profoundly transformed by the multiplication of new tools for duplicating books in fifteenth-century Europe. The communications shift altered the way Western Christians viewed their sacred book and the natural world. It made the word of God appear more multiform and his handiwork more uniform. The printing press laid the basis for both literal fundamentalism and modern science.

By making the Bible more accessible, printing undermined the power of the Catholic Church and its priests to act as intermediaries in delivering religion to the people and led to mounting support for a restructuring or 'reformation' of Church doctrine and to the development of Protestantism.

Both the Reformation and the Renaissance were brought to a close in Europe during the sixteenth and seventeenth centuries by the Counter-Reformation, a **conservative** backlash that re-established monarchical absolutism in Church and state. Its most extreme manifestation was the Spanish Inquisition. During the Counter-Reformation, European states, recognizing the powerful role of ideas, writing, printing, and communication in general, placed severe controls on printing to limit the dissemination of humanistic ideas. Particular printers and writers were branded as heretics and were tortured and executed. Nevertheless, writers and printers persisted. In 1644 in England, writer John Milton penned his anti-censorship essay, *Areopagitica*, advocating the free flow of ideas. His essay was motivated by a 1643 decree that renewed a ban on type founding and maintained the monopoly of Oxford, Cambridge, and London over printing. Only in 1695, with the lapse of the Licensing Act, did printing in England gain its freedom—a freedom later confirmed in the first copyright act, the Statute of Anne, in 1710. Nonetheless, attempts to restrict publishing continued for some time. For instance, freedom to publish in France was granted with the Revolution in 1793 but was lost under Napoleon and not restored until 1870.

The backlash against humanism that characterized the Counter-Reformation did not last, and in the early eighteenth century a new attempt at humanism that combined logic and empiricism introduced the Age of Reason, otherwise known as the Enlightenment. The Enlightenment was distinguished by an intellectual approach based on a scientific and rational perspective on the world, a fundamental shift in world view that championed science over religion and justice over the abuse of power, and a social contract that specified individual rights and freedoms over the absolutist rule of kings and popes.

The writings of Enlightenment philosophers such as John Locke (1632–1704), Voltaire (1694–1778),

The printing process has changed dramatically since this Gutenberg Bible was published, circa 1455.

War of Independence (1775–83), and later, with the French Revolution (1789–99), Europe and North America were gripped in conflict as a new social order took shape. The result was a massive upheaval in European society that laid the ground for yet another change in social structure, the shift from an agrarian to an industrial society—a transformation that, again, was fertilized by communication.

From the invention of the printing press onward, the spread of knowledge based on a humanist understanding of the world laid the foundation for the profound political and social change from feudalism to capitalism, from farming to industry, from medieval to Renaissance and then to an Enlightenment world view. In the realm of politics, the acquisition of such knowledge allowed a new class of citizens to emerge and gain enough education to compete with the aristocracy for the right to govern. Similarly, in culture, talented and knowledgeable creative artists brought forward secular literary, musical, and artistic works that were appreciated by the viewer for their visions and understandings of the world. In this context, knowledge, reason, and information-based institutions became, and have remained, essential to the larger process of government because they inform the public about the important issues of the day and the various solutions proposed by those who wish to govern. (For discussion of what Habermas termed 'the public sphere', see Chapters 2 and 10.)

In summary, the printing press informed citizens on matters both important and trivial. Printers were among the first groups of capitalists—skill-based entrepreneurs who printed news sheets, pamphlets, and books to sell to booksellers and the public. At first, printers busied themselves with the dissemination of ancient knowledge, but as that was assimilated and individualism began to take hold, authorship by contemporary people emerged. The established struggle between those in power and a world view that supported other perspectives and understandings was intensified. A wealth of documentation prior to and including the beginnings of copyright tells us much about the various attempts by those in power to control the output of information by their rivals, especially when it was directed

Jean Jacques Rousseau (1712–88), and Adam Smith (1723–90) worked to undermine the inherited right of kings and the Church to control government. They argued that people possessed natural, inalienable social rights, and they upheld the market over feudal forms of production and exchange. These shifts in social ideas that characterized the Enlightenment were fuelled by an emerging elite competing for power with the aristocracy. This expanding, materialist, prosperous, and educated **bourgeoisie**—or new land-owning class—had been working to build a market economy and colonial trade from about the sixteenth century onwards. Through the eighteenth and early nineteenth centuries, the Enlightenment's legacy of scientific reason combined with the growing wealth of the bourgeoisie to fuel change in social and political structure. First, with the American at the general population. In the main, those who wished to gain power spoke in the name of the bourgeoisie and the manufacturers who required greater freedoms to operate. As they achieved these freedoms, others began to speak in the interests of workers and other social interests. A great cacophony of voices could be heard.

The Industrial Revolution, Communication, and Social Form

Just as the Enlightenment gave rise to new ways of thinking about people's relations to each other and to the world, so the Industrial Revolution introduced a major change in social organization. With the application of growing scientific knowledge to production, industry began to dominate in the late eighteenth century in Western Europe. As landlords moved to turn their lands to commercial agriculture, serfs, tenant farmers, and others dependent on those lands for their livelihoods were forced to migrate, either into the swelling cities and towns where the new 'manufactories' were being built or across the oceans to developing colonies, which increasingly served as sources for raw materials for industrial production. New forms of transportation—such as railways and steamships—provided means for moving people, raw materials, and finished goods, while new forms of communication—such as the telegraph and newspapers—provided vehicles for co-ordinating buyers and sellers, workers and employers, and governments and citizens.

The growth of industry complicated social relationships as urbanization and migration stamped the landscape with the spatial and temporal edifices and rhythms of industrial production. Industrial production demanded the co-ordination of social action across increasing physical distances, as both raw materials for factory processes and foodstuffs for rising populations converged on burgeoning urban centres. Industrial life also redrew the dimensions of family life. The traditional extended family, whereby mother and father, children, grandparents, and aunts and uncles might live in close proximity—even in the same home—gave way to the nuclear family, a more flexible form of social organization that was more easily moved from place to place in pursuit of work opportunities. Industrial production also shifted the temporal dimensions of social life. Work in a rural, agricultural setting is ongoing, requiring a paced way of life in which the work and daily living must adjust to seasonal cycles, structured by the necessary tasks of animal husbandry, raising crops, and sustaining and maintaining the family and the household. Industrial production demanded a different temporal division of the day so that a different distinction arose between work and leisure time.

It was in this context that modern communications media took form. In the face of the changes wrought by the new industrial way of life, the media developed what Raymond Williams has called 'specialized means' to close the geographical and social distances created by industrial production and to serve new social interests and needs. As Williams (1974: 22–3) illustrates, in this context 'the press [developed] for political and economic information; the photograph for community, family and personal life; the motion picture for curiosity and entertainment; [and] telegraphy and telephony for business information and some important personal messages.'

As discussed in Chapter 1, in the context of developing industrial society the telegraph greatly enhanced the co-ordination of people and goods across vast distances. It was a key advance in what Karl Marx described as people's abilities to 'shrink space through time'. It forestalled the necessity of physically sending messages from one place to another and enabled communication literally at the speed of light. Both government and industry could respond much more quickly to developing events, accomplishing so much more in shorter periods of time that it seemed as though space—or the distances between places and things—had actually become smaller. Governments more quickly learned of revolts in far-flung parts of their territories, responded with troops, and thereby secured more readily the supply of resources and markets.

Manufacturers could order raw materials from suppliers a continent away, while orders for goods could be taken from cities and towns scattered across the country. The telephone built upon and enhanced the economic relations created by the telegraph, and although today we think of the telephone as primarily for personal communication, it was, first and foremost, and generally remains, a business tool.

The photograph, on the face of it, was a simple technique for capturing images on light-sensitive glass or paper; but it became a way of constructing family and community socially at a time when traditional kin and friendship ties were being torn apart. As Susan Sontag (1999: 177) points out:

> Photography becomes a rite of family life just when, in the industrializing countries of Europe and America, the very institution of the family starts undergoing radical change. . . . Those ghostly traces, photographs, supply the token presence of dispersed relatives. A family's photograph album is generally about the extended family—and often it is all that remains of it.

With the rise of large commercial newspapers in the late nineteenth century, the photograph also becomes a way of familiarizing readers with political and business leaders—of 'putting a face to the name'—as well as, through images, linking them with far-off events. In this way, photography helped sew the seams of the emerging industrial-based social fabric.

While the photograph was woven into the context of new familial and community relationships, motion pictures—an extension of the photographic image—were given cultural freedom to grow by the new rhythm of the industrial day that divided time between work and leisure. Through the early twentieth century, an increasing number of urban dwellers had free time and disposable income. Entrepreneurs worked to find ways to capitalize on these circumstances, and new products or **commodities** (Box 3.1) were created to sell to this growing body of consumers, among

Source: © istockphoto.com/Mikhail Pogosov

Two young sisters pose in an early photograph. 'Camera' in photography initially meant a room: a photographic device that could hold one or more people inside it. The nineteenth-century studio camera that took this photo was much less bulky, and became very popular from the 1880s. Large plates coated with light-sensitive chemicals were replaced at the back of the camera for each succeeding photograph. Most photographers developed their own plates and images until in 1888 John Eastman developed the Kodak camera with celluloid film that could be returned to the manufacturer for developing.

them the motion picture. The motion picture was also the product of the economies of scale engendered through industrial production. Many copies or prints of the same film could be shown simultaneously in widely scattered cities and towns, thereby spreading the cost of production among many audience members.

Of all the modern media given both form and function by the development of industrial society, however, the newspaper was both the earliest to develop and the most pervasive.

⸭ BOX 3.1   THE COMMODITY AND COMMUNICATION

One of the most dynamic features of capitalism as an economic system is the way it works to convert things for which we find need and uses in our lives into products for which we must pay market prices. Critical commentators call this the commodification of everyday life—that is what Karl Marx highlighted as the process of turning 'use value' into 'exchange value' (see Mosco, 1996). Others celebrate this process as the entrepreneurial spirit of capitalism.

Think of all the different elements of the process of communication that have been commodified over the last few years. Television and radio used to arrive free over the air. Now the monthly cable or satellite bill can eat up a day's pay. Time spent in movie theatres—particularly the time between when people take their seats and the film starts—has been commodified as the theatre owners have used advertising to turn that time into a product they can sell to advertisers. Internet access is now sold in a range of different speeds. Telephone service has evolved into an ever-increasing array of products such as voice mail, text messaging, and various web-based telecom services. Even the ring tones for cellphones have become products for sale. And, increasingly, information itself—such as news, government reports and statistics, and course readings—is becoming a product for sale.

As we shall see in the following chapters, this ongoing commodification of communication products and processes lies at the heart of what people call the 'communication economy' or the 'communication revolution' and is seen as a key factor in economic growth. However, it creates a growing divide between the communication 'haves' and 'have-nots', between the 'information rich' and the 'information poor'. And, given that communication products and processes play key roles in our knowledge and understanding of the world, the commodification of communication and information—or turning both information and access to it into products we have to pay for—can't help but undermine people's abilities to exercise their full rights and responsibilities as citizens.

The Beginnings of the Modern Press

In the eighteenth and early nineteenth centuries, some degree of organization was brought to the cacophony of publishing voices created by the printing press as newspapers began to be aligned with (and sometimes even owned by) political parties. This pattern—the emergence of many voices, then their reduction to a few, often politically aligned, newspapers—has been repeated in many Western countries at various points in their histories. And just as this pattern has repeated itself, so has the subsequent transition of control of newspapers from political parties to business interests. In books and magazines a variation on the same pattern can be seen, with control first being established in the hands of wealthy patrons; then, among liberal members of the elite; and, finally, passing—sometimes first through political hands—to business enterprises.

In Canada, newspapers in the early to mid-1800s were generally under the control of partisan political interests. As Robert Hackett and Yuezhi Zhao (1998: 20) observe in *Sustaining Democracy: Journalism and the Politics of Objectivity*:

> Often owned by a group of wealthy partisans . . . papers had the explicit purpose of representing a political party. Overall, they tended to serve the ruling political and business elites. . . . Newspapers often counted on financial support from government patronage or direct party subsidies. Shaped by party affiliations, the journalism of the time was replete not only with special pleading for the politicians who financially supported each paper, but also with vicious personal attacks on political foes.

By the early twentieth century, however, the cost of producing newspapers drove them into the control of business. Perhaps the largest influence on this shift in ownership was the development of industrial society. Around the end of the nineteenth century, the growth in industry and urban populations led to developments in both mass production and mass marketing. As Minko Sotiron (1997: 4) explains in *From Politics to Profit*, the modern newspaper in Canada is rooted in the period '1890–1920, when, among other things, a rapidly expanding urban population, increased literacy, the economic boom of the Laurier era, and a growing national market of consumer markets contributed to the profitability of new newspaper ventures.'

Newspaper publishers found that providing marketers with a vehicle to reach the increasing numbers of consumers was more profitable than direct alliances with political parties, and advertising soon became their major source of revenue. As modern newspapers evolved in the context of industrial society, they crossed the boundary between the public life of work and community and the private home. In this redaction they began to serve multiple roles. Not only were they the source of political and community news, but they provided a wide range of other information important to a population confronted with an increasingly complex society. Want ads linked job seekers and employers, merchandise and service ads linked growing numbers of workers with a growing number of products, and personal ads helped people locate partners and friends in the increasingly impersonal urban environment. New technologies animated these changes. Cheap newsprint and faster printing presses lowered the cost of newspapers, while the telegraph and later the telephone were plentiful conduits for the information needed to fill pages and attract readers. Thus, just as the photograph, the motion picture, the telegraph, and the telephone took form and function in the emerging structure of industrial society, so, too, did newspapers (Schudson, 1978).

Journalism also changed to meet the new industrial regime. In news, 'objectivity' replaced partisan reporting as papers sought to reach a wider readership and increase circulation and profits (see Hackett and Zhao, 1998; Schudson, 1978). The use of headlines and photographs to capture the attention of potential readers became popular, as did partitioning newspapers into different sections and offering a range of different features—such as serialized novels—to attract a diverse readership.

As the press became more a business than a service, publishers also promoted their own interests, emphasizing the freedom to pursue profitability in the marketplace unencumbered by state restrictions (Chapter 8). Journalists developed a complementary ethic by stressing their need for independence from the state for reportage and analysis. This dual business and journalistic thrust has allowed the press to establish some distance from the politicians of the day. This is not to say that in claiming their independence newspapers, and the media as a whole, represent the interests of all citizens. On the contrary, as we will see in the following chapters, the media generally represent the interests of the power elites in society—mostly business interests, but also the interests of the political and intellectual elites.

Perspectives on the Press

Since its inception the role of the printing press in developing and circulating ideas has been controversial. In Martin Luther's day, it was used to undermine the traditional power of the Catholic Church. As newspapers developed through the seventeenth and eighteenth centuries, governments in Britain and Europe used a range of measures to censor and control the circulation of news in order to maintain social and political control. Through the late eighteenth and early nineteenth centuries, however, early liberal writers such as Jeremy Bentham, James Mill, and John Stuart Mill advocated that a press independent from government regulation (a 'free' press) was central to good government and democracy. It was in this context that in a speech to the British House of Commons, Edmund Burke referred to the press as the **fourth estate**, meaning that alongside the other 'estates' or institutions of social governance—the clergy, the nobility, and the commons—the press played an important role as a kind of political watchdog, guarding the rights of citizens through publicly reporting on affairs of state. In the wake of the long struggle to wrest political control from the hands of monarchs, as John Thompson (1999: 122) points out, 'There is considerable force in the argument that the struggle for an independent press, capable of reporting and commenting on events with a minimum of state interference and control, played a key role in the development of the modern constitutional state.' Consequently, over the last several centuries **freedom of the press** from government interference became an important political ideal and is reflected in the Constitution of the United States, the United Nations' Universal Declaration of Human Rights, and the Canadian Charter of Rights and Freedoms.

But while newspapers did contribute to political freedoms, as they came to be operated as commercial enterprises there has been a growing concern that corporate interest—that is, the pursuit of private profit—has dominated over the public interest in their operation. Press barons of the late nineteenth century were known to sensationalize news, and sometimes even to make it up, in their efforts to attract readers. And today there are many examples of how news production and, sometimes, perspectives in news media are tilted towards the interests of the shareholders of media companies rather than to the general public.

Still, defining the exact social role of the press, and subsequently that of the media, is a matter of some debate and depends largely on one's theoretical perspective. In liberal theory the function of the mass media is to preserve liberal democracy—in other words, the political system within which the media now exist. The media are expected to monitor abuses of power and to attempt to ensure that the will of the people is carried out. They assist in ensuring that governments and institutions are flexible and sensitive to the changing needs and desires of society. According to this theory, the media provide the information necessary for public participation in the political process and aid in the dissemination of information about public programs and services. In short, they provide citizens with information about matters that are part of the political and socio-economic system in which they live—information that most citizens would not otherwise receive.

In contrast to liberal political theory, the Marxist approach (Chapter 4) describes the media's activities not as working on behalf of the community as a whole, but rather as promoting the ideology and the interests of the dominant classes of society. Marxists point out that while the media may propose

revisions and small reforms, such as the election of an opposition party in place of a continuation of a current government, they do so to preserve the existing political system rather than opting for a new, more equitable system that serves the interests of all citizens equally. In putting forward a limited range of ideas and analysis, the media present different manifestations of the same basic political perspective and thus reinforce existing power relations and ideology. In short, the media reflect the interests of their capitalist owners in maintaining a politically stable society.

Critical scholars James Curran (1990) and John Fiske (1987, 1989a, 1989b, 1989c) have carved out a middle ground in describing the role of the media in Western society. Like the Marxists, they claim that the media are intimately involved in relations of social power, but they see them as contributing information and analysis on a wide variety of subjects and from a fairly broad set of perspectives. The media do so in the context of various competing groups and individuals and, sifting through these different perspectives, seek to interpret the 'real' meaning of events. For example, in the case of Aboriginal land claims one can, at various times, see the point of view of First Nations, the provincial and federal governments, business, residents on the land, or ordinary Canadians who are not direct stakeholders. At times the contributions of the media are made with the interests of the public in mind; at other times they are more self-interested or represent the interests of a particular group. If major reforms are called for on a particular issue, the media may eventually present and discuss that possibility. In the end, however, for a variety of reasons we will examine in following chapters, Fiske and Curran claim that the media generally entrench the status quo.

Which of these theoretical perspectives is the true or correct one? Indeed, all three approaches provide insight on media operations. As we saw in Chapters 1 and 2, the social role and structure of the media are complex. But to understand what role they play in any specific instance we need to examine the relations of power in which they are implicated.

Given the various conceptions of the media, considerable attention and debate have been directed at the ownership and control of the media: where does it or should it rest? Analysts have identified four different sites where the power of media ownership and control may be located in society:

- within the state;
- as part of social or political movements or parties;
- as private enterprises;
- as public or government enterprises at arm's length from the government of the day.

Each of these locations tilts the interests and the orientation of the media in a particular direction.

Scholars have discussed the implications of the media operating from each site, in terms of ownership, content production, and societal functioning (Chapter 9). When run by the state or government the media tend to strengthen state control, as has been the case in one-party totalitarian states and in certain developing countries where the state maintains close control over the media. In the hands of social and political movements they tend to fragment and politicize society, as in Italy, unless a delicate balance of interests and a calm political climate prevail, as in the Netherlands. In media held by business, the profit motive, the interests of business, and the interests of advertisers are advanced at the expense of the interests of the community as a whole. When run as a public enterprise, such as the CBC or British Broadcasting Corporation (BBC), education, enlightenment, and, sometimes, talent development tend to become the primary values, with the interests of advertisers becoming secondary. In the Canadian context, nation-building was also a high priority (Box 3.3).

The Traditional Mass Media and Canadian Realities: History and Structure

Just as larger social, political, and economic events such as the Enlightenment and the Industrial Revolution have shaped communications media in general, so, too, have the development and structure of the Canadian state, as well as a distinctive Canadian culture, nuanced the struc-ture and operation of media in Canada.

In the early nineteenth century, European settlement of the geography that is now Canada took the form of a collection of colonies scattered across the vast northern half of North America. Industry, such as it was, was largely devoted to the export of staples or raw materials for manufacturing in Great Britain and the United States. In this context, the lines of communication followed the lines of commerce and ran either overseas to Britain or north–south into the US. But by the mid-1800s, both Britain and the US had enacted trade restrictions on the colonies, forcing them to look to themselves for development. In the face of these pressures, Confederation in 1867 was the first step to building an economic unit out of these colonies.

In 1879, Prime Minister John A. Macdonald introduced Canada's first National Policy, a set of initiatives designed to turn the idea of an east–west economy into a reality. The National Policy had three particularly important components:

1. the building of a transcontinental railway;
2. a tariff designed to limit the entry of manufactured goods from the US and Britain;
3. efforts to entice immigrants to settle the prairies.

The railway was to provide a reliable line of transportation for people and goods across the country, and particularly to move raw materials from the margins of the country to the industrial heartland in central Canada where they would be manufactured into goods and shipped back out to market. In other words, the railway was to bind the country into a cohesive political economic unit with a 'ribbon of steel'. The tariff was used to tax materials and manufactured goods entering the country. Its purpose was to protect 'infant' Canadian industries by keeping cheap competitive goods outside the country. At the same time, it encouraged foreign investment, as non-Canadian companies wishing to tap into the expanding Canadian market were encouraged to build factories and produce goods here in order to avoid the tariff. The tariff was necessary because Canada had a much smaller population than either Britain or the US and did not have the **economies of scale** (Box 3.2) necessary to produce goods at a price that could compete with similar goods produced in those countries. Finally, immigration policy actively sought settlers from Central and Eastern Europe to populate the Prairie provinces, both to develop the land and raise grain for the central Canadian market and to serve as a market for the manufactured goods of Ontario and Quebec.

Despite these measures, because of the large size of the country and the small population, it was often difficult to wring profits from business in Canada and the government often had to step in to encourage private investment. For instance, the Canadian Pacific Railway (CPR) was issued a wide range of government payments and subsidies to encourage the building of the transcontinental railway. Similarly, because of the large investment necessary, Bell Telephone was given a monopoly on long-distance telephone service in central Canada so that it might exploit economies of scale when building that system.

Still, it was all but impossible for the government to attract private investment for some activities. In these instances, both federal and provincial governments frequently undertook these activities themselves, often in the form of Crown—or government-owned—corporations. For instance, Canada's second national railroad, which served to bolster service to some areas and bring service to others not served by the CPR, was government-owned. Canada's first transcontinental airline—now Air Canada—was a Crown corporation, as was the first national broadcaster—the CBC. Later, Canada's first satellite company—Telesat Canada—was also a government initiative.

In short, historically, because of the unique features of the Canadian state, the government has often taken a strong hand in shaping the economy. At the federal level, these efforts have been motivated by a strong nationalist sentiment. This tradition of nation-building is reflected in the structure of Canada's media industries. For instance, just as the railway was seen as binding Canada physically, so in the 1930s broadcasting was envisioned as binding the country together through a common Canadian consciousness or perspective on the world (Box 3.3). Consequently, the government set up the Canadian Radio Broadcasting Commission and later the Canadian Broadcasting Corporation to create a national broadcasting network and Canadian programming—two activities that the private sector was unable to undertake profitably at the time. Later, various policy measures in the magazine, newspaper, publishing, music, film, and telecommunications industries were undertaken with similar objectives in mind—to help build and strengthen a common Canadian culture. In other words, they were enacted with nationalist purposes

BOX 3.2 ECONOMIES OF SCALE

Economies of scale reflect the fact that the greater the quantity of a particular product is made, the less each one costs to produce. Much of the cost of an industrial product is in setting up the factory that will produce it. Whether one is producing cars, stoves, or matches, buying the real estate on which the factory is located, building the building in which it will be housed, and then designing and creating the machinery that will make the product represent a much greater investment than the raw materials that go into the product. For instance, if putting together a factory for making stoves costs $1 million and the labour and raw materials that go into each stove cost $100, then the cost of manufacturing one stove will be $1,000,100. If 10,000 stoves are produced, then the cost of each stove would be $200 ($1,000,000 divided by 10,000 equals $100 + $100 in raw materials). However, if 1,000,000 stoves are produced, the cost falls to $101 each ($1,000,000 divided by 1,000,000 equals $1 + $100 in raw materials). Consequently, because the United States over the years has had a population roughly 10 times the size of that of Canada, manufactured goods coming out of the US have been cheaper than those made in Canada.

❖ BOX 3.3   BROADCASTING AND NATION-BUILDING

In the face of an overwhelming spillover of American programming into Canada, the government set up the Canadian Radio Broadcasting Commission (CRBC) and later the Canadian Broadcasting Corporation (CBC) to build a national broadcasting network and create Canadian programming. In introducing the 1932 Broadcasting Act to the House of Commons—the legislation that created the CRBC—Prime Minister R.B. Bennett outlined what the government saw as the purposes of that legislation:

> . . . this country must be assured of complete Canadian control of broadcasting from Canadian sources, free from foreign interference or influence. Without such control radio broadcasting can never become a great agency for communication of matters of national concern and for the diffusion of national thought and ideals, and without such control it can never be the agency by which consciousness may be fostered and sustained and national unity still further strengthened. . . . No other scheme than that of public ownership can ensure to the people of this country, without regard to class or place, equal enjoyment of the benefits and pleasures of radio broadcasting.

Source: © istockphoto.com/HuttonArchive

Early on, Canadian legislators recognized radio's ability to operate on the principle of free speech and its potential to create a national community.

in mind. However, as we shall see, the government record in building and strengthening Canadian culture is patchy at best, and while government policy has often been framed by strong language that claims concern for Canadian culture, it has not always been backed with strong action.

Before considering some of the larger political principles and cultural concerns that underpin the Canadian media, we need to understand the distinctive characteristics of the Canadian state that have shaped the development of its communication system. We have already looked at two of these characteristics: the *vastness of the country* and the *small size of Canada's population*. These geographic and demographic facts have pressed Canada to invest in expensive national transmission systems so that Canadians can stay in touch with each other.

A third significant characteristic, derived in part from the size of the country, is Canada's *regionalism*. Canada is not just a country of physical geographic variety; it is a country of regional cultures. From the disparate French and British colonies scattered throughout what is now Canada grew a 'confederation'. This nation required means of internal communication, but not those in which messages would be generated only from a central point and fed to outlying regions. Each region needed to generate its own information such that the region's particularities might be reflected to the whole. This would help bring the country together—or such has been the ideal.

Canada is also a nation of *two official languages*. The right to speak either English or French is now enshrined in our Constitution. But Canadians have committed themselves to more than a freedom of language choice for individuals. They have committed themselves to providing federal government services, including broadcasting, in both official languages. Bilingual government services and bilingual broadcasting channels (not just programs) are a testament to the right of any Canadian to live and work wherever she or he may wish. They are also a continual reminder to all that we are officially a bilingual country.

In 1971, during Pierre Trudeau's first term as prime minister, Canada also officially became a *multicultural country* and, although it was long in coming, an increasing number of media programming services are tailored to various ethnic communities.

A final, never-to-be-forgotten characteristic of Canada's communications environment is its proximity to the US. Economies of scale in media production, coupled with our acceptance, particularly in anglophone Canada, of some similar basic political and economic philosophies and this proximity, have led to a massive penetration of US products and ideas into Canada. In Canada, more

American television programming is available to the vast majority of Canadians than is Canadian programming. On most Canadian commercial radio stations, more American material than Canadian material is available to listeners. On virtually all magazine racks in Canada, more American magazines are available to the reader than Canadian magazines, in spite of the fact that more than 2300 magazines are published in Canada. More than 95 per cent of the films screened in Canadian theatres are foreign, mainly American. More American authors than Canadian authors are read by the average Canadian schoolchild. Our proximity to the US and the resultant spillover of American cultural products comprise a major factor to be taken into account in considering Canada's communications environment. Because, unlike many Canadian media companies, for economic reasons US media companies are primarily interested in distributing products produced in the US rather than imported products, the US has less tolerance for products that are not recognizably American, and the counter-flow—Canadian ideas into the US—has been very limited.

BOX 3.4   THE ECONOMICS OF MEDIA REPRESENTATION

Economies of scale also underlie media production. For instance, much of the cost of producing a magazine or book is in paying the writers, editors, photographers, and typesetters to create the 'first copy'. After that, these initial expenses are spread across the number of copies produced. So, if the cost of gathering and putting together all of the material that goes into a particular magazine is $50,000, if 50,000 copies of that magazine are printed, the editorial cost of each magazine is $1.00. However, if 500,000 magazines are printed, the cost falls to only 10 cents per copy. Similar economics apply to film and television, where the 'cost per viewer' is spread over the number of audience members.

Because the market for media products in the United States is roughly 10 times the size of the market in Canada, the cost per reader or cost per audience member for those products is often significantly less in the US than it is for Canadian production aimed primarily at a Canadian audience. Consequently, it is often much more profitable for Canadian distributors of media products to sell American books, magazines, TV shows, and films than those made specifically for the Canadian market. As a result, American media products are often more common in Canada than homegrown versions. It is not because Americans make better media products than Canadians that our markets are overrun with them; it's simply because more money can be made selling them in Canada than producing our own.

In the face of the challenges posed by these characteristics of Canadian media markets, Canada has a fairly strong record of achievement in forging a national communications system. Table 3.1 provides a chronology of dates of important communications achievements, including many Canadian firsts.

Each of these developments was cause for some rejoicing and some sense of pride. Each in its own way strengthened east–west links from the Atlantic to the Pacific and was a factor in nation-building and cohesion. As important as the technological achievements in building the system are the legislative achievements behind that technological expansion: the 1932 Broadcasting Act and the 1993 Telecommunications Act. These statutes gave voice to the public interest in the development of these communication systems and set in law the public goals and ambitions that underlie them. Still, addressing the needs of all the different regions and peoples of the country has been difficult, particularly in the North, where, as Lorna Roth (2005: 221) notes, 'When first introduced in the 1960's and 70's, television temporarily stalled indigenous self-development by introducing yet another Southern medium devoid of First People's images, voices, and cultural activities.'

These realities continue to present challenges to government, business, and other social groups for creating communication systems that serve all the peoples of Canada in a fair, equitable, and comprehensive manner.

TABLE 3.1   Some Important Achievements in Canadian Communication History

YEAR	ACHIEVEMENT
1885	A transcontinental railway
1901	A transatlantic radio link
1927	A trans-Canada radio network
1932	A trans-Canada telephone network First Broadcasting Act
1948	World's first commercial microwave link
1956	World's first tropospheric scatter transmission system
1958	A transcontinental television service A transcontinental microwave network
1959	First Canadian communications satellite experiment including use of the moon as reflector
1968	Canadian Film Development Corporation
1970	Beginning of fibre optic research
1972	A domestic geostationary communications satellite
1973	First nationwide digital data system World's first digital transmission network (Dataroute)
1976	Bill C-58: legislation to help Canadian magazine industry
1990	Completion of a 7,000-kilometre coast-to-coast fibre optic network, the longest terrestrial fibre network in the world
1991	Canadian Broadcasting Act
1993	Canadian Telecommunications Act
1996	Launch of the first North American commercial digital radio service
1999	Aboriginal Peoples Television Network established
2005	Canadian Television Fund
2010	Canadian Media Fund

An inukshuk is a stone cairn or landmark used by the Inuit either on its own or as part of a larger set of inuksuit as a mode of communication. They are used for a variety of purposes such as aids to navigation, memorials, and marking hunting sites.

Canada: The State, the Market, and the Individual

In theory, freedom of the press is founded on the notion of free speech. From an audience perspective, freedom of the press translates into exposure to an ideological spectrum within which a range of ideas and policies are considered. As we have pointed out, freedom of the press developed in Europe from a power struggle between the nobility and the Church on the one side and printers and entrepreneurs of newly developing businesses and manufacturers on the other side. Canadian press history is distinctive because of the degree to which the British colonial government accepted liberal principles of press operation and press freedom prior to the evolution of strong, separate interest groups in early Canadian society. Thus, while printers depended on government printing contracts, the colonial government tolerated, to some degree, their printing of anti-government commentary.

Oddly enough, Canada's tolerance was founded both on its colonial status and on the country's proximity to the United States. That is, as leaders in colonies of Great Britain the Canadian political elites were enfranchised by their class connections to the mother country. Hence, the colonies in what is now Canada strove to remain abreast of changes in the United Kingdom, which, when the Canadian press was developing, were towards modern liberal democracy. When the enactment of liberal principles became too slow in Britain, Canada turned to the United States for models, which were even more radically focused on the rights of individuals and freedom of enterprise without state interference.

Despite the strong role of the state in shaping and supporting the Canadian economy, Canadian media were from the outset the product of private enterprise. Consequently, Canadian media pioneers created a press and media culture committed to the individualism inherent in liberal principles. In more concrete terms, the Canadian media were and are strong supporters of **freedom of speech**, but less enthusiastic about the role of the government in the economy. The support of the media for free trade and against regulation of the economy in the interests of Canadians and Canadian institutions is a case in point.

What are the limitations on your freedom of speech?

It could be argued that this theme of the media—on one hand, being supported and protected by government regulation, while, on the other, championing market freedoms—is present throughout the history of Canadian media. For instance, in the broadcasting field support for private broadcasters and Canadian ownership of broadcast outlets has been a constant theme of successive Broadcasting Acts and broadcast regulation. However, with the exception of the CBC, private broadcasters have been more interested in importing and distributing US programs than in producing Canadian programs because that is where the profits lie. Certainly, there is evidence to support such a viewpoint in various broadcasting histories (see, for example, Armstrong, 2010; Vipond, 2000; Raboy, 1990; Weir, 1965; Babe, 1990; Rutherford, 1990; Peers, 1979, 1969).

Robert Babe (1990), a communications political economist, identifies an additional factor that contributed to this scenario. He argues that, in part, the configuration of our broadcasting and telecommunications systems is a result of deals made in the US to split patents there among companies in such a way that telecommunications became a separate industry from broadcasting. Patents for radio and telephone transmission in Canada were split in the same way, and hence Canadian subsidiaries of US telecommunication companies controlled the same patents as did their parent companies in the US and operated in parallel with them. In broadcasting, ownership restrictions prevented parallel home-office/branch-plant operations. But they did not stop broadcasters from continually pushing for the right to import US programs in bulk and run essentially parallel operations.

The Mass Media and Canadian Culture

We can now turn to examining the relationship between Canadian culture and Canada's mass media—including government's administration and regulation of them. This relationship is interesting and complex.

As discussed in Chapter 2, set at the intersection between people and the different social groups, organizations, and institutions that make up our society, the media are primary vehicles in communicating the depth and breadth of the ways of life—or culture—of Canadians. Building on some of the definitions of culture discussed in the last chapter, the federal government notes that culture 'includes the knowledge, beliefs, art, morals, customs and all other capabilities acquired by a particular society' (from a report on Canada's cultural industries titled *Vital Links* [Canada, 1987: 11]). To this schema we might add the laws, institutions, and organizations that give society form. From this perspective, culture is a way or ways of life. In Canada, we have a distinctive set of institutions—such as governments, schools, universities, media, the health-care system—that give Canadian culture form, as well as the distinctive ideas, values, and beliefs that exist within that larger framework of social institutions.

Media, of course, are central to how we come to understand and share culture, and, in a large industrial nation such as Canada, the media are intricately woven into the social fabric. They are the means through which the exchange of ideas, experience, images, and interpretations and perspectives on the world takes place. Indeed, it is generally through the media that we come to know our society, its institutions and organizations, and the other people with whom we share our national culture. For this reason, the media industries—such as those involved in radio and television broadcasting, digital media, film, music, newspapers, magazine and book publishing, and more—are often called cultural industries. As discussed in Chapter 8, Canada's cultural industries provide an information base around which various communities and other social groups that make up our society can coalesce and interact, at the best of times contributing to social cohesion, and a sense of belonging on the part of all members of society.

Canada's modern communications system is historically rooted in transportation. While it is true that Sir John A. Macdonald and his government had the CPR built primarily to ensure the flow of goods and immigrants, with the flow of both came the flow of information—through the mail and the telegraph. The post office instituted inexpensive second-class mail rates to encourage the circulation of newspapers and magazines, which helped knit the country together. These, and other commercial communications—for example, the Eaton's department store catalogue—gave Canadians a sense of connection with their compatriots elsewhere in the country. For instance, people on the Prairies or the west coast, ordering a pump organ from Clinton, Ontario, or a wood stove from Sackville, New Brunswick, gave western Canadians an economic link and a social connection to eastern Canada.

From these humble beginnings, the federal government has instituted a range of policies to encourage the development of Canadian media and a media system operating on an east-west axis. Today, many of the laws and regulations dealing with the cultural industries are administered by Heritage Canada (Figure 3.2), the federal government department responsible for this field of legislation.

While Canadian governments have nodded to the importance of media and cultural products in the life of the nation, Babe (1990), Grant (2004), and others have argued that they have not been consistent protectors and supporters of Canada's cultural industries. One of the main points of concern has been competition from American media products.

Foreign content has always been a part of the flow of information within the Canadian nation, but it has also been the subject of controversy. Tables 3.2 and 3.3 list the top programs in the English and French television markets for the weeks 6–20 September 2010. The figures provide a sense of the size of the audiences for each program. In Quebec, Quebec-made television dominates the schedule. But in the rest of Canada, US shows dominate overwhelmingly—so much so that if we were to take Table 3.2 as an indication of what English Canadians know about themselves and others through television, we would have to conclude that anglophone Canada must be suffering from an identity crisis from the infusion of American-made programming. Economically, this large-scale presence of mainly American media products has drawn criticism for taking away jobs from Canadian media workers and undermining Canadian industry in general. Culturally, as discussed in Chapter 2, such foreign media products have worked to make Canadians and their public institutions strangers in their own land.

Canadian government investment in communications has traditionally stressed telecommunications transmission and technology. In the 1990s, amid budget cuts to public broadcasting, the federal government spent millions upgrading transmission networks. More recently, the government's focus has been on developing a Canadian digital policy to create 'a safe and reliable environment that encourages citizens, content providers, governments and businesses to engage in online transactions and electronic commerce' (Canada, 2010e).

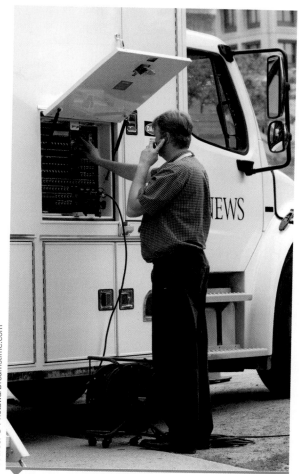

Source: © Photawa/Dreamstime.com

The media is central to how we come to understand and share culture. For this reason, media industries, such as television broadcasting, are often called cultural industries.

FIGURE 3.2 Maximum Allowable Foreign Ownership of a Canadian Broadcaster

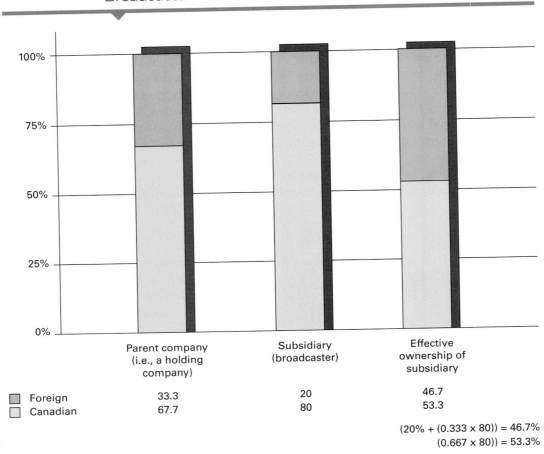

	Parent company (i.e., a holding company)	Subsidiary (broadcaster)	Effective ownership of subsidiary
Foreign	33.3	20	46.7
Canadian	67.7	80	53.3

$$(20\% + (0.333 \times 80)) = 46.7\%$$
$$(0.667 \times 80)) = 53.3\%$$

As free trade between nations increases, so does foreign ownership. As this figure illustrates, according to Canadian law effective ownership of a broadcaster can be as much as 46.7 per cent through indirect ownership (of a holding company) and direct ownership of the broadcaster that is a subsidiary of the holding company. Any increase in allowance of foreign ownership would give majority control to a foreign owner. Within political economic theory, the role of foreign ownership looms large as a factor affecting cultural sovereignty.

This commitment to current technology and effective, rapid transmission has been a mixed blessing (Charland, 1986). In spite of the rhetoric used to justify each new major expenditure, the technology has provided a conduit for foreign media to reach Canadian audiences that has not necessarily served the cultural needs of Canada and Canadians. Within Canada, the telecommunications infrastructure has served private-sector growth, including the formation of national newspapers such as *The Globe and Mail* and the *National Post*, which have taken advantage of satellite and other communications technologies to print regional editions of their newspapers simultaneously in different parts of the country. In the case of broadcasting, through the insistence of the CRTC, some cultural benefits have emerged from private-sector growth, but the

TABLE 3.2 Top Programs, Total Canada (English), 6–20 September 2010*

RANK	PROGRAM	BROADCAST OUTLET	WEEKDAY	TOTAL AUDIENCE (000S)
1	Big Bang Theory	CTV	...T...	3,112
2	House	Global	M......	2,699
3	The Mentalist	CTV	...T...	2,643
4	Criminal Minds	CTV	..W...	2,639
5	Survivor: Nicaragua	Global	..W....	2,589
6	Grey's Anatomy	CTV	...T...	2,528
7	Dancing with the Stars 11 PRF	CTV	M......	2,479
8	Amazing Race 17	CTV	......S	2,438
9	C.S.I. New York	CTV	....F..	2,325
10	Glee	Global	.T.....	2,244
11	Hawaii Five-O	Global	M......	2,136
12	Blue Bloods	CTV	....F..	2,126
13	Dancing with the Stars 11 RES	CTV	.T.....	2,086
14	Castle	CTV	M......	1,921
15	The Defenders	CTV	..W....	1,915
16	Bones	Global	...T...	1,876
17	C.S.I.	CTV	...T...	1,863
18	NCIS: Los Angeles	Global	.T.....	1,708
19	Dragons' Den	CBC	..W....	1,582
20	CTV Evening News	CTV	MTWTF..	1,578
21	The Simpsons	Global	......S	1,536
22	Undercover Boss	CTV	......S	1,519
23	Battle of the Blades	CBC	......S	1,511
24	$#*! My Dad Says	CTV	......S	1,485
25	NCIS: Los Angeles	Global	.T.....	1,373
26	Dancing with the Stars 11	CTV	.T.....	1,346
27	Two and a Half Men	'A'	M......	1,326
28	Desperate Housewives	CTV	......S	1,284
29	CTV National News	CTV	MTWTFSS	1,259
30	Rick Mercer Report	CBC	.T.....	1,222

*Based on confirmed program schedules and preliminary audience data. Demographic: All Persons 2+.
Source: © 2010 BBM Canada.

private broadcasters have been reluctant contributors to national cultural goals.

The usual rationale for government investment in communication infrastructure is that technological development creates jobs—numerous spin-off technologies lead to the creation of new industries, products, and hence jobs in the information sector. In the language of economists, there are significant **multiplier effects**, meaning that such investment leads to direct and indirect jobs. It is certainly the case that a ready infrastructure has assisted Canadian business to embrace the internet as a business tool. New internet businesses have been founded and traditional businesses have been able to take advantage of Canada's robust technological infrastructure.

TABLE 3.3   Top Programs, Québec French, 6–20 September 2010*

RANK	PROGRAM	BROADCAST OUTLET	WEEKDAY	TOTAL AUDIENCE (000)
1	Banquier, Le - Spéciale 50 ans TVA	TVA	......S	2036
2	Occupation double à Whistler	TVA	......S	1641
3	Tout le monde en…	SRC	......S	1436
4	Yamaska	TVA	M......	1188
5	Parent, Les	SRC	M......	1171
6	Enfants de la télé	SRC	..W....	1114
7	Poule aux oeufs d'or, La	TVA	..W....	948
8	Auberge chien noir	SRC	M......	943
9	J.E.	TVA	....F..	916
10	Destinées	TVA	..W....	908
11	Jean-Marc Parent : urgence de vivre	TVA	M......	899
12	SP: Bloopers TVA	TVA	M......	880
13	Tranches de vie	TVA	..W....	877
14	Promesse, La	TVA	.T.....	868
15	TVA Nouvelles (18h - LV)	TVA	MTWTF..	866
16	TVA Nouvelles (18h - SD)	TVA	.....SS	850
17	Galère, La	SRC	M......	842
18	Providence	SRC	.T.....	837
19	SP: Bloopers TVA	TVA	.T.....	837
20	Mauvais Karma	SRC	..W....	830
21	Rescapés, Les	SRC	.T.....	815
22	TVA Nouvelles (17h)	TVA	MTWTF..	807
23	Dr House	TVA	.T.....	794
24	Caméra café	TVA	.T.....	779
25	Cercle, Le	TVA	MTWTF..	772
26	Fièvre de la danse, La	TVA	...T...	719
27	Du talent à revendre	TVA	....F..	684
28	Facture	SRC	.T.....	682
29	Ciné-Extra	TVA	.....S.	676
30	Gags, Les	TVA	M......	641

*Preliminary data.

Source: © 2010 BBM Canada.

Historically, the country's small population has created a dearth of investment in the technological infrastructure of communications. Canadians have never been in a position to produce enough programs to fill the transmission capacity we have developed. Even if Canadian producers could somehow produce the programs, there would not be enough money in the pockets of advertisers, the public, and governments to pay for the range of choice available in the infrastructure. In other words, we have created an information environment that keeps us abreast industrially of the most advanced nations but that opens us to inundation by foreign cultural products. We neglected to design a system that would guarantee the development of Canadian culture and cultural production. The reason, it would seem, is a belief on the part of policy-makers in the liberal doctrine of free enterprise—an extension of the idea of liberal individualism. This idea has overshadowed our abilities to represent the distinctive elements of a Canadian culture in our media venues.

The Americans, who happen to be close by and also happen to be the world's most successful entertainment and information producers, can step into our cultural complacency. The selection—and, perhaps most importantly, the price—they offer in such areas as television and film is too attractive for private business to refuse. For one-tenth the cost of producing a season of half-hour television dramas in Canada, US producers can provide a high-quality program with high ratings and ever-so-attractive stars, complete with press attention and magazine commentary that spill over the border in American media products. While Canadian governments at times have accepted the role of patron in the name of cultural sovereignty or national development and have provided subsidies and enacted legislation to protect Canadian media products and support producers, they have been reluctant to impose heavy restrictions on private enterprise or to restrict the ability of foreigners to do business in Canada. Consequently, only in Quebec is the regional culture thoroughly reflected in the media (Table 3.3). In the rest of the country, the result of this focus on technology, liberal market principles, and lack of determination to ensure a dominance of Canadian media products has been, for decades, a cultural low road (Chapter 7).

Politics and the Canadian Media Today

As we have seen, the media traditionally are portrayed as playing an important role in the governance of society. This section considers the distinctive role of the media in Canadian politics.

The modern nation-state is a sophisticated information apparatus, with government and the traditional mass media acting as two of its major information arms. More recently, web-based media have provided a considerably enhanced opportunity for ordinary citizens to obtain information and to exchange it with others. The government, in order to govern effectively and to perpetuate itself,

both collects and produces information. The traditional mass media collect and produce information to inform the public and the state and to maintain successful commercial ventures. The interactive media allow people who possess the skills and equipment to produce, seek out, and exchange information.

The role of the news media in carrying information between people and the government makes for extremely close relations with government. The news media depend on the government for information and for advertising. The government depends on the news media to disseminate that information. But the government's desire to keep certain information from the media, such as information that might undermine the popularity of the government of the day, imbues that relationship with ambivalence. At the same time, the desire of the media to maintain their independence and periodically to demonstrate their integrity transforms that ambivalence into a love-hate relationship on the part of politicians. The dependence of the media on government for information makes that love-hate relationship mutual (see, for example, Rose and Kiss, 2006; Nesbitt-Larking, 2001; Hayes, 1992; Cocking, 1980; Gratton, 1987; and the proceedings of the Canadian Study of Parliament Group, Canada, 1980.)

In theory, the media act as a counteractive force to potential abuse of power by the state. The media also help, along with the opposition parties in Parliament, to monitor government policy and action (see, for example, Fletcher, 1981). The parliamentary press gallery deserves some direct attention in this context. The gallery is the sum of all journalists who are working on political stories in Ottawa or the provincial capitals and who become members of the Ottawa or of provincial capital galleries. It is also, as the federal Task Force on Government Information (Canada, 1969, vol. 2: 115–19) noted, 'the most important instrument of political communication in the country'. The press gallery performs two essential roles: to disseminate government information and to assess the wisdom of government policy and action by reporting and analyzing House debates.

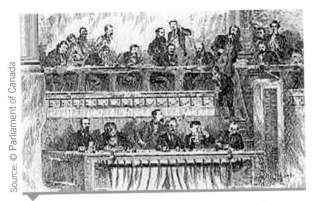

Source: © Parliament of Canada

The press gallery in the original chamber. The parliamentary press gallery is a group of approximately 350 journalists assigned to report on the business of Parliament and government. They are afforded access to parliamentary proceedings through the press gallery in the parliamentary chamber, as well as offices on Parliament Hill.

The press gallery and the media more generally do not have free rein to carry out their roles. They are constrained by a set of laws, standards, and professional approaches that govern their activities. For instance, professional codes of ethics, press councils in some provinces, **libel** law, and limited **access to information** are factors in how and what the media report (Chapter 9). Restrictions also emerge from the manner in which journalists operate. Political scientist Fred Fletcher (1981) has noted the effect on news reporting of the workings of press galleries. Until the 1960s, when they came to be seen as compromising standards of reporting, if not in direct conflicts of interest, press galleries benefited from such incentives as retainers paid by governments to journalists, preferred access, and other perquisites of their profession. In recent decades the galleries have striven to become as independent as possible from the control of government; consequently, they have become more professional. In turn, their independence from government has been compromised by *pack journalism*. The term derives from the tendency of journalists to hang around in groups while all pursue the same story. As a result, vast areas of government activity are inadequately covered, such as the courts, regulatory agencies, parliamentary committees, and policy-making and adjudication within the civil service. A further shortcoming of the press gallery is that many journalists lack the training to understand certain elements of government. Finally, in the face of recent efforts by large media chains to cut down on expenses, the size of the parliamentary press gallery is shrinking. It is now more clearly dominated by a few larger papers and wire services, as well as the major broadcast networks. Most noticeable is the decreased number of regional members whose function was to report on matters from the perspective of the region they represented.

In addition to the controls exercised upon the media, the media themselves can act in ways that impede their role of keeping the public informed. The public's right to know as opposed to the media's tendency to create stories is one such issue. For instance, every decision a government makes that involves the spending of money can be questioned after the fact. Should the government be spending that money? Is it getting good value for its dollar? Who is benefiting? When the media become intent on defeating a government they need only ask such questions continuously to place the government on the defensive, potentially interfering with its ability to govern, as perhaps was the case with the Liberal sponsorship scandal that led to the fall of Paul Martin's Liberal government in 2005. Meanwhile, the public may be ill-informed about the intent of the government, the context of spending and its relative prudence, and the ways in which government programs actually benefit citizens.

Specific regulations govern media behaviour in some areas to ensure fair reporting—especially of the media's coverage of elections. Regulations control aspects of political advertising; for example, they prohibit dramatization and forbid political ads to be broadcast within 48 hours of an election. There are restrictions on who can advertise what during a political campaign. For instance, interest groups are restricted from advertising in favour of one party based on their stance on one issue, such as abortion.

There are also less direct measures the government can use to control the media. When the government perceives that the structure or operation of the media may be moving against the public interest, it can establish a public inquiry to examine media operations, as it did with the 1970 Special

Senate Committee on the Mass Media, the 1980 Royal Commission on Newspapers, and the 2001 House of Commons Standing Committee study of broadcasting. However, while such inquiries are a good vehicle for developing an understanding of the forces shaping the media, they have not proven effective in achieving change (Skinner et al., 2005).

Since government is the largest advertiser in the country, the withdrawal of advertising can hurt media organizations, especially the print media. The government can seek to control journalists by giving selective access to people or information and by exercising favouritism in its monopoly over government-created information. For example, inconsistencies in dealing with access to information can easily be exploited for political motives. Releasing news at 4 p.m. on a Friday afternoon allows the information to make the evening news programs, but with little opportunity for comment. The next morning, when the news is old, the newspapers get their shot at interpreting the event or announcement. The soft form of this sort of media manipulation by government is termed 'news management'. Provincial governments also have some power in this regard. For example, attorneys general can order investigations into what they perceive as media interference with the court system and trials (Canadian Press, 1993).

Individual politicians can put their stamp on relations between the government and media. For instance, as the CBC program *The Press and the Prime Minister* documented, Pierre Trudeau was continually engaged in matching wits with the press. On a day-to-day basis, he was neither an unsophisticated nor a mute observer of the role and failings of the press in Canadian society. At election times he was a master of media manipulation in his presentation of issues and persona. During Jean Chrétien's time in office, he was known for his waffling on issues with the press, often leaving reporters and pundits unsure of where he stood on issues of the day. Stephen Harper is particularly noted for avoiding the media altogether.

Recently, some writers have argued that the line between government and the media is blurring as more and more journalists 'cross over' to take well-paid jobs in government (Rose and Kiss, 2006). Politicians are hiring former journalists to work as public relations people or 'handlers' to help manage their images and the issues faced by government. This raises questions over whether issues are being fairly and accurately presented by governments, or whether they are subject to 'spin' or interpretation that serves the personal political agenda of politicians. As Jonathan Rose and Simon Kiss (2006: 336) ask, 'who is producing the content that we consume in our daily lives? Perhaps public relations officials—whether they are government, industry, or otherwise—are gaining the upper hand?' In the US, one of the most extreme (or clever, depending on one's point of view) recent examples of 'spinning' a world-changing event was the American government's embedding of journalists with their troops during the invasion of Iraq in 2003. As one critic noted, they did a fine job of reporting both sides—both sides, that is, of the soldiers protecting them, not of the adversaries.

Amid the shifting relations between government and the media, the internet, with its many sources of information and capacity for information-sharing, appears to be challenging the role of the traditional mass media as the 'voice of the people'. For instance, web logs, or 'blogs', have played an increasingly important role in political communication, particularly in the US. For instance, Matt Drudge's blog, *The Drudge Report*, broke the story of President Bill Clinton's affair with White House intern Monica Lewinsky, seriously hampering the president's political effectiveness during his last days in office. Bloggers also discovered that documents used by CBS news to claim that President Bush 'had shirked his duties as a member of the National Guard during the Vietnam War' were 'of questionable veracity', leading CBS 'to apologize and launch an internal inquiry into how the story had passed internal checks' (ibid., 139). Drawing on the work of blog researchers Drezner and Farrell (2004), Rose and Kiss (2006: 340) point out that 'blogs have significant advantages in the opinion-formation process, often shaping important political events early on. Whereas members of the traditional media must go through some basic processes of vetting and editing before their accounts can be put forward, these constraints are non-existent for bloggers.' At this point, exactly what the impact of new web-based media will be on traditional media in the political sphere is difficult to say, but blogs and other online media are playing an expanding role in the political process.

When placed in the context of the history of the media outlined earlier in this chapter, contemporary tensions, shifts, and changes in the relations among the government, the media, and the public illustrate one thing for sure: the relationship between government and the media is one of on-going negotiation and change.

Information Needs, Communication Actualities, and the United Nations

Because of our proximity to the US and our frequent contact with American media products, you may tend to believe that the US behaves in its trading relations in a manner consistent with its ideology of free enterprise and free trade; but this assumption is wrong. You may be surprised to learn that other countries are similar to Canada in their concern over the flow of American cultural products inside their borders. You may be further surprised to hear that other countries have stronger restrictions on the importation of cultural goods than does Canada. As well, the US Congress is extremely protectionist. The US engages in judicial harassment by tying up foreign producers with legal challenges when it refuses to accept negative rulings in trade disputes, such as with the long-running argument over US tariffs on softwood lumber.

The United States is the richest and most powerful nation on earth. Moreover, it has an overall ideology that reflects its position of prominence and a tenacious ideological adherence to individual freedom and freedom of enterprise. These and other factors have created a society that is materially richer than Canada and more able to foist its products on the rest of the world. (Nevertheless, it has, at the same time, a very weak social safety net and public health-care system and has become fiscally vulnerable through heavy indebtedness to China.)

In Chapter 5 we will explore in more detail the impact of cultural products on audiences, but for now let us advance a few simple concepts. Continuous exposure to American cultural products presents us with a set of attitudes, perceptions, and ideas—a world view—inherent in those products. That effect is basic in all communication, not just propaganda. It is also the reason why the Motion Picture Association of America attempts to persuade US film producers to use American rather than Japanese automobiles on their sets (Rever, 1995). The problem with continuous exposure to foreign cultural products is that if we lack exposure to other products, other perspectives, other ways to understand the world, other alternatives for making choices, then we are open to blindly adopting (or rejecting) the values presented, which may clash with the values and institutions that inform our own ways of life. Moreover, continuous exposure to foreign media products also affects our sense of media forms, formats, and styles. For instance, we have become so accustomed to the fast-cut, high-action style of Hollywood feature films that those films that don't adopt Hollywood conventions often are rejected as slow, boring, or too intellectual.

The impact of foreign cultural products has been a long-standing issue for many people and communities. It arises from a commitment to preserve, develop, and represent one's own culture and nation. The focus on American cultural products derives from the fact that the US is by far the dominant producer of cultural products. While such concern can develop into extreme protectionism, intolerance, and political self-interest, it may also be a commitment to a pluralistic world society being represented in all its heterogeneity. For some time the United Nations Educational, Scientific and Cultural Organization (UNESCO) served as a focus for the articulation of these concerns and for the desirability of nations favouring their own artists, authors, and cultural producers. With the withdrawal of the US and the UK from **UNESCO** in the early 1980s, entailing the loss of one-third of its budget, this agency tended to steer away from playing such a role. Only recently has the organization managed to regain some of the political momentum it lost during that period (Warnica, 2005).

⁂ BOX 3.5 INTRODUCING UNESCO: WHAT WE ARE

UNESCO works to create the conditions for dialogue among civilizations, cultures and peoples, based upon respect for commonly shared values. It is through this dialogue that the world can achieve global visions of sustainable development encompassing observance of human rights, mutual respect and the alleviation of poverty, all of which are at the heart of UNESCO's mission and activities.

The broad goals and concrete objectives of the international community—as set out in the internationally agreed development goals, including the Millennium Development Goals (MDGS)—underpin all UNESCO'S strategies and activities. Thus, UNESCO'S unique competencies in education, the sciences, culture and communication and information contribute towards the realization of those goals.

UNESCO'S mission is to contribute to the building of peace, the eradication of poverty, sustainable development and intercultural dialogue through education, the sciences, culture, communication, and information. The Organization focuses, in particular, on two global priorities:

- Africa
- Gender equality

And on a number of overarching objectives:

- Attaining quality education for all and lifelong learning
- Mobilizing science knowledge and policy for sustainable development

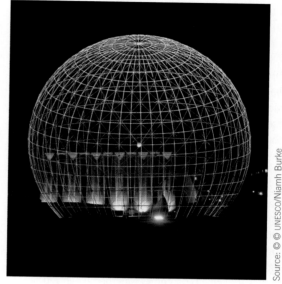

Source: © © UNESCO/Niamh Burke

UNESCO's Symbolic Globe.

- Addressing emerging social and ethical challenges
- Fostering cultural diversity, intercultural dialogue, and a culture of peace
- Building inclusive knowledge societies through information and communication

Source: UNESCO, at: www.unesco.org/new/en/unesco/about-us/who-we-are/introducing-unesco.

As discussed in later chapters, the position developed by UNESCO on communications problems and prospects, at first with the MacBride Report (1980) and more recently with the Convention on the Protection and Promotion of the Diversity of Cultural Expressions (2005), is that each nation has the right to a national culture or communications policy. A nation must have the capacity to take information produced either by itself or by the world community and analyze it according to its own national needs and priorities. In practice, Canada has not fully committed itself to this need. Yet our investments in high technology, such as the information highway, demonstrate that neither are we entirely without commitment to this end. Canada is in the position of being economically able to work towards an information infrastructure oriented to its national needs and the maintenance of its independence. Being already committed to technological development in communications, being economically well-off, and being so near and so like the US, we are in a position to lead in setting boundaries on the US cultural barrage for our own benefit and for the benefit of other nations. Whether or not the federal government will take comprehensive measures to meet such challenges is still open to question.

⁑ SUMMARY

The evolution of the modern mass media began in the mid-fifteenth century with Gutenberg's development of printing by means of movable type. Printing with movable type facilitated a social movement that saw the eclipse of feudalism and the dawning of the Renaissance, followed by the Reformation, the Enlightenment, and the Industrial Revolution. The divine right of kings was replaced with the notion of the *consent of the governed*. The printing press served an important social role from the fifteenth century onward in gathering information and informing citizens.

In making their contribution, the press and, subsequently, other communication media have been influenced by their social and historical location; that is, they have been given form and function by a larger set of social circumstances and events. The rise of industrial society, along with urbanization, increased literacy, and the eight-hour workday, provided the context within which contemporary media evolved their forms and functions. In Canada, the development of modern media was further shaped by basic geographical and social realities such as our vast, sparsely populated, bilingual, multicultural, and regional country, which lies next to the United States—the world's largest economy and most aggressive exporter of entertainment and information products.

Moreover, while the role of the media in society can be conceived from various ideological perspectives—as the fourth estate, as liberal, as Marxist—in Canadian society the press and then the electronic mass media have developed, to a large part, under market principles. And while Canadians have invested a great amount of public funding in the electronic media to assist in nation-building, and this investment in technological infrastructure has provided Canadians with a high level of communication services, it has also paved the way for the importation and distribution of a vast amount of foreign content.

As we shall see in Chapter 8, after years of subsidies and support, magazine and book publishers, filmmakers, and sound-recording artists are, to a degree, increasing their domestic market share and making a mark on the world stage. However, these successes are fragile and require the ongoing support of governments. At the same time, technological change has raised the possibility of giving a greater voice to the people—not only to express themselves but also to own and control information sites that may demand greater responsiveness from government and the traditional mass media. But whether the potential of this technological capacity will be realized or whether it will weaken the traditional mass media remains to be seen.

Canadians must remind themselves that, in taking action to regulate the mass media and to stimulate cultural industries, they are not alone. While efforts to define and protect cultural industries have weakened in the face of growing transnational trade and trade agreements, the struggle to maintain control over their own cultural development remains a concern for many nations and is still being fought in various venues.

⁑ KEY TERMS

access to information, p. 80
Areopagitica, p. 61
bourgeoisie, p. 62
commodities, p. 64
conservative, p. 61
economies of scale, p. 69
Enlightenment, p. 59
fourth estate, p. 66

freedom of speech, p. 73
freedom of the press, p. 67
ideology, p. 59
Industrial Revolution, p. 59
libel, p. 80
multiplier effects, p. 77
Renaissance, p. 59
UNESCO, p. 82

⫸ RELATED WEBSITES

Access to Information and Privacy Acts: www.tbs-sct. gc.ca/atip-aiprp/index-eng.asp
These two Acts provide a sense of Canada's legislation in these areas.

Canada's Privacy Act: http://laws-lois.justice.gc.ca/eng/ acts/P-21/index.html
As you will see, the Privacy Act covers much more than internet privacy.

Media History in Canada: mediahistory.ca
This central bibliographic source provides information on Canadian media history.

Canadian Heritage: www.pch.gc.ca
Every Canadian student concerned with culture, the media, and heritage should visit the website of the federal government's Canadian Heritage site.

John Locke: www.orst.edu/instruct/phl302/philosophers/ locke.html
Many universities have taken it upon themselves to provide texts free of charge to the world. Many are in the US. This site provides information on and texts written by John Locke.

Milton's Areopagitica: www.buddycom.com/reviews/ areopag/index.html
This important work on censorship by the English poet can be found on a variety of sites that are accessible by doing a Google search on 'Areopagitica'.

rabble.ca
A vibrant online source of alternative news and views.

Institute for Alternative Journalism: www.alternet.org
A valuable alternative news website.

⫸ FURTHER READINGS

Armstrong, Robert. 2010. *Broadcasting Policy in Canada*. Toronto: University of Toronto Press. A comprehensive account of the history and dimensions of broadcasting policy in Canada.

Canada. 1981. *Report of the Royal Commission on Newspapers*. Ottawa: Supply and Services. This dated but most recent Royal Commission on the press brings forward many issues. Its background papers are also very informative.

Canada, House of Commons. 2003. *Our Cultural Sovereignty: The Second Century of Canadian Broadcasting. Report of the House of Commons Standing Committee on Canadian Heritage*. Ottawa: Communication Canada. This report provides good background on the history, structure, and problems facing Canadian broadcasting.

Vipond, Mary. 2000. *The Mass Media in Canada*. Toronto: James Lorimer. This book provides a historical perspective on the development of the Canadian mass media.

Wagman, Ira, and Ezra Winton. 2010. 'Canadian cultural policy in the age of media abundance: Old challenges and new technologies', in Leslie Regan Shade, ed., *Mediascapes*, 3rd edn. Toronto: Nelson, 61–77. Provides an overview of some of the contemporary challenges facing Canadian cultural policy.

Weir, Ernest Austin. 1965. *The Struggle for National Broadcasting in Canada*. Toronto: McClelland & Stewart. As the title suggests, the author presents an account of the development of public broadcasting in Canada and of the political and cultural milieu out of which this regime was established.

Williams, Raymond. 1979. *Television, Technology and Cultural Form*. Glasgow: Fontana Collins. Focusing on the development of television, Williams illustrates how technological development is the product of a broad set of social forces.

❯ STUDY QUESTIONS

1. What was the essence of the Enlightenment?

2. How do Enlightenment values influence the mass media?

3. Describe how modern media can be seen as a cultural form inherent to industrial society.

4. Describe some of the ways in which the federal government has played a central role in developing both the Canadian economy and the Canadian media?

5. Provide some examples of 'economies of scale' in media organizations.

6. Explain why or why not governments should be able to control the information environment. If so, in what ways?

PART II

Theoretical Perspectives

CHAPTER 4

Theoretical Perspectives on Media Content

The philosophers have only interpreted the world, in various ways;
the point is to change it.

— KARL MARX

OPENING QUESTIONS

- What are 'representation' and
  'signification' in communications?
- What is 'social theory'?
- What are some of the main
  theoretical perspectives on
  media content?
- What is media 'genre analysis'?
- Do the media provide a full,
  unbiased perspective on the
  world?

Learning Objectives

- To be able to use terms for the analysis of content, including
  signification, indeterminacy of representation, intertextuality,
  polysemy, rhetoric, sign, signifier, and signified.
- To recognize social theory as a means of uncovering the
  complexity of social communication.
- To be able to use various theoretical perspectives, including
  literary criticism; structuralism, semiotics, and post-structuralism; discourse analysis; content analysis; critical political
  economy; and media form/genre analysis.
- To be able to discuss the constraints within which the media
  operate.

Introduction

Chapters 4 and 5 introduce communication theory and illustrate some of the main approaches to the study of media content and audiences. This chapter begins by introducing terms that describe some basic characteristics of the process of communication and media content. It then introduces a number of theoretical and methodological perspectives communication theorists use when studying content. Finally, it considers some of the dimensions of the interaction between media content and society.

Representation and Signification

When we study communication, and particularly communication content, we are generally studying practices or processes of **representation**. What is representation? It's the act of putting ideas into words, paintings, sculpture, film, plays, television programs,

or any other medium of communication. A picture of a plane crash is not the crash itself, obviously, but a 're-presentation' of that crash. A map is a representation of the actual place that it seeks to describe. An advertisement for a sports utility vehicle (SUV) is a representation or way of thinking about such a vehicle. Even a 'live' television broadcast of a hockey game or some other sporting event is not the game itself but a series of carefully chosen and constructed images, camera angles, and commentary that represent the event in an audiovisual package.

In putting ideas into any medium of communication, a person selects certain elements of reality to describe the object, event, person, or situation he or she wishes to represent. In other words, representations are, to a large part, simplifications and interpretations of the objects and events they describe. The person receiving or decoding that communication then uses what he or she knows of what is described and what he or she knows of the system

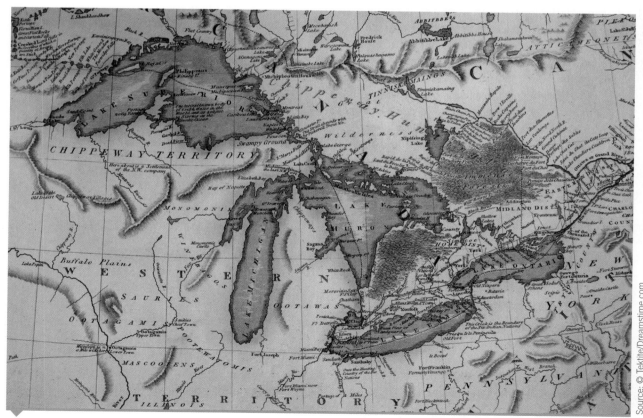

Maps are icons because their directional relations and distances between landmarks physically resemble what they 'stand for.'

of representation—most often language—to come to an understanding of what was encoded by the sender.

A more rigorous way of thinking about representation is as a process of signification. Signification is using signs to make meaning. What's a **sign**? Anything with meaning: a word, an image, a sound, a painting, even things themselves like dark clouds on the horizon. The Swiss linguist Ferdinand de Saussure—sometimes considered the founder of **semiotics** or the science of signs—posited that signs are composed of two elements: the signifier and the signified. The **signifier** is the thing that we see, hear, or feel: the image on a screen, sounds, or small bumps on paper. The **signified** is the idea or mental concept we draw from those signifiers: the ideas in a blog, music, or words written in Braille. The process of signification is a process of making meaning. Indeed, from this perspective the whole of our experience of the world is a process of signification as we translate the signs we encounter into meaning: dark clouds mean rain; a short chapter means less homework; an angry parent means trouble.

C.S. Peirce categorized signs into three different types: icon, index, and symbol. An icon looks like the object it describes. For instance, maps and photographs both are icons. An index is related to the object it represents. Smoke is an index of fire and a sneeze is an index of a cold or allergy or irritant. A **symbol** is a sign that bears no direct resemblance to what it signifies. Words are symbols, as is the image of an apple when it is used to represent something other than fruit, such as knowledge or a particular brand of electronic products.

Intertextuality, Polysemy, and the Indeterminacy of Representation

The idea that a sign can represent or signify more than one thing raises the indeterminacy of representation. To some the image of a sporty SUV might signify or represent luxury, adventure, or sex appeal; to others, environmental disaster. The sound of falling rain might signify or represent a soothing summer's

What does this image signify to you? What do you think it was intended to signify to audiences?

evening or an impending flood. The meaning of any particular sign is not guaranteed but is dependent on the context of its use and interpretation.

In other words, signs do not exist in isolation. Rather, they are either explicitly or implicitly part of larger 'texts' or sets of signs and symbols. Images of SUVs are often found in advertisements that portray them as part of mountain adventures or happy family outings. The melodic splash of rain is often used to establish a mood in music, film, or television programs. In other words, the meaning of these signs is itself given form by its relation to other signs in the context of a larger symbolic system. If we are confronted by images and sounds without this kind of grounding, to make meaning out of them we often supply our own context, drawn from memory and imagination.

The idea that meaning is made in the context of larger symbolic systems draws our attention to two other important elements of the process of signification. The first is the 'intertextuality' of the process of making meaning. Intertextuality refers to the meaning we make of one text depending on the meanings we have drawn from other sets of signs we have encountered (Kristeva, 1969; Barthes, 1968). That is, meaning is grounded in the relationships we find between different texts. Our understanding of the ad for the SUV as a family vehicle is dependent on our combining knowledge of the SUV as a mode of transportation and the representation of the people in the image as a family. Folding the two signifiers together—SUV and happy family—creates the signified 'family vehicle'. Similarly, our understanding of the ways vehicle exhaust emissions are related to global warming might also lead us to interpret the SUV as an instrument of environmental degradation. Thus, our past experience—our individual histories—provides the backdrop for interpreting the signs and symbols we encounter in everyday life.

Second, making meaning is an active process. Making the connection between signifier and signified, joining past and present experience, requires active participation. Even when the meaning of things appears obvious, even natural, it requires active work. We make or create meaning.

Because signs can be open to a variety of interpretations, they are 'polysemic', that is, having 'many meanings' (Jensen, 1990). The different types or levels of meaning drawn may be denotative and connotative, where **denotative** meaning refers to the literal or most obvious interpretation of the sign and **connotative** meaning refers to the range of other, less obvious, or more subjective meanings that may be drawn.

Advertisements exemplify the purposive use of signs to create different levels of meaning. For instance, by using seemingly 'ordinary' women in their ads instead of professional models that generally represent the standards of beauty in soap and cosmetic advertising, the Dove Real Beauty Campaign (Appendix to this chapter) apparently attempts to re-signify the usual advertising meaning of 'beauty'.

The fact that signs are polysemic highlights the importance of context for the creation and interpretation of meaning. The social and cultural conditions surrounding the production of media texts, as well as those involved in their consumption, play into the meaning generated from them. Similarly, the fact that any given sign can have many meanings illustrates **the indeterminacy of representation**. On one hand, the meaning of signs and the messages of which they are a part is indeterminate because there is an indeterminable number of ways of representing an object, action, or event—another representation can always be made. On the other hand, they are indeterminate because there is no *necessary* correspondence between the meaning encoded in a particular message by the sender and that decoded by the receiver. Nevertheless, each representation is grounded in a specific context as the person and/or medium doing the representing works to guide the audience or receiver of the message towards a specific or preferred meaning.

There are many factors determining polysemy, or the grounded indeterminacy of representation. For instance, different media provide different systems for making meaning. Moreover, one system of representation cannot encompass the full spectrum of the meaning of another. A painting cannot be fully translated into a prose essay, or even poetry. Nor can a sculpture be completely transformed into a photograph or even a hologram. Inevitably, something is lost. In short, a multiplicity of meanings can be generated within one medium, and meaning can be generated within the multiplicity of media.

Polysemy and the indeterminacy of representation tend to lead the study of communication away from the foundations of science and social science towards the foundations of interpretation we find in the humanities. It is concerned more with **rhetoric** (how things are said) and hermeneutics (how things are interpreted) than with 'truth' per se.

In the study of communication, the importance of a statement is not limited to whether it

Source: Dove/PA Wire URN: 8069588
Press Association via AP Images

What are the polysemic representations of these young women? What does this presentation mean to you? How do you think other viewers interpret it? In what ways do these women differ from conventional models?

⁝ BOX 4.1   DEVELOPING PERSPECTIVE

No doubt many in the West assume that the owners of Al Jazeera satellite television were secret allies of Osama bin Laden and al-Qaeda. Much in the same way, one might say that the US television networks were dancing to the tune of the American government when they agreed to block the transmission of al-Qaeda videotapes in response to the demand of the US National Security Adviser, Condoleezza Rice. Al Jazeera's senior producer puts the matter this way: 'It would be wild to claim that we are friends of al-Qaeda, but at the end of the day we do not answer to such people as Condoleezza Rice....We do not talk about what the king ate for breakfast or how many people kissed his hand like the rest of the Arab media. We are more likely to ask those who didn't kiss his hand why they didn't. That's why all the security chiefs in the West monitor every word of our output.'

predicts events, can be refuted by others, or generates other interesting hypotheses—all standards used in science. What is interesting is how an act of communication selects and re-presents or re-constructs something, and what gives a particular representation its force, its ability to persuade, or its attractiveness. Whatever makes a particular novel, painting, or film more popular or revered than another, or even a novel more 'powerful' than a film, cannot be satisfactorily discussed by reference to the relative 'truth' of each communication. Such media and individual works are discussed by communication scholars in terms of their rhetorical force or in terms of the nature or style of their representation.

For instance, if we compare media, the visual dimension of film and television quite consistently adds a specific sense of reality that another medium, such as print, cannot provide. However, what film and television gain in that dimension they often lose in subtlety, character development, and room for imaginative play when compared to print. Similarly, the discussion of abstract ideas changes when one moves from books to the popular press or to television. Television demands a pluralism of sight, sound, and personage that is partially present in radio and absent in print—more than a few minutes of the same person talking, no matter what the visuals, tends to undermine the speaker's credibility or, at least, the viewers' interest. Just the opposite seems to hold for print—a single 'voice' will more readily elicit a reader's trust and understanding. The characteristics of different media tend to nuance in particular ways the crafting of content.

Communication Theory as Social Theory

In studying the process of communication we often draw on social theory, and particularly communication theory, for helping us to understand how processes of communication are nuanced and operate. What is social theory? Generally, it is a representation of the social world; a set of ideas about how the world is organized and functions. While we all have ideas about how the world works, often our assumptions are fragmentary and contradictory. Take, for instance, common-sense proverbs such as 'many hands make light work' and 'too many cooks spoil the broth'. While they both purport to provide a way of understanding and approaching work, they offer contradictory perspectives on how to do so. In contrast, social theory strives to offer rigorous, logical explanations of elements of the social world. It is a representation of the world that attempts to provide a systematic and comprehensive explanation of the relationships between individuals, social groups, and the world around them.

What is the purpose of social theory? At one level, it provides explanations of how things work and why things are the way they are. At another level, such explanations guide action: to alleviate social problems and improve the quality of life or to construct social policy. To paraphrase Karl Marx, 'The purpose of social theory is not simply to understand the world but to change it', and change it in a progressive manner that makes things more egalitarian and provides more equal access to the fruits of our society for all citizens.

As a kind of social theory, communication theory is a way of representing the complex process of communication. It is a way of trying to understand the different forces that contextualize and give form to human communication and, particularly for our purposes, mass communication.

There are, however, a wide variety of com-munication theories. Some are elements of larger theories of society (liberal and Marxist theories, for instance) and offer broad claims of the role and purpose of various forms of communication in society as a whole, such as theories of the press. Others offer only partial explanations of the process of communication, such as the semiotic explanation of the process of signification discussed above. Some provide simple, highly abstract perspectives, such as Shannon and Weaver's model of communication that was outlined in Chapter 1 (Figure 1.2), which asserts that communication both begins and ends with individuals. Others, such as the social model of communication (Figure 1.3), illustrate the process of communication as given form by a great many factors and variables.

To provide a better understanding of the variety of ways different theories approach and envision the process of communication we will now turn our attention to another model of communication.

The Encoding/Decoding Model

As we have seen, mass communication is a process that involves both **encoding**, or creating media messages, and **decoding**, or interpreting them. While these are active processes, in each of these moments a range of social institutions and forces serve to frame or contextualize the ways in which messages are constituted and the ways in which people make meaning from them. Drawing from Stuart Hall's (1993) discussion of this process, Figure 4.1 illustrates some of the key elements involved in it. Please note, however, that although the diagram displays these pieces of the

FIGURE 4.1   Encoding and Decoding

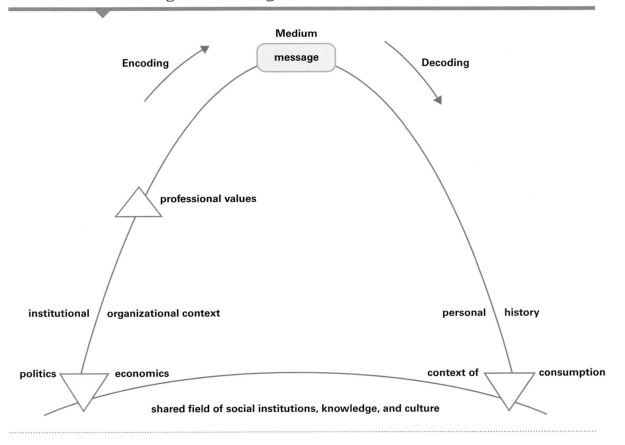

process as individual parts, in reality all of these parts are interrelated. For instance, as we saw in Chapter 3, communication media are integral to the societies of which they are a part, not separate or distinct technical systems. Similarly, the professional values of media workers are woven between organizational and technical imperatives, not ideas separated or distinct from social context. However, for purposes of illustration, we have abstracted the process of communication from this larger social context and exploded its pieces to highlight the different roles that each plays. Each of these pieces is described below.

First is the shared field of social institutions and knowledge, or culture, within which the media system operates—the general social milieu in which we live. It is comprised of language and social customs: ideas we hold about gender, family, and work as well as the laws, regulations, and other social processes and structures that frame and animate society and the ways we think and act in the world. To a large part these are the elements of what we referred to as 'industrial society' in Chapter 3. Or, they might be thought of as 'culture', or the 'ways of life' that make up our society. Certainly, the ways that each media producer and consumer experiences and draws on this larger social milieu are not the same; often they are quite different. However, this milieu does provide a common field of referents for people to draw on and to make meaning from.

Second, the broad political and economic processes contextualize how the process of media production is undertaken. On the political side, we would include specific laws and regulations that frame the way media organizations operate and what media professionals do: libel laws, copyright, and media ownership regulations. In the case of broadcasting, we would include the Broadcasting Act and the regulations promulgated by the CRTC; for film, distribution regulations; and for newspapers, ownership regulations. As we saw in Chapter 3, each medium operates in a specific legal and regulatory context that informs the way its products are created. On the economic side, we are concerned with the ways in which the drive for profits or commercial forces impinge on production. As we have seen, the economies of scale enjoyed by American producers help flood Canadian markets

with American media products. All of these political and economic circumstances influence the ways media products in Canada represent the world.

Third is the institutional or organizational context within which media messages are created. Here we might consider the ways in which organizational mandates or imperatives frame what media organizations do and the products they create. For instance, the National Film Board is guided by its mandate to 'represent Canada to Canadians'. This purpose underlies all of the products it produces. Similarly, as laid out in the Broadcasting Act, the CBC's mandate guides that organization's actions. Private broadcasters and other media have profits as their motive. Hence, both the ways their resources are organized at the organizational level and the media products they produce reflect that imperative.

A fourth dimension of influence on the way media represent the world is the professional values that guide media producers. Media professionals are guided in their practices by specific ideas about the characteristics of the products they create. Journalists go to journalism school to learn how to identify newsworthy events and produce news reports. Similarly, writers working on situation comedies, soap operas, and other program genres are governed by assumptions and guidelines as to how those programs are structured.

Fifth, as we have discussed, the medium through which representations are communicated can have great influence on the form and structure of ideas and information. Telling a story in a novel is quite different from telling it in a film. Radio addresses audiences quite differently compared with television or newspapers. News is often presented quite differently on the web than in traditional media.

Finally, at the level of decoding, the context of consumption—where and by whom media products are consumed—has impact on the meaning that is made from them. Age, education, family background, religion, gender, race, ethnicity: all of these elements of one's background or 'history' can play on how media messages are decoded. Moreover, much of this personal experience is social experience, that is, experience drawn from the larger field of social institutions, knowledge, and culture. For Stuart Hall, these factors could result in interpretations or 'readings' of messages that range from 'dominant'—such as those that are in complete agreement with the ideas/perspectives contained in the message—to 'oppositional'—such as those that are in total disagreement with those ideas.

Again, while the encoder's and decoder's experiences of this field may be vastly different, it does provide a common set of 'referents'—that is, ideas, situations, and circumstances that can be referred to or represented in media products. Consider the television program *The Simpsons*, which is broadcast in a large number of countries and a number of different languages around the world. The culture and institutions found in these countries are often quite different, yet people in these different places are able to decode the meaning from this program and share in its humour. How so? To a large extent this is because the show's writers draw on a set of characters and circumstances familiar to all those people. The program focuses on a typical nuclear family—father, mother, and three children—who live in a typical American town and lead a typical life: homemaking, working, going to school, getting into trouble. In other words, both the characters and

the situations they encounter are stereotypes of lives in an industrial society that many recognize and to a degree understand, even though they may not live like that or approve of the stereotyping. In creating the program, its writers draw on ideas familiar to a very diverse group of people. And, in large part, the wide appeal of that program depends on their ability to find common points of knowledge and understanding in the midst of that diversity.

As a social model of communication, the encoding/decoding model draws our attention to the fact that the process of communication is given form by social factors. Individuals who work in a particular institutional and organizational context employ professional values to construct media messages that draw on social knowledge supposedly shared by their intended audience; then, the messages are delivered through particular technical systems to audience members with particular social backgrounds. In turn, these individuals draw upon social knowledge accrued through their personal histories to decode the messages and deploy that information in their lives.

This model is useful for understanding how certain theories envision the process of

---

⁝ BOX 4.2   MEDIA/CULTURE BINDING

The media interact with everyday life in various ways. Catchy tunes played countless times or repeatable phrases played frequently float through one's head at the oddest times—and are intended to. The media inform us about politics, life in other cultures and places, how people kiss, how people smoke, how people rob banks, how children and others play with toys, how people dance. The list of human behaviours modelled in media is endless (see Meyrowitz, 1985, and his 'effects loops'). But the interaction is not a one-way process. The media draw their content from the real lives of particular real individuals and groups. In an example that captures this relation well, the famous writer and semiologist, Umberto Eco, looked at it this way:

1. A firm produces polo shirts with an alligator on them and it advertises them.
2. A generation begins to wear polo shirts.
3. Each consumer of the polo shirt advertises, via the alligator on his or her chest, this brand of polo shirt.

4. A TV broadcast (program), to be faithful to reality, shows some young people wearing the alligator polo shirt.
5. The young (and the old) see the TV broadcast and buy more alligator polo shirts because they have 'the young look'.

- *Which is the mass medium*? The ad? The broadcast? The shirt?
- *Who is sending the message*? The manufacturer? The wearer? The TV director? The analyst of this phenomenon?
- *Who is the producer of ideology*? Again, the manufacturer? The wearer (including the celebrity who may wear it in public for a fee)? The TV director who portrays the generation?
- *Where does the (marketing) plan come from*? This is not to imply that there is no plan, but rather that it does not emanate from one central source.

Source: Eco (1986: 148–50).

communication. Few theories claim to explain the influence of all of these different dimensions on that process. Rather, they focus on how a number of those elements work to determine how the media operate and the influence they have.

A central consideration of media and communication theory is the relationship between agency and structure. To put this another way: can people generally encode whatever ideas and meanings they want into media messages and programs? Or, do the structures and processes in which people live and work determine the range and character of the messages and ideas they can produce? This is a pivotal question for trying to explain how media systems operate. However, as a number of researchers have pointed out, social structure is both 'enabling' and 'constraining' (see Giddens, 1984). For instance, language provides a structure for communication, a set of words and rules for communicating. While that structure is constraining in that we can only communicate in that language if we correctly enact its vocabulary, it is also highly enabling because it allows the communication of a vast range of ideas. Similarly, while working as a reporter at a large newspaper is constraining in that one has to adhere to editorial policies and professional values regarding what kinds of events constitute news, how to write a news story, etc., as well as organizational rules and deadlines, it also is enabling because it allows one to write about changing events and circumstances on a daily basis, from a range of perspectives, and because the material one writes will be read regularly by thousands of people.

Theories of the Media, Theories of Society

As noted, different theories take different approaches to the study of the media. In this section we consider four perspectives on the media and society. The first two—the libertarian theory of the press and social responsibility theory—draw on liberal theories of society to consider what they believe to be the social conditions necessary to create a responsible press. The second two perspectives—political economic theory and the mass society thesis—are to a large part themselves theories of

society and thereby illustrate what they see as the dominant social influences on the structure of the media and media content. The point to consider here is not which of these theories is the right or 'true' perspective on the media and society, but rather the insight that each brings to the analysis.

Libertarian Theory

The notion of freedom to express one's beliefs, which spread across Europe during the Reformation with the invention of the printing press, was advanced in England by John Milton's *Areopagitica* (Chapter 3) and the English Bill of Rights accepted by William III. Such philosophers as John Locke (1632–1704), David Hume (1711–76), and John Stuart Mill (1806–73) nourished those concepts of agency and the free will of individuals, and they were further expanded during the eighteenth century, the Age of Enlightenment. The modern **libertarian theory** of the press derived from these precursors its fundamental assumption that individual freedom is the first and foremost social goal to be sought. Despite the fact the government can play social roles that are enabling and constraining (e.g., 'enabling' in that it supplies education, etc.; 'constraining' in terms of taxation and laws and regulations governing behaviour), libertarians are highly suspicious of the state—some to the point of anarchy. Limiting the powers of the state and other impediments to individual action, libertarian philosophers maintain, will create the most advantageous situation for all. Of course, what they overlook or downplay is that under this arrangement some people—those with more wealth and power—are 'more equal'— that is, have far more opportunities—than others.

Libertarian theory sees the mass media as an extension of the individual's right to freedom of expression and, hence, as an independent voice that helps to make government responsible to the people. The media do so by feeding information to people so that, come election time, performance can be rewarded or punished. In a non-political context, libertarians see the mass media as assiduous pursuers of free speech. Freedom of speech is considered one of the most important of all freedoms; and while it may result in problems and difficulties in the short term, as in the case of pornography and of hate speech, libertarians maintain it is the best way to preserve freedom and the rights of all citizens.

In striving to ensure distance between the government and the mass media, the libertarian places media in the hands of private citizens. The rights to publish and to free expression are fundamental rights of citizenship and must not be tampered with, particularly by government. However, in the face of the overarching importance placed on freedom of expression, there is little concern for the fact that in the course of media production and operation, the private sector promotes its own interests—those of developing markets and of accruing profits—which are placed above the interests of the people, of society, and of the government of the day. Consequently, rather than allowing journalists to dedicate themselves to 'serving the people', privately controlled media tend to maximize their own interests as private, profit-oriented corporations, thereby undermining the libertarian ideal they claim to uphold.

Social Responsibility Theory

While also drawing on liberal theories of society and the libertarian theory of the press, **social responsibility theory** arises from the perception that the libertarian arrangement fails to produce a press that is generally of benefit to society. The concept was originally put forward by a non-governmental US commission, the (Hutchins) Commission on the Freedom of the Press (1947).

In Canada, the Kent Royal Commission on Newspapers (Canada, 1981: 235) explained the social responsibility theory well, pointing out that as newspaper publishing began to be taken over by big business, the notion of social responsibility was born of a need to fight against the potential of a new authoritarianism by big-business ownership of the press. The Kent Commission defined the concept of social responsibility as follows:

The conjoined requirements of the press, for freedom and for legitimacy, derive from the same basic right: the right of citizens to information about their affairs. In order that people be informed, the press has a

critical responsibility. In order to fulfill that responsibility it is essential that the press be free, in the traditional sense, free to report and free to publish as it thinks; it is equally essential that the press's discharge of its responsibility to inform should be untainted by other interests, that it should not be dominated by the powerful or be subverted by people with concerns other than those proper to a newspaper serving a democracy. 'Comment is free', as C.P. Snow, one of the greatest English-speaking editors, wrote, 'but facts are sacred.' The right of information in a free society requires, in short, not only freedom of comment generally but, for its news media, the freedom of a legitimate press, doing its utmost to inform, open to all opinions and dominated by none. [C.P. Snow was, for years, editor of the *Manchester Guardian*—a British newspaper known for its rigorous reporting and social conscience.]

Ironically, although an American commission into press freedom (led by university president Robert Hutchins) coined the term 'social responsibility', it is a concept much better accepted in Canada and in Europe than in the US. This is because, in the US, the First Amendment to the Constitution states that 'Congress shall make no law…abridging the freedom of speech, or of the press.' Being the first of the constitutional amendments, it sits at the top of the hierarchy of rights. The Canadian Constitution does not allow for such a hierarchy of rights whereby one right takes precedence over another, for instance, the freedom of the press versus the right to a fair trial. Thus, in Canada and Europe it is possible to limit free speech based on a consideration of its consequences—reporters must be careful not to discuss a crime in such detail as to jeopardize a person's right to a fair trial (Chapter 9). However, despite the fact that the social responsibility theory of the press might be seen as the dominant theory of the media in Canada (Chapter 8), exactly what the dimensions of press responsibility are in Canada and how they might be either taken up by or imposed on the private corporations that make up the large part of Canada's media remain the subject of public debate.

The Mass Society Thesis

As a consequence of industrialization in the nineteenth century, people were uprooted from traditional rural ways of life to live in cities (Chapter 3). For many writers of the time this new way of life was without cultural foundation. Cut free from a traditional (feudal) agricultural way of life and the social values, customs, and bonds that gave that life form and function, people in the new industrial context became a collection of isolated individuals—an undifferentiated 'mass' society within which no assumptions about social order and people's place and function in it were held in common. Broom and Selznick (in DeFleur and Ball-Rokeach, 1989: 160) describe the new urban society thus:

> Modern society is made up of masses in the sense that there has emerged a vast mass of segregated, isolated individuals, interdependent in all sorts of specialized ways yet lacking in any central unifying value or purpose. The weakening of traditional bonds, the growth of rationality, and the division of labor, have created societies made up of individuals who are only loosely bound together. In this sense the word 'mass' suggests something closer to an aggregate than a tightly knit kinship group.

In this state of social atomization and potential moral disorder, the masses were regarded by the social **elite** of the day as somewhat threatening, as though through their new-found political and economic power—the extending franchise or right to vote, their increasing importance in the industrial division of labour, and their rising power as consumers to whom manufacturers are increasingly directing the outputs of their production—they posed a severe threat to the existing cultural order and the abilities of intellectuals and other elites to sustain their ways of life. The nature of this perceived threat varies from writer to writer. For some it is viewed as a potential state of anarchy, a breakdown of social order. Others express concern that these people are easily subject to manipulation and easy targets for totalitarian social and political movements. From this perspective the rise of the Nazis in Germany and of Stalin in Russia were attributable to the rise of mass society. In this context, media are seen as a unifying force in society, a means of conjoining minds in common cause and action, although not necessarily towards positive ends.

Through the early twentieth century this elitist perspective wound its way through a range of academic disciplines and had a strong impact on early communication theory. To a large extent, it framed new media such as radio and film as part of a new 'commercial' or mass culture where media content is simply an unsophisticated commercial product designed to placate the masses with cheap entertainment and, through advertising, incorporate them into a more consumer-oriented way of life. As we shall see in Chapter 5, underlying these conceptions of the purpose of mass media was a rather unsophisticated vision of audiences.

Political Economy and Marx

Before economics became a free-standing social science, it was seen by early proponents, such as Adam Smith (1723–90), as inexorably tied to politics. In the same way that the management of a family's resources and the power dynamics associated with it might be called domestic **political economy**, so the organization of a nation's resources, involving as it does both overall political decisions and economic management, could be called national political economy. As capitalism became entrenched in the nations of the West, capitalist political economy first came to be called 'capitalist economics' and then, simply, 'economics'. The argument for separating politics and economics, to oversimplify matters, was that the market should operate as a system of resource **allocation** independent of political systems. Hence, the term for economics: *tout seul*. However, not all writers agreed with this premise. In the early to mid-nineteenth century, as capitalist industry was introducing massive social change in Europe, Karl Marx argued that the capitalist system was premised on a set of social relations in which politics and economics were inextricably linked.

Modern Western societies, Marx argued, were characterized by a new and revolutionary mode of production—industrial capitalism—in which scientific techniques, applied to the mass production of an ever-increasing range of goods (or commodities, in Marx's terms), created wealth for the owners of capital. In Marx's analysis, industrial society is organized around the reproduction of capital, that is, the creation of 'surplus' or profits from productive activities. This tends to create two main classes: capitalists, the owners of the means of production (factories, commercial property, etc.); and workers, those who, because they don't own productive property, must sell their labour power to capitalists. Marx argued that this system of production generally serves the interests of the capitalists—a tiny fraction of the population—and that workers, the vast majority of people, are exploited by the capitalists. They can be fired at any time and for whatever reason, and they have to fight to squeeze a living wage out of industrialists.

As Marx saw it, modern capitalism transformed all aspects of life, particularly at the political level, as government and the structure of the state increasingly came to represent the interests of capital. New laws were enacted to protect private property, particularly the productive property of capitalists. Labour legislation laid the legal framework for relations between capital and labour. Taxation raised funds for creating infrastructure—roads, railways, canals, harbours, and communication systems—that kept the wheels of commerce moving. Schooling was redefined along industrial models in order to teach people the skills necessary to become productive workers. And when workers rebelled through strikes or some other form of civil disobedience, the police force could be called upon to restore order.

At the heart of a **Marxist analysis** of modern society is a belief in the possibility of a better life that could be shared by all—a life that is blocked by the private appropriation of wealth. On the one hand, techniques of mass production seemed to offer the possibility of the end of scarcity. Material abundance could be available to all if the techniques of modern manufacturing were somehow regulated with everyone's interests in mind. On the other hand, Western society has not realized this possibility. A bitter paradox is created when huge quantities of grain sit in prairie elevators; powdered milk, in storage; and butter, in freezers while thousands of people live in hunger in Canada and millions live in extreme hunger or near famine elsewhere in the world.

Marx's ideas have shaped the political life of the twentieth century throughout the world. In most European democracies, the development of the political parties of the masses tended to be split in two—those who represent the interests of the owners of property and those who represent the interests of workers. Experiments in communism (a political application of Marx's ideas) lasted for 70 years in Russia and continue in China and Cuba. Although the Russian system of authoritarian state socialism clearly has failed, Marx's ideas have not been entirely discredited and Communist and socialist parties still command strong showings in elections in European countries and elsewhere in the world. Marx's emphasis on the fundamental importance of economic life on the structure and other elements of social life remains a substantial and important contribution to social theory.

Writers working from Marx's analytic legacy are critical of the ways in which the structure of society affords benefits—wealth and power—to some groups of people over others; hence the term 'critical' political economy. In particular, critical political economy focuses on the ways in which the allocation, production, distribution, and consumption of social resources enable and constrain social action. That is, it is concerned with the way the ownership and control of society's resources—particularly productive resources—give owners a larger say in the form and direction society takes than to those lacking such controls.

Critical political economy is concerned with the ways in which the media support dominant interests in society, helping them maintain power and control (Chapter 5). In contrast to the libertarian and social responsibility theories of the press, which argue that the media can and should have a relatively independent place in the political and economic processes that govern society, critical political economy argues that in capitalist societies the media are a key institution in promoting capitalism and in helping maintain social inequality (Mosco, 2009).

Perspectives on the Study of Content

A number of perspectives have been developed and used to study media content. A few of the more popular perspectives are discussed in this section—literary criticism, structuralism, semiotics, and post-structuralism; discourse analysis; critical political economy; content analysis; and media form or genre analysis. For the most part, these perspectives are drawn from other theories of communication and of communication media. Here, however, we will generally consider how they address the encoding of media messages and the larger social and linguistic forces that they see as coming to bear on the production process. Again, the existence of this multiplicity of perspectives underscores the importance of the notion that it is not which one of these is the correct perspective, but rather what useful insight each brings to the analysis of media content.

Literary Criticism

Literary criticism is the study and interpretation of texts. It explores the different ways that texts can be analyzed and understood. Its roots reach back to when written records first emerged. As soon as something is recorded, it becomes open to interpretation and discussion. Major movements and changes in world history have focused on examinations and re-examinations of particular texts. For example, Martin Luther challenged the interpretation of the Bible by the Roman Catholic Church and the right of the Catholic Church to control access to and to be the sole interpreter of the scriptures. Similarly, in China from the Sung dynasty (AD 900) forward, there existed official interpretations of classic Confucian texts and unofficial versions were banned.

Debates in literary criticism have been particularly important for communication studies and for the study of content because they draw our attention to the various ways meaning might be drawn from texts. Should texts be read simply in terms of the intentions of the author? Or might meanings other than what the author intended be considered legitimate 'meanings' of the text? Might texts be viewed as the product of forces that impinge on the author, like language and culture? What weight may one put on the reader who 'decodes' the text?

One of the traditional modes of criticism is to view texts in terms of the presumed intention of the author. From this perspective, interpretation tries to uncover what the author consciously had in mind, as expressed in the text. Freudian analysis purports to explain, furthermore, what the author had subconsciously in mind. The text is treated only as the specific product or vehicle of an individual author-creator, whose other works may be cross-compared in the same light—e.g., the novels of Jane Austen, the plays of Shakespeare. This approach spread to film studies (e.g., a comparison of the films of Alfred Hitchcock) and became known as auteur theory, which focuses on the creative control of the director and treats the director as the creative originator of the film.

Adbusters often employs semiotics to create 'subvertisements', ads slightly changed or 'subverted' to expose the negative effects of the products they promote. Here the 'signifier'—the vodka bottle—has been modified to shift its 'signified' from the usual party atmosphere depicted in liquor ads to something less alluring.

In the early twentieth century a variant of literary criticism, New Criticism, gained prominence. From this perspective analysis is confined to the texts per se and authorial intention is disregarded. Readings of the works aim to discover ambiguities and multiplicities of meanings. More recently, the new literary criticism has incorporated concepts from linguistics, sociology, and anthropology to extend debates into a wide range of factors (including language and culture) that can be drawn into the interpretation of content.

Structuralism, Semiotics, and Post-structuralism

In the 1950s and 1960s, a perspective known as 'structuralism' became dominant in the social sciences and humanities, especially in the fields of linguistics, anthropology, sociology, psychology, and literature. In the analysis of media content, the aim of **structuralism** is to discover underlying patterns or structures that shape both texts and genres; to try to uncover common linguistic or thematic patterns that give them form. Here, the author is viewed primarily as a vehicle who enacts the extant rules of language and culture in the creation of her/his work (or life). From a structuralist perspective, to a large extent, we do not speak language so much as language speaks us.

An early and seminal work exemplifying structuralist principles was that of the Russian folklorist Vladimir Propp. In the 1920s, Propp collected over 400 traditional tales from Europe and showed how they all had a similar narrative structure. First, he identified a set of basic (lexical) elements (all stories have certain, similar items): a hero or heroine, a villain, a helper. Second, he described the motifs that propel the narrative from beginning to end. Thus, something must happen to set the hero (usually male) in motion: at some point the villain will disrupt the hero's plans; and at some point the hero will receive aid from a helper (who may or may not be female) to overcome the obstacles in his way. Propp was able to reduce the apparent complexity of a great number of different stories to a simple set of underlying narrative elements that could be combined in a strictly limited number

of ways (see Propp, 1970). The structural analysis of narrative has subsequently been applied to all manner of stories, including James Bond novels and films (Eco, 1982; Bennett and Woollacott, 1987), romantic novels (Radway, 1984), and soap operas (Geraghty, 1991). Figure 4.2 illustrates structuralism at work in the romance genre.

Once narrative structures and surface elements were identified, Propp and other structuralists were able to identify common themes that recurred in stories from all over the world. The magical union of strength and beauty, power in two forms, is a good example of a myth to be found in virtually all cultures. Structuralists would attend to its basic structure. The male embodiment of spiritual and bodily strength (usually a prince) grows up in his kingdom. The female embodiment of beauty and perceptiveness (a princess) grows up in her kingdom. One or both may be disguised in a certain way (a frog prince, a pig princess) or confined (Sleeping Beauty, Cinderella), sometimes as a result of immature vulnerability (plotting by unworthy usurpers, innocence). An event, story, or intervention of some sort induces one (usually the male in a patriarchal society or the female in a matriarchal society) to set out on a quest, sometimes purposeful, sometimes not. The less purposeful the quest the more the coming union is written in the stars or blessed by the gods in the form of an unconscious urge in the seeker. The seeker finds the sought (the object of his or her dreams, again evidence of divine blessing) and recognizes her or him by virtue of her or his or both of their inner senses, inherent kindness, or nobility. This something not only confirms the union but confirms the special qualities of both seeker and sought, which befits them to rule others (divine right of kings). The children of the union are, of course, very special, since they inherit the qualities of both.

Such myths live on. The most obvious twentieth-century example of the myth of the prince/princess ascending the throne would be the courtship and marriage of Charles, Prince of Wales, and Diana, a commoner who became Princess of Wales. However, as with so many myths, the story ended tragically.

FIGURE 4.2   The Narrative Logic of the Romance

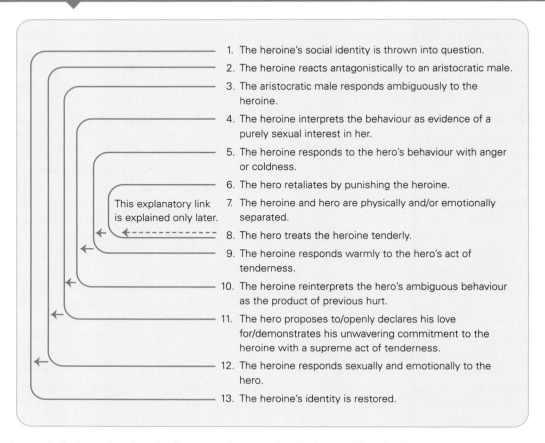

1. The heroine's social identity is thrown into question.
2. The heroine reacts antagonistically to an aristocratic male.
3. The aristocratic male responds ambiguously to the heroine.
4. The heroine interprets the behaviour as evidence of a purely sexual interest in her.
5. The heroine responds to the hero's behaviour with anger or coldness.
6. The hero retaliates by punishing the heroine.
7. The heroine and hero are physically and/or emotionally separated.
8. The hero treats the heroine tenderly.
9. The heroine responds warmly to the hero's act of tenderness.
10. The heroine reinterprets the hero's ambiguous behaviour as the product of previous hurt.
11. The hero proposes to/openly declares his love for/demonstrates his unwavering commitment to the heroine with a supreme act of tenderness.
12. The heroine responds sexually and emotionally to the hero.
13. The heroine's identity is restored.

This explanatory link is explained only later.

From Janice A. Radway. *Reading the Romance: Women, Patriarchy, and Popular Literature.*

So powerful are such myths that US film stars have handlers who build up their mythological identity by counselling them only to accept certain roles. Some pursue a particular type of character—e.g., Arnold Schwarzenegger, Bruce Willis—while others pursue versatility—e.g., Brad Pitt, Robert De Niro.

Another influential scholar in the field of structuralism was the Swiss linguist Ferdinand de Saussure, mentioned earlier. Saussure developed what was later seen as the structural analysis of language (1974). Saussure proposed that language could be scientifically studied in the abstract, as an underlying set of linguistic structures (langue, in his terms) that could be combined together by any native speaker to produce an utterance (parole). As

he argued, 'Language is a system of signs that express ideas, and is therefore comparable to a system of writing, the alphabet of deaf-mutes, symbolic rites, polite formulas, military signals, etc. But it is the most important of all these systems' (Saussure, in Silverman, 1983: 4–5). To better understand this system he proposed a science of signs—semiotics. For Saussure, 'meaning' is made in the difference between signs. Given that symbols bear no necessary relation to what they represent, the only way to identify the symbol is by knowing what it is not; a red light at a traffic intersection is not a green light (see Silverman, 1983). Anthropologist Claude Lévi-Strauss extended the structuralist formula into social interaction and claimed to show in his work 'not how men think in myths, but how myths operate in men's minds without their being aware of the fact' (Lévi-Strauss, 1969: 12). The point is that words carry preconceived ideas, or 'signifieds', about things and thereby provide a frame or screen for interpreting the world. From this perspective, one can begin to see why structuralism sometimes claims that people are 'spoken' by the language they use rather than the other way around.

As we have seen, based on the sign (signifier/signified), a semiotic analysis distinguishes between two levels of meaning: the denotative and the connotative. Using this schema, Roland Barthes (1972) has famously decoded ideological meanings in everything from wrestling and striptease, to the paintings in the Louvre, television, popular novels, and advertisements. By making connections between the images found in everyday media and the ideologies of bourgeois capitalist society, Barthes strove to uncover the ways that popular culture promotes dominant ideas and values.

Consider the ad that portrays the SUV as a family vehicle that can be used for city transportation and country adventure. From Barthes's perspective, the ad not only represents the SUV as a part of family life, but also draws on a deeper more subtle set of assumptions and values—another order of connotations. Based on the notion that the meaning of the ad is found in the differences between the images that it contains and possible alternatives, underlying the ad are ideas such as: the nuclear family is the natural and dominant social unit; private vehicles are a preferred mode of transportation; and the domination of nature is both a legitimate and pleasurable leisure activity. Social issues such as what comprises a 'family' in this day and age and the forms of environmental damage caused by private vehicles are ignored, buried under contemporary social myths. In other words, the text positions the reader in reference to the objects in the ad in particular ways and encourages a very specific reading, or understanding, of those objects. From this perspective, by accepting the idea that the SUV is the perfect family vehicle, not only are you accepting the obvious premise of the ad, but you are absorbing the baggage of these underlying ideas as

well. Through the 1970s and 1980s semiotic analysis, à la Barthes, became the preferred way of reading cultural texts (see, e.g., Williamson's analysis of advertisements, 1978).

While both structuralism and semiotics provide useful insights into the ways in which language structures the form and content of communication, perhaps their biggest shortcoming as modes of analysis is how they underplay the importance of the particular in favour of the general—of langue in contrast to parole. The roles of the individual speaker and listener (or producer and consumer) of communication and the context of the message in the process of communication are ignored.

Beginning in the 1960s, post-structuralism emerged as a critique of the idea that a consistent structure to texts exists and that the process of encoding somehow fixes or solidifies meaning for the decoder. A number of the main proponents of post-structuralism had been structuralists earlier, among them Roland Barthes.

For post-structuralists, 'meaning' is made in the act of decoding and, thereby, is the purview of the reader or audience member. Whatever sense is to be made of any particular word, image, or sound is the product of those persons interpreting those signs and depends on the perspective(s) they bring to the task. For instance, women may interpret content differently from men, gays differently from heterosexuals, children differently from adults. Understanding texts involves 'deconstructing' them to uncover the possible play on differences they contain. Meaning is never fixed in content. It remains as fluid as the next reader makes it. In semiotic terms, post-structuralism argues that signs have come undone and that signifiers can no longer be said to have specific 'signifieds'. Take, again, the SUV ad. Who cares about the happy-heterosexual-family symbolism seemingly bestowed on the vehicle by the advertising company? With one look at the ad's description of its spacious interior and stylish appointments, perhaps a gay environmentalist group will decide that this is the perfect mode of transportation for getting its members to their latest waterfowl habitat recuperation project in the mountains.

This is the point made by Barthes in his famous essay, 'Death of the Author' (1977). 'Auteur theory' has not died but has become understood as only one window on the reality of the text. Since the text becomes meaningful only in the act of being read and understood, the source of meaning, Barthes argued, is the reader. The effect of this startling reversal was the 'empowerment' of the reader or audience. No longer chained to the dull task of trying to find out what Shakespeare 'had in mind' when he wrote Hamlet (an impossible task anyway, argued Barthes), the reader was free to create his or her own meanings, to open up rather than close down the meaning of the text. Gone was any notion of a 'true' or 'authentic' meaning of the text. Texts were 'polysemic' and had a number of different possible meanings. The conception of reading also changed from the passive absorption of the text's imposed meaning to an active exploration of the text's possibilities.

As illustrated in Chapter 5, this shift in interpretation parallels a shift in the ways audiences are viewed in terms of their relation to media content.

Discourse Analysis

Discourse analysis is another perspective with a long history, dating back more than 2,000 years to the discipline of *rhetorica*. *Rhetorica* was oriented to effective persuasiveness and dealt with the planning, organization, specific operations, and performance of speech in political and legal settings (van Dijk, 1985, vol. 1: 1). A passage, speech, or performance can succeed or fail based on the impact it makes on its audience.

Drawing from structuralism, discourse analysis focuses on how language, as a system of representation, provides us with a particular perspective or 'position' in the social world. It posits that language is a kind of structure, and that by being inside that structure, language provides us with a particular view of the world. Today there are many strands of discourse analysis at play in communication studies (see van Dijk, 1997). A major stream focuses on specific instances of language use and their relationship to social power. Another, following the work of Michel Foucault, considers how specific modes of language use bind our ways of thinking and become 'sedimented' into specific institutions and relations of social power.

The first of these modes of analysis points to how particular patterns and conventions of language usage become taken for granted and considers how these patterns serve as larger frames of reference to shape our experience and understanding of the world. For instance, discourse analysis has been used to illustrate the gendered character of language—chair*man*, fire*man*, fisher*man*—and to demonstrate through historical referents how this kind of language has supported patriarchal forms of domination in society. Hence, today, to promote more egalitarian relationships, we use gender-neutral language—chair, firefighter, fisher. This type of analysis also provides a way of understanding how particular elements of media content work together to create a larger perspective on, or way of seeing, social events and circumstances. For example, a discourse analysis of federal election coverage might look at all of the different kinds of media content focusing on the election—coverage of debates, polls, editorials, news stories—and analyze the ways in which different leaders and parties are treated in that coverage. Were they given equal time/space? Were the views of one party or leader given more favourable or sympathetic treatment than others?

Discourse analysis also provides a framework for understanding how specific kinds of language use fit into larger social practices—for example, how prime ministerial television appearances are discursive elements in a larger political struggle. Here, a discourse analyst might note that beyond the content itself, political debates represent a challenge mounted against the incumbent to dislodge that incumbent from a discourse of power. On the other side, it is the job of the incumbent to constrain the pretender in a discourse of questionable power-seeking. From this perspective, language is a system of power that is utilized to help enact or create a new set of social relations. It is a key stepping stone on the path to changing relations of social power; in this instance, changing the government.

This second type of discourse analysis has a more structuralist character and argues that, in the form of ideas or sets of ideas, discourse (language) becomes a way of knowing the world and, in turn, a way of controlling it. In a series of studies that includes histories of madness, prisons, and sexuality, Michel Foucault (1995, 1988, 1980) illustrates how, through making crime, madness, and sex into objects of scientific inquiry and discipline, the 'knowledge' or ideas generated from these inquiries become a vehicle to control action and behaviour. As ways of thinking and being in the world, discourses become 'sedimented', or structured, into institutions and organizations. They become rules and regulations that govern our lives and our ways of thinking, seeing, and being in the world. In this way, words move from being simply ideas to becoming disciplining social practices. Consider how the idea of 'education', for instance, has become sedimented or structured into particular practices, objects, and institutions, such as classes, textbooks, and schools or universities. By this account, we live immersed in discourse, like fish in water, with its invisible currents shaping and determining much if not all of our lives as language, in the form of ideas, takes on a life of its own. At the personal level, larger social discourses frame our ideas, hopes, and desires. Our identities are given form by the discourses of which we are a part: what it means to be male, female, Canadian, etc. From this perspective, media content can be seen as part of these larger discursive formations, part of the social mechanism through which norms, values, and other ideas about how the world 'should be' are circulated and reproduced.

Critical Political Economy

Working from the Marxist perspective that the media generally support private capital and the dominant interests in society, writers in the field of critical political economy have approached the media from a number of directions (see Mosco, 2009). For instance, in the 1970s Dallas Smythe pointed out that in contrast to the seeming fact that the purpose of the media is to serve the interests and tastes of audiences, that is, to inform and entertain people, the product from which private broadcasters and newspapers draw the balance of their income is 'audiences' and that the real business of commercial media companies is selling audiences to advertisers. From this perspective, media serve the interests of owners, not the public at large. As he argues:

> The capitalist system cultivates the illusion that the three streams of information and things are independent: the advertising merely 'supports' or 'makes possible' the news, information, and entertainment, which in turn are *separate* from the consumer goods and services we buy. This is untrue. The commercial mass media *are* advertising in their entirety...both advertising and the 'program material' reflect, mystify, and are essential to the sale of goods and services. The program material is produced and distributed in order to attract and hold the

Dallas Walker Smythe (1907–92) was a groundbreaking Canadian political activist and researcher in the field of the political economy of communication.

attention of the audience so that its members may be counted (by audience survey organizations which then certify the size and character of the audience produced) and sold to the advertiser. (Smythe, 1994: 9)

Taking a somewhat broader perspective in their book *Manufacturing Consent: The Political Economy of the Mass Media,* Edward Herman and Noam Chomsky (2002: 2) argue that there are five political, economic, and organizational 'filters' screening the US news media to ensure that the news works in favour of political and economic elites:

1. the concentration of ownership of the media in the hands of a few large private corporations;

2. the media's dependence on advertising as their principal source of revenue;

3. the media's reliance on government and business elites as sources of news and opinion;

4. 'flak', or negative feedback from powerful established interests when the news plays against their interests;

5. strong belief in the 'miracle of the market' as a means to satisfy social needs and desires. As they argue, the model 'traces the routes by which money and power are able to filter out the news fit to print, marginalize dissent, and allow the government and dominant private interests to get their messages across to the public'.

The political economy of communication has been employed to illustrate how disparities in information and media hardware underlie disparities in wealth between countries of the global North and South (Hamelink, 1995), why the Canadian media are generally dominated by American product (Pendakur, 1990), and how corporate media generally represent a rather narrow range of perspectives and opinions (Hackett and Gruneau, 2000).

In sum, the main point made by critical political economy is that the larger political and economic relationships that govern society reach down to structure not only the ways in which the media operate but also in the ways they represent the world to us.

Content Analysis

Although often used as a method for analyzing media content, 'content analysis' is not a theory. Rather, it is used in conjunction with such approaches as discourse analysis to identify the specific characteristics of media content, such as how particular people, social groups, or places are framed or treated in news stories and what is either included or left out of particular stories or television programs (Krippendorf, 2004).

Content analysis emphasizes the quantitative aspects of media content, specifically, the number of occurrences of a particular category of phenomenon. For instance, what places (cities, provinces, or countries) are covered in news stories? What kinds of subjects are covered? What sources do reporters quote or draw on in writing a story? (Are some politicians quoted more than others? Are some think tanks called on more than others?) How often are minorities covered in news stories? How are they covered?

The system of analysis works this way. First, the analyst determines the variables to be measured. Variables may include things like the general subject or theme of a story; the particular people, places, or events represented; whether these things are framed or treated in a positive or negative light; and the sources or experts quoted. The researcher then sets up units of analysis—phrases, sentences, paragraphs, column inches, etc.—and counts these variables and perhaps their relation to other aspects of content, such as pictures or long pieces with prominent placement. On the basis of frequencies of occurrence in one or more media products (newspapers, TV news programs, etc.), the analyst can provide a reading of the media treatment of an issue over time. What has been left out of a story might be just as important as what is included. For instance, a 1996 study by NewsWatch Canada illustrated that over a six-month period on CBC and CTV television newscasts, 'right-wing think-tanks received 68 per cent of all references while left-wing think-tanks received 19.5 per cent' (Hackett and Gruneau, 2000: 204). While these statistics don't tell us what the news stories were about, they illustrate that during that period right-wing sources were consulted or referred to more than three times to one. Similarly, a content analysis of the online editions of Canada's self-described national newspapers—*The Globe and Mail*, *National Post*, and *Le Devoir*—showed that their coverage was not national at all, but largely confined to the cities and provinces in which they were based and the activities of federal government institutions (Gasher, 2007).

In another instance, a content analysis focusing on the coverage of Latin America in the US press over time revealed that the dominant definition of news—what was most often reported about Latin America—was natural disasters, such as earthquakes and volcanoes. During the 1970s there was a gradual shift towards a focus on dictators and banana republics. More recently, there has been a further shift towards a broader collection of information. Such an analysis is revealing not only in terms of the triviality of the 'news' definition for an entire continent but also in terms of the significant absences—the failure to offer any serious account of the economic, political, or social developments of that region of the world. Likewise, content studies of social representation in media products have pointed to the fact that the people identified by reporters as 'experts' on subjects are mainly white, professional males. In contrast, black males are often portrayed as criminals, athletes, or musicians. Other studies illustrate both a general lack of representation of people of colour in mainstream Canadian media, and that when they are represented it is often in the form of stereotypes (Jiwani, 2006). As can be seen from these examples, content analysis is generally used as a method to uncover evidence of some kind of bias in news reports or other media content (Jiwani, 2010; Hackett and Gruneau, 2000; Gans, 1979; Tuchman, 1978; Schlesinger, 1978).

> ## ❖ BOX 4.3   ON ORSON WELLES
>
> Paul Heyer has created an interesting text/audio analysis of Orson Welles's War of the Worlds that is a media form analysis in that it deals with the intuitive understanding Welles had of radio as a medium. Heyer's article is in *Canadian Journal of Communication* 28, 2 (2003): 149–65. Or go online at www.cjc-online.ca

Genre or Media Form Analysis

Another framework of analysis that can be used as a complement to any of the above frameworks is derived from McLuhan's notion of the medium as the message. The presentation of meaning is constrained by the medium itself and how it structures and carries content. Beyond that, meaning also is constrained by the genre within a particular medium, e.g., action movies or chick flicks as subsets of all movies.

Each medium organizes and encourages particular elements of content and particular relations between those elements. These elements and relations are distinct to each medium and forever are shifting with the creativity of the practitioners. A good comparative example (which combines both genre and media form) is the television news team of on-air reporter and camera operator versus the single newspaper reporter. The news team intrudes more on the event and operates within the constraints of a television news story, which demands compelling visuals and a story that can be told quickly and simply. On the other hand, a newspaper story depends for its strength on elements such as a logical presentation of the facts and thorough analysis. The following subsections consider the characteristics of a number of major media forms such as news stories.

The News Story

The news story is a distinctive genre that differs in its structure according to the medium within which it appears. Nevertheless, all news stories share certain fundamental characteristics. Canadian sociologists Richard Ericson, Patricia Baranek, and Janet Chan (1989) developed a set of criteria to describe the characteristics that make events newsworthy. Peter Desbarats (1990: 110), former dean of journalism at the University of Western Ontario, summarizes these criteria:

- Simplification: an event must be recognized as significant and relatively unambiguous in its meaning.
- Dramatization: a dramatized version of the event must be able to be presented.

- Personalization: events must have personal significance to someone.
- Themes and continuity: events that fit into preconceived themes gain in newsworthiness.
- Consonance: events make the news more readily when they fit the reporters' preconceived notions of what should be happening.
- The unexpected: unexpected events that can be expected within frames of reference used by reporters are newsworthy.

Soap Operas

Developed at the beginning of the 1930s in the early days of commercial radio, soap operas were a popular cultural form designed to socialize a home-confined, female audience with disposable income into the art of consuming, especially household cleaning products (Williams, 1992; LaGuardia, 1977). Televised French and Spanish-language versions—téléromans or télénovellas—are particularly popular in Quebec and Central and South America. Along with news, soaps are the most analyzed kind of narrative genre on television. They have been of particular interest to feminist scholars because they are a preferred form of entertainment for female viewers in many countries. Analysis has concentrated on the form and content of soaps and on the pleasures they offer viewers.

Over time and after much study, academic perceptions of soaps have changed. At first, they were considered the epitome of that commonly criticized aspect of television that echoes the mass society thesis: trivial, mindless entertainment. Gradually, however, just as the pleasures offered by other forms of popular culture such as films, magazines, sports, and other forms of television were legitimized as valid pastimes, so too soaps were viewed in a more positive light (Geraghty, 1991; Radway, 1984).

Music Videos

In a fashion similar to the soaps, music videos, particularly rock videos, emerged because producers wanted to socialize an audience into purchasing their product. The difference between the soaps and music videos is that, with videos, the product to be purchased is part of the promotional vehicle used to bring it to the attention of the audience. Music videos are visually enhanced versions of the recorded music that audiences are intended to purchase. They provide a visual track to the sound recording and sometimes, as in the case of Michael Jackson's *Thriller*, or, more contemporarily, some of Lady Gaga's videos, they are highly crafted works of art in their own right.

⁘ BOX 4.4   PLUGGING, FAVOURABLE COVERAGE, AND PUFF EDITORIALS

In advertising terms, 'plugging' refers to the way newspapers and other media sometimes work to promote their advertisers. In fact, favourable coverage of advertisers is often expected of media producers.

If you look at the real estate sections in newspapers, they are little more than promotional sections for various parts of the housing industry. So accepting are most Canadians of such favourable coverage that in face of the scandal surrounding leaky condominiums in British Columbia, no one took the newspapers to task publicly for not having exposed this problem, which had been growing over the years through a lack of responsibility on the part of builders and building inspection codes. One journalist lost his job after

writing a critical article on the subject years before it became a public issue. Of course, his employer denied the connection between the reporter's forthrightness and loss of job.

Not only do commercial media shy away from critical coverage, they often supply quite positive coverage to complement ads. Newspapers regularly run 'special editorial supplements' or 'advertorials' as separate sections of the paper in which the positive attributes of everything from cars to movies to whole industries are trumpeted in what look very much like 'news' stories. And on television, video press releases advertising new products such as detergents and movies can be found masquerading as news items on news programs.

As media content, rock videos provide viewers an entry point to popular culture. They provide examples of clothes and accessories to buy, how to behave, what expressions to use, and so forth. In providing material for imaginative creation, music videos complement fashion photographs and magazines. Viewers provide individual interpretation and inject a dynamism built on popular music, ridding the pictures of their frozen-in-time quality (see Goffman, 1959; Fornas et al., 1988). As James Curran (1990: 154) has remarked, 'rock music is viewed as a laboratory for the intensive production of identity by adolescents seeking to define an independent self.'

Reality TV

A genre that has enjoyed increasing popularity over the last 10 years is reality-based television. As a program category, reality TV encompasses a range of different types of programming including game shows, talent searches, cooking and food programs, sports, lives of celebrities, talk shows, hidden cameras, hoaxes, and a 'day or week in the life' of prominent personalities.

Reality TV sometimes assumes a documentary style and focuses on 'real-life', unscripted situations. Other times, plot and narrative structure are achieved through editing and/or having subjects participate in contrived scenarios. Other traditional narrative techniques, such as characterization, are achieved through focusing on people with outlandish personalities and jobs or by careful casting of participants.

For producers and television networks, a prime attraction of reality TV is its low cost. With neither expensive actors to pay nor high-priced sets and special effects to create, reality-based television is an antidote to the fragmenting market and the shrinking viewers and ad dollars accruing to individual broadcast stations in the sea of choices now available. Most of the cast members of these programs work for nothing, and the sets or locations require little preparation. Meanwhile, on the decoding side of the equation, reality TV shrinks the distance between program and audience as ordinary people become television stars and videos and other material

⫸ BOX 4.5   MEDIA AND REALITY

Some social theorists argue that the distinction between media representation and reality has blurred, or even collapsed altogether. Working in the 1960s Guy Debord argued that we had begun living in a 'society of the spectacle'—that is, a media and consumer society 'organized around the consumption of images, commodities, and spectacles' (Best and Kellner, 1997: 84). As he points out, much of how we understand life, much of what we know and enjoy, is created by others and presented to us in commodity form. The watching of sports events substitutes for the actual playing of games. Our knowledge of world events is mediated through newspaper stories and what we see on TV. Our experience of nature is gleaned through theme parks, zoos, aquariums, and travel programs on television. Our experience of other cultures is generally confined to travelogues and 'ethnic' restaurants and festivals. Computers and the web have accelerated this process. Cards and other games are played online as simulations of real events. Even sex slips into the realm of the virtual. Indeed, as Debord points out, 'in the modern conditions of production, life presents itself as an immense accumulation of spectacles' (in Best and Kellner, 1997: 84), almost all of which are sold to us—'mediated' through the market. At the heart of this system, of course, are the media: the source of myriad representations of the real.

Writing some years later, Jean Baudrillard pushed Debord's thesis even further. He thinks that the line between the real and its representation has become so blurred that it is now impossible to tell the difference between them (Baudrillard, 1995). As he argues, modern life has been taken over by simulation, and the 'real' world folded in among so many representations, that it is not possible to tell where one begins and the other ends. From this perspective we are living in a 'simulacrum', a hyperreal world where reality has been substituted by symbols and signs that refer only to other symbols and signs rather than to a grounded, objective reality. How true is Baudrillard's thesis? How will you decide?

created by non-professionals are used in television programs.

The Advertisement

Advertising has profound significance in our market-based, consumer society. It animates much of the economy, linking producers and consumers by creating awareness and demand for products and services, and advertising lies at the very foundation of the commercial mass media, financing the production and distribution of most information and entertainment. For a surcharge paid on consumer products (the cost of ads is built into the cost of products), advertising has become the central means for financing the media. With media such as newspapers, television, radio, and websites, as well as cable, satellite, and mobile delivery systems, consumers pay only a small portion, if any, of the cost of content. Rather, the bulk is paid by advertisers, who hope that audiences *pay attention*. Dallas Smythe (1981: 111), the political economist who identified the media audience as a product sold to advertisers, argued provocatively: 'The mass media of communication...were a systemic invention of capitalism, developed since the last quarter of the nineteenth century. They were innovated to aid in the mass marketing of consumer goods and services produced by giant oligopolistic corporations using science both in managing production and marketing.'

Media's dependence on advertising has a profound impact on the content and design of media products. For instance, products are designed to attract audiences with particular demographics or characteristics. Whether a newspaper like *The Globe and Mail* that is tailored to catch the interest of high-income professionals, a magazine such as *Chatelaine* designed to attract young women, or a television station such as *Spike* geared specifically to young men, the main consideration of publishers and producers is who, exactly, will read or watch their content. And, by extension, will advertisers pay for the attention of that audience? Consequently, content is tailored to attract particular people.

The design of media products also reflects this commercial imperative. After the front page of a newspaper, the pages are generally designed so that the first place the readers' eyes fall is on advertising. Television programs, which generally have a climax or plot confrontation just before a cut to commercial, are written to pull audiences through commercial breaks. Online content, too, is placed and designed to ensure that the viewer's eyes meet with the sponsoring advertisers.

Modern advertising developed with the mass media and as Johnston (2010) notes, '(t)he first newspaper published in Canada, the *Halifax Gazette* (1752) contained ads for a grocer, a job printer, and a tutor located in Halifax itself.' Advertising as we know it today, however, took form with the rise of contemporary industrial society, from about 1880 through the 1920s, as industry was developing large economies of scale, workers, wages were increasing with the rising efficiencies in production, literacy rates were rising, and a consumer society was emerging. It was during this time that advertising agencies were founded and began to supply industry with creative services and market research. Together these services helped propel the industry to new heights (see Box 4.6).

But while advertising is sometimes celebrated as essential to the affluence of consumer society because it stimulates demand, it is also criticized as the major impetus behind environmental degradation and shrinking natural resources. The continuous bombardment of flashy and seductive ads is seen as fuelling an increasing array of false needs and driving a lifestyle characterized by an escalating frenzy of consumption (Leiss et al., 2005: 83–7). In a world where shopping is celebrated as a form of recreation—sometimes described as 'retail therapy'—the inevitable outcome is depleted forests, diminishing oil supplies, and global warming.

Today, advertising is a multi-billion-dollar industry. In 2009, advertisers spent more than $14 billion advertising their wares in Canadian newspapers, magazines, television, radio, and online media. Online advertising is very quickly taking on increasing importance, rising from $98 million in 2000 to $1.82 billion in 2009. All this expenditure adds up to an environment where we are bombarded with commercial messages. Some writers claim that people living in cities see up to 5,000 ads per day—in the media, on billboards, on posters, and even on personal clothing.

❖ BOX 4.6   ADVERTISING AND CONSUMER SOCIETY

In a 1930 address to the Association of National Advertisers, US President Herbert Hoover captured the key importance of advertising to consumer society.

Advertising is one of the vital organs of our entire economic and social system. It certainly is the vocal organ by which industry sings its songs of beguilement. The purpose of advertising is to create desire, and from the torments of desire there at once emerges additional demand and from demand you pull upon increasing production and distribution. By the stimulants of advertising which you administer you have stirred the lethargy of the old law of supply and demand until you have transformed cottage industries into mass production. From enlarged diffusion of articles and services you cheapen costs and thereby you are a part of the dynamic force which creates higher standards of living. You also contribute to hurry up the general use of every discovery in science and every invention in industry. It probably required a thousand years to spread the knowledge and application of that great human invention, the wheeled cart, and it has taken you only 20 years to make the automobile the universal tool of man. Moreover, your constant exploitation of every improvement in every article and service spreads a restless pillow for every competitor and drives the producer to feverish exertions in new invention, new service, and still more improvement. Incidentally, you make possible the vast distribution of information, of good cheer and tribulation which comes with the morning paper, the periodical, and the radio. And your contributions to them aids to sustain a great army of authors and artists who could not otherwise join in the standards of living you create.

Source: John T. Woolley and Gerhard Peters, *The American Presidency Project* [online]. Santa Barbara, CA. Available at http://www.presidency.ucsb.edu/ws/?pid=22428.

While in its early incarnations advertising was a way to increase sales by supplementing or making known consumer satisfaction, it has become the means whereby producers create needs, launch products, and maintain sales. Industry has a great capacity to produce, and the health of those industries—and, by extension, our market economy—becomes dependent on consumption keeping pace. Because so much is at stake, and the constraints of space or time are so great, an astonishingly high investment is involved in the making of advertisements. It is not uncommon for a 30-second television advertisement to cost more to produce than a 30-minute program. Millions of dollars of production investment in the advertised product hang in the balance. And, of course, there are the residual costs paid to media outlets and actors to have the advertisement seen or heard again and again.

Advertisements attempt to create a relationship between products and potential consumers, particularly when the products are essentially identical in their basic defining characteristics, such as taste and alcohol content for beer or cleaning capacity for detergent. As Leiss et al. illustrate in their book *Social Communication in Advertising*, advertising companies have used various strategies to try to imbue their products with qualities that they think are particularly attractive to consumers and/or are important to their self-image and lifestyle. In this way they try to build a relationship between the product and the would-be consumer.

Source: © istockphoto.com/ItchySan

Today, advertising is everywhere, even on our clothing.

Apart from straightforward broadcast and display and classified advertising, four other types of advertising are significant. The first includes advertisements for a company rather than its products—usually called institutional advertising. These ads are designed to propagate a favourable corporate image and promote the virtues of a corporation rather than a particular product or product line. In some cases, such as in advertisements for the energy industry, the responsible nature of the individual company or the industry as a whole is put forward explicitly with regard to concerns that have either been expressed by the public or that the corporations have discerned through market research. Think of how many companies try to portray themselves today as 'green'.

The second type of advertisement includes those that masquerade as reporting. They have been called a variety of names, including infomercials and advertorials. Advertorials, typically offered to clients for placing a conventional advertisement, present descriptive material on, for example, the contribution of a company to the larger economy. They are usually prepared for print publications, sometimes written by a journalist, but sometimes written by an employee or agent of the company or agency that is the subject of the article. Television infomercials, half-hour programs pushing particular products, are similar to advertorials. They now account for over $1 billion in sales in the US.

Another type of advertising is **product placement.** Hollywood films have long had plugs for products written into their scripts. For instance, in the 1932 Marx brothers film *Horse Feathers*, there is a famous scene (in bad taste) where Groucho Marx tosses another character a roll of Lifesavers candies

⁞ BOX 4.7   LOOKING FOR AD SPACE

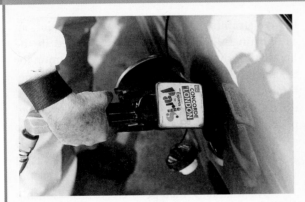

As if the space over urinals were not enough, *Time* magazine used escalator handrails in the Metro Toronto Convention Centre to remind people of its existence. The ING bank used the floor of a major walkway serving all three of Vancouver's Seabus, Skytrain, and West Coast Express public transit systems. Some enterprising entrepreneurs, operating seemingly on the wrong side of the law, scattered ads for fake photo IDs on the streets and sidewalks in the nightclub district of Vancouver, and boxers and other athletes sometimes temporarily tatoo their backs and chests with ads that will reach audiences while they are under the camera's gaze.

when she falls out of a canoe and calls for help. However, in recent years the practice has accelerated considerably. Car manufacturers pay big bucks to have their vehicles showcased in action adventure films, such as the James Bond series, and cereal and liquor manufacturers pay to have both visual and oral references to their products woven into television scripts.

The expansion of product placement both in movies and on television illustrates how the basic relationship between content and advertisement has been distorted over the years—a change that has been sometimes underplayed by communication researchers. Advertisers buy audiences—everyone acknowledges that. What they do not generally acknowledge is that they purchase audiences in certain frames of mind. No advertiser is going to support a publication, broadcasting program, or website with content that conflicts with their products or that may cause the audience to adversely

react to their products. For instance, airlines have regularly stipulated that newspapers and magazines not run airline ads next to copy describing plane crashes or hijackings. Such advertiser interference upsets journalists, program producers, and editors, but as direct government funding for public broadcasting continues to dry up and as the drive to make greater profits in film and other media increases, the influence of advertisers continues to grow.

Finally, a growing form of advertising production is sourced from audience members as companies call on audiences to craft commercials themselves. Frito-Lay, for instance, has run consumer-produced ads on the Super Bowl broadcast for several years and companies such as Starbucks and General Motors' Chevrolet have also tried to capitalize on this trend. If nothing else, the hype around such contests itself generates an excitement for the brand and strengthens audience attention to those ads.

BOX 4.8 MEDIA CREATING MEANING: POSSIBILITIES AND LIMITATIONS

In drawing on the larger field of social knowledge and events the media are constantly influencing us: they select certain events to bring forward; they create an image of those events; and they create a discourse within which events and issues are defined (see Coulter, 2010; Mills, 2004; Mitchell, 1988). But beyond influencing our view of reality, do the media have the ability to create a reality quite at odds with the facts? Such a scenario is explored in the movie *Wag the Dog*, in which a Hollywood producer is commissioned to wage a small, bogus war to divert attention from the domestic difficulties of an American president. Though this movie perhaps exaggerates the lengths to which the media will go to 'create' meaning, they have at times attempted to create meaning that conflicts with common perceptions.

Perhaps a more disturbing scenario played out in the United States following the attack on the World Trade Center in 2001 and the US invasion of Iraq in 2003. A series of polls conducted in the summer of 2003 in the US found that 48 per cent of respondents incorrectly believed that links between Iraq and al-Qaeda had been found, '22 per cent that weapons of mass destruction

had been found in Iraq, and 25 per cent that world opinion favoured the US going to war with Iraq' (PIPA/Knowledge Network, 2003). However, no evidence has ever been found to support any of these assertions. In other words, the poll illustrated that the American people were badly misinformed as to the circumstances surrounding the invasion of Iraq. The poll also found that people's misconceptions varied significantly depending on their source of news, with 80 per cent of those reporting the Fox network as their major source having one or more of these misconceptions, while only 23 per cent of those depending on public broadcasting networks (e.g., PBS, NPR) had one or more. In excess of 50 per cent of respondents were found to believe also that Iraq was at some level involved in the attacks—a perception that US intelligence agencies say is unfounded. Moreover, people holding these misconceptions were more likely to support the war. Can the US media be held directly responsible for promoting these misconceptions? The poll provides no direct evidence that they have done so. However, it does suggest that the media have done a very poor job of informing the American public on a matter of global political importance.

❯ SUMMARY

Social models of communication attempt to understand the variables or larger social context affecting the encoding and decoding of media messages. This chapter has examined a number of different theories and perspectives on the social elements of communication—the dynamics of meaning-creation and of interpretation.

The study of the creation and interpretation of media content is the study of representation, or, as the semioticians say, signification. Such study examines how symbols, such as the words and ideas contained in language, are constructed and used to interpret the world of objects, events, persons, and even representations.

The study of representation involves understanding the nature of polysemy, intertextuality, and grounded indeterminate systems. In less technical words, it involves understanding how messages are open to a variety of interpretations, how interpretations depend on other representations, and how there are bound to be a finite but unpredictable number of interpretations of the object, event, or phenomenon being represented.

Several approaches are used to understand and analyze media content. Some of the main categories are literary criticism; structuralism, semiotics, and post-structuralism; discourse analysis; critical political economy; content analysis; and genre/media form analysis. Each has particular strengths and draws out various forces playing on content.

The media are integral elements of our society, bound through a process of the interpenetration of media content and lived reality. Often they massage and present material from the margins of society to make it acceptable and available to the mainstream. The media are not free to create non-existent social values even though they may affect the manner in which social values are played out. The interpenetration of reality and media representation is problematic, especially with regard to violence and pornography. The simplification, reductionism, and dramatization of issues also create unacknowledged problems.

❯ APPENDIX: DOVE REAL BEAUTY CAMPAIGN: CHALLENGING THE CODE?

Selling Soap: Is Dove's 'Campaign for Real Beauty' the Real Deal?
Nicole Cohen

You could say that advertising is soap's dirty little secret. It started during the colonization of North America, when European settlers pushed Aboriginal populations off the land that is now Canada and the United States. According to Andrea Smith, who wrote *Conquest: Sexual Violence and American Indian Genocide*, in order to justify the elimination of indigenous people, settlers had to construct Aboriginal bodies as 'dirty' and 'impure'. An advertisement for Proctor & Gamble's Ivory soap helped popularize the myth of the 'dirty native'. The ad read:

We were once factious, fierce and wild,
In peaceful arts unreconciled
Our blankets smeared with grease and stains
From buffalo meat and settlers' veins.
Through summer's dust and heat content
From moon to moon unwashed we went,
But IVORY SOAP came like a ray
Of light across our darkened way
And now we're civil, kind and good
And keep the laws as people should,
We wear our linen, lawn and lace
As well as folks with paler face
And now I take, where'er we go
This cake of IVORY SOAP to show
What civilized my squaw and me
And made us clean and fair to see.

The ad suggested that Ivory soap 'civilized' Aboriginal people, while furthering the colonists' racist ideas about them being dirty and uncivilized. In the mid-nineteenth century, soap companies Pears, Lever, Proctor & Gamble, and Kirk's continued to market their soap as a way to achieve 'whiteness', which was associated in these ads with being gentle, soft, and civilized.

Unsurprisingly, soap advertising was also used to tell women how to behave, promoting traditional gender roles. A 1937 Palmolive ad shows an image of a bride and groom on their honeymoon and advised the woman that 'romance comes to girls who guard against dry, lifeless... middle age skin', reminding the happy bride that her marriage was dependent on her preserving her youthful, soft skin. Soap ads directed at women have since made their message a little less blatant, relying instead on visual signifiers that reinforce the notion that women are expected to stay thin, soft, supple and flawless. Then, in October 2004, one company changed its tune. Dove, which makes soap and other beauty products, launched its global Campaign for Real Beauty to appeal to folks tired of seeing unrealistic representations of women used in advertising, and to spread a feel-good message based on watered-down feminist notions of empowerment.

Dove launched its Campaign For Real Beauty through images. It set up a photography exhibit in a shopping mall, for which 58 female photographers submitted an image they thought captured female beauty—a group of teenagers carefully applying makeup, a woman standing in the shadows wearing a burka, a girl having her 'before' photo taken at summer weight-loss camp, old women, young women, women from around the world. The exhibit was designed to spark a conversation about the representation and meaning of beauty, which, on the surface, it did well: it showed women of different shapes and sizes doing all sorts of activities in front of various backdrops. Every woman who viewed the exhibit could likely identify with at least one of the images.

The 'Wall of Sentiments' featured quotes from viewers. 'I love that the photographs capture the real essence of beauty and not what the media throws at us day after day', wrote one visitor. 'Thank you for showing that true beauty is not just a small waist and large breasts, it's something that comes from within', wrote another.

While viewers could walk out of the exhibit filled with positive feelings about women and beauty, the message was not without a sales pitch: at the exit, a Dove employee was handing out samples in a blue-and-white box that read: 'Beauty has nothing to do with perfection and everything to do with care.'

Dove is a major brand owned by Unilever, a multinational corporation that sells food, home, and beauty products, with profits in the billions of dollars. Dove's marketing push focused on 'real' beauty is a clever twist on traditional advertising approaches: it has brought the company loads of free publicity as newspaper writers buzz about seeing 'real women'—as opposed to modelling agency ideals—being promoted as beautiful.

And it seems that Dove's commitment to 'real' beauty is more than skin deep—the company has set up the Dove Self-Esteem Fund to support programs that boost young women's self-image. It also made a donation, at the time of the mall exhibit, to the National Eating Disorder Information Centre (NEDIC), an organization concerned with the socio-cultural factors that can influence disordered eating, including the damaging messages of beauty and fashion ads.

Dove even commissioned a study that surveyed 3,300 girls and women aged 15 to 64 in Brazil, Canada, China, Germany, Italy, Japan, Mexico, Saudi Arabia, the UK, and the US to 'explore self-esteem and the impact of beauty ideals on both women's and girls' lives.' It's impressive coming from an industry that's usually only interested in what shade of red gets women most excited.

The report found that 90 per cent of women want to change something about their physical appearance, usually their weight. Sixty-seven per cent said their negative body image prevented them from participating in 'life-engaging' activities such as going to school or speaking out about issues they care about. Enraging stuff; and Dove has based its confidence-boosting efforts on this information.

Still—and product pitches at the end of thoughtful photo exhibits are an obvious reminder of this—it's difficult to believe that Dove's efforts are entirely altruistic. After all, they're doing this to sell soap. And when you take a deeper look at the brand, underlying corporate contradictions begin to emerge. Dove's parent company, Unilever, also owns the Slim Fast meal-replacement milkshake brand, which encourages people to skip meals to lose weight. Then there is Fair and Lovely, a skin-lightening cream marketed heavily in India, which capitalizes on privileged notions and imagery of Western beauty. Finally, there is the male fragrance Axe, another member of the Unilever family whose advertising campaigns feature ultra-thin, hyper-sexualized women uncontrollably lusting after a guy wearing Axe.

You will likely never see a Dove model in an Axe ad. The print-ad component of the Dove campaign has featured the faces and bodies of real women (read: not models) on billboards around the world, selling the idea that this is a brand that cares about the kind of beauty that comes from within. A visit to www.campaignforrealbeauty.ca greets you with: 'For too long, beauty has been defined by narrow, stifling stereotypes...we believe real beauty comes in many shapes, sizes and ages.' A series of billboard advertisements featured women with so-called flaws, images that don't represent traditional signifiers of female beauty: 'Ugly spots or beauty spots?' asked the ad featuring a freckled woman. 'Wrinkled or wonderful?' asked another.

Many people were impressed that ads were finally featuring women that look less like femme-bots and more like themselves. After all, feminist researchers and academics have been critiquing advertising's unrealistic and objectified vision of women for years. As Salon.com writer Rebecca Traister put it, Dove's campaign was 'a little ray of sanity in this anorexic world'.

Another of Dove's advertising blitzes was titled 'Real Women Have Real Curves' (as if we'd forgotten). The ads featured women ranging from size 6 to size 12, wearing nothing but plain white underwear and big smiles, looking pretty pleased to be flaunting their bodies. Dove says the ads weren't airbrushed (which later turned out not to be true). The American models were recruited while at university, at work, or in coffee shops and asked to appear in the ads just the way they were. In Canada, Dove held a casting call for women who wanted to show off their natural bodies, an event that made national news.

While it was exciting to see these gorgeous, diverse women on billboards, something seemed odd. The taglines for the ads read, 'Let's face it, firming the thighs of a size 2 supermodel is no challenge' and 'New Dove Firming. As tested on real curves.'

Firming cream is, of course, a product designed to make women feel bad about themselves so that they'll buy something they don't need. Love your curves, women are told, as long as they're tight and firm. (And, by the way, firming cream isn't some magic potion that will give you runner's legs without the effort. Dove marketing manager Sharon MacLeod even admitted in a press release that 'Dove is using these ads to show that using a skin firming product is not about transformation, but rather about taking care of your skin and feeling great about your curves.') When it comes down to it, the Dove ads and all the buzz they've generated keep reminding us that being beautiful is the most important thing a woman can be.

So what happens when an advertisement for beauty products exposes the tricks-of-the-trade other advertising companies use to sell similar products? Does the positive representation in the Dove campaign counter all the negative representation women and girls are faced with in advertisements? Do these images really break from the traditional 'code' of beauty product marketing? Do they signify alternative ideas about what makes a woman beautiful? And, finally, can a business that exists solely to make money sincerely promote social change? How excited should we get over a campaign like Dove's—no matter how socially conscious it appears to be—when at the end of the day, the goal is to move product? If there is one thing that can be said about the images in Dove's campaign, it's that they really have us thinking about the power of images.

Nicole Cohen is the co-founder and former co-editor of *Shameless* magazine, a magazine for young women and trans youth. This article first appeared in *Shameless*.

> KEY TERMS

allocation, p. 98
connotative, p. 91
content analysis, p. 106
decoding, p. 93
denotative, p. 91
discourse, p. 104
elite, p. 98
encoding, p. 93

indeterminacy of representation, p. 91
libertarian theory, p. 96
Marxist analysis, p. 99
political economy, p. 98
product placement, p. 112
representation, p. 89
rhetoric, p. 91
semiotics, p. 90

sign, p. 90
signifier, p. 90
signified, p. 90
social responsibility theory, p. 97
structuralism, p. 101
symbol, p. 90

> RELATED WEBSITES

Advertising Standards Canada: www.adstandards.com/en
A listing of Canadian advertising codes and guidelines, as well as information and reports on public complaints, can be found at this site.

Media Awareness Network: www.media-awareness.ca
The Media Awareness Network provides information and insightful analysis of various media issues, including violence in the media.

The Semiotics of Media: www.uvm.edu/~tstreete/ semiotics_and_ads/contents.html
A website on semiotics created by Professor Tom Streeter of the University of Vermont.

Theory.org: www.theory.org.uk/lego-hall.htm
Who says that academics don't have a sense of humour? This site offers a respectful play on social theory.

> FURTHER READINGS

Eco, Umberto. 1986. 'The multiplication of the media', in Umberto Eco, *Travels in Hyperreality*. New York: Harcourt Brace Jovanovich, 148–69. This essay and the others provide delightful insights into the unrealities of representation.

Jiwani, Yasmin. 2010. 'Rac(e)ing the nation: Media and minorities', in Leslie Regan Shade, ed., *Mediascapes: New Patterns in Canadian Communications*, 3rd edn. Toronto: Nelson Education, 271–86. A very good discussion of the representation of race in Canadian media.

Johnston, Russell. 2010. 'Advertising in Canada', in Leslie Regan Shade, ed., *Mediascapes: New Patterns in Canadian Communications*, 3rd edn. Toronto: Nelson Education 104–20. A good, brief history of the development of the advertising industry in Canada.

Leiss, William, S. Kline, Sut Jhally, and Jacqueline Botterill. 2005. *Social Communication in Advertising*, 3rd edn. New York: Routledge. This is an excellent history of advertising and the different ways advertising constructs relationships between people and products.

Media, Culture and Society. This journal is the pre-eminent British media studies journal, founded in the 1970s by five young media scholars.

Mosco, Vincent. 2009. *The Political Economy of Communication*, 2nd edn. Thousand Oaks, Calif.: Sage. A good overview of the history and application of the political economy of communication.

❯ STUDY QUESTIONS

1. Use the encoding/decoding model to analyze a popular TV program such as *The Simpsons*. What kinds of shared ideas and social values do the programs' writers draw on to tell the story? Why do you think the writers picked these to include in the program? How do the scheduling and structure of the program reflect the fact that it is a commercial television program?

2. Perform a semiotic analysis on a magazine advertisement for an automobile, cologne, or company. What are the signifiers used in constructing the ad? What are the signifieds? How do these work together to construct meaning? How many different meanings can be taken from the ad?

3. Compare the libertarian, social responsibility, and political economic theories of the media. Which theory provides the most accurate perspective on how the media operate in our society?

4. Make a content analysis of a major news story (the story may be covered over a number of days, in a number of articles, in a number of publications). Who are the major sources quoted in the story? What perspectives appear to have been left out?

5. Select a news story in a broadsheet newspaper (for example, *The Globe and Mail*) and the same story in a tabloid (for example, one of the Sun chain of newspapers). Identify the major differences in treatment. Then turn to the various theoretical perspectives in this chapter and apply the most appropriate model to your understanding of these differences. If your work is done as part of a group, compare and discuss your selections of theoretical models and findings.

6. 'Calvin Klein is a pernicious influence on society. The ads of this company demean and exploit human beings.' Discuss this statement. Be sure to include a consideration of polysemy.

7. Following Baudrillard, to what extent do you think that reality has been replaced by symbols and signs that refer only to other symbols and signs rather than to a grounded objective reality?

CHAPTER 5

Theoretical Perspectives on Audiences

> What the media are selling, in a capitalist society, is an audience.
>
> — 1970 SPECIAL SENATE COMMITTEE ON THE MASS MEDIA

Learning Objectives

- To explain the interaction between media and audiences as a dynamic interaction in which audience members actively and selectively interpret media content based on frameworks of understanding they bring to that content.

- To appreciate that media–audience interaction is not predictable but can be explained after the fact.

- To differentiate ways of studying relations between media and audience members: effects research, uses and gratifications research, Marxist analysis and the Frankfurt School, British cultural studies, feminist research, reception analysis, and industry audience research.

- To know what industry members measure about audiences and to explain how they measure those characteristics such as reach, share, and viewing time.

OPENING QUESTIONS

- How do media relate to their audiences?
- What theories study those relationships?
- How are audiences researched?
- What are some of the shortcomings of media industry audience research?

Introduction

As we have seen, media weave through our lives at many levels. At the political level, they help frame and animate our understanding of the events and circumstances that define citizenship, how society is organized politically, and our role and purpose in that organization. At the level of culture, media play on our knowledge of social groups, gender, and racial and ethnic distinctions. They also collude in our understanding of social roles (e.g., mother, child, teacher), organizations, and institutions. They address us as fans and devotees of particular media personalities and types of programs. And economically, they position us as consumers. In all these ways media frame and animate our sense of identity and provide an understanding of ourselves in relation to others and the world. By and large, however, the media address us as audiences, that is, as sets or groups of individuals for whom their content is designed. Media seek audiences: sometimes to inform, sometimes to enlighten, other times to entertain, and usually to sell to advertisers, or pay a fee for the receipt of content.

With the explosion of new, often interactive media choices, people are able to set the terms of their participation as audience members and even contribute to media production. In both traditional and new media, user-generated content is providing an expanding part of our media choice. Still, the overarching relation is one where content is designed for consumption by specific groups or types of individuals, generally with a profit motive in mind.

Media audiences are of interest to academic and industry researchers. Scholars and social scientists seek to understand the nature of the interaction between the media and their audiences; what audiences do with media content; how they engage with television, books, magazines, and music; how media influence perceptions and understandings of the world; and how they guide or influence social action. Members of the industry have a different agenda. They want to know the size and the **demographic** characteristics (age, gender, ethnicity) as well as other attributes of particular audiences, such as education, income level, and purchasing patterns, so they can define the product they are selling (the audience to

Source: Library and Archives Canada/Richard Harrington/National Film Board of Canada. Prototeque collection/Accession 1971-271/PA-111390

Ever since the television became a common household item, researchers have been interested in studying how audiences interact with this medium

the advertiser). Industry members also want to know how audiences respond to audience-building techniques so they can understand how to attract larger audiences or audiences with specific characteristics.

This chapter explores approaches to the audience. It begins with the academic perspectives and then turns to a discussion of industry measures of audiences. It ends with an appendix, a case study of audience measurement practices in the Canadian consumer magazine industry.

Making Meaning in Context: Culture, Media, Audience

Audience members do not accept all of what they see or hear—whether the facts of a news story or the general portrayal of society and its values that a film, television show, or novel may contain. Not everyone who sits down in front of a screen brings all of her or his critical faculties to bear on every program watched or to every piece of pulp fiction. Neither is it the case that audiences are generally composed of fragile beings desperately seeking simulated social contact and meaning through the media. Watching television, reading books or magazines, listening to music, and so on are largely casual or leisure activities. No research has ever shown that the media have the power to induce audience members to act against or outside their will.

Media–audience interaction is probably best thought of as a sometimes energetic, sometimes passive engagement between audience members and the media. Insofar as the media draw relations between audiences and a larger set of social values and institutions, this interaction also takes place at a social or cultural level. From this perspective, audience members, the media, and cultures can be conceived of as a closely woven meaning-generating system.

Let us consider the example of a young woman, home early from classes, who tunes into WWE on TV to find Undertaker and Kane throwing each other around the wrestling ring. No one is home, least of all her brother, who left the television on this channel the day before. Though normally not a fan of wrestling, she can't find the remote so she watches for several minutes. Within those few minutes she finds that the bout is nothing special. 'Boring', she thinks, and looks more carefully for the remote. This example illustrates many of the elements of meaning-generation. As our protagonist is confronted with this program, she immediately recognizes the scene and the characters and can sense if anything appeals to her in this action soap opera directed at young men. She analyzes the material on the screen by interpreting the events in her terms and then reacting accordingly.

Is this interaction complex and multidimensional? Yes. Implicitly, our protagonist knows that wrestling is not targeted at her. The fact that none of the advertising accompanying the program is relevant to her proves it. The interaction is also mediated by the context, and the choices found in the moment. Were she at a friend's house and they wanted to watch, she might stay with the program a while longer. But here at home by herself, she wonders what the other channels have to offer. What is in the fridge? How soon is her next assignment due? In assessing whether or not to watch, her perspective is framed by her degree of engagement with the subject matter (very small) and her knowledge of wrestling (what it is generally about and what tends to happen). Her action in looking for the remote, her sighs of boredom, her flopping down on the couch in the first place all are part of the meaning she is making of the situation she is in.

Given these media–audience dynamics, where does culture as an active, meaning-generating system figure in this scenario? Cultural dynamics play themselves out in the woman's vision of herself and the relevance of the program to her. Also, the fact that the program is aired and commands vast audiences is part of a cultural dynamic. Finally, the very scene of these modern gymnasts/gladiators heaving each other around in a sensational action theatre draws on a wide range of cultural ideas and values.

Because the relation between media, audiences, and cultures is based on interaction and is not predetermined, any consideration of the interaction of audience behaviour, media content, and cultural form must take place within a very broad framework—one that has the potential to encompass any and all elements of the interaction. Audience interpretations of media content derive from at least the following factors: (a) the social background or 'history' of the audience member; (b) her/his current state of mind; (c) the social situation, or context, within which the media consumption is taking place; and (d) the text or content. Given these criteria, we are able to understand the possible roots of our female viewer's behaviour. Nevertheless, a particular part of her individual personality or attitude in that moment might have caused her to behave differently. We cannot know exactly how she will react. However, the point of analyzing media audience relations is not to predict audience behaviour but rather to understand it.

Culture is a key element in this meaning-generating system. The individual's cultural milieu works to help create identity through acting as the reference point to a host of factors, including social and familial customs, laws, various institutions that mediate interaction, governing structures, and opportunities afforded by cultural and physical geography. As discussed in Chapter 2, culture is a set of ideas and values or 'way of life' through which people understand and relate to the larger set of organizations, institutions, and relationships within which they live. It is a dynamic derived from the wealth, history, and present-day attitudes and actions of groups and individuals that comprise the social milieu of which they are a part. Through interactions based in this context, people generate meaning through a constant process of selection, re-stylization (or appropriation), and transformation.

The study of audiences can be approached in many different ways. We will examine six academic approaches to the audience: effects research; uses and gratification research; Marxist analysis and the Frankfurt School; British cultural studies; feminist research; and reception analysis (see also Murray, 2010; Ruddock, 2007; McQuail, 2000; Alasuutari, 1999; Lindlof, 1991; Jensen and Rosengren, 1990). As with the perspectives on content we examined in the last chapter, the point here is to provide an overview of some of the main ways audiences have been

⟩ BOX 5.1   A TREATISE ON FAME

Is fame simply a media-induced phenomenon or do the roots of celebrity predate modern media?

In a three-part series in *The Globe and Mail* (18 Dec. 2000, A11) columnist Doug Saunders traces fame back to Goethe, who with the publication of his novel *The Sorrows of Young Werther* in 1774 caused Germans to imitate the dress and mannerisms of the protagonist and to become obsessed with the author's

Source: Courtesy of MuchMusic

Teens camp out for days in Toronto in hope of getting tickets to an awards show featuring Justin Bieber and Drake.

private life. But fame is probably as old as humanity. What about Jesus Christ? His wrestling with fame was framed in a confrontation with the Evil One in the wilderness before he stepped into public ministry. What about other religious figures such as Mohammed or Buddha? What about Ulysses and, for that matter, the Greek pantheon of gods?

Saunders suggests some other historical figures who had the quality of fame. Franz Liszt, in 1841, hired Gaetano Belloni to handle his tours, perhaps the first example of agents and managers. In turn, Liszt was hired by Phineas T. Barnum, a man of fame himself, for millions of dollars to tour with 'The Greatest Show on Earth'. Charles Dickens experienced fame in 1858 in his author tour of Britain, the US, and Canada. Florence Lawrence also earned it in 1910 when she became the first actor to receive a movie credit in her own name. In 1911 the first fan magazines were launched, which helped intensify fame for such actors as Toronto-born Mary Pickford. In 1942, singer Frank Sinatra started near-riots with his appearances and became arguably the first pop star. Orson Welles rose to fame overnight as a radio star with the 1938 broadcast of 'War of the Worlds'. In 1948, Milton Berle became a TV star. In 1960, John F. Kennedy became as much a political celebrity as a US president. In 1968, Pierre Trudeau followed suit in Canada. In 1990, following in the footsteps of other sports celebrities such as Babe Ruth, Michael Jordan signed a $100 million contract for endorsements of other products. And in 1997, US TV networks split their coverage between two celebrities, Bill Clinton giving his State of the Union address and the verdict on the trial of O.J. Simpson.

More recently, in a clear illustration of how fame and media are intertwined, kids lined up for days to try to get tickets to the MuchMusic video awards in Toronto in the summer of 2010 to see stars such as Justin Bieber and Drake.

approached by researchers, as well as illustrate some of the key issues audience research has raised, not to present a comprehensive review of these perspectives.

Effects, Agenda-Setting, and Cultivation Analysis

Early studies of the media following World War I (1914–18) presupposed media to have direct **effects** on human behaviour and attitudes. Fuelled by the success of propaganda campaigns during the war, which seemed to indicate that the masses would believe almost anything they were told, researchers posited the 'magic bullet' or 'hypodermic needle' theory of communication, built on the idea that media could inject ideas into people's heads. This perspective was supported by the social science of the day, which, on one hand, subscribed to the mass society thesis of vulnerability and, on the other, was animated by early behaviourist conceptions of psychology that saw human behaviour as a simple response to external stimuli. The early success of newspaper and radio advertising, which stimulated demand for the growing range of products generated by industry during the interwar period, added credence to this idea.

While the success of war propagandists and early advertisers seemed to demonstrate that people were easily swayed by media suggestion, studies conducted after World War II (1939–45) found that the impact of media messages on individuals was weak and, if anything, acted to reinforce existing ideas and beliefs rather than to alter opinions. In a review of effects research published in 1960, Joseph Klapper, a respected media researcher of the day, concluded that 'mass communication does not ordinarily serve as a necessary or sufficient cause of audience effects, but rather functions through a nexus of mediating factors' (cited in McQuail, 2000: 415).

Having found weaker effects than anticipated, researchers undertook the task of reanalyzing the relations between media and audiences and began

Source: © Gruffyddthomas/Dreamstime.com

What effect do you think large-scale advertising has on the things we buy?

to look for more diffuse, indirect effects. Working in this vein in the early 1960s, Bernard Cohen argued that news 'may not be successful in telling people what to think, but it is stunningly successful in telling its readers what to think about' (cited in Croteau and Hoynes, 2003: 242). For example, the front page of *The Globe and Mail* (and presumably, to a lesser extent, the *National Post* and the *Ottawa Citizen*) plays a significant role in what questions are asked that day in the House of Commons, as does the CBC news. This idea that the media serve an **agenda-setting** function, that they work, selectively, to draw the public's attention to particular events and circumstances, has gained a measure of credibility among media researchers.

Beginning with George Gerbner (1969, 1977), researchers have also examined the effects of viewing behaviour on people's conception of social reality, a perspective that has evolved into what is called **cultivation analysis**, wherein content is studied for its ability to encourage or cultivate particular attitudes in viewers towards particular persons or perspectives (see Signorelli and Morgan, 1990). For instance, Gerbner's work illustrated that people who watch a great deal of television overestimate the amount of violence in society and tend to have a 'bunker mentality' to protect themselves from what they perceive to be a violent world. However, in spite of the broad acceptance of Gerbner's work, certain British studies (e.g., Wober and Gunter, 1986) have not been able to replicate his findings.

Effects analysis has been greatly criticized, essentially because researchers have not been able to identify clear, strong effects from media exposure, which abstracts the process of communication from its social context and tries to draw a straight line between sender and receiver. Just as the Shannon and Weaver model of communication discussed in Chapter 1 was shown to be too simplistic to account for the myriad influences on the ways media messages are constructed, so the effects model does not illustrate the many influences on decoding. From this perspective, human agency is reduced to a simple reaction to content without consideration of how a larger set of social characteristics and forces—age, gender, education,

mental condition, etc.—bear on media reception.

Research on agenda-setting suffers from similar defects. It offers no explanation for how or why the media select what they will cover or what forces might be at play to help sensitize audience receptivity to messages. As the encoding/decoding model outlined in Chapter 4 illustrates, the media draw their material from a larger set of social circumstances. Perhaps the news agenda is set in this context, by local, national, and world events. On the other hand, perhaps the agenda is set by public or audience demand, or possibly it is an interaction between media institutions, audiences, and this larger set of social circumstances. In short, the effects tradition of media research raises more questions than it answers.

Moreover, when concerns over media effects are raised, it is interesting who is or is not condemned for putting forward certain media constructions. German film director Leni Riefenstahl, who died at the age of 101 in September 2003, was never forgiven for her movies *Triumph of the Will* (1934–5) and *Olympia* (1936–8), which portrayed Hitler's Nazis in a heroic light. In contrast, D.W. Griffith, whose *Birth of a Nation* (1916) portrays African Americans as ignorant and crude, is considered a pioneer of American film. Oliver Stone has also escaped condemnation for his movie *Natural Born Killers* (1994) even though copycat crimes were committed in its wake. Stanley Kubrick, on the other hand, withdrew *A Clockwork Orange* (1971) from circulation in Britain after some of its violence was re-enacted in real life (*Globe and Mail*, 22 Aug. 2002). The debate around such movies often reproduces effects theory simplistically. Little attention is paid to the social circumstances—such as poverty, inequality, racial discrimination, alcoholism, child and sexual abuse, or extreme misogyny—that animate real-life violence.

Uses and Gratification Research

Uses and gratification research (U&G) began both as a response to findings of limited effects and as a reaction to the growing concern, rooted

⠿ BOX 5.2 THE LANGUAGE OF MOVIES AND TV

Part of the structuring process of each media form is that it develops a language the audience comes to understand. The following are examples of 'languages' the audience has come to learn through TV and film content.

- All police investigations require at least one visit to a strip club.
- All beds have L-shaped sheets to allow the man to bare his chest and the woman to hide hers.
- Ventilation systems are perfect hiding places. They reach to every part of a building, are noiseless to enter and easy to move along both horizontally and vertically, and no one thinks to look there.
- German accents are sufficient should you wish to pass for a German military officer.
- When alone, foreigners speak English to one another.

- All women staying in haunted houses are compelled to investigate strange noises in their most revealing underwear.
- Cars that crash almost always burst into flames.
- Any person waking from a nightmare sits bolt upright.
- All bombs are fitted with large time displays that indicate exactly when they are to go off.
- You can always find a chainsaw if you need one.
- Having a job of any kind ensures that a father will forget his son's eighth birthday.
- Any lock can be picked easily unless it is on a door to a burning building in which a child is imprisoned.
- The more a man and woman hate each other initially the greater the chance they will fall in love in the end.

Source: Adaptation of 'A sampler of one-liners and true facts', by Gary Borders, *The Daily Sentinel* (Nacodoches). (Gary B. Borders)

in the mass society debates, that 'popular culture'—the wide variety of new television, radio, and musical content that started to gain popularity in the 1950s—was undermining or debasing audience tastes (Blumler and Katz, 1974). Based in social psychology, instead of the question 'What do media do to audiences?', the central question of this approach is, 'What do audiences do with the media?' The underlying premise was to focus on the agency of audience members and explore their motivations in the active selection of media content. Take, for example, two university students who decide to see an action movie after their last exam of the semester. They are not yet at the theatre, but uses and gratification theory is relevant. Going to a movie provides a good chance to relax, get together with friends, enjoy whatever is of interest in the movie, and go out for a coffee afterwards to socialize. Movies give people a chance to talk about other, related interests.

In contrast to effects research, the uses and gratifications approach is more attentive to audience variables, that is, the orientations and approaches audience members bring to their selection and interpretation of media content. Given its roots in

social psychology, U&G has concentrated on the micro (personal) and meso (group or institutional) levels of social existence, with little attention paid to the macro level—the social, ideological, cultural, or political orientations of the audience. Work during the 1980s spoke of never-ending spirals of uses and effects in which audience members look to the media for certain kinds of information (Rosengren and Windahl, 1989). Having gained this information, they behave in a particular way and then return to the media for further information, and so on. In fact, the two fields—effects research and uses and gratification research—have been growing closer together and are, to a degree, complementary.

But while U&G theory puts more emphasis on agency than does effects theory, it still focuses on abstracting media consumption from the larger social context. Media consumption is reduced to an individual desire, process, or relationship. The influences of larger social factors are not fully explored. Moreover, U&G theory is functionalist: it is built on the assumption that media function to serve some kind of audience need and then set out to discover what that need is. No account is taken of the larger social origins of this supposed need or of how the process of media consumption plays into a larger set of social forces and institutions. The larger social purposes of media and how audience uses and understandings of media are shaped by other social conditions are not considered.

Marxist Analysis and the Frankfurt School

Marxism sees society as animated by a set of social forces based on capitalist forms of production (Chapter 4). Working from this larger frame, Marxist perspectives on the media generally focus on how the media support dominant interests in society, helping them maintain power and control over time. Consequently, Marxist perspectives don't focus on media–audience relations per se and/or on the ways media interact with or impinge on the agency of individual audience members. Rather, Marxist critics consider the ways in which media integrate audiences into the larger capitalist system.

One of the most far-reaching and influential Marxian critiques of twentieth-century media and culture comes from a group known as the **Frankfurt School**. The leading members of this group of intellectuals were Max Horkheimer, Theodor Adorno, and Herbert Marcuse; their ideas were formed in the interwar period (1920–40) (Jay, 1974). At first they worked at the Institute for Social Research attached to the University of Frankfurt, but when Hitler came to power, because they were Jews and their ideas were fundamentally out of step with fascism, they had to leave Germany, eventually settling in the US. Adorno and Horkheimer found faculty positions at Columbia University, where they remained until after World War II. In the late 1940s, Adorno and Horkheimer returned, with great honour, to Frankfurt, where they continued to work in the university until the 1970s. Marcuse (1954, 1964) settled in San Francisco, where he made his major contributions, remained in the US, and became an intellectual hero of the counterculture in the 1960s.

These intellectuals argued that capitalist methods of mass production had profound impacts on cultural life. Capitalist methods had been applied, in the nineteenth century, to the manufacture of the necessities of life, that is, to material goods like machinery and clothing. Beginning in the 1920s, although interrupted by the Great Depression and World War II, capitalism was applied to the production of what we call consumer goods—to a new range of goods, products, or commodities. With the help of advertising, families were persuaded that the acquisition of cars, household appliances, and fashionable clothing and accessories was essential to modern life. New forms of mass communication such as cinema, radio, and photography (in newspapers and magazines), complete with formulaic and commercial content, became woven into this way of life. These new forms, on one hand, were subject, in their development, manufacture, and distribution, to capitalist methods of mass production; on the other hand, they displaced older, high-cultural forms of leisure and entertainment such as symphonies, the ballet, theatre, poetry, and great literature. At the same time, the media also served as a key vehicle for celebrating and helping integrate people into this new commercial way of life. Adorno and Horkheimer pooled these developments together under an umbrella term: 'the culture industry' (Adorno and Horkheimer, 1977 [1947]).

The Frankfurt School argued that, through such developments, industrial capitalism penetrated deeper into cultural life and began creating a ready-made way of life. Thus, people's wants and desires were both created and satisfied through the marketplace. Building on the concerns of the mass society theorists that industrial society heralded a loss of social and cultural values, Adorno and Horkheimer saw marketers rushing to fill this void with an endless parade of commodities. However, this new way of life was devoid of any deeper meaning or understanding of the world. The pleasures derived from consumption lasted only as long as it took for new commodities to come on the market. The distinctions between different makes, models, and brands are largely illusory and based on quickly shifting styles rather than substantive qualities or characteristics. Popular films and music are formulaic, their plots and rhythms easily recognized and understood. And in the ongoing churn of the market, no lasting relationships or deeper understandings of the world might be made.

From this perspective, culture and the media serve only one master: capital. All culture becomes a product of industrial capitalism and the guiding logic is one of profit for the capitalist. With no active audience the possibility of the media acting as a venue for democratic discussion of issues of public concern disappears. Media effects, uses, and gratifications are buried under the domination of culture and the media by the rhythms and needs of capital. Audience members are seen as little more than cultural dupes, or as Smythe (1994: 9) puts it, unpaid 'workers' for the capitalist 'consciousness industry' who are inexorably drawn, via the media, into a prepackaged world where choice is simply an illusion that supports this domination. (For a critique of this reading of Adorno and Horkheimer, see Gunster, 2004.)

The Frankfurt School members have been accused of cultural elitism and of pessimism. Perhaps most importantly, their perspective provides little room for human agency. The audience is simply a tool of the capitalist economy, and very few people today would suggest that the culture industry (a useful term) has the entirely negative effects that the Frankfurt School claimed it did. Nevertheless, the members of the Frankfurt School rightly pointed out the importance of analyzing cultural industry as integral to capitalism and questioned critically its impact and effect on contemporary cultural life. The issues they addressed have continuing relevance. Since they first developed their analysis, the expansion of certain cultural industries circulates their particular influence throughout the world; from blue jeans to films to Disneyland-type theme parks, particular cultural icons and narrow cultural expressions have been spread globally. The *Lord of the Rings* movie trilogy, for instance, was not only a movie of special effects and important ideas; it was a marketing extravaganza. Thanks to TV we've all been there and done that, and it all looks the same, because

> ## ❖ BOX 5.3 ON THE BIRMINGHAM SCHOOL
>
> An article by Norma Schulman on the beginnings and impact of the Centre for Contemporary Cultural Studies at the University of Birmingham can be found on the website of the *Canadian Journal of Communication*: www.cjc-online.ca. For Schulman's article, follow the links through back issues to vol. 18, no. 1 and to the full text of the article: www.cjc-online.ca/viewarticle.php?id=140&layout=html.

you can stay in the same hotels and buy the same things in the same shops in the same shopping malls at locations around the world. The trends the Frankfurt School identified years ago today pepper the globe.

British Cultural Studies

British cultural studies began as a reaction to Marxist and other media theories' downplaying of the role of human agency while discounting the apparent pleasures of popular culture. The impact of the growing mass culture in post-war Britain, particularly on the working class, was of interest to a number of intellectuals in the 1950s, including Richard Hoggart (1992 [1957]) and Raymond Williams (1958). To advance his concerns, Hoggart established a small post-graduate Centre for Contemporary Cultural Studies at the University of Birmingham, which his colleague Stuart Hall took over in the late 1960s. Hall's work in the 1970s with graduate students in what came to be called the **Birmingham School** of cultural studies was increasingly influential and largely defines what is today known as 'cultural studies'.

Two main lines of development can be identified in the short history of British cultural studies from the 1950s to the present: the analysis of working-class culture, particularly the culture of young working-class males, and then, in response to feminist critiques at the Centre, the analysis of young working-class females (Women's Studies Group, 1978) (see Turner, 1990; McGuigan, 1992;

Storey, 1993; Schulman, 1993). A central concern was the use of mass culture, by both sexes, to create and define gendered identities. What clothing you chose to wear, the kind of music you listened to, whether you had a motorcycle or a scooter—these things helped create your image and define your personality. Instead of individuals being manipulated by the products of mass culture—as the Frankfurt School had argued—it was the other way around. Individuals could take these products and manipulate them, subvert them, to create new self-definitions. The classic study of this process is Dick Hebdige's *Subculture: The Meaning of Style* (1979), which looked at how young, white, working-class males created identities for themselves through music: from mods and rockers in the 1950s and 1960s through to punk and beyond in the 1970s. Cultural studies paid particular attention to the ambiguous relationship between musical styles and social identities and to the embrace of black music and the culture of young, black males by young, white, working-class males. This trend is captured beautifully in the 1991 film *The Commitments*, based on the Roddy Doyle novel, when the protagonist, Jimmy Rabbitte, assembles a group of working-class Dublin youth in an R&B band and asks them to repeat after him, 'I'm black and I'm proud.' While cultural studies illustrated that the appropriation of meaning was much more complex than previously thought, it also demonstrated that social forces and institutions worked in complex ways to help reproduce the dominant order. For instance, in his classic study of an English high school, Paul Willis (1977) shows how rebellion against established authority leads working-class youth to working-class jobs.

An important strand in the study of contemporary culture has been analysis of film and television. In the 1970s the British Film Institute's journal *Screen* put forward a structuralist-inspired analysis of film arguing that how a story is told (through techniques of editing, visual images, and so forth) controls and defines the viewer. The narrative techniques of cinema subtly but powerfully imposed their meanings on the spectator, who cannot avoid being 'positioned' to see the film in a particular way. The notion of 'position' refers particularly to the point of view constructed for the viewer through filmic techniques—how the viewer is 'put in the picture'. In a classic analysis of Hollywood movies, Laura Mulvey (1975) argued that the pleasures of this kind of cinema were organized for a male viewer and that women (both in the storyline and as objects to be looked at) were merely instruments of male pleasure—objects of a male gaze.

Stuart Hall and his students, undertaking an analysis of how television and other media work, develop a more open kind of analysis. They argue that media content is structured to relay particular meanings—preferred readings—to audiences, but that it is quite possible for audiences to refuse that meaning and develop their own interpretation of what they hear and see (Glasgow Media Group, 1976).

The key concept in such analysis is ideology. The meaning of ideology has been much discussed (see Johnston, 1996; Eagleton, 1991; Larrain, 1979, 1983; Thompson, 1980 [1963]). Several different definitions of ideology include a coherent set of social values, beliefs, and meanings that people use to decode the world, for example, neo-liberalism and socialism. Marxist ideology refers to a particular set of ideas, values, and beliefs that question support for the dominant or ruling class. From the Marxist viewpoint, capitalism promulgates such ideas as 'the poor are lazy', 'capitalism is the only viable economic system', and 'unions and strikes are bad for society'. Through this ideological misrepresentation of social reality, the working class is prevented from understanding how they are exploited or oppressed and come to accept the values of the ruling class. In other words, they have been lured into a 'false consciousness' of how capitalist society works. From this perspective, 'ideology' is a way of representing the world to oneself, a set of ideas that one uses to impose order on society and to decide what place different people and groups should occupy in the social order. By presenting versions of social reality that represent the existing order as natural, obvious, right, and just—in short, as the way things are and ought to be—the effect of ideology is to maintain the status quo, that is, the domination of the powerful over the powerless.

In the face of the social unrest of the 1960s and 1970s—the civil rights movement in the US, the rise of feminism throughout the Western world, and the student movement in Canada, the US, and several European countries—some social scientists began to argue that there was more than one form of ideological oppression at play. Not only did ideology keep the workers in a subordinate position, but it also did the same for women, people of colour, and other social groups. Indeed, through their acts of protest, these groups illustrated that they had their own ideas about how the social world should be structured and what their positions in that world should be—they had their own ideologies. Hence, the question became, 'Amid all of these possible competing ideologies, why is it that the one that generally helps keep wealthy white males in positions of power seems to prevail?'

Exploring this question in the British context, cultural studies researchers argued that British television reproduced the dominant value system—loosely understood as a paternalistic, class-based consensus that believed in the monarchy, the Anglican Church, Parliament, and the rule of law, among other things (Hall, 1978, 1980). For instance, television news and current affairs programs are major vehicles for reproducing dominant values: powerful **primary definers** (interviewed politicians, experts, the military) are routinely allowed to define the issues, express their opinions, and offer interpretations of events and circumstances (Hall et al., 1978). Alternative or oppositional interpretations of events are seldom, if ever, allowed expression. An extreme example of this in Britain was the banning of members of Sinn Fein (the political wing of the Irish Republican Army [IRA]) from British television (see Curtis, 1984; Schlesinger, 1983). Television dramas, films, song lyrics, popular novels, etc., all can all be seen as a set of morality tales from which we are to take lessons in what constitutes desirable and undesirable behaviour. Moreover, when media products fail to conform

to dominant values they are often seen to cause negative effects, which illustrates the point that a **dominant ideology** helps to define these other perspectives as 'dangerous'.

Hall argues that, despite the fact that they reflect the dominant ideology, these media presentations can be decoded by viewers in very different ways (Hall, 1978). Indeed, as protesters from the 1960s to today demonstrate, not all people decode either the media or social life in general in the same way. Depending on their social background—gender, class, race, ethnicity, culture—people often hold different and/or competing ideologies and articulate meaning differently. Although a dominant ideology may be reflected in media products, media content need not be read or understood that way. A study by David Morley (1980)—a graduate of the Birmingham School—was an important step in establishing this perspective. Morley looked at how viewers of a 1970s BBC program called *Nationwide* interpreted, made sense of, or decoded the program. He found, as Hall had suggested, three different responses: dominant, negotiated, and oppositional. Some viewers accepted the values of the program, which stressed national unity and strong family values, suggesting that Britain was essentially a nation of white, middle-class families living in suburbia. These viewers accepted the program's preferred meaning, this consensual representation of British society that systematically filtered out conflicting interests of marginalized social groups (that is, marginalized by this definition). Other viewers took a rather more critical or negotiated view of the program; while a few groups of viewers (notably young blacks) rejected it altogether.

Spurred by the work of the Birmingham School, through the 1980s and 1990s the cultural studies approach concentrated on how audiences made sense of the media (Lee, 2003). The approach rejected the strongly deterministic view of the Frankfurt School and the journal *Screen*, stressing that media consumption was an active process. It also illustrated how popular culture was a rich and dynamic field, filled with a complex range of social meanings.

Feminist Research

Feminist media studies have much in common with cultural studies (see Franklin et al., 1992). The feminist approach developed from French writer Simone de Beauvoir's *The Second Sex* (1957 [1949]) and the writings of Betty Friedan (1963) in the US. Like Marxism, feminism is deeply critical of the character of modern societies, which, it argues, are based on fundamental inequalities. But where Marxism locates the roots of inequality in capital ownership and class division, feminism points to the male domination of society (patriarchy) as the root of profound human inequalities and injustices. These inequalities are pervasive aspects of modern life; men have economic, political, and cultural power, women do not. Men generally control public life, while women occupy the marginal spaces of private life and domesticity.

How is it that patriarchal values continue to have such power? Critics studied how cultural products can contribute to normalizing the oppression of women. Advertisements were one obvious place to look (Williamson, 1978), and film, television, and popular fiction provided other avenues (Media Education Foundation, 2002). Feminist researchers developed the idea of gendered narratives (Laura Mulvey's work on film was influential here); types of stories (narrative genres) appeal or speak to male readers or viewers (adventure stories like the Western or James Bond novels are classic examples), while other types appeal to female readers and viewers (Radway, 1984, is the key text). Likewise, they looked at gendered television; feminist audience studies discovered the kind of radio and TV programs that women preferred (see, e.g., Hobson, 1980, 1982). David Morley (1986) studied TV viewers in family settings and discovered a consistent profile of male and female preferences. One principal program category was TV soap operas with their largely female viewing audiences, and many studies have since examined what women enjoy in such programs (Seiter et al., 1989, review previous work).

While providing key insights into the structure of media texts, some of this early work has been criticized for its lack of theorization of the ways in which women 'read' media texts and incorporate them into their lives. For instance, Ien Ang and Joke Hermes (1991) argue that certain feminists seem to have accepted a crude inoculation model of media effects on women derived from effects theory (i.e., the media inject audiences with meanings) and underline the necessity of investigating how women negotiate with the 'texts' they encounter in the media.

Since its early days, **feminist research** on the media has expanded. For instance, Andrea Press (2000: 28–9) observes that feminist scholarship has at least three, sometimes overlapping, dimensions. The first looks at '[f]eminism, difference and identity' and 'highlights the experiences of those who have remained unheard and gives voice to that which has remained unspoken.' Here, analysis focuses on how media representation and social discourse override or frame out particular perspectives and voices. A second strand of research, 'feminism and the public sphere', emphasizes the 'role of the media in facilitating—or hindering—public debate', particularly in terms of 'giving voice to those previously unheard, such as women, under-represented groups, and others whose ideas have not previously entered public debate.' For instance, in the context of new media, Shade (in Grossberg et al., 2006: 291) points out, 'There are tensions in gender differences, whereby women are using the Internet to reinforce their private lives and men are using the Internet for engaging in the public sphere.' The third dimension, 'new technologies and the body', considers 'broader questions about media, technology, and the relationship of both to the body' (Press, 2000: 29).

At a more general level, recent feminist scholarship examines how media consumption is woven into patterns of everyday life and how women and other social groups deploy media, along with other facets of their experience, to make meaning of their lives (Hermes, 2006).

Reception Analysis

In the 1980s, cultural and feminist studies of the mass media increasingly looked at how audiences made sense of cultural products, how they

Source: © istockphoto.com/Rich Legg

Research has shown that men and women prefer different types of movies and respond differently to the same movies.

interpreted what they read, saw, and heard. But it became apparent that to do this, it was necessary to attend not simply to the product itself (the novel, the film, the TV drama), but also, more generally, to the context in which the consumption of the cultural product took place. **Reception analysis** thus takes into account the social setting in which audiences respond to the products of contemporary popular culture and in this way is somewhat similar to uses and gratifications theory. However, rather than emphasizing what use or gratification an audience member gains from media exposure, reception analysis focuses on how he or she actively interprets what the media text has to offer and how media consumption is re-integrated into the personal dimensions of her or his life. As Gray (1999: 31) puts it, this work 'place[s] media readings and use within complex webs of determinations, not only of the texts, but also those deeper

structural determinants, such as class, gender, and…race and ethnicity. These studies have also shed light on the ways in which public and private discourses intersect and are lived out within the intimate and routine practices of everyday life.'

Reception analysis has been of particular interest to feminist scholars in a number of ways. For one thing, the household is a prime site for cultural consumption by women. When US researcher Janice Radway studied American women readers of romantic fiction she found that they emphasized how the activity of reading became a special, personal time when they left behind domestic chores, responsibilities to husbands and children, and created a time and space for themselves and their own pleasure. They saw it as a moment of self-affirmation (Radway, 1984). This discovery points to the importance of attending to what lies outside the cultural products themselves. The meaning of romance fiction for Radway's readers was something more than the form and content of the stories themselves. It resonated with integral elements of their lives.

In the same way that Radway examined romance reading, work was undertaken on how family members use radio, TV, newspapers, magazines, VCRs, and satellite dishes. It showed that these media can be used for a range of purposes that have little to do with their content. Parents may watch a TV program with a child to nourish their relationship rather than to learn what the program is about. The dynamics of power relations between males and females, parents and children, and older and younger siblings have been studied in relation to, for instance, who has access to the remote control for the TV or who can operate the VCR (Morley, 1986). Here, the attention is directed towards what the audience brings to a viewing or decoding, the social context, and the act of viewing. Media researchers J. Bryce (1987), Peter Collett and R. Lamb (1986), D. Hobson (1980), and Tania Modleski (1984) have described how various groups—women, men, families—watch television. Women, for instance, often juggle television-watching with domestic chores. Children often play while watching TV and look up only when

❖ BOX 5.4 FAN STUDIES by Steve Bailey, Ph.D.

Dressed as Storm Troopers, a man and his five-year-old son Ronan attend Fan Expo, a three day conference for sci-fi, anime and horror show lovers held in Toronto.

One important recent development in the study of media audiences has been the development of the distinct field of 'fan studies' that emerged in the 1980s and 90s. Fan studies has roots in a number of earlier scholarly perspectives in the study of communication and culture, most notably work in the 'British Cultural Studies' tradition. Scholars such as Paul Willis and Dick Hebdige became interested in the role that passionate attachments to forms of media culture played in the composition of a social identity and in the behavior of individuals with such deep interests in particular performers, programs, and other cultural objects. Hebdige, for example, looked at the ways that 'subcultures' formed around appreciation for certain styles of clothing or genres of music. Another important influence was the work of literary scholar Janice Radway, author of *Reading the Romance*, who studied avid female readers of romance novels, a genre considered to be of low quality and little interest by mainstream work in literary studies. The recognition that this mode of consuming mediated messages required specific forms of research and had distinct characteristics was then extended into a recognized field of fan studies. Part of this effort was designed to move the study of fandom way from one that view fans as pathological or stereotypically obsessive in their interests and study them as manifestations of one segment of a larger audience community.

Scholars of media fandom, or 'fanthropologists' as they are sometimes jokingly called, tend to rely on research methods associated with anthropology and qualitative sociological approaches, especially ethnography. They often study fans in natural social situations, such as concerts, fan conventions, or other social gatherings and tend to favour methods such as interviews and detailed questionnaires to gather data on fan behaviour. Increasingly, scholars of fandom have examined a range of 'secondary texts' produced by fans such as fan fiction, artwork inspired by a particular cultural object or performer, and other forms of cultural production. The crucial work in the development of fan studies was Henry Jenkins's 1992 book *Textual Poachers*, which explored these types of activities in considerable detail. The creative work of fans is analyzed to help understand how they relate to the objects of their interest and passion and to make better sense of the importance of fandom in the development of worldviews, forms of identity, and social behavior. This area of fan research has become increasingly intertwined with scholarship examining 'participatory culture', which involves the examination of a variety of forms of cultural consumption that involve productive activities on the part of consumers, such as recording comical 'filke' songs that parody mainstream culture or performing unauthorized modifications of commercial video games.

Most recently, scholars of media fan cultures have focused a great deal of attention on the impact of the internet on fan communities. The rise of virtual culture has allowed for the formation of large international fan communities connected through websites, email lists, and other forms of new media communication. This technological shift has greatly expanded the number of individuals who participate in some form of fan culture and has also allowed for the development of a wide range of cultural practices, such as the making and distribution of video and audio 'mashups' of popular culture, works by fans. An important early work in this area was Nancy Baym's 2000 book *Tune In, Log On: Soaps, Fandom, and Online Community*, which examined the use of the internet by soap opera fans, and has continued in the work of a number of contemporary researchers.

Steve Bailey is author of *Media Audiences and Identity: Self-Construction in the Fan Experience* (New York: Palgrave Macmillan, 2005). Reproduced with permission of Palgrave Macmillan.

their ears tell them that the plot is thickening. Men often watch programs not of their own choosing. In some families and at some times, a switched-on television functions as a conversation stopper or mediator rather than as a source of watched programming.

British media scholar Paddy Scannell (1988) has analyzed the manner in which broadcasting works at the level of individual audience members to sustain the lives and routines of whole populations, while researchers Roger Silverstone (1981) and John Hartley (1987) have discussed how television provides the basis for symbolic participation in a national community, or sometimes, as in the cases of Belgium, Switzerland, and Canada, an international linguistic community.

More recently, researchers have begun to explore how new media are changing people's perception of themselves, offering new avenues for identity formation. For instance, through a series of case studies, Sherry Turkle (1995) illustrates how computers with their access to chat rooms, online games, and other web offerings are providing what Andrea Press and Sonia Livingstone (2006: 189) describe as 'a more malleable notion of "self"'.

Thus, from the perspective of reception analysis, an 'audience' is not so much a group as a variable set of individuals whose lives (and conceptions of the meaning of media consumption) are structured between media texts and the shifting dimensions and determinants of their own lives. In other words, media are seen as one element in a larger set of institutions, technologies, and discourses that provide the means through which people live their lives.

BOX 5.5   LEND ME YOUR EARS AND I'LL GIVE YOU WHITE BREAD

Why are radio stations as bland as sliced white bread? The answer, according to Bill Reynolds, former editor-in-chief of *eye Weekly* in Toronto, is corporate concentration and vertical integration. Reynolds (2002: R1, R5) notes, 'This interpretation is really a political-economic analysis of content' (see Chapter 4).

'In Canada', Reynolds continues, 'Corus radio has 52 stations reaching 8.4 million Canadians per week. Corus controls both the classic rock and new rock formats in two major markets—Q107 and Edge 102 in Toronto, and Rock 101 and CFOX in Vancouver.... The corporate motivation is to keep those lists [playlists] as tight and familiar as possible, right across the country.... Research shows that tight formatting works. Stations carry only 35 'currents', or new songs, and change between three and five songs per week.... [For radio] losing one percentage point of market share can mean as much as $1.5 million in lost annual revenue.'

The 'research' of which Reynolds speaks is industry research on the size and nature of the audience, how long people listen, when they listen, what they're doing while they listen. Reynolds goes on to explain that it falls to the radio-promotion representatives of the record companies and, in the US, independent promoters to get untried and untested songs played. In the US, independent promoters actually pay radio stations between $100,000 and $400,000 for the right to represent them and in turn the record companies pay these promoters $800 to $5,000 for each song added to the station (depending on market size). Reynolds notes that most claim that pay-for-play does not exist in Canada, but he also notes that if one overlooks the 35 per cent Canadian content requirement, the playlists of Canadian and US radio stations look remarkably similar.

This side of communications businesses does not receive as much attention as it should. The vast majority of the material that audiences see in newspapers or on television, in movie theatres or in magazines, as well as what they listen to on radio, is the result of major marketing efforts of producers.

Of course, in any business things never stand still. University-based radio stations, co-op stations such as CFRO in Vancouver, Radio CINQ in Montreal, and the Beat at 94.5 FM in Vancouver, are breaking the mould. And deejays at clubs also are a separate force in the music world. But like the big beer makers, in contrast to the microbreweries, in terms of availability and market advantages mainstream product continues to dominate.

Industry Audience Research

While academics have had their own reasons for studying mass media audiences, media institutions themselves have long been keenly interested in finding out what people read, listen to, and watch. Such information has practical value. It enables TV or radio stations, for instance, to identify their audiences and discover their listening or viewing habits and preferences. Industry-led research on audiences attends to basic issues, such as when people are available or not to listen or watch, and when exactly they are watching or listening (audience habits). Given this, they can also find out what audiences like or dislike (audience tastes). This information has obvious economic value: the more precise the information they have about their own and their competitors' audiences, the greater the possibilities to sell these audiences to advertisers or to improve their product (to attract even more advertisers).

Traditionally, such research concentrated on audience size: the bigger the audience for a TV program, the more attractive it would be to advertisers. But since the 1970s, industry researchers have tried to provide more accurate information about what kinds of viewers are attracted to which programs. A program could have a very large audience, but a large portion of this audience may have limited disposable income, and thus not appeal to advertisers. A program with a smaller audience with greater spending power may be more valuable to advertisers than a large general audience. For instance, a program may not reach a mass prime-time audience, yet it may have a strong viewership among young, affluent professionals, and hence can command premium prices on advertisements. The specific makeup of an audience can also attract advertisers. For instance, for the makers of Barbie, an audience of prepubescent girls and their mothers is of great value. Targeting audiences with very specific demographics is called **narrowcasting**.

Narrowcasting has been given impetus by the explosion of new broadcast channels. Over the last 25 years, the number of television channels available to Canadian audiences has mushroomed from less than 20 to several hundred. This has led to severe audience fragmentation, as the available television audience has been scattered across this expanding television landscape, not to mention the increasing draw of the internet. For instance, in 1969, 35 per cent of the English-speaking television audience watched the CBC while 25 per cent watched CTV. By 2007–8, the CBC share had fallen to 5.4 per cent, and, together, CTV, Global, and other non-specialty channels garnered less than 24 per cent of the viewing audience. Fragmenting audiences have put pressure on broadcast companies to find innovative ways to reach large numbers of people. This has led to concentration of media ownership as companies work to reach or re-aggregate audiences by owning a number of different television channels or media outlets. Audience fragmentation has also led media companies that have traditionally owned broadcast and newspaper outlets to buy web-based media, such as News Corporation's 2006 purchase of MySpace.com. More recently, the proliferation of mobile media has led to a convergence of telecommunications and broadcast companies as telecommunications companies strive to obtain content for the new mobile services they are offering.

Three concepts basic to institutional audience research are:

1. **reach**: the number of actual or potential audience members during a particular program period;

2. **share**: the percentage of the audience 'reach' who are watching a particular program during a specific time period;

3. **viewing time**: the time spent viewing during a day, week, or longer period of time.

'Share' is generally the most important statistic as it describes what percentage of the available audience is tuned in to a particular program.

Formative research and summative research (Withers and Brown, 1995) are other approaches to measuring the appeal of TV programming. **Formative research** is undertaken during production, usually by means of focus groups, to obtain reactions to programs in the making. **Summative research** measures the effectiveness of a program after its completion.

Both commercial media outlets and public media institutions conduct audience research. By 1936, for instance, the BBC had set up its own listener research department to answer questions about listener habits and preferences, such as when people get up, go to work, return from work, and go to bed. The same department took responsibility for television once it was established. Do people watch more TV in winter than in summer? Do people in certain locations watch more or less than viewers elsewhere? As they answered such questions, media managers could schedule programs to conform to the daily habits and routines of the British people (Scannell, 1988). The BBC also undertook research into audience preferences: what kinds of music did people prefer to listen to—dance-band music or orchestral music, opera, chamber music, or other? BBC audience research provided answers to such questions and helped broadcasters determine how much of each kind of music they ought to air (Pegg, 1983; Scannell and Cardiff, 1991).

In Canada, the CBC took on many of the same research tasks as the BBC, but its studies are of a slightly different context (Eaman, 1994). As early as the 1920s in North America, individuals were attempting to set up procedures to measure radio audiences. There was even an early electronic device, the audimeter, designed to record the stations that were being heard in the home.

In October 1936, one month before the CBC began operations, Montrealer Walter Elliott set up an independent market research operation with a partner, Paul Haynes, to serve both the CBC and commercial broadcasters (ibid.). Various other individuals and companies followed over the years, but while they were successful in a commercial context they did not serve the interests of the CBC very well. The most obvious example of their failings came in the form of the ratings of a CBC radio station operating out of Watrous, Saskatchewan. Even though it was well-known that this station was listened to throughout the Prairies and even into British Columbia, surveys carried out by Elliott-Haynes showed the audience share to be almost zero. The main reason for this inaccuracy seemed to be that only the urban areas were surveyed, and

within a limited time period and by telephone. Later work showed that the CBC in Watrous was the most listened-to station in Saskatchewan.

For years the CBC attempted to use commercial audience research services, though it realized their shortcomings. By 1954, the need for high-quality audience research for public broadcasting had become more than obvious. Moreover, the conceptualization of what information was needed had advanced beyond audience share to qualitative information. So, following the lead of the BBC, the CBC set up its own research department.

Eaman has summarized the types of research undertaken by the CBC over the years:

- the impact of cable on television viewing;
- methodological analysis;
- critiques of other studies;
- indirect indicators of audience demand;
- program balance analysis;
- analysis of Canadian content and gender roles;
- effects analysis;
- awareness analysis;
- research on audience maximization;
- audience composition;
- special broadcasts audiences;
- audience behaviour, that is, how often people listen to and/or watch what and when;
- habits and interests of certain age groups;
- comparisons of certain audiences to the general population;
- opinions of programs by audiences;
- opinions of what programs should be broadcast.

Understanding television consumption is important if policy-makers are to ensure there is an ongoing presence of Canadian television products available to Canadians in the current, shifting technological environment. Research illustrates that despite the growing presence of computers and the web, on average per-person television viewing actually increased from about 22 hours per week in 1994–5 to 27.1 hours per week in 2007–8

(CBC, 2009). However, as Figure 5.1 shows, foreign programming dominates prime time on English-language television. Alternatively, as Figure 5.2 illustrates, on French television Canadian programming is by far the viewers' favourite in prime time. As Figure 5.1 also illustrates, even though about 25 per cent of the programming on the private English networks, CTV and Global, is Canadian, it accounts for far less of audience viewing time.

This disparity is at least in part the product of the economics of the Canadian market As the CBC (2003: 2) notes:

> Simulcast rights to popular US sitcoms and dramas can be purchased for between $100–125,000 per hour, which is roughly a third of the cost of licensing a Canadian program. Purchases of these rights also benefit—at no cost—from aggressive publicity that the US networks use to promote these American shows. The popular US series attract large audiences and command premium advertising rates in Canada; the most successful ones

generate revenues of between $350–450K per hour, which amounts to three to four times their cost, and five times the revenue that top Canadian programming can generate.

In other words, in English Canada cheap foreign programming is much more profitable for broadcasters than original Canadian programs. Not because it is of better quality or because Canadians can't make good programs, but simply because it is so much cheaper for broadcasters to build audiences to sell to advertisers using foreign programming than using Canadian programming. The CBC also exploits this disparity. However, rather than counting the returns on foreign programs as private profit, all of that revenue is focused towards producing Canadian programming. In French Canada, it would appear that audiences generally prefer programs that reflect local perspectives on the world, although one network, TQS, does focus on delivering foreign programming.

Table 5.1 illustrates that in the face of this problem the CBC is the dominant provider of

FIGURE 5.1   English Conventional TV and Canadian Programming, Prime Time %

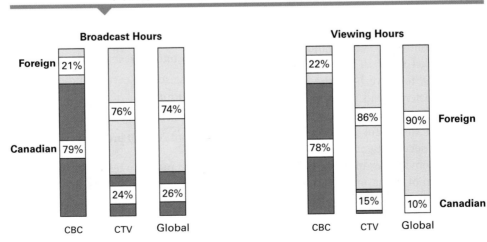

'September 2007 to August 2008'
Source: BBM Nielsen
The Broadcasting Environment — CBC/Radio-Canada's Audience Performance

Source: © 2009 BBM Canada

FIGURE 5.2   French-Language TV Stations and Canadian Programming, Prime Time %

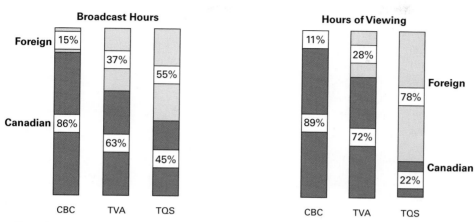

'September 2007 to August 2008'
Source: BBM
The Broadcasting Environment — CBC/Radio-Canada's Audience Performance

Source: © 2009 BBM Canada

TABLE 5.1   Top 20 Canadian Drama/Comedy Series*

RANK	NETWORK	PROGRAM	AMA
1	CTV	Corner Gas (Monday, 8 p.m.)	1,234,000
2	CBC	Little Mosque (Tuesday, 8:30 p.m.)	826,000
3	CBC	Just for Laughs (Sunday, 8 p.m.)	740,000
4	CBC	Rick Mercer Report (Tuesday, 8 p.m.)	710,000
5	CBC	Little Mosque (Wednesday, 8 p.m.)	686,000
6	CTV	Robson Arms (Monday to Wednesday, 8:30 p.m.)	652,000
7	CBC	The Tudors (Tuesday, 9 p.m.)	636,000
8	CBC	The Border (Monday, 9 p.m.)	598,000
9	CBC	Air Farce Live (Friday, 8 p.m.)	590,000
10	Global	The Guard (Tuesday, 10 p.m.)	572,000
11	CBC	This Hour Has 22 Minutes (Tuesday, 8:30 p.m.)	553,000
12	CBC	Rick Mercer Report (Friday, 8:30 p.m.)	546,000
13	CTV	Corner Gas (Tuesday, 8:30 p.m.)	495,000
14	CBC	Sophie (Wednesday, 8:30 p.m.)	452,000
15	CTV	Degrassi: Next Generation (Monday, 7:30 p.m.)	432,000
16	CBC	Halifax Comedy Fest (Monday, 8:30)	430,000
17	CBC	Winnipeg Comedy Fest (Monday, 8 p.m.)	424,000
18	CBC	Halifax Comedy Fest (Tuesday, 9 p.m.)	400,000
19	CBC	Heartland (Sunday, 7 p.m.)	392,000
20	CTV	Instant Star (Tuesday and Sunday, 8:30 p.m.)	373,000

*Note: Prime time shows only, 27 Aug. 2007–6 Apr. 2008.
Source: © 2009 BBM Canada

TABLE 5.2   Top 20 Drama/Comedy Series on French-Language Television*

RANK	NETWORK	PROGRAM	AMA
1	RC	Les Lavigueur, la vraie histoire	1,343,000
2	RC	Les Boys	991,000
3	TVA	Annie et ses hommes	942,000
4	TVA	Les Sœurs Elliot	912,000
5	TVA	Taxi 0-22	857,000
6	TVA	Les étés d'Anaïs	849,000
7	TVA	Destinées	813,000
8	RC	L'Auberge du chien noir	761,000
9	TVA	La Promesse	751,000
10	TVA	Nos étés	743,000
11	TVA	KM/H	692,000
12	RC	Providence	691,000
13	TVA	Histoire de filles	633,000
14	RC	Belle-Baie	630,000
15	TVA	Le Négociateur	622,000
16	RC	Rumeurs	592,000
17	RC	Casino	583,000
18	RC	Virginie	505,000
19	RC	C.A.	504,000
20	TVA	Le cœur a ses raisons	503,000

*Note: Prime time shows only, 27 Aug. 2007–6 Apr. 2008.
Source: © 2009 BBM Canada

English-Canadian drama and comedy programming. As the table points out, 14 of the top 20 Canadian drama/comedy programs were aired by the CBC in 2007–8. Consequently, in English Canada the CBC plays a particularly important role in delivering Canadian drama and comedy to audiences.

As Table 5.2 illustrates, on French-language television, Radio-Canada (RC), the CBC's French counterpart, is not the only substantive supplier of Canadian programming. In the time frame represented here, only nine of the top 20 programs were provided by Radio-Canada. The other 11 were aired by TVA, a private network.

Today, normal industry or institutional research (the terms are synonymous) adds information on media consumption to survey data obtained through various sampling procedures. Traditionally, media consumption has been measured by means of diaries kept by audience members, in which people log in and out as they watch or cease to watch. In 1993, BBM Canada (formerly the Bureau of Broadcast Measurement) introduced the **people meter**, a sophisticated electronic device to measure listening/viewing every 12 seconds. These devices had a significant impact on audience data and caused some turmoil in the industry. For instance, we now know that far fewer audience members have their eyes and minds glued to the tube than was claimed by those selling audiences. The data from the people meters therefore caused ad rates to be readjusted. In 2009, BBM introduced portable people meters that track audience members through recording inaudible codes embedded in broadcast programming. The impact that these will have on the industry is being assessed.

FIGURE 5.3 How PPMs Work

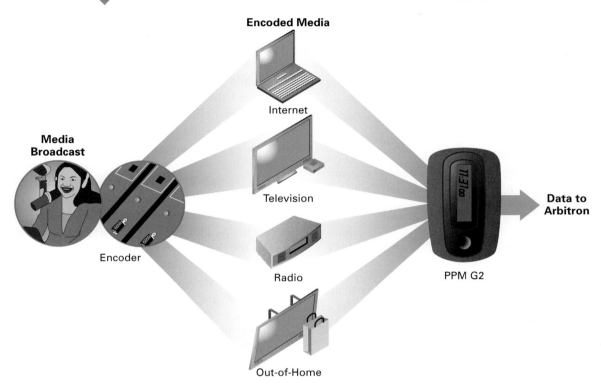

The portable people meter (PPM) can determine what consumers listen to on the radio; what they watch on broadcast, cable, and satellite TV; what media they stream on the internet; and what they hear in stores and entertainment venues.
Source: © Arbitron, Inc.

Industry research also introduces categories within which programs are measured. Such categories allow for greater precision in assessing success, but they also demand that programs conform to the categories that are measured. For instance, commercial radio can be divided into the following categories. (Those listed here are categories revised in 2000. They are contained and elaborated on in Public Notice CRTC 1999-76.)

- Category 2 (Popular Music)
  - Subcategory 21: Pop, rock, and dance—includes all types of rock music.
  - Subcategory 22: Country and country-oriented—includes country & western, traditional country, new country, and other country-oriented styles.

- Subcategory 23: Acoustic—music composed and performed in an acoustic style by the chansonniers and singer/songwriters of our time.

- Subcategory 24: Easy listening—'cocktail' jazz, soft contemporary jazz, middle-of-the-road, and 'beautiful music'.

- Category 3 (Special Interest Music)
  - Subcategory 31: Concert—includes the whole spectrum of classical music traditions.
  - Subcategory 32: Folk and folk-oriented—authentic, traditional folk music as well as contemporary folk-oriented music that draws substantially on traditional folk music in style and performance.

– Subcategory 33: World beat and international—music that draws heavily from the traditional music styles of countries throughout the world. It also includes music from the popular, folk, and classical music traditions of countries throughout the world that are played in instrumental form or sung in languages other than English and French.

– Subcategory 34: Jazz and blues—historic and contemporary music in the jazz and blues traditions.

– Subcategory 35: Non-classical religious—music of the church or religious faiths; gospel, hymns, contemporary Christian.

Audience Research and the Public Interest

Industry research has its limitations, particularly when it comes to understanding the needs and desires of audiences. Ien Ang discusses such limitations in her book, *Desperately Seeking the Audience* (1991), and captures the problem with the chapter title, 'Audience-as-market and audience-as-public'. Ang notes how industry research tells producers how successful they have been in reaching their audience but leaves them profoundly ignorant about the precise ingredients of their success or failure. Indeed, industry audience research offers little understanding of the motivations, understandings, or relationships audience members bring to bear on programs.

In an article in the *Canadian Journal of Communication*, Toronto media researcher Liss Jeffrey (1994) explores this issue in greater detail. What, she asks, are audience members? Are they individuals with particular psychological traits? Members of specific social, ethnic, age, or religious groups? Members of a society that allows for a fair amount of leisure time? Income earners? People with jobs that are repetitive and not very fulfilling? Persons who can benefit from positive role models? Commodity units to be sold to advertisers? Citizens? Obviously, they are all of these. Yet, as Jeffrey points out, when audiences are conceived by programmers as something to be sold to advertisers, only some of these audience characteristics are served by the media. True, their demographic characteristics may be known and their degree of attentiveness estimated, but because they are not conceived as citizens who could benefit from certain information and entertainment, they, the public and commercial sectors of programming, and the country all suffer. For instance, in this context, do the media in general impart values that reflect the ideals of society and contribute to its improvement and survival? Do they adequately inform citizens about domestic and international affairs? Do they allow us to see our own achievements or to know about ourselves so that we understand how we can make a contribution to society?

Such questions are important because the greater use that society and individuals make of the media, the greater are the media's responsibilities. If audiences are seen only within limited frameworks—for instance, to be entertained but not enlightened—then the media's contribution to society is very limited. Moreover, increasingly, access to the media—particularly television broadcasting—is costly, leaving many people with reduced access and some altogether without. As illustrated in the next chapter with our discussion of the Broadcasting Act, such questions are particularly relevant in Canada where broadcasting has been traditionally viewed as a public service and charged, by Parliament, with specific public duties. Reducing broadcasting service to a simple calculus of the marketplace serves to undermine our knowledge and understanding of the many dimensions of public life, as well as our abilities to participate in it.

The Transforming and Vanishing Audience

As discussed in earlier chapters, audiences and audience members are being transformed by the internet into users and user groups. Increasing levels of choice and different degrees of interactivity are changing the ways both media and audiences are being thought of. True, website owners often treat users like audiences, bombarding them with all kinds of advertising. But media organizations are

❯ BOX 5.6   THE AUDIENCE AS MEDIA PRODUCER

As people increasingly turn to the web for entertainment, information, and socializing, large media corporations are turning to audiences themselves to create media content. In October 2006, Google announced that it had agreed to buy YouTube for $1.65 billion. At the time, YouTube was delivering over 100 million video views per day and had 65,000 new videos being uploaded daily. Finding ways to 'create value'—or make money—from those people and the videos they contribute to the site was the main impetus to the acquisition.

Earlier in 2006, News Corporation—one of the world's largest media corporations with holdings in film, newspapers, television, magazines, cable, and book publishing—purchased the social networking site MySpace.com for approximately $580 million in cash. With more than 25 million visitors per month, MySpace users put their lives on line through blogs, photo galleries, music, and a wide range of information about their likes and dislikes. It is also a favourite of advertisers. News Corporation plans to integrate MySpace with its news, sports, and entertainment offerings to create a comprehensive interactive commercial media site (see www.youtube.com and www.myspace.com).

working to find ways to integrate user-generated content into their products. At the same time, the distinctions between media producer and audience member are being eroded as audience members are becoming participants in the production of 'mass' media. For instance, on television's *Battle of the Blades*, *Canadian Idol*, and other programs, the audience participates in deciding contest winners; on some sports programs, audiences can choose the camera angles they want to watch from; and on other programs people contribute video and other material they have made to the program content (see Lessig, 2008).

On the web, the distinction between producer and audience is even blurrier as people create blogs, podcasts, games, web-cam sites, and other material for public consumption. User-generated videos on YouTube can garner millions of views. As P. David Marshal (2004: 22–3) points out, 'Through interactivity, the old division between media form and viewer is broken down more completely as the former viewer is included into the "guidance" of the program, game or Internet browser and its outcomes.' Indeed, with these interactive forms of media content the audience 'vanishes', drawn up into the program itself. What do these developments have in store for definitions of audience and audience research? Stay tuned to find out.

❯ BOX 5.7   MACHINIMA

Machinima (pronounced muh-sheen-eh-mah) is filmmaking in a real-time, 3-D computer-generated environment, often using video-game technology. Working within a shared video game, people work either on their own or together to create a film. Action within the game is scripted and then recorded by the various 'actors' from their points of view on the resulting scene. These different shots are then brought together and edited to create the film.

Machinima is an example of 'emergent game play', or the creative use of video-game technology in ways that differ from the designers' intent. Machinima films have won awards in numerous film festivals, but because of the ways they subvert the intended purposes of the game they are not always welcomed by game companies (see www.machinima.org).

❖ SUMMARY

Media–audience interaction might usefully be conceived of as interaction between active, meaning-seeking entities and meaning-generating systems—persons, groups, the media, and cultures. Such a perspective provides a framework for explaining how media, audiences, and culture interact in an orderly but non-deterministic fashion.

The various theoretical approaches reviewed in this chapter bring out different elements of that interaction. Effects research highlights the direct impact of the media on the behaviour of audience members. Marxist research and the Frankfurt School draw attention to the ways production of media and cultural products have the potential to advance the interests of the producers and the elites in society over those of ordinary people. Uses and gratification research tells us what audience members tend to do with media content. Cultural studies describe how audience members select features from the media and use them as meaningful elements in their lives. Feminist research brings forward the gendered nature of narratives and, like cultural studies, explores how the audience member is positioned by the narrative. Reception analysis emphasizes the interpretive structures of audience members, which may derive from personality, content, situation, and/or other variables.

All approaches to the audience offer information and insight for explaining and understanding, but not predicting, audience behaviour, which depends not only on what the audience brings to the text, but also on the culturally specific references contained in the material. In academic research, the earliest analyses emphasized what the media did to the audience. More recent studies have asked what audiences do with media content. While cultural studies oriented to textual content have been dominant for some time, greater attention is now being paid to audience dynamics. Consideration of the social context of viewing, listening, and reading adds yet further elaboration to the articulation of audience variables.

Industry research generates information in precise quantitative measures on the nature of audiences, their size, age, location, education, family income, use of certain products, use of leisure time, and so on. However, the limitations of industry audience research are demonstrated by their inability to understand and meet audience needs with respect to enlightening and socially fulfilling programming.

Understanding internet users and usage is a growing area of inquiry. Already, advertisers have found that certain modes of advertising are largely ineffective and others produce annoyance. How advertisers will meet with internet users on terms acceptable to both has yet to be determined. Meanwhile, while it is clear that new communications technologies and the growing convergence between broadcasting and the web are having dramatic impacts on notions of audience and the role of media in identity formation, as well as the role of media in forms of communication and citizenship, the role and purposes of new media are ongoing sites of struggle among industry, audiences, public interest groups, and policy-makers (see, e.g., Ruggles, 2005; Moll and Shade, 2004). How this struggle will play out remains to be seen.

❖ APPENDIX: THE WORLD'S BEST READERSHIP DATABASE—PMB, A CASE STUDY

Though our discussion on audience research has focused on the broadcast media, such research is also pursued for print media. In fact, Canada is home to a rich print audience database. It is controlled by the Print Measurement Bureau (PMB), an industry organization run as a non-profit entity by Canadian magazine publishers, advertising agencies, advertisers, and other companies and organizations in the media industry. Industry members sit on the board of directors and various committees and offer guidance in many aspects of the research. PMB's annual study has grown since its first year (1983)—it now evaluates the readership of 118 print publications. Each annual PMB study reports data from a two-year rolling sample of 24,000 individuals aged 12 and over. This means that the results of 12,000 individuals interviewed in 2005 and 12,000 interviewed in 2006 would form the basis of the data reported in the year 2007.

The study's results are based on a nationally representative, stratified, random sample of Canadians. Of the 47,000 census enumeration areas in Canada, 2,000 are chosen that are representative. Variables taken into account include location, ethnicity, age, socio-economic status, and language. Within each enumeration area, 10 households are selected at random and interviewers customarily succeed in getting an average 6.5 to agree to a one- to two-hour, face-to-face interview and the subsequent completion of a printed questionnaire. One respondent is selected from each household in such a way that each member of a household has an equal chance of being chosen.

Readership data are collected for various Canadian English-language and French-language publications such as *Maclean's, Reader's Digest, Flare, TV Guide,*

L'Actualité, Elle Québec, and *Chatelaine.* The at-home personal interview gathers information on reading habits: what publications respondents have scanned/read; the number of times they have read them; the time spent reading an issue; the degree of interest in the publication. Also compiled in the interview are the demographic characteristics of respondents (age, gender, level of education, household income and size, and personal income and occupation) and their habits with respect to other media (TV, radio, public transit, Yellow Pages, newspapers). In a questionnaire completed after the interview, respondents provide information about the products and services they use, their lifestyle and leisure activities, and their shopping habits. Examples of the areas covered are drugs, groceries, home entertainment products, alcohol, other beverages, cars, financial services, home furnishings, and so on. A PMB member can sponsor the questionnaire: in such cases, questions about the purchase and use of certain brands of products would be included (PMB, n.d.). Figure 5.4 summarizes how this information can be interrelated.

FIGURE 5.4   Interrelationships of Data from PMB Surveys

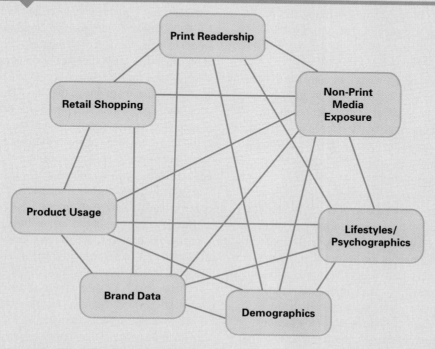

Source: Print Measurement Bureau, Total Canada Age.

In addition to access to a comprehensive database with useful information on readers' habits, values, and attitudes on a variety of subjects/products, members of PMB can also request that previously interviewed respondents be contacted again to answer a set of specific questions tailored to the member's interests. These additional data, combined with the annual database, can provide a fuller account of people's tastes and preferences and help members of PMB—whether advertisers, publishers, or other industry organizations—know their market, improve their product/service, design an advertising campaign, and so on. PMB, however, does not collect all the information pertaining to readership. Additional research conducted elsewhere in the industry can tell you what time of day people read magazines, what locations have the most number of readers (hair salons are the top), and so forth.

Magazines use PMB's annual data to understand more fully the nature of their readership. By monitoring their readership, they can, for example, mount subscription campaigns aimed at market segments attractive to advertisers. They may even complement such campaigns with a reorientation of their editorial content and approach. Magazines also use PMB data as a primary tool in selling advertising space to advertisers and ad agencies. The data also allow magazines to gain a sense of the characteristics of the readership of their competitors.

Magazines and ad agencies can carry their use of the data even further. If, for example, an ad agency is buying space on behalf of a computer company, such as Apple, it can statistically establish not only the number of people in a particular city, such as Windsor, who read a particular magazine, but also highly reliable probabilities of how many own a Macintosh, and indeed how many own a Mac, a MacBook, an iMac, Power Mac, or any other Apple product. For that matter, the agency can establish how many readers own other types of computers and how many do not own one at all. Given this information, the agency can determine how best to access a particular audience and then buy, for example, a series of ads in one magazine, ads in several magazines, or some other combination.

Just to give a sense of the reality of the business, we analyzed some of the data published in 2009. The following discussion is based on Table 5.3.

We have selected five magazines and one newspaper for analysis: *Canadian Geographic, Chatelaine, Flare, Maclean's, Reader's Digest*, and the Saturday edition of *The Globe and Mail*. We will look at readership (and make mention of circulation). From these figures, taken from PMB *2009 Readership Volume* (PMB, 2009), we have selected four variables to examine: age, education, region, and gender. The unweighted figures (column 2) represent the actual number of respondents interviewed. The weighted figures (column 4) represent an adjustment of the numbers so that they more accurately reflect the population as a whole. The sample (row 1) represents the projection of the unweighted figures onto the population as a whole, while the population (row 2) represents the projection of the weighted figures onto the population as a whole. So, for example, the unweighted number of readers of *Canadian Geographic* projected from the actual interviews is 2,905,000. The projection of readership based on the weighted sample is 3,458,000. All the figures given below the top two rows of figures (sample and population) are based on weighted figures.

V% represents a percentage of the population (calculated vertically in the table) within the individual variable being examined. To take the simplest example, 1,896,000 males read *Canadian Geographic*, which amounts to 55 per cent of all readers and hence a V% of 55; while 1,562,000 females or 45 per cent read the magazine for a V% of 45. A comparison of the V% of an individual magazine to the V% of the weighted population figures indicates how much difference exists between the general population and the readership of the magazine. For instance, while women account for 51 per cent (V%) of the population, only 45 per cent of *Canadian Geographic's* readers are women. The value I represents much the same thing as V%, only more accurately: PMB defines I as 'a measure of the relative degree of association between the two variables (for example, between readership of the publication and a demographic characteristic) relative to a base of 100' (PMB, 1998: n.p.). For example, persons aged 12–17 show an I of 154 for *Canadian Geographic*, which means any sample of persons aged 12–17 would be 1.54 times more likely to be readers of *Canadian Geographic* than if the sample were selected from the population as a whole. And finally, H% is the percentage of the population calculated horizontally in the table within the individual variable being examined. Thus, for example, readers of *Canadian Geographic* aged 25–34 represent 10 per cent of the overall population of readers aged 25–34 of all magazines surveyed.

A sense of the variability in readership of these five magazines and one newspaper can be obtained from the population figures (row 2). *Reader's Digest* leads readership with 6,423,000, which is the highest of any magazine in Canada, followed by *Chatelaine* with 3,549,000, *Canadian Geographic* with 3,458,000, *Maclean's* with 2,341,000, *Flare* with 1,429,000, and *The Globe and Mail* with 1,232,000.

Readership alone, however, does not always tell the full story. Circulation and readers-per-copy (RPC) figures (not included in Table 5.3) can be quite different from readership. For the titles presented in Table 5.3, RPCs are as follows: *Canadian Geographic* 16.4, *Chatelaine* 6.0, *Flare* 9.2, *Maclean's* 6.2, *Reader's Digest* 6.9, and *The Globe and Mail*, 3.1. (PMB, 2009: 1).

Let us take a closer look at some basic characteristics of the readership of these magazines and some interesting variations from the norm. Later, we will turn to readers themselves. One last thing to bear in mind: readership is affected by language, as is apparent in the figures of readership of English-language magazines in Quebec. But do not forget that there are populations of French-language speakers elsewhere in the country.

For *Canadian Geographic,* the following points are interesting to note. Examining readership by age shows that in absolute terms the largest group of readers (948,000) consists of those aged 35–49. In fact, the magazine has a substantial readership with those aged 25 and above. But it also is very successful with those aged 12–17—481,000 of that age group read the magazine and, as noted above, it has an I of 154. The lower I values for age groups 18–24, 25–34, and especially 65+ indicate that the magazine is less popular among those age groups. In terms of education, again, while the magazine has a lot of readers with no certificate or diploma (785,000), the I values demonstrate that it is relatively more successful in attracting a healthy share of people having a bachelor's degree (118) and some post-graduate training (144). In terms of region, while

the main market is in Ontario (1,407,000 readers), it is relatively more successful west of Ontario with I of 162 in Manitoba and Saskatchewan (but only 367,000 readers), 146 in Alberta, and 130 in BC. The magazine's stronger appeal among males compared to females can be seen in the absolute numbers, the V%, the I, and even the H%.

Chatelaine and *Flare* are most interesting if examined together. The success of *Flare* with young women is apparent in the I figures for those aged 12–34 (120, 168, and 132). But the substantial numbers of readers aged 35–49 (430,000, or 30 per cent of its overall readership) cannot be ignored. As the I values indicate, *Flare* is relatively more successful in attracting young readers than those 50 and older (where the I values drop below 100). However, *Chatelaine* actually has more readers in the 12–34 age range than *Flare* and its I values stay above 100 for the two age groupings from age 35 to 64. In terms of numbers of readers, *Chatelaine* attracts the most readers (3,549,000). The largest percentage of readers (31 per cent) is in the 35–49 age group. The figures also show that *Chatelaine* has relatively greater appeal to those with some post-secondary education (I = 133) while *Flare* wins out with those who hold bachelor's degrees (I = 129). Looking at the numbers by region, in 2002 those in Atlantic Canada had the greatest tendency to be readers of *Chatelaine* (I = 134) and those in Manitoba and Saskatchewan had the greatest tendency to be readers of *Flare* (I = 141); in 2006, Albertans led in the percentage readership of both magazines (I values are 135 and 150); and in 2009 those in Manitoba and Saskatchewan led in percentage readers (I = 151 for *Chatelaine* and 174 for *Flare*). Given this migration of market penetration, one wonders whether the magazines, which are owned by the same company, Rogers, conduct regional subscription campaigns that differ from year to year. In interpreting these figures, it is always important to bear in mind absolute numbers of readers in comparison with the relative I values: Ontarians account for about 40 per cent of English-language readers, whereas Manitoba and Saskatchewan account for less than 10 per cent. And, surprisingly enough, 681,000 men read *Chatelaine* and 180,000 read *Flare*, 19 and 13 per cent of all readers respectively.

TABLE 5.3 Characteristics of readership of five magazines and one newspaper sold in Canada (Fall 2009, All 12+)

	Unweighted	V%	Weighted	V%	CANADIAN GEOGRAPHIC				CHATELAINE			
					000	V%	H%	I	000	V%	H%	I
Sample	24,841	100	24,841	100	**2,905**	100	12	100	3,230	100	13	100
Population	24,841	100	28,703	100	**3,458**	100	12	100	**3,549**	100	12	100
Age												
12–17	1,944	8	2,591	9	**481**	14	19	**154**	233	7	9	73
18–24	1,876	8	3,147	11	396	11	13	105	281	8	9	72
25–34	3,140	**13**	4,524	16	459	13	**10**	84	510	14	11	91
35–49	6,662	27	7,726	27	**948**	27	12	102	1,105	**31**	14	**116**
50–64	6,288	25	6,270	22	796	23	13	105	927	26	15	**120**
65+	4,931	20	4,445	15	379	11	9	71	494	14	11	90
Education												
No Cert. or Diploma	4,942	20	6,726	24	**785**	23	12	96	569	16	8	68
Sec./High School Grad.	5,523	22	7,332	26	761	22	10	86	889	25	12	98
Trade Cert./Diploma	2,272	9	2,928	10	355	10	12	101	330	9	11	91
University/Other Cert	5,567	22	5,961	21	684	20	11	95	979	28	16	**133**
Bachelor's Degree	4,014	16	3,624	13	514	15	14	**118**	515	15	14	115
Post Grad. +	2,523	10	2,072	7	359	10	17	**144**	267	8	13	104
Region												
Atlantic	1,408	6	2,058	7	292	8	14	118	338	10	16	133
Quebec	7,454	30	6,790	24	262	8	4	32	179	5	3	21
Ontario	8,730	35	11,143	39	**1,407**	41	13	105	1,793	51	16	130
Man./Sask.	1,350	5	1,878	7	**367**	11	20	**162**	352	10	19	**151**
Alberta	2,298	9	2,944	10	519	15	18	**146**	420	12	14	115
BC	3,601	14	3,890	14	612	18	16	**130**	467	13	12	97
Gender												
Male	11,327	46	14,142	49	**1,896**	55	13	111	**681**	**19**	5	39
Female	13,514	54	14,561	**51**	1,562	45	11	89	2,868	81	20	159

Source: Print Measurement Bureau (2009).

FLARE				MACLEAN'S				GLOBE &MAIL (SAT)				READER'S DIGEST			
000	V%	H%	I	000	V%	H%	I	000	V%	H%	I	000	V%	H%	I
1,132	100	5	100	2,145	100	9	100	1,341	100	6	100	5,015	100	20	100
1,429	100	5	100	**2,341**	100	8	100	**1,232**	100	4	100	**6,423**	100	22	100
155	11	6	**120**	113	5	4	54	73	6	3	66	518	8	20	**89**
263	18	8	**168**	252	11	8	98	90	7	3	67	711	11	23	**101**
296	21	7	**132**	274	12	6	74	175	14	4	90	758	12	17	**75**
430	**30**	6	112	659	28	9	105	324	26	4	98	1,744	27	23	**101**
220	15	4	71	650	28	10	**127**	374	30	6	**139**	1,523	24	24	**109**
64	5	1	29	393	17	9	108	197	16	4	103	1,169	18	26	**118**
239	17	4	71	293	13	4	53	92	7	1	32	1,358	21	20	89
409	29	6	112	511	22	7	85	170	14	2	54	1,743	27	24	**106**
134	9	5	92	248	11	8	104	67	5	2	53	679	11	23	**104**
330	23	6	111	509	22	9	105	205	17	3	80	1,524	24	26	**114**
233	16	6	**129**	462	20	13	**156**	375	30	10	**241**	685	11	19	84
83	6	4	81	317	14	15	**187**	323	26	16	**363**	434	7	21	94
88	6	4	86	187	8	9	112	98	8	5	**11**	692	11	34	**150**
41	3	1	12	79	3	1	14	70	6	1	**24**	268	4	4	18
783	55	7	141	1,241	53	11	**137**	666	54	6	**139**	2,762	**43**	25	111
163	11	9	**174**	245	10	13	**160**	55	4	3	68	711	11	38	**169**
165	12	6	113	360	11	9	108	112	9	4	89	860	13	29	**131**
189	113	5	98	329	14	8	104	230	19	6	**138**	1,129	18	29	**130**
180	**13**	1	26	1,184	51	8	103	692	56	5	**114**	2,913	45	21	92
1,248	87	9	172	1,157	49	8	97	540	44	4	86	3,509	**55**	24	108

Maclean's and *Time* also made for an interesting comparison in 2006, which was made easier by the fact that both their readership figures are somewhat less than 3 million overall. But with the demise of the Canadian edition of *Time*, that comparison has disappeared. Moreover, *Maclean's* has not picked up readership as a result. The 2009 data indicate that *Maclean's* appeals particularly to those 50–64 (I = 127) who have a bachelor's degree or more education (I = 156 and 187) and particularly to those living in Saskatchewan and Manitoba (I = 160) followed by Ontarians (I = 137). In comparison, there is a far more marked appeal of *The Globe* to men (I = 114) aged 50–64 (I = 139) with a bachelor's degree (I = 241) or more education (I = 363) and particularly to those living in Ontario (I = 139) and BC (I = 138). It is difficult to know why Manitoba and Saskatchewan readers have edged out Albertans and taken more strongly to magazine reading since 2006. It may be accountable to marketing, or increased wealth, but if it is, it is not company specific: the same I differentials show up in *Reader's Digest* (I = 169) and *Canadian Geographic* (I = 162) as in the Rogers-owned titles.

Both absolute numbers and relative success with certain parts of the population (based on variables like age, education, region, and gender) are important for advertisers (as well as for the magazines themselves). Reaching readers is one thing, but reaching them in a particular environment is also important. The appeal and impact of an ad will be affected by the publication in which it appears. To make the point strongly, it would be surprising to find an ad directed exclusively at the 681,000 male readers of *Chatelaine*. Yet if it were to appear, it would probably gain attention by virtue of its novelty. *Reader's Digest* deals with this issue all the time; in spite of its ability to deliver more readers, and across many groups, some advertisers are reluctant to advertise in the magazine because they see it as an inappropriate editorial environment. This view stems from various reasons, such as the magazine's condensation of the work of respected writers, its conservative politics, and the dentist office/barber shop/beauty parlour associations some have with the magazine.

Which brings us to a quick analysis of *Reader's Digest* figures. First, while the actual numbers are formidable for those aged 12–17 and 25–34, they are below the par of 100. Among 18- to 24-year-olds and 35– to 49-year-olds, readership is average (I = 101 in both cases), while I climbs to 109 and then 118 for the top two age categories. The magazine is also relatively more successful than other magazines in reaching those with less rather than more education. I values are above 100 for those with secondary school education, a trade certificate or diploma, or some university or post-secondary training. By region, even though Ontario accounts for 43 per cent of its readership, the magazine appears to do slightly better, according to I values, in all other regions (except Quebec, where the French-language edition is strong). As noted, more women than men read the magazine.

Table 5.3 only touches on some of the variables that are of interest and that PMB monitors. For instance, PMB tracks average number of reading occasions, the average number of minutes spent reading, a scaled average editorial interest, and the average percentage of the population that has looked into a copy of the title, the last category of which is called 'reach' (PMB, 2009: 65, 67). Table 5.4 presents the data for the titles discussed in this section. Comparing *Flare* and *Chatelaine* is instructive in that, in all cases *Flare* has weaker readings. Note the high measures for *Reader's Digest*. But also note that lack of correlation between the circulation and reach of *Maclean's* (Tables 5.3 and Table 5.4) compared to the circulation and reach of *Canadian Geographic* and *Chatelaine*. The reach of *Maclean's* at 34 per cent is greater than both these higher circulation magazines, the reach of which is 25.3 and 26.2, respectively, even with their 50 per cent extra circulation (PMB, 2009: 1, 67). How is this explained? It is probably not the genre difference, nor differential newsstand presence. Most likely, it is the fact that *Maclean's* publishes 52 issues per year whereas the others publish 12.

The time spent reading per issue, along with publication frequency, are important for both the advertiser and the magazine in calculating how much to charge for ad space. PMB calculates the levels of media exposure to radio and television and to daily, community, Saturday, and Sunday newspapers, as well as time spent using the internet. Cross tabulations can thus be made and the relative salience of the magazine environment approximated.

In some of its instructional materials, PMB provides examples of how its database can be used to determine a plan for, and the cost of, reaching a certain population

TABLE 5.4 Reading Occasions, Time Spent Reading, Average Editorial Interest, and Reach

TITLE	AVERAGE NUMBER OF READING OCCASIONS PER ISSUE	AVERAGE NUMBER OF MINUTES SPENT READING PER ISSUE	AVERAGE EDITORIAL INTEREST	PERCENTAGE OF POPULATION THAT LOOKED INTO TITLE OVER THE PAST 12 MONTHS
Canadian Geographic	2.11	43.47	7.2	25.3
Chatelaine	2.11	39.86	6.38	26.2
Flare	1.66	28.63	6.11	13.8
Maclean's	2.14	43.67	6.89	34
Reader's Digest	3.03	62.18	7.34	40.3
The Globe and Mail (Sat. edn)	*	41.58	*	*

*DATA not available

Source: Print Measurement Bureau (2009: 65, 67).

(PMB, 1998). Figure 5.5, for example, demonstrates how to determine the cost of reaching a certain percentage of the known population of a particular target group. The various important elements of the table are explained in the boxes surrounding the central table.

Based on the data in Figure 5.5, an advertiser might choose to place ads in *Canadian Living*, *Homemakers*, and *Reader's Digest*, reasoning that these three magazines would provide good coverage of the target population with some (but not a great deal of) overlap. On the other hand, if the product were strongly home-oriented, *Homemakers* and *Canadian Living* might be chosen instead. All the variables have to be assessed to match an advertiser's product and goals with suitable advertising venues.

Another example, Figure 5.6, illustrates the power of the database to identify the amount and nature of product usage, the exact characteristics of those who are users, and, subsequently, how an advertiser might best reach the market he or she wishes.

As you can sense by the nature of the data and the terms in which it is presented, the magazine enterprise, like most commercial media enterprises, focuses on serving advertisers. The numbers tell the important stories to advertisers and to the financial and advertising sales managers. These numbers, however, are of little importance to readers, contributors, and editors, who are more interested in the content of a magazine and its image.

FIGURE 5.5   How to Read a Cost Ranking (Crank) Report

Target:
A specific user-defined segment of the base population against which all magazines on this run are evaluated. It can be defined by demographics, product usage, or even psychographics.

Projected Population (000):
The projected actual population of the target (e.g., there are 5,279,000 women 25–54 living in Canada).

Cost ($):
The cost of a single insertion in a magazine. This cost can be changed to reflect ad size, colour or b/w, regional rates, or specially negotiated rates. Shown here are national, full-page, four-colour rates.

Percent of Base:
The target market as a percentage of the total base population (e.g., 29.47% of all English adults 18+ are women 25–54).

Rank:
The position of each magazine in the specified category (e.g., with 1,078,000 average issue readers, Canadian Living ranks 3rd in composition). Rankings are also shown for CPM and can be interpreted in a similar way.

CPM (Cost Per Thousand):
The cost for each magazine to reach 1,000 women 25–54 (e.g., Canadian Living's CPM is $25.25—calculated by dividing the per insertion cost of $27,220 by the net reach per average issue in thousands: 1,078).

Composition (%):
The percentage of readers of a magazine's average issue who are in the target group (e.g., of all English adults 18+ who read Canadian Living; 51.95% are women 25–54).

Coverage (%):
The average issue audience of a magazine as a percentage of the target population (e.g., Canadian Living reaches 20.42% of women 25–54—1,078,000 Canadian Living readers, divided by the target population of 5,279,000).

Average Audience (000):
The total number of respondents in the target market who are reached by one insertion in a magazine (e.g., 1,078,000 women 25–54 read an average issue of Canadian Living).

English Adults 18+

Target: Women Age 25–54
Population (000): 5279

Percent Base: 29.47%

Media	Cost ($) 4C	Avg Aud (000)	Coverage (%)	Composition (%)	Rank	4C CPM	Rank
Canadian Living	27220	1078	20.42	51.95	3	25.25	1
Chatelaine (Eng)	35695	992	18.79	51.53	4	35.98	6
Reader's Digest	28610	953	18.05	30.57	7	30.02	4
Homemakers	20640	766	14.51	53.19	2	26.95	2
TV Times	61540	632	11.97	29.27	8	97.37	10
TV Guide	19775	597	11.31	33.79	5	33.12	5
Leisureways/ Westworld	37900	510	9.66	30.72	6	74.31	9
Maclean's	29995	488	9.24	27.20	9	61.47	8
Time	20530	443	8.39	27.11	10	46.34	7
Cdn. House & Home	12435	430	8.15	57.87	1	28.92	3

Source: 1998 PMB Two-Year Readership Study: Weighted by Population

Source: Reprinted from PMB Media School (Toronto: PMB Print Measurement Bureau), by permission of PMB Print Measurement Bureau, Total Canada Age 12+.

FIGURE 5.6 Sample Products Profile Table

Personally Eat Chocolate/Candy Bars   Base: Total Canada—Age 12+

	Total		Non-User Past 6 Months				User Past 6 Months				Light (1-2)				Heavy (6+)			
	000	V%	000	V%	H%	I	000	V%	H%	I	000	V%	H%	I	000	V%	H%	I
Sample	20415	100	4889	100	24	100	14320	100	70	100	7121	100	35	100	1261	100	6	100
Population	24998	100	5876	100	24	100	17601	100	70	100	8750	100	35	100	1641	100	7	100
Male	12301	49	3198	54	26	110	8194	47	67	95	4033	46	33	94	804	49	7	94
Female	12696	51	2687	46	21	90	9406	53	73	105	4717	54	37	106	837	51	7	106
Age 12–17	2400	10	307	5	13	54	2019	11	84	120	890	10	37	106	355	22	15	225
Age 18–24	2857	11	459	8	16	68	2281	13	80	113	1205	14	42	120	226	14	8	120
Age 25–34	4953	20	1026	17	21	88	3681	21	74	106	1922	22	39	111	268	16	5	82
Age 35–49	7058	28	1591	27	23	96	5064	29	72	102	2609	30	37	106	447	27	6	97
Age 50–64	4139	17	1224	21	30	126	2646	15	64	91	1303	15	31	90	186	11	4	68
Age 65+	3591	14	1268	22	35	150	1911	11	53	76	822	9	23	65	159	10	4	68
EDU - No Cert or Dipl	7957	32	1883	32	24	101	5557	32	70	99								
- Sec/High Sch Grad	6208	25	1404	24	23	96	4458	25	72	102								
- Trade Cert/Dipl	2680	11	707	12	26	112	1816	10	68	96								
- University/Other Cert	4691	19	1036	18	22	94	3418	19	73	103								
- Bachelors Degree	2338	9	571	10	24	104	1635	9	70	99								
- Post Grad +	1124	4	275	5	25	104	716	4	64	91								
Married/Living Together	13888	56	3483	59	25	107	9609	55	69	98								
Single/Wid/Div/Separated	11096	44	2393	41	22	92	7980	45	72	102								
Principal Wage Earner	14757	59	3908	67	26	113	9763	55	66	94								
Principal Grocery Shopper	15558	62	3876	66	25	106	10699	61	69	98								
Professionals	1109	4	287	5	26	110	719	4	65	92								
Sr. Management/Owners	743	3	212	4	28	121	464	3	62	89								
Other Managers	2302	9	502	9	22	93	1630	9	71	101								
Tech/Sales/Teachers/Others	2014	8	440	7	22	93	1448	8	72	102								
Clerk/Secretarial	2786	11	507	9	18	77	2170	12	78	111								
Skilled/Unskilled/Prim	5879	23	1268	22	22	95	4106	23	72	103								
All Other	10364	41	2661	45	26	109	7064	40	68	97								
Employed Full Time	11682	47	2674	46	23	97	8237	47	71	100								
Employed Part Time	3011	12	545	9	18	77	2353	13	78	111								
Atlantic Region	1953	8	400	7	20	83	1553	9	76	108								
Quebec	6265	25	1483	25	24	101	4414	25	70	100								
Ontario	9388	38	2371	40	25	107	6520	37	69	99								
Manitoba/Saskatchewan	1772	7	385	7	22	92	1280	7	72	103								
Alberta	2278	9	432	7	19	81	1654	9	73	103								
British Columbia	3244	13	805	14	25	106	2180	12	67	95								
Montreal	2876	12	700	12	24	103	2028	12	71	100								
Toronto	3682	15	979	17	27	113	2550	14	69	98								
Calgary	706	3	140	2	20	85	528	3	75	106								
Edmonton	725	3	142	2	20	83	537	3	74	105								
Vancouver	1598	6	401	7	25	107	1108	6	69	98								
Comm Size Under 100M	8960	36	1984	34	22	94	6284	36	70	100								
Comm Size 100M–1MM	7881	32	1813	31	23	98	5633	32	71	102								
Comm Size 1MM +	8158	33	2080	35	25	108	5684	32	70	99								

There are 17,601,000 people 12 years of age or over in Canada who have eaten a chocolate/candy bar in the past 6 months.

70% of the 24,998,000 people 12 years of age or over in Canada have eaten a chocolate/candy bar in the past 6 months.

The greatest number of chocolate/candy bar eaters is in the 35–49 age group (29%). 5,064,000 people aged 35–49 have eaten a chocolate/candy bar in the past 6 months.

On a per capita basis, people aged 12–17 are the most likely to eat chocolate/candy bars. They have an index of 225 meaning that they are 125% more likely to eat chocolate/candy bars than their incidence in the general population.

The absolute, unweighted, number of respondents.

000 = Thousands
V% = Vertical Percentage
H% = Horizontal Percentage
I = Index

Source: Print Measurement Bureau, Total Canada Age 12+.

❯ KEY TERMS

agenda-setting, p. 124
Birmingham School, p. 127
British cultural studies, p. 127
cultivation analysis, p. 124
demographic, p. 120
dominant ideology, p. 129
effects, p. 123

feminist research, p. 130
formative research, p. 134
Frankfurt School, p. 126
narrowcasting, p. 134
people meter, p. 138
primary definers, p. 129

reach, p. 134
reception analysis, p. 131
share, p. 134
summative research, p. 134
uses and gratification research, p. 124
viewing time p. 134

❯ RELATED WEBSITES

Audience Dialogue: http://audiencedialogue.net/
As the website says, it 'exists to provide useful information for communicators of all kinds—broadcasters, publishers, aid agencies, arts organizations, webmasters, and anybody else who's interested in using research-based techniques to make their organizations more effective.'

BBM, the Bureau of Measurement: www.bbm.ca/
This site contains all kinds of interesting information on who watches TV and who listens to radio, at what time of the day they listen, how much time they spend listening, in what location, and so forth.

Canadian Journal of Communication: www.cjc-online.ca
CJC provides links to back issues of the journal, including the Norma Schulman article cited in this chapter (vol. 18, no. 1).

Cultural Theory: British Cultural Studies: www.youtube.com/watch?v=zyUYG1J3tKI
This short lecture by Professor Ron Strickland of Illinois State University provides a good introduction to British cultural studies.

The Frankfurt School: www.marxists.org/subject/frankfurt-school/index.htm
This website provides a history of the Frankfurt School and discusses some contemporary theorists carrying on their legacy. See particularly the entries for Theodor Adorno and Max Horkheimer.

Print Measurement Bureau (PMB): www.pmb.ca/
The print equivalent to the BBM, this site is a bit more difficult to navigate but it does provide basic magazine circulation statistics and readership by men and women. You can also download a presentation.

❯ FURTHER READINGS

Ang, Ien. 1991. *Desperately Seeking the Audience*. London: Routledge. This book offers a good summary of audience research.

Jensen, Klaus Bruhn, and Karl Erik Rosengren. 1990. 'Five traditions in search of an audience', *European Journal of Communication* 5: 207–38. This article provides an orientation to the various schools of thought that guide audience research.

Murray, Catherine. 2010. 'Audience-making: Issues in Canadian audience studies,' in Leslie Regan Shade,

ed., *Mediascapes: New Patterns in Canadian Communication*, 3rd edn. Toronto: Nelson, 83–103.

Radway, Janice. 1984. *Reading the Romance*. Chapel Hill: University of North Carolina Press. Radway's book is a classic analysis of how women readers use romantic fiction and demonstrates the contribution scholars can make to understanding the interaction between the media and people's lives.

Ruddock, Andy. 2007. *Investigating Audiences*. London: Sage. A valuable analysis of how media audiences are analyzed.

⫶ STUDY QUESTIONS

1. Define each of the following in fewer than 50 words:

   - Effects research
   - Reception analysis
   - Uses and gratification research
   - Cultural studies
   - The Frankfurt School

2. Some reception studies (for example, Radway) appear to describe the interaction between audiences and content as secondary to the tangential actions surrounding the interpretation of content. The act of reading counts more than what the person derives from the content itself. Comment on this observation in relation to other methods of analysis.

3. Which of the perspectives on audiences would you use for writing an essay about the impact of media violence on society? Why?

4. Which of the perspectives on audiences corresponds most closely to your own views, and why?

5. Is there anything to be concerned about in regard to the information that industry organizations collect on audiences, which advertisers consult? Have you ever responded to a market survey? If so, have you always 'told the whole truth and nothing but the truth'? Discuss.

CHAPTER 6

Communication Technology and Society: Theory and Practice

The computer is no more than an instantaneous telegraph with a prodigious memory.
— CAROLYN MARVIN, 1988

OPENING QUESTIONS

- What is 'technology'? What are some approaches to defining the term?
- What is the relationship between technology and social change?
- What is the relationship between public policy and technological development?
- What is 'open software'?
- What is 'technology transfer'?
- How does copyright bear on information technology?
- What are some key issues regarding new information and communications technologies?

Learning Objectives

- To understand that technology is the product of a broad set of social and historical circumstances.
- To discover how, rather than solving problems, technology changes conditions.
- To review how policy, both in the past and at present, has influenced and is influencing the development of technology.
- To learn about open software and technology transfer.
- To learn about some key areas of technology policy, specifically, individual rights and collective rights, piracy, and trading regimes governing trade in intellectual property.
- To appreciate some recent technological changes and their influence on society.

Introduction

We live in interesting times. It is common to hear that we are in the midst of one of the most dramatic cultural shifts since the Industrial Revolution—an Information Revolution. And Western society, indeed much of world, is in the midst of major changes facilitated by information and communication technology. But exactly how 'new' or 'revolutionary' these changes are is open to debate. The communication technology being implemented today was, to a large extent, being discussed in the late 1960s and early 1970s (Dutton et al., 1986). Consequently, today's technological transformation of communication has been at least 40 or 50 years in the making. And if one considers that 40 to 50 years prior to these ideas being developed—that is, in the 1920s and 1930s—radio was just being introduced and television was very futuristic, we can see that the last 80 to 100 years have also seen great technological change. If we go back still another 40 to 50 years—to the 1870s and 1880s—when the telephone was starting to push the communicative boundaries recently set by the telegraph, we can begin to appreciate that the last 120 years have all been marked by significant, and continual, changes in information technology.

Moreover, as illustrated in both Chapter 3 and Chapter 11, these changes in technology have not taken place in a vacuum. Rather, they have been accompanied by profound political and economic changes. From the rise of industry-based society in the late nineteenth century and the urbanization that followed, to the two World Wars and Great Depression that characterized the first half of the twentieth century, to the post-war economic boom and birth of contemporary consumer society in the second half of that century, technology, and particularly information technology, has been both shaped by, and given form to, sweeping social change. Today the ways in which computing technology and digital media are working with other political, economic, and social forces to restructure society is only partially understood. In 2010 and 2011, in places like Tunisia and Egypt cellphones and

The authors wish to thank John Maxwell for his work on previous iterations of this chapter. John is assistant professor in the Master of Publishing Program at Simon Fraser University.

Source: © Ianpoole/Dreamstime.com

An antique telegraph key from which Morse code would have been sent.

the internet were key to helping organize political dissent and bringing down totalitarian governments. Only with time will we come to fully appreciate the new realities, new opportunities, and new challenges presented by the digital age.

This chapter begins by examining some different perspectives on technology in general and communication technology in particular, and by discussing how communication theorists view technology. It then provides an overview of the development of communication technology and explores some recent technological developments in communication, reviewing the categories of activity these developments are affecting. The chapter concludes with some observations on communication technology and society.

Perspectives on Technology

The word 'technology' is from the Greek 'techne', meaning art, craft, or skill. From this perspective we can see that technology is considered to be more than simply tools, gadgets, or devices. Rather, it is devices or machines *plus* a knowledge or understanding of their use or operation, that is, an understanding of how they fit into a larger set of social circumstances or way of life. From this perspective, technology is seen as complexly woven into the circumstances and rhythms of social life.

Canadian physicist Ursula M. Franklin points out that technology is about 'the organization of work and people', and that it involves 'procedures, symbols, new words, equations, and, most of all, a mindset'. This perspective reminds us not to look at technology in isolation, as a kind of thing that has specific effects on people, but rather to see technologies as parts of an ongoing way of life, with deeply tangled causes, effects, interpretations, and motivations.

Working from a similar perspective, US communication scholar Langdon Winner (1977) notes that technology encompasses at least three elements:

1. pieces of apparatus;

2. techniques of operation to make the apparatus work; and

3. social institutions within which technical activities take place.

Here, technology is part of a larger social system. Something as simple as an overhead projector, found in almost every university classroom, is of no use in a forest or a farmer's field. In the classroom, however, it becomes a useful pedagogical tool for communicating ideas to a large group. In this context it is also part of a much larger process of education, replete with social ideas and values that foreground the process of education as a valued social practice and the classroom as a place contextualized by power relations in which one person imparts knowledge to a group of attentive students.

In *Television: Technology and Cultural Form*, Raymond Williams (1974) makes a similar point, arguing that technology reflects the overall

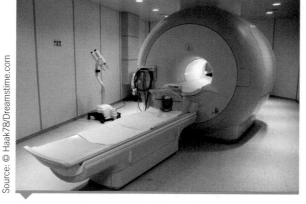

Source: © Haak78/Dreamstime.com

A CT scanner is a specialized piece of equipment, but its use benefits people in many different ways.

organization of society (Chapter 3). In and of itself, for instance, the telegraph is simply a wire with an electric current running through it. But, in the context of developing industrial society, it is a means of co-ordinating the movement of people and goods across vast distances. Similarly, offering programs to fill our leisure time and advertising to drive the consumption of a vast range of goods and services, television feeds and maintains the mass society that industrialization created.

These perspectives on technology are clearly not about specific kinds of tools or electronic devices, but rather about the complex network of ideas and practices of which they are a part.

Thinking about Technology

In *Questioning Technology*, philosopher Andrew Feenberg (1999) provides an account of the major conceptual frameworks and orientations social scientists and philosophers have used to think about technology. His analysis provides four main perspectives on technology: instrumentalism, determinism, substantivism, and critical theory. A fifth perspective, constructivism, is closely related to critical theory.

Instrumentalism sees technology as a value-neutral tool that can shorten the path to natural ends or, alternatively, social goals. For example, if we need a drink of water, a cup works better than either our hand or putting our face in a pool of water. If we need to get from Long Beach on Vancouver Island to The Beaches in Toronto, a plane or two in combination with cars and buses gets us there faster and more easily than walking and swimming. Conversely, **technological determinism** holds that technology operates according to an inexorable logic inherent in the technology itself. Technology here is seen as part of the natural evolution of a better world and that the effects of technology are imposed by the technology itself, rather than through human decisions about how it is employed. It is easy to see examples of **determinist** thinking in the trends towards miniaturization and mobility: the mobile phone you carry today will inevitably be replaced by one that is smaller or lighter and allows you to do more with it—or so we commonly think.

From the determinist perspective, human control over the exact direction of technological development is minimal; the technology, in a sense, has a life of its own.

In a stance related to technological determinism, **substantivism** claims that not only does technology operate according to its own inherent logic, but also that this logic is at the expense of humanity. The harsh social realities of the Industrial Revolution, the development of nuclear weapons, and more recently the threat of environmental disaster have given substantivist critics much to think and write about to bolster their perspective. Take the automobile, for example: the availability of mass-produced cars in the early twentieth century led to the development of large-scale infrastructure (roads, highways, suburbs, shopping malls) designed with cars and car travel in mind. But we now live in a world where the urban sprawl (not to mention air pollution and dependency on foreign oil reserves) brought on by a car-oriented culture is very difficult to escape; more efficient and more environmentally friendly modes of mass transit are notoriously difficult to design and build, simply because urban density is so low in the suburbs (compared with urban density in Europe or Asia, where rail travel is much more economically feasible). The structure has become self-reinforcing: the only way to live in car-oriented suburbs is to drive a car.

Taking their position to a logical conclusion, Feenberg reports that substantivists view the modern condition as reflective of the essence of modern technology—its rationality, its efficiency, its priority on control and calculability. The more pessimistic or dystopian of the substantivists argue that technological thought and action threaten non-technological values as they extend ever deeper into social life. We become slaves to the machine. Thus, it is not uncommon in universities and other institutions for rules to be built around the capacity of the technology to keep processing information in an orderly way—and not around what is best for professors and students. For instance, graduate students working full-time on their theses instead of taking classes may find themselves not classified as full-time students and hence may be faced with loan repayment. Even when solutions for working around particular regulations are put in place, with staff changes the rationales for these solutions may be forgotten or deemed not to be worthwhile as the years go by. As Jacques Ellul, one of the foremost theorists working from this perspective expressed it, technique has become autonomous. McLuhan made the same point by saying that human beings are 'the sex organs of the machine world'.

Consider this summary Dizard has written of Ellul's position (best exemplified in Ellul's book, *The Technological Society* (1964):

1. All technological progress exacts a price—while it adds something, it subtracts something else.

2. All technological progress raises more problems than it solves, tempts us to see the consequent problems as technical in nature, and prods us to seek technical solutions to them.

3. The negative effects of technological innovation are inseparable from the positive. It is naive to say that technology is neutral, that it may be used

Ellul's points about technology are exemplified in catastrophic events such as the disaster at Fukushima Daiichi nuclear power plant following the 2011 tsunami in Japan.

Source: © istockphoto.com/Sherwin McGehee

for good or bad ends; the good and bad effects are, in fact, simultaneous and inseparable.

4. All technological innovations have unforeseen effects. (Dizard, 1985: 11)

While these points have a ring of truth, they also express inevitability and pessimism that have been challenged. A complementary viewpoint to Ellul's can be found in the writings of Canadian philosopher George Grant. In *Technology and Empire*, Grant argued that the foundation of all modern, liberal, industrial, and post-industrial societies is to be found in technique and technology. In 1969 he claimed that the dominant doctrine of modern **liberalism** was 'the belief that human excellence is promoted by the homogenizing and universalizing power of technology' (Grant, 1969: 69).

But neither instrumentalism nor substantivism is adequate. Technology is *not* neutral as the instrumentalists claim. Our ways of life *are* changed even when we purchase something as small as an iPod or a cellphone. Edwin Black (2001) has described how IBM made it possible for the Nazis to undertake censuses that provided both ethnic background and addresses—allowing the Nazis to round up Jews and send them to the gas chambers. **Critical theory** claims we do have choices to develop technology, to shape its development, to use it, and to engage with it to a greater or lesser extent. IBM did not have to facilitate the collection and storage of data to increase the efficiency of rounding up Jews. But in playing the particular role it did, it contributed to a world in which technology can be criticized as dehumanizing and even murderous.

Feenberg (1999) argues that theorists Herbert Marcuse and Michel Foucault—scholars who were part of the 'New Left' movement of the 1960s—opened up the opportunity to think about technology and technological development as something other than an outside force that could only be slowed or quickened by society. Rather, they made it possible to conceive of technology as existing inside society. In other words, technology is integral to society like religion, education, culture, economics, and political systems, and is thus subject to the same kinds of criticism.

This twofold notion—that technology exists within society and that social forces and political decision-making can control both the nature of the machines that emerge and their usage—means that technology develops in what Feenberg calls a **socially contingent** manner. In other words, technology arises and takes a particular form depending on the dynamics of the society in which it emerged—which may include rejection, as happened with fax machines when they were first invented, and with movable type in China (prior to Gutenberg). Rather than pointing to a good or a bad essence of technology, critical theory sees technology as offering possibilities of which society must choose a course of action. Such sites of struggle raise issues of power, control, and freedom that society must address.

Constructivism has emerged from the shortcomings of both instrumentalism and substantivism. Today, a constructivist framework largely prevails in studies of technology. Constructivists argue that technology is socially constructed and shaped by social forces. They argue that the contest for the site is addressed and that many potential paths lead out from the first forms of a new technology. There are always viable alternatives to our research and development priorities, the form technology will take, and the uses to which it will be put. They go on to say that to succeed, technology must have a technical and a social logic; in other words, new tools (or systems) succeed where they find support in the social environment.

Once a tool or system finds a supportive environment it usually undergoes a process of closure. Closure refers to the fixing of a product or system into a socially recognized object, producing a 'black box', an artifact or way of doing things that is no longer called into question. And once a black box is closed, or 'naturalized', as sociologists Bowker and Star (1999) define the situation, its social origins and alternatives are quickly forgotten and the artifact or system appears purely technical and inevitable—as if it were bound to emerge in the form it has taken. It becomes part of the taken-for-granted environment. This notion both of purity (independent from social forces) and of inevitability (that it would emerge in the form it did) is, Feenberg claims, a **determinist illusion**. In a different society, or at a different time in history, or in the hands of different developers, a certain piece of

Source: © Bettmann/CORBIS

Technology brought myriad manufacturing applications to the assembly line.

technology might have been differently configured. Differently configured, the telephone could readily have served as a broadcast receiver for musical events (Box 6.3) just as phones have become news cameras; cameras, sound recording devices; and computers, burglary tools.

The constructivist view of technology maintains that technology arises within and under the control of society; specific practical and political choices are involved in development of technical systems. For example, the **deskilling** of work is neither inevitable nor an accident of technological advance. Deskilling results from developers breaking down workplace tasks into a series of simple steps or components. This allows an employer to replace people doing complex tasks with less skilled people, each performing one simple part of a complex task. Simplification allows the employer to pay less. While deskilling may actually increase the reliability of production, decent wages for workers may be undermined and job satisfaction may plummet. Deskilling systems is not inevitable or inescapable. Rather, it has a particular history in the development of mass production and factory management. The constructivist motto is, thus, 'it could have been otherwise.'

The nature of a constructivist view has been captured by Wiebe Bijker (1993). In fact, as Felczak

(2006: 6) notes, Bijker actually extends the constructivist formulation:

> Society is not determined by technology, nor is technology determined by society. Both emerge as two sides of the sociotechnical coin, during the construction process of artifacts, facts, and relevant social groups.

Bijker claims that what we call a machine is a **Socio-Technical Ensemble** and, 'it should, in principle, be possible to sketch the (socially) constructed character of that machine.' Similarly, the term 'social institution' is short for a different socio-technical ensemble and 'it should be possible to spell out the technical relations that go into making that institution into a stable setup' (Bijker, 1993: 125).

This means that any machine—from a chainsaw or hair dryer to a space station or the Hubble space telescope—arose in a socially defined intention of its developers, who were able to create a particular technical device for intended and sometimes unintended uses, hence a socio-technical ensemble.

Felczak makes two further points. One is derived from sociologists John Law and Michel Callon (1988). If machines are socio-technical ensembles, then it follows that engineers are social activists. They design machines that reconfigure social relations and hence change society. On the other side of the equation, in the context of information technology, social scientific investigation can embrace an activist element just as some scientific inquiry does, for example, in the health sciences. Imagine the health sciences limited to describing and addressing symptoms without looking for the causes and means of neutralizing them (see Lorimer et al., 2000). Rather than being after-the-fact commentators on socio-technical ensembles, social scientists can engage in the development of socio-technical ensembles and, by participating in defining their nature, can contour them for the benefit of society.

Source: © Espion/Dreamstime.com

In technologically-advanced countries, people are convinced that we should be continuously looking for new and better technologies. This desire is also seen in young people's interest in new and innovative video games.

Technology and Western Society

Is Western society unique in its relationship to technology? Probably not—all cultures and societies can be seen as being based on tightly integrated technologies. Sociologist of science Bruno Latour suggests that what distinguishes modern society from so-called traditional societies may be the size and scope of our socio-technical ensembles, rather than any qualitative difference in the way people think or cultures act.

As successive layers of technology have taken root in Western society and successive layers of infrastructure have been laid down, we should not be surprised to find that our dependency on these systems has grown. So enthusiastic is the acceptance of technology by Western, especially North American, society that some would argue that the world is increasingly in the firm clutches of the **technological imperative**, that is, we have

convinced ourselves that we should continuously develop new technologies and apply them broadly for a better life. Furthermore, development of technology in Western society is usually a deliberate attempt to create material objects, interventions, or systems that, in changing or improving situations, allow the developer to reap financial reward. In this sense, technological development is a business—and the economies of Western nations are wrapped up intimately with the innovation, development, and promotion of new technologies. One result is that the technological distance between countries of the global north and global south in communication has been generally increasing. This gap, which from time to time is brought forward for discussion, is often called the **digital divide**.

Recalling Winner's three-part definition of technology, we can see that technologically oriented societies affirm and embrace machinery, the social organization necessary to adopt that machinery, and the acquisition of the requisite skills and techniques needed for its operation for private financial benefit, largely without social or political interference. The enthusiastic acceptance of technology is sometimes so complete that both analysts (e.g., Gilder, 1991) and the general public fully believe the projections about the future of society based on technological capacity. This is a straightforward

---

⁖ BOX 6.1 THE DIGITAL DIVIDE

'Digital divide' is a term used to describe the differences in access to information and communication technology by different social groups. For instance, in Canada, low-income families typically have less access to up-to-date computers and high-speed internet connections. There are also digital divides along the lines of gender, race, and ethnicity, as well as between Aboriginal and non-Aboriginal populations. As Figure 6.1 illustrates, at the international level the digital divide is even more pronounced. The question is, as more and more of our lives are lived online and dependent on computers, to what degree are particular groups and communities disadvantaged by the digital divide?

FIGURE 6.1   The Global Digital Divide

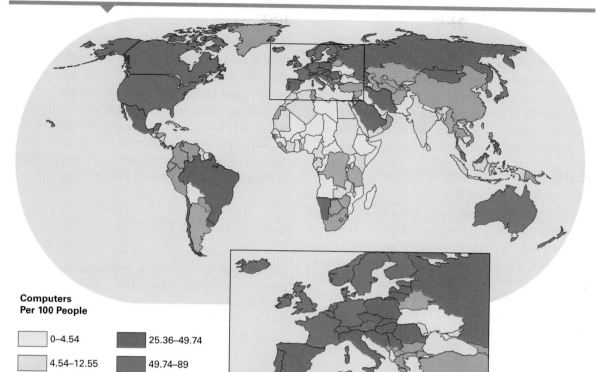

Source: United Nations Global Development Goals Indicators (Robinson Project). Cartography by Derek Boogard.

example of technological determinism: if technological development (usually conceived of as developing and adopting some kind of apparatus) can do something, society will take full advantage of this technological capacity and will be shaped fundamentally by the apparatus.

For instance, technological determinism would argue that landing a man on the moon changed society fundamentally: it was seen as the beginning of the colonization of space by humanity. Similarly, the internet was presumed to democratize the world more completely than ever before. Of course, sociotechnical ensembles have had profound impacts on society, but the extent to which they have met these expectations is not borne out and remains contested. This is the kind of technological determinism we all tend to engage in and this perspective glosses over the fundamental complexity of the real world.

Determinism fails to consider that the technology does not drop out of the clear blue sky or from the head of some genius. Rather, it is derived from specific efforts to solve problems or find opportunities. For instance, the very neutral (if gendered) statement 'man went to the moon' could be more accurately framed as 'the US government contributed enormous funding to military-industrial contractors in order to establish American technological superiority in the Cold War with the Soviet Union by putting a human being on the moon.' Technological determinism also ignores the role of state and institutional control over the industrialized application of technology. As is apparent, the internet can as easily be used for dictatorship or terrorism as for democracy; it can further bigotry as easily as enlightened debate. In the early days of the internet users fought against its commercialization; today it is a powerful conduit for all kinds of e-commerce. If politicians wish, they can enact policy so that a certain technology (e.g., the internet) can only be used in certain ways (e.g., for legal forms of communication), and hence, with certain consequences (e.g., clamping down on child pornography or organized crime). Such control is not just in the hands of governments; more often corporate interests exercise their power to shape technological systems in order to preserve market influence.

The Dangers of Technology and Technological Hubris

Implicit in our everyday perspective on technology is the notion that technology can transform society for the good, in other words, that it contributes to progress. But as Ellul points out, the consequences of the transformative dynamic of technology usually go unrealized in its initial application. Antibiotics are a well-known example. While antibiotics have been a godsend to public health, we now understand that strains of antibiotic-resistant bacteria have emerged precisely because of our use of antibiotics. Each winter, following the SARS scare of 2004–5, health officials worry that a drug-resistant strain of flu may cause a world pandemic. Similarly, the development of monocultures—single varieties of plants that are most productive and produce the most economically harvestable crop—makes food supplies extremely vulnerable to failure. Likewise, genetically modified crops and animals (Box 6.2) have the potential for great harm as well as good. The 1912 sinking of the *Titanic* was a famous example of technological hubris. The *Titanic* was viewed as unsinkable because it was an example of the latest and greatest technology.

In communication, similar issues surround the limitations of technology. While more people are able to access vast amounts of information, economies of scale come to dominate; thus, information attracting only a limited audience tends to disappear. Specialty magazines disappear from newsstands, and scholarly monographs that focus on narrow yet important subjects—such as the influence of ethnicity on modern farming communities—have a very difficult time getting published. The control systems of the large producers tell them

that they can make more money elsewhere. Some kinds of national, provincial, and regional news, as well as information about our neighbours down the street, become harder to find as the news media shift their focus to what will sell news. Finally, elements as mundane as the number of hours one might spend sitting in front of a computer or TV, or the lack of socialization involved in working from home, may have considerable unanticipated health consequences when multiplied throughout society. Again, this is what Ellul meant by the inseparability of the good and bad effects of technology.

Centralization, Decentralization, and Control

The question of who owns and controls technologies was a critical issue before Karl Marx wrote about the means of production. Before the Industrial Revolution the means of production were agricultural. Landowners controlled the means of the production of food—that is, they owned the land—while peasants worked the land to pay a large portion of their crops to the owners, who became rich while the peasants barely stayed alive. Communication technologies have traditionally been owned and controlled by large corporations and/or governments (Chapter 2). Although large, privately owned media corporations still dominate the mediascape, some shift has occurred, away

Source: © Indy2320/Dreamstime.com

In this portrait, on display at the National Portrait Gallery in London, England, Thomas Edison poses with his phonograph. The round objects beside the machine are wax cylinders, on which the music was recorded. It is said that the phrase 'canned music' came from the cans in which wax cylinders were stored to protect them.

❖ BOX 6.2   GLOWING PIG PASSES TRAIT ON
By Christopher Bodeen

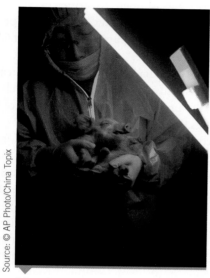

Source: © AP Photo/China Topix

When lit up in the dark, the pigs glow green. In daylight, their eyes and skin are green-tinged.

Beijing – A cloned pig whose genes were altered to make it glow fluorescent green has passed on the trait to its young, a development that could lead to the future breeding of pigs for human transplant organs, a Chinese university reported.

The glowing piglets' birth proves transgenic pigs are fertile and able to pass on their engineered traits to their offspring, according to Liu Zhonghua, a professor overseeing the breeding program at Northeast Agricultural University.

'Continued development of this technology can be applied to…the production of special pigs for the production of human organs for transplant,' Liu said in a news release posted Tuesday on the university's website.

Calls to the university seeking comment Wednesday were not answered.

The piglets' mother was one of three pigs born with the trait in December 2006 after pig embryos were injected with fluorescent green protein. Two of the 11 piglets glow fluorescent green from their snout, trotters and tongue under ultraviolet light, the university said.

Robin Lovell-Badge, a genetics expert at Britain's National Institute for Medical Research, said the technology 'to genetically manipulate pigs in this way would be very valuable.'

Lovell-Badge had not seen the research from China's cloned pigs and could not comment on its credibility. He said, however, that organs from genetically altered pigs would potentially solve some of the problems of rejected organs in transplant operations.

He said the presence of the green protein would allow genetically modified cells to be tracked if they were transplanted into a human. The fact that the pig's offspring also appeared to have the green genes would indicate that the genetic modification had successfully penetrated every cell, Lovell-Badge added.

But he said much more research and further trials—both in animals and in humans—would be necessary before the benefits of the technology could be seen.

Other genetically modified pigs have been created before, including by Scotland's Roslin Institute, but few results have been published.

Tokyo's Meiji University last year successfully cloned a transgenic pig that carries the genes for human diabetes, while South Korean scientists cloned cats that glow red when exposed to ultraviolet rays.

Source: Bodeen, C. (2008, 9 January). 'Glowing Pig Passes Genes to Piglets'. *Association Press*. http://news.nationalgeographic.com/news/2008/01/080109-pig-glow.html

---

from a centralized model (the mass media) in which a single entity owns and controls both the generation of content and the technology that produces it. Meanwhile, large corporations ferret out investments for vertical and horizontal integration, looking towards the aggregation of content and of audiences sufficiently large to run a viable, attention-selling business. In short, new media constitute a highly contested site and media entrepreneurs will be looking for ways to shape the organization of technology to their financial advantage.

Technical Convergence: Old Myth, New Reality

Traditionally, communication has been divided into several different industries based on the 'siloing' or enclosure (see Chapter 10) that came to exist around a particular communicative process. For example, telephone systems were designed to facilitate point-to-point communication offering limited quality or **fidelity** in the sound they carried (telephones need only transmit a recognizable voice) but developed sophisticated switching. Broadcast technology was designed not only to carry signals from a single point to multiple points but also to have a satisfactory level of fidelity so that listening to voice and music would be enjoyable. No switching between senders and receivers was required, just a stream of signals flowing outward from a single source. Sound recording technology was developed to yield the highest possible sound fidelity, but distribution was determined by consumer purchase. And just as recording technology increased in its fidelity over the years from wax cylinders to various qualities of magnetic tape, and from shellac-surfaced and vinyl records to polycarbonate-and-aluminum optical compact discs and DVDs, so radio improved as stations migrated from AM (amplitude modulation) to FM (frequency modulation) bands, and then to digital radio.

No doubt many assumed there was a technological basis to the division of responsibilities between telephone and broadcast, as Babe (1988, 1990) has pointed out (see also Winseck, 1998); however, no such technological determinism existed. Telephone systems could easily have been turned into broadcast instruments as they were in the very first example of voice telephony by Reginald Fessenden (Fessenden, 1974) and in early radio forms and as they were used in the former Soviet Union. Social and political forces achieved several different technical closures to allow the formation of viable communication industries (Chapter 2).

The separation of communication functions into separate industries and the development of technology that best suited the functions of telephony, broadcasting, and sound and video recording have served society well. This separation is now many decades old, and government regulation largely takes the resulting industry structure for granted. Such industrial and technological separation prevented the overall control of communication by one set of companies by spreading ownership somewhat broadly. With **digitization** and the development of digital media infrastructure, the traditional technological separation of telephony, broadcasting, and cable as well as music and movie purchase for home consumption ceases to make sense, leaving an industrial and regulatory structure that is open to criticism and change. Telephone companies now provide TV programming, and cable companies are offering telephone and internet service.

Digital media devices such as cameras, computers, musical instruments, radio, television, cable, GPS units, and telephones are information machines that essentially do the same job—collect and code, thereby transforming information (sounds and images) into digital form. They are merely specialized, computerized transceivers (transmitters *and* receivers). For instance, through sampling and/or synthesis, an electronic keyboard can reproduce almost any sound. A digital audio file is essentially the same as a digital image file; no technical reason prevents you from manipulating a song in an image-editing program or from adding effects like reverberation to a photograph (or the series of photographs formerly recorded on film for movies). Each reading device is a computer specialized to a particular sound and/or image and/or text format. They have digitization in common; hence, the ability of one device to send output or to receive input from another is called **convergence** (see Chapter 10). Where, historically, we have seen communication industries arranged around significantly different technological underpinnings, the advent of digital media means everyone is working with the same foundational technologies—everything mediated by computers, computer codes, and computer networks—and by the internet itself). The resulting reconfiguration of communication industries presents considerable challenges for policy and policy-makers.

Technology and Policy

Early in the twenty-first century, two central issues are: (1) to ensure that the needs of the public and of cultural and national groups are met, and (2) to ensure that certain businesses do not become too powerful and thwart the participation of others

✧ BOX 6.3 FIRST BROADCASTERS USED PHONE

Source: From *Popular Science*, September 1933, p. 39

Who were the earliest broadcasters? Ten years before the first radio programs were put on the air, a group in Chicago, Ill., regularly delivered musical programs and news bulletins over the telephone lines of many subscribers. The rare old photograph shows these pioneers broadcasting from their studio. Each singer is holding a microphone, while other individual microphones are attached to the instruments. To listen to the music, a subscriber had merely to sit beside the telephone and hold the receiver to his ear. If he received a phone call while listening, the musical program was automatically disconnected.

and prevent further social and technological development. The attempt by Microsoft to dominate in nearly every software market is a case in point. Some feel that the success of Google is equally threatening.

While allowing for both convergence and competition sounds like a good idea, regulatory agencies like the Canadian Radio-television and Telecommunications Commission cannot easily forge appropriate policy. For example, telephone and cable companies provide internet access to consumers and are known as 'backbone providers'.

They also provide connectivity to small internet service providers (ISPs), who also sell internet access to the public. Similarly, the cable companies own some of the specialty TV channels and provide access to these not only to the public but also to their competitors. Clearly, there are conflicts here: first, between the large and small ISPs; and second, between the cable companies and the independent specialty channels. Arguably, these conflicts are exploited by the larger companies to the degree they can get away with it. Government policy sets the rules of the game, determining whether, for instance, cable companies can own specialty channels. But the CRTC's powers are limited by a number of factors, including the number of corporations willing to create products for sale (see also Chapter 7).

Satellite radio is an interesting case in point. In the fall of 2005, the CRTC licensed two services in Canada, Sirius radio and XM Radio Canada, both American companies. The CRTC initially ruled that the services would be required to carry at least eight original channels produced in Canada, 25 per cent of which were to be in French, and a maximum of nine foreign channels for each Canadian one. After some protest by citizens' groups and a referral back to Cabinet, the services agreed to increase their Canadian content. However, in 2007 the two American parent companies merged, causing a merger of their Canadian branch services. Consequently, the companies controlled outside of Canadian jurisdiction left the Canadian government no say in the restructuring of the industry and less control over the operation of the industry here.

Policy issues can have a significant international component and getting a foreign company, particularly one running a monopoly service, to adhere to the regulations in all the different countries in which it co-operates can be a difficult task. Yet more challenging to policy-making is the internet; while different countries have different laws on free speech, privacy, access to information, and so forth, the internet undermines those laws by being available everywhere and based nowhere. While, on the internet, **geoblocking** (Box 6.4) can be used to stop unauthorized reception to some extent, satellite broadcasting presents greater challenges.

The Internet

The internet presents challenges for traditional conceptions of communication technology and industries, in its starting assumptions, its structure, and the ways in which people are using it. The sheer size of the internet today means that how it differs from older communication models represents a major shift in the way we must think about communication media. For instance, by some estimates almost 30 per cent of the world's population now use the internet (www.internetworldstats.com/stats.htm) (see Figure 6.2).

The foundations of the internet were laid in the United States in the 1960s, when large amounts of Cold War–era government funding were poured into the new computer science departments at American universities. Researchers at the time were interested in developing an interactive computer network. The original ARPANET project (*circa* 1969) connected computer systems at five US universities, enabling information exchange and message-sending between them (Figure 6.3). One of the key ideas behind the network was that if, in the event of a nuclear attack, one or more of its nodes were destroyed, unlike a point-to-point communication system, it could still function. This project grew into the 'internet' through the 1970s and early 1980s, by which time most of the underlying technological infrastructure in use today had been worked out.

Demonstrating a particular socio-technical ensemble, a number of interesting features of the early internet shaped how it works today. First, the internet was developed as a *peer-to-peer system*; there is no central control point in the network, unlike even the telephone system, which maintains centrally managed switching. The internet is arranged like a web, in which points on the network are redundantly interconnected; the route by which any particular piece of information travels is decided by software rather than by the physical connections, and all points on the internet are equals or peers, at least in theory. The internet trades information units called **packets**, which are something like envelopes with 'To:' and 'From:' labels on them. Network software reads these address labels and makes decisions about how to transfer packets along the web. Furthermore, these packets are like sealed envelopes; the contents are important only to the computer systems at either end of a transmission. The internet is described as an end-to-end architecture, with the network itself remaining ignorant or, at least, neutral about what is being transferred. This feature is called **network neutrality** and ensures that the data being transferred receives equal treatment.

An interesting feature of the internet is that it has existed for much of its life as a publicly funded

❖ BOX 6.4   GEOBLOCKING

Putting Limits on Who Can View Online Video: How It Works and Why It's Done

By Grant Buckler, CBC News

Source: © Artushfoto/Dreamstime.com

To protect rights agreements, many broadcasters allow only local audiences to view video online.

'The requested video cannot be displayed in your region.'

Many online video devotees have seen this message on their screens. Some know how to find ways around it. For many others, irritated resignation is the only avenue available. And quite a few probably wonder why and how they are denied access to certain online content based solely on where they are.

Geoblocking or geofencing is a technique for making sure only the people within (or sometimes outside) a specific geographical region can view online content such as a video stream. It's the result of a clash between the global reach of the internet and the balkanized way commercial content is often licensed.

Geoblocking can be used for various purposes, not all of which involve licensed content. One common use for the technology is to avoid legal problems tied to online content or services that are legal in some jurisdictions but not in others, notes Michael Geist, Canada research chair of internet and e-commerce law at the University of Ottawa. A primary example is online gambling. Cyber-casino operators can stay out of legal trouble by denying access to users in jurisdictions where it's illegal.

When would-be viewers are denied access to mainstream audio or video content such as TV shows being streamed online, legal issues are usually involved, too. But in this case the issues surround the way rights to such content are sold. For instance, the CBC bought from the International Olympic Committee (IOC) the rights to broadcast the 2008 Summer Olympics on television, along with digital rights to stream video of the events online. But those rights applied only to Canada. The IOC sold similar rights to NBC in the US. 'We as the

Canadian rights holder are privy to certain digital rights', explains Bob Kerr, director of business development at, 'but we have to make sure we don't leak into the States.'

International sports events, the rights to which are usually controlled by governing bodies such as the IOC or the Fédération Internationale de Football Association (FIFA), are where geoblocking most often comes into play. But it can also occur when television networks sell international rights to their entertainment programming, or when independent production companies sell rights market by market.

If a US broadcaster sells a Canadian network a series that is also available on the US network's website, for example, the US company may prevent Canadians from watching its streaming video to avoid infringing the rights it has sold to the Canadian network.

This may happen even if the Canadian network didn't actually buy online rights to the show, notes Alan Sawyer, principal consultant at Two Solitudes Consulting, a Toronto-based new media consultancy.

That's because the foreign network that sold the Canadian broadcast rights doesn't want to annoy its customer by having an international online video stream draw potential viewers away from the Canadian television broadcast—which could affect the program's Canadian television ratings and hence the advertising revenue it generates.

How It Works

To plug those types of leaks, online broadcasters employ software that can determine a website visitor's location by looking at his or her computer's Internet Protocol (IP) address. This is a numeric code assigned to every computer connected to the internet, whether it's an individual user's laptop or a large corporation's web server.

Depending on the type of internet access you have, that number may change every time you connect to the net (a 'dynamic' IP address) or remain the same for as long as you stay with your internet service provider (a 'static' address).

Either way, your IP address by itself can't identify you personally or give your exact location to an outsider on the internet. But just as a telephone number has an area code, an IP address roughly indicates the location of the computer to which it is assigned. IP addresses are given to internet service providers in blocks, so the first digits of the address identify the provider and, thus, the country of origin.

Source: Buckler, G. (2009, June 8). 'Putting limits on who can view online video: How it works and why it's done.' *CBC News*. Available at http://www.cbc.ca/news/technology/story/2009/02/04/f-tech-geoblocking.html.

FIGURE 6.2   Internet Users in the World, Distribution by World Regions, 2010

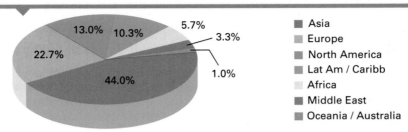

- Asia
- Europe
- North America
- Lat Am / Caribb
- Africa
- Middle East
- Oceania / Australia

22.7%   13.0%   10.3%   5.7%   3.3%   44.0%   1.0%

❖ BOX 6.5   KNOWLEDGE FRAMEWORKS AND UNDERSTANDING

An article in *The New Yorker* tells the story of Ted Ames, who was born into a fishing family on the Maine coast. On account of his small stature his parents encouraged him to obtain an education. He pursued biology in the hope of obtaining a job related to the fishery. In the course of his studies he realized that the centralized knowledge that science brought to the east coast fishery neglected the wisdom of generations of fishers. Sampling techniques, for example, took no account of spawning grounds and fish behaviour. It was as if any patch of fish habitat was equal to any other patch. Ames's research led him to some work done at Memorial University of Newfoundland that identified the spawning grounds of cod. The findings were surprising in that, just like salmon, it seems that cod return to their place of birth to reproduce. The problem is that bottom-dragging trawlers have been destroying the spawning grounds, and those that are left, or that have recovered to some degree, are less and less known to modern fishers with their sonar. In short, both scientists and fishers were losing the local (or traditional) ecological knowledge of fish behaviour so neither group had any particular wisdom on how to rebuild the cod fishery.

Ames decided that this knowledge could be and needed to be captured. By interviewing older fishers, he combined their wisdom with his knowledge of biology and, as an ethnobiologist and practising fisherman, received a half-million-dollar 'genius' award from the MacArthur Foundation in the process. The result: a fuller understanding of the factors influencing the reproduction and survival of cod and more informed efforts towards the recovery of the fishery in the Gulf of Maine.

Source: Wilkinson (2006). See also www.fishhistory.org/publicPapers. php.

system, first in the US, and today in most other countries as well. However, since the mid-1990s, more of the internet is made up of corporate, for-profit components, while substantial chunks worldwide still are run by governments and/or academic institutions. This has given the internet a different character from large-scale corporate media like television, and effective corporate control of the internet is still limited, though this status is in flux as corporate interests make larger and larger investments in internet infrastructure. The internet certainly is not free from large corporate involvement. The dot-com boom of the late 1990s was a gold rush of stock market speculation in companies that were founded to computerize anything capable of being computerized. Investors flocked to ideas rather than to viable business models and lost a tremendous amount of money doing so. When the dot-com movement ended (the bubble of speculation and hopes for instant riches burst) in 2001, because there were no viable businesses behind many companies, the largest corporations maintained their investments and profit-making in the internet. The areas of economic growth so far have to do with network provision—that is, the companies that own the connections and charge for access—and the web search engines. In 2005, Google became the largest media company in the

FIGURE 6.3 ARPA Net Map, circa 1977

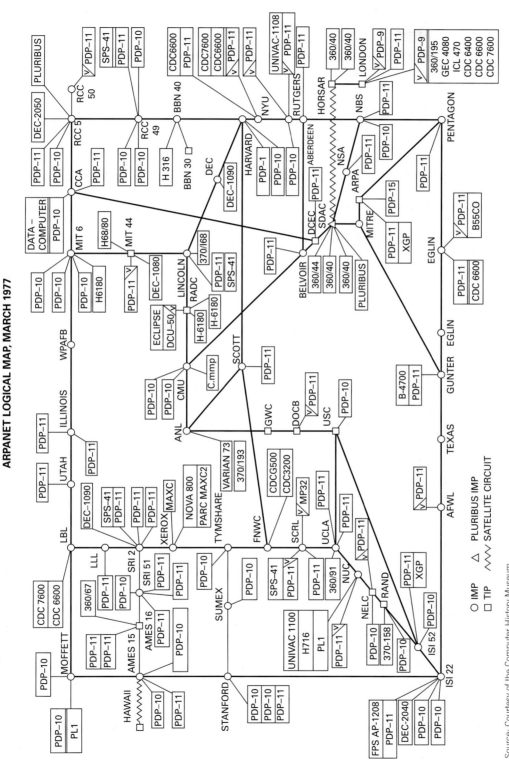

ARPANET LOGICAL MAP, MARCH 1977

Source: Courtesy of the Computer History Museum

world by market valuation (the total value of all shares held): at $80 billion US, it was larger than Time Warner, Disney, or Viacom. It is interesting to consider that this value resides in a company that most of us use every day without paying a cent.

A second significant feature of the internet is that its underlying technologies have for the most part been developed and released non-commercially as open systems and more recently as **open-source software**. This means that the software, standards, and protocols that make the internet run are not owned or controlled by any one party, but, rather, are publicly available just like published academic research. The major internet engineering process has for decades revolved around a system of requests for comments or RFCs. The RFC is effectively a peer-review system where contributions of software and system design are openly circulated, reviewed, and improved on by a community of engineers in much the way Wikipedia is open to participation in its content. The result is that anyone wanting to contribute to the process can do so. Over the past decade, this process has grown into a general strategy for software development, with a rich variety of components available as open source—that is, free for examination, modification, use, and distribution, without typical commercial trappings such as licence fees, trade secrets, or usage restrictions.

This model of systems development has proved enormously successful for the internet itself, but it also has cultural implications. In a world in which works—text, music, video, and so on—are stored and transferred digitally, and consequently can be copied and distributed globally in an instant and for almost no cost, traditional conceptions of copyright and intellectual property have become increasingly problematic, especially for century-old industries that have grown up around a more traditional copyright landscape. Into the legal battles that result from technological change comes the open-source movement, bringing with it a completely different sensibility about how and by what terms works should be circulated and exchanged.

With regard to internet usage by the general public, the World Wide Web emerged as an internet application in the early 1990s and quickly grew to be the largest user of internet **bandwidth**—the capacity of a network for carrying information. The web provides a friendly interface to the internet, and grew in its first decade to the point where it allowed for an almost infinite number of niche audiences to access content of interest to them. For much of the web's first decade, its basic model was a simple page-delivery system. However, its increasing interactive capability, in terms of both web content being served up by user choices and other applications acting more like desktop computer software, has transformed users into webmasters. The biggest trend in recent years has been the rise of social networking (Chapter 1).

The web's status as a new mass medium comes to the fore when we consider the impact of **blogging** on journalism. It is easy enough to see bloggers as journalists—or at least reporters or editorialists—and the mainstream media have had to take note of this fact, either by attempting to distance themselves from blogging by appealing to ideals of quality, objectivity, and journalistic ethics or by incorporating bloggers in their offerings. A segment of the blogging community (or 'blogosphere' as it has been called) has responded to this challenge by branding itself as 'citizen journalism' and noting that the combined voices of thousands of observers (some expert) have at least as good a claim to objectivity and accuracy as does the journalism profession. However, the main difficulty with the blogosphere is, like the internet itself, that there is no guarantee of truthfulness or validity of any single contribution. In the journalism profession there is a commitment to certain procedures aimed at objectivity, fairness, reliability of sources, and so on (Chapter 9).

The web is not the same thing as the internet, and dozens of other applications or services are used by millions of people daily, from older—electronic mail and online discussion forums—to newer forms such as multi-participant role-playing games, peer-to-peer file-sharing systems, instant messaging, and distributed computing systems. Increasingly, we are seeing traditional media formats, such as video and telephone services, appearing as internet-based applications. There are few technical obstacles to these developments; internet-based television content seems mostly slowed by copyright and licensing ambiguities, and internet telephony, or VOIP (voice-over internet protocol) is becoming more widely used.

Perhaps the most intriguing characteristic of the internet is that no single trend is at work; rather, innovation and creativity seem to be occurring in hundreds of directions at once. Cable TV proponents once promised an imminent 500-channel universe. The internet offers millions of possibilities. And, while the internet introduces a new level of decentralization of services and control, it is important to remember that a unified network is a tool that can at the same time facilitate an even greater concentration of databases, brands, and discourses.

Technology Transfer

The export of new technologies from one country to another is usually referred to as **technology transfer**. The problem with most of the thinking behind technology transfer is the tendency to reduce technology to 'machines' or 'devices' and to ignore the wider social and cultural contexts in play. Indeed, the 'problems' of 'technology transfer' (both problematic terms) have themselves contributed to the development of the richer definitions of what technology actually is, which were introduced at the beginning of this chapter.

Research on technology transfer reveals a number of insights. Generally speaking, direct causal correlations between the introduction of a technology into developing economies and changes in social behaviour (for example, between the availability of birth control devices and actual use) cannot be easily identified. Combinations of technology with other changes can modify behaviour. For example, economically speaking, in many rural and agricultural settings it is seen as a net asset for families to have more children, whereas in a city they are a net expense. Hence, birth control information with a change of circumstances may have an effect as urbanization gradually changes the orientation to size of family.

Technical approaches to the introduction of technology (skills training, explanation of the equipment) are limited in their effectiveness because the socio-cultural element is missing in the ensemble. E.F. Schumacher's classic work, *Small Is Beautiful* (1973), has elaborated much of this dynamic. Nor does the local manufacture of equipment in developing economies, designed to give people insight into how it is assembled and a sense of ownership, necessarily remove barriers to its adoption and maintenance. Equipment can be assembled under direction and without any understanding of its operation or how it might fit into the practices and contexts of daily living. The importation of 'turnkey operations'—where the importing country simply opens the box and turns the machine on—often proves of limited value due to lack of prior study of the social context. Such transfers, if they do work, often create substantial long-term dependency relationships as the receivers of the technology continue to rely on those supplying it for instruction on its use and maintenance. Perhaps most importantly, many of the people working in factories in developing countries cannot afford to buy the products they make. Those products are destined for export markets in the richer 'post-industrial' countries of the Global North. While China is striving to be an exception to this rule, in many instances technology transfer in today's global economy tends to wrap the receiving country in a net of political and economic dependency.

In the end, this discussion leads us right back to the beginning. Technology is not merely machinery—each artifact or system, in Bijker's words, is a socio-technical ensemble or, in Franklin's conception of technology, is a social practice.

Technology, International Law, and Copyright Law

By international covenant, countries currently have the right to participate in communication development and also to protect themselves from it, a protection that has been set aside in free trade agreements such as those that apply within the European Union. For example, should an unwanted satellite signal spill over so that it is transmitting across boundaries, a country can object. Japan has adjusted some of its satellite footprints in response to such objections. Shaping the footprint of Rupert

Murdoch's Star TV satellites is just one of the restrictive conditions under which the Murdoch conglomerate operates in China.

Countries have the power also to forbid the importation or exportation of any other form of information, either material or immaterial. These rights to protect groups, which are largely dependent on national status, are termed **collective rights**.

Balanced by these collective rights are **individual rights**. The United Nations' Universal Declaration of Human Rights (Article 19) states all individuals have the right to 'seek, receive and impart information'. The collectivity has the right to act in its own interests, yet individuals within the collectivity have the right to do so as well, and their interests may be contrary to those of the collectivity. Thus, while Canadians want regulation to ensure a predominance of Canadian broadcast signals, many individual Canadians want the freedom to choose what broadcast signal to receive. Once individual rights to 'seek, receive and impart'—especially to 'impart'—are extended to commercial information producers and then extended to corporations on the basis that corporations have the status of persons (in most legal respects), problems arise. The force of individuals who do not want the state to interfere with individual freedoms is pitted against corporations avidly pursuing their 'individual freedom'. This puts the political, social, and cultural interests of the collectivity against the demands of producers, whether individuals or business interests.

Technological developments represent a continual challenge for legal systems and policy-makers (Chapter 7). The foremost challenge is to respect collective and individual rights and to ensure that the greatest number of citizens gain the maximum benefit. At times and in some countries, creating universal benefits means assisting dissemination. At other times or in other countries it may mean denying people access to certain technologies and content in order to promote a more universal distribution of other content via alternative technology. For example, one reason cable TV was not introduced earlier in Europe is that it would have undermined state monopolies and the economies of scale that underlay the 'quality' of programming that public broadcasters produced (Collins, 1992).

Other rights enter into the picture in technological development. Personal privacy is one. As Valerie Steeves (2010) argues, privacy can be regarded simultaneously as a 'human right', a 'democratic right', and an important 'social value' and, in the current information environment, privacy is under attack on all three fronts. The most obvious example of invasion of privacy is that which takes place when someone with a scanner intercepts a cellphone conversation. Similarly, someone may intercept your credit card number as it is being transmitted along the internet. But other aspects of privacy are equally important. Profiles of individual consumer behaviour gained by tracing a consumer's spending patterns potentially infringe on personal privacy because they describe a unique profile from a wide range of personal preferences and activities in which one is involved. Indeed, an industry has developed for obtaining such data because we have the technological capacity to monitor people's personal computers. This activity is commonly called **data mining**. Determining the level of privacy to be protected and then protecting personal privacy are complex matters for policy-makers.

Protection of intellectual property has also become a salient issue with the digitization of content and the incredible opportunities that now exist for distributing that content. **Copyright**, a legal and commercial framework that emerged in the era of print, when it was relatively difficult (i.e., capital-intensive) to produce and distribute copies of works, now faces major conceptual challenges in a digital world where copies can be made and distributed at little or no cost.

Technology and Copyright Law

Digital technology, which allows for easy, inexpensive, and almost perfect copying and distribution of digital files over the internet, has brought a new dynamic that powerfully challenges copyright law. As many people provide content to the internet with no wish or expectation for financial gain, this technological capacity has encouraged an emergent

⁑ BOX 6.6   PRE-EMPTING DISSENT: COLLABORATIVE VIDEO-MAKING SITE

While corporations and governments struggle to tame the internet to the rules of copyright, the internet and open-source software are enabling new forms of artistic collaboration. In the video at www.infoscapelab.ca/preemptingdissent, the filmmakers are creating a public archive of material they are using to make their film *Pre-empting Dissent* while encouraging people to contribute relevant material themselves. The site and the materials it holds will then be available to anyone who wants to use it for future projects.

culture of sharing. Everything from the design of web pages to software source code to digitized music and video is shared online—sometimes on an enormous scale.

Copyright law begins with a different premise than does the internet, dating back to a time when monarchs and church leaders wanted to control (not to facilitate) the circulation of ideas. Copyright in England began with the Statute of (Queen) Anne of 1710 (see www.copyrighthistory.com/anne.html). Copyright law vests in the creator, not outright ownership, but the right to control the copying of a work. In other words, it is a temporary monopoly property right—the right to benefit financially from the sale of copies of a created literary work—and a more long-lasting, **moral right**—the right to be associated with the work, i.e., named as the author. In Canada, this includes the right to restrict use of the work in association with other events, products, organizations, and so forth. Copyright law also establishes public or user rights as a way of balancing the rights of society with the rights of the creator. This balance is based on the notion that ideas emanate from the social whole and the individual gives expression to them through the intellectual work of articulating them in written form, photographic reality, or any other copyrightable form. The most important manifestations of user rights are two. First, copyright limits the term of the monopoly property

right. Second, it circumscribes creators' rights by protecting only the expression of the idea, not the idea itself; hence, others may paraphrase. It also introduces a user right called fair dealing—in the US the equivalent right (which is not identical to the Canadian right of fair dealing) is fair use. Fair dealing allows users to quote a passage in reviewing or studying a work; it allows a person to make a copy for purposes of study. The fair-dealing principle represents a balancing of freedom of speech (to talk about a copyrighted product) with the property right of the creator—to benefit from the dissemination of his or her work.

In short, there is an inherent conflict between copyright law and the internet and other digital technologies that ease and affirm the sharing of information. Indeed, the operation of computers—which make temporary copies of materials that you see on your screen—is to some degree in conflict with copyright law. So powerful has been the desire for free sharing of information that actual internet practice is in clear conflict with copyright law, so much so that schoolteachers have been cautioned against using any internet materials for fear of a lawsuit against their school boards by Access Copyright, the main rights collective of creators and copyrights holders (Murray, 2005: 652).

The copyright industries reacted to the internet and digital copying technologies with assiduous lobbying to strengthen copyright laws and controls on behalf of rights holders because they perceive their interests to be under threat. In recent years, in various countries, waves of new copyright laws have emerged with an aim to vest greater control with the rightsholder and less with users. A common example is the DVD, which is presented as a 'black box' medium that can only be played on a licensed playback device. In the US, attempts to circumvent the technological barriers built into DVDs and playback devices, even for legitimate purposes, are potential grounds for legal action under the **WIPO copyright treaty**. Canadian law allows for circumvention for legitimate purposes, but changes may soon give our laws similar provisions to those of the US (Bradley, 2010).

Copyright holders have been successful in some jurisdictions, notably the EU and the US, in extending the length of time the copyright holder has to benefit from his/her temporary monopoly.

Rights holders and their organizations tend to mount their lobby efforts in the name of fighting personal and commercial **piracy** and distribution of illegal copies by many in the first instance and by fewer larger-scale operations in the second instance. They have been successful in establishing Digital Rights Management (DRM) mechanisms that do not just put a lock on content but involve monitoring and data collection of individual user behaviour without the user's knowledge. This kind of eavesdropping is forbidden in other contexts, for example, wire-tapping telephone conversations, and raises privacy concerns for users (Murray, 2005). It is also worth noting who the negotiators are in setting user rights and what their positions are. As Murray (ibid., 653) points out, they are most often large public institutions and organizations, such as the Council of Ministers of Education of Canada (CMEC), that both counsels against internet use in schools (because some uses may infringe) and also is prepared to bow to strong assertions of creators' rights by Access Copyright (which is wide open to legal interpretation). The CMEC might better stand up for user rights by, for example, 'contributing to legal clarification by defending reasonable interpretations of users' rights, [rather than bowing] to assertions about the law made by...Access Copyright' (ibid., 654).

Adjudicating the matter is not simple. Protection that is either too strong or too weak in ensuring creators' rights could disrupt communication and cultural industries. Lack of protection of intellectual property allows cheap consumption of products and deprives creators of reward for their intellectual effort. Without reward, the creative industries—writers, artists of many kinds, book and magazine publishers, television and movie producers, sound recording and distribution companies—could wither and die. Lack of protection also stands in the way of legitimate business in intellectual property in countries that turn a blind eye to piracy. In India in the early 1990s, so many small theatres were screening pirated videos that the state introduced a licensing system in an

Illegal DVDs are displayed in a marketplace in Spain. Despite ongoing attempts to curb the illegal manufacturing and sale of digital products, issues with piracy and illegal distribution continue to be an uphill battle.

attempt to garner revenues. Although this was done, the videos shown continued to be illegal copies. However, as Urvashi Butalia (1994) notes, this should not lead to the conclusion that piracy is rampant in all media in India. On the contrary, at least in book publishing, countries such as India have come to realize that their interests are better served by enforcing copyright laws. The film industry of Egypt, for example, is severely crippled by the numerous bootleg copies made as soon as any film is finished. Nevertheless, the motivation for many countries to take decisive action is not strong—the effect of legislation would be primarily to protect the interests of US industries.

So what is being done about copyright and what does the future hold?

Alternatives to Copyright

Lawrence Lessig, a Stanford University law professor, has spearheaded a movement to create a legal framework for the sharing, rather than exploitation, of intellectual property. For several years Lessig was on the US university lecture circuit speaking out against the tendency of large corporations to overly restrict the use of copyrighted materials, including cartoon characters. At the same time, he pointed out that those same corporations, specifically Disney, had drawn inspiration from the folklore of the past for the characters they were trying to forbid others to use. In a lecture entitled 'Free culture: How big media uses technology and the law to lock down culture and control creativity' (see www.free-culture.cc/freeculture.pdf), Lessig articulates four main points:

1. Creativity and innovation always build on the past.
2. The past always tries to control the creativity that builds upon it.
3. Free societies enable the future by limiting the power of the past.
4. Ours (the US and, by extension, the world) is less and less a free society.

Lessig convinced many that there should be an alternative to copyright and his persuasiveness allowed him to form a foundation to which many have donated. That not-for-profit foundation is called Creative Commons and its main activity has been the creation of a legal alternative to copyright (see http://creativecommons.org/). Creative Commons has developed a number of symbols that can be attached to a work to signify what rights are claimed. A double-c inside a circle indicates that it is being made available under a Creative Commons licence. The Canadian version of the full licence can be downloaded from: http://creativecommons.org/worldwide/ca/. Contained in that agreement is this key section:

3. Licence Grant. Subject to the terms and conditions of this Licence, Licensor hereby grants You a worldwide, royalty-free, non-exclusive, perpetual (for the duration of the applicable copyright) Licence to exercise the rights in the Work as stated below:

(a) to reproduce the Work, to incorporate the Work into one or more Collective Works, and to reproduce the Work as incorporated in the Collective Works;
(b) to create and reproduce Derivative Works;
(c) to distribute copies or sound recordings of, display publicly, perform publicly, and perform publicly by means of a digital audio transmission the Work including as incorporated in Collective Works;
(d) to distribute copies or sound recordings of, display publicly, perform publicly, and perform publicly by means of a digital audio transmission Derivative Works;

The above rights may be exercised in all media and formats whether now known or hereafter devised. The above rights include the right to make such modifications as are technically necessary to exercise the rights in other media and formats. All rights not expressly granted by Licensor are hereby reserved, including but not limited to the rights set forth in Section 4(e).

The above section is followed by another section on restrictions, and creators are able to restrict use in a variety of ways. As well, Creative Commons has developed a set of symbols that creators can affix to their material (see http://creativecommons.org/about/licenses/meet-the-licenses).

Creative Commons is not the only game in town. GNU, which stands for Gnus Not **Unix**, issues a General Public Licence (GPL) and is generally used by software developers.

The actions of large copyright corporations are also being challenged in the music industry in Canada. Terry McBride, the CEO of Nettwerk Music Group in Vancouver, takes issue with the manner in which the music industry is managing itself in the face of a clear desire of fans to be able to choose the music they want and have it readily available to download. McBride has undertaken a variety of projects, including financing the legal defence of a girl in Texas who was charged with illegally downloading and sharing music files. In September 2006, he masterminded the multi-layered release of a Barenaked Ladies album. As well as placing the CD in music stores, McBride sold the individually recorded vocal, guitar, drum, and other tracks so that fans can actually remix the songs according to their own liking (O'Brian, 2006). Nettwerk sells individual songs from its website, but unlike other services there are no Digital Rights Management restrictions, leaving the consumer to do what he or she likes with the music. The website states:

> Litigation is destructive, it must stop… as per Nettwerk copyrights, we have never sued anybody and all our music is open source to encourage fans to share it with others and help us promote our Artists. As per those Artists we manage on other labels (Majors), we take issue with those labels claiming that litigating our fans is in our interest, as it clearly is not.

Achievements in the Information World

Beyond doubt, communication technology is changing the world. Over the past decade many new devices, services, and capacities have emerged to enhance our ability to communicate and handle information. In the process, social dynamics have changed.

Increased Communication Capacity, Speed, and Flexibility

With satellites, optical fibres, sophisticated switching technologies, and data communication engineering, rather than merely having an ability to get a message from A to B, we now speak in terms of bandwidth and nanoseconds. When applied to radio-based communication systems (like broadcast TV), bandwidth used to mean the proportional amount of a particular band of frequencies allotted to any given station or transmitter. The wider the band, the greater the amount of information—and generally the higher the image or audio quality—that can be effectively communicated. With newer packet-switched systems like the internet, bandwidth refers to the number of digital **bits** sent per second and is a function of how fast the switching machinery can operate. More bits result in more information per second (or nanosecond). For example, CD-quality stereo audio is sampled (digitized) at 44,000 times per second, 16 bits per sample, for each of the two (left and right) stereo channels. Without **compression**, a communication system needs to be

capable of sending about 1.4 million bits per second to transmit music effectively. Digital compression reduces the number of bits required to represent the information mathematically. The MP3 format, for instance, reduces the requirements for CD-quality audio to about one-tenth (128 or 192 thousand bits per second), which is easily handled by common 'high-speed' or 'broadband' internet services. Hence, we now have the ability to transmit music that sounds perfect to our analogue ears, an ability that, as noted in the previous section, changes music consumption patterns and threatens the traditional manner in which the music industry has operated.

Canada is and always has been at the forefront of communication technology, beginning with such events and people as the first phone call made in the world by Alexander Graham Bell from Brantford to Paris, Ontario, on 10 March 1876; the first transatlantic telegraph message from Poldhu, England, to Signal Hill in St John's, Newfoundland, at noon on 12 December 1901; and the first radio broadcast, by Canadian Reginald Fessenden, on Christmas Eve, 1906. We were the first nation to launch a domestic communication satellite and the government of Canada has maintained a commitment to both speed and capacity. According to *Computer*

> ## ⟫ BOX 6.7 REGINALD FESSENDEN
>
> Christmas Eve 2006 marked the 100th anniversary of the world's first voice broadcast, by Reginald Aubrey Fessenden (1867–1932), a Canadian inventor born in Knowlton, Quebec. Fessenden's technical achievement was the development of the heterodyne principle, a process of mixing modulated radio signals that is still basic to modern AM radio. By the time of his death Fessenden had developed 500 patents that were effectively infringed on by emerging large corporations such as RCA (the Radio Corporation of America). In 1928, the US Radio Trust finally acknowledged Fessenden's contribution in an admission of what would be seen as patent infringement today and granted him the enormous but—relative to his vital invention—paltry sum of $2.5 million. He died in Bermuda four years later.

Industry Almanac (2005), there are over 6.7 million broadband subscribers in Canada, ranking eighth in the world (behind much more populous countries).

Increased Flexibility in Production and Distribution

In the last two decades, the traditional, centralized, capital-intensive model of communication media has been eroded by digital media. In the late 1980s, desktop publishing brought layout and design of books and magazines to anyone with a computer and a laser printer. In the mid-1990s, the web brought a new form of almost zero-cost global distribution online. In the late 1990s and early 2000s, inexpensive digital tools transformed music and video production and independent producers were increasingly able to reach audiences directly via social networking sites such as MySpace and FaceBook. Producers are bypassing the traditional middlemen and connecting directly with consumers in a phenomenon known as **disintermediation**.

But a counter-trend is developing. Some call it re-intermediation, in which a new breed of filtering agencies is emerging. A good example is Apple Computer's iTunes music store, which presents a new mechanism for filtering, sorting, and, more importantly, promoting music available online. YouTube provides another example, whereby hundreds of millions of pieces of video are available free. These re-intermediators have established their own brand identity and presence. With the burgeoning of content, the traditional challenges of producing, manufacturing, and distributing product are being replaced by the provision of a wide range of content filtered, organized, and capable of being sampled and remixed in new ways. What makes this possible is not just a wealth of content, but an enormous increase in the amount of readily available information *about* the content, through blogs, reviews, tags, comments, and cataloguing data. As Chris Anderson points out in his 2006 book, *The Long Tail*:

> Consumers…act as guides individually when they post user reviews or blog about their likes and dislikes. Because it's now so easy to tap this grassroots information when you're looking for something new, you're more likely to find what you want faster than ever. That has the economic effect of encouraging you to search farther outside the world you already know, which drives demand down into the niches. (Anderson, 2006: 56)

Production services markets also are changing. China and India have become powerhouses of production to Western specifications. It is only a matter of time before they take over an increasing amount of content creation and design and go directly to the market for confirmation.

Models and Databases: Controlling Things and Processes

Computers are and always have been about **models**; the earliest computers were used to construct a model to allow projections of reality. Today, the mother of all information technologies is the **database**—most commonly, the relational database that structures information as collections of rows and columns and the web of interrelations between them. By collecting a large amount of real-world data as they are produced, and placing this material in a database, one can develop a sophisticated model with an immense amount of power to analyze what has gone before, understand what is happening currently, and predict what will happen next. Google's statistically improbable phrases (SIPs) allow discourse communities to be identified and publications of interest to be brought to the attention of consumers. (Perhaps the best explanation of statistically improbable phrases is to cite some examples. Phrases such as 'content analysis' and 'mass communication' are highly probable in documents dealing with analysis of communication and, although occasionally used, are highly improbable in normal discourse.) No doubt, the spy services of various nations use the same techniques to try to identify and track terrorists or political and ideological enemies. In the aftermath of the 13 September 2006 shooting at Dawson College in Montreal, in which one woman was killed and

19 other people were wounded by a gunman who then killed himself, some wondered whether analysis of websites might allow prior identification of potential murderers. Others, quite rightfully as well, worry about intrusive government monitoring of the communications of citizens.

Developing and analyzing databases of information in an effort to create new systems and processes of control is a growing field of study. Manufacturing relies on computer modelling and feedback. The emerging field of bioinformatics merges computer science with genetics, as researchers populate vast databases with genetic information, seeking to understand genetics through constructing computer-based models of the human (and many other species') genome. The combination of anthropological techniques (ethnography) with biological data into ethnobiology is allowing two different realms of information to be merged.

Such activities are sometimes referred to as 'topsight' and the pursuit of topsight is one of the major thrusts of high technology today. Every electronic transaction is recorded and the sum total of transactions creates a body of data, which, in turn, can be mined for valuable information. This information can then be used by the person who collects it or it can be sold to another party. The direct recording of information also results in a net decrease in the costs of the transactions. No longer is paying for an item one function, assessing the store's stock levels another, counting cash yet another; with electronic transactions all this and more are rolled into one. Yet, effectively, such activities represent a scaling up of processes normal to small business. The small business often knows its customers intimately: 'The usual, Mr Wodehouse?' Computerization of information allows the intimacy of such interactions to be synthesized. Some feel uncomfortable with such machine synthesis, and many would claim it makes a poor (as well as alienating) attempt at knowing the customer or, for that matter, of knowing its product. For example, people who have ever purchased anything online from Amazon have probably recognized the ludicrous suggestions of what else they might be interested in buying.

Nuisances, Problems, Dangers

With new capabilities and advantages come new challenges and dangers. Though plenty has been achieved in the past few decades thanks to communication technology, a number of interesting problems have arisen.

System Vulnerability

Moving to a computer-dominated, digital world introduces certain vulnerabilities, some a result of human intervention, others a result of nature. A major cosmic event involving substantial electromagnetic disturbances could wipe out the increasingly delicate computer systems on which we rely. Gophers have been known to chew through the coatings on optical cables! Satellites are vulnerable to the forces of the universe, as Canada learned when two of its communication satellites were hit with cosmic particles. Just as thieves exist in the real world, they populate cyberspace. Systems exist to protect sensitive data like credit card numbers (as well as passwords, pins, and other identity tokens). Usually, such tokens are encrypted before being transmitted over the network. **Encryption** technology uses complicated mathematics to scramble a message and render it as incomprehensible as possible. Only with the correct key (a number or string of characters) can the message be unscrambled. But, as with locks on doors, whatever can be encrypted can also be cracked, given enough effort. Most day-to-day encryption (such as that which protects your communication with your bank online) is crackable. Practical, real-world data security—as with physical locks—is concerned with making things *secure enough* to make it not worth an attacker's while. Nothing is ever 100 per cent secure.

Computer users—especially those using Microsoft Windows—spend a good deal of time and trouble dealing with viruses. While several companies make anti-virus tools, they are only able to barely keep up with new viruses; one can never be 100 per cent safe. Viruses in combination with encryption-cracking schemes can be particularly nasty, with thousands of virus-infected computers being hijacked to participate in a distributed cracking project.

In January 1999 the Air Miles program and its customers were shocked to find thousands of

❖ BOX 6.8   CANADIAN SCIENTISTS CRACK CODE FOR TRACING ANONYMOUS EMAILS
By Lesley Ciarula Taylor

Engineers and computer scientists at Concordia University have cracked the code for tracing anonymous emails.

For the first time, said data-mining expert Benjamin Fung, analysts have used the complex algorithms and almost imperceptible human quirks that make up the concept of 'frequent pattern' to work out each person's unique email fingerprint or 'write-print'.

'The people who wrote the email don't even recognize what they are doing', Fung told the *Star*. 'One of the features we break down is vocabulary richness. That would be hard to increase quickly.'

Other telltale evidence of the mystery writer can come from common grammatical mistakes, an unconscious extra space between each paragraph or patterns in punctuation.

'We've collected thousands of features to find the different combinations', Fung said.

The combinations are the key. All of the suspects may misspell 'consensus', but not all of them misspell 'consensus', use commas instead of periods, and think 'none' takes a plural verb.

'Everyone has a unique combination. We see it as quite useful in criminal investigations.'

The cyber-forensic tool, reported in the journal *Digital Investigation*, can ferret out the author of emails used for phishing, spamming, cyber bullying, email bombing, child pornography and sexual harassment, among others.

Right now, said Fung, it's a first-stage tool in a criminal investigation with an ability far beyond [what] simple humans have to pick up the author's 'write-print'.

It does have its limits. An investigator can capture the Internet provider (IP) of an email and thus trace it to one house or one office. From there, the 'frequent pattern' system can weed out other users and find the culprit.

But can it trace an anonymous email sent from an internet café?

No, said Fung. 'We can at most infer the gender and the nationality.'

Still, researchers' tests produced an 80 to 90 per cent success rate in finding the author from a field of about 10 people and 70 per cent from a pool of about 20 suspects.

The next stage of research will be to apply the data-mining method to the even shorter texts of instant messaging, chat rooms and social media, said Fung.

Source: 'Canadian scientists crack code for tracing anonymous emails', by Lesley Ciarula Taylor, March 8, 2011. Reprinted with permission by Torstar Syndication Services.

'confidential' customer files open for viewing to passing web browsers. While the problem was fixed quickly, the vulnerability of information collected by others is illustrated by this unintentional breach of security—and this example did not even involve outside hackers breaking into the site. Even though the files do not contain credit card numbers, to make them publicly available is an invasion of privacy. Or is it? Has Air Miles not invaded the privacy of the consumer in the same way in which that privacy obviously has been violated through its public availability? To frame the question differently, does the number of people who see the information determine whether the privacy is invaded? Air Miles and other organizations with which you deal usually collect information with your agreement. It is part of the fine print that you will find in many products and services agreements. Air Miles rewards you

with points for giving them this information. Many organizations sell their data lists to others. That, too, can be seen as an invasion of privacy even if

Source: © istockphoto.com/Yong Hian Lim

Unsolicited bulk email messages—known commonly as 'spam'—are a common means for spreading computer viruses.

the intent of such organizations is not illegal. These are issues that must be broached if we are going to address adequately the issue of system vulnerability.

As if attempts to disrupt normal internet activity by technically defeating a system via spam, viruses, and encryption-cracking were not enough, we must also consider the role of human beings in the techno-social internet ensemble and examine the vulnerabilities of millions of online users.

One of the most common examples of online fraud is 'phishing'. You receive an email message from your bank or other company with which you have a relationship in which you are told of some new feature or change to their service. All you need to do, it tells you, is to click on the provided link, log in, and update your account. The problem is that the site you are asked to connect to is not the bank, and so when you type in your identification number and password, you are unknowingly giving this information to the people behind the scam. For very little investment (it costs little to send an email to hundreds of thousands of people), even a small percentage of people who respond by following the link and 'logging in' can pay off for these crooks.

Extreme fraud involves stealing the identity of another. According to the Ontario Privacy Commissioner, Ann Cavoukian, identity theft is 'an epidemic' in the US. Identity theft involves collecting enough information on someone that the fraud artist can begin to assume that person's identity. Knowing this to be a possibility, people who make extensive use of the internet routinely provide false information in response to the requirement by certain sites and internet services to provide a user identity, in order to protect themselves. The relative instability of identity and authentication schemes on the internet leads to opportunities for fraud on both small and large scales. More robust identification systems have not yet been developed, though various parties are working on an 'identity 2.0' system to replace the tangle of accounts, passwords, and partial identities most of us must contend with online, and that make easy work for the fraud artists.

Privacy

As our lives become increasingly mediated by electronic technologies information regarding our health, financial status, preferences, and other personal information is being monitored and stored in massive databases. Every time we visit a medical facility, fill out an application, give out our social insurance number, or even sit down at a computer, the chances are that information about the nature of that activity is being monitored and recorded. These records reveal much about ourselves and are often used by organizations to exact economic and political control over our lives.

For instance, companies often mine their customer lists in search of prospective customers for new services and products. Much of the junk mail and spam we receive by both snail mail and email finds us in this manner. A more sinister version of this scenario involves insurance and health records. For instance, pharmacists have been caught selling information to insurance companies about what prescriptions people were buying. Such information might be used to deny people certain types of medical insurance as our health-care system becomes increasingly 'user-pay'. Similarly, law enforcement agencies collect and maintain data on thousands of people who have never committed crimes. The reasons for keeping such files, as well as the implications they may have for those people, is not always clear. But 'no fly' lists that keep people from using public transportation without any explanation as to why they have been banned and similar types of exclusionary actions are a logical extension of such lists. And, in connection with both work and school, ICTs are often used to monitor people's performance, ensuring they behave in ways that employers and other officials deem 'appropriate'. There have been a number of cases, for instance, where employers and school administrators have used Facebook posts and other online materials to bar people from work and educational opportunities.

At the heart of these infringements on personal privacy is the issue of self-determination. As both public and private institutions enhance their abilities to shape and/or control the actions of private individuals, the individual's capability to negotiate the conditions under which she/he both works and lives is undermined. Consequently, personal freedom and the human interactions that flow from it are reduced to a series of heavily constrained choices—choices orchestrated by commercial and political forces outside of the individual's knowledge or control.

⠶ SUMMARY

This chapter began with some perspectives on technology that emphasize the practical, social, situated nature of technology. We reviewed several complementary theoretical perspectives of technology, including instrumentalism, determinism, substantivism, critical theory, and constructivism. We discussed the limitations of the first four and how theorists increasingly see technology as a phenomenon that, like other areas of social practice such as business, education, health, and families, exists within society and can be controlled by society for its own purposes. We noted how machines can be seen as socio-technical ensembles, as phenomena that have technical elements but are social in their application or manifestation. We emphasized how technology changes things rather than solves problems—positive and negative consequences of technology are always intertwined and, to some extent, unpredictable. We examined closure and how closure on a particular socio-technical ensemble leads to a determinist illusion that the machine/system/black box could only have developed in the way it finally did.

Communication technology is closely linked to control, and public policy in the past century has had a major impact on the particular socio-technical ensembles and the resulting industries with which we now live. Digitalization and **technological convergence** have reopened the same policy problems in the twenty-first century. How to provide for the greatest social benefit, given the technologies and industries currently emerging, is a question that may not be answered with replications of twentieth-century solutions. We also described the fundamentally different dynamic the internet brings to the fore and how this dynamic is changing the copyright law.

The social rationales most often used in favour of technological development highlight health and education. On the other hand, the realities of technological communication systems, once they are introduced, involve commercial exploitation. Communication technology, like all technology, does not immediately transfer to developing societies. Some basic concepts in the regulation of communication technology are individual rights, collective rights, privacy, and intellectual property.

Communication technology has come a long way since the simple electric current in a wire that powered the telegraph 150 years ago. Optical fibres can be impregnated with rare earths to serve as natural amplifiers, a process called *rare-earth doping*; cable signals can ride free on power lines; children's toys have more computing power than the desktop computer of a decade ago; and hundreds of thousands of individuals can come together to create vast information resources or to lobby for socio-economic change.

Computers have combined with communication to make location irrelevant to the efficacy of personal communication. Video, audio, data—any kind of information—can be transmitted with ease to any location in the world and into outer space. Production need no longer be highly centralized because high-quality transmission technologies (hardware) is relatively portable and inexpensive, so much so that protection of intellectual property has become problematic. Ease of communication gradually is creating both a global village and a global marketplace of producers in which dominant economies can outsource production to inexpensive labour pools.

Previously complex tasks have been simplified and made less expensive, and new tasks have emerged hitherto undreamt of. Objects can be located on maps that are drawn with ease. Vast pools of information are readily available. Behaviour of many different kinds can be monitored and patterns identified that are a surprise even to those whose behavioural patterns are being monitored.

These developments come at a cost. Communication systems that people have come to need and rely on can be shut down by natural forces and by sabotage. No information is entirely secure because, just as computers can build walls, other computers can knock them down. Active internet users can become unwitting victims of spam and viruses. Not only individual computers, but whole systems can be shut down. With copying being so difficult to control, corporations are vulnerable to piracy and sabotage. Individuals can have their identities stolen and any electronic transaction can be accessed by a determined cracker/hacker.

Although communication has a cultural component, the development of communication technologies is firmly within the political and economic domain.

Canada, France, and certain other nations continue to attempt to preserve cultural communication against the ravages of information and entertainment exporters led by the US. What the next balancing of interests will be cannot easily be forecast. Indeed, the evolving shape of society as affected by the dynamics of digital communication technologies remains a matter of speculation.

As McLuhan said: 'We shape our tools....' Through innovation and the enactment of policy, especially in the context of the evolving power of communication technology, we shape technology, as well as its industrialization. McLuhan added: 'thereafter our tools shape us.' Yet, there has been very little consideration of the macro implications of the development of the information sector. This lack of prior consideration is part of the technological imperative, which assumes that any unforeseen problems can be solved in time by still newer technological solutions. Today, for example, we hear such arguments in regard to climate change and environmental degradation. The blithe acceptance by society of technology because it means economic gain, at least for some, blinds us to considering the desirability of technological developments for society as a whole, whether those developments involve health, entertainment, war, fashion, or life itself.

KEY TERMS

RELATED WEBSITES

Backbone Magazine: www.backbonemag.com
Backbone is a Canadian magazine with insights into technology and the web.

Book distribution: www.amazon.com; www.chapters.indigo.ca
Competing with the huge American online bookseller Amazon.com is Chapters/Indigo.

CANARIE: www.canarie.ca/en/home
The CANARIE website carries a wealth of information on Canada's data network.

Convention on the Protection and Promotion of Diversity of Cultural Expressions: www.pch.gc.ca/pgm/ai-ia/rir-iro/gbll/convention/index-eng.cfm
This site provides background and analyzes Canada's interests with respect to the convention.

Lawrence Lessig's Creative Commons: http://creative commons.org
Lessig's Creative Commons site is a good lead into any discussion of copyright in the context of new technologies.

RiP! A Remix manifesto: **www.nfb.ca/film/rip_a_remix_manifesto**
This major award winning film explores issues of copyright and intellectual property in the information age.

Open Source Cinema: www.opensourcecinema.org
As the site explains, it 'lets you create your own videos online, remix media that you have on your computer,

as well as remix other people's media from places like YouTube and Flickr.'

Wired **magazine: www.wired.com**
Wired is an influential source of opinion on new media. It touts Marshall McLuhan as its patron saint.

❖ FURTHER READINGS

Anderson, Chris. 2006. *The Long Tail: Why the Future of Business Is Selling Less of More*. New York: Hyperion. An examination of market transformations in cultural goods such as books and music when display/retailing costs are reduced to negligible amounts.

Barney, Darin. 2005. *Communication Technology*. Vancouver: University of British Columbia Press. A good historical discussion of the relationships between ICTs and democratic processes in the Canadian context.

Bradley, Dale. 2010. 'Balance or betrayal: Copyright reform and the right to culture in the digital age', in Leslie Regan Shade, ed., *Mediascapes*. Toronto: Nelson. 356–71. A good overview of the issues of copyright reform in Canada.

CRTC. 2010. *Navigating Convergence: Charting Canadian Communications Change and Regulatory Implications*. Ottawa: CRTC. A CRTC report on trends

and development in media convergence in the Canadian context and some of the regulatory issues it raises.

Feenberg, A. 1999. *Questioning Technology*. New York: Routledge. An analysis of the nature of technology, including a review of various theories that attempt(ed) to explain technology.

Lessig, Lawrence. 2001. *The Future of Ideas: The Fate of the Commons in a Connected World*. New York: Random House. Lessig argues that established corporate interests are moving with considerable speed and force to shut down the creative and innovative space that the internet created through such means as copyright law.

Steeves, Valerie. 2010. 'Privacy in a networked world', in Leslie Regan Shade, ed., *Mediascapes*. Toronto: Nelson, 341–55. A good discussion of some of the central issues regarding privacy and ICTs.

❖ STUDY QUESTIONS

1. Using a concrete example, such as broadcasting, radio, the internet, or computers, outline the three elements of technology and how they interact to influence society.

2. Open software strives to take control of technological development out of the hands of big corporations. What is the state of open-source software development and is it a viable alternative to proprietary software?

3. If technology is developed according to humanistic concerns, such as serving the health and

education needs of society, why does technology seem to serve industry? Provide examples in your discussion.

4. What new communication technology has affected your work or personal life?

5. Is the legitimate use of technology impinging on our personal privacy? In what ways?

6. Which theories of technology have most to offer?

CHAPTER 7

The Formation of Public Policy

No other country is similarly helped and embarrassed by the close proximity of the United States.

— ROYAL COMMISSION ON
BROADCASTING, 1957

OPENING QUESTIONS

- In what structured environment does communication occur?
- What is 'communications policy'?
- How is communications policy developed?
- What role does the public play in policy development?
- Why was communication subject to regulation internationally?
- What ideas guided communications policy development in Canada for most of the twentieth century?

Learning Objectives

- To understand what communications policy is.
- To realize that all countries establish rules by which communication is organized.
- To understand that communications policy results from a political process and is developed both by local governments and international governing bodies.
- To know the broad history of communications policy development globally and within Canada.
- To learn about the ideas on which Canadian governments based their communications policy for most of the twentieth century.
- To learn why these themes began to lose their force in the latter part of the twentieth century.

Introduction

Mass communication is a highly structured activity that takes place in a constructed environment, informed by communication technologies as discussed in the preceding chapter, but also by laws, policies, conventions, economic imperatives, guiding ideals, and public pressures. **Communications policy** establishes the rules of the game as laid down by international regulatory bodies and national and regional governments to ensure that media serve not only their owners and content creators, but individual citizens and society as a whole. The policy realm establishes rights and responsibilities individually and collectively. If media workers have the right to freedom of expression, they also have a responsibility to respect individuals' privacy and laws pertaining to libel, copyright, hate speech, etc. If media owners have the right to a reasonable return on their investment,

they also have an obligation to exert responsibly their market power and to respect the larger social and cultural goals of their community.

Policy development in any one jurisdiction is always part of a larger, international policy context because mass communication takes place across borders. Copyright laws are believed to have been introduced in the late fifteenth century, and international telephony has been regulated since the early 1900s. Policy is particularly germane today when digital technologies enable media content to penetrate every region of the globe in an instant.

The policy discourse in Canada, articulated through a series of **Royal Commissions**, task forces, public hearings, and committee reports, serves as the country's collective response to the question: What is communication for? All countries use the same basic radio technology, for instance, but

---

⫶ BOX 7.1   RATIONALE FOR MARKET INTERVENTION

Aside from the particularities of the Canadian case, there are a number of common reasons for market intervention—why the state intervenes in the communications sphere. These are summarized in the Report of the Federal Cultural Policy Review Committee (Canada, 1982a). The most common of these is **market failure**, that is, the inability of the market to serve properly the needs of society. For one thing, markets do not recognize the longevity of cultural products, and particularly those products that come to be regarded as classics in their genre. Typically, these works do not satisfactorily compensate their creator during the creator's lifetime; their value may not be recognized until decades after their creator's death (pp. 64–6).

Second, governments recognize that 'infant industries' may need state support until they can build their own markets. This is particularly the case in Canada, where a market is so dominated by foreign products— e.g., Hollywood films—that a competing domestic industry struggles to get off the ground in a marketplace that has been established and served by preceding producers (pp. 66–7).

Third, governments argue that cultural goods are 'merit goods', and deserve to be produced whether or

not there is a market to sustain them. Literary forms like poetry and some branches of the performing arts— symphony orchestras, opera companies—have 'manifest value' and would be very difficult to sustain without government subsidy. In other words, merit goods generate 'positive externalities', which are positive benefits to society, the value of which cannot be captured in the market relationship (pp. 67–8). For example, despite filling Toronto's Four Seasons Centre for 70 performances during the 2009–10 season and selling more single tickets than ever before, the Canadian Opera Company (COC) reported an operating loss of $194,000 for the year (Everett-Green, 2010). A *Globe and Mail* story reported that COC ticket sales, which were up 6 per cent, accounted for just 41 per cent of the company's revenues of $32.5 million. Fundraising and sponsorships made up 28 per cent, government grants accounted for 19 per cent, and production and space rentals made up a further 12 per cent. The deficit was made up with a cash infusion from the COC Foundation.

Other factors motivating communications policy development are the 'limitless variability of tastes' of the public, the large element of risk involved in cultural production, and the substantial investments of resources required to produce cultural goods (p. 69).

The Canadian Opera Company.

organize their radio systems in particular ways—who can own radio stations, how many stations they can own, over what geographical expanse they can broadcast, what kinds of programming they can carry, etc. Governments frequently intervene when they believe the market will not adequately serve their goals, as Box 7.1 explains; communications policy decisions reflect changes in social thinking.

In Canada, communications policies can be developed by governments in committee, subject to usual parliamentary procedures, or by public agencies like the Canadian Radio-television and Tele-communications Commission (CRTC). Depending on their impact, they may or may not generate much media or public attention or feedback. More significant policy initiatives, the emergence of new problems in the communications field, or the advent of new media technologies typically prompt federal and provincial governments to call for public hearings, either through Royal Commissions, task forces, or parliamentary committees. This allows governments to collect information, to gauge opinion from the public, from the business community, and from people directly involved, and to receive specific recommendations.

These consultative exercises inform, but do not determine, communications policy in any simple way. Typically, the resulting reports contain background information, valuable data, arguments from various perspectives, and pertinent recommendations to governments and government departments that emerge from months, often years, of study. The recommendations range from the pragmatic to the idealistic, from those that represent mere tinkering with the status quo to much more radical propositions. The government of the day weighs the political, economic, legal, and socio-cultural implications of these recommendations and decides if and how to act. Many of our most prominent cultural institutions—the National Film Board, the Canada Council, Tele-film Canada, the Canadian Radio-television and Telecommunications Commission, the Canadian Broadcasting Corporation—emerged from such recommendations.

Canadian government interventions in the communications field have been guided for most of the past century by a logic that frames the media, culture, and society in terms of the nation-state. While these interventions, and this logic, have never gone unchallenged (see Woodcock, 1985), they have faced particularly strong opposition in recent years on three fronts: the fiscal, the technological, and the philosophical (Gasher, 1997). First, can Canada afford to promote and protect Indigenous cultural activity? In an era of deficit reduction at all levels and in all departments of government, the cultural sector has not been spared budget cuts. The severity of these cuts means some cultural programs have disappeared and those that survive strain to fulfill their mandates. The flip side of this question is, of course, can Canada afford *not* to intervene? Second, with the rise of new, powerful, pervasive, and global communication networks, is it technologically feasible, even possible, for

The CRTC is Canada's regulatory body for radio, television, and telecommunications.

The CBC's headquarters in downtown Toronto.

Source: © Sarah Affleck

governments to intervene in communicative activities that stretch beyond their borders? For the time being, at least, Ottawa has answered affirmatively, but the question becomes more pertinent daily. Finally, should Canadian governments be involved in cultural production in the first place, given the costs, the private-sector alternatives, the global climate of liberalized trade, and concerns about what state intervention means for the independence of cultural producers?

In order to address these questions properly, we need to understand how and why Canada's communications policy structure emerged. This chapter situates the Canadian policy discussion within a global context, then addresses public involvement in Canadian policy development. Next, it traces the historical trajectory of com-munications policy in Canada through four defining twentieth-century policy documents. This section reveals the bases on which communications policy was forged until the 1980s: the project of building a nation and a national culture, and the concern that a strict

market approach to communications would lead to further dominance of the Canadian mediascape by the United States. The chapter concludes with a discussion of how those themes, while they remain pertinent, no longer resonate as they once did with the public, cultural producers, or governments. In Part III, Chapter 8 will look at the policy picture from the perspective of each of the communication sectors in turn, particularly as digitization and the emergence of the internet have raised new challenges and are breaking down the clear distinctions between sectors.

Back to the Future

The instantaneous global communication enabled today by ubiquitous digital technologies resurrects communication policy themes that have been played out for more than 500 years, at least since the invention of the printing press in the mid-fifteenth century. For example, we hear regular news reports that countries like Iran, North Korea, Myanmar (Burma), China, and Cuba seek to prevent or strictly control cross-border communication flows—e.g., banning foreign journalists, shutting down wireless networks, blocking access to certain websites, conducting surveillance on private email correspondence—particularly when those communications concern political subjects. However, all countries patrol their communications borders: to protect national security, to prevent the illegal circulation of materials (e.g., child pornography), to ensure the integrity of financial data, to protect national cultural industries, etc.

International communications scholar Cees Hamelink (1994) describes communications policy as a by-product of global contact between peoples, companies, and governments. Most of this contact prior to 1800 came about through meetings of individual traders, merchants, and diplomats. But following the expansion of trade markets during the Industrial Revolution—that led to the expansion of trade markets within and beyond Europe—and the French Revolution—that fostered nationalism throughout Europe and reinforced the sovereignty of nation-states—there was created greater need for multilateral state governance (ibid., 5–6).

Each of the communications actors required its own forms of international governance. As early as the sixteenth century, the postal system in Europe was regulated by bilateral agreements to facilitate and standardize the circulation of letters across borders. Expanding shipping and railway networks necessitated a more formal, multilateral agreement. The first meeting was held in Paris in 1863 and a subsequent meeting in Berne, Switzerland, led to the founding of the General Postal Union in 1874 (renamed the Universal Postal Union in 1878). 'The 1874 Berne conference introduced basic norms and rules that still hold today' (ibid., 7). These include the freedom of postal transport within countries belonging to the Union and the standardization of charges collected by each country for mail service between members.

Similarly, the development of telegraphy in the early nineteenth century required standardization and co-operation across borders. Again, this began with bilateral agreements, and the agreements between European countries in the 1850s provided the template for the 1865 International Telegraph Convention. The Convention adopted Morse code as its first international standard, and agreed to protect the secrecy of telegraph correspondence, to respect the right of all to use international telegraphy, and to reject liability for telegraph service providers (ibid., 7–8). Telephony was incorporated into the agreement in 1903 and in 1932 the International Telegraph Union and the International Radio-Telegraph Union merged to become what we know today as the International Telecommunications Union (ibid., 8–9).

The first international conference to discuss radio communication ('wireless radio-telegraphy'), held in Berlin in 1903, led to the 1906 Berlin Radio Convention, adopted by 29 countries. The Convention allocated frequency bands within the earth's electromagnetic spectrum for use by specific services (e.g., marine communication, emergency communication) at a time when radio was used for two-way, point-to-point communication rather than the broadcasting we are familiar with today. A subsequent radio conference in Washington in 1927 drafted a new Radio Convention and Radio Regulations to address a range of issues raised by radio broadcasting, from **frequency allocation** to station ownership and state control (ibid., 9–10).

The printing press prompted the notion of **intellectual property**, and it is believed that the first copyright laws emerged in Vienna in the late fifteenth century. Most of the earliest copyright laws protected only national citizens' works. The US Copyright Act of 1790, for example, did not protect foreign authors' works, which led to the rampant pirating of books by best-selling English authors, most famously Charles Dickens (Box 7.2) (ibid., 11). Some argue discriminatory US copyright law laid the economic basis for a burgeoning US publishing industry. A series of bilateral agreements on intellectual **property rights** were signed between 1840 and 1866, when the First International Convention on Copyright in Berne—the **Berne Convention**—granted protection to foreign published works. Further discussions produced the Berne Treaty on copyright in 1886.

> In the development of authors' rights the basic principles have been to ensure remuneration for an author by protecting his [*sic*] work against reproduction (for 50 years after the author's lifetime), to demand respect for the individual integrity of the creator, to encourage the development of the arts, literature and science, and to promote a wider dissemination of literary, artistic and scientific works. (ibid.)

Included within the definition of intellectual property is industrial property; national patent protections emerged in the late eighteenth and early nineteenth centuries. The first multilateral negotiations took place in Vienna in 1873 and led in 1883 to the Convention for the Creation of the Union for the Protection of Industrial Property (ibid., 14–16).

The founding of these international governing institutions was fraught with struggles over questions of political and economic sovereignty, and over questions of communicative power, as they continue to be today. As cultural production became large-scale cultural industry in the twentieth century, there were both cultural and economic concerns about media imperialism; already by the last half of the nineteenth century, three news agencies dominated the production and circulation of international news around the world, dividing global territories among themselves and

⋮⟩ BOX 7.2   CHARLES DICKENS

Source: © istockphoto.com/Ralf Hettler

The United States passed its first copyright legislation in 1790, but did not sign the Berne Convention, initially drafted in 1886 to provide mutual recognition of copyright between sovereign nations, until 1988 (Association of Research Libraries, 2010). For the most part, US copyright law recognized only the works of US authors.

Mass pirating of English-language books by foreign, especially English, authors persisted throughout the nineteenth century, despite the urgings of British (and some American) authors and politicians for Congress to recognize international copyright. Charles Dickens's *A Christmas Carol,* for example, sold for the equivalent of $2.50 in England and for six cents in the United States (Vaidhyanathan, 2001: 50). In January 1837, 55 British writers petitioned Congress, but a proposed bill to protect their intellectual property on US soil was opposed by US publishing houses and went nowhere (ibid., 51).

In 1842, Dickens himself toured the United States. 'At many stops, Dickens pleaded for international copyright. Yet his audiences were filled with fans who had happily paid very low prices for American-printed, leather-bound copies of his work, from which Dickens earned nothing. Dickens was asking his readers to pay more money for his product, and they were in no mood to do so' (ibid.). Dickens's account of his US tour, *American Notes* (1843), sold 50,000 pirated copies in the US in three days.

By the 1890s there was a veritable 'cheap books' movement in the US. While some major publishing houses, like Henry Holt (who published Thomas Hardy's books), operated on a 'courtesy principle' and respected foreign authors' copyrights, they were competing with less scrupulous cheap-books publishers who created 'chaos' in the US publishing industry (ibid., 52–3).

The historical American recalcitrance with respect to international copyright seems ironic today, when the US, one of the world's largest producers of cultural materials, chastises, and pursues legal remedies against, countries like China that flaunt intellectual property agreements.

---

thus monopolizing the framing and definition of current events. By 1914, the major Hollywood film companies had captured 85 per cent of the world film audience (McChesney, 1997: 12–14). The United Nations Educational, Scientific and Cultural Organization (UNESCO) became the principal forum for discussion about how to resolve political tensions produced by the expansion of the world communications system, particularly between east and west during the Cold War and between the Global North and Global South that persist today. The World Trade Organization (WTO) has become the venue for discussions of the economic implications of communicative exchange.

It should be noted that provincial governments also develop policy particular to their needs, Quebec being the most obvious example. If governments privilege the collective concerns of their jurisdictions—sovereignty, identity, the economy—non-governmental organizations (NGOs) like Amnesty International and Reporters Without Borders foreground basic individual human rights, including the **right to communicate**, privileging the universal application of such rights according

Source: © Bidermann/Dreamstime.com

Students march in an Amnesty International demonstration. With a presence in over 150 countries, Amnesty International works to protect human rights worldwide.

to such conventions as the **Universal Declaration of Human Rights** (Box 7.3).

All democracies respect rights such as freedom of expression and freedom of the press, but in practice these rights are heavily constrained when so much of our public communication takes place through mediated forms, and when so few of us have access to those forms. Thus, a push emerged in

the late 1960s advocating the right to communicate, an attempt to further democratize communication in general and the media in particular. As Marc Raboy and Jeremy Shtern (2010: 31) explain: 'The movement to establish a right to communicate is largely based on the premise that freedom of expression does not comprehensively address the social cycle of communication in modern, technologically mediated societies.' A right to communicate would ensure that everyone has the right to the information she or he needs, provide for a balanced information exchange between persons, regions, and countries, insist communication structures promote two-way communication, ensure that people acquire basic communication skills, and guarantee room for active social participation as well as individual privacy. The right to communicate was recommended by the UN's MacBride Commission in 1980, but largely disappeared from the policy agenda until it was resuscitated by civil society groups in 2001 as part of discussions of the World Summit on the Information Society (ibid., 34–5; Ó Siochrú, 2010: 41–2; see also Chapter 11).

❖ BOX 7.3 UNIVERSAL DECLARATION OF HUMAN RIGHTS

The Universal Declaration of Human Rights was the first global statement outlining the basic elements of non-negotiable human rights and the foundation for international human rights law. Its first draft was written by a Canadian, John Peters Humphrey, a legal scholar who was appointed the director of the Human Rights Division of the UN Secretariat. The 30-article document was adopted by the United Nations General Assembly on 10 December 1948. Canada was one of 48 countries voting in favour of the declaration.

Article 19 of the declaration speaks most directly to communication: 'Everyone has the right to freedom of opinion and expression; this right includes freedom to hold opinions without interference and to seek, receive, and impart information and ideas through any media and regardless of frontiers.' The full document can be found at: www.ohchr.org/EN/UDHR/Pages/Introduction.aspx.

Source: Eliza Massey / McGill University Archives, 2002-0086.04.186. Provided for research purposes only. Copyright Eliza Massey.

John Peters Humphrey.

The Public in Public Policy Formation

The formation of communication policy necessitates a tricky balancing act between individual and collective needs, and between universal principles and national and regional exigencies. For a country as diverse as Canada, it is doubly perilous. How do you accommodate the individual and collective communications needs of a relatively small population occupying the world's second-largest country, most of whom live close to the border with the United States, the world's richest and most powerful media empire? How do you balance the needs of individuals with the collective needs of francophone and Aboriginal Canadians and other minority groups? How do you ensure Canadian voices are heard without foreclosing Canadians' access to the international mediascape? And how do you ensure Canadians' voices are heard on all of these questions in the policy development process?

The issue of whether public opinion matters to policy formation is an important one in a country that has gone to considerable effort and expense establishing task forces and Royal Commissions to study issues ranging from foreign investment to national cultural development. While most analysts would agree that public opinion matters, *how* it matters is not clear (Gasher, 1998). Is public consultation merely a public relations exercise, or does it play a part in policy decisions?

A consideration of who constitutes 'the public' participating in such inquiries must be central to any discussion of this policy institution. While hearings are open to anyone wishing to participate, they most often attract interested parties—industry stakeholders, labour leaders, organized pressure groups—rather than disinterested citizens. While this recognition does not negate the importance of public consultation to policy formation, it qualifies substantially the extent to which such inquiries can be seen as impartial surveys.

In a study of the adoption of federal Royal Commission and task force recommendations on the national question from 1951 to 1987, Sylvia Bashevkin insists that policy research remains inconclusive about the relationship between public opinion and policy formation. What the research has suggested, Bashevkin argues, is that public opinion may serve as both an antecedent to and outcome of formal public consultations. First, 'a strong reservoir of public support' makes it easier for governments to implement recommendations (Bashevkin, 1988: 394). Second, and conversely, clear-cut divisions in public attitudes render policy implementation more difficult. Finally, Bashevkin maintains, 'policy research in Canada and elsewhere suggests that governmental action frequently coincides more closely with elite- than mass-level opinion', especially when mass-level opinion is polarized (ibid., 394). From her particular study, Bashevkin concludes that 'opinion matters depending on who expresses it' (ibid., 407).

Paul Litt (1992) and Marc Raboy (1995b) reach very different conclusions about public input into the policy process from their respective case studies of the Massey-Lévesque Commission (the Royal Commission on National Development in the Arts, Letters and Sciences, 1949–51) and the Broadcasting Act of 1991. In spite of the Massey-Lévesque Commission's boast of having heard 'the voice of Canada' (Canada, 1951: 268), Litt depicts the Commission's proceedings as exclusive to an elite group of cultural nationalists and academics. Raboy, on the other hand, maintains that the transparency of public debate on broadcasting between 1986 and 1991 allowed certain social groups to be included in the rewriting of the Broadcasting Act. Litt (1992: 4) argues that Massey-Lévesque was commandeered by Canadian cultural nationalists and interest-group politics, and dismisses as 'hogwash' the Commission's suggestion that it heard a representative sample of public opinion— let alone 'the voice of Canada' (Litt, 1992: 53–4). 'The commission had mobilized a constituency that would generate interest in its report and maintain political pressure for government action in cultural affairs. In the process the commission itself was transformed from a stolid official investigation into something of a national crusade. The highbrows were on the march' (ibid., 55).

Raboy concluded from a five-year study of the process that led to the revised Broadcasting Act that 'the transparency of public debate [was] essential in giving access to social groups who would otherwise have little influence on the process' (Raboy, 1995b: 457). Specifically, public input was responsible for enshrining the rights of women, ethnic groups, First Nations, and disabled persons in the new Act and for reinforcing the public-service principle of Canadian broadcasting. In this case at least, argues Raboy, the policy process was 'an important site of public action'.

The studies by Bashevkin, Litt, and Raboy underline the case-specific nature of the relation-

ship between public input and policy formation. If, in general terms, the policy process remains a site of contest, negotiation, and power, each of these contests produces a particular conjuncture of contestants exercising varying degrees of power—such as cabinet ministers, commissioners, lobbyists, and individual members of the public—wrestling with issues in an atmosphere that may be more or less politically charged. At the same time, the consultations are informed by the historical juncture at which they take place. As we will see in the reading of four key twentieth-century

❖ BOX 7.4   MAJOR COMMUNICATIONS POLICY DOCUMENTS

The following are key communications policy documents that have informed governments for the past 80 years. The reports, available through most public and university libraries, are written in a clear and accessible style and are valuable to researchers for the data and analysis they contain, but also for the language they use to talk about the respective roles of the public and private sectors in producing and delivering communications services to Canadians.

1929: Report of the Royal Commission on Radio Broadcast
1951: Report of the Royal Commission on National Development in the Arts, Letters and Sciences
1957: Report of the Royal Commission on Broadcasting
1961: Report of the Royal Commission on Publications
1968: Report on Book Publishing
1969: Report of the Task Force on Government Information
1971: Mass Media, The Uncertain Mirror: Report of the Special Senate Committee on Mass Media
1977: The Publishing Industry in Canada
1977: The Film Industry in Canada
1978: English Educational Publishing in Canada
1978: French Educational Publishing in Canada
1981: Report of the Royal Commission on Newspapers
1982: Report of the Federal Cultural Policy Review Committee
1984: The National Film and Video Policy

1985: Report of the Film Industry Task Force
1986: Report of the Task Force on Broadcasting Policy
1986: Sex-role Stereotyping in the Broadcast Media: A Report on Industry Self-regulation
1987: Vital Links: Canadian Cultural Industries
1988: Canadian Voices, Canadian Choices: A New Broadcasting Policy for Canada
1995: Competition and Culture on Canada's Information Highway: Managing the Realities of Transition
1996: Report of the Information Highway Advisory Council
1996: Making Our Voices Heard: Mandate Review Committee (CBC, NFB, Telefilm)
1996: Building the Information Society: Moving Canada into the 21st Century
1997: Preparing Canada for a Digital World: Information Highway Advisory Council
1999: Report of the Feature Film Advisory Committee
2000: From Script to Screen
2002: Canadian Content in the 21st Century: A Discussion Paper about Canadian Content in Film and Television Productions
2003: Our Cultural Sovereignty: The Second Century of Canadian Broadcasting. Report of the Standing Committee on Canadian Heritage
2006: Final Report on the Canadian News Media: Report of the Standing Committee on Transport and Communication
2006: Final Report of the Telecommunications Policy Review Panel

policy documents, answers to the question 'What is communication for?' are both important and subject to change.

The Aird Commission, 1929

The Aird Commission—officially, the Royal Commission on Radio Broadcasting—represents a watershed moment in communications policy history because it was the first public consultation of its kind and it resulted in the recommendation that a national and publicly owned broadcasting **network** be introduced into a field that up until then was dominated by local and privately owned radio stations (Vipond, 1992). As Marc Raboy (1990) has noted, after the Aird Commission, broadcasting policy in Canada became *national* policy. But the Aird Commission has significance beyond broadcasting. Besides proposing the initial blueprint for a Canadian radio network, Aird recommended, and helped to initiate, a particular pattern of cultural governance. Historian Mary Vipond (1992: 219) comments: 'A new view of the role of the government vis-à-vis culture and the media was thereby implied. Never before had the state been assigned such control over a cultural field.'

The first regulatory authority in Canada was the Ministry of Marine and Fisheries, administering the 1913 Radio-telegraph Act. The ministry licensed both transmitters and receivers. The first Canadian radio station to obtain a licence was XWA in Montreal in 1919, an experimental broadcaster established by the Canadian Marconi Co. By 1928, there were more than 60 radio stations operating across Canada under minimal regulation, many of them affiliated with newspapers and electrical appliance dealers (ibid.).

As the airwaves became more crowded through the 1920s, prompting disputes over both signal interference (from powerful American stations) and the content of broadcasts (especially religious broadcasts), the Canadian government recognized the need for a more comprehensive approach to broadcast policy. The Aird Commission was estab-lished in December 1928 by Minister of Marine and Fisheries P.J. Arthur Cardin. Earlier, Cardin had asked ministry officials to prepare a report with recommendations for federal broadcasting policy. That departmental report, submitted 15 November 1928, recommended the establishment of a Royal Commission (Bird, 1988: 37). Less than a month later, Sir John Aird, president of the Canadian Bank of Commerce, was appointed chair, and he was joined by two other commissioners: Charles A. Bowman, editor of the *Ottawa Citizen*, and Augustin Frigon, an electrical engineer who was director of Montreal's École Polytechnique and director-general of technical education for the province of Quebec (Canada, 1929a: 2). The Commission held public sessions in 25 Canadian cities between 17 April and 3 July 1929, during which time it received 164 oral statements, 124 written submissions, and held conferences and received written statements from all nine provinces (Canada, 1929b, 5–6, 18–21).

Vipond (1992: 213) argues that 'the genesis, mandate, and personnel of the Aird Commission predetermined its conclusions to an important extent.' First, Vipond points out that the Aird Commission's agenda was largely set by the Radio Branch of the Department of Marine and Fisheries when it established the terms for the Royal Commission in 1928. Second, she notes the biases of the Aird commissioners, especially those of commissioner Charles Bowman, who had written a series of editorials in the *Ottawa Citizen* in 1927 and 1928 advocating a public-service model for Canadian broadcasting, and Commission secretary Donald Manson, the chief inspector of the Radio Branch, who was dissatisfied with radio's status quo. Third, Vipond remarks that before the public hearings began, the commissioners—John Aird especially—were perturbed by NBC's assumption that Canada was part of its market.

Finally, Vipond (ibid., 207) notes that the social context of the late 1920s was conducive to the federal government's intervention in radio broadcasting. Nationalists in both English and French Canada had throughout the decade remarked (ibid., 207–8;

see also Raboy, 1990: 18–19, 29) on the threat posed to Canadian identity by 'the flood of American popular culture pouring over the border' (Vipond, 1992: 207).

Marc Raboy (1990: 7) has argued that the significance of the Aird Commission is that it 'infused broadcasting with a *national* purpose'. That is, 'Canadian broadcasting policy would be a national policy and the system it directed would have a clearly national vocation'. If the Aird commissioners described the purpose of their inquiry as 'to determine how radio broadcasting in Canada could be most effectively carried on in the interests of Canadian listeners and in the national interests of Canada' (Canada, 1929b: 5), they were invoking the the order-in-council that established their mandate. The Aird report, in other words, was neither the Canadian government's first word on radio broadcasting, nor were the commissioners starting from scratch in their attempts to develop Canada's first comprehensive broadcasting policy.

Source: Alexandra Studio/Library and Archives Canada/PA-122227

Members of the Aird Commission. From left to right, Charles Bowman, Sir John Aird, Donald Manson, Dr. Augustin Frigon.

The Aird Commission remained faithful to the agenda that had been established in its mandate. Most significantly, the Commission rendered radio a government institution, citing a European precedent. 'Everywhere in Europe we found inquiries being conducted under government auspices for the purpose of organizing broadcasting on a nation-wide basis in the public interest' (Canada, 1929b: 5). The Commission's order-in-council had proposed three options for action, all of which required state intervention in some form: private enterprise with government subsidy; a federally owned and operated system; or, a provincially owned and operated system. Citing public support for placing broadcasting 'on a basis of public service', the commissioners argued that only some form of public ownership could satisfy 'both the interests of the listening public and of the nation' (ibid., 5–6). Not only would radio broadcasting in Canada be a public service national in scope, but it would be federally owned and operated with 'provincial authorities' exercising full control over programming (ibid., 6–7):

A national company would own and operate all stations in Canada, each province would have a Provincial Radio Broadcasting Director 'who will have full control of the programs broadcast by the station or stations located within the boundaries of the province for which he [sic] is responsible', and each province would have an advisory council. The national company—the Canadian Radio Broadcasting Commission—would have a 12-member board of directors, three directors representing the Dominion and one from each province (ibid., 7). The proposed CRBC would also have the capacity for chain broadcasting to permit national broadcasts (ibid., 8). In addition to the existing licence fees on radio receivers—a user-pay system—the CRBC would be financed by a federal subsidy, a proposed $1 million for five years (ibid., 10).

If Aird's vision of the structure of radio was a likeness of federalism itself, the medium was also perceived as an instrument of national purpose. 'In a country of the vast geographical dimensions of Canada, broadcasting will undoubtedly become a great force in fostering a national spirit and

BOX 7.5   CANADIAN RADIO LEAGUE

The release of the Aird report in October 1929 coincided with the beginning of the Great Depression, which delayed serious consideration of its recommendations. The Canadian Radio League, founded in 1930 by Graham Spry and Alan Plaunt, led a campaign to support the Aird Commission's central recommendation of a national public radio system under Spry's famous slogan, 'The State or the United States'. The Canadian Radio League lobbied politicians and government officials and mustered public support for public broadcasting in the face of counter-arguments by the private broadcasting industry. R.B. Bennett's Conservative government passed the Canadian Radio Broadcasting Act in 1932, establishing the Canadian Radio Broadcasting Commission, which took over the radio facilities of the Canadian National Railway and established a rudimentary network of private and public stations broadcasting in French and English. The CRBC, however, struggled from a lack of funding, a weak mandate, and administrative problems. A new Canadian Radio Broadcasting Act was passed in 1936, establishing a restructured Canadian Broadcasting Corporation as a Crown corporation and ensuring its financial stability through a $2.50 radio licence fee.

interpreting national citizenship' (ibid., 6). Cited as one of the reasons radio should be subsidized by Ottawa was its potential to promote national unity (ibid., 10).

Programming, too, would be categorized in the terms of the nation-state. It would be predominantly Canadian and would have a considerable educational component, unlike the local and regional programming that had characterized private radio in Canada up to that point. Aird had determined that the primary purpose of the CRBC 'would be to give Canadian programs through Canadian stations' (ibid., 10). The reported stated: 'There has…been unanimity on one fundamental question—Canadian radio listeners want Canadian broadcasting' (ibid., 6).

Closely tied to the issue of Canadian programming was Aird's call for an emphasis on educational programming, and *national* education would be

central to this. Public education is, of course, part of the state's purview, and under the Canadian constitution's division of powers, it is the provinces' responsibility. By educational programming, Aird meant 'education in the broad sense, not only as it is conducted in the schools and colleges, but in providing entertainment and of informing the public on questions of national interest'. Educational broadcasts would include exchanges of programs with other parts of the country, but also foreign programming. Aird recommended that specified time slots be set aside for 'educational work' (ibid., 6–11).

The Aird report attributed its findings to 'the people' and thus asserted that the report spoke for the people of Canada. Aird posits the people as constituents and the Royal Commission as their representative body, even though the consultation process was limited in scope and attracted primarily interested parties (e.g., radio station owners and managers, broadcasting equipment manufacturers, radio club spokespeople). The report is full of attributions to public opinion.

Through their public consultation process, the Aird commissioners felt confident they could represent the interests of the Canadian public, in the same manner that politicians represent and speak for their constituents.

Besides its recommendation to nationalize radio, the Aird Commission raised two themes that would surface in subsequent reports and which inform Canadian communications policy to the present day: the relationship between communications media and commerce; and the cultural menace represented by close proximity to the United States.

Radio in Canada in the 1920s was run by local, private enterprise. Aird detected two related problems with this structuring. First, the private stations suffered from a lack of revenue, which 'tended more and more to force too much advertising upon the listener'. Second, stations were crowded into urban areas, where the revenue potential was greatest, resulting in the duplication of service in some areas and in other, less-populous areas being 'ineffectively served' (ibid., 6). Aird was especially critical of the commercialization of the radio airwaves through advertising, and the report recommended the elimination of 'direct advertising', defined as 'extolling the merits of some particular article of merchandize or commercial service'. Aird was more tolerant of 'indirect advertising', or sponsored programs. But, the 'ideal program should have advertising, both direct and indirect, entirely eliminated' (ibid., 10).

The distaste of the Aird Commission for advertising was matched by its displeasure that the majority of programs heard by Canadians originated in the United States. 'It has been emphasized to us that the continued reception of these has a tendency to mould the minds of young people in the home to ideals and opinions that are not Canadian' (ibid., 6). By international agreement, Canada had in 1929 only 6 exclusive and 11 shared broadcast wavelengths, and Aird recommended a more equitable division of the broadcast spectrum with the United States (ibid., 11).

In sum, Aird took a huge step in advocating state intervention in the cultural sphere. By endorsing the idea that radio broadcasting should be established on the basis of a national public service and governed by a national institution, the Aird report proposed a framework patterned after that of the nation-state itself and dramatically extended the state's power into cultural affairs. Aird also introduced into the policy discourse two recurrent topics: commercialization and Americanization. These themes would form the central tenets of communications policy formation in Canada.

The Massey-Lévesque Commission, 1949–51

The Louis St Laurent government commissioned the most sweeping study of the cultural field in Canadian history in 1949, a study that was to include within its scope museums, libraries, archives, historical sites, monuments, scholarship, voluntary societies, crafts guilds, and the mass media. The co-chairs of what was officially named the Royal Commission on National Development in the Arts, Letters and Sciences, 1949–51, were Vincent Massey, chancellor of

the University of Toronto, and Georges-Henri Lévesque, dean of the Faculty of Social Science at Laval University in Quebec City. The Massey-Lévesque Commission held 224 meetings, 114 of them public, received 462 briefs, and heard 1,200 speakers. The briefs included submissions from 13 federal government institutions, 7 provincial governments, 87 national organizations, 262 local bodies, and 35 private commercial radio stations and drew on a series of background research studies (Canada, 1951: 8).

The order in council establishing the Massey-Lévesque Commission, like the Aird Commission two decades earlier, gave it an agenda that situated the broad spectrum of cultural activity within the 'national interest'. The commissioners were asked to examine and make recommendations upon six areas: the operation and future development of such federal agencies as the National Film Board, the National Gallery, the National Museum, the Public Archives and Library of Parliament; Canada's relations with the United Nations Educational, Scientific and Cultural Organization (UNESCO) and other international bodies; relations between the government and national voluntary associations; methods to make people in foreign countries more aware of Canada; measures to preserve historical monuments; and 'the principles upon which the policy of Canada should be based, in the fields of radio and television broadcasting' (ibid., xxi, see also Shea, 1952: 10–11).

If Aird was careful to attribute to 'the people' the recommendation that radio broadcasting in Canada be organized on the basis of national public service, the Massey-Lévesque Commission took for granted the government's appropriation of the cultural sphere in the national interest. At one point, in fact, the report questioned whether culture and citizenship could even be distinguished as separate realms (Canada, 1951: 31). Consistent with the order-in-council from which it received its mandate, the Commission perceived cultural activity as a state responsibility.

In a sense, Aird served as inspiration for the Massey-Lévesque report; the commissioners credited Aird with providing the foundational rationale for radio as a national public service, and endorsed the results (ibid., 279). Invoking what Maurice Charland (1986) has called a logic of 'technological nationalism', the Commission made an analogy between the all-Canadian railway of the late nineteenth century and radio, positing them as the material bases for nationhood. 'Many Canadians in the 1920s...began to fear that cultural annexation would follow our absorption into the American radio system just as surely as economic and even political annexation would have followed absorption into the American railway system fifty years earlier' (Canada, 1951: 24).

Massey-Lévesque restated the principles on which national public radio had been established; it even recommended that the new broadcast medium, television, follow radio's model (ibid., 301–2). Massey-Lévesque not only reinforced the cultural policies that had turned radio and, subsequently, cinema—with the establishment of the National Film Board in 1939—into government institutions, but greatly broadened state jurisdiction in the cultural sphere. The Commission recommended, for example, the establishment of a new federal institution, the Canada Council, to lend funding support to the arts, humanities, and social sciences (ibid., 377–8). As the Canada Council's proposed mandate suggested, Massey-Lévesque brought a number of activities within the purview of the 'national interest'. Universities, for example, were assigned 'special responsibility for certain national problems' and were seen as 'recruiting grounds for the national services'. Massey-Lévesque further recommended the establishment of a national botanical garden, a national zoological garden and a national aquarium (ibid., 326). Even voluntary associations were cast as national institutions.

As with Aird, Massey-Lévesque applied a federalist model to culture. The National Gallery, for example, would serve not only Ottawa but the provinces as well, 'and to see its work as a whole one must leave the capital and visit the local galleries in the provinces' (ibid., 81). In other sectors, cultural activity was portrayed as complementary to federal ministries. For example, culture was to serve an external affairs function through exports and cultural exchanges. In a cold-war climate, Massey-Lévesque reminded us, culture is also national defence. 'Our military defences must be secure; but our cultural defences equally demand national attention; the two cannot be separated' (ibid., 275).

Culture, the report emphasized, is also part of what it means to be a self-respecting nation-state; it is a manifestation of civilization attained. Massey-Lévesque referred to national cultural institutions as part of our 'national equipment as a civilized country' (ibid., 380) and lamented the lack of two essential items from this store: a national library and a national historical museum (ibid., 323). 'It has been suggested to us that one measure of the degree of civilization attained by a nation might fairly be the extent to which the nation's creative artists are supported, encouraged and esteemed by the nation as a whole' (ibid., 182).

Cultural institutions not under state control were portrayed by Massey-Lévesque as potentially harmful influences. Most of the Commission's angst was reserved for cinema, which it described as 'not only the most potent but also the most alien of the influences shaping our Canadian life' (ibid., 50). What is not explained in the report is why it recommended no action in the feature-film sector, given the Canadian industry's domination by Hollywood.

Perhaps the most important national service provided by cultural activity in the Massey-Lévesque Commission's view was its capacity to engender a sense of the national among Canadians. Cultural activities, the report stated, 'lie at the roots of our life as a nation' and they are 'the foundations of national unity' (ibid., 284). Even handicrafts and handicrafts exhibitions 'can and do exert an important influence on our national unity' (ibid., 237). Massey-Lévesque accepted uncritically the concept of a national culture and that cultural production should be perceived in national terms. 'Canada became a national entity because of certain habits of mind and convictions which its people shared and would not surrender. Our country was sustained through difficult times by the power of this spiritual legacy.' Tradition is always in the making, the report noted, 'and individuals interested in the arts, letters and sciences throughout our country are now forming the national tradition of the future' (ibid., 4–5).

Cultural expression in the Massey-Lévesque report (ibid., 271) is the search for essence, the search for a 'Canadian spirit', a bond which defines as Canadian in their soul the constituents of the nation-state, no matter what their language, ethnicity, race, etc.

> We thought it deeply significant to hear repeatedly from representations of the two Canadian cultures expressions of hope and of confidence that in our common cultivation of the things of the mind, Canadians—French and English-speaking—can find true 'Canadianism'. Through this shared confidence we can nurture what we have in common and resist those influences which could impair, and even destroy, our integrity.

Such institutions as archaeological, art, and historical museums 'help to develop a Canadian spirit without raising questions of race, religion, or political convictions' the commissioners averred (ibid., 94).

Massey-Lévesque concluded that in painting, Canada has most closely approximated a sense of 'Canadian' art. 'Canadian painting, through its honesty and its artistic value, has become above all the other arts the great means of giving expression to the Canadian spirit' (ibid., 211). Yet, what had been achieved in painting had not been achieved in writing; Canada hadn't produced, the report regretted, a 'national literature' in either English or French. Canadian writers, critics told the Commission, 'are subject to the pull of a variety of forces', among them Canadians' 'historical ties' to Great Britain and their proximity to the United States (ibid., 223–5).

The Commission acknowledged differences within Canada, but it was divided as to their significance. Canada's demographic and geographical diversity inspired creativity; but difference was perceived as a potential threat to national unity.

'Through all the complexities and diversities of race, religion, language and geography, the forces which have made Canada a nation and which alone can keep her one are being shaped' (ibid., 4–5).

Regional difference, however, must contribute to national unity rather than 'sectionalism'. Acknowledging complaints that the CBC was 'excessively centralized' (ibid., 33, 298), Massey-Lévesque nonetheless upheld CBC radio as an example of a unifying cultural force.

> Canadian sectionalism is not yet a thing of the past, but it is certain that the energetic efforts of the Canadian Broadcasting Corporation in providing special regional programmes and informative talks, and in introducing a great variety of Canadians to their fellow citizens, have done much to bring us nearer together. From Vancouver Island to Newfoundland and from the Mackenzie River to the border, Canadians have been given a new consciousness of their unity and their diversity. (Ibid., 280)

A case in point was the Commission's position on native culture. Massey-Lévesque confessed an interest in Native arts and crafts 'for its own sake and because it affects the well-being of an important group of people' (ibid., 239), but endorsed the suggestion that 'the Indian can best be integrated into Canadian life if his fellow Canadians learn to know and understand him through his creative work' (ibid., 243). In this formulation, Native culture becomes a force for national unity.

As Aird had done, Massey-Lévesque placed the educational dimension in the foreground of cultural activity, and assumed responsibility for it. The Commission's explicit intention was that Ottawa support and promote cultural work of 'merit'. For example, the report discussed film 'chiefly as a means of furthering national unity and popular education' (ibid., 50), which may partly explain its neglect of the feature-film sector. The Commission expected a higher standard of programming from public radio than from private radio (ibid., 286). One of the dangers the Commission perceived in private commercial broadcasting was that such a system may produce 'many programs which are trivial and commonplace and which debase public taste' (ibid., 280–1).

Like Aird, Massey-Lévesque purported to speak for the people; many of its comments were attributed to the oral and written submissions it received. 'We believe we have heard the voice of Canada. We should like to think that we have recorded and reproduced this voice as clearly and as honestly as it came to us throughout our country and from so many of our fellow-citizens.' Despite this enthusiasm, the report notes, on the same page, that most of the evidence came from organized groups and, 'We heard very little from the citizen who represented no one but himself' (ibid., 268).

Massey-Lévesque also spoke to the issues of commercialization and Americanization. Faced with complaints from the private sector about government monopolizing film production and radio and television broadcasting, the report responded that the NFB and the CBC were protecting the nation 'from excessive commercialization and Americanization' (ibid., 58). The Commission was particularly forceful in answering criticism from private broadcasters. Claiming that the Canadian Association of Broadcasters was operating on 'a false assumption that broadcasting in Canada is an industry', the report stated bluntly: 'Broadcasting in Canada, in our view, is a public service directed and controlled in the public interest by a body responsible to Parliament' (ibid., 282–3).

The Commission shared Aird's distaste for broadcast advertising, while acknowledging its importance as a source of revenue, particularly with the introduction of the more costly medium of television to the CBC's portfolio. Massey-Lévesque, for instance, recognized that complete elimination of advertising from the national radio network was 'impracticable', depriving Canadian companies of a national audience for its advertisements and depriving the CBC of more than $2 million in advertising revenue. To ban commercial advertising from the national radio network, the commissioners argued, risked lowering the standard of programming and

might divert listeners to American stations (ibid., 290–1). These comments were echoed with regard to television.

Again, it may have been this anti-commercialism that explains the Commission's fleeting interest in commercial cinema. The report made no recommendations that government intervene in the commercial feature-film sector, and even registered its approval of Hollywood producing films in Canada that addressed Canadian themes (ibid., 367–8). As in radio, the Commission saw film in terms of a mixed economy, combining private and public investment in film production (ibid., 311).

With the exception of feature film, Massey-Lévesque was apprehensive about the US cultural presence in Canada. The report argued that Canada is culturally dependent in its 'uncritical use of American educational philosophy' (ibid., 16–17), in reading more foreign than domestic periodicals (ibid., 17–18), and in the reliance of Canadian newspapers on foreign, principally American, news services for their international news coverage (ibid., 62–3). The ultimate danger of such dependence was cultural annexation. The Commission's insistence that 'any network of private stations in Canada would inevitably become small parts of American systems' supported its recommendation to prohibit private radio networks in Canada (ibid., 288).

If the Commission revisited the themes of commercialization and Americanization that characterized the Aird Commission, Massey-Lévesque introduced the topic of financing to the cultural debate, a topic that has become central to policy discussions in our time. Unlike today, however, the financial bind was confined to the cultural institutions themselves and wasn't a reflection of the government's fiscal health. The Commission referred to a 'financial crisis' affecting both the CBC and Canadian universities; it recommended stable, long-term state funding to address the CBC's problem and to maintain its independence from government (ibid., 293–4). Similarly, the Commission recommended Ottawa assist the universities through annual contributions based on provincial population figures (ibid., 355).

In sum, Massey-Lévesque endorsed the federal government's initial cultural interventions and recommended Ottawa expand its responsibility in this field, framing the arts, letters, and sciences in terms of Canada's national interest. Not only specific media like radio, television, and documentary film were deemed part of the state's cultural dominion, but cultural activity in general was appropriated within the federal government purview. The Commission defined cultural production as a requisite element of nationhood, and thus perceived the cultural sphere as state jurisdiction. Even the sciences were given a national cast, as evidenced by the report's call for a *national* aquarium, botanical garden, and zoological garden.

Massey-Lévesque posited private enterprise as antagonistic to the nation-building project in Canada and counterproductive to its framing of culture as national culture. The Commission cited as proof the contrast between the meritorious and educational programming of the CBC and the 'trivial and commonplace' output of private radio. More importantly for the Commission, the commercialization of culture would mean its Americanization, casting the very project of nationhood itself in peril.

The Fowler Commission, 1956–7

The Fowler Commission—officially, the 1957 Royal Commission on Broadcasting—resulted from a Massey-Lévesque recommendation, that the subject of television broadcasting be reconsidered by an independent investigating body within three years of the beginnings of television broadcasting in Canada. Again, the Commission's agenda was largely set; the 2 December 1955 order-in-council establishing the Fowler Commission insisted that 'the broadcasting and distribution of Canadian programmes by a public agency shall continue to be the central feature of Canadian broadcasting policy' (Canada, 1957: 293).

Chaired by Robert Fowler, a Toronto lawyer who had previously sat on the Royal Commission on Dominion–Provincial Relations from 1937

to 1940 (the Rowell-Sirois Commission) and the Wartime Prices and Trade Board (established in 1939), the Commission held 47 days of hearings in 1956 in 9 of the 10 provinces (bad weather cancelled the hearings in Newfoundland). It heard 276 briefs from individuals and organizations and received an additional 600 submissions by letter. The Commission was asked to make recommendations on seven points, including CBC television policy, the provision of adequate programming for both public and private television, financing (how much and from what sources), and the licensing and control of private television and radio 'in the public interest' (ibid., 293–4).

As of December 1956, Canada had 189 radio stations, 167 of them private and 22 owned and operated by the CBC. Forty-two stations broadcast in French, the remaining 147 in English. The CBC was operating three radio networks: the 45-station Trans-Canada (17 stations owned by the CBC); the 50-station Dominion (one CBC-owned); and the 25-station French network (four CBC-owned) (ibid., 32–3). Canada had 38 television stations in operation, 9 of them owned and operated by the CBC and all of them tied either to the CBC's French or English networks. More than half of Canadian households (i.e., 2.3 million) had TV sets (ibid., 17, 34–5).

If the Massey-Lévesque Commission took state governance of culture for granted, as an obvious extension of Ottawa's authority, Fowler was much more reflective. By 1957 there were four international agreements pertaining to broadcasting in Canada (ibid., 17–18). Broadcasting in Canada was governed by two federal statutes: the 1938 Radio Act, amended several times; and the 1936 Canadian Broadcasting Act. The Fowler report noted: 'In Canada, Parliament has long since decided that there should be some degree of public control not only on *how* broadcasting will be conducted but also on *what* may or may not be transmitted by radio and television stations' (ibid., 20).

Prompted in part by private commercial broadcasters (represented by the Canadian Association of Radio and Television Broadcasters (CARTB)),

Fowler's initial question was: Is there a need for the state regulation of broadcasting in Canada? The Commission responded in the affirmative and cited public support for this conclusion. 'We are satisfied that for Canada this is a legitimate and proper function of the state, and under our constitution it is a function of Parliament' (ibid., 81).

Fowler explained its conclusion in four ways. The first was technological imperative. Rejecting the 'freedom of the press' analogy, which the CARTB had used to push for a devolution of state control of broadcasting, Fowler noted that the limited number of radio and television frequencies necessitated allocation and a state licensing system (ibid., 100–2). Second, Fowler portrayed broadcasting as too powerful a medium to permit a laissez-faire approach. 'Broadcasting is too important and its influence too great, to have the basic decisions as to those persons who shall be in charge of broadcasting removed from the control of those who are directly responsible to the Canadian people' (ibid., 100–2). On this basis, Fowler rejected CARTB's proposal to delegate broadcast regulation to an independent board of broadcast governors (ibid., 133). A third justification for state regulation was 'to restrain commercial forces from the excesses to which they may go' (ibid., 84–5). This meant prohibiting too much advertising and encouraging a stronger commitment on the part of private broadcasters to 'the public interest'. Re-asserting the primacy of the public interest, the Commission argued that 'it is not the freedom of the private station operator or the commercial sponsors that is important; it is the freedom of the public to enjoy a broadcasting system which provides the largest possible outlet for the widest possible range of information, entertainment and ideas' (ibid., 86). Finally, Fowler argued (ibid., 110) that state-regulated broadcasting was the only way to ensure Canadian broadcasting.

> If we want to have radio and television contribute to a Canadian consciousness and sense of identity, if we wish to make some part of the trade in ideas and culture move east and west across the country, if we seek to avoid engulfment by American cultural forces, we must regulate such matters as importation of programmes, advertising content and Canadian production of programmes.

There was, in other words, 'no choice' for Canada.

> We cannot choose between a Canadian broadcasting system controlled by the state and a Canadian competitive system in private hands. The choice is between a Canadian state-controlled system with some flow of programmes east and west across Canada, with some Canadian content and the development of a sense of Canadian identity, at a substantial public cost, and a privately owned system which the forces of economics will necessarily make predominantly dependent on imported American radio and television programs. (Ibid., 109)

As Massey-Lévesque had done six years earlier, Fowler restated the national public service basis upon which broadcasting in Canada had been defined since Aird. Fowler perceived Canadian radio and television as 'a single broadcasting system made up of both publicly owned and privately owned stations, under the control and supervision of a single agency responsible to Parliament, and that we think this is a unique and positive Canadian achievement' (ibid., 117). In this schema, Fowler saw private broadcasters as 'valued and essential partners with the CBC in the single Canadian broadcasting system' (ibid., 136).

While defending the national public service structure of broadcasting, the Fowler Commission nevertheless revealed some cracks in its foundation: the growing hostility of private broadcasters; complaints about the CBC's centralization in Montreal and Toronto; and the subsumption of difference—regional, French-English, ethnic—within the national whole.

The Fowler report acknowledged that Canadian broadcasting had to be representative. Regional needs had to be met and the Commission emphasized the need for programming 'as diversified and designed to satisfy as many different tastes (minority as well as majority) as economics and practicability may allow' (ibid., 75). Consistent with this, Fowler proposed a Board of Broadcast Governors that would be representative, with at least one of the 15 members from each of Canada's five regions: the Maritimes, Quebec, Ontario, the Prairies, and British Columbia (ibid., 94).

Fowler gave little weight to criticisms of the CBC's concentration in central Canada, describing Montreal and Toronto as 'necessarily' being 'the two principal programme production centres in Canada' (ibid., 71). Conceding that 'ideas' programs could more easily be decentralized, Fowler maintained that 'arts' programs benefited from central Canadian concentration. 'From the purely artistic point of view, the national audience deserves the best and in almost every case the best will be found in the larger centres.' A policy of 'indiscriminate decentralization' would mean 'the Canadian public will have to pay more money for less quality' (ibid., 70).

Fowler's auto-critique was similarly evident in its admission that state regulation defies 'nature', but is nevertheless essential to Canadian statehood.

> We are trying to do something that is not easy. The natural pressures are against us; the flow runs north and south and we are trying to make some part of it run east and west. The forces of economics are against us too, as they have been against many odd Canadian dreams and aspirations in the past. But this is one we had better work at, for it is really important if we are to keep a Canadian identity and culture; if there is, in fact, to be a Canadian force in the world. And that may be important to many people—both inside and outside Canada. (Ibid., 287)

The broadcasting system Fowler envisaged was not without cost, and the Commission saw 'its primary duty' as 'to deal with problems of business administration and finance' (ibid., 1–2), particularly as television service meant substantially higher

costs. The Commission portrayed national public broadcasting as a necessity for Canada, and similarly deemed the broadcasting system it favoured as worth the expense, especially in the context of a prosperous economy. 'It is…clear that we could have had cheaper radio and television service if Canadian stations became outlets of American networks. However, if the less costly method is always chosen, is it possible to have a Canadian nation at all?' (ibid., 9). Fowler's major recommendation was increased and stable multi-year financing, based on 10-year forecasts of cost estimates (ibid., 265–6).

The Fowler Commission adopted a pragmatic, yet condescending, view of the commercialization of Canadian broadcasting. By the mid-1950s, selling goods had become one of the 'four principal functions' of the broadcasting system (ibid., 44), yet the alliance of these four functions clearly was uneasy. Fowler described as 'a conflict of interest and motives' the private broadcaster's 'uncomfortable conflict between his desire to render a public service and his sound business instincts' (ibid., 85).

Fowler maintained the rhetoric of Aird and Massey-Lévesque in portraying the United States as a threat to Canadian culture. Repeating Massey-Lévesque's point that Canada's relationship to the US was unique—in terms of proximity, Canada's small, scattered population strung along the American border, and a shared majority language—Fowler noted: 'No other country is similarly helped and embarrassed by the close proximity of the United States' (ibid., 7–8). Like Aird and Massey-Lévesque, Fowler posited the **privatization** of broadcasting as the Americanization of Canadian radio and television (ibid., 230–3).

In sum, the Fowler Commission further reinforced the three themes that had legitimized state intervention in the cultural sphere in Aird and Massey-Lévesque. Fowler insisted that broadcasting remain a national service governed by the state, equating the interest of the nation-state—national unity, national identity—with the interests of the public in all regions of Canada. Fowler rejected the private-enterprise alternative by casting the full-scale commercialization of Canadian broadcasting with its Americanization. Fowler, however, also hinted at a new force in the communications policy debate: economics. With television, the costs of state governance had risen dramatically and thus state intervention in the cultural field was meeting increased resistance.

The Applebaum-Hébert Committee, 1981–2

The Federal Cultural Policy Review Committee was established in August 1980 by Minister of Communications and Secretary of State Francis Fox. Fox insisted the scope of Applebaum-Hébert be 'broad and include all the main programmes of the Federal Government' (Canada, 1982a: 369). Its mandate was to pick up where Massey-Lévesque had left off three decades earlier (ibid.,. 3–5).

Like the commissions discussed above, Applebaum-Hébert was not without an agenda. The committee published and distributed 50,000 copies of a discussion guide in December 1980 in order to stimulate public participation in its hearings. The guide introduced the 18-member committee, 'defined the field of inquiry', provided an historical overview of federal cultural policy, 'outlined challenges and options facing Canadian cultural policy in the years ahead', and invited submissions (ibid., 370). Some intervenors expressed dissatisfaction with the committee's restriction on policy options (Canada, 1982b: ii). Applebaum-Hébert held public hearings in 18 cities in every province and territory in 1981 (Canada, 1982a: 370).

The Applebaum-Hébert report represents a significant shift in thinking about the state's cultural role in general, and in attitudes towards the specific guiding principles by which state intervention had to this point been motivated and justified. While Applebaum-Hébert endorsed a role for the state, it re-directed it. Conspicuously absent from the report was the anti-commercial and anti-American rhetoric characteristic of the Aird, Massey-Lévesque, and Fowler reports.

The Applebaum-Hébert report was circumspect with regard to the principle of state intervention in the cultural field; its first three chapters provided a critical assessment of the history of cultural policy in Canada. The report sought to balance what it perceived as a continuing need for an active state role in the cultural sphere with a concern for cultural producers' independence from state influence and control. In a radical departure from this concern for cultural autonomy and the threat of 'official censorship' (ibid., 30–1), Recommendation 1, for example, called for the stipulation of the independence of federal cultural agencies in a Cultural Agencies Act 'in recognition of the fact that government activity in culture and the arts is subject to special considerations requiring a distinctive measure of autonomy' (ibid., 34). The committee insisted that federal agencies such as the Canada Council, the CBC, the National Arts Centre, the NFB, and the Canadian Film Development Corporation should be exempt 'from political direction in the form of ministerial directives of either a general or a specific nature' (ibid., 35–8).

Another element of the committee's insistence on the independence of cultural producers related to funding. 'If cultural life is to be autonomous and self-directed, it is important that it not become excessively dependent on one source of support—and especially on one government source' (ibid., 57). In the performing arts, for example, Applebaum-Hébert envisaged the following income sources: 'box office receipts, governments at all levels, and private donations from individuals, corporations and foundations' (ibid., 174).

Yet, the committee was not completely consistent on the autonomy question. Applebaum-Hébert endorsed collaboration between cultural affairs and international trade promotion, and between travelling performing artists and Canadian business interests abroad. The committee proposed a Canadian International Cultural Relations Agency to administer international cultural relations under the Secretary of State for External Affairs (ibid., 334–7).

Applebaum-Hébert is striking, too, for the absence of a national identity or a national unity discourse. This did not, however, preclude a commitment to maintaining Canadian heritage and to advocating greater representation of Canadian creations in existing cultural institutions. Applebaum-Hébert tied the preservation of heritage properties to Canadians' 'sense of place and continuity with their past' (ibid., 110). And the committee regretted the absence of Canadian materials in Canadian cultural institutions.

Nevertheless, Applebaum-Hébert maintained state governance as a central tenet. The committee was not deterred by the economic recession of the early 1980s, which created pressure on governments to curtail spending. Reflecting its support of a cultural role for the state, it recommended the creation of a federal ministry of culture (ibid., 46–7), the establishment of a Contemporary Arts Centre (ibid., 148), the introduction of a depreciation allowance and purchasing incentives to stimulate private demand for contemporary visual art (ibid., 151), and greater support for Canadian magazines (ibid., 225–6).

With regard to two central cultural institutions, however, the Applebaum-Hébert report advocated a retreat by the state. The committee recommended that the National Film Board be transformed into a research and training centre, delegating the bulk of its production activities to independent producers (ibid., 256–5); and it recommended that the CBC relinquish all of its television production activities, with the exception of its news programs, in favour of acquiring shows from independent producers (ibid., 292–4).

The Applebaum-Hébert report is particularly noteworthy for the break it made with the neat equation between the state's interests and those of the Canadian public in the cultural domain. Besides divorcing cultural producers from the nation-building project, Applebaum-Hébert acknowledged, and portrayed positively, regionalism and multi-ethnicity, referring in its opening chapter to 'the different cultural traditions that Canadians so cherish' (ibid., 8).

Applebaum-Hébert also signalled an important shift in attitudes concerning the private sector's place in cultural production. The report placed new emphasis on building audiences and markets for Canadian cultural products. Applebaum-Hébert was less interested in resisting capitalism's encroachment than in devising means by which to create space for Canadian voices. Building audiences was proposed as a strategy to increase public support for both culture and federal cultural policy.

Applebaum-Hébert cannot be described as fully embracing market principles and the commodification of culture. Rather, the report took a pragmatic stance. Cultural policy needed to nurture and enlarge audiences, but it also had to respond to cultural sectors that were not adequately served by market economics. Publishing was probably the best example of an area in which free-market principles did not serve the interests of Canadian culture. The committee conceded that it was possible for companies to profit from the publication of *certain* kinds of books, but it was more difficult 'to make any money or even to survive financially by publishing original Canadian books or periodicals of cultural significance' (ibid., 211–14). Nevertheless, there was growing acceptance in Applebaum-Hébert of the notion of 'cultural industries': a market-oriented, industrial-scale approach to cultural production (ibid., 80–2).

Finally, Applebaum-Hébert demonstrated none of the anti-American sentiment of previous commissions. The report lamented the dominance of American cultural products in the Canadian marketplace, not because of any pernicious American influence, but because Canadian cultural works were correspondingly under-represented—in publishing (ibid., 224), in sound recording (ibid., 240), in television broadcasting (ibid., 249–50), and in cinema (ibid., 252–8). In spite of this, Applebaum-Hébert refused a protectionist stance, preferring to recommend pro-active strategies by which Canadian cultural products could capitalize on the American-dominated industrial infrastructure, which the committee accepted as part of the cultural landscape.

Applebaum-Hébert maintained to a considerable extent the logic of state governance of the cultural sphere, but it did not do so unquestioningly. It shifted the state's role away from that of proprietor and regulator of culture towards the more comfortable roles of custodian, patron, and, especially, catalyst. Applebaum-Hébert is also remarkable for the extent to which it abandoned the three motivating themes that had been the basis of Canadian cultural policy for the preceding half-century. The committee discarded the schema that equated state governance of culture with its Canadianization, and the market governance of culture with its Americanization.

Re-evaluating Canadian Communications Policy

What we have seen through the evolution of Canada's communications policy discourse is a broad and fundamental re-evaluation of state involvement in the cultural sphere. What were once almost sacred cultural institutions—the CBC, the NFB—increasingly are perceived by some as expendable. There has been a shift in social values that applies specifically to three of the ideological pillars on which Canada's cultural policies have been based. The first of these pillars has equated the interests of the state with the interests of the Canadian public. The second has rejected the wholesale commercialization of cultural production in Canada. The third conceives of the United States as a force of **cultural imperialism** to be resisted. In this formulation, Canadian state intervention ensures Canadian sovereignty over cultural expression in the belief that the commercialization of culture would result in its Americanization and threaten Canadian culture and the bonds of nationhood.

The first signs of a shift could be detected in the Fowler Commission's report, which noted the rise of private-sector opposition to state intervention, concerns about the centralization—in Toronto, Montreal, and Ottawa—of Canada's principal cultural institutions, and the problem of satisfying regional and minority cultures within a larger national communications policy apparatus. The Applebaum-Hébert report may have best encapsulated the policy

shift in its credo that 'the essential task of government in cultural matters is to remove obstacles and enlarge opportunities' (ibid., 75). While we hesitate to generalize—each of the communications sectors faces very particular obstacles and opportunities, as we will discuss in Chapter 8—that would seem to be the prevailing theme of approaches to policy development since the 1980s.

There is no single reason for this shift, but it is clear that the equation positing the interests of the Canadian state with the interests of the Canadian people no longer holds. If the immediate post-war period and the years leading up to centennial celebrations in 1967 could be described as a period of strong Canadian nationalism, that sentiment was rivalled in the 1960s and 1970s by a growing regionalism. The 1960s saw the emergence of a strong Quebec nationalist movement that had both militant—the Front de Libération du Québec (FLQ) and the October

Source: CP Photo/La Presse files – Alain Roberge

Michel Tremblay, writer and playwright.

Claude Jutra, film actor, writer, and director.

Crisis of 1970—and progressive—the Parti Québécois forming the provincial government in 1976—elements. The sense of Quebec's distinctiveness grew through the 1980 referendum on sovereignty, the repatriation of the Canadian constitution in 1982, and the Meech Lake (1987) and Charlottetown (1992) constitutional accords. Quebecers' sense of themselves as a distinct people was fuelled, too, by early successes at finding a French-speaking voice in popular music (Robert Charlebois, Beau Dommage, Offenbach), film (Claude Jutra, Pierre Perrault, Gilles Carle), literature (Hubert Aquin, Anne Hébert, Réjean Ducharme, Marie-Claire Blaise), theatre (Michel Tremblay, Robert Lepage), and television. Protected by language and promoted by a star system that English Canada has never been able to imitate, Quebec's communications sector is another mark of the province's distinct status.

This period, too, marked the rise of Western regionalism, particularly in Alberta and British Columbia. The Trudeau government's National Energy Program of 1980—a unilateral attempt by Ottawa to assert federal control over an industry under provincial jurisdiction—confirmed the view that the resource-based industries of the Western and Atlantic provinces were economically subservient to central Canada's manufacturing sector, producing intense resentment especially in provinces like Alberta and British Columbia, who were seeking to assert their growing economic

and political power. A new federal party, the Reform Party, was formed in Alberta in 1987 with the motto 'The West Wants In' (Bright, 2002). British Columbia was always a reluctant member of the Canadian federation, feeling distinct and isolated from the rest of Canada. It had a distinct, two-party political system, polarized between Social Credit on the right and the New Democratic Party on the left, and it had a cosmopolitan population of migrants from across Canada and from other parts of the world. In the 1980s and 1990s, 80 per cent of immigrants to BC came from Asia, so that by 1995, English was the first language of less than half the students (44 per cent) in the Vancouver public school system, with 31 per cent speaking Chinese as a first language (Resnick, 2000: 7–8).

As so many of Canadians' communication needs have been served by commercial media, the argument that commercialization threatens Canadian culture becomes harder and harder to sustain. Even Canada's public television broadcaster, the CBC, has come to resemble a commercial service. Recessions in the mid-1970s and the early 1980s compelled governments to rethink their spending on cultural programs and organizations. As both the Fowler and Applebaum-Hébert reports signalled, economics had become a significant factor in policy discussions, and fiscal restraint has been a predominant theme of every government since the 1980s. Political ideologies have become much more fiscally conservative. After years of state intervention under the Trudeau Liberals, the Mulroney Conservatives declared Canada open for business, embracing free trade with the United States and less state intervention—what is misleadingly termed 'de-regulation' (see Box 7.6)—in all sectors of the economy. International agreements liberalizing trade in this period had significant implications for government communications policy, because national policies were subject to scrutiny by international trade bodies such as the World Trade Organization. The Mulroney government privatized a number of former **Crown corporations**, including the national airline Air Canada, the aerospace

❖ BOX 7.6 DE-REGULATION OR RE-REGULATION?

The term used most commonly to describe governments' retreat from intervening in the marketplace—whether in communications, health care, education, or anywhere else—is de-regulation. The term de-regulation implies that these sectors of the economy are gradually being freed from regulation because governments are withdrawing their powers of surveillance and control to allow market forces to hold sway.

But market forces are also a form of regulation, producing simply an alternative form of governance. Some commentators prefer to use the term re-regulation, because it more accurately and precisely captures the process that is taking place. The term re-regulation suggests that these sectors continue to be regulated, but market regulation is being substituted for state regulation.

manufacturer Canadair, the aircraft manufacturer De Havilland, and the telecommunications carrier Teleglobe Canada.

Even if Canadian governments had wanted to vilify American cultural producers, they would have had a tough time convincing most Canadians; by the late 1960s and early 1970s, American popular culture had to a great extent become *our* popular culture, and Canadian producers had made breakthroughs in popular music and television—thanks largely to Canadian-content regulations—as well as in literature. Still, American movies, television programs, popular music, magazines, and books were less 'foreign' to Canadians than most indigenous products and programs. The domination of the Canadian communications marketplace by US cultural products continued to be cited in policy documents as a problem, but there were no longer any political points to be scored with the Canadian people in framing the United States as a cultural menace, as there had been in the time of Aird and Massey-Lévesque.

SUMMARY

Communication is a structured activity, taking place within an environment constructed by laws, policies, conventions, economic imperatives, guiding ideals, and public pressures. Communications policy establishes the rules by which mediated communication occurs, and dates back to the first days of the printing press in the fifteenth century, when books began to be produced on a large scale and were traded across borders. Policy is developed at both the local and global levels, as governments need to respect international covenants dealing with the circulation of cultural products while addressing their own particular exigencies.

Communications policy in Canada frames the media, culture, and society in terms of the nation-state, so that communications policy is always also national policy. Priorities, though, can shift through time and the chapter traces policy development through four

pivotal moments of the twentieth century. If policy was driven initially by the need to develop within Canadians a strong sense of nation and national culture, which treated commercialization and Americanization as threats to those aims, the thematic rationale began to shift in the 1960s and 1970s. The financial burdens of state intervention became much more apparent and worrisome, regionalism became a rival sentiment to nationalism, and Canadians became accustomed to the commercialization and the Americanization of media. To a great extent, by the 1970s American commercial popular culture was less foreign to Canadians than the products of their own indigenous culture. While American domination of the Canadian communications marketplace continues to be defined as a problem by policy analysts, it no longer resonates the same way with Canadian governments or with the Canadian people.

KEY TERMS

Berne Convention, p. 188
communications policy, p. 185
Crown corporations, p. 206
cultural imperialism, p. 205
frequency allocation, p. 188

intellectual property, p. 188
market failure, p. 185
network, p. 193
privatization, p. 202
property rights, p. 188

right to communicate, p. 189
Royal Commissions, p. 185
Universal Declaration of
    Human Rights, p. 189

RELATED WEBSITES

Canadian Radio-Television and Telecommunications Commission: www.crtc.gc.ca
The CRTC governs broadcasting and telecommunications in Canada and its website is an excellent source of information about recent decisions and upcoming hearings.

Department of Canadian Heritage: www.pch.gc.ca/
This is the government ministry responsible for communications and culture. Its website contains information on all of the cultural industry sectors as well as news releases and speeches pertaining to the ministry.

Friends of Canadian Broadcasting: www.friends.ca/
Friends is a lobby group dedicated to the preservation and promotion of Canadian identity and culture on radio and television. Its website is a good guide to current broadcast policy changes and the issues raised by those changes.

Canadian Centre for Policy Alternatives: www.policyalternatives.ca/
This is an independent research centre advocating policies for social and economic justice. Its series of policy papers includes studies touching on communication and culture.

⋗ FURTHER READINGS

Hamelink, Cees J. 1994. *The Politics of World Communication*. London: Sage. This book provides a comprehensive summary of global communications policy development from its earliest manifestations to the late twentieth century.

Raboy, Marc. 1992. *Missed Opportunities: The Story of Canada's Broadcasting Policy*. Montreal and Kingston: McGill-Queen's University Press. This book provides a history of broadcast policy development in Canada and a critique of its framing as national policy.

Raboy, Marc, and Jeremy Shtern, eds. 2010. *Media Divides: Communication Rights and the Right to Communicate in Canada*. Vancouver: University of British Columbia Press. This book situates Canadian communications policy within the larger movement dedicated to the democratization of communication and establishing the concept of communication rights.

Vipond, Mary. 1992. *Listening In: The First Decade of Canadian Broadcasting, 1922–1932*. Montreal and Kingston: McGill-Queen's University Press. The brief but fascinating history of Canadian radio prior to the establishment of a national broadcaster is detailed in this work.

⋗ STUDY QUESTIONS

1. Why is communications policy necessary?
2. In what ways are Canada's policy questions similar to those of other countries, and in what ways are they different?
3. What were the predominant ideas motivating communications policy development through the first half of the twentieth century? Why were these ideas predominant?
4. What is the argument against market solutions as the way to address Canada's communication and cultural needs?
5. Do you agree that American popular culture has to a significant extent been adopted by most Canadians? If so, why is the domination of the Canadian mediascape by US cultural products a problem?
6. Why did attitudes towards policy development change in the 1960s?

PART III

The Communications Environment

CHAPTER 8

Communications Policy: Sector by Sector

... industrial activity cannot be equated with culture, a national sense of self, or even opportunities for domestic expression; sales merely signify achievements in producing, marketing, and exporting goods.

— RYAN EDWARDSON, 2008

OPENING QUESTIONS

- What features are common to the communications policy sectors, and what features distinguish them?

- What does it mean to say that media technologies, media forms, and media industries have converged?

- What is the Broadcasting Act and how does it define Canada's broadcasting system?

- Why has the Canadian Radio-television and Telecommunications Commission decided not to regulate new media?

Learning Objectives

- To learn the commonalities and particularities of the communications policy sectors.

- To understand convergence among the communications sectors, and the consequent regulatory and policy implications.

- To learn about the central characteristics of Canada's cultural industries.

- To realize that, while all sectors are affected by digitization, traditional media forms remain important to these sectors' economic viability.

Introduction

If, as we discussed in Chapter 7, the development of communications policy must always take into account the constructed environment in which a particular form of mass communication takes place—technologies, laws, existing policies, conventions, economic imperatives, guiding ideals, public pressures—policy formulation must also adapt to change. One of the most significant changes of the past two decades has been **convergence**, which in the context of communication means the merging of previously distinct technologies, media forms and media industries. A second dramatic change has been pressure for countries like Canada to revise and formulate communications policy in conformity with new international trade covenants. What has not changed, though, is a central policy priority: ensuring that Canadians have the full citizenship, cultural, and economic opportunities mass communication affords.

Digitization is the translation of information from various analog formats into patterns of 1s and 0s that can be transmitted along cables, fibre optic networks, telephone lines, and over the air, then reconstructed by various kinds of electronic receivers, such as computers, cellular phones, DVD players, MP3 players, and so on. In the past it made sense to talk about distinct media forms—magazines, radio, television, cinema—as completely separate industries. But these media **silos** are breaking down. Almost all media content today is produced digitally, with the result that it can be distributed both in its conventional form—e.g., hard-copy magazines, over-the-air radio and television, celluloid film—and digitally, typically via the internet. The internet, though, is not simply an alternative delivery mechanism, but a media platform in its own right that encourages the transformation and bundling of media content.

As the accompanying illustration demonstrates, this convergence of media forms has been aided and abetted by the convergence of media companies themselves, which are no longer in the newspaper or television business exclusively, but are producing content for online audiences as well. The CBC, for example, which we have come to know as a broadcaster, announced in 2009 that it would become a multimedia company, meaning that it intended to integrate more fully its radio, television, and online operations. The Montreal media company

FIGURE 8.1 Competition Landscape in the Era of Convergence for Today's Major Players

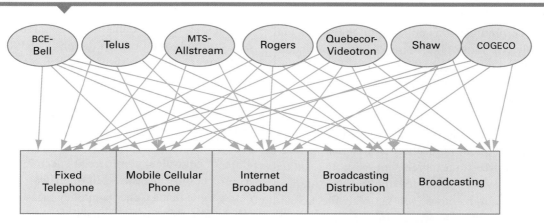

Communications companies that began as broadcasters, publishers, or cable or telephone companies have become multi-platform media conglomerates, creating a much more complicated, and concentrated, picture of media ownership in Canada.

Source: Canada. House of Commons, 'Canada's foreign ownership rules and regulations in the telecommunications sector', June 2010. At: www.parl.gc.ca/HousePublications/Publication.aspx?DocId=4618793&Language=E&Mode=1&Parl=40&Ses=3&File=123.

Quebecor, which began as a newspaper company, owns magazines, newspapers, a book publisher, a web portal, and a television network (among other media properties); it uses its portal—http://fr.canoe.ca—to showcase news-related content from a range of its media holdings.

As consumers of these communication products, we are quickly adapting to a mediascape in which we have increasing choice about how—and when and where—we listen to music or watch television or read a book. We can listen to music on our home stereo system or car radio, as we've always done, or we can listen via personal computer or MP3 player. We can watch television at home at the scheduled time, or record it with a PVR system for later viewing, or call up a streamed version on our personal computers. The way we use media, and consequently our vocabulary, are changing.

One of the most attractive features of digital technology is its capacity for **interactivity**. If there has always been a participatory element to audiences' consumption of media products, digital technology allows more and more people to become producers, whether in creating their own videos, music compilations, web pages, or blogs, or in manipulating the output of media professionals. In a similar vein, it has lowered the barriers to entry for more sustained communications projects like citizen journalism and other alternative media formulations (see Lessig, 2008).

If communications policy is to be relevant and effective, it must take these changes to what is called the 'media ecology' into account. A second significant change to the policy environment since the 1980s has been pressure to liberalize international trade and to eliminate protectionist legislation, including rules and regulations pertaining to the fields of communication and culture. Canada signed a free-trade agreement with the United States in 1987, and signed the North American Free-Trade Agreement (NAFTA) with the US and Mexico in 1994. Canada is also a member of the World Trade Organization (WTO), which has its own international framework for multilateral trade dating from 2007. These agreements seek to encourage international trade in goods and services across all sectors, and in so doing, strive to

create a 'level playing field' by abolishing national policies perceived as discriminatory. One of the most contentious areas in these trade deliberations is cultural policy, which is designed precisely to discriminate on the basis of nationality in order to protect and promote indigenous cultural activities and industries.

The US is not only Canada's largest trade partner and closest neighbour, but the world's foremost advocate for breaking down trade barriers, particularly in industries like television, film, music, and publishing where it is a net exporter. (The US is less enthusiastic about free trade in areas in which it is a net importer, such as softwood lumber.) The enormous quantity of cultural materials US companies produce and their ability to recover their costs of production in their own domestic market—the world's richest—provide American **cultural industries** with tremendous advantages in the global marketplace. It is generally 10 times cheaper for Canadian television networks to buy and broadcast American programs than it is to produce their own; the star power and promotional heft behind those American productions only compound this structural advantage. If there were no measures to promote the production and distribution of Canadian cultural products, there would be little room for Canadian creators in their own marketplace; we would, in a sense, be back where we started in the early to mid-twentieth century.

For this reason, Canadian negotiators insisted on a cultural exemption in the original 1987 free-trade agreement with the US and in NAFTA. This 'exemption', however, is highly qualified, and not really an exemption at all. Not only does the agreement allow several exceptions, but the exemption itself comes with a key proviso that allows for one of the signatories to take a form of retaliation 'of equivalent commercial effect' in response to protectionist measures. In other words, the US could argue that a Canadian policy measure causes a US cultural industry financial damage, and seek redress from the Canadian government. One ongoing trade irritant between the two countries is Canada's subsidization through tax credits of US film and television producers shooting on location in Canada (see Armstrong, 2010: 227–8).

There is no general exemption for cultural industries under the WTO either, although this sector has been subject to discussions. The United Nations Educational, Scientific and Cultural Organization (UNESCO) has adopted a Convention on the Protection and Promotion of the Diversity of Cultural Expressions, and Canada was the first country to ratify it (in 2005). But this convention has not been signed by the United States and to date has no bearing on international trade law (ibid., 229–30). There will continue to be pressure on countries like Canada to conform to strict market regulation of the cultural industries, rather than adhering to a regulatory regime that sees in these industries both economic and cultural dimensions.

This chapter provides profiles of the major communications sectors and examines sector-specific policy challenges in full recognition of the convergence of media forms and media industries currently underway. But it also picks up where Chapter 7 left off, recognizing, too, that policy priorities are shaped not only by technological and industrial exigencies, but are subject as well to responses generated by one persistent question: what is communication for?

Telecommunications

The historical core of the telecommunications sector is the telephone industry, but the telecommunications sector has become the veritable backbone of a growing range of applications, from conventional and wireless telephony to the provision of internet services. There is no better illustration of media convergence, and how telecommunications has evolved, than the new generations of 'smartphones', which act as telephones, cameras, video and audio players, and personal computers all in one small, hand-held device. Telecommunications is a $41 billion industry with six sub-sectors: local wireline telephone service, long-distance wireline telephone service, internet services, data transmission, private line, and wireless services. Almost all Canadians (99.1 per cent) have some form of telephone service; interestingly, fewer Canadian households have landlines than previously (91.1 per cent, compared to 97 per cent in 2002) and an increasing

number (8 per cent) have wireless only (CRTC, 2009a: 117). Wireless has become the largest sector of the telecommunications industry, accounting for 41 per cent of revenues (ibid., 114).

Telecommunications is governed in Canada by the Telecommunications Act (1993), which pertains to matters of technology, infrastructure, and distribution networks, but not the content of the communications they deliver. The **Canadian Radio-television and Telecommunications Commission** (CRTC) is charged with enforcing the rules laid out in the Telecommunications Act, although this is one area in which the Canadian government has decided that market forces should be the principal regulator. The Telecommunications Act requires the CRTC to rely on market forces 'to the maximum extent feasible' and to regulate 'where there is a need to do so, in a manner that interferes with market forces to the minimum extent necessary.' In all of its activities, the CRTC is guided by four basic principles: transparency, fairness, predictability, and timeliness. Since 1994, the CRTC has refrained from regulating mobile services, retail internet services, long-distance telephony, international services, and satellite services (CRTC, 2010c: 5). The CRTC regulates only where market competition does not meet the objectives of the Telecommunications Act, but it can intervene in the areas of tariffs and the licensing of international telecommunications services. The CRTC holds regular public consultations to obtain feedback on telecommunications issues.

Telecommunication companies are service providers, offering transmission services for a fee. There are two types of telecommunications carriers. Common carriers are obliged to carry any message (content) that a company or individual wishes to send at equitable cost. Telephone companies, for example, are common carriers, merely transmitting our voice messages. **Contract carriers**, on the other hand, provide transmission services to specific companies or individuals, but are not obliged to provide those same services to other individuals or companies. The banks, for example, contract for telephone and data communication services and obtain bulk rates unavailable to the average citizen. The internet is not subject to **common carriage** rules (Box 8.2).

❖ BOX 8.1   TELECOMMUNICATIONS ACT, SECTION 7*

The foundation for Canadian telecommunications policy is contained in section 7 of the 1993 Telecommunications Act. It states:

7. It is hereby affirmed that telecommunications performs an essential role in the maintenance of Canada's identity and sovereignty and that the Canadian telecommunications policy has as its objectives:

(a) to facilitate the orderly development throughout Canada of a telecommunications system that serves to safeguard, enrich and strengthen the social and economic fabric of Canada and its regions;

(b) to render reliable and affordable telecommunications services of high quality accessible to Canadians in both urban and rural areas in all regions of Canada;

(c) to enhance the efficiency and competitiveness, at the national and international levels, of Canadian telecommunications;

(d) to promote the ownership and control of Canadian carriers by Canadians;

(e) to promote the use of Canadian transmission facilities for telecommunications within Canada and between Canada and points outside Canada;

(f) to foster increased reliance on market forces for the provision of telecommunications services and to ensure regulation, where required, is efficient and effective;

(g) to stimulate research and development in Canada in the field of telecommunications and to encourage innovation in the provision of telecommunications services;

(h) to respond to the economic and social requirements of users of telecommunications services; and

(i) to contribute to the protection of the privacy of persons.

* Notes omitted.
Source: Government of Canada Telecommunications Act, section 7 http://lois.justice.gc.ca/PDF/T-3.4.pdf 2010. Reproduced with the permission of the Minister of Public Works and Government Services Canada, 2011.

❖ BOX 8.2   NET NEUTRALITY: TWENTY-FIRST-CENTURY COMMON CARRIAGE?

Building on regulatory concerns of common carriage, **net neutrality** refers to internet service providers (ISPs) treating all content and applications equally, without degrading or prioritizing service based on their source, ownership, or destination (see Milberry, forthcoming). Concern over a non-neutral network rises from fears that internet service providers have a financial interest in discriminating against competitors or different classes of users. Indeed, this is what early telecommunications policy surrounding common carriage sought to prevent: imbalanced power relations stemming from control over communication resting with those who own the networks of communication.

As it stands, existing laws may not prevent wholesale ISPs from offering new services that prioritize some content (either that of their subscribers, or of particular applications) over other content. This would authorize a two-tier internet with a 'fast lane' for those willing or able to pay higher fees—namely corporate clientele—and a 'slow lane' for the public—small content providers (e.g.,

alternative media outlets), content creators (e.g., bloggers, artists) and regular users. While this creates a more profitable system for incumbent ISPs, it also has the effect of creating a closed, non-neutral network requiring additional fees for priority access.

A related issue is that of 'throttling' or traffic shaping. Here, ISPs control the speed over which particular types of traffic travel the internet. Some have already begun to slow traffic originating from peer-to-peer (P2P) applications, creating a de facto two-tiered internet. Using deep packet inspection (DPI) technology, P2P downloads are identified and slowed down, ostensibly to make space for other traffic on a congested network, while those transmitting 'approved' content remain in the fast lane. P2P traffic uses similar amounts of bandwidth as the proprietary services such as iTunes or Bell Video Store. However, no punitive measures against 'bandwidth hogging' have been undertaken against these services (Mezei, 2009). For more information, see: http://saveournet.ca/sites/default/files/SON_FvF.pdf.

Source: Milberry (forthcoming).

The major telecommunications issue of the last decades of the twentieth century was the transition from monopoly services to competing services. Until the 1980s, private telephone companies were granted monopoly status in designated territories, with the understanding that they would provide equitable telephone service at reasonable rates to both urban and rural markets, subsidizing toll-free local calling with the long-distance rates they charged.

That system was gradually transformed and, in September 1994, in what has come to be known as Telecom Decision 94–19, the CRTC ruled that competition must be the basis for the provision of all telecommunication services, including local telephone service. This decision required companies to separate the costs of providing any single service (e.g., local phone service) from those for any other service (e.g., long-distance phone service), meaning that companies would no longer be allowed to cross-subsidize services.

The issues confronting telecommunications today concern technological convergence, market regulation, **spectrum allocation**, and network neutrality. The Telecommunications Policy Review Panel of 2005–2006 proved to be a strong advocate of market forces regulating the telecommunications sector in its recommendations to the Minister of Industry (Canada, 2006b). The panel outlined three kinds of regulation: economic, technical, and social. Under economic regulation, the panel recommended the establishment of a Telecommunications Competition Tribunal 'as a transitional mechanism to expedite the change from the traditional

❧ BOX 8.3   SATELLITE COMMUNICATION

Canada has been a pioneer of non-military satellite application since the early 1960s. In 1964 Canada joined INTELSAT, the international **consortium** that operated the first satellite communication service with the mandate to provide international communication linkages. The possibility of improving trans-Canada communication links using satellites has appealed to federal policy-makers since at least 1965. A White Paper on satellite policy, issued in 1968, stated: 'A domestic satellite system should be a national undertaking stretching across Canada from coast to coast, north to Ellesmere Island and operating under the jurisdiction of the Government of Canada' (Canada, 1968b).

In 1969, the Telesat Canada Act established the joint public-sector/private-sector corporation that was given the responsibility to own and operate the Canadian satellite communication system and to provide communication services to Canadian locations on a commercial basis. Telesat's first satellite was launched in 1972 and shortly thereafter the company initiated the first domestic satellite communication service in the world. By 1995, Telesat had launched five series of satellites.

Telesat is the 'carriers' carrier', a reference to the fact that most of the signals carried on satellite are transmitted on behalf of another carrier, such as a telephone or cable-TV company. Historically, the primary use for satellites was telecommunications traffic (mostly voice telephony and data communication). However, by 1987 it was apparent that broadcasting services were becoming at least as important to Telesat. The vast majority of broadcasting services consisted of the delivery of video signals across the country.

Satellite technology was the key to integrating Canada's North into the larger telecommunication and television networks of the south, beginning with the Anik satellite program of the 1970s. If, initially, this meant the delivery of more sophisticated telephone service to some northern communities, it also meant the one-way delivery of CBC programming in French and English to the North, with no Native-language or culturally relevant programming on offer (Roth, 2005: 74–88). The first step towards the true 'televisual joining of Canada's North and South' occurred with the establishment of the Inuit Broadcasting Corporation in January 1982 (ibid., 134–5). Aboriginal broadcasting was not enshrined in Canada's Broadcasting Act until 1991, and it achieved two-way flow with the licence approval of the Aboriginal Peoples Television Network (APTN) in February 1999; APTN received mandatory carriage on basic cable throughout Canada and satellite delivery to 96 northern communities (ibid., 204).

Canadian approach to telecommunications regulation to the more competitive deregulated approach recommended in this report' (ibid., 6). This tribunal would be a joint decision-making body involving the CRTC and the Competition Bureau. Technical regulation 'should ensure safe and efficient use of telecommunications facilities and promote rapid deployment of advanced telecommunications and ICT networks throughout Canada' (ibid., 7). Social regulation should be devoted to ensuring affordable access to telecommunications services in all regions of Canada as well as 'meeting the needs of the disabled, enhancing public safety and security, protecting personal privacy and limiting public nuisance through telecommunications networks' (ibid., 9).

The industry is pressuring government to allocate more space for mobile data traffic in the atmosphere's electromagnetic spectrum, and space at cheaper rates (CWTA, 2010). This request is due to the growing demand for wireless services and the growth in the number and kinds of devices employing connectivity to wireless networks. Wireless traffic is expected to double every year until 2014. The list of devices

Source: © Route66/Dreamstime.com

Satellite technology played an important role in closing the gap between Canada's regions.

with wireless connectivity already includes basic cellphones, smartphones, laptops, netbooks, e-book readers, tablets, digital cameras, and in-car safety and entertainment systems. Toy manufacturers are expected to be among the next to employ wireless features in their products (ibid., 9–10).

Broadcasting

Broadcasting in Canada is a $14 billion industry that includes radio and television, as well as the distribution services of cable, satellite, and, increasingly, the internet and mobile devices (CRTC, 2010c: 26). There are more than 1,200 audio services in Canada, 75 per cent delivering service in English, 22 per cent in French, and another 3 per cent in a third language. Canadians listened to radio an average of 19.5 hours per week in 2009 (ibid., ii). Radio in Canada comprises private commercial, national public, community, campus, Aboriginal, and religious broadcasters. Private commercial radio accounts for 79 per cent of the audience in an average week, with the public broadcaster, CBC/Radio-Canada, accounting for 12.7 per cent (ibid., 31–6).

Canadian television offers more than 700 services across conventional, pay, pay-per-view, video-on-demand and specialty TV services. The average viewer watched 26.5 hours of television per week in 2009 (ibid., 51). Specialty services in English accounted for 29.4 per cent of the Canadian television audience in 2009, followed by private conventional services (22.2 per cent), pay-TV (5.1 per cent) and the CBC (4.9 per cent). Non-Canadian television services accounted for 21 per cent of viewing (ibid., 55–6), but it is important to remember that a great deal of US television programming is carried, and viewed, on Canadian channels, meaning Canadians watch more American television than this figure suggests.

Radio and television broadcasting content has migrated to online and mobile platforms in recent years. One-quarter of anglophone Canadians reported watching television online in 2009, as did one-fifth of francophone Canadians. Nineteen per cent of anglophones and 5 per cent of francophones reported listening to podcasts, while 17 per cent of anglophones and 13 per cent of francophones listened to radio programming streamed online in 2009 (ibid., 102–4).

Every country in the world regulates broadcasting, in part because the over-the-air broadcast spectrum is finite and requires management of assigned airwaves, not only for standard radio and television services but as well for emergency services used by such agencies as police, fire, ambulance, and the military. As we discussed in Chapter 7, however, the Canadian government, like many others around the world, regulates broadcasting as well because it serves national cultural and political goals. While Canada considers the broadcast airwaves public property, all broadcasters require a licence from the federal regulator, the CRTC, an independent public authority reporting to the federal Department of Canadian Heritage. The CRTC's broadcast policy guidelines are set out in Section 3 of the Broadcasting Act (1991) and are tied to 'the cultural, social, political and economic fabric of Canada' (ibid., 5). This section of the Broadcasting Act is in Box 8.4. Access to content produced by Canadians is 'the underlying principle of the broadcasting objectives'. The CRTC states: 'Canadian content must not only exist, it should also be available to all Canadians both as participants in the industry and as members of the audience' (ibid.).

BOX 8.4 BROADCASTING ACT, SECTION 3 BROADCASTING POLICY FOR CANADA

3. (1) It is hereby declared as the broadcasting policy for Canada that

(a) the Canadian broadcasting system shall be effectively owned and controlled by Canadians;

(b) the Canadian broadcasting system, operating primarily in the English and French languages and comprising public, private and community elements, makes use of radio frequencies that are public property and provides, through its programming, a public service essential to the maintenance and enhancement of national identity and **cultural sovereignty;**

(c) English and French language broadcasting, while sharing common aspects, operate under different conditions and may have different requirements;

(d) the Canadian broadcasting system should
 (i) serve to safeguard, enrich and strengthen the cultural, political, social and economic fabric of Canada,
 (ii) encourage the development of Canadian expression by providing a wide range of programming that reflects Canadian attitudes, opinions, ideas, values and artistic creativity, by displaying Canadian talent in entertainment programming and by offering information and analysis concerning Canada and other countries from a Canadian point of view,

(iii) through its programming and the employment opportunities arising out of its operations, serve the needs and interests, and reflect the circumstances and aspirations, of Canadian men, women and children, including equal rights, the linguistic duality and multicultural and multiracial nature of Canadian society and the special place of aboriginal peoples within that society, and

(iv) be readily adaptable to scientific and technological change;

(e) each element of the Canadian broadcasting system shall contribute in an appropriate manner to the creation and presentation of Canadian programming;

(f) each broadcasting undertaking shall make maximum use, and in no case less than predominant use, of Canadian creative and other resources in the creation and presentation of programming, unless the nature of the service provided by the undertaking, such as specialized content or format or the use of languages other than French and English, renders that use impracticable, in which case the undertaking shall make the greatest practicable use of those resources;

(g) the programming originated by broadcasting undertakings should be of high standard;

⁘ BOX 8.4 *(continued)*

(h) all persons who are licensed to carry on broadcasting undertakings have a responsibility for the programs they broadcast;

(i) the programming provided by the Canadian broadcasting system should

(i) be varied and comprehensive, providing a balance of information, enlightenment and entertainment for men, women and children of all ages, interests and tastes,

(ii) be drawn from local, regional, national and international sources,

(iii) include educational and community programs,

(iv) provide a reasonable opportunity for the public to be exposed to the expression of differing views on matters of public concern, and

(v) include a significant contribution from the Canadian independent production sector;

(j) educational programming, particularly where provided through the facilities of an independent educational authority, is an integral part of the Canadian broadcasting system;

(k) a range of broadcasting services in English and in French shall be extended to all Canadians as resources become available;

(l) the Canadian Broadcasting Corporation, as the national public broadcaster, should provide radio and television services incorporating a wide range of programming that informs, enlightens and entertains;

(m) the programming provided by the Corporation should

(i) be predominantly and distinctively Canadian,

(ii) reflect Canada and its regions to national and regional audiences, while serving the special needs of those regions,

(iii) actively contribute to the flow and exchange of cultural expression,

(iv) be in English and in French, reflecting the different needs and circumstances of each official language community, including the particular needs and circumstances of English and French linguistic minorities,

(v) strive to be of equivalent quality in English and in French,

(vi) contribute to shared national consciousness and identity,

(vii) be made available throughout Canada by the most appropriate and efficient means and as resources become available for the purpose, and

(viii) reflect the multicultural and multiracial nature of Canada;

(n) where any conflict arises between the objectives of the Corporation set out in paragraphs (l) and (m) and the interests of any other broadcasting undertaking of the Canadian broadcasting system, it shall be resolved in the public interest, and where the public interest would be equally served by resolving the conflict in favour of either, it shall be resolved in favour of the objectives set out in paragraphs (l) and (m);

(o) programming that reflects the aboriginal cultures of Canada should be provided within the Canadian broadcasting system as resources become available for the purpose;

(p) programming accessible by disabled persons should be provided within the Canadian broadcasting system as resources become available for the purpose;

(q) without limiting any obligation of a broadcasting undertaking to provide the programming contemplated by paragraph (i), alternative television programming services in English and in French should be provided where necessary to ensure that the full range of programming contemplated by that paragraph is made available through the Canadian broadcasting system;

(r) the programming provided by alternative television programming services should

(i) be innovative and be complementary to the programming provided for mass audiences,

(ii) cater to tastes and interests not adequately provided for by the programming provided for mass audiences, and include programming devoted to culture and the arts,

(iii) reflect Canada's regions and multicultural nature,

(iv) as far as possible, be acquired rather than produced by those services, and

(v) be made available throughout Canada by the most cost-efficient means;

⟫ BOX 8.4 *(continued)*

(s) private networks and programming undertakings should, to an extent consistent with the financial and other resources available to them,

   (i)   contribute significantly to the creation and presentation of Canadian programming, and

   (ii) be responsive to the evolving demands of the public; and

(t) distribution undertakings

   (i)   should give priority to the carriage of Canadian programming services and, in particular, to the carriage of local Canadian stations,

   (ii) should provide efficient delivery of programming at affordable rates, using the most effective technologies available at reasonable cost,

   (iii) should, where programming services are supplied to them by broadcasting undertakings pursuant to contractual arrangements, provide reasonable terms for the carriage, packaging and retailing of those programming services, and

   (iv) may, where the Commission considers it appropriate, originate programming, including local programming, on such terms as are conducive to the achievement of the objectives of the broadcasting policy set out in this subsection, and in particular provide access for underserved linguistic and cultural minority communities.

(2) It is further declared that the Canadian broadcasting system constitutes a single system and that the objectives of the broadcasting policy set out in subsection (1) can best be achieved by providing for the regulation and supervision of the Canadian broadcasting system by a single independent public authority.

Source: Government of Canada Broadcasting Act Section 3 http://laws. justice.gc.ca/PDF/B-9.01.pdf 2010. Reproduced with the permission of the Minister of Public Works and Government Services Canada, 2011.

The CRTC ensures that content produced by Canadians is broadcast through a number of policies, including Canadian content regulations for radio and television broadcasters, the carriage of Canadian services by cable and satellite providers, and minimum Canadian ownership of broadcast networks (Box 8.5). The CRTC's regulatory duties derive from Section 5(2) of the Broadcasting Act, requiring the Commission 'to regulate and supervise the broadcasting system in a flexible manner that, among other things, takes into account regional concerns, is adaptable to technological developments, and facilitates the provisioning of broadcasting programs to Canadians' (CRTC, 2010c: 5). Today, the CRTC's duties in the broadcasting field include:

- defining categories of broadcasting licences;
- issuing and renewing licences, up to a maximum of seven years;
- modifying existing licence conditions;
- suspending or revoking licences (the CBC licence excepted);
- licensing cable distributors and satellite delivery systems;
- hearing complaints about the broadcasting system;
- reviewing mergers of media companies.

The CRTC is not simply a rubber-stamp agency. In 1999, the Commission reduced the length of the licence of Montreal AM radio station CKVL from seven years to three. The CRTC punished the station for the insulting and vulgar remarks of 'shock jock' André Arthur and the failure of the station's owner, Metromedia CMR Montreal Inc., to take seriously numerous public complaints about Arthur (Canadian Press, 1999). In 2004, the CRTC denied the licence renewal application of Quebec radio station CHOI-FM, arguing that the station, and radio host Jeff Fillion in particular, repeatedly aired derogatory comments about women, people of colour, and psychiatric patients, a decision that was subsequently affirmed by the Federal Court of Appeal (Thorne, 2005; Armstrong, 2010: 89–92).

⁂ BOX 8.5 CORPORATE CONVERGENCE, MEDIA DIVERSITY, AND MEDIA OWNERSHIP REGULATIONS

In the face of corporate mergers between companies like Canwest newspapers, *The Globe and Mail,* CTV, Global Television, and Bell Canada, the CRTC formulated new ownership policies in 2008. Broadcasting Public Notice CRTC 2008–4 issued new regulations regarding 'cross-media ownership; the common ownership of television services, including pay and specialty services; and the common ownership of broadcasting distribution undertakings'. These new policies include:

i) a prohibition on cross-media ownership that prevents a company from owning a radio station, a local television station, and a local newspaper serving the same market;

ii) a policy that prevents one company from controlling more than 45 per cent of the total national television audience share;

iii) a policy that prohibits one company from owning all of the 'distribution undertakings' (i.e. cable, satellite, etc.) in any given city.

While these regulations do provide for some measure of media diversity, there are several problems with them. First, in terms of one company owning 'a radio station, a local television station, and a local newspaper serving the same market', television and newspapers are by far the most influential in terms of news as well as the most likely for common ownership. Hence this prohibition does little to ensure diversity in terms of one of the most important elements of media content. Second, the regulation addressing television audiences speaks only to national audiences. It says nothing about local or regional shares. Hence, one company can monopolize as many markets as it likes, just so long as it doesn't exceed 45 per cent of any one national market. As for the prohibition against one company owning all the distribution undertakings in a given city, this doesn't account for the ways in which companies that own both distribution outlets and content providers such as television channels and web portals might discriminate against channels and web portals that provide competition to their own properties.

For more information, see: www.crtc.gc.ca/eng/archive/2008/pb2008-4.htm.

But to say that the CRTC merely regulates the broadcasting system to achieve policy objectives set by Parliament understates the extent to which the CRTC has been obliged to interpret policy. It also understates the extent to which the CRTC has established policies of its own in areas such as cable, specialty TV, and new media. In March 2010, for example, the CRTC ruled that private television networks have the right to negotiate 'fee-for-carriage' compensation, a fee for the use of their signals by cable and satellite distributors. This ruling came with the proviso that if the networks opt to negotiate such a fee, they forgo the regulatory protection that requires all cable and satellite distributors to carry conventional networks, as well as forgoing their guarantee of a preferred location on the dial. The TV networks were seeking this new revenue stream after having posted an operating loss ($118 million) for the first time since the Commission began tracking the industry's finances in 1996. In making the ruling, the CRTC asked the Federal Court of Appeal to ensure the ruling is within the CRTC's jurisdiction (Krashinsky, 2010a).

In recent years, a major shift in broadcasting policy has occurred pertaining to the issue of access, from an original emphasis on signal coverage to an emphasis on participation. From as early as 1936, one of the fundamental principles of Canadian broadcasting policy has been the extension of service to all Canadians, and private broadcasters' place in the national broadcasting system has been to help in providing Canadians in all areas of the country access to the reception of radio, and later television, broadcast signals (Canada, 1986: 5–14).

The notion of 'access to broadcasting' began to assume another dimension in the 1960s, once extensive territorial coverage of radio and television had been achieved and a private television network (CTV) had been established. Access came to mean the inclusion of all Canadians in the content and production of programming. While the issue of Canadian content has been significant since the first decade of

Source: © CP Photo/Tobin Grimshaw

Jeff Fillion, former CHOI-FM radio host.

radio, the idea of requiring a minimum percentage of broadcast time to be used for transmitting Canadian television productions was instituted by the Board of Broadcast Governors in 1959 (see Box 8.6).

Today, **Canadian content** regulations stem from the CRTC's obligation under the Broadcasting Act to ensure that each licence-holder makes 'maximum use... of Canadian creative and other resources in the creation and presentation of programming'. The CBC's programming, according to the Act, should also be 'predominantly and distinctively Canadian'.

The Canadian content quota has never been well received by the private broadcasters, who have protested each requirement vigorously and sought to minimize their carriage of Canadian-produced materials (see Babe, 1979). The CRTC requires conventional television licensees to have at least 60 per cent of all programming hours given to Canadian productions; the requirement for specialty and pay-TV channels is typically 50 per cent. Radio regulations require English-language commercial AM and FM radio stations to play at least 35 per cent (raised from 30 per cent in 1998) Canadian musical selections, both as a weekly average and between 6 a.m. and 6 p.m., Monday to Friday. French-language stations are required to program 65 per cent of their vocal recordings in the French language between 6 a.m. and 6 p.m., Monday to Friday (Armstrong, 2010: 62–3, 97–9).

The principal battleground for disputes over Canadian content quotas has been English-language television, where Hollywood productions are readily available, cheap to buy, and popular with audiences and advertisers. Since the early 1980s, several events have improved the situation significantly. The first of these was the establishment of Telefilm Canada's Broadcast Program Development Fund, which encouraged independent producers to create high-quality TV dramas and series. These productions, in a number of instances, have shown a strong potential for export sales as well. The second event was the licensing of a number of specialty and pay-TV services, to be distributed via satellite and cable. All the new services were required to spend a portion of their revenues on programming production. The third development was the establishment by the private sector of a number of production funds in the 1980s and 1990s, increasing the pool of capital available to production companies and making it easier for them to get airtime.

BOX 8.6 CANADIAN CONTENT

The commonly used phrase 'Canadian content' is an unfortunate misnomer because, for regulatory purposes, it refers not to the content of a song or film or television program, but to the people who produce it. In other words, the content itself can touch on any subject, and does not have to concern Canada at all. For music or audiovisual programming to qualify as Canadian content, it must be produced by Canadian citizens according to specific requirements by the Canadian Audio Visual Certification Office (CAVCO), for film and television content, and the CRTC's MAPL criteria for musical content.

TABLE 8.1 The Canadian Audio Visual Certification Office (CAVCO) Points System

For a creative series to be recognized as a Canadian production, a total of at least six points must be allotted according to the following scale. Points are awarded for each Canadian who rendered the services.

NON-ANIMATED PRODUCTIONS (LIVE ACTION)	POINTS AWARDED
Director	2
Screenwriter	2
Lead performer for whose services the highest remuneration was payable	1
Lead performer for whose services the second highest remuneration was payable	1
Director of photography	1
Art director	1
Music composer	1
Picture editor	1
ANIMATED PRODUCTIONS	
Director	1
Design supervisor (art director)	1
Lead voice for which the highest or second highest remuneration was payable	1
Design supervisor (art director)	1
Camera operator where the camera operation is done in Canada	1
Music composer	1
Picture editor	1
Layout and background where the work is performed in Canada	1
Key animation where the work is performed in Canada	1
Assistant animation and in-betweening where work is performed in Canada	1

Source: Report of the Auditor General of Canada, November 2005, Office of the Auditor General of Canada. Reproduced with the permission of the Minister of Public Works and Government Services, 2011.

Canadian producers spent $2 billion on television production in 2007–8 (the latest year for which figures are available), amounting to just over 8,000 hours of programming. The average budget for the English-language fiction genre was $1.5 million per hour, an all-time high. Funding from Canadian broadcasters and federal and provincial tax credits accounted for almost two-thirds (64 per cent) of total financing (CFTPA, 2009: 34–6). Three-quarters of this production took place in Ontario and Quebec (ibid., 45). Three Canadian series were among the top 10 shows based on audience ratings during the 2007–8 television season: *Les Lavigeur, la vraie histoire* (third overall, with an average audience of 2.2 million per minute), *Canadian Idol 5—Results* (fifth, 2.08 million), and *Canadian Idol 5—Performance* (seventh, 1.99 million). Five of the top seven most popular Canadian TV series were French-language productions (ibid., 57).

The federal Department of Canadian Heritage initiated a review of Canadian content in March 2002, inviting submissions from the public and interested parties in the film and television industries. In a discussion paper entitled *Canadian Content in the 21st Century* (Canada, 2002: 1), the department said 'the time has come to reassess the definition of Canadian content and ensure that the approach that is chosen is up to date and well suited to the challenges ahead.'

The range of Canadian programming has already undergone considerable refinement. In the 1970s and 1980s, there was an increasing recognition of Canada's multicultural makeup and demands were made that the broadcasting system should reflect this reality. As Lorna Roth (1998: 493–502) notes, by the early 1980s, one in three Canadians was of non-British, non-French, and non-Aboriginal descent, and the federal government began to enshrine guarantees of cultural and racial pluralism in the Constitution, for example, in sections 15 and 27 of the Canadian Charter of Rights and Freedoms (1982), and in legislation, for example, the Multiculturalism Act (1998).

Inclusion was one of the central themes informing discussions leading up to the adoption of a revised Broadcasting Act in 1991. Marc Raboy (1995b: 457) argues that the 'transparency of public debate' between 1986 and 1991 was responsible for enshrining the rights of women, ethnic groups, Native peoples, and disabled persons in broadcast legislation. In section 3 (1) (d)(iii), the Act states that the Canadian broadcasting system should:

> through its programming and the employment opportunities arising out of its operations, serve the needs and interests, and reflect the circumstances and aspirations, of Canadian men, women and children, including equal rights, the linguistic duality and multicultural and multiracial nature of Canadian society and the special place of aboriginal peoples within that society.

Subsequent clauses call for the provision of programming that 'reflects the aboriginal cultures of Canada' and programming 'accessible by disabled persons'. As Lorna Roth (1998: 501) has stated: 'Though it still faces multiple challenges, we might say that the Canadian attempt to deal with "cultural and racial diversity" in broadcasting represents its political willingness to symbolically weave cultural and racial pluralism into the fabric of Canadian broadcasting policy and human rights legislation.'

A signal achievement in the diversification of Canadian broadcasting was the establishment of the Aboriginal Peoples Television Network, which was licensed as a national network in 1999, a world first. APTN provides a range of news, variety, and dramatic programming, and broadcasts in English, French, and a variety of Aboriginal languages: Inuktitut, Cree, Inuinaqtuun, Ojibway, Inuvialuktun, Mohawk, Dene, Gwich'in, Mi'kmaq, Slavey, Dogrib, Chipewyan, Tlingit, and Michif. More than 80 per cent of its programming originates from Canadian producers (APTN, 2010; Roth, 2005).

The CRTC is not broadcasting's only regulator. The Canadian Broadcast Standards Council (CBSC) and Advertising Standards Canada (ASC) are industry associations providing a measure of self-regulation. The CBSC, for example, has policies on equitable portrayal, violence, and ethics, although it only investigates when complaints are made. The ASC administers the Canadian Code of Advertising Standards, which includes a Broadcasting Code for Advertising to Children. The Broadcasting Code for Advertising to Children contains guidelines pertaining to the factual presentation of products and services, product prohibition, sales pressure, comparison claims, as well as limits on the amount of advertising per program (Advertising Standards Canada, 2010). In Quebec, television advertising on children's programming is prohibited under the Quebec Consumer Protection Act (Armstrong, 2010: 153–4).

The policy area that warrants the most attention in coming years will be internet broadcasting, which the CRTC is not currently regulating (Box 8.7). As Robert Armstrong argues, the distribution of audiovisual content online is drawing listeners and viewers away from advertising-funded radio and television and thereby undermining the revenue base on which broadcasting depends. Audiences for commercial broadcasting are slowly declining, and perhaps in response, broadcasters are favouring low-cost television formats: news, talk, variety, reality, and live events (e.g., sports and award shows). Three kinds of content predominate online: user-generated videos, relatively inexpensive commercial programming, and relatively expensive drama and documentary. Armstrong writes: 'To date, the Internet is recycling high-cost, high-quality audiovisual programming without participating in its development and financing. Thus, while new media are drawing viewers and revenues away from licensed broadcast media, in part by recycling such programs, they are undermining the financial model that has permitted their creation, particularly high-quality drama, documentaries, and children's programs' (ibid., 242).

Recorded Music

A great proportion of radio broadcasting is, of course, recorded music, and there is a significant symbiosis between radio broadcast policy and policies designed to encourage the production and dissemination of Canadian music. Surveys indicate Canadians listen to music an average of 27 hours

❯ BOX 8.7   THE FUTURE OF BROADCAST REGULATION?

Both the CRTC and the Supreme Court of Canada are wrestling with the question of broadcast regulation in a digital environment. Faced with a growing number of web-based services such as Netflix and Google TV that offer film and television programs that compete with traditional broadcast, cable and satellite companies, the CRTC held a meeting of industry members and other stakeholders in Ottawa in March of 2011 to consider the impact of these services on existing media markets and regulation (CRTC, 2011). Some of the questions considered at that meeting were:

How to ensure Canadians continue to have access to an evolving communications system and to broadcasting content that reflects Canadian culture.

How to recognize the complete convergence between 'telecommunications' and 'broadcasting'.

How to ensure the communications system benefits all Canadians.

How to foster the continued production and promotion of Canadian content, and Canadians' access to that content in a global environment.

Whether Canadian legislation is outmoded.

How to understand the manner in which the statutes governing the communications industry will evolve.

The Supreme Court announced the same month that it will render a decision on whether internet service providers are broadcasters when they distribute media content and video material online. Hearings were expected to begin in 2012 (*Mediacaster*, 2011).

To date, the courts have decided that internet service providers are not subject to CRTC regulation under the Broadcasting Act. A number of industry groups—e.g., the Alliance of Canadian Cinema, Television and Radio Artists, the Canadian Media Production Association, the Directors Guild of Canada, and the Writers Guild of Canada—have argued that ISPs are behaving like broadcasters and should be subject to the same regulations as broadcast companies.

per week, and radio is the single most popular media platform, accounting for 35.8 per cent of listening time (Canada, 2010a). Historically, the most important policy development for Canadian recorded music was the CRTC's establishment in 1971 of Canadian content quotas for radio. The quotas were a response to the under-representation of Canadian recording artists on Canadian radio stations at the time; as of 1968, for example, Canadian music accounted for between 4 and 7 per cent of all music played on Canadian radio, in a period when the popular music scene was exploding and when Canadian musicians like Gordon Lightfoot, Neil Young, Joni Mitchell, and The Guess Who were part of the explosion (Filion, 1996: 132). A points system known as MAPL was devised to determine whether or not recordings qualify as Canadian, based not on their actual content, but on who produces them (Box 8.8).

Although the quota system recognizes the importance of radio airplay to music sales, radio's primacy as a promotional vehicle has been challenged since the 1980s, first by music video stations (MuchMusic and MusiquePlus in Canada) and,

Canadian singer-songwriter, Neil Young.

Source: © AP Photo/Lisa Poole

⁑ BOX 8.8   THE MAPL SYSTEM—DEFINING A CANADIAN SONG

Canadian content regulations focus on the factors of production and work to ensure that Canadians have the opportunity to participate in media production.

The CRTC defines a Canadian musical selection in its Radio Regulations. Within these regulations, four elements are used to qualify songs as being Canadian: Music, Artist, Performance and Lyrics (MAPL).

To qualify as Canadian content, a musical selection must generally fulfil at least two of the following conditions:

- M (music): the music is composed entirely by a Canadian
- A (artist): the music is, or the lyrics are, performed principally by a Canadian
- P (performance): the musical selection consists of a live performance that is recorded wholly in Canada, or performed wholly in Canada and broadcast live in Canada
- L (lyrics): the lyrics are written entirely by a Canadian

Source: www.crtc.gc.ca/eng/info_sht/r1.htm.

more recently, by a combination of MP3 players and internet sites, including online radio. Websites permitting bands to upload and promote their music provide a much more diverse spectrum than conventional radio, with its limited, mainstream genres, can muster. CBC Radio 3 (http://radio3.cbc.ca), for example, streams music from independent Canadian musicians, many of whom receive little or no mainstream radio airplay.

The Canadian recording companies, represented by the Canadian Independent Record Production Association (CIRPA, www.cirpa.ca), have always insisted that the Canadian content rules are essential to their survival and those of the artists they record. This is because the commercial music market is structured against Canadian interests; commercial Canadian radio stations, if given the choice, would prefer to play American recordings that have been made popular by the publicity they generate in the US media market (e.g., through music magazines, celebrity news, televised talk shows, and awards shows). The major recording careers of some Canadian performers and composers were launched through significant airplay on Canadian radio and, more recently, on music video television. If it can be argued that Céline Dion and Bryan Adams no longer need to rely on quotas for airplay, it must also be acknowledged that less mainstream acts and up-and-coming performers do. Providing exposure to bands through radio and

Canadian indie rock group Arcade Fire poses for photographers after the 2011 Grammy Awards ceremony.

TV in their home markets gives them wider exposure, legitimacy, a fan base, and a financial foundation to pursue international recognition.

The problem for the Canadian recording industry is that the international success of Canadian performers has not always meant success for Canadian recording companies. Most often, emerging international stars leave their original label behind. If necessary, a major recording company will buy out an artist or band's contract and offer them far more investment than a small Canadian company could ever afford. Hence, Canadian labels depend for their survival on the new Canadian artists they discover and for whom they can get exposure through Canadian content supports.

A second significant policy measure was the establishment in 1982 of the Fund to Assist Canadian Talent on Record, which became known as FACTOR/MusicAction when a French-language component was added (www.factor.ca, http://musicaction.ca). With the encouragement of the CRTC, the fund was created by several radio broadcasters (CHUM Ltd, Moffatt Communications, Rogers Broadcasting Ltd) in partnership with two major industry associations (CIRPA and the Canadian Musical Reproduction Rights Agency Ltd, www.cmrra.ca) to channel money into the Canadian music industry; together, FACTOR and MusicAction contributed about $22 million in support to Canadian musicians in 2009. The funds provided are used, for example, to produce demo tapes and promotional video clips and to organize promotional tours by musicians.

The 1996 Task Force on the Future of the Canadian Music Industry acknowledged that gaps in the federal government's policy apparatus compromised the effectiveness of Canadian content regulations and the 1986 Sound Recording Development Program. Specifically, the Task Force identified three areas of future policy concern: 'grossly inadequate' copyright legislation; the absence of incentives to strengthen independent recording companies (which are responsible for more than 80 per cent of Canadian content recordings); and the absence of Investment Canada guidelines for the industry.

In May 2001 the Department of Canadian Heritage announced a new Canadian Sound Recording Policy, entitled From Creators to Audience. Its goal is to provide support at every level of the sound-recording process—from the development of creators to the building of audiences, as its title suggests. The policy established the Canada Music Fund, which absorbs the pre-existing Sound Recording Development Program and promised to:

- build community support and skills development of creators;
- support the production and distribution of 'specialized music recordings reflective of the diversity of Canadian voices';
- provide project-based support to new emerging artists;
- develop the business skills of Canadian music entrepreneurs;
- ensure the preservation of Canadian musical works;
- support recording industry associations, conferences, and awards programs;
- and monitor industry performance.

The government renewed and restructured the Canada Music Fund in 2009, increasing its annual funding to $27.6 million until 2014. It eliminated the programs in support of musical diversity and sector associations, but added monies for digital market development and international market development (CBC News, 2009).

If radio remains the primary dissemination platform for recorded music, almost everything else about how we listen to music has changed in the digital age, and this is prompting a major restructuring of the music industry. As Patrik Wikström notes, in less than a decade, the music industry 'has completely shifted its centre of gravity from the physical to the virtual—from the Disk to the Cloud' (Wikström, 2009: 4). The sale of physical recordings—i.e., CDs, DVDs—is decreasing world-wide; sales were $18.4 billion US in 2008, compared to a peak of $26 billion US in 1999. Digital sales, however, are growing, accounting for almost 21 per cent of world-wide industry revenues. The picture is the same in Canada, which is the world's sixth-largest market for recorded music (Canada, 2010a: 7).

This has impacted significantly the position and the fortunes of the world's four major recording companies—Universal Music Group, Sony Music Entertainment, Warner Music Group, EMI Group—who have each shed one-quarter of their workforce since 2000 (Wikström, 2009: 65). While these companies still account for 72 per cent of the global music-recording market, they don't exert the industry power they once did. For one thing, most artists today have access to their own sophisticated recording equipment and can produce their own recordings. For another, artists today can reach the listening public directly through the internet.

But the biggest threat to the fortunes of the recording industry is illegal **file-sharing**. According to the International Federation of the Phonographic Industry, for every legal music download there are 20 instances of illegal file-sharing (ibid., 101). And it is estimated that in China, 90 per cent of recorded music is traded illegally (ibid., 70). The industry is combating music piracy through information campaigns, lawsuits, the lobbying of international trade organizations and technological security measures (ibid., 152–3), but its battle is part of a larger struggle all of the 'copyright industries' face. Copyright, which recognizes and protects artists' creations as 'intellectual property', will be a central policy issue for a number of media industries in the years to come.

Cinema

The film industry has the same kind of symbiotic relationship with television as the music industry has with radio. Given the longstanding difficulty Canadian-made feature films have had in penetrating Canadian movie theatres, television has been their most reliable means of distribution. And yet, like music, digital platforms—online and wireless mobile—are becoming more and more significant outlets for all forms of audiovisual production. To what extent Canadian films will succeed in reaching audiences this way, and whether their producers will be adequately compensated, remain open questions.

The Canadian theatrical film industry is relatively small, generating just $273 million in spending during the 2007–8 fiscal year, producing 75 theatrical films (45 in English) and seven shorts. The average budget for English-language features was $3.8 million, and $2.8 million for French-language features. Most of this production took place in Ontario and Quebec (CFTPA, 2009: 60).

Governments' principal policy contributions have come in the production sector of the film industry, rather than in distribution or exhibition. More than half of the financing of Canadian feature films comes from government funding programs: the Canadian Feature Film Fund (25 per cent), provincial tax credits (15 per cent), federal tax credits (7 per cent), and other public funding sources (8 per cent). The Canadian Feature Film Fund, established in 2000, is administered by Telefilm Canada and contributes about $90 million annually to film development, production, distribution, and marketing (ibid., 68–9).

Federal and provincial governments in Canada have been sponsoring motion-picture production in one form or another since the earliest years of the twentieth century, and Ottawa has operated a national film production organization continuously since 1918. Canada, however, has been much more successful in the spheres of industrial and documentary film production—e.g., films produced by the National Film Board, founded in 1939, have won 12 Academy Awards (see Table 8.2)—than in the higher-profile domain of dramatic, feature-length film production, the kinds of movies we see in our theatres. There, Hollywood is the dominant player in the Canadian market, occupying better than 90 per cent of screen time in Canada's commercial movie theatres. Even though directors like Atom Egoyan, François Girard, Denis Villeneuve, Deepa Mehta, Mina Shum, Léa Pool, and Denys Arcand have given renewed vigour to Canadian feature filmmaking since the early 1980s, domestic films have averaged only between 3 and 6 per cent of box-office revenues in Canadian cinemas.

Source: © AP Photo/The Canadian Press, Paul Chiasson

Director Denis Villeneuve's film *Incendies* was nominated for an Academy Award in 2011. Despite their success with critics, few Canadian films make a splash at the box office.

TABLE 8.2   The National Film Board's Academy Awards

FILMS	
Year	Title (Director)
1941	Churchill's Island (Stuart Legg)
1953	Neighbours (Norman McLaren)
1978	Le Château de sable (Co Hoedeman)
1979	Special Delivery (John Weldon, Eunice Macaulay)
1980	Every Child/Chaque enfant (Eugene Fedorenko)
1983	If You Love This Planet (Terre Nash)
1984	Flamenco at 5:15 (Cynthia Scott)
1995	Bob's Birthday (Alison Snowden, David Fine)
2004	Ryan (Chris Landreth)
2007	The Danish Poet (Torril Kove)
OTHER CATEGORIES	
Year	Award
1989	Honorary Oscar in recognition of NFB's fiftieth anniversary
1999	Technical achievement to NFB scientists Ed H. Zwaneveld and Frederick Gasoi and two industry colleagues for the design and development of the Film Keykode Reader

Source: www.nfb.ca.

In a sense, our own domestic cinema is foreign to Canadian audiences. For most of its history, the Canadian film market has been treated as an extension of the US market. The industry has been characterized by **vertical integration**, in which the same Hollywood studios that produce feature films also own film distribution companies and movie theatres. Vertical integration ensures the distribution and exhibition of Hollywood studio films, making it very difficult for independent film producers to compete. Until 2004–5, the same companies that owned major Hollywood studios also owned Canada's principal theatre chains—Famous Players and Cineplex Odeon—and the distribution companies that supplied those theatre chains with films. Famous Players was owned by Viacom Inc. of New York, which owned the Hollywood studio Paramount Pictures. Cineplex Odeon merged with Sony Inc.'s Loews Theatres in 1998 to form Loews Cineplex Entertainment (LCE). LCE's principal shareholders at the time were the Hollywood studios Sony Pictures and Universal Studios.

In March 2002, Loews was purchased by the Canadian companies Onex Corp. and Oaktree Capital. Onex and Oaktree subsequently sold Loews in 2004, but Onex retained an ownership interest in its Canadian theatre properties through Cineplex Galaxy LP. In 2005, Cineplex Galaxy LP purchased Famous Players from Viacom in a $500-million deal that merged Canada's two largest theatre chains under the new name Cineplex Entertainment LP. Today, Cineplex Entertainment LP is owned by the publicly traded Cineplex Galaxy Income Fund (www.cineplex.com).

Canada has three major theatre chains, which own about two-thirds of the country's cinema screens. Cineplex Entertainment is by far the largest chain, with 129 theatres and 1,342 screens across the country (www.cineplex.com). Independently owned Empire Theatres is the second largest, with 51 theatres and 390 screens (www.empiretheatres.com). The third big player is AMC Entertainment Inc., with eight theatres in the greater Toronto area, Montreal, and Ottawa, with 184 screens. A North American movie exhibition company, AMC Entertainment is a subsidiary of Marquee Holdings of Kansas City (www.amctheatres.com).

After decades of Hollywood dominance of Canadian theatre screens, Canadians have come to associate cinema with Hollywood cinema, rendering 'foreign' all those films made by other countries, including Canadian-made films. In 2007–08, the most recent year for which figures are available, Canadian films accounted for almost one-fifth of the movies playing in Canadian movie houses, but a meagre 2.8 per cent of the box office. Canadian films earned a 13.8-per-cent share of the French-language market, but just 1.1 per cent of the English-language market. There was one Canadian film among the top 10 earners in the French-language market—*Cruising Bar 2*, which earned $3.5 million—but none among the top 10 in the English-language market. Only one English-language Canadian feature film earned more than $1 million at the box office (*Passchendaele*, $4.34 million) (CFTPA, 2009: 72–5).

Although at the federal level the primary policy concern in the post-war period has been increasing the production and distribution of Canadian feature films for theatrical, home video/DVD, and television release, provincial governments—most notably in Quebec, Ontario, and British Columbia—have instituted programs to encourage Hollywood producers to locate their film and television productions in such cities as Montreal, Toronto, and Vancouver (see Gasher, 2002; Elmer and Gasher, 2005). This foreign location service production accounted for $1.8 billion in spending in 2007–8, two-thirds of it in British Columbia alone. US producers were responsible for three-quarters of the 210 foreign location service productions that year (CFTPA, 2009: 76).

In the early years of the last century, Ottawa perceived cinema as a medium of nation-building. The first state-sponsored films in Canada were tools to promote immigration from Britain to settle the Prairies; motion pictures are believed to have played a key role in Canada attracting three million immigrants between 1900 and 1914. Early films were also used to lure industry and investment capital (Morris, 1978: 133–5). The use of film as a medium of propaganda during World War I led governments to play an increasing role in film production, and Canada became the first country in the world with government film production units, although Ottawa consistently rejected calls to curtail American monopolization of the commercial film sector. A distinction was made by state

officials between the purposeful films of government production and entertainment films (Magder, 1985: 86). The establishment of the National Film Board of Canada under the direction of John Grierson in 1939 entrenched the state as a producer of films for nation-building purposes.

Increasingly in the post-war period, the federal government has been called upon to address the commercial film sector. The first serious attempt by the Canadian government to stimulate indigenous feature-film production was the establishment of the Canadian Film Development Corporation (CFDC, now Telefilm Canada) in 1967. The CFDC was mandated to: invest in Canadian feature-film projects; loan money to producers; present awards for outstanding production; support the development of film craft through grants to filmmakers and technicians; and 'advise and assist' producers in distributing their films (ibid., 148).

Private investment in film production had been encouraged by Ottawa since 1954 through a 60 per cent capital-cost allowance, a tax deduction available to investors in any film, no matter the source. The law was revised in 1974 to increase the write-off to 100 per cent, but only for investments in Canadian feature films. The impact of the capital-cost allowance is debatable in terms of the program's cultural and economic objectives. The 1985 *Report of the Film Industry Task Force* (Canada, 1985: 28–9) concluded that the capital-cost allowance, in fact, 'widened the gap between production and market'. Because the introduction of the 100 per cent capital-cost allowance coincided with the CFDC's decision to drop its demand for a distribution agreement as a funding prerequisite, the capital-cost allowance in effect reduced the importance of distributor participation in Canadian film projects. As a result, 'while the supply of Canadian theatrical properties increased considerably, many were totally unmarketable'. Investors proved to be more interested in tax savings than in cinema; when returns on investment were not forthcoming and the economic recession of the early 1980s hit, private investment in film production dried up.

Canadian governments have been reluctant to impose protectionist measures on the film industry, even though Ottawa heard repeated calls for screen quotas in Canadian movie theatres throughout the twentieth century. Part of the problem, certainly, is that the operation of movie theatres falls under provincial jurisdiction, and a nationwide screen quota would demand co-ordination among the 10 provinces. But there really is no public appetite for reducing in any way Hollywood's stranglehold on the Canadian market. Most Canadians—including francophones in Quebec—believe that going to the movies means going to Hollywood movies, and until at least the late 1980s there was probably not a large enough stock of quality Canadian features to warrant a quota.

Neither the 1984 *National Film and Video Policy* (Canada, 1984), introduced by the Liberal government, nor the 1985 *Report of the Film Industry Task Force* (Canada, 1985), delivered to the Conservative government of Brian Mulroney, favoured quotas, preferring instead to target the structural issues of distribution and vertical integration. Distribution is the key sector in the industry because it is a critical source of film financing and it is the pipeline that controls the supply of films to theatres. The 1985 Task Force report was on the mark, recommending that all film distribution in Canada be carried out by Canadian-controlled companies, that measures be adopted to prevent the vertical integration of distribution and exhibition companies, and that the bidding system for films be changed to ensure that all exhibitors can compete fairly for all films. While the Mulroney government talked tough about taking back control of Canada's commercial film industry, it was also negotiating a free-trade agreement with the United States. At the end of the day, it was decided that restructuring the Canadian film industry ran contrary to the spirit and the letter of the free-trade agreement (see Gasher, 1988).

As a result of Canadian cinema's difficulty in penetrating Canadian movie theatres, television has become since the 1980s the largest source of revenue for private Canadian film and video companies. Television is a friendlier platform for Canadian movies, thanks to Canadian ownership and Canadian content regulations, the CBC's inherent interest in Canadian content, and the licensing in the 1980s of pay-television and specialty

channels devoted to broadcasting feature-length films. In recognition of the promise television held, the federal government in 1983 altered the mandate of the Canadian Film Development Corporation. The federal Department of Communications introduced the $35-million Canadian Broadcast Development Fund, to be administered by the CFDC, which later that year changed its name to Telefilm Canada to reflect its new emphasis on television. While the sum of money in the Broadcast Fund may not appear significant, it increased considerably the ability of production companies to access other sources of investment and it encouraged Canadian film producers to look more and more to television production. Magder (1985: 211) argues: 'In a very real sense the Canadian government had solved the problem of distribution and exhibition by gearing production activities to the regulated market of Canadian television.'

Building audiences was the central theme of a new feature-film policy introduced by the federal Heritage Ministry in October 2000 (Canada, 2000). The ambitious goal of this policy, entitled *From Script to Screen*, was to capture 5 per cent of the domestic box office within five years—compared to a paltry 2.1 per cent in 1999—and to increase audiences for Canadian features abroad. The policy amounted to a doubling of the Canadian government's investment in the industry, from $50 million to $100 million annually. The new Canadian Feature Film Fund, administered by Telefilm Canada, supports screenwriting, production, marketing, and promotion. The biggest investment—$40 million annually—goes to the Project Development, Production and Marketing Assistance Program. A 'performance-based component' to this program allocates money to producers and distributors based primarily on their track records of success at the box office, but also recognizes the degree of Canadian content and critical acclaim achieved. A 'selective component' funds the production and distribution of innovative and culturally relevant projects by new filmmakers. The policy also supports screenwriting, professional development, promotion, and film preservation.

Since the early 1980s, Ottawa has been gradually ceding its leadership role in the film policy field to the private sector and the provinces. Even though Telefilm remains the single most important source of film funding, no film can be made with Telefilm money alone. Filmmakers find themselves tapping half a dozen sources of funding to get their films made. Canada's major banks and broadcasters have become important sources of financing for both project development and film and television production. These funding sources include Astral Media's Harold Greenberg Fund, Bell Broadcast and New Media Fund, Bravo!Fact, Film Finances Canada, Independent Production Fund, and Quebecor Fund.

Canada's provincial governments have adopted a two-track film strategy. Every province in the country has a film office to promote it as a location for film and television production, primarily to Hollywood producers. In addition, the provinces provide development, production, and/or post-production support to indigenous producers through such funding vehicles as grants, loans, direct investment, and tax credits on labour costs. *Playback*, the Canadian film industry trade magazine, provides current listings of public-sector and private commercial funding sources and programs (see http://bluepages.playbackonline.ca/).

Digitization is compelling theatre companies to convert their projection systems from 35-mm film to digital, which allows for closed captioning and language choice, and 3D. Their business includes online ticket and DVD sales, in-house media (pre-show advertising, film magazines), and merchandising.

Reminiscent of the late 1940s and early 1950s when television arrived, movie theatres today compete with increasingly sophisticated, high-definition and wide-screen home theatres, as well as a growing number of online movie services. For example, iTunes has been offering movie downloads since 2008, and two new download services were introduced to Canada in 2010: Netflix and Cineplex. Cineplex is part of the Digital Entertainment Content Ecosystem, an initiative by the Hollywood studios to establish a standard system to allow films to be stored and played on any digital device. Disney is establishing its own system

(Mah, 2010; Krashinsky, 2010b). As they did at the dawn of television, filmmakers are seeking ways to make the cinema experience distinct from rival viewing platforms (e.g., by experimenting with 3D, huge screens, digital sound).

New Media

Many new features compose the present media landscape. We are referring in broad terms to **new media** technologies, new media forms, and new media applications that have emerged since the 1990s and are associated with the production of digitized information and its distribution through converged computerized communications networks. Such technologies include the internet, CD-ROMs, DVD hand-held mobile devices of all kinds, and portable computers of all kinds. These entail forms that only recently have become familiar, like World Wide Web pages, blogs, podcasts, RSS feeds, fan fiction, and wikis. New media applications include interactive gaming, text messaging, video conferencing, mash-ups, and social networking (Burkell, 2010: 314–17). Because new media are digital, they allow for a converged and networked architecture, and they permit—even encourage—interactivity and content manipulation. NewMedia TrendWatch (2010) reports 26 million internet users in Canada as of June 2010 (77 per cent of the population), accessing the internet via desktop and laptop computers, netbooks, smartphones,

A decade ago, text messaging was an uncommon practice, but today it is one of the most widely used methods of communication.

mobile phones, MP3/MP4 players, and video-game consoles.

Industry Canada (2009) groups 31,500 companies within a $155 billion information and communication technologies (ICT) sector. Almost 80 per cent of these companies are involved in the software and computer services industry, which comprises software publishing, computer systems design, data processing, telecommunications services, and program distribution. The sector is characterized by small companies (most have fewer than 10 employees), a well-educated workforce (more than 40 per cent have university degrees), and considerable private-sector spending on research and development.

The Canadian government does not regulate new media, other than to enforce existing laws that apply universally. This decision stems originally from a CRTC policy consultation in 1998–9 that addressed three questions:

1. Do any of the new media constitute services already defined by the Broadcasting Act or the Telecommunications Act, and if so, how should they be regulated?

2. How do the new media affect the regulation of the traditional broadcasting undertakings of radio, television, and cable?

3. Do the new media raise any other broad policy issues of national interest?

The CRTC determined that, for the most part, the internet is not subject to either the Broadcasting Act or the Telecommunications Act. For those materials that do fall under the legal definition of 'broadcasting'—e.g., digital audio services and audiovisual signals—'the Commission has concluded that regulation is not necessary to achieve the objectives of the Broadcasting Act.' There was already a wealth of Canadian content on the internet at the time and the Commission ruled that new media were having no detrimental impact on either radio and television audiences or advertising. The Commission further determined that websites specializing in 'offensive and illegal content', such

BOX 8.9   THE VIDEO-GAME INDUSTRY

The sub-sector of the information and communication technologies industry with the highest profile in Canada is the video-game industry, a $1.7 billion industry with 247 companies and 14,000 employees, concentrated primarily in Vancouver and Montreal (Hickling Arthurs Low Corp., 2009). An export-intensive growth industry, the sector entails video-game production, the provision of tools, applications, and software for game developers, and support services for video-game players. The best-known and largest of these companies are EA Canada in Vancouver and Ubisoft in Montreal. Industry activity in Vancouver benefits from its proximity to the Hollywood film and television industry, which is increasingly integrating its products into video games. Montreal earned its reputation through the 3D animation work of Softimage in the 1990s, software that was used, for instance, in the Hollywood blockbuster *Jurassic Park*. The biggest companies in Montreal today are Ubisoft and EA Mobile. The video-game industry benefits from government support in the form of labour tax credits in five provinces: Prince Edward Island, Nova Scotia, Quebec, Ontario, and Manitoba.

The key issue confronting the video-game industry is talent development. To that end, Ubisoft established in 2005 a campus in Montreal that offers college and university-level courses in collaboration with the Cégep de Matane and l'Université de Sherbrooke. EA donated $1 million in 2007 to establish a master's degree program in Digital Media at the Great Northern Way Campus in Burnaby, BC, in collaboration with the University of British Columbia, Simon Fraser University, the British Columbia Institute of Technology, and the Emily Carr Institute of Art and Design. The Ontario College of Art and Design was also reported to be developing a digital media program (ibid.). The Entertainment Software Association of Canada (www.theesa.ca/) tracks developments in the industry and is a good source for information. Nick Dyer-Witheford of the University of Western Ontario leads a research team investigating the Canadian video game and computer industry, and its website—http://publish.uwo.ca/~ncdyerwi/—provides data and analysis.

as pornography and hate messages, were already covered by Criminal Code provisions (see www.crtc.gc.ca/eng/archive/1999/PB99-84.htm).

The CRTC revisited this question in 2008–9 by conducting a public consultation on the subject of new media broadcasting. In announcing its 2009 New Media Policy, the CRTC reaffirmed its 'hands-off' policy, but called on the government of Canada to devise a national digital strategy (CRTC, 2009b). In a speech to the Banff World Television Festival in June 2009, CRTC chairman Konrad von Finckenstein insisted that 'we do not see new media today as a threat to the audience numbers of licensed broadcasters.' The 2009 New Media Policy exempts from licensing all providers of audio or video programming on the internet or through mobile devices using point-to-point technology. The CRTC referred to the Federal Court of Appeal the question of whether internet service providers (ISPs) constitute broadcasters—and hence should be licensed—when they provide online access to broadcast content.

The internet is not entirely beyond government regulation. The Montreal teenaged hacker Michael Calce (known as Mafiaboy) pleaded guilty to 56 charges and served eight months in a group home for his February 2000 denial-of-service attacks on five major websites, including Yahoo!, eBay, and CNN (CBC News, 2008). Officials are also patrolling the web for fraud and privacy violations, including identity theft (Box 8.10).

Further, as Vanda Rideout and Andrew Reddick (2001: 265) point out, new media are subject to the regulation of the market economy, effectively depriving Canadian citizens of policy input. One of their central concerns is the corporate power that converged media corporations can exert in the digital marketplace. 'What is somewhat different is that whereas particular firms may have dominated one or a few parts of the communications sector [in the past], now, with corporate, technical and content convergence, a handful of firms are dominating the whole communications marketplace' (ibid., 273).

Until Canada establishes a national digital strategy, the federal government's principal involvement in new media is through support programs that seek to ensure 'a dynamic and diverse Canadian cultural presence in both English and French on the Internet' (Canada, 2008). The Department of Canadian Heritage's Canadian Culture Online Strategy takes the form of a series of funding programs established between 2001 and 2005. The Partnerships Fund assists partnership initiatives between private and public not-for-profit organizations making available to Canadians online the cultural collections of local and provincial cultural organizations. The Gateway Fund aims to increase the amount of Canadian cultural content available on the internet. The Canada New Media Fund supports the development, production, and marketing/distribution of original and cultural interactive or online new media works.

⁂ BOX 8.10   ONLINE PRIVACY CONCERNS

Users gaining access to free online services can be valuable to web companies who either sell, or allow others to collect, information about their users. According to a research study by a Toronto social media technology firm, the average 'Facebook fan'—a user who endorses a company, product, or cause on the world's most popular social networking site—was worth $136.38 to marketers in 2010. Google and Yahoo! have been gathering and selling user data for years. Facebook, however, had to increase its users' privacy protections following a 2009 investigation by Canada's Privacy Commissioner. In a July 2009 report, the Privacy Commissioner accused Facebook of a series of privacy breeches, the most serious of which was 'a charge that Facebook was allowing application developers to temporarily scrape personal information, including names, e-mail addresses, birthdates, relationships and education history, every time a user clicked on a game or advertisement.' Canada was a leader in establishing in 2010 the Global Privacy Enforcement Network, a group of 17 privacy offices from around the world (El Akkad and McNish, 2010).

The Department of Canadian Heritage has also teamed up with Canada's museums to establish the Virtual Museum of Canada (www.museevirtuel-virtualmuseum.ca/) that brings together online collections from museums across the country.

Publishing

Digitization is the biggest challenge confronting the book, magazine, and newspaper publishing industries. For more than 500 years, publishing has meant the printing, transportation, and storage of physical and relatively bulky reading materials, and most of the costs associated with publishing are contained in the physical production and distribution of these materials: printing presses, paper, ink, transport, and the tradespeople who carry out these processes. These costs are exacerbated in a country like Canada, with a huge land mass and a relatively small and widely dispersed population. As more and more people access reading materials electronically—through the internet, through tablets, through e-readers—there is great potential for publishers to reduce production costs and, at the same time, expand their audiences. In this transitional period, though, publishers are having to produce *both* hard-copy and electronic editions with no assurance that the burgeoning market for electronic publications will generate the revenues that hard-copy publishing has provided, at least any time soon. The newspaper industry is discussed in considerable detail in the next two chapters, so our focus here is on book and magazine publishing.

Book publishing is a $2 billion industry in Canada, consisting of 1,500 publishing houses. Canadian-controlled publishers are responsible for 56 per cent of industry revenues, employ two-thirds of the industry's workers and publish more than 75 per cent of Canadian-authored books. There are 10,000 new books by Canadian authors published each year and the average Canadian household spent $108 on books in 2008. Most Canadian publishing houses are located in Ontario (63 per cent) and Quebec (30 per cent). Foreign-owned publishers control 44 per cent of the Canadian book market, specializing in mass-market titles, including Canadian best-sellers. The global book-publishing market is growing and electronic publishing is the biggest growth area; this sector grew by more than 50 per cent in 2009 (Canada, 2010a: 3; Ontario Media Development Corporation, 2010: 3–5).

Like all of the communications industries described in this chapter, the book industry is confronting the implications of digitization. Digitization is a promising development; whether through online book sales, on-demand publishing, direct orders, or electronic publishing, digitization holds out the promise to reduce printing, storage, and transportation costs; facilitate book promotion; and make more books available to more Canadians. However, digitization entails significant investment in new technologies for publishers and thus gives an advantage to the largest publishing houses; and it can create considerable distinctions between the

An increasing number of people have put their printed books on a shelf and turned instead to e- readers.

prices online booksellers can offer and the prices bookstores demand in order to remain profitable.

The biggest task facing Canadian publishers is, as always, accessing appropriate shelf space in bookstores to display their titles. The retail sales sector has changed dramatically since the 1990s as independent booksellers, which typically offered specialized lines and informed customer service, have been largely replaced by large retail chains. There are more than 3,000 bookstores in Canada, but there is only one national retail chain for English-language books—Chapters/Indigo, with about 45 per cent of the market—and two major chains for French-language books in Quebec—Archambault and Renaud-Bray, with 48 per cent of the market. Independent booksellers occupy about 20 per cent of the retail sales market (Canadian Heritage, 2010a: 4; Ėdinova, 2008: 74). New sales channels are emerging—e.g., online sales, e-books, non-traditional retailers like Wal-Mart and Costco—and will offset somewhat the concentration of the retail sales sector. But this shift to large retailers could diminish the range of books offered to Canadian readers: the large publishing companies will have the greatest access to these channels, because they produce the most popular books and their market share will allow them to withstand the aggressive price discounting that tends to be a feature of these outlets (Turner-Riggs, 2007: 8–9). Canadian publishers are already challenged by the impact a strong Canadian dollar has had on book prices. Aside from the overall increase in the price of new books, a strong Canadian dollar can make the Canadian list prices of books uncompetitive with those offered by US retailers even before the discounts typically offered by the major retailers (Turner-Riggs, 2007: 9–11).

Distribution, too, can be a bottleneck in getting books to readers. Book distribution in Canada is characterized by rising transportation costs, more rigorous inventory management, and the advantageous position of the largest publishers, who, as we noted above, offer the most profitable book lines (Turner-Riggs, 2008: 62). Canada lacks a national wholesaler who can match the scale and efficiency of the major US book wholesalers. Large-volume publishing companies, which tend to publish non-Canadian titles, are better positioned than smaller publishers, who are less attractive to distributors because they are more expensive to serve, especially if they are located outside the Greater Toronto Area where most of the book inventories are stored. 'Given that Canadian-owned firms are responsible for publishing a majority of Canadian-authored titles, this in turn indicates that the wide availability of a diverse selection of Canadian titles is heavily dependent on the ability of Canadian publishers to access effective distribution' (ibid., 53–4). As digital books sales increase, distribution problems for smaller publishers likely will worsen.

French-language publishers have been far more successful in getting their books to audiences; better than 90 per cent have access to national distribution and close to 90 per cent of Canadian French-language titles are distributed across the country (Ėdinova, 2008: 8). This advantage is due in part to the fact that they do not face the same head-to-head competition from the US as English-language publishers. But there are two other factors. One is Quebec's Bill 51, passed in 1981 to protect Canadian-owned booksellers. Bill 51 establishes an accreditation system whereby public institutions like schools and libraries are required to order their books from accredited local retailers (rather than directly from publishers or through wholesalers). Accredited publishers, distributors, and retailers are also eligible for Quebec government assistance programs (ibid., 20–2). The French-language publishing industry also uses an efficient book-ordering system, called the *système d'offre*. Based on agreements between distributors and retailers, newly published books are automatically shipped to bookstores in predetermined numbers. The distributors assume the shipping costs and the retailers assume the costs of returning unsold books (ibid., 19). This system ensures the timely and consistent diffusion of new French-language books by Canadian authors.

The federal government supports book publishing through a number of funding programs. The Canada Book Fund (formerly the Publishing Industry Development Program) had its funding of $39.5 million per year renewed in April 2010 for another five years. The Book Fund has two components: Support for Publishers, which aids the production and promotion of Canadian-authored books through financial assistance to Canadian-controlled publishers; and Support for Organizations, which assists the promotion of Canadian-authored books by industry organizations and associations through programs for marketing, professional development, strategic planning, internships, and technology projects. The Canada Council provides $19 million in grants each year to Canadian writers in a variety of genres. The National Translation Program for Book Publishing is a $5 million fund to support the translation of Canadian-authored books from English to French and French to English. The Public Lending Right provides $10 million annually to Canadian authors based on the presence of their books in libraries (Canada, 2010b, 2010c; Ontario Media Development Corporation, 2010). The federal government also protects the Canadian book industry through ownership restrictions with policy dating from 1974. The current investment policy restricts foreign investment in new businesses to Canadian-controlled joint ventures, prohibits the direct acquisition of a Canadian-controlled business by a non-Canadian, reviews indirect acquisitions based on the net benefit to Canada, and requires non-Canadians wishing to sell an existing book-industry venture to ensure that Canadian investors have full and fair opportunity to bid (Canada, 2010b: 8). The review committee for foreign investment policy affirmed that: 'Canadian control of Canadian book publishing is a key and long-standing tenet of the Government's policy in this area given the demonstrated commitment of Canadian-owned firms to the identification, development, and support of a wide range of Canadian writers' (ibid., 9). This policy came into play in the 2010 decision to approve the establishment of a Canadian distribution centre by the American company Amazon, one of the largest online booksellers, judging it to be in the best interests of Canada (ibid., 11–12).

As in other communications spheres, the provinces have their own support systems for book publishing. Ontario, for example, has the Ontario Arts Council, a book publishing tax credit, the Trillium Award to reward excellence among Ontario writers, and the Ontario Media Development Corporation's Book Fund and Export Fund (see Ontario Media Development Corporation, 2010: 7).

Revenu Québec offers a tax credit for book publishers and does not impose provincial income tax on writers' royalty payments. Quebec's Société de développement des entreprises culturelles (SODEC) has funding programs for book exports, publishing, the production of special editions, book fairs, libraries, book transportation, digitization; and it supports collectives and associations in the book publishing sector (SODEC, 2010).

Magazine publishing in Canada is a $1.5 billion industry producing 2,500 titles and employing the equivalent of 8,000 full-time workers. Like Canadian books, Canadian magazines compete with American titles, but Canadian magazines' share of the market has risen over the past 30 years, from 20 per cent to 40 per cent (Magazines Canada, 2008: 1–4). US magazines dominate newsstand shelves, with 95 per cent of shelf presence and a corresponding 95 per cent of the sales; of the top 40 English-language magazines sold on Canadian newsstands, only six are Canadian (ibid., 5). But Canadian magazines dominate subscription sales, with a 70-per-cent share (ibid., 10).

Faced with significant competition and high distribution costs, the magazine industry is one of Canada's most volatile, and most diverse, media sectors. Some magazines are published by large media corporations like Transcontinental, Quebecor, and Rogers, while others are produced by foundations, associations, and artists' collectives. New magazine titles appear each year, but many of these titles don't last long. According to Statistics Canada data, about one-third of Canadian magazines do not make a profit. The average profit for the industry as a whole is modest, ranging from 6 to 8 per cent (ibid., 21–4). That said, there is considerable optimism in the industry overall. In the last five years, 256 new magazines have been launched, advertising revenue is growing, and readership numbers are stable; the time Canadians spend reading magazines each month remains steady at just over 40 minutes (ibid.). Canada's general-interest magazines earned $692 million in advertising revenues in the recession year of 2008, their first decline after 10 years of steady increases (Canadian Media Directors' Council, 2010: 13).

While almost all magazines have an online presence, few magazines in any country have been financially successful with their online editions due to uncertainty about revenue streams. With so many free choices for online audiences, there is little appetite for paying subscription fees and online advertising spending remains low compared to other media. The Ontario Media Development Corporation (2008: 21–2), in a study of the province's magazine industry, noted 'there is little consensus around how magazine publishers can derive revenue from their investments in the Internet, beyond certain benefits in terms of marketing and promotion which most have been quick to seize.'

As a general rule, Canadian magazines earn about two-thirds of their revenue from advertising and just under 20 per cent from subscriptions. However, this varies greatly from magazine to magazine. The key source of government funding comes from the Department of Canadian Heritage's Canada Periodical Fund, which provides to the industry $75.5 million annually. The Canada Periodical Fund replaced both the Canadian Magazine Fund and the Publications Assistance Program in 2010. The fund contains three elements: Aid to Publishers, which supports content creation, production, distribution, online activities, and business development for Canadian magazines (print, online) and non-daily newspapers; Business Innovation, which provides monies for small and mid-sized magazines (print, online); and Collective Initiatives, which funds organizations' efforts to increase the overall sustainability of the Canadian magazine and non-daily newspaper industries (Canada, 2010d). The new fund provides the same amount of money as the programs it replaced, but with some differences. First, it caps grants to any one magazine at $1.5 million (with the exception of farming magazines), meaning some of the biggest beneficiaries in past years will receive less, while others will receive more. Second, qualifying publications must have circulations of 5,000 copies or more annually (with the exception of ethnocultural, Aboriginal, official language minority magazines, and magazines serving the gay, lesbian, bisexual, and transgender communities), meaning some small-circulation arts and literary magazines will be cut off. Third, magazines published by professional associations—e.g., the Canadian Medical Association—will no longer be eligible (Masthead, 2010).

The biggest change, however, is the cancellation in 2009 of the $15 million annual subsidy that Canada Post used to provide to support the Publications Assistance Program (PSP). Given the magazine industry's reliance on subscriptions mailed to readers, Magazines Canada had described the Canada Post–subsidized PAP as 'the most successful cultural industry policy of the Government of Canada' (Magazines Canada, 2008: 10). Distribution has become the fastest-rising cost for magazine publishers. Not only do postal rates continue to rise, but in 1998 the World Trade Organization overturned Canada Post's preferential rates for Canadian magazines (ibid., 11).

Postal Service

The postal system typically is overlooked by communications scholars, even though it is our oldest mass medium and its history remains closely bound to the history of transportation in Canada (see Gendreau, 2000) The post office was one of the first federal government departments established after Confederation in 1867, but both the French and British colonial regimes had postal service in the earliest days of the colony. The French relied on ships to transport mail across the Atlantic Ocean from France and along the St Lawrence River valley in the seventeenth and eighteenth centuries. Mail was carried overland by travellers and fur traders forming a 'human network of communication' (Willis, 2000: 36–7). The British established a formal postal system along the St Lawrence River valley in 1763 under the governance of a deputy postmaster general. Service was introduced to

Although this rural mailbox is a nostalgic reminder of a much more agricultural Canada of the past, mail has not been entirely displaced by email and other electronic means of communication.

Nova Scotia in 1785 (Willis, 2000: 39–40). Canada Post was created as a Crown corporation in 1981 after having been run directly as a department of the federal government since 1868.

While email has no doubt replaced a great deal of personal and business letter-writing, there remains a need for the physical delivery of letters, documents, greeting cards, catalogues, parcels, books, magazines, newspapers, and commercial advertising. Canada Post operates more than 6,500 post offices across the country and in 2009 moved 11 billion pieces of mail to 15 million addresses. It has the exclusive right to collect and deliver letters up to 500 grams in Canada, and is mandated by the Canada Post Corporation Act (1985) to deliver to every Canadian address five days per week (Canada Post, 2009: 2–6). The corporation has three core business sectors: letter mail and courier service, parcel delivery, and direct marketing (e.g., advertising flyers). Canada Post competes with other, private direct-marketing and courier companies in these growing industry sectors.

An international agreement established the General Post Union in 1874 (later renamed the Universal Postal Union), ensuring the free transportation of mail within member countries and the standardization of charges collected by each country for mail service between members (Hamelink, 1994: 7). As a Crown corporation providing what is considered to be a key communications service, Canada Post is required by the federal government to undertake special obligations. These include: the provision of free mail service between Canadian citizens and designated members of government; reduced postal rates for the shipping of books between libraries; the transportation of nutritious, perishable foods and other essential items to isolated northern communities; and the free mailing of materials for the blind (Canada Post, 2009: 28). As noted, in 2009, Canada Post cancelled its $15 million annual subsidy to support Canadian magazine postal distribution.

⠂ SUMMARY

This chapter began by outlining two significant changes impacting the media landscape in recent years, changes that have far-reaching implications for Canadian communications policy: the convergence or merging of previously distinct technologies, media forms, and media industries; and trade liberalization, which puts pressure on Canada to make its policies, laws, and regulations conform to international trade agreements. What has not changed is Canada's central policy priority of ensuring that Canadians benefit from the opportunities that mass communication affords.

The chapter provided a profile of each of the major communications sectors—telecommunications, broadcasting, recorded music, cinema, new media, publishing, postal service—and outlined their respective policy challenges, providing current information about

these industries and policy responses by governments. Each of the sectors had things in common—e.g., new services, digitization—as well as distinctions particular to their field.

It is clear that each of these sectors finds itself in a transitional phase between analog or hard-copy platforms and new, digital platforms. This transition implicates communications companies seeking emergent revenue streams while still reliant on traditional income sources; it implicates individuals transitioning to new ways of communicating; and it affects policy-makers striving to serve the interests of Canadian communications industries and Canadian citizens in an environment characterized by an increasing amount of global governance.

⠂ KEY TERMS

Canadian content, p. 223
Canadian Radio-television and Telecommunications Commission, p. 215
common carriage, p. 215
consortium, p. 217

contract carrier, p. 215
cultural industries, p. 214
cultural sovereignty, p. 219
file-sharing, p. 228
interactivity, p. 214
net neutrality, p. 216

new media, p. 233
silos, p. 213
spectrum allocation, p. 217
vertical integration, p. 230

⠂ RELATED WEBSITES

Canadian Radio-television and Telecommunications Commission: www.crtc.gc.ca
The CRTC website contains a wealth of information about the broadcasting and telecommunications industries, as well as industry studies, press releases, and current decisions rendered.

Canadian Video Game and Computer Industry: http://publish.uwo.ca/~ncdyerwi/
This site contains current research—statistics and analysis—on the Canadian video game and computer industry produced by a University of Western Ontario team led by Nick Dyer-Witheford.

Department of Canadian Heritage: www.pch.gc.ca/
This site is that of the government ministry responsible for communications and culture. It contains information on all of the cultural industry sectors as well as news releases and speeches pertaining to the ministry.

Music in the Cloud: http://musicinthecloud.wordpress.com/
Produced in support of the 2009 Patrik Wikström book *The Music Industry*, this site contains updated news, information, and analysis on the global music industry.

Playback's BluePages Directory: http://bluepages. playbackonline.ca
Produced by *Playback*, Canada's trade magazine for the film, television, video, and interactive media industries, this guide provides information about companies

working in the industry. It also provides a guide to both government and non-government funding sources for audiovisual producers.

⋙ FURTHER READINGS

Armstrong, Robert. 2010. *Broadcasting Policy in Canada*. Toronto: University of Toronto Press. This is an accessible, comprehensive, and current portrait of the policy picture for broadcasting in Canada. It covers every aspect of broadcast regulation in detail, and situates Canadian policies with respect to international trade and cultural agreements.

Canadian Journal of Communication. Canada's premier source for current research on communication issues in all areas. Current and back issues can be accessed online at: www.cjc-online.ca/index.php/journal.

Playback Magazine. Canada's trade magazine for the film, television, video, and interactive media industries, this weekly publication provides up-to-date industry news, information, and analysis. Current

issues and its news archive can be accessed online at: http://playbackonline.ca/.

Shade, Leslie Regan, ed. 2010. *Mediascapes: New Patterns in Canadian Communication*, 3rd edn. Toronto: Nelson Education. This book comprises a series of chapters on contemporary communications issues, focusing on media practices and content.

Wikström, Patrik. 2009. *The Music Industry*. Cambridge, UK: Polity Press. As its title suggests, this book provides an analysis of the structures of the international music industry, and what changes in the way music is distributed and consumed imply for producers and distributors.

⋙ STUDY QUESTIONS

1. Why are Canada's media companies not moving more aggressively into digital platforms?
2. Why has net neutrality become an important issue?
3. Robert Armstrong points out that internet providers are contributing to the decline in radio and television audiences, but are not contributing economically to the creation of audiovisual programming. What is the solution to this problem?
4. The CRTC has decided not to regulate new media. Does this mean that new media are not subject to any form of regulation?
5. How have your media consumption habits changed in recent years?
6. What are the most important communications concerns facing Canadians? What can be done about those concerns?

CHAPTER 9

Ownership and the Economics of Media

> You can say that at times freedom in our kind of society amounts to the freedom to say anything you wish, provided you can say it profitably.
>
> — RAYMOND WILLIAMS, 1989

Learning Objectives

- To understand that there is no natural or inevitable way to organize the media.
- To understand how, and the extent to which, media organizations participate in the economy.
- To recognize the fundamental distinctions between public and private forms of ownership.
- To be able to explain the implications for media content of public and private ownership.
- To be able to identify media reform initiatives and the emergence of alternative media movements that seek to alter the Canadian mediascape.

OPENING QUESTIONS

- How does economics impact mass communication?
- In what ways do media organizations participate in the economy?
- What roles does advertising play in mass communication?
- What fundamental distinctions are there between publicly owned and privately owned media?
- Why does it matter who owns the media?

Introduction

Though we use the term 'mass media' quite often, we can easily forget how diverse a sector this is, especially in these times. A mass medium can be a small, co-operatively run alternative magazine or a national television network. There is no natural or inevitable way to organize the mass media; their structures evolve through time, and different societies organize their media in particular ways. The United Kingdom, France, the United States, and Canada—all Western, liberal democracies—structure their mass media in distinct ways in response to particular social needs, desires, and pressures. Even within the same country, different rules are applied to different media, as we discussed in Chapters 7 and 8. Our mass media institutions are not simply products of technology, but are organized according to the particular characteristics of the given medium, the resources it draws upon, and the socio-political context in which it operates.

Nevertheless, all media organizations have something in common. No matter how they are organized, they participate in the economy, the sphere of society in which, in the words of media economist Robert G. Picard (1989: 8–9), 'limited or scarce resources are allocated to satisfy competing and unlimited needs or wants.' This is the heart of economics: how we pay for the things we need and want. Producing things requires money, labour, and material resources, and what economists seek to understand is how the money, labour, and resources interact.

Picard identifies four groups served by the media: media owners, audiences, advertisers, and media workers (ibid., 9)—to which we would add, governments. Each of these groups is multi-layered and requires some elaboration. The category of media owners, for instance, can range from the complex management groups of large, converged, and publicly traded corporations—such as Quebecor or BCE—to community groups or individuals with their own websites. Some of these groups are motivated primarily by profit, others by some kind of **public service** or social purpose. Media owners include governments (e.g., the National Film Board of Canada), labour organizations (e.g., the Ontario Teachers' Pension Plan investment in CTVglobemedia), political groups (e.g., the Communist Party of Canada's newspaper *The People's Voice*), non-profit foundations (e.g., *The Walrus*, published by The Walrus Foundation), non-government organizations (*Greenpeace Magazine*), co-operatives (e.g., Atlantic Filmmakers Cooperative), and individual businesspeople (e.g., Brunswick News). Regardless of who they are or what their motivation is, they participate in some way in the economy.

We used to think of audiences as passive consumers of media products and services. But as we discussed earlier, research has demonstrated that audiences are much more active in the ways they choose, receive, draw meaning from, and make use of media than was previously understood or appreciated. These audiences have become much more active in the era of digital media, which allow media consumers to also become media producers—hence the term 'prosumers'—whether by engaging in online discussion groups, putting together music compilations for their MP3 players, sharing commercial TV or film on YouTube, alerting followers to breaking news via Twitter, or going much further in producing mash-ups, sampling music, or documenting their own daily lives on Facebook. Regardless of the nature of their media use, members of the audience are crucial to the economic vitality of the media.

Advertisers use media not only to promote the goods and services they want to sell, but as well to project a certain kind of brand identification. Think of the number of companies using advertising to foster a 'green' image. From an economic standpoint, advertisers generate revenue for media organizations in their quest to speak to audiences about the products and services they want to sell; they buy access to audiences (Box 9.1).

Media workers comprise a heterogeneous group ranging from the star directors and actors of a Hollywood blockbuster to those who make their living in the film industry as carpenters, electricians, drivers, and hairdressers. Some media workers, in other words, have a central and direct role

⁙ BOX 9.1   ADVERTISING

Advertising is a medium of communication in and of itself, and serves a number of purposes. Its most obvious purpose is to provide consumers with information about goods and services available in the marketplace. Advertisements can also be used to provide information of general public interest; governments, for example, are among the biggest media advertisers and use advertising both to inform citizens—about new programs, changes in laws or regulations, public health warnings, etc.—and to persuade citizens about government policy. Advertisements can also be read for what they say about predominant social and cultural values (e.g., gender roles, notions of beauty, health, happiness, and success).

Less obvious, perhaps, is the role of advertising in the overall economy. A capitalist economy requires perpetual and ever-increasing consumer spending. Advertising, in this way, is an important driver of the economy, acting as a catalyst for consumer spending. Advertising is believed by economists to create demand for products and services (Leiss et al., 2005: 32–3), and without 'a mechanism for mass distribution of information about products', the economies of scale of mass marketing may be unattainable (ibid., 16). Companies, as actors within the larger economy, advertise in order to maintain and expand revenue flows, to generate new and repeat business, to create new markets by informing consumers about new products and services, and to compete with rival companies and brands.

The media are advertising's principal vehicles of delivery. As communications theorist Dallas Smythe (1977) observed, the media's principal commodity is the audience, which is sold to advertisers. If advertising first appeared in newspapers, magazines, and catalogues, and on flyers, posters, and billboards in the last half of the nineteenth century, all media serve advertisers today and 'the business of advertising structures media operations in a capitalist economy' (Johnston, 2010: 104). Russell Johnston argues that 'every media outlet tries to produce an audience sought by advertisers' (ibid., 105).

For media companies, advertising is a critical revenue source. In the case of commercial, over-the-air radio and television, free newspapers and magazines, and many websites, it is their sole revenue source. Other media combine subscription fees with advertising. Most daily newspapers and monthly magazines derive 60 to 80 per cent of their revenues from advertising, which greatly subsidizes the newsstand or home-delivery price. Even media that previously relied solely on retail sales are turning to advertising for additional revenues. For example, if the previews that are screened prior to the feature attraction in movie theatres can be seen as a form of advertising, it is common today to present paid advertisements prior to the previews in Canadian movie theatres. Companies often pay film producers a fee for 'product placement' within the movies: the use of a recognizable brand by the characters or as a visible element of the backdrop.

Advertising is turning all public spaces into advertising vehicles, into media for commercial messages: bathroom walls, handles of self-serve gas pumps, the floors in subway transit systems. Even the logo on your sweater, your jeans, or your running shoes is an advertisement.

to play in the creation of the content we see on our screens, while many others play indispensable roles in media support networks: running printing presses, entering data, selling advertising, applying makeup, maintaining servers. Some of these workers are paid royalties or have an ownership stake and, therefore, have a clear and direct financial interest in the welfare of the enterprise. Others are hired project by project and are paid an hourly wage for a contract of limited duration. Thus, media workers can have very different stakes in the operation, the mission, and the overall welfare of the media organization.

Through their cultural policy apparatus, governments adopt guidelines and laws that compel media organizations to serve the needs and wants of national or regional constituencies, as we saw in Chapters 7 and 8. This has meant ensuring Canadians have access to the cultural and economic opportunities that participation in the media affords.

It is amid these currents and counter-currents that we consider media economics and the various forms of ownership in this chapter: their goals, methods of operation, and strengths and shortcomings within the context of the interests of the society as a whole.

Advertising is around us every day.

Motion picture crews are made up of a large group of people, each with highly specialized skills.

Allocating Resources

Resources are the ingredients media organizations require in order to generate and disseminate their product or service; media economics studies how these resources are acquired and paid for. Typically, these resources fall into four categories: labour; technology; capital; and material resources. Some media forms are more resource-intensive than others and therefore demand greater investment. Motion picture production, for example, typically requires large crews encompassing a diverse collection of highly skilled workers, elaborate costumes and sets, considerable amounts of advanced technology, and, therefore, significant levels of capital investment. The major film companies also have their own distribution networks. Few have access to such resources. While low-budget films do get made and distributed, film production remains a resource-intensive form of art. Other media forms have much lower barriers to entry; a novel can be produced primarily through the labour of a lone individual and a website can be produced single-handedly with a personal computer.

The matter of what resources are required for media production is significant because it speaks directly to the questions of how mass media are organized, who owns the media, and whether they are owned for profit, for public service, for advocacy, or some combination of these. Questions about resources have a direct bearing on the kinds of books, music recordings, video games, films, and magazines that are produced and made available to us.

The category of 'labour' includes all of the 'human resources' required. This can range from a single individual writing and uploading a daily blog, to the dozens of people required to produce a weekly TV drama series, to the hundreds involved in the production of a big-budget feature film. The number of people and their skill level will have a noticeable impact on the quality of the production. The mass media bring together people specialized in particular creative processes with those skilled in the business side of the operation. The larger the media company, the greater the divide between these groups tends to be.

'Technology' refers partly to the equipment and, increasingly, to the specific software applications media organizations require. Clearly, some mass media—e.g., film, television, sound recording, computer games—require more investment in hardware and software than others. But technology also refers to the particular step-by-step processes by which production and dissemination are organized, and how, or whether, labour is divided among the various production tasks. Typically, large media organizations divide the production process into a series of specialized tasks—like an assembly line—while smaller organizations commonly require workers to perform several separate tasks. Digitization has made multi-tasking easier, allowing large media companies to cut staff and either outsource production tasks or combine them in-house, as a cost-saving measure. Computerization, for example, allowed newspaper companies in the 1970s and 1980s to eliminate some of their production departments—e.g., inputting and coding data, sizing photographs, page design, and makeup—and turn those production tasks over to journalists working with user-friendly software applications (see McKercher, 2002).

Capital refers not simply to money, but to money that is invested in media enterprises with the expectation of a return on investment. Most commonly the return is financial, but there are other kinds of returns. In the case of **commercial media**, investors are seeking a financial return at least comparable to what they would receive for investing in any other enterprise. But they may also be interested in the prestige that accrues from owning a media company or from being involved in a media project. Power and influence are other forms of return for commercial investors. Governments that own, or invest in, mass media have a primary interest in returns such as cultural development, regional industrial development, nation-building, job creation, or the expansion of the variety of cultural products and the range of voices within their jurisdictions. Governments may also turn their media into avenues for promoting their platforms and showcasing their achievements, especially prior to elections. Non-profit societies, co-operatives, and interest groups may participate in media to fill what they perceive to be gaps in media content or for the sole purpose of advocacy.

The media use *material* resources, too: paper to print books, magazines, and newspapers; plastics to produce CDs, DVDs, video games, and cellphones metals to produce TV sets, computers, DVD players, and sound systems; chemicals to produce ink and to fuel delivery vehicles. These materials not only cost money, but they link media economies to other economies and to the rules, regulations, and challenges affecting those economies. The attraction of electronic publishing is that it avoids the significant costs of paper, ink, and fuel for delivery vehicles, and at the same time extricates publishers from the environmental implications of paper, ink, and fuel production.

Much of the excitement about digital media, in fact, is that they are much less resource-intensive than their old media cousins. This translates into significant cost savings for old-media producers, but they also lower what economists call the **barriers to entry** for new participants in media production. Establishing a website, for instance, requires relatively few technological and capital resources, although it can require human resources comparable in number and skill level to old media if the site is to maintain quality standards and compete with all the other similar websites to generate an audience.

Markets consist of products—i.e., specific media products and services—and places. The Canadian market has a number of distinguishing features that must always be taken into account in considering the economics of mass communication in Canada, as Box 9.2 explains.

Source: CP Photo/Frank Gunn

Grammy-winning Canadian singer-songwriter Diana Krall poses for photographers as she receives her star on Canada's Walk of Fame.

BOX 9.2   THE CANADIAN MARKET

The very particular characteristics of the Canadian media market inform all of the economic decisions made by media companies, governments, and labour organizations. Although Canada constitutes an attractive market based on its relative affluence and technological sophistication, we have a small population—33 million—dispersed across a huge land mass, with most of us clustered within 100 kilometres of the border shared with the world's most productive and lucrative media market: the United States. If most Canadians share a common language with the US, we also have a significant French-language population concentrated in Quebec, which constitutes a media market of its own. We are a diverse population, based on race, ethnicity, and religion, as well on the regions in which we live. These characteristics of the Canadian market speak to our limited market power.

As users and consumers of media, we want access to the best the world has to offer, and in that sense we belong to a world market for popular culture. We want our artists and musicians and writers to be able to participate in that world market. And a great number, among them Oscar Peterson, Diana Krall, Margaret Atwood, Alice Munro, Atom Egoyan, Céline Dion, and Robert Lepage, have succeeded internationally.

But we also need a distinct and viable market for Canadian media products and services, those which may not have much reach beyond Canada's borders, but remain invaluable. As all peoples do, we want books and films and songs that speak to, teach us about, and keep a lasting record of our unique experiences. We want news and information that keeps us abreast of what is happening here—locally, regionally, nationally—and that reflects our own views and interests. We want to be able to see ourselves—literally, figuratively—in poems and plays and in the visual arts.

When we look at how mass communication in Canada is structured, we need to consider these particularities of the Canadian market.

Satisfying Needs and Wants

Each society makes decisions about how to structure its economy to satisfy its needs and wants. Western democracies are founded on a number of fundamental freedoms, including freedom of the individual, both as a political actor and as a participant in the economy. Western democracies have predominantly free-market economies, in which individuals are at liberty to engage in private enterprise, producing and consuming according to their own interests. But no economy is completely free; governments at all levels participate in the economy, in some instances providing the infrastructure that allows private enterprise to thrive—e.g., building roads, delivering water and hydroelectricity, funding public education, establishing favourable tax rates—and at other times tempering market forces when they feel it is in the public interest, however that interest may be defined. Typically, governments temper market forces both through restrictions and through incentives.

For most of the twentieth century Canadian governments took an interventionist stance towards the cultural industries. But, since the early 1980s, governments have become much more willing to let markets dictate prices and costs of production, not only in the communications realm, but also in the fields of health care and education. For another, free-market economics are becoming more popular world-wide and even former Communist countries are keen to become part of international organizations devoted to freer trade. Third, the crumbling of international trade barriers and advancements in technology have increased the global flow of communication services across borders, resulting in the availability of many more cultural choices from abroad than we've ever had before. Fourth, the globalization process, which is producing what David Morley and Kevin Robins (1995: 1) describe as 'a new communications geography' (Chapter 11), calls into question conventional notions of community: people's sense of how they belong to the national community has changed. All in all, it is becoming more and more difficult for governments to assume control of cultural production on behalf of their constituents.

These changes pertain to matters of how mass communication is structured, and for what purpose. Some media organizations are privately owned—by individuals, by companies—and respond to the profit motive, negotiating a compromise between the most profitable products and consumer demand. Others are publicly owned—by governments, by non-profit societies, by co-operatives—and respond to what they perceive to be collective needs and wants, mostly in areas of the economy where private enterprise cannot satisfactorily meet collective needs and wants.

The basis for **private ownership** derives from both classical and contemporary economic theory. In his classic study *The Wealth of Nations* (1937 [1776]), Adam Smith sought to explain how a free-market society manages to secure and to produce peoples' material needs—food, clothing, shelter—without any form of central economic planning. Smith formulated a set of basic 'laws' of the marketplace, and is perhaps best known for identifying the market's **invisible hand**, whereby 'the private interests and passions of men' are directed to serving the interests of society as a whole. As the political economist Robert Heilbroner (1980: 53) explains, Smith's laws of the marketplace 'show us how the drive of individual self-interest in an environment of similarly motivated individuals will result in competition; and they further demonstrate how competition will result in the provision of those goods and services that society wants, in the quantities that society desires, and at the prices society is prepared to pay.' Smith argued, in other words, that self-interest directs people to whatever work society is willing to pay for, and that this self-interest is regulated by competition with other self-interested parties. No one participant in the market can become greedy, because prices for goods and wages for workers are kept in line by competition. Similarly, competition regulates the supply of goods, preventing both overproduction and underproduction. Smith 'found in the mechanism of the market a self-regulating system for society's orderly provisioning' (ibid., 55).

While even in Smith's day—the earliest days of capitalism—there were price-fixing combines and **monopoly** producers who disrupted the competitive balance among producers, for the most part, eighteenth-century England conformed to Smith's model. Contemporary society, however, does not conform to Smith's model. For one thing, market competition has given way to market dominance—hence, the term **monopoly capitalism**—as huge corporations seek to minimize, even eliminate, competition among producers and as large labour unions seek to minimize competition among workers. Governments have entered the marketplace on the basis of the public interest, often set in contradistinction to self-interest, disrupting the neat functioning of Smith's 'invisible hand'. Government intervention, that is, has been quite visible in deliberately seeking to direct the economy to serve particular social interests, whether those interests are job creation for its citizens or maximizing export opportunities for domestic producers.

While neo-classical economists appeal to societies to revive the laissez-faire credo—leave the market alone to regulate itself—Smith's model has become increasingly divorced from economic reality as his 'laws' of the marketplace have been consistently violated by all parties over the past two centuries. The idea that the mass media simply serve the needs and wants of audiences, who base their consumption decisions on universally accepted notions of merit, is an attractive one. But the evidence suggests that in the cultural sector of the economy, too, Smith's 'laws' of the marketplace have limited application. Too often we associate TV and box-office ratings and book, magazine, and record sales as indicators of merit in the cultural market; as Box 9.3 explains, economic success is not always a reliable gauge of value.

BOX 9.3 THE MYTH OF MERITOCRACY

Myths are stories we tell ourselves to help us understand the way the world works. The myth of meritocracy is a story about the egalitarian nature of the media marketplace, whereby consumers discriminate among cultural products solely on the basis of universally accepted conceptions of worth. It asserts, in essence, that those books or records or movies that deserve to be made will be made and find an appreciative audience in the marketplace (see Gasher, 1992). While we might all like to believe that the media marketplace works without bias, the myth of meritocracy discounts completely the political economy of cultural production.

Merit, of course, is not completely irrelevant; audiences don't simply watch happily everything that's put in front of them, and we can all point to fine works that we've read or watched or heard and that have proved immensely popular. But the notion of merit is greatly overstated. For one thing, consumer demand is a product of industry supply. When we choose a television program or a movie to watch, our choice is restricted to what's available. When we browse the magazine racks, our choices are limited to what's being displayed. Most often, we have no say in what is produced.

Second, the myth of meritocracy denies the market power behind certain cultural producers. The major Hollywood film companies, for example, are tied into international distribution networks and theatre chains, ensuring themselves screen time in movie theatres around the world and narrowing the field of competition considerably by erecting significant barriers to entry. Their market power also allows them to hire the greatest star actors and directors to create, produce, and publicize the film.

Finally, the myth of meritocracy ignores the question of whose tastes determine the qualitative norm against which all other productions are measured, and how those tastes are determined. Commercial radio,

for instance, sets constraints pertaining to the length of songs, the language used in lyrics and the subject matter, which clearly favour easy listening over more challenging or provocative selections. We tend to buy the music we hear on the radio. Similarly, commercial television favours 30- or 60-minute dramatic programs with recognizable personalities and formats, and accessible, non-threatening story lines. Programming that doesn't fit these broadcast parameters usually isn't aired, and certainly not during prime time.

The World Wide Web has vastly increased the size of the marketplace and created at least some room for alternatives (see Anderson, 2006). This innovation addresses our first point about audience choice, in part, but does nothing to address either the question of market power or of qualitative norms.

The media market most certainly has a commercial bias; the greater the size of the audience a book or movie or album is likely to appeal to, the greater the chance it will be produced and benefit from its producer's market power. But commercialism is only one particular kind of worth, rendering cultural production as commodity production and appealing to the tastes of the majority. Other values—e.g., cultural worth, educational worth, minority taste, intellectual challenge—are largely excluded from this equation.

There can be other kinds of biases, too, when, for instance, decision-makers determine that audiences aren't interested in works about women, or about people of colour, or stories that address explicitly people in exotic places like . . . Canada. Canadian popular music and Canadian literature fought such biases half a century ago; we don't think twice now when a Canadian artist wins a Grammy or a Canadian writer wins a Booker Prize. But Canadian dramatic television and, especially, Canadian feature film still face hurdles in international screen markets, in large part because they tend to be distinctly Canadian.

Market Economics and Cultural Production

A fundamental problem is the tendency of many people, especially economists, to apply the free-market perspective to sectors of the economy in which it may not be entirely appropriate. Economists often argue that if films, books, TV

programs, magazines, and sound recordings cannot survive in the marketplace, then they do not deserve to survive. To intervene to support what large audiences are not interested in, the argument goes, is to use the state to subsidize the tastes of an elite. While the merits of **economism**—the perception of cultural production as commercial enterprise

—can certainly be debated, further consideration takes us back to our earlier discussion of returns on economic investment. Not all returns are financial. Not all returns are immediate. For that matter, not all costs are financial. This point is important because it goes to the heart of how we perceive cultural production and what role we assign the mass media in society. Economists talk about market externalities. **Market externalities** are the costs and benefits of economic activity that are not accounted for by—that are external to—the immediate economic transaction between buyer and seller. For example, critics of graphically violent films and video games claim that such films and games exact social costs—in law enforcement, in health care, in social welfare—that are not part of the production cost or sale price of these items. Instead, those costs are assumed by society at large. On the flip side, externalities can be positive; the benefits of a good public education—literacy, numeracy, critical thinking skills, specialized knowledge, etc.—spread beyond the tuition-paying student and the school to society at large.

Market economies have a number of other limitations. In its comprehensive survey of state involvement in cultural activity in Canada, the Applebaum-Hébert Committee (Canada, 1982a: 64–71) noted that governments often intervene in the cultural sphere in cases of market failure, when the market does not or cannot serve adequately the cultural needs of society. Markets typically do not recognize the longevity of cultural products, which may be produced by one generation and maintain their value through subsequent generations. Think of the number of artists—Van Gogh, Rembrandt, or our own Emily Carr—who are today recognized for their genius, but who were not adequately compensated for their creations in their own lifetimes. Markets may also fail to accommodate **infant industries**—new, domestic industries that cannot compete right away with well-established and large-scale transnational industries. Canadian feature film and television are good examples of industries that continue to struggle to find markets in the context of Hollywood's dominance of this country's commercial theatre and television screens. Cultural

production also confounds market economics because it entails a large element of risk and requires a substantial investment of a society's resources, and because the public has a 'limitless variability of tastes'. The most common instance of market failure in the cultural sphere, however, involves the market failing 'to register the full benefits conferred' by cultural activity.

Free-market or laissez-faire economics reduces all goods and services to the status of commodities, objects that attain their value through marketplace exchange. While we often believe a market economy to be responsive to consumer demand for choice, the cultural theorist Raymond Williams (1989: 88) reminds us that the organization of communication within a capitalist economy imposes 'commercial constraints', so that 'you can say that at times freedom in our kind of society amounts to the freedom to say anything you wish, provided you can say it profitably.' Commodities, by definition, are 'validated' strictly through sale (Chapter 3). As Yves de la Haye (1980: 34–5) observes, when cultural activities are organized commercially, their purpose becomes the generation of profit. If we perceive books as, first and foremost, commodities of exchange, then their value is measured in retail sales.

Economism confines the notion of value to *exchange* value, and dismisses as externalities the *use* value of cultural goods and services. Economism also casts individuals as consumers playing a narrow role in the economy, rather than as citizens with a larger role to play in democratic society. Television programs, theatrical performances, and museum exhibits are not simply goods or services that we buy and sell, but opportunities for the kind of communication that is fundamental to the understanding of culture. They are expressions of a way of life and of a system of beliefs and values. They are expressions of ideas and perceptions that help people to imagine themselves within the culture and to articulate their personal contributions to its priorities.

The same logic works in cinema. Canada's commercial theatre chains benefit from both audience familiarity with what Hollywood produces and the publicity these films generate through fan magazines and televised entertainment programs like *Entertainment Tonight* and *E-Talk Daily*. English Canada has never succeeded in developing a comparable celebrity culture that would turn Canadian actors and directors into household names. In Quebec, however, French-language magazines like *7 Jours* and *Dernière Heure* and television programs like *La Fureur* and *Tout le monde en parle* generate sizable audiences and have turned Québécois performers into stars. *Tout le monde en parle*, for instance, is a hugely popular Sunday evening television talk show on Radio-Canada, attracting audiences of almost 1.5 million for two hours of talk about current events, the arts, and popular culture, featuring each week high-profile newsmakers, artists, and celebrities. English Canada has nothing comparable.

In other cultural industries, the private sector's reluctance to invest in Canadian cultural production is less easy to quantify, but as illustrated in Chapter 3, economies of scale give book and magazine publishers marketing their wares in both Canada and the US tremendous cost advantages over those selling only in the Canadian market, rendering distinctly Canadian products much less profitable for book and magazine retailers. In other words, even in cases where Canadian media products are profitable, more money can sometimes be made from distributing US products than Canadian ones. The success Canada has had in developing, with considerable state intervention, a popular music industry and a vibrant literary tradition since the 1960s seems to suggest that a certain amount of prejudice is at play in the private sector as well. That is, in spite of all evidence to the contrary, some media owners simply do not believe Canadians can produce popular and profitable forms of entertainment, and thus prefer to take the safer route of importing cultural products for which someone else has already done the work of building a market.

There is no denying the tensions between the public good and the private commercial interest. Canada's Broadcasting Act recognizes these tensions by assigning social responsibilities to all licence-holders, including minimum Canadian-content regulations and special additional responsibilities for the public sector. Section 19 of the Income Tax Act provides recognition in the form of effectively restricting majority ownership of Canadian newspapers, magazines, and broadcasting stations—i.e., any medium that accepts advertising—to Canadians; although this requirement has been diluted considerably and there is pressure on the federal government to ease this restriction further to increase the pool of potential buyers and thereby decrease the number of Canadian properties owned by concentrated media companies. The public goals of communication are also recognized in the form of postal grants to qualifying Canadian publications and in the support policies of the Department of Canadian Heritage for cultural industries, even if these programs are under review by a federal government committed to balancing its books and under pressure from the United States through World Trade Organization challenges. In the area of film, support policies, targeted programs, and public agencies such as the National Film Board and Telefilm Canada recognize film's public goals. Complementary provincial support policies demonstrate how deeply felt these public goals are. In telecommunications, the notion of common carriage also reflects public goals.

The Historical Context

Historically, cultural production is associated with both Enlightenment values and the emergence of a capitalist economy. As noted in Chapter 3, the Enlightenment was distinguished by an intellectual approach based on a scientific and rational perspective of the world, a fundamental shift in world view that championed science over religion, justice over the abuse of power, and a social contract that specified individual rights and freedoms over the absolutist rule of kings and popes. Capitalism, which traces its roots to the late fifteenth century, is an economic system based on the private ownership of the **means of production** (Box 9.4) and the clear separation of capital—owners of the means of production engaged in the pursuit of profit—and labour—workers who satisfy their material needs (food, shelter, clothing) by exchanging their labour for a wage.

⁖ BOX 9.4   THE MEANS OF PRODUCTION

When economists refer to the means of production, they are talking about the mechanism or process by which we satisfy our material needs for food, clothing, and shelter, and thus ensure our survival and the survival of our dependants. The means of production are, bluntly, the means of life.

In older, agrarian societies, peasants had direct access to the means of production; by working the land they could literally live off the land, eating what they grew and gathered, slaughtering livestock for food, leather, fur, and other necessities; felling trees for fuel and collecting stones to use with wood to construct shelters. By controlling the means of production they had direct access to, and control of, the means of their own survival. Most of us today would regard this means of survival as meagre and not particularly appealing. But the point we want to make is that peasants' relation to the means of production was fundamentally different from our own living today. Capitalism is a very specific economic and political system. A capitalist economy is an exchange economy mediated always by market relations.

Capitalism separates workers from the means of production. Instead of having direct access to the means by which to produce our life needs, we exchange our labour for wages and in turn exchange those wages for food, clothing, and shelter. If we cannot sell our labour—i.e., we are unemployed—we are cut off from this exchange economy. As the historian Ellen Meiksins Wood (2002: 7) explains: 'Material life and social reproduction in capitalism are universally mediated by the market, so that all individuals must in one way or another enter into market relations in order to gain access to the means of life.' When we apply for a job, for instance, we are entering the job market, offering our labour in exchange for wages. In turn, we take those wages and enter the housing market, the food market, and the clothing market, exchanging our wages for our life needs. This is the sense in which we mean the market mediates between individuals and the necessities of life.

If our access to the means of production is governed by market relations, so is our access to the products of our own and of others' labour. Even when our work is devoted to the production of food, clothing, or home building supplies, we don't own those products, but must purchase them as we would any other commodity.

Why is this important?

Some people today argue that digital communication technologies return ownership of the means of production to ordinary people. The inference is that those who wish to engage in media production themselves no longer need to work for the corporate media conglomerates, but can set up shop themselves. The further inference is that corporations no longer wield the economic power they once did, that corporate concentration in the media industries is no longer the concern it once was.

But this is where an important distinction must be made between the means of production and workplace tools. A carpenter who owns his or her own set of tools, no matter how extensive, does not own the means of production. He or she must engage in the capitalist economy by exchanging his or her specialized labour for a wage. Only when the carpenter establishes his or her own business—which requires all of the infrastructure necessary to secure and fulfill contracts, and ultimately to make a living—can he or she be said to own the means of production, to own the means of satisfying his or her material needs. Even then, all of the carpenter's business relations are conducted through the market, where he or she must compete with all of the other woodworking businesses for customers.

Similarly, someone with a website or a blog does not own the means of production, only the tools with which to produce that website or blog; those tools do not constitute the means of production in and of themselves, nor do they necessarily constitute the means with which to satisfy the blogger's material needs of survival.

Yes, personal computing grants individuals unprecedented access to the mediasphere, as the millions of personal blogs, Facebook pages, Twitter accounts, and small websites attest. But a distinction must be made between communicating as a hobby, a pastime, or some other kind of personal project, and communicating to make a living.

Communications media share these historical roots. Mass communication enables the kind of social, cultural, economic, and political opportunities we associate with the Enlightenment and capitalism. At the same time, communications media serve the needs of modern states to circulate information about rights, duties, responsibilities, obligations, and freedoms. Gutenberg's printing press was revolutionary because it responded to a social structure that could accommodate individual initiative, to a thirst for learning, to a growing literacy, and to an opportunity to make the Bible and other manuscripts available to an increasingly literate public (Eisenstein, 1979).

Canadian values and ideals have their roots in these same traditions, and our institutions bear clear traces of this history: combining elements of both private and public enterprise. The establishment of the commercial press in Canada, for example, was a response by entrepreneurial printers to the opportunity to publish, under contract, official government information and to make such information widely available. Taking Britain and the United States as its models, the press in Canada soon evolved into an institution capable of responding to other social and political pressures for the distribution of information and ideas.

From the beginning of printing to the present day there has been a struggle between 'the media' and 'the state' for control of communications. Each has compelling reasons to want control of the generation and distribution of content. The state needs to communicate in order to govern, to command allegiance from its citizens, and to generate a sense of community among its inhabitants. Reading a newspaper, for example, keeps us informed about our government's activities and offers us a depiction of the place in which we live: who our fellow citizens are, what they look like, what they think, what they value, etc. (see Anderson, 1989). The battle for press freedom was fought on the foundation of individual freedom and the relation between freedom of speech and democracy, with the press putting itself forward as a separate estate representative of a distinct set of interests, not those of church, business, or landowners, but those of

'the people' (see our discussion of the 'fourth estate' in Chapter 3).

Simultaneously, the press was fighting for the economic interests of private press owners. The press won recognition, at least in part, on the basis of the conjoined interests of individual free speech and the generally accepted liberal theory and commercial practice of the day; intellectuals like John Milton, John Locke, and John Stuart Mill were the early proponents of the libertarian theory of the press, maintaining that the freedoms of expression and of the press were inextricably linked to democratic government (see Osler, 1993).

Within the context of liberal-capitalist economic theory, the press asked for nothing more than any other business. But in dealing with information, which even during the Industrial Revolution was recognized as somehow different from other commodities, the press found it prudent to fight and win the battle on non-economic grounds, on the basis of the rights of individuals to free speech. The state never did give up its right to produce and disseminate information, and, indeed, well into the twentieth century the so-called 'free press' was closely aligned with political parties, as well as church groups and labour organizations (see Sotiron, 1997). Even today, the Canadian press cannot be said to be completely independent of government. For one thing, governments are among the largest advertisers in newspapers and magazines, providing them with an indispensable revenue source. For another, journalists are heavily dependent on politicians and state bureaucrats for the production of news. The relationship between journalism and the state is largely symbiotic rather than adversarial.

Organizing Structures

No media industry in Canada is governed exclusively by free-market economics. Governments, both provincial and federal, are implicated in one form or another in the structure of every media industry: as proprietors (CBC, NFB); custodians (museums, galleries, theatres); patrons (commissions, grants, sponsorships); catalysts (tax incentives, subsidies); or regulators (CRTC) (Canada, 1982a: 72). The result is that our mass media are organized as a complex mixture of public and private enterprise.

Newspaper publishing comes closest to an exclusively private enterprise, but even here section 19 of the Income Tax Act ensures that Canadian newspapers remain Canadian-owned; the newspaper industry is protected by the state from foreign takeover and foreign competition. Newspapers are considered by the state to be relatively untouchable because they are so closely associated with the historical struggle for freedom of the press (and, subsequently, other mediated forms of expression). In the post–World War II period, governments in Great Britain, the United States, and Canada all have ignored reasoned calls to intervene in the newspaper industry to ensure a better balance between the press's freedom to publish and its responsibility to keep citizens properly informed. Both the Davey Committee (Canada, 1971: 255–6) and the Kent Commission (Canada, 1981: 237) raised concerns about ownership concentration in Canada's newspaper industry

and proposed legislative mechanisms to address the problem. The Standing Senate Committee on Transport and Communications (Canada, 2006a) revisited this question in 2003 and, besides echoing previous commissions on the topic of corporate concentration, added corporate consolidation and cross-media ownership to the list of concerns about conglomerate ownership. The Kent Commission proposed a Canada Newspaper Act to balance the rights and responsibilities of a free press and recommended legislation both to correct the worst cases of corporate concentration and to prohibit the further **concentration of ownership**. Magazine publishing in Canada is distinguished from the newspaper business in this regard by its dependence on both government subsidies (e.g., preferred postal rates, direct grants) and protectionist legislation (the Income Tax Act) for its survival in a marketplace dominated by American publications (see Dubinsky, 1996).

Table 9.1 summarizes the Canadian daily newspaper ownership groups, testifying to the high level

TABLE 9.1 Daily Newspaper Ownership Groups (as of September 2009)

PUBLISHER	NUMBER OF NEWSPAPERS (2010)	SHARE OF CANADIAN DAILIES (2009)	TOTAL WEEKLY CIRCULATION (2009)	SHARE OF TOTAL WEEKLY CIRCULATION (2009)
Glacier Ventures International Corp.	6	0.9%	210,569	0.9%
Brunswick News Inc.	3	2.2%	547,162	2.0%
FP Canadian Newspapers LP	2	3.5%	999,246	3.7%
Transcontinental Inc.	10	2.6%	650,749	2.4%
Postmedia Network Inc. (formerly Canwest)	13	30.8%	8,198,501	30.5%
Halifax Herald Ltd.	1	2.6%	751,474	2.8%
Power Corp. of Canada	7	11.1%	3,064,518	11.4%
CTVglobemedia Inc.*	1	7.7%	1,891,629	7.0%
Black Press	4	0.6%	147,287	0.5%
Continental Newspapers Canada Ltd.	3	1.2%	332,984	1.2%
Alta Newspaper Group LP/ Glacier Ventures (AB) Ltd.	3	0.8%	210,348	0.8%
Torstar Corp.	4	11.6%	3,181,200	11.8%
Sun Media (Quebecor Inc.)	36	23.3%	6,354,458	23.7%
Sing Tao Newspapers	1	n/a	n/a	n/a
Independents	3	1.3%	310,423	1.2%
Totals	97	100.2%	26,850,548	99.9%

*In September 2010, BCE Inc. assumed full ownership of CTV and sold *The Globe and Mail* to Woodbridge, thus breaking up CTVglobemedia.
Source: Newspapers Canada

of corporate concentration in this segment of the economy (up-to-date statistics can be found at www.newspaperscanada.ca/). Postmedia Network Inc. (formerly CanWest), with 13 daily newspapers including the *National Post*, accounts for more than 30 per cent of all weekly newspaper circulation, while the top five companies together—Postmedia, Quebecor, Torstar, Power Corp. and CTVglobemedia—control almost 85 per cent of weekly circulation. The country's three independent newspapers together account for slightly more than 1 per cent.

The state presence is much more apparent in the broadcasting sector. Radio, for example, has private, commercial stations operating alongside publicly owned broadcasters (i.e., CBC and the French-language Radio-Canada) and community stations. CBC and Radio-Canada compete with the commercial broadcasters for audiences, but they do not compete for advertising. Public radio in Canada has been commercial-free since 1974, leaving the public broadcaster wholly dependent on federal government funding for its operations. Community radio stations are run by non-profit societies with a democratic management structure, and raise money from a combination of advertising, government subsidies, and fundraising activities such as radio bingo. As discussed in Chapter 8, all radio stations—private, public, and community—are regulated by the CRTC; they are required to meet the specific conditions of their broadcast licence as well as Canadian-content quotas. The domestic sound recording industry, though owned by private interests, has been the principal beneficiary of Canadian-content regulations on radio.

Whether publicly or privately owned, all media need to generate, maintain, and grow their audiences, as discussed in Box 9.5 on marketing.

Television, too, is a mix of private, public, and community broadcasting stations. A significant difference is that the stations of CBC and Radio-Canada, including the CBC News Network and Le réseau de l'information (RDI), compete with the commercial broadcasters for both audiences and advertising. This competition for advertising has long been a sore point with the private broadcasters, who feel the CBC encroaches on their

business, specifically when the public broadcaster goes after programming particularly attractive to audiences and advertisers—e.g., professional sports, American game shows, blockbuster Hollywood films—but seemingly unrelated to the CBC/Radio-Canada's public-service mandate. Even supporters of public broadcasting sometimes argue that advertising competition distorts the public broadcaster's mission. However, the CBC contends that, due to cuts in government funding, it needs this revenue to make ends meet while producing quality Canadian programming. Besides, as Leonard Brockington, the first chair of the CBC, argued in the 1930s, the CBC is the only broadcaster that delivers 100 per cent of the revenues it earns from advertising back to taxpayers in the form of Canadian programming. The profits of private broadcasters go to shareholders, not to the public.

Both private and public television in Canada are regulated (e.g., licensing, Canadian-content quotas, advertising limits) and both private and public broadcasters benefit from federal and provincial subsidies for the creation of Canadian film and television programming. Specialty channels form the sector of the ownership picture that will bear closest scrutiny in the years ahead; as audiences fragment, these services have become particularly attractive properties and a growth area for both public and private broadcasters and for cable and satellite distribution companies.

The film industry in Canada is a special case because it has both public and private production houses, but the distribution and exhibition sectors of the industry are organized along principles of private enterprise. Governments in Canada have been involved in film production—as patrons, catalysts, and regulators—since early in the twentieth century (Chapter 8). Hollywood began to dominate the burgeoning commercial film industry in the 1920s, which did not sit well with Canadians in the period of strong Canadian nationalism following World War I. The federal government established the National Film Board of Canada in 1939 as a means of asserting a greater Canadian presence on cinema screens. The NFB, though, has largely been confined to producing the kinds

⁖ BOX 9.5   MARKETING

Whether or not media organizations are structured as commercial enterprises, great effort is expended in identifying audiences, determining their needs and consumption habits, maximizing their numbers, maintaining their loyalty, and, in the case of media that carry advertising, matching audiences to appropriate advertisers. Audiences, in other words, are not already pre-assembled, simply waiting for the show to start. Audiences need to be built through a number of activities that fall under the general category of marketing. Marketing includes surveys of actual and potential customers, analysis of ratings, circulation and/or attendance data, advertising of all kinds, other forms of publicity, and promotional campaigns.

Media organizations conduct regular surveys to determine who their audiences are (their age, sex, income bracket, education level, media usage, etc.), what their needs are, and to what extent they are satisfied with the services they're receiving (Chapter 5). Television and radio stations subscribe to ratings services, newspapers and magazines subscribe to circulation auditing services, movie companies track box-office receipts, and websites count page views to get a measure of their connection to audiences and users, and who exactly they are connecting with. These data form a feedback mechanism by which audiences communicate to media organizations through their consumption activities.

Media organizations don't have exclusive audiences, but must constantly compete for attention with all the other media products and services vying for peoples' screen time. Advertising is one way of doing this. A second is promotion, and the two often work hand-in-hand. If you look at the entertainment section of any daily newspaper, you will see advertisements for CDs, DVDs, films, and upcoming concerts and shows, with related review articles and celebrity interviews. The advertisements are paid for, but the articles result from promotional activities that encourage arts journalists to report on their products and interview their stars. Film festivals, for example, provide an opportunity for movie-makers to create buzz around a film; journalists play along by reviewing the films and interviewing and photographing the stars. Concert tours, similarly, give both fans and journalists live access to musicians while promoting their latest recording.

Maintaining audiences has become increasingly difficult with the explosion of communicative activities now competing for people's time and attention because such products and services are what media economists call 'experience goods'; we can only measure the true worth of a movie or a book or a magazine after we have consumed it. The recommendations of friends, colleagues, or opinion leaders in a given community can go a long way in promoting a media product or service.

Besides advertising and promotion, media companies have devised a number of strategies to maintain audience allegiance. The most benign means is through branding. Branding is the creation of an identity for a company or a specific product that generates clear and positive associations among consumers. Through branding, a media company is depending on its reputation to ensure repeat, and growing, business. Media companies use their brand identifications to differentiate themselves from competitors. The CBC, for example, through its slogan 'Canada lives here', reminds people that its services are produced by Canadians for Canadians.

There are more assertive means as well. One way to keep people coming back is through so-called loyalty programs. Books stores like Chapters and Indigo, for example, sell membership cards that give buyers discounts on all of their purchases. Once you've signed up, it is in your financial interest to keep buying books through their stores rather than shopping elsewhere.

If such loyalty programs encourage repeat customers, a second, more devious, means is to wall people in, to compel them to keep using your products and services. Wireless phone companies, for example, typically offer customers free or discounted phones only if they sign an exclusive, set-term service contract with that provider. E-book producers similarly restrict the sources from which e-books can be purchased and downloaded. This is the strategy employed by Apple (see Lyons, 2010); iPads, for example, will only play videos downloaded from the iTunes Store.

of films that tend not to be shown in commercial theatres—documentary, experimental, animation, and sponsored films—leaving the production of dramatic feature-length films to the private sector. If there has been competitive tension between the NFB and private-sector producers, it has been over contracts for sponsored films, which are films commissioned by government departments and corporations for educational and marketing purposes. Even the private producers of feature films in Canada rely heavily on government subsidies and tax breaks for production, distribution, and marketing, and public television has been one of Canadian cinema's most dependable exhibition venues.

Until recently, telephone service was defined by Ottawa as a 'natural monopoly' and Canada had both private (e.g., BC Telephone, Bell Canada) and provincial state monopolies (e.g., Sasktel, Manitoba Telecom Services) operating side by side. The CRTC, however, began to deregulate the industry in the 1980s, first opening up long-distance telephony to competition and in 1994 opening all telephone services to competition. Similarly, the Crown corporation Canada Post monopolized mail service until the 1980s when private companies created a market for specialized courier services.

Even art galleries, theatres, concert halls, and museums, insofar as they can been seen as mass media, are characterized by a mix of public and private ownership, with content generated by both public-sector and private-sector sources. The international web of computer networks we call the internet has no single owner, but it, too, counts on both public- and private-sector initiatives for its operation and its content. Cyberspace is a medium of exchange for all kinds of communication and defies any simple structural category.

Communications scholar Ted Magder (1993: 10–11) argues that state intervention in the cultural sphere has been motivated by two objectives: national identity and economic growth. The Canadian Pacific Railway remains a powerful symbol in Canada because it was one of the first national institutions asked to serve both goals simultaneously; the building of the railway was a private enterprise heavily subsidized by Ottawa and designed to bind a sparsely populated, vast country together. If the CPR permitted the transportation of people and goods back and forth across Canada, the federal government imagined that a national radio broadcasting network would allow for the transcontinental dissemination of ideas, values, and images. In fact, the metaphor describing the CBC as a 'railway of the airwaves' has been evoked many times.

The goals of creating a Canadian national identity and stimulating economic growth remain in perpetual tension in the communication sphere, and the various ownership structures of the media in Canada speak to Ottawa's ongoing struggle to keep both objectives in view. Where the Canadian people fit into this picture is an important question. Canadians are, at the same time, citizens, audience members, workers, consumers, and taxpayers, and their support for both private enterprise *and* public service contributes to the tension around ownership structures.

Public Ownership

The central difference between public and private forms of ownership relates to the question of return on investment. If private enterprises are interested primarily in a financial return, public enterprises seek other kinds of return: cultural development, industrial development, job creation, national identity formation, etc. **Public ownership** is devoted to providing communication as some kind of public service based upon public goals: to enable citizenship, to foster a sense of community on regional and national scales, to promote regional and national cultures. Private ownership is devoted to providing communication for profit. Regardless of the mix of private and public enterprise described above, this distinction is fundamental and needs always to be kept in view if we are to make the link between the ownership structure of a medium and the purpose of the communication it provides.

The idea of public service is to employ the mass media for social goals. This can mean the provision of universal and equitable service to all Canadians, as in the telecommunication, postal, radio, and television industries. It can mean foregrounding the educational component of communication, which informs all cultural policy to some extent. Or it can mean ensuring a Canadian voice in film, radio, TV, publishing, and popular music, where there has been, and remains, a clear risk of being drowned out by American voices. Communication as public service is inherently inclusive, addressing audiences as citizens rather than as consumers, and asserting citizens' rights to communicate and to be informed.

The public service ideal, of course, is not without shortcomings when it comes to putting principles into practice. In Canada, public service has often meant *national* service—i.e., communication in the service of nation-building. As Marc Raboy (1990: xii–xiii) notes, in the broadcasting sector this has meant the subordination of other social and cultural goals to national economic and political interests, specifically, 'the political project of maintaining "Canada" as an entity distinct from the United States of America and united against the periodic threat of disintegration posed by Quebec'. It has also meant the concentration of film, radio, and television services in central Canada, creating a hierarchical distinction between the 'national' preoccupations of Ontario and Quebec and the 'regional' concerns of the other provinces and territories.

The central ethic of the public corporation, though, is connected to the democratic ideal. More specifically, it is to provide a public service to both the users of the service and to the population as a whole. If private enterprise operates on a simple user-pay basis, public enterprise employs a much more complex cost structure, in which the users of the public service do not pay the full cost of providing that service. The costs are shared by all taxpayers. For example, visitors to the National Gallery in Ottawa pay an admission fee, but that fee does not recover the full costs of operating the gallery or of purchasing and maintaining the art collection contained therein. The remaining costs come from federal government tax revenues, tax money collected from every Canadian, most of whom have never visited and are unlikely ever to visit the

The National Gallery of Canada in Ottawa.

National Gallery. The rationale for such a cost structure is the need to promote national culture and the conviction that a strict user-pay system would not meet this objective. The government-owned mail system, Canada Post, has a slightly different cost structure, but the same principle applies; we all share in the costs of maintaining a basic and essential communications service. For example, rather than determine the cost of posting a letter on the basis of the costs of delivery—i.e., less to send a letter across town than across the country—Canada Post charges us the same rate for the same stamp whether our letter is mailed across three blocks or across three time zones within Canada. The rationale for this cost structure is the need to provide equitable mail service to all Canadians, whether they live in concentrated urban centres or remote northern communities.

Canada Post provides the same service to all Canadians.

Public enterprise has a long and distinguished tradition in every Western country. As Herschel Hardin (1974) points out, Canada has made extensive use of public enterprise throughout its history, with the most common form being the Crown corporation. But it is not without its drawbacks. As noted by Marc Raboy on the previous page, national communications services can become nationalist services, catering to the goals of the nation rather than to the divergent and possibly contrary goals of the various regions of the country. The CBC, for example, struggles constantly to accommodate the great diversity of perspectives that constitute our national culture. Similarly, the production headquarters of these services tend to be centralized—in Toronto for English Canada, in Montreal for French Canada—distancing them from the communities they are mandated to serve. In a country as large and diverse as Canada, this can have repercussions for access to these institutions—as audiences, as cultural producers—as well as for the interests and concerns they serve. That said, privately owned media operating on a national stage face similar challenges (e.g., the national newspapers *The Globe and Mail* and *National Post* and the private TV networks CTV, Global, and TVA).

Public ownership removes the element of choice from our decisions about media consumption, and can cause resentment among those who have to pay for services through their tax dollars but don't use them. We all pay for CBC radio and television broadcasts, National Film Board documentaries, and performances at the National Arts Centre, but not all of us are faithful consumers and some of us may very well object to their programming choices.

Public ownership grants a tremendous amount of responsibility and power to governments in deciding when, where, and how to intervene in the communications economy. As governments change, so can the state's cultural priorities. More importantly, public ownership creates an opportunity for political interference. Even though public media companies are managed at arm's-length from the government of the day, they nonetheless depend upon governments for their mandates and their operating budgets. The CBC, for example, has seen its annual appropriation from Parliament—its largest revenue source—shrink dramatically over the past 15 years, from about $1.5 billion in the early 1990s to $1.2 billion in 2008–9, while at the same time being made responsible for more services (CBC, 2009).

Though direct political interference is rare—and can also be brought to bear on privately owned media companies—a number of high-profile incidents serve as a reminder that the state retains this power to pressure public institutions. In 1990, the National Gallery drew heavy criticism for its $1.8 million purchase of a modernist painting by the New York artist Barnett Newman called *Voice of Fire*, which had hung in the US pavilion at Expo '67 in Montreal. Among the critics was Conservative MP Felix Holtmann, the chair of the House Communications and Culture Committee (Geddes, 2010). In 1992, CBC Television attracted the ire of Canadian war veterans and Senator Jack Marshall, the chairman of the Senate Subcommittee on Veterans Affairs, for its three-part World War II series *The Valour and the Horror*, produced by the Montreal documentary filmmakers Terence and Brian McKenna (Nash, 1994: 526–33). Parts two and three of the series were particularly critical of Canadians' participation in the blanket bombing of German cities and in the Normandy invasion. During Senate subcommittee hearings the CBC was condemned for airing the series, and the CBC ombudsman produced a report concluding that the series was 'flawed and fails to measure up to CBC's demanding policies and standards' (ibid., 531). In 2008, Stephen Harper's Conservative government adopted Bill C-10, an amendment to the Income Tax Act allowing the federal government to deny tax credits to film and television projects considered offensive for reasons of violence, hatred, or sexuality. The bill was reportedly prompted by the release in 2007 of a Canadian dramatic comedy entitled *Young People Fucking*.

ON THE OTHER HAND, ANY "ARTISTE" OUT THERE WHO WANTS TO LIVE AND WORK IN AFGHANISTAN...

Source: © Terry Mosher

Prime Minister Stephen Harper announces $5 million in cuts to arts and culture funding.

Private Ownership

Private-sector ownership assumes two basic forms. The ownership of a company can be closely held, either by an individual or by a very small group (often family members). Or the ownership of a company can be widely held by a large group of shareholders, who buy and sell their interest in the company through the stock market. In the latter case, a company will form a board of directors answerable to its shareholders. There can be some confusion about distinctions between types of public ownership (Box 9.6).

The general ethic of the private or commercial media outlet is survival and growth in a marketplace driven by profit. This ethic does not derive merely from the personality traits of private-sector owners; it is structural. Commercial corporations are organized for the purpose of earning returns for their owners, based on their ability to find a market for a product or service and their ability to meet, and ultimately expand, that market. If publicly owned media have an obligation to serve *all* Canadians, private media serve only those who constitute their target market—those audiences most attractive to advertisers.

Because the bottom line in the private sector is profit, private media companies have considerable

latitude in changing course to maximize their economic returns. In radio broadcasting, this can mean a re-positioning in the market, either through the introduction of new program segments, or through a complete change in format, from, say, all-news to golden oldies. A book publisher might decide to get out of the business of publishing poetry or avant-garde fiction and focus on how-to books or celebrity biographies. More radically, a communications company can move into other industries altogether, whether those markets are in the sphere of communications or not. Consider the example of Thomson Corp. Now known as Thomson Reuters, Thomson Corp. started as a small newspaper company in Timmins, Ontario, in the 1930s, became one of Canada's two largest newspaper owners by the 1980s, and boasted significant newspaper holdings in the United States and the United Kingdom by the 1990s. The company that was primarily a newspaper publisher for half a century had completely abandoned the newspaper industry by 2003 for what its directors perceived as greener pastures in other industries: financial, legal, scientific, and health-care publishing, medical publishing, travel, etc. Thomson only returned to journalism when it merged with Reuters, one of the world's largest news services, in 2008 (Thomson Reuters, 2009). The Thomson family returned to the newspaper business in 2010 when its Woodbridge subsidiary reacquired an 85 per cent stake in *The Globe and Mail* (Ladurantaye, 2010).

Within the private sector exists a considerable variety of ownership structures. The single enterprise is, as its name suggests, a business form in which owners confine themselves to one business with no connections to other companies. It is a single, independent firm that usually operates on a small scale. Some examples persist, particularly among magazines, community weekly newspapers, and small-town radio stations; but single enterprises are fewer and fewer as chains both large and small gobble them up or force them out of business.

Chain ownership, a common form of media organization in Canada, is the linking, or **horizontal integration**, of a number of companies in the same business—typically, newspapers, radio stations, or

❖ BOX 9.6   PUBLIC OWNERSHIP

'Public ownership' is a slippery term used in two contradictory ways by economists: sometimes to mean ownership by the state on behalf of its citizens—'the public'—and at other times to mean ownership by a group of self-interested shareholders. These are very different kinds of ownership.

The first sense of public ownership refers to Crown corporations like Canada Post or the Canadian Broadcasting Corp., which are owned by the state on behalf of the Canadian people.

The second sense of public ownership refers to private corporations whose shares are publicly traded through the stock exchange. They are 'public' in the sense that shares in these companies can be bought and sold by anyone with the means to do so. Rogers Communications is an example of a publicly traded company; anyone can buy an ownership share.

Economists use the term 'public' to mean 'publicly traded' because there are also 'private' companies owned privately—typically by a family or a small group of owners—and shares in the company are not for sale through stock exchanges. Brunswick News, for example, is a private media company owned by J.K. Irving of New Brunswick. Another privately held company is the Jim Pattison Group of British Columbia, which owns a number of communications properties including radio and television stations, an outdoor advertising company, and a periodical distribution company.

In this book we use 'public ownership' to mean state-owned, and 'private ownership' to mean either shareholder-owned or privately held.

---

television stations—occupying different markets. Chains are usually geographically dispersed, but sometimes members of the chain will occupy the same location and aim for distinct audiences. Vancouver's two daily newspapers, the *Sun* and *Province*, for example, are both part of the larger Postmedia Network, but they seek different readers and advertisers within the Lower Mainland of British Columbia. Member companies in a chain may have agreements to buy and sell services from each other. Postmedia newspapers, for instance, share editorial content (stories and pictures) among member papers and have their own wire service. In addition, chains often consolidate administrative resources, so that accounting and marketing services or departments responsible for technological innovation will be able to serve all members in the chain. Television networks are also chains; CTV, for example, has **affiliate** stations in eight provinces, co-ordinating programming through its Toronto headquarters (CTV, 2010). Such sharing of resources offers chain operations tremendous cost advantages over single enterprises. Typically, chain ownership provides the advantages of reducing competition and creates economies of scale (see Rutherford, 1992).

Vertical integration is the concentration of firms within a specific business that extends a company's control over the entire process of production. A vertically integrated company, for instance, will have subsidiary companies involved in every aspect of an industry. The most common example of vertical integration is the commercial film industry, in which the major Hollywood companies not only own production studios and distribution companies, but have subsidiaries involved in theatrical exhibition, television, and video/DVD rental to ensure their films reach audiences and generate revenues. The advantages inherent to vertical integration are substantial. A vertically integrated company ensures itself of resource supplies and sales markets, and it minimizes other uncertainties, such as competition, related to the circuit of production (Mosco, 1996: 175–82).

Conglomerate ownership is characterized by large companies with a number of subsidiary firms in related and unrelated businesses. Besides the advantages of scale, shareholder risk is reduced because the conglomerate is not dependent for its profits on any one industry. Convergence is the name given to the economic strategy media conglomerates employ in an attempt to create synergies among their media properties (see Table 9.2). One of Canada's most converged conglomerates is Quebecor Inc. Through Sun Media and Osprey

Media, Quebecor owns 20 daily newspapers and 34 non-dailies, as well as magazines and shopping guides. Quebecor is also in the businesses of television (TVA), telecommunications and cable distribution (Videotron), new media (CANOË), publishing (books, magazines), and retailing (Archambault, SuperClub Vidéotron) (Quebecor, 2010).

Implications of Private Media Ownership

For those who believe that communication in all its forms involves much more than satisfying markets, the appropriation by private enterprise of a greater and greater share of the mass communication sphere is of great concern. While economists argue that the free-market organization of cultural production is the most efficient means of giving consumers what they want, political economists maintain that the commercial organization of cultural production limits choice and discriminates between those members of the public who have disposable income to spend on advertised products and those who don't. This is particularly the case when corporate concentration limits the number of, and distinctions between, producers and distributors (see Mosco, 1996: 182–205).

In the realm of the mass media, private enterprise is seen as having two particular social benefits. First, it is said to stimulate the provision of affordable goods and services for which consumers have expressed a need or desire through their purchasing decisions. Second, because advertising subsidizes the media, consumers are able to receive content either free (e.g., radio) or at minimal cost (e.g., daily newspapers). These benefits, of course, are not as straightforward as they may seem. First of all, anticipating what consumers will buy is an inexact science, notwithstanding polls and focus groups. Consumers can only make choices among those already offered—supply to a large extent governs demand—and media managers have been frustrated time and again in trying to determine which new services will attract consumers. Media economists have demonstrated, for example, that most major Hollywood movies lose money, and the

studios depend on their blockbuster hits to make up for their far more numerous flops (Leblanc, 1990: 287). The same applies to television series; each new fall season introduces more losers than winners, shows that are cancelled after only a few weeks. Advertising and other forms of publicity, of course, play a role in generating excitement and consumer demand around new films, TV shows, music recordings, and book releases, but consumer tastes remain very hard to anticipate.

Second, it is simply not accurate to say consumers receive some media programming free, thanks to advertising. Instead, consumers pay for it in a roundabout way. Even if we do not directly hand over any money to a radio station to listen to its programming, we pay for that programming nonetheless every time we buy an advertised product. Advertising costs, in other words, are built into the sale price of potato chips and breakfast cereal, so that a share of the money we spend on groceries, snacks, clothing, beer, gasoline, and cosmetics pays for media programming.

Media economists also argue that we pay with our time—we literally pay attention—whenever we consume media services and that time and attention is what advertisers seek (Picard, 1989). This key point to understanding how commercial media work within the economic system is that to generate profits, managers of commercial media seek to attract audiences to their programming to sell those audiences to advertisers. Communications theorist Dallas Smythe (1994: 270–1) points out that what advertisers buy is not simply air time or newspaper space, but 'the services of audiences with predictable specifications who will pay attention in predictable numbers and at particular times to particular means of communications'. Through increasingly sophisticated audience measurement techniques, media managers collect data on their audiences—not only the size of the audience is determined, but demographic factors such as income, education, age, and sex—and sell advertisers access to the kinds of audiences that will be interested in buying their product or service. Mass media content, therefore, is merely 'an inducement (gift, bribe or "free lunch") to recruit potential members of the audience and

TABLE 9.2   Converged Conglomerates in Canada

QUEBECOR INC.

PUBLISHING

-Newspapers: Sun Media Corporation newspaper chain with 8 metro dailies, 7 free commuter dailies, 9 local dailies in Ontario and western Canada and approximately 150 weeklies, buyers guides, and speciality publications. Sun Media acquired Osprey Media in 2007. The newspaper chain has 20 daily newspapers and 34 non-daily newspapers.

-Magazines: *7 jours, Clin d'oeuil, Dernière Heure, Échoes Vedettes* among others

TELEVISION

-Vidéotron: cable TV provider with 1.7 million subscribers in Quebec; its cable network covers 80 per cent of the province and is the largest in Quebec

-TVA: owns 6 of 10 stations in the TVA network, as well as the speciality channel Le Canal Nouvelles, among others. It is the largest French-language TV network in North America.

-Sun TV News: Quebecor acquired the Toronto-based English-language station CKXT in 2004 and rebranded the station as SUN-TV, to identify with the *Toronto Sun* newspaper. The new network launched in April 2011.

NEW MEDIA

-Canoe.inc: operates CANOE network of internet properties, including canoe.ca portal, and reaches 7.8 million users monthly.

-Nurun: web business applications

-Vidéotron: internet service provider for over 90 per cent of Quebec

RETAIL

-Archambault: retail chain of 15 books and music stores; owns Camelot-Info chain of stores specializing in computer and other reference books, Paragraphe bookstore in Montreal, 13 general literature publishing houses, two music and video distributors, and a music label

-SuperClub Vidéotron: retail chain of video sales and rentals with over 278 locations

SHAW COMMUNICATIONS INC.

TELEVISION

-Shaw Cablesystems G.P.: cable TV provider with 2.1 million cable customers

-Shaw Direct: satellite television provider with 840,000 customers across Canada

-Shaw Broadcast Services: one of the largest commercial signal distribution networks in North America. Provides more than 460 English, French, and multilingual video and audio signals through 52 satellite transponders to US and Canada.

(acquired Canwest Global's TV assets, pending CRTC hearing in September 2010 this includes:)

-Global TV Network: 12 stations in 8 provinces

-Speciality channels Dejaview, Fox Sports World, Movietime

RADIO

- Shaw Broadcast Services: Provides more than 460 English, French, and multilingual video and audio signals through 52 satellite transponders to US and Canada.

NEW MEDIA

-Shaw Cablesystems G.P: over 1.7 million internet customers and 900,000 digital telephone customers

OTHER

-Shaw Tracking: mobile communications for transportation industry, with 700 customers and 40,000 vehicles

POSTMEDIA NETWORK INC.

PUBLISHING

-Newspapers: *National Post* national daily newspaper; 11 metro dailies, 27 community newspapers

-Magazines: *Financial Post Business* (*National Post*); *Living Windsor, Swerve, TVtimes*

-Postmedia Editorial Services: provides 24-hour newspaper pagination services to newspapers across America who want to outsource their pagination

NEW MEDIA

-Postmedia News: wire service providing 24-hour content in print, digital, and online; collaborates with Postmedia Network Inc. newspapers

-canada.com: internet portal for news and information

-Online shopping: on canada.com and local shopping through newspaper websites

-FP Infomart

TABLE 9.2 Converged Conglomerates in Canada (*continued*)

POSTMEDIA NETWORK INC.

-FP DataGroup

-working.com

-driving.ca

-remembering.ca

-celebrating.com

-househunting.com

-shopping.com

-faceoff.com

-Software: Quicktrac (add tracking database) and Quickwire (newswire management program)

ADVERTISING
-Flyerforce

-Go!Local

ROGERS COMMUNICATIONS INC.

PUBLISHING
-Rogers Publishing: over 70 periodicals, including *Maclean's, Chatelaine, Flare, L'Actualité*, and Canadian business and trade publications.

TELEVISION
-Rogers Cable Inc.: Canada's largest cable TV provider, with 3.5 million customers in Ontario, New Brunswick, and Newfoundland and Labrador.

-Rogers Media Inc.: OMNI Television: free, over-the-air and multilingual stations OMNI.1 and OMNI.2 (Ontario) and OMNI BC, and OMNI Alberta (75 hours of ethnic programming per week)

-Citytv Network

-Shopping Channel

-Rogers Sportsnet

-Infomercial producer mix productions (Quebec)

-Minority interests speciality channels Viewers Choice Canada, Outdoor Life Network, Biography Channel Canada, and others.

RADIO
-Rogers Broadcasting: 53 radio stations across Canada, including all-news stations in Toronto, Vancouver, Calgary, Kitchener, Saint John, Moncton, and Halifax.

TELEPHONY
-Rogers Cable Inc.: 770,000 telephony customers

Rogers Wireless: serves 7.3 million wireless telephone subscribers as of 31 December 2007.

NEW MEDIA
-Rogers Yahoo! Hi-Speed Internet: cable-based internet service provider

-advisor.ca

-moneysense.ca

*CTVGLOBEMEDIA INC.

PUBLISHING
-*The Globe and Mail*, national daily newspaper

-*Report on Business Magazine*

TELEVISION
-CTV: national television network of 21 owned stations and two independent affiliates.

-/A\: digital cable and satellite provider, with customers in British Columbia, Alberta, Ontario, and Atlantic Canada

-interests in 30 specialty channels, including TSN, MTV, and The Discovery Channel.

RADIO
-CHUM Radio Division: 34 radio stations across Canada

NEW MEDIA
-CTVNEWS.com, ctv.ca

-GlobeAdvisor.com, GlobeandMail.com

-thecomedynetwork.ca

-Workopolis.com

-TSN.ca

-talktv.ca

-autohound.ca

*In September 2010, BCE Inc assumed full ownership of CTV and sold *The Globe and Mail* to Woodbridge, thus breaking up CTVglobemedia.

TABLE 9.2   Converged Conglomerates in Canada (*continued*)

ROGERS COMMUNICATIONS INC.	*CTVGLOBEMEDIA INC.

RETAIL

-Rogers Video: chain of video sales and rentals in over 450 locations.

OTHER

-Sports Entertainment group: combined operations of the Rogers Centre entertainment venue (formerly known as the SkyDome) and the Toronto Blue Jays

to maintain their loyal attention'. Smythe writes that 'the free lunch consists of materials which whet the audience members' appetite and thus (1) attract and keep them attending to the programme, newspaper or magazine, and (2) cultivate a mood conducive to favourable reaction to the explicit and implicit advertisers' messages.'

The explosion of free media sites on the internet has necessitated new thinking about how to pay for the production and distribution of media content, as we discuss in Boxes 9.7 and 9.8.

Private ownership of the communications media raises four particular concerns. The first is that private enterprise casts cultural production

⠿ BOX 9.7   FREE CONTENT

Media organizations remain economically viable when the revenues they generate from producing and distributing content at least match and, preferably, exceed the costs required to obtain the resources necessary for content production—labour, technology, capital, and materials. One of the new economic challenges for media organizations is how to pay for those resources when consumers expect to receive content free. If once we had to pay for newspapers or magazines or recorded music or films, we can now find almost everything we want free on the web. How, then, can media companies afford to keep providing content that we increasingly expect not to have to pay for? As *Wired* magazine editor Chris Anderson argues in his book *Free: The Future of a Radical Price*, in the digital marketplace, 'Free is almost always a choice.' He adds: 'Sooner or later, most producers in the digital realm will find themselves competing with Free' (Anderson, 2009: 72).

Free is not entirely new. We have always received over-the-air radio and television as well as community newspapers and some kinds of magazines without having to pay a subscription fee. The costs to those radio and TV stations and newspapers and magazines were covered by the advertising they could sell. They still work that way. One difference today is that almost all media content comes to us free over the internet, and advertisers are not yet willing to pay the same amount for online advertising as they have paid for advertising

in the traditional media. As more and more of us opt for online content, radio and TV ratings and the circulation of hard-copy newspapers and magazines fall, as do the advertising rates they can charge, rendering the old media model less and less viable. A second difference is that the range of content available free online is limitless; every kind of media content is available, from countries all over the world, and in hundreds of languages. Our local radio, television, magazine, and newspaper providers are now competing with thousands of other content providers.

How is the provision of free media content economically sustainable?

Anderson maintains that providing media content free can be the basis of a successful business model, provided that it is matched with some form of payment.

Source: © Grandmaisonc/Dreamstime.com

Who pays for the 'free' newspapers?

▶ BOX 9.7 (continued)

'Free may be the best price, but it can't be the only one' (ibid., 240). He provides four models of 'free'. The 'three party' model is the most familiar to us; it works by having advertisers pay the costs of providing us with free content. The 'direct cross-subsidy' model works by combining free services with pay services. For example, your wireless provider may give you a free cellphone, but only if you buy a subscription to its telephone service. The 'freemium' model works by offering customers a free basic service while charging others for a premium or enhanced service. This is the model used by some online newspapers and magazines, which offer some of their articles free, but charge a subscription fee for access to exclusive content and to archived editions. Finally, there is what Anderson calls the 'non-monetary' model. In this case, the media organization benefits from the time we spend or the attention we pay to a particular website. Google, for example, collects data every time we use its search engine, data that ultimately improves its PageRank algorithm, and that ultimately increases the value of Google search to advertisers (ibid., 23–9).

The idea of making money by giving away content may be counter-intuitive, but consider the example of the alternative rock band Radiohead. In 2007, Radiohead released its seventh album *In Rainbows* as a digital download, asking people to name their own price.

While a number of people downloaded it without paying anything, the average price paid online was $6 (US), and the band made more money from the digital downloads than from the total sales of its previous album. When *In Rainbows* was released on DVD, it sold another 3 million copies worldwide, making it the band's most commercially successful album. Radiohead's subsequent concert tour, its biggest ever, sold 1.2 million tickets, bringing in yet more money (ibid., 153–4).

This media economy is driven by a shift from scarcity to abundance of all kinds of media content; where once we had a choice between a finite number of radio stations, television channels, newspapers, magazines, books, recorded music, and films, we are now faced with an infinite array of media products and services from all over the world. This abundance is driven in part by the increasing cheapness of computer processing power, digital storage, and bandwidth (ibid., 77). But if the supply of content has grown, demand, which is governed by how much time we can spend consuming media, has not kept pace, intensifying the competition among content suppliers (ibid., 140–2). In the online world, Anderson argues, attention and reputation are the currencies most in demand (ibid., 238). Content providers vie for our limited amount of attention, often relying on their reputation—their brand—to attract that attention.

▶ BOX 9.8 MAKING MONEY ON THE WEB
By Stephany Tlalka

On the internet, popularity does not translate directly into profitability. YouTube is a case in point. The website was created in 2005 by three former PayPal employees, with the vision of sharing home-made videos on-line. The site was an instant hit, and less than a year later, it was purchased by Google for $1.65 billion US (Kehaulani Goo, 2006). YouTube's on-line popularity has skyrocketed: two billion videos are watched per day, it regularly makes celebrities out of its users, and even co-hosted the 2007 presidential debates with CNN (Chapman, 2010). While YouTube accounts for 40 per cent of all videos watched on-line in the United States, the website has yet to translate its user traffic into prof-

its (Heflet, 2009). In 2009, a Credit Suisse report projected that YouTube generated just $240 million US in revenues, with operating costs of $711 million US—representing a loss of almost half a billion dollars (Waters, 2010). Only in 2010 did Google project YouTube would turn a profit. Google's chief financial officer triumphantly announced that select YouTube videos with advertising were viewed one billion times per week. But it appears even web-page advertisements are not generating enough revenue. Google announced YouTube will collaborate with companies like Universal Music and Sony Music entertainment to power Vevo, a website for music videos. YouTube has also launched a search tool for advertisers, allowing

⠶ BOX 9.8 *(continued)*

them to target content by age and topics like politics and fashion (Learmonth, 2010).

Unlike its subsidiary, Google's financial success is established, with revenues in 2010 totalling $6.82 billion US (Miller, 2010). However, Google's popularity differs from YouTube, as its presence extends beyond an entertainment domain. Ninety per cent of Google's advertising revenue comes from search advertising, advertisements that appear while users are performing searches or using e-mail (ibid.). While Google's revenues increased by $1 billion US since 2009, competing search engines are gaining ground and more sophisticated advertising techniques are surpassing Google's search–advertising software, AdWords. In an attempt to supplement its non-search business, Google is experimenting with expandable advertisements on YouTube, and mobile advertisements on its Android mobile phone (ibid.). Google also announced a partnership with Omnicom Media Group to build an advertising trading desk. The deal will allow Omnicom to harness Google's analytic tools to fit its clients with advertising space across a range of websites. Industry executives predict the partnership will be as lucrative as the $1.3 billion US search–advertising market itself (Steele, 2010).

The internet has become something of a holy grail in the newspaper industry, where revenues have dwindled since classified advertising and audiences migrated on-line. The news industry in general is experimenting with ways to generate revenue through on-line advertising. However, advertising on the web is much cheaper than advertising in print. While newspapers can charge thousands of dollars for a single printed-page advertisement, on-line advertising rates are about $7 US for 1,000 impressions (Learmonth, 2010). Even worse, digital advertising revenues for newspapers fell from 16.2 per cent in 2005 to 11.4 per cent in 2009, and PriceWaterhouseCoopers predicts a further decline by 2014 (ibid.). This trend is partially due to increased competition on-line. A newspaper like the *Montreal Gazette* now competes for audiences with the *New York Times*, CBC.ca, and Wikipedia. It even competes with pornography and gambling websites, the kings of on-line advertising. On-line pornography revenues are estimated at $57 billion US, with revenues in the United States alone around $12 billion US—larger than the combined revenues of television networks ABC, CBS, and NBC (Rosenberg, 2010). The 2007 industry estimate for global on-line gambling was $21 billion US (American Gaming Association, 2010).

All news organizations are attempting to brand themselves on-line, in an attempt to maximize audiences and traffic to their domain. For instance, in 2009 *Sports Illustrated* published a story in its on-line edition, SI.com, before the print edition. The exclusive story revealed that New York Yankees' star Alex Rodriquez had been taking performance-enhancing drugs while playing for the Texas Rangers. *Sports Illustrated*'s goal was to attract audiences to the website by having the story first—a key, 'first-past-the-post' mentality that provided high profits for newspapers for centuries. However, the logic did not create the website traffic expected. Individuals searching for the Rodriquez story went through Google, and ended up with search results for articles published by competing organizations, or even attributed rewrites of the news story (Osnos, 2009).

News aggregators and on-line companies like Google, Yahoo!, and AOL are adjusting to the on-line advertising climate by collaborating with other businesses, refining their advertising software, and increasing their original content by staffing blogs and news sections. Newspapers, on the other hand, have responded by putting up (and taking down) paywalls to online content, cutting staff, and blurring the distinction between their product and the competition (Ives, 2010). The rising legitimacy of the internet over newspapers was exemplified in Canada in March 2010. Prime Minister Stephen Harper did an exclusive interview on YouTube's 'Citizen Tube', surpassing mainstream journalists who were eager to interview him about proroguing parliament and his Throne Speech (Murphy, 2010). Mr Harper even has a YouTube channel.

Source: Stephany Tlalka is an MA student in the Department of Journalism, Concordia University.

as commercial enterprise, whereby the goal of communication becomes the generation of profit. This form of organization imposes commercial constraints on communication. Communication as commercial enterprise creates pressures to maximize entertainment value and to minimize difficulty and complexity, and to provide communication in an advertising-friendly or consumption-friendly environment. In the medium of television, for example, competing programs are only a click of the remote away. Programming that is difficult, challenging, or slow-paced may have trouble holding audiences, and could be hard for broadcasters to support. This includes newscasts, which, according to the expectations of commercial enterprise, need to maximize ratings in a competitive environment even if that means sacrificing the quality and integrity of their journalism.

A second concern is that the increasing convergence of media properties reinforces the profit motive and moves owners further and further from their core areas of business. That is, conglomerates are in business to make money rather than to make movies or newspapers or books or video games. The goal of the conglomerate is to serve shareholders and paying customers, rather than society at large. By privileging the profit motive above all else, the creation of conglomerates weakens the owners' commitment to core areas of business; media properties may become a lesser priority within the conglomerate than, for example, its real estate holdings. Managers can revise the conglomerate's mandate, or abandon media industries altogether for more lucrative industries.

Related to this is a third concern. The broader a conglomerate's reach, the more businesses it is involved in, the greater the chance for a conflict of interest between its media business and its other holdings. Critical themes—e.g., environmentalism, labour practices, poverty—in newspaper and magazine stories, TV documentaries, or radio programs could threaten the earnings or community standing of the conglomerate's other holdings. In such cases, the conglomerate's media properties will feel pressure to avoid certain subject areas, depriving the public of a full airing of important social issues or confining their discussion within safe parameters.

Finally, the trend towards corporate concentration has reduced substantially our sources of information at precisely the point in history when our dependence on communications media for our knowledge of the world has increased. The plethora of TV and radio channels, websites, books, magazines, newspapers, music recordings, and video cassettes available to us is largely illusory; it disguises the fact that many of these media are the products of a mere handful of large corporations, and that others—e.g., websites—are primarily distribution channels for other media, rather than generators of original content. If we are to take seriously our role as citizens in democratic society, we should be encouraging the greatest variety of information sources possible, as well as an increase in distinct media channels for us to express ourselves. Taken together, these trends of private ownership have reduced our sources of information and narrowed the range of what can be said and how it can be expressed.

Media Democratization

The barriers to media ownership have decreased considerably with digitization and the greater accessibility of a range of communication technologies, from personal computers to digital cameras and sound recorders. Individuals with minimal skills and a small amount of relatively inexpensive equipment can establish their own media projects on the World Wide Web, whether for personal amusement, artistic expression, or some form of political activism. Similarly, groups ranging from schools to aid organizations can establish websites to communicate their activities and their points of view to the world. This new citizen engagement in media is widely heralded as a democratization of mass communication or **media democratization** (see Gillmor, 2004; Shirky, 2008).

The idea of democratizing the media has a history dating back at least to the 1960s and

The Vancouver Public Library hosted Media Democracy Day in November, 2010.

1970s, when co-operative radio stations, film and video collectives, and alternative or 'underground' newspapers were established. Recently, however, the relative accessibility of the internet, the inadequacies of both public and private forms of ownership described above, and the hyper-commercialism that has accompanied globalization have combined to reinvigorate movements for media reform and the establishment of alternative media organizations.

Proposals for reforming the existing media—especially in the field of news and information—include: imposing limits on ownership concentration, and especially cross-media ownership; amending the Competition Act to account for diversity in the expression of news and ideas;

legislating a code of professional practice or a code of ethics for media organizations; restructuring provincial press councils and/or establishing a National Media Commission; and enacting right-of-reply legislation, which would permit editorial redress for persons misrepresented in the media (Skinner, 2004: 16–17). David Skinner argues that 'these reforms would help ensure some diversity in corporate news voices, provide journalists some independence from their corporate employers and provide some checks on the relationship between the media and the public' (ibid., 18). Reform initiatives, however, leave standing the fundamental structures of public and private media institutions.

The other means by which groups seek to democratize the media is through the establishment of alternative media outlets, defined as 'independent and/or community-minded media with a self-espoused mandate to serve a particular range of social groups and/or interests' (ibid., 23). Examples include Co-op Radio in Vancouver and the myriad of independent media centres sprouting on the World Wide Web. If these are to be viable alternatives, Skinner argues, they need to create an infrastructure based on sound economic models and strategies, for example, by forming associations and strategic partnerships to combine production and distribution resources (ibid., 24–5).

:> SUMMARY

There is no natural or inevitable way to organize mass communication. The media are social institutions structured in various ways according to their technological characteristics, the resources they draw upon, and the socio-political context in which they operate. If all media organizations have something in common, however, it is that they participate in the economy by generating revenues for media owners, by providing communication services to their audiences, by advertising goods and services, and by providing employment.

The mass media in Canada are owned both privately and publicly, but all operate in a mixed economy. No media industry in Canada is governed exclusively by free-market economics. Even newspaper publishing, which comes closest to an exclusively private enterprise, is subject to federal government regulations regarding ownership intended to protect newspapers from foreign takeover and foreign competition. Nor is any media organization in Canada immune to the demands of the marketplace; even the publicly owned CBC must pay attention to ratings and advertising revenues.

The critical difference between public and private forms of media ownership pertains to their bottom lines. Public ownership is devoted to providing communication as a public service, to employ the mass media for social and/or national goals. Private ownership is devoted to providing communication for the profit of media owners. These distinctions are fundamental because they speak to the role communication is assigned in Canadian society. The economistic view perceives communication, first and foremost, as commercial enterprise, subjecting all forms of cultural production to commercial criteria of supply and demand. The **culturalist** view regards cultural products as much more than commodities to be exchanged in the marketplace. They are expressions of a culture as a way of life and as a system of beliefs and values. They are expressions of ideas and images that help a culture to imagine itself and to articulate its priorities. As private enterprise has encroached on more and more areas of mass communication in Canadian society, concerns have been raised over the commercialization of cultural production, conglomerate ownership of media organizations, conflicts of interest between media companies and other businesses owned by the same parent, and corporate concentration.

Moves to democratize the media have assumed two forms: media reform, which seeks to find ways to diversify and render existing media organizations more accountable; and alternative media, that is, the establishing of new independent media outlets dedicated to serving defined communities.

:> KEY TERMS

affiliate, p. 262
barriers to entry, p. 247
capital, p. 247
commercial media, p. 247
concentration of ownership, p. 254
conglomerate, p. 255
culturalist, p. 271
economism, p. 250
horizontal integration, p. 262
infant industries, p. 251

invisible hand, p. 249
market externalities, p. 251
means of production, p. 253
media democratization, p. 269
monopoly, p. 249
monopoly capitalism, p. 249
private ownership, p. 249
public ownership, p 258
public service, p. 244

RELATED WEBSITES

Broadcast Dialogue: www.broadcastdialogue.com
This site offers directory and contact information for all Canadian radio and television stations, as well as news from the broadcasting industry.

Newspapers Canada: www.cna-acj.ca
This site provides a wealth of industry news and ownership information.

Quebecor Inc.: www.quebecor.com
This site provides a detailed look at one of Canada's largest media companies and its principal champion of media convergence.

FURTHER READINGS

Anderson, Chris. 2009. *Free: The Future of a Radical Price*. New York: Hyperion. This engaging and thought-provoking book is about the economics behind free media content.

Heilbroner, Robert L. 1980. *The Worldly Philosophers: The Lives, Times, and Ideas of the Great Economic Thinkers*. New York: Simon & Schuster. This very readable reference guide is to history's leading economic theorists.

Mosco, Vincent. 2009. *The Political Economy of Communication: Rethinking and Renewal*, 2nd edn. Los Angeles: Sage. Mosco's theoretical work applies contemporary political-economic thought to communication and cultural industries.

Skinner, David, James Compton, and Mike Gasher, eds. 2005. *Converging Media, Diverging Politics: A Political Economy of News Media in the United States and Canada*. Lanham, MD: Lexington Books. This collection of essays provides a current comparison, overview, and critique of the political economy of the news industries of the United States and Canada.

STUDY QUESTIONS

1. Why are the same media organized differently in similar countries such as Canada, the US, Great Britain, and France?

2. What did Adam Smith mean by the 'invisible hand' of the market? To what extent does his economic thinking apply to communications media today?

3. What is the rationale for state intervention in the cultural economy?

4. What are 'externalities' and how are they pertinent to the discussion of media economics?

5. How does advertising on CBC television affect the public broadcaster's central mission?

6. What are the principal distinctions between public and private forms of ownership?

7. Name three forms that private ownership of the media can assume.

8. What is media convergence and what does it imply for media content?

9. Why is it often more beneficial for Canadian television networks to buy US programs than to produce their own?

10. How do media 'sell audiences to advertisers'?

11. In what ways have the media been democratized?

CHAPTER 10

Journalists as Content Producers

The power which the media derive from their reality-defining capability is attributable to the service they perform in making us the indirect witnesses to events of which we have no first-hand knowledge or experience.

— TONY BENNETT, 1996

Learning Objectives

- To understand that journalism, like all other forms of media content, is produced, but under particular conditions.
- To discover how news production is governed by professional ideals; by the use of language; by socio-cultural, legal, and economic contexts; and by the emergence of new journalism forms.
- To be able to analyze the ways in which structural features affect the kind of journalism produced.
- To learn about the place of new, primarily digital, forms of producing and delivering news within the larger mediascape.

OPENING QUESTIONS

- ⟫ Why is it important to understand that news stories, like other kinds of media content, are produced or constructed?
- ⟫ Why is 'framing' better than 'gatekeeping' for understanding the way journalists produce news stories?
- ⟫ What does it mean to describe journalism as a practice of representation?
- ⟫ How do news stories produce meaning?
- ⟫ To what extent do new media forms provide new opportunities for journalism?

Introduction

Content producers are central to mass communications. Radio hosts, magazine photographers, web designers, television producers, film editors, songwriters—all have vastly different job descriptions and work environments, but they all manufacture media content. The stories and images we see and hear, whether based on fact or fiction, are never presented simply or 'naturally', but are instead highly constructed by people with particular sets of technical and aesthetic skills, organized within a specific production environment, and guided by ideals, ideologies, conventions, regulations, and institutional demands. This process of construction involves a series of choices about what content to create, how, and for whom, and whether those choices are made consciously or unconsciously.

This chapter posits journalism as a particular practice of content production, and an especially interesting one given the new ways it is evolving in our time, the new openings being created for people to participate in the production of news and commentary, and the challenges this presents to the mainstream or commercial news industry. We have seen movements devoted to new journalism, public or civic journalism, alternative journalism, advocacy journalism, citizen journalism, peace journalism, global journalism. But regardless of its particular form, journalism operates within a specific environment, with a set of ideals, storytelling conventions, and audience expectations that distinguish it from other kinds of content production. In its simplest definition, journalism provides the public factual information and informed commentary about current events, by addressing the most basic questions of who, what, when, where, why, and how.

News as Content Production

Like all forms of content, news is produced and, much like other mass media forms, news is produced and presented in story form. News items are typically referred to as 'stories', and, like all stories, they consist of characters, conflicts between characters, temporal and geographical settings, and a narrative that takes us from a beginning to an end, even if the story is updated in subsequent editions and newscasts. News production has implications for how we think about news and for the role journalism plays in society. News stories, while based on actual events and real people, never simply 'mirror' reality, as some journalists would contend. A mirror, after all, shows us only what is placed before it, nothing more and nothing less, and in the proportions presented to it; the person holding the mirror may have control over where to point it, but the depiction the mirror offers is always a simple, direct, and unorganized reflection. The mirror metaphor and the associated notion of 'reflection' do not adequately describe the role of journalists as content producers.

Nor is news simply gathered. Such a conception of journalism underestimates the degree of selection that goes into producing a news report and the extent to which events must meet a news organization's particular standards of 'newsworthiness'. Each day reporters and their editors or producers face an infinite number of events from which to fashion their news stories. They receive far more invitations to press conferences than they could possibly cover and they receive far more press releases than they could ever use. Journalists make choices about what to cover based on what they perceive to have 'news value', what fits within their organization's

Source: © istockphoto.com/Joel Carillet

All news stories are told from someone's perspective.

particular areas of coverage (politics, business, sports, crime, the arts), and what they believe will interest their audience. Deciding what is news is a subjective operation, involving reporters and their editors or producers in a complex and consultative process of selection. While news judgment is most often exercised intuitively by journalists under time pressure in the field, based on their experience and expertise, media scholars have identified a number of criteria that render some events news and others not news. Melvin Mencher (2000: 68–76), for example, identifies seven determinants of

newsworthiness: *timeliness* (events that are immediate or recent); *impact* (events that affect many people); *prominence* (events involving well-known people, places, or institutions); *proximity* (events that are geographically, culturally, or 'emotionally close' to the audience); *conflict* (events pitting two sides against one another); *peculiarity* (events that deviate from the everyday); and *currency* (long-simmering events that suddenly emerge as objects of attention).

Figure 10.1 illustrates the process by which an event becomes news. It demonstrates that within

FIGURE 10.1   International News Flow via a News Service

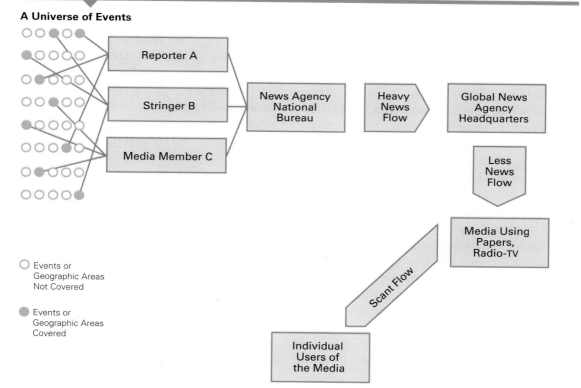

Of the many prospective news events, only some are covered by reporters, 'stringers', or members relaying stories to the bureau of a global news agency. Bureau editors forward important news items to the world headquarters of the agency. Editors at world headquarters select what they think newsworthy and submit them to the member news organizations, who choose which stories they believe will interest their audiences. Finally, individual readers, listeners, or viewers decide what international news they will be attentive to. What began as hundreds of events and items has gradually dwindled to only a handful.

Source: Al Hester, 'International news agencies', in Alan Wells, ed., *Mass Communications: A World View* (Palo Alto, CA: Mayfield Publishing, 1974). Reproduced with permission of the author.

a veritable galaxy of daily events going on around the world, only some are selected by journalists as worth reporting, based on the criteria italicized above. As Jaap van Ginneken (1998: 31) makes clear, journalists' perceptions inform these decisions. 'News is something which is (perceived as) "new" within a specific society, and not something which is (perceived as) "nothing new". It is something which is (perceived as) unexpected, extraordinary, abnormal, not something which is (perceived as) expected, ordinary, normal.' To cite a simple example, normal rush-hour traffic volume on a local urban freeway is not news, while a seven-car pileup that kills three people and closes several lanes of the freeway for a number of hours is.

This process of selection has compelled some theorists to perceive journalists—especially editors and news directors—as gatekeepers, people who sift through a huge number of events and decide which will be covered and which stories will be broadcast or published. But **gatekeeping** is only a partial explanation of the news production process, applicable only to some stages of selection. A newspaper assignment editor, for example, chooses among an assortment of scheduled daily press conferences, meetings, and speeches and decides which will be staffed by a reporter and which will not. This, admittedly, is a form of gatekeeping. Similarly, wire editors will sort through hundreds of wire-service stories from around the world each day to select those to be considered for publication. This, too, is gatekeeping.

Gatekeeping accounts for the question of *what* the news organization will cover, but it leaves aside the equally important issue of *how* an event will be covered. It ignores, for example, the extent to which wire-service stories are revised by copy editors and the different 'play'—length and prominence—they receive from one news organization to the next. The same news item may occupy the first two-and-a-half minutes of the six o'clock news on one channel, complete with interviews and illustrative footage, and warrant only 15 seconds of the anchor's narration on another channel. Same event, but different news stories. Newspapers, too, assign relative importance to news stories by how they

play them—whether as a front-page story with a bold headline above the fold or as a back-page brief item. Again, the same event may receive completely different treatment from one newspaper to the next.

The gatekeeping metaphor also ignores the creative nature of content production. Every news organization establishes a brand: an identity for its audience and its advertisers through the style of journalism it practises—serious and thorough, entertaining and concise, etc. Developing and maintaining that identity is achieved by establishing a certain kind of editorial presence through the assignment of resources and the shaping of content. Tabloid newspapers like the *Toronto Sun* and *Le Journal de Montréal*, for example, pay a considerable amount of attention to crime stories, covering the police beat and the courthouse quite heavily. Their news stories are relatively short and written in a lively and provocative style, and their pages are filled with bold headlines and lots of photographs. **Tabloids** are typically populist newspapers, devoted to what they perceive to be the interests of the everyday person. More sober **broadsheets** like *The Globe and Mail* and *Le Devoir*, on the other hand, pay much more attention to political, foreign affairs, and cultural reporting. They tend to feature much longer, in-depth stories. These newspapers are interested in very different kinds of stories and news presentations, catering to what they perceive to be a more discriminating audience and aspiring to be read by society's opinion leaders. Examining how this editorial style is created opens up the selection process to many more factors than the notion of gatekeeping can accommodate. The gatekeeping metaphor, nonetheless, draws our attention to what gets left out of the selection process.

A more precise way to think of journalists as content producers is through the metaphor of the frame. Through words, images, sounds and story themes, journalists 'frame' reality. If we think of the empty page or the blank screen as an empty frame, it is journalists who decide how to fill that frame each day, by inserting into the frame particular stories, visuals, and graphics and by leaving out much more material. They decide not only which events to include in the news frame, but also how to depict those events and what prominence to assign

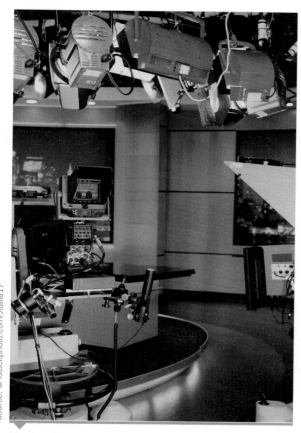

Source: © istockphoto.com/Jitalia17

The 'gatekeepers' of a newsroom are the journalists, editors, and news directors who decide which stories to report.

the story in the newspaper or broadcast or website; what aspects or angle of the story to emphasize; whose voices are heard; what meanings they encourage audiences to take away from the story.

The metaphor of the frame implies, first of all, that there are limits to what a news organization can properly present as news. These limits are defined by such practical considerations as the size of the 'news hole' (the amount of editorial space available in print journalism) or 'news block' (the amount of air time available in a news broadcast), the costs involved in producing the coverage (does it involve travel and hotel accommodation?), and the availability of reporting staff. Even the producers of online news sites, with much more capacity for content, make decisions about what to include and exclude, and which content to feature prominently on their home page. These limits are also governed by the

more subjective criteria of an event's news value and how well it suits the news organization's particular areas of coverage. We would expect a news organization specializing in arts coverage to send its own reporter to the Toronto International Film Festival or the Juno Awards presentations, rather than rely on the Canadian Press wire service, just as we would expect a news organization specializing in sports to send its own reporter to the Stanley Cup final, regardless of which teams are playing.

News coverage is also governed by a given news organization's particular political stance, whether or not this position is ever explicitly stated. Think about how news organizations may react differently, even if the distinctions are subtle, in their coverage of labour–management disputes, same-sex marriage legislation, cuts in social spending, or international trade disputes. In her groundbreaking study of news practices, media scholar Gaye Tuchman (1978: 1) used the frame metaphor to emphasize the necessarily restricted view of the world journalism provides:

> Like any frame that delineates a world, the news frame may be considered problematic. The view through a window depends upon whether the window is large or small, has many panes or few, whether the glass is opaque or clear, whether the window faces a street or a backyard. The unfolding scene also depends upon where one stands, far or near, craning one's neck to the side, or gazing straight ahead, eyes parallel to the wall in which the window is encased.

No news organization can cover every event from every possible angle. Therefore, what stories it includes and excludes can reveal a great deal about the news judgment it applies when producing its daily news package. This judgment is exercised subjectively; it is not uncommon, in a newsroom production environment that brings together a diverse mix of individuals, for reporters and editors to disagree, sometimes vehemently, about whether an event is newsworthy at all, or if it is, how it should be covered and how it should be played.

It was the best of times.
It was the worst of times.

(Depending upon which paper you read.)

Same day.
Same story.
Two points of view.
Which one represents you?

THE TORONTO STAR

As demonstrated by this *Toronto Star* advertisement, individual media organizations, as well as individual journalists, can tell vastly different stories about the very same event.

As we have suggested, this practice of **framing** occurs within a production environment shaped by a number of factors: the ideals that distinguish journalism from other kinds of content production; the use of language—whether textual, aural, or visual—and the shaping of news reports into stories that give news events meaning; the specific socio-political culture in which news stories are produced;

the laws and regulations that govern journalism; the economics of news production; and the technological infrastructure available to journalists.

Ideals of Journalism

If news is constructed, it is also subject to particular ideals that distinguish journalism from other forms of storytelling—and distinguish journalism as it is practised in Western democracies like Canada from the way it might be practised elsewhere. We may be justifiably skeptical about how well journalists and the news organizations they work for live up to the ideals of their profession. Ideals, after all, are lofty principles, even standards for perfection, but they do provide the yardsticks by which critics, practitioners, and audiences alike evaluate performance. These ideals form the set of values that distinguish journalism from other communication practices.

Journalism has a fundamental guiding ideal: the quest for truth. This quest is idealistic because the truth is not always accessible to us as fallible human beings, and certainly not readily accessible within the constraints most journalists have to work with. Even the most conscientious, hard-working, and ethical journalists face time constraints, but journalists are also constrained by access—to people, to documents, to events—and by their own limits of expertise. The seemingly simple task of reporting on what happened—during a meeting, during a battle, during a public demonstration—is always inflected with people's perception and interpretation. Increasingly, we recognize that there is usually more than one truth at play; we might agree on a basic set of facts, but how those facts are made meaningful can produce many truths. Nonetheless, journalism derives its authority from providing the public with *credible* accounts of current affairs. Credibility is the currency in which the news media deal, and no news organization wants to be perceived as not credible.

The performance of journalism's truth-seeking function is related to a second ideal: serving democracy. Truth-seeking is the foundation for **freedom of the press**, a fundamental freedom for all democracies that is explicitly noted in Canada's Charter of Rights and Freedoms (s. 2[b]). Journalism is tasked with the production and circulation of information and ideas for the benefit of all, extending the basic democratic right of freedom of expression granted to all individuals into the realm of the mass media. As scholars Robert Martin and Stuart Adam (1991: 27) note, freedom of expression can be seen as 'an essential pre-condition to the creation and maintenance of democracy itself.... A democratic society must not only permit, but encourage, the widest possible participation of all its members in its economic, social, and cultural affairs. The flip side of the *right* to freedom of the press is the news media's *responsibility* to inform Canadians as engaged citizens—rather than as consumers or spectators—in a democratic society.

The struggle for freedom of the press is ongoing and journalists are at the forefront of efforts to extend public **access to information** in both formal and informal ways, as Box 10.1 addresses.

Journalists are often highly dependent on official sources and their own contacts for information, and the news media's role as 'fourth estate' grants journalists their moral authority to gain access to the people and institutions that populate their reportage: politicians, bureaucrats, police officers, community leaders, celebrities, Parliament, the court system, the stock exchange, and so on.

As was discussed in Chapter 3, the term 'fourth estate', which refers to the role the news media play in the governing of a democratic society, originated with journalists' struggle to gain access to the proceedings of the British Parliament in the late eighteenth and early nineteenth centuries. The role of the press in Parliament was institutionalized with the physical construction of a press gallery in 1831 (Osler, 1993: 61). This was a recognition of the place of journalism in representing citizens as a kind of watchdog over their governors.

The news media today fulfill the role of a fourth estate by reporting on legislative debates and other government business, and by pressuring governments to increase access to information. All

⫸ BOX 10.1   FREEDOM OF THE PRESS

Constitutional guarantees and universal declarations are important, but they define freedom of the press in largely abstract terms. The real, concrete meaning of freedom of the press is derived from its daily exercise by those journalists who push at the boundaries of what can be screened and what can be published.

Journalists exercise freedom of the press when they report what is truly new and important to the public interest; when they broaden the range of debate; when they expand the horizons of what can be reported, imagined, revealed, criticized. Journalists also exercise freedom of the press when they hold their own news organizations to the standards and ideals of their journalistic calling, especially when that news organization may have to pay a political or economic price for its reportage.

Freedom of the press would be meaningless as a human right if journalists never exposed scandal; if they never revealed information government officials preferred not to divulge; if they never quoted critics of powerful people and powerful institutions; if they never drew attention to hypocrisy, greed, or arrogance—if, in other words, they never gave anyone cause to restrict press freedoms. As journalism educator John Miller (1998: 115) puts it: 'Freedom is like muscle: use it or lose it.'

The right to freedom of the press is exerted not only in exceptional, headline-grabbing cases—e.g., the Somalia affair, Shawinigate, the Pentagon Papers, the Watergate scandal—but on a daily basis, in countless small ways. Journalists are giving meaning to freedom of the press every time they reveal more than their sources are willing to share with the public, every time they undermine the propaganda disseminated by corporate and political communications officers, every time they introduce factual evidence to accompany decision-makers' opinions.

To exercise freedom of the press, then, is to give it concrete meaning, when it means discomforting news sources, antagonizing public officials, prompting court challenges, even irritating fellow journalists.

legislatures in Canada have press galleries populated by print, radio, television, and online reporters, and journalists also regularly attend the public meetings of municipal governments. Of all the coverage the news media provide, political reportage is considered to be the most closely related to journalism's role in democratic society: providing citizens with the information they need to be free and self-governing (see Kovach and Rosenstiel, 2001).

This notion of the news media as a fourth estate is connected to journalistic independence. Ideally, journalists are independent agents in service to the public, concerned only with the public good and beyond the influence of powerful private interests. This is, of course, a fantasy. For one thing, journalists are subjective beings with their own values and beliefs, and they are not above serving their own ideological or political interests, whether consciously or unconsciously. But even the most conscientious and self-reflexive journalist is not immune to the influences that can be brought to bear by the political and/or commercial agenda of his or her own news organization; by the public relations industry serving governments, corporations, and other organizations; and by the motivations of the actors in the story who supply information and commentary, often for their own purposes. And as we will discuss further below, our mainstream news organizations are not at all independent from either corporate Canada or political Canada, but have instead become closely intertwined with these institutions of power. A principal raison d'être of alternative news providers is precisely to reassert journalistic independence from political and economic power.

Perhaps the most contentious ideal of journalism is **objectivity**. Journalists are supposed to report objectively, which means separating clearly the reporting of verifiable facts from the assertion of values and opinions. In a conventional news report, facts are declared in the reporter's voice and values are attributed to others, whether as direct quotations or as paraphrased statements. In most mainstream newspapers, news reports are physically distinguished from commentaries: columns, editorials, letters to the editor, op-ed submissions. Radio and television newscasts, news magazines,

and news-based websites apply similar measures to distinguish for their audiences facts and values.

Separating facts from values or opinions is much easier said than done, which is why many people reject the notion of objectivity altogether. For one thing, as we noted above, journalism involves selection, which immediately brings into play a number of subjective judgments: what's news, why is it newsworthy, what angle to the story should be pursued, who should be interviewed, what does this news event mean to the public? For example, the verifiable facts of nearly 500 Sri Lankan refugees arriving by boat off the coast of British Columbia in August 2010 produced a range of very different news frames, from terrorist threat to humanitarian crisis. Second, as discussed in the next section, the use of language to describe news events unavoidably attributes meaning to those events. And news, by definition, is what is perceived by journalists to be important or significant to the public interest; that is the first meaning given to any story, and is

Source: The Canadian Press/Jonathan Hayward

A ship containing an estimated 500 Tamil refugees. They weren't all illegal migrants – that had to be decided by courts, and many were released as genuine refugees arrives in Colwood, BC, on 13 August 2010. How many journalistic points of view, in addition to those mentioned in the text, can you associate with this news photo?

further amplified by the amount and the type of coverage the story is granted.

But rather than reject objectivity altogether, as if it were some kind of absolute value, it is more useful to understand it in relative terms. As communications scholar Jaap van Ginneken (1998: 43) writes: 'Complete objectivity or subjectivity are only extremes on a scale; they are never reached, because most observation reports are governed by varying degrees of inter-subjectivity, that is to say, by varying degrees of agreement between subjects about the characteristics of the object.' Journalism, it is worth noting, is not the only institution in Canadian society that subscribes to objectivity, on seeking impartial, verifiable truths. The judicial system and the scientific research community also seek to produce objective knowledge, to separate fact from opinion, to pursue the truth.

There are more sophisticated ways to think about journalistic objectivity. Communications scholars Robert A. Hackett and Yuezhi Zhao reject the traditional 'positivist' model of objectivity, which perceives truth as the relatively simple product of direct observation and accurate recording. The positivist model asserts that all that stands between reality and journalistic accounts of that reality is good reporting practice, an assertion that fails to account adequately for the mediating presence of the journalist, the language he or she employs, and the socialization he or she has undergone (Hackett and Zhao, 1998: 109–66). Hackett and Zhao, however, also reject the postmodern position, which dismisses objectivity as unattainable because the real world cannot be perceived directly without the mediation of conventional concepts, theories, ideologies, and values, without the mediation of language (in all its forms), and, often, without the mediation of people describing the world on our behalf. Instead, they propose a critical realist approach to objectivity, a position that acknowledges the limitations of both positivism and postmodernism, but nonetheless insists that the real world is accessible, knowable, and describable. Coming to know the truth about the world, they maintain, is a never-ending process, with knowledge constantly produced and revised, subject to the mediation of our categories,

concepts, values, and conventions, and emerging only as a result of 'the interactive or dialectical to and fro between subject and object, concepts and reality' (ibid., 129). In other words, if knowledge about the real world cannot be taken at face value through direct observation, and if knowledge production is always subject to various layers of mediation, knowledge and truth can nonetheless emerge through careful and reflexive investigation. 'The world is knowable—but not at first sight' (ibid., 130).

Some journalists prefer to substitute the values of balance and fairness as a means of dodging the objectivity question, but these qualities are equally problematic. Balance typically means presenting both sides of the story, a common practice in mainstream news reports. It makes a number of presumptions, however, that cannot be sustained. For one thing, there can be many more than two sides to a story, and limiting the presentation to two often means choosing the most polarized positions, leaving aside more moderate views, and rendering the two polarized positions irreconcilable; this is one of the contentions of peace journalism (Lynch and McGoldrick, 2005). For another, the concept of balance can create the impression that the two views presented in a story are equally valid. News coverage of climate change, for example, often creates the impression that there is a serious debate about whether climate change exists by giving voice to both scientists and those who dispute their claims, granting comparable weight to both sides' positions. By refusing to discriminate among opinions, journalists do not bring us closer to the truth.

Similarly, fairness is a poor substitute for objectivity. Fairness is most often exercised in journalism by providing people with an opinion a fair hearing. Those opinions, however, may not be fair to the truth.

Journalism as a Textual Practice

As discussed earlier, journalists do not simply mirror or reflect the world in their news reports, but instead produce or construct stories about the events they believe are most newsworthy. And, as the saying goes, no story tells the full story, no picture gives the whole picture. News stories are told through the medium of language, that is, a range of symbolic systems: written or spoken words, images, sounds, symbols, gestures, even colours. News stories are texts; rather than faithful *reproductions* of the world, they are highly constructed *representations* or depictions of the world through language. Hall (1997: 16) defines **representation** as 'the production of meaning through language'. In other words, journalists re-present the objects of their reportage. As we discussed in Chapter 4, to re-present is to make present, or depict, or symbolize, through language(s): news photos, audio clips, television reports, newspaper articles. In so doing, journalists unavoidably give those objects meaning.

At the simplest level, deciding to cover an event *as* news in the first place defines it as important, significant, relevant, and/or interesting. A second level of meaning pertains to precisely how the story is covered. How, for instance, should the story be framed? Why is it newsworthy? Is it good news or bad news, positive or negative, a natural disaster or a human-made tragedy? Is it a business story, a consumer affairs story, or a labour story? Is it worth front-page treatment or simply a news brief? Finally, what words are chosen to label the event, what images are selected to depict the event and its principal actors? Whose voices are heard?

If language is the medium through which meaning is produced, how does the process work?

The Swiss linguist Ferdinand de Saussure demonstrated that language works to produce meaning in the relationship between a signifier—an utterance of language (e.g., a word, an image, a symbol, a gesture, a sound)—and a signified—the image in our heads that is created when we see or hear a specific language utterance. This is precisely the process we engage in when we acquire language skills as an infant, and what we might do if we later decide to acquire a second or third language. To cite a simple example, when we hear or see the word 'tree' (the signifier), we picture in our minds a woody, leafy plant (the signified), even if we may not know which specific tree is being referred to.

This process quickly becomes more complicated—and contentious—when we read or hear

FIGURE 10.2

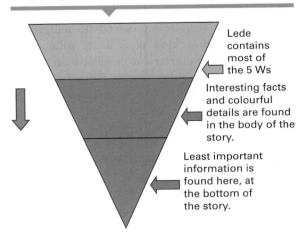

News stories tend to follow a formulaic and hierarchical story structure known as the inverted pyramid. As the diagram illustrates, a story written in this manner puts the most essential information in the first few paragraphs, with less important details and comment further down. The lead, or introduction, provides 'who', 'what', 'when', and 'where' information. Subsequent paragraphs seek to provide answers to the 'how' and 'why' questions.

Source: Newspapers Canada

everyday words like 'family' or 'marriage'. What do these words mean—and not mean? For some of us, 'family' denotes a nuclear family, for others an extended family. We might exclude from that association other kinds of family: same-sex parents with an adopted child; unmarried parents with children, etc. When journalists use the word 'family', then, what exactly do they mean, and what do they *not* mean? Similarly, what do we think of when we see the word 'marriage'? What kinds of couplings does this include and exclude? Can two people of the same sex be married? Can two people who have been living together for years without having any kind of official wedding ceremony or marriage licence be considered married? The very definition of marriage is frequently the subject of news stories. In Quebec news reports, the term 'Québécois' can have an inclusive meaning—all residents of Quebec—or an exclusive meaning—French-Canadian residents of Quebec. The distinction is significant, particularly during media discussions of Quebec sovereignty and nationhood.

Let's consider the flip side of this process. Journalists typically begin with the signified—the event or person or institution they are covering—and need to assign the object of their coverage signifiers or language descriptors. Thus, they choose language to label and describe what they are covering, and those labels have meaning. Think about the ways in which journalists describe demonstrators, for example. Are they portrayed as engaged citizens exercising their democratic rights or as rabble-rousers and troublemakers? Which demonstrators are chosen to illustrate the event in news photographs, the peaceful, conservatively dressed marchers, or black bloc protestors breaking plate-glass windows and confronting police? The same demonstrators, and the same demonstration, can be made to mean, through news stories and images, a range of things.

While some journalists may make these choices deliberately, more often these meanings are produced unconsciously by simply following news conventions—e.g., the violent demonstrator makes a more compelling photo than the peaceful marcher—or by subscribing to what they perceive to be their audience's common-sense viewpoint—e.g., a labour–management dispute as a disruptive inconvenience to the public. Regardless of whether we can establish intent, journalists' subjectivity once again comes into play.

The point here is that journalists are implicated in this process of meaning production in three specific ways:

- Journalists decide what is news.
- Journalists attach relative importance to news events.
- Journalists interpret those events through the language choices that constitute their coverage.

This production of meaning is significant because, as communications scholar Tony Bennett (1996: 296) observes, 'the power which the media derive from their reality-defining capability is attributable to the service they perform in making us the indirect witnesses to events of which we have no first-hand knowledge or experience.'

Journalism as a Socio-Cultural Institution

Journalism is a socio-cultural institution in the sense that it both informs and is informed by the society and culture in which it is practised. As a social institution journalism is integrated politically because, in a democratic society such as Canada, it assumes the role of serving democracy through its fact-finding mission. Journalism is integrated economically because it is an industry in and of itself, the news media are a key advertising vehicle, and the structure of news organizations within a large-scale news industry is consistent with the larger economic organization of Canadian society where predominantly corporate and commercial enterprises comprise and determine the nation's economy.

Journalism is also cultural because journalists produce texts that describe the communities in

Source: The Canadian Press/Jake Wright

A news photograph of a demonstration captures only a fragment of the entire event at a precise moment in time. But it nonetheless becomes the picture of that event for the news consumer. Think about which demonstrators are depicted in this news photograph, how they are depicted, and how this image shapes our understanding of the larger event.

which we live, privilege certain community values and behaviours, and situate our community within the larger world. News reportage identifies society's central institutions of power and its most influential players; news reports are often about those institutions—governments, the courts, the police, the schools, businesses—and the people who run them—politicians, lawyers and judges, police officers, educators, business leaders.

Through the media we are presented with a picture of our community, its members, and their central preoccupations. The media also offer value judgments about right and wrong, legitimate and illegitimate, whether concerning how we behave, what we wear, how we drive, what we eat and drink, or what political beliefs we hold. Similarly, news coverage draws boundaries around 'here' and 'there', and determines what is considered important and relevant to a particular community of people. In this way, journalism makes distinctions between community insiders and community outsiders, establishing a sense of 'us' and 'them'. As communications scholar John Hartley (1992:

207)) argues, the news 'includes stories on a daily basis which enable everyone to recognize a larger unity or community than their own immediate contacts, and to identify with the news outlet as "our" storyteller.' The boundaries between those defined as 'us' and 'them' are not coterminous with any formal political boundaries or citizenship but can be drawn from any number of bases: gender, race, class, ethnicity, etc. News media, then, according to Hartley, not only help to define and constitute communities, but in doing so they also draw boundary lines that divide communities into domains of 'us' and 'them'.

Providing a picture of our community—who constitutes that community, what its history is, what its most pressing issues are, and what its norms and values are—is a complex task for journalists. There is always a gap between the reality of community life as we experience it and the constructed reality the news media provide us, between the real world and the news world. Nonetheless, in mass societies such as Canada, where most of us live in large and diverse cities, journalism remains a key component

❖ BOX 10.2 STATUS OF WOMEN IN THE NEWS MEDIA

A comprehensive global study by the International Women's Media Foundation (2011) found there are equal numbers of men and women working for news media companies in Canada, but women are under-represented in the highest levels of media management and their average salaries are lower than men's in most occupational categories. The IWMF surveyed 11 Canadian news companies—five newspapers, three television stations, three radio stations—and collected data on close to 14,000 employees (ibid., 159).

The study determined that women accounted for approximately half of the positions in junior-level (54.8 per cent) and senior-level (45.5 per cent) professional positions, categories that include writers, editors, anchors, directors, producers, researchers, reporters, and correspondents. Women occupied half of the middle management positions (senior editors, chiefs of correspondents, design directors, creative directors, senior human resources and finance staff) and 55.1 per

cent of senior management positions (news directors, editors-in-chief, managing editors, executive editors, human resource directors, bureau chiefs, administrative directors). Women hit the glass ceiling, though, at the top level of management (publishers, chief executive officers, chief financial officers), accounting for 39.4 per cent, and governance positions (members of governing boards), where they accounted for 26.3 per cent. Women predominated in sales, finance, and administrative positions (61.7 per cent), but were under-represented in production and design (23.6 per cent) and technical professional jobs (13.1 per cent) (ibid., 160).

With respect to salary, the study found that men tended to earn more than women in top-level management, senior-level management, middle management, senior- and junior-level professional positions, and in sales, finance, and administration. Most of the positions occupied by women in the news industry were full-time, regular jobs (ibid., 161).

of what the political theorist Jürgen Habermas (1996: 55) termed 'the public sphere':

> By 'public sphere' we mean first of all a domain of our social life in which such a thing as public opinion can be formed. Access to the public sphere is open in principle to all citizens. A portion of the public sphere is constituted in every conversation in which private persons come together to form a public. They are then acting neither as business or professional people conducting their private affairs, nor as legal consociates subject to the legal regulations of a state bureaucracy and obligated to obedience. Citizens act as a public when they deal with matters of general interest without being subject to coercion; thus with the guarantee that they may assemble and unite freely, and express and publicize their opinions freely. When the public is large, this kind of communication requires certain means of dissemination and influence; today, newspapers and periodicals, radio and television are the media of the public sphere.

Habermas traces the emergence of an idealized public sphere to the eighteenth century, a period in the development of democracy when private persons gathered as peers in salons, cafés, and pubs to consider and discuss the issues of the day and come to some determination about them. This public sphere mediated between society and the state in the sense that it provided a forum for private citizens without formal political power to come together and influence political authority through rational argument. The newspapers of the day became 'the vehicles and guides of public opinion' (ibid., 58). Habermas regrets that the public sphere in contemporary society no longer operates on the basis of rational argument among private citizens coming together as equals, but has become instead 'a field for competition among interests in the cruder form of forcible confrontation' (ibid., 59). If the media provide some space for citizens to speak, through letters to the editor, op-ed commentaries, call-in radio and television

programs, and online discussion forums, the focus of news coverage is almost exclusively on what are usually termed 'opinion leaders'—politicians, businesspeople, administrators pollsters, public relations spokespeople, think tanks, and other assorted experts and officials. These people are not speaking for themselves or impartially, but on behalf of society's most powerful vested interests. This, again, explains the potential significance of alternative journalism forms, such as blogs and citizen journalism sites, that seek to restore citizens' voices to the mediascape, by relating opinions and points of view we don't normally hear and by giving voice to people not often provided the opportunity to speak through mainstream media.

The news media's role in the public sphere is significant, given the extent to which we depend on the media for knowledge about our world. When, as citizens, we are confronted with the prospect of sending Canadian troops to fight in Iraq or

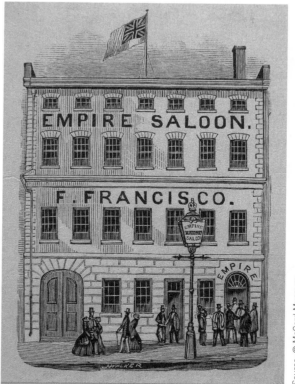

Do you see Habermas's notion of private citizens coming together as equals in this public gathering?

Afghanistan, we often rely on the media for our knowledge of those countries and it is through the media that the reasons for fighting, or not fighting, are proposed to us by the opinion leaders. Similarly, when a boatload of Sri Lankans arrives on the coast on British Columbia seeking asylum, we depend on news reports to learn who they are, why they fled Sri Lanka, and what their arrival means for Canadians. The media serve as socializing institutions for all kinds of public attitudes about race, ethnicity, immigration, gender roles, the aged, youth culture, etc.

Roger Silverstone sees the media as constituting an environment and emphasizes 'the significance of the media for our orientation in the world.... The media are both context and contextualized. They both construct a world, and are constructed by that world' (Silverstone, 2007: 6). What he calls the 'mediapolis' is a significant moral space where we confront, and make judgments about, others:

> [The media] orient the reader and viewer to a world that embodies the primary values of the society that produces them, notwithstanding the inevitable differences and contradictions within and between societies in such matters. They inscribe judgements of good and evil, of benevolence and malevolence, both in the narratives of global and national reporting, as well in the dramatization of fiction. There is in all of these frameworks a narrative of us and them, of origins and futures, of boundaries and the articulation of difference, without which our culture, indeed any culture, could not survive. (Ibid., 62)

Journalism, like all media forms, is both text and context, a site upon which beliefs and values are developed and communicated, and where they can be reinforced or challenged. Journalists, in this sense, are social actors heavily implicated in this process.

Journalism is often described as a profession, even though, unlike the medical and legal professions, it has no regulatory body and requires no mandatory formal training. Anyone who practises journalism, whether as a freelancer, an internet blogger, or a staff member of a news organization, is a journalist. Unfortunately, we have little current data on who Canadian journalists are, and the task of gathering this information has become ever more complicated as the mainstream media reduce the size of their newsrooms through layoffs and buyouts and contract out more work, and as a vast array of alternative media groups devoted to news and commentary emerge. That said, there is widespread concern that journalism continues to be an exclusive occupation and that newsrooms fall far short of reflecting the make-up of the Canadian population.

In the state-regulated broadcasting sphere, inclusivity is a prominent theme of the Broadcasting Act (1991). Section 3(d)(iii) of the Act declares that the Canadian broadcasting system should:

> through its programming and the employment opportunities arising out of its operations, serve the needs and interests, and reflect the circumstances and aspirations, of Canadian men, women and children, including equal rights, the linguistic duality and multicultural and multiracial nature of Canadian society and the special place of aboriginal peoples within that society.... (Canada, 1991)

As discussed in Chapter 7, federal broadcast legislation has shifted its priority from the extension of radio and television services to all parts of Canada to the enshrinement of the 'broadcasting rights' of three specific groups: women, Native peoples, and multicultural/multiracial communities. Lorna Roth (1996: 73) writes: 'Each has the right to be fairly portrayed on the airwaves and equitably represented on staffs throughout all broadcasting services—public, private, and community.' Research, however, indicates that the Canadian news media remain far from attaining this goal.

A 2004 study by the Task Force for Cultural Diversity on Television found that visible minorities comprised just 12.3 per cent of anchors and 8.7 per cent of reporters and interviewers in English-language news. Another study determined that more than 90 per cent of television news directors were white (Khakoo, 2006).

Inclusivity is an important issue in a period of globalization and in a country as culturally and racially diverse as Canada, and newsmaking should bear some resemblance to the composition of Canadian society, both in the content generated and in the people employed. Clearly, *who* reports the news has implications for *what* gets covered, *how*, and *to whom* news reports are addressed (see Nielsen, 2009).

As noted earlier, there is considerable room for interpretation in judging the news value and the appropriate presentation of a particular event or issue. Therefore, journalists' life experiences—their assumptions, their biases, their prejudices, their values—affect their reportage. In a report to the Canadian Race Relations Foundation, researchers Frances Henry and Carol Tator (2000: 169) concluded that journalists were not objective, detached, or neutral in their reporting. 'They are highly selective in their writing. Often their own sense of social location, experiences, values and world views, as well as the interests and positionality of publishers and newspaper owners, act as an invisible filter to screen out alternative viewpoints and perspectives.' A relatively young reporting staff, for example, may be less aware of, and less sensitive to, issues that pertain to an aging Canadian population, such as the future of the Canada Pension Plan or the costs of prescription drugs. A predominantly male newsroom may be less receptive to issues of particular relevance to women, such as child care, reproductive rights, and sexism, and may be prone to patriarchal views of certain issues that especially involve women, such as sexual assault, spousal abuse, and pay equity (see Meyers, 1997).

Henry et al. (2000: 296–310) argue that the media are particularly important sources for information about Canada's visible minority communities. But because few Canadian journalists are non-white and because Canadians of colour are rarely interviewed by journalists unless the news item directly concerns race, minority men and women are largely invisible in Canadian newsrooms and Canadian news coverage. This invisibility 'communicates the message that they are not full participants in Canadian society.' Communications research has repeatedly determined that when people of colour are visible in news reportage, they are often depicted in negative and stereotypical ways. Henry et al. write: 'A pervasive theme of both news and [dramatic] programming is the portrayal of people of colour as "the outsiders within," reinforcing the "we–they" mindset.' People of colour lack access to the media to make their voices heard. Journalism educator John Miller (1998: 137) argues that this also results in 'blind spots' in news coverage: 'If few women or visible minorities are in positions where they can determine what newspapers cover and how, issues affecting them are probably not going to receive proper attention or get on the agenda for public debate.'

The point is not to turn the news media into organs of advocacy for the disenfranchised. Instead, Kovach and Rosenstiel (2001: 108) explain: 'The ultimate goal of newsroom diversity is to create an intellectually mixed environment where everyone holds firm to the idea of journalistic independence. Together their various experiences blend to create a reporting richer than what they would create alone. And in the end that leads to a richer, fuller view of the world for the public.'

Legal Parameters Governing Journalism

Freedom of the press is one of the most fundamental rights of a democratic society, and journalism in Canada is practised in a free press environment. Section 2 of the 1982 Canadian Charter of Rights and Freedoms protects both freedom of expression and freedom of the press under the heading 'Fundamental Freedoms':

2. Everyone has the following fundamental freedoms:
   (a) freedom of conscience and religion;
   (b) freedom of thought, belief, opinion and expression, including freedom of the press and other media of communication;
   (c) freedom of peaceful assembly; and
   (d) freedom of association.

This does not mean, however, that journalists are free to report whatever they want. Press freedom in Canada is constrained by laws that ensure journalists' freedoms do not compromise the security of the state or the freedoms of other Canadian citizens. As journalist and legal scholar Michael G. Crawford (1990: 3) notes: 'The danger in the term "freedom of the press" is that it implies a special right has been imparted upon the news media which is above the rights of the general public. That is not the case.' The news media have no greater privileges than the average citizen. Journalists, instead, are recognized by the Canadian courts as 'members and representatives of the public'. In law, freedom of the press is a right of media proprietors. While journalists in the field produce the stories, it is their employers who exercise the constitutional power of freedom of the press, deciding whether or not to run a particular story and, deciding how any given story might be handled.

Freedom of the press is a core right of all modern democratic states. But this tenet of liberal democracy is not interpreted exactly the same way by all democracies, compelling journalists to work within both national and international legal and policy frameworks. At the international level, Article 19 of the Universal Declaration of Human Rights (1949) provides the ethical foundation. It states:

> para. 1: Everyone shall have the right to hold opinions without interference.
>
> para. 2: Everyone shall have the right to freedom of expression; this right shall include freedom to seek, receive and impart

⠶ BOX 10.3   ETHICAL CODES FOR JOURNALISTS

In the electronic media, the Canadian Association of Broadcasters has a Code of Ethics, a Code Regarding Violence in Television Programming, and an Equitable Portrayal Code administered by the Canadian Broadcast Standards Council. The Code of Ethics contains 18 clauses dealing with such issues as: the diversity of the audience; abusive and discriminatory material; the vulnerability and impressionability of children; participation in worthwhile community activities; the nature of educational efforts; the accuracy of news; the presentation of public issues; the content of advertising; subliminal devices; conformity with advertising codes; the distinction between advertising and news and public affairs programming; portrayal of each gender; and the public responsibilities of broadcasting. In addition, Advertising Standards Canada administers voluntary codes on advertising, including advertising to children (www.adstandards.com/en/Standards/canCodeOfAdStandards.aspx#advertising).

The Association of Electronic Journalists (RTNDA) also has a 14-point Code of Ethics (www.rtndacanada.com/ETHICS/codeofethics.asp). Its preamble states: 'Free speech and an informed public are vital to a democratic society. The members of RTNDA Canada recognize the responsibility of broadcast journalists to promote and to protect the freedom to report independently about matters of public interest and to present a wide range of expressions, opinions and ideas.' To that end, RTNDA members follow a code pertaining to: accuracy, equality, authenticity, privacy, independence, integrity, conflict of interest, corrections of errors, decency and conduct, fair trial, violent situations, intellectual property, impediments, sources, and respect and enforcement. For example, Article 8 states:

> Broadcast journalists will treat people who are subjects and sources with decency. They will use special sensitivity when dealing with children. They will strive to conduct themselves in a courteous and considerate manner, keeping broadcast equipment as unobtrusive as possible. They will strive to prevent their presence from distorting the character or importance of events.

The written press is guided by a different set of institutions. Canada has six regional press councils—representing British Columbia, Alberta, Manitoba, Ontario, Quebec, and the Atlantic provinces—to address public complaints (Saskatchewan and the territories have no press councils). However, press councils have no regulatory authority, relying instead on publicity and moral suasion to encourage ethical behaviour by member newspapers and their journalists.

information and ideas of all kinds, regardless of frontiers, either orally, in writing or in print, in the form of art, or through any other media of his/her choice.

para. 3: The exercise of the right provided for in para. 2 of this article carries with it special duties and responsibilities. It may therefore be subject to certain restrictions, but these shall only be such as are provided by law and are necessary for the respect of the rights or reputation of others or for the protection of national security or of public order or of public health or morals.

Article 12 of the Declaration also deals with press functioning by addressing infringement of privacy and attacks on honour and reputation: 'Everyone has

the right of protection of the law against such interference and attack.' These two rights, free speech and the right to privacy, always exist in tension with one another. Journalists may have rights, but they also have legal obligations and ethical responsibilities.

While enjoying freedom of the press, Canadian journalists are also subject to national and international law, and they are compelled to subscribe to a variety of ethical codes that deal with the business of news production. These codes serve as guidelines rather than regulations, and while they may indeed encourage responsible journalism, their primary goal is to ward off legislative intervention.

In addition to the codes of ethics and regulatory bodies that guide Canadian newsmakers to provide fair and accurate reporting, particular Canadian laws aid or constrain the newsmaking process.

Newspaper companies in the past have adopted their own codes of ethics, but this practice has largely been abandoned for fear that it increases publishers' legal liability. In a study of Canadian journalism ethics conducted in 2001–2, researcher Bob Bergen (2002: 10–11) could identify only one daily newspaper, the *Toronto Star*, that operated according to a set of well-publicized principles. More typical, Bergen said, was the *Ottawa Citizen*, which had a 19-page Ethics and Policies manual that its journalists were expected to follow. Bergen also examined 65 collective-bargaining agreements and found that 59 contained clauses allowing journalists to take specified actions when ethical issues arose (ibid., 33).

In the present climate of increased concentration of ownership and increased commercialization of the news media, governments are pressuring converged media companies to make public statements of their journalistic principles. For example, when the CRTC renewed the television licences of CTV and CanWest Global in August 2001, it imposed a number of conditions, including the requirement that the two networks adhere to a Statement of Principles and Practices governing the cross-ownership of TV stations and newspapers (CRTC, 2001).

The Quebec government, which is particularly sensitive to the high levels of **corporate concentration**

among French-language news media—two companies, Quebecor and Gesca, between them own all but one of Quebec's French-language dailies—is also pressing news organizations in the province to publish ethics codes as part of a larger attempt to ensure 'the quality and diversity of information'.

As discussed in Chapter 7, a study in 2003 of the Canadian broadcasting system by the Standing Committee on Canadian Heritage (the Lincoln Committee) expressed concern about both corporate concentration and cross-media ownership, particularly as it threatened news organizations' editorial independence. Most recently, the June 2006 report of the Standing Senate Committee on Transport and Communications (Canada, 2006a) made a number of recommendations to limit corporate concentration and cross-ownership across the media spectrum. Noting that Canada was 'atypical among large democracies', the Committee encouraged the federal government to develop the same kind of regulatory mechanisms that impose ownership restrictions in Britain, France, Australia, Germany, and the United States (ibid., 24). The report concluded: 'Excessive levels of concentration and the domination of particular markets by one media group engender distrust in the very institutions that Canadians rely upon for their news and information' (ibid., 63).

These statutes are designed to protect the public interest and cover areas such as access to information, libel, privacy, and contempt of court.

Access to information laws have recently been enacted in North America as a way of extending the right to freedom of information. The basic principle is that, in the name of democracy, most government information should be available to the people. Exceptions should be rare and are justified only when public access to information might pose a risk to national security, the privacy of individuals, or the confidentiality of certain political discussions (e.g., the advice of public servants to cabinet ministers). The federal government and all the provincial governments have access to information legislation, which outlines what kinds of government information are subject to scrutiny and how journalists and ordinary citizens can obtain access.

Access to information laws are important to journalists and the general public for two reasons. First, governments are ravenous collectors of information and have considerable data at their disposal, ranging from budget and expenditure documents to tax returns and detailed census statistics. This information is required by journalists to ensure a full understanding of the social, political, and economic issues they cover. Journalists, for example, comprise one of the groups impacted negatively by the Conservative government's 2010 decision to abandon the mandatory long-form census; census information is invaluable to anyone—journalists, researchers, policy analysts, local governments—interested in a detailed and comprehensive portrait of the Canadian population. Second, much of a government's daily work and decision-making occurs outside of public meetings. In order for journalists to monitor government activities and report them to Canadians, they need to know what happens beyond public forums. Again, this access to information is required to report on and evaluate government performance.

While freedom of expression laws define the positive foundation of journalism, libel and other restraint laws define the negative constraints within which journalists must operate. **Libel** is the publication or broadcasting of 'a false and damag-

ing statement'. Such a statement must be seen to discredit or lower the public perception of an individual, corporation, labour union, or any other 'legal entity' (Crawford, 1990: 15; Buckley, 1993: 112). In most countries, responsibility for libel extends beyond the author to editors and producers in their role as people who review submissions and decide what to include and not to include in putting reports together for publication or broadcast. Libel law serves to protect against falsehood the reputations of those who are the subjects of published or broadcast reports. At the same time, it seeks to ensure that journalists live up to the ideals of fairness and accuracy in their pursuit of truth.

Libel and personal privacy are closely connected, and often the trade-off between personal privacy and public interest is the central issue behind libel cases. Section 7 of the Charter of Rights and Freedoms states: 'Everyone has the right to life, liberty and security of the person and the right not to be deprived thereof except in accordance with principles of fundamental justice.' Section 8 protects against 'unreasonable search or seizure'. In addition, the federal government, all 10 provinces, and all three territories have legislation to protect privacy, pertaining to such issues as eavesdropping, surveillance, wiretapping, and use of personal documents.

Contempt of court also is connected closely to invasion of privacy. Canadian controls on the media in commenting on cases before the courts are generally less stringent than in Britain, but much more stringent than in the United States. In Canada, the courts can prevent ongoing news coverage in order to protect citizens. In May 1999, for example, a Calgary court ordered *Alberta Report* magazine to stop publishing stories about genetic, late-term abortions, i.e., those prompted by prenatal diagnoses of abnormality, at Foothills Hospital. The Calgary Regional Health Authority had complained to Alberta's Court of Queen's Bench that the stories were endangering the lives of hospital staff (Foot, 1999: A4).

An April 1998 Canadian Supreme Court ruling expanded considerably the bounds of privacy legislation. The Court ruled that 'it is against Quebec law to publish an identifiable picture of a person no matter

BOX 10.4 LIBEL CHILL

The term **libel chill** refers to the effect that the threat of libel action can have on the news media, particularly in the coverage of powerful individuals and organizations. This threat can be effective in discouraging journalists because, under Canadian libel law, the burden of proof rests with the accused (known as 'reverse onus'). Once a libel action is mounted, in other words, the onus is on the journalist to defend him or herself. Free comment about powerful people can exact a hefty price if those powerful people choose to contest journalists' reports about them in the court of law. Whether or not the court decides in favour of the plaintiff, the journalist must endure the anxiety associated with such an action.

The plaintiff, on the other hand, risks little from a libel suit, beyond increased publicity and general speculation about guilt or innocence.

A more recent concern about 'online chill' involves the legal liability of websites that publish reader comments and host discussion forums. The BC-based website P2Pnet.net was hit with a **defamation** suit for comments posted to the site by its readers. The legal question raised was whether websites could be compelled to remove allegedly libelous content under the threat of legal liability. Legal scholar Michael Geist writes: 'Under current Canadian law, intermediaries can face potential liability for failing to remove allegedly defamatory content once they have received notification of such a claim, even without court oversight' (Geist, 2006).

The easiest way for journalists to avoid libel suits is to avoid publishing or broadcasting contentious material. While libel law can be seen to work as a censoring device (hence the term, 'libel chill'), others argue that libel law contributes positively to the reporting of what would be agreed upon by a community of fair-minded people as the truth.

how harmless, taken without his or her consent, unless there is an overriding "public interest". The Supreme Court was upholding a 1991 Quebec court decision to award $2,000 to a Montreal woman whose picture was taken without her consent while she sat in the doorway of a building. The photograph was published in the Montreal literary magazine *Vice Versa* as part of a story on urban life (Cherry, 1998: A4). The ruling means that individuals' privacy is protected even when they are in a public place. Journalists must walk a fine line between notions of personal privacy and public interest. People's lives are not fair game for journalists, unless a clear case for the public's right to know can be argued.

Contempt of court refers to instances when the judicial process is interfered with and/or the courts are disobeyed (Buckley, 1993: 110). Here again, two fundamental democratic rights come into conflict: the right to freedom of the press and the right to a fair trial. Section 11(d) of the Charter of Rights and Freedoms states that any person charged with an offence has the right 'to be presumed innocent until proven guilty according to law in a fair and public hearing by an independent and impartial tribunal'. To ensure these conditions are met, the justice system has at its disposal a number of measures, some of which affect the ability of journalists to report the news in its entirety. For example, judges in Canadian courts can impose publication bans on court proceedings and the press is not permitted to identify juveniles involved in court cases or to identify the alleged victim in a rape trial (see ibid., 96–111).

The Supreme Court of Canada ruled in May 2010 that journalists do not have a constitutional right to protect the identity of their information sources during police investigations, but the Court agreed that some sources may warrant protection on a case-by-case basis (MacCharles, 2010). The decision upheld a 2001 judgment against editors of the *National Post* to release a document received by reporter Andrew McIntosh, who was investigating the role of then–prime minister Jean Chrétien in the Shawinigate affair.

Clearly, there is no simple, or universal, definition of freedom of the press. In Canada, freedom of the press is defined in the context of existing laws and judicial interpretations of constitutional guarantees informed by legal precedents.

Economics of News Production

Besides being affected by the legal and ethical imperatives described above, most journalists in Canada work for commercial news organizations and, as such, are also implicated in the process of generating profits for their owners. Decisions about what a comprehensive news package entails in a commercial news industry will always be made in concert with the need to maximize audiences and attract advertising. Advertising, after all, pays most of the bills of mainstream news organizations and pays all of the bills in the cases of freely distributed community newspapers and commuter dailies. Even the CBC, a public broadcaster that receives about two-thirds of its operating funds from government, must pay attention to audience ratings to maintain public confidence and to attract television advertisers, even though advertising accounted for less than one-fifth of CBC's radio and television services' revenues in fiscal 2008–9 (CBC, 2009).

Like all other commercial media, news organizations target particular market segments in order to assemble an audience that will be attractive to advertisers. For example, tabloid newspapers like the *Ottawa Sun*, the *Vancouver Province*, and *Le Journal de Montréal* aim for younger, blue-collar readers and give extensive coverage to crime stories, popular entertainment, and sports. Their judgment of news and their writing style is tuned accordingly. On the other hand, broadsheet newspapers like *The Globe and Mail*, the *Toronto Star*, and *La Presse* aim for a more sophisticated readership and give much more coverage to politics, business, high culture, and world affairs.

No news organization has an unlimited budget. This means that the news value of an event must always be weighed against the costs required for coverage, particularly if the story necessitates travel. The maintenance of permanent news bureaus, whether in Beijing or Ottawa, is expensive and the coverage those bureaus produce has to warrant the costs involved, in terms of the quality of the reportage and/or the prestige that accrues to the news organization for having far-flung correspondents. At the same time, no news organization has unlimited time or space to tell its stories, and news judgment must also account for this. A television or radio newscast is always the same length, whether it is a slow news day or a busy one. Newspapers vary in size from day to day, but this is primarily a product of how much advertising they sell. Online news providers are much less constrained in this regard, and can base the quantity of their content package on what is regarded as necessary to provide adequate coverage on a day-to-day basis and what their staffs can produce.

Besides these structural factors affecting news decisions, ideological factors also come into play. Owners, managers, and journalists all subscribe to certain beliefs about how the world works and, regardless of how objective and fair a journalist tries to be, these beliefs influence what gets covered and how. The *National Post*, for example, strongly supported the Unite the Right movement in the late 1990s and early 2000s, leading to the unification of the Canadian Alliance (previously Reform) and Progressive Conservative parties. Editorialists at Gesca papers in Quebec (e.g., *La Presse*) are required by its owners to take a federalist political position (Gingras, 2006: 111).

More often, though, such bias in the judgment of news assumes subtler forms and may not be readily discernable to readers and viewers, many of whom may share the bias. Jaap van Ginneken (1998: 60–3) identifies five categories of 'values' that are promoted widely and continuously and, hence, tend to predominate in the news coverage of the Western democracies:

1. The economic values of free enterprise and a free market.
2. The social values of individualism and social mobility.
3. The political values of pragmatism and moderation.
4. The lifestyle values of materialism and autonomy.
5. The ideological values that the West's point of view is based on scientific reason, while

the views expressed in developing and non-Western countries are based on dogma.

These values, van Ginneken asserts, are widely shared among Western journalists, with the result that they are taken for granted and through news media discourse become 'naturalized'. As these perceptions are subscribed to, particularly by those in power, they form a society's 'dominant ideology'. Alternative views, such as the belief in the necessity of market regulation or the balancing of individual with collective rights, thereby are positioned as deviant or 'unnatural'.

As we have suggested throughout this chapter, news stories are selective representations of the universe of daily events going on around us. Both the stories that are told and how they are told owe something to the prevailing values that define newsworthiness, the particular style and budget of the news organization, and the beliefs and ideas that tend to predominate in society (see Figure 10.3). In any consideration of the question, 'What is news?', a number of factors are at play.

A specific economic constraint in commercial news production is corporate concentration.

FIGURE 10.3 Defining the News

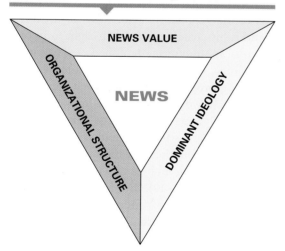

News can be seen as a product of the complex tension among: the factors that inform news value; the economic, time, and space constraints of organizational structure; and the beliefs that comprise the dominant ideology in society.

As discussed in Chapter 9, our news comes from a handful of corporations that have media outlets in a number of Canada's major cities and that are increasingly committed to convergence, or the delivery of news and information across a range of media platforms—newspapers, magazines, radio, television, internet.

Media ownership confers control over the content of news at two levels. *Allocative control* is exercised by publishers, shareholders, and directors, who allocate resources—labour and capital—to a news organization. They determine such things as the overall mandate or philosophy of the news organization, its annual operating budget, its anticipated profit margin, and its capital expenditures for technological upgrades. They also hire senior managers who share their views on the mandate of the news organization and will ensure that it is enacted. **Operational control** is exercised by editors and producers who decide on a day-to-day and story-to-story basis how to employ the resources allocated. Such decisions include who to hire (at entry levels), who to assign to which news production tasks, and which stories to cover (Murdock, 1990: 122–3). Of course, these two levels are not mutually exclusive and some owners are more involved than others in daily news production.

It must be acknowledged, though, that newsrooms are complex work environments and the time pressures associated with daily journalism limit the amount of *direct* influence owners and managers can reasonably exercise over the journalists in their employ. Reporters, who spend much of their time in the field gathering information and conducting interviews, enjoy considerable latitude in generating ideas and developing their stories. Control over reporting staff is best seen as *indirect*. That is, it consists of a socialization process in which individual journalists—once hired and assigned to a particular department—learn what kinds of stories their supervisors want, and, more importantly, what kind they do not want (see Schulman, 1990). Every reporter has a tale to tell of producing a tantalizing story that was never published.

Corporate concentration is a growing concern around the media world and has attracted renewed attention in Canada in recent years. Thanks to mergers, takeovers, buyouts, and closures, fewer and fewer companies control the production of news. This has a number of implications for the process of newsmaking and the quality of information we receive (see Skinner et al., 2005). First, critics argue that as the sources of news and comment diminish, so does the diversity of such information. Alternative and oppositional voices risk being ridiculed, marginalized, or ignored altogether. Second, corporations are responsible to shareholders who are primarily interested in profit maximization. This can affect the quality of news coverage if managers are stingy with their newsroom budgets and/or their news organization avoids provocative, yet important, stories for fear of antagonizing audiences and/or advertisers. A third concern is the potential for conflict of interest between a corporation's news business and the other businesses it owns.

Quebecor, for example, which owns *Le Journal de Montréal*, the city's most popular daily newspaper, the TVA television network, and the canoë.ca internet portal, has been the subject of a number of news reports in recent years because of its labour practices (see Box 10.5). Other conflicts of interest can arise relating to ownership. For instance, the Montreal newspaper *La Presse* has long been suspected of compromise in its coverage of the federal Liberal Party because the president of the company that owns the newspaper, André Desmarais, is married to former prime minister Jean Chrétien's daughter. In a specific instance, Chrétien's chief of staff, Jean Pelletier, complained directly to Desmarais about criticism of the prime minister by *La Presse* columnist Chantal Hébert (see Richer, 1999).

Conflict between the rights and the responsibilities of the news media characterized much of the twentieth century, and governments in the UK, the US, and Canada have all conducted investigations into patterns of media ownership in the post–World War II period. As discussed in Chapter 4, the report of the Hutchins Commission on Freedom of the Press in the United States is recognized as a foundational document for what is known as the social responsibility theory of the press (Commis-sion on Freedom of the Press, 1947). This theory extends the core democratic right of freedom of the press to include the right of citizens to be adequately informed by the news media.

Canada's Special Senate Committee on Mass Media, known as the Davey Committee (Canada, 1971: 3), concluded that media diversity defied the logic of market economics: 'More voices may be healthier, but fewer voices are cheaper.' Among the Davey Commission's principal recommendations was a press ownership review board, 'with powers to approve or disapprove mergers between, or acquisitions of, newspapers and periodicals' (ibid., 71). But, given the federal government's refusal to regulate either Canada's free press or the free enterprise in which news organizations engage, no such panel was ever established.

In 1980, the Royal Commission on Newspapers, known as the Kent Commission, was created in direct response to a 'rationalization agreement' between Canada's two premier newspaper chains of the period, Southam and Thomson, which left Southam alone in the Ottawa market and Thomson alone in the Winnipeg market. In line with the social responsibility theory of the press, the Kent Commission concluded that freedom of the press is not the owner's or editor's right to free speech, but is part of the people's right to freedom of expression and is 'inseparable from their right to inform themselves'. In the aftermath of the Royal Commission hearings, federal Consumer Affairs Minister Jim Fleming proposed a Canada Newspapers Act (1983), which would establish a national press council, offer grants to encourage newspapers to open bureaus across Canada, and impose ownership restrictions. But the legislation was opposed by the vocal publishing lobby and was never adopted (see Miller, 1998: 37–40). The Kent Commission's critique of the newspaper industry was sound, but to regulate the press is to redefine the legal meaning of freedom of the press, which democratic governments have so far refused to do.

As mentioned above, the 2003 Lincoln Committee report on broadcasting in Canada contained a number of recommendations to shore up editorial independence, particularly in instances of cross-

⁖ BOX 10.5 JOURNALISM WITHOUT JOURNALISTS?

Working conditions for journalists at mainstream news organizations have changed dramatically over the past 40 years; newsroom staffs have been decreasing in size owing to frequent layoffs and buyouts, while the quantitative demands on those who remain have risen. In 2008 alone, for example, the *Toronto Star* cut 270 jobs, Sun Media cut 600 jobs (10 per cent of its workforce), CTV cut 105 positions, and CanWest cut 560 jobs (5 per cent of its workforce) (Dubrowski, 2008; Friend, 2008).

All media are affected, but the newspaper industry has emerged as the principal battleground between news workers and media managers. Managers are continually pressured to cut costs while maintaining revenues. Journalists—reporters, photographers, editors—are pressured to maintain standards of quality while being asked to produce more.

Computerization in the newspaper industry in the 1970s and 1980s meant journalists had more qualitative control over their work, but it also meant more of their workday was spent on page design and layout: cosmetics rather than content. Digitization has facilitated research and reporters' ability to file stories from the field, but it also has led to the convergence of previously distinct media platforms; reporters are now expected not only to file to the daily newspaper but to the website as well, keeping the web versions of their stories up-to-date. Further, reporters are being asked to blog and appear on the radio or television stations also owned by their parent company. Newspaper chains are looking to centralize some journalism tasks, such as page layout and copy editing. And they are using their websites as a catch-all for content produced throughout the company.

Journalists are resisting these changes because they see the working conditions, and consequently their work, deteriorating.

Journalists at the *Montreal Gazette* had been without a collective agreement since June 2008, after failing to get anywhere in negotiations with then-owner Canwest Global Communications. Montreal's largest-circulation newspaper, *Le Journal de Montréal*, owned by Quebecor, locked out its workers on 24 January 2009 when negotiations for a new collective agreement broke down. Quebec has anti-scab legislation; the paper was put out by management, some non-union contract writers (columnists), and others who crossed the picket line electronically. Among other things, the company wanted to cut jobs, increase the length of the work week, and allow content from its other media platforms into the newspaper. The dispute was finally settled in February 2011, when the members of the Syndicat des travailleurs du Journal de Montréal voted 64 per cent in favour of a proposal that would see the company hire back just 62 of the 253 locked-out workers (24 of them journalists), the rest sharing a $20 million severance package. Workers at Quebecor's sister newspaper in Quebec City, *Le Journal de Québec*, were locked out for 16 months between 2007 and 2008 in a dispute over similar contract conditions.

Source: The Canadian Press/Ryan Remiorz

Locked-out *Journal de Montréal* workers.

media ownership (Canada, 2003). Similarly, the final report of the Standing Senate Committee on Transport and Communications (Canada, 2006a) encouraged the federal government to enforce more diligently existing regulations concerning corporate concentration and cross-media ownership, and to expand the mandates of the CRTC and the Competition Act to include mechanisms for both the open review of media company mergers and for greater restrictions on media ownership.

In their defence, news media owners assert that a wealth of information sources—print, radio, television, magazines, and especially today the internet—makes corporate concentration less of a concern than it was when the Davey and Kent Commissions conducted their hearings. There is some merit to this argument. More newspapers, magazines, radio stations, and TV channels are available to us than ever before, and the internet gives users access to websites from around the world. Alternative sources of information are available—at least on some subjects and for most of us.

But we need to be cautious in accepting this argument at face value. First, there is considerable information-sharing among news media. That is, print and broadcast organizations depend heavily on the same wire services—Canadian Press, Associated Press, Agence France Presse—for regional, national, and international news, so that frequently the same story is used by various newspapers, radio stations, television outlets, and websites. Chris Paterson argues, in fact, that convergence has resulted in the increased concentration of information delivery on the internet.

> Comparative analysis of international news stories from major news Web sites with wire stories reveals a dearth of original journalism (or even copy-editing) and near total dependence by major Web news providers (like MSNBC, CNN, Yahoo and others) on wire service reporting and writing. (Paterson, 2005: 146; see also Paterson, 2001)

In other words, an increase in the quantity of news sources does nothing to ensure an increase in the diversity of news sources or in the quality of interpretive journalism.

Distinctions among print, broadcast, and online coverage of local stories are similarly minimized because competing news organizations often set the news agenda for each other: they monitor each other's coverage, they cover the same local events, and they cite the same information sources. We may think we are benefiting from a broad range of news coverage, but all too often these media are getting their stories from the same source. For example, the Pew Research Center's Project for Excellence in Journalism (2010) conducted a study of Baltimore's news ecosystem, accounting for 53

providers of local news across all media platforms. The study determined that 83 per cent of the stories recorded were essentially repetitive, and of the remaining 17 per cent that contained new information, almost all of it originated with traditional news providers. In only two instances did new media organizations break new information.

In addition, a considerable amount of internet information comes from the same government and corporate sources used by the conventional media, and this information is often packaged by websites established by traditional print and broadcast outlets.

While a promising development in this regard is the emergence of a number of alternative and independent news sources, particularly online, these newcomers cannot match the news-production resources that the mainstream commercial news organizations can muster, nor, yet, can they boast the authority that the mainstream news sector has won through many decades of service.

Corporate concentration is considered to be less of a problem in radio and television news because two important features of Canada's broadcasting industry mitigate against its domination by one or two companies. The first is the existence of the CBC/Radio-Canada as Canada's public broadcaster, for which there is no parallel in the newspaper or magazine industries. With radio, television, and online services in French and English, the CBC serves Canada well with news and information programming, even if some would argue that it could do a much better job in these areas. The second difference, as discussed at length in Chapter 7, is that the broadcast industry is regulated by the CRTC, which, in enforcing the Broadcasting Act, can impose ownership restrictions and broadcasting standards on licence-holders. Some questions remain, however, about how much power the CRTC has to interfere with corporate mergers.

Not everyone accepts that corporate concentration denigrates journalism. David Demers (1999), for example, maintains that corporate ownership and good journalism are not mutually exclusive. Newspaper chains, Demers maintains, benefit from 'economies of scale and superior human and capital resources', which can result in both quality reporting and industrial stability. Such chains can afford to hire the best journalists and best editors, and provide them with resources to produce original reporting. He argues as well that the size of such corporations protects them from pressure that can be brought to bear by governments or from major advertisers.

One clearly positive result of corporate concentration is its pooling of considerable capital resources. This permits newspapers like *The Globe and Mail* and *La Presse* to establish the kind of editorial budgets that an independent news organization simply could not afford. These two dailies, for example, have permanent news bureaus across the country and around the world and they have the resources to send their reporters and columnists wherever the action is. Very few metropolitan dailies, however, have foreign correspondents, relying instead on wire services to supply them with both national and international news and analysis from a relatively small stable of **syndicated** columnists. But size does not always mean better coverage. For instance, if we compare Canada's national television networks, the CBC does a much better job than either CTV or Global of bringing a distinct, Canadian perspective to regional, national, and international news coverage.

New Journalism Forms

Alternatives to mainstream journalism have existed since at least the 1960s: campus radio stations and newspapers, non-profit community radio, community-access television, documentary film co-operatives, 'underground' or alternative weekly newspapers (see Skinner, 2010: 225–31). These media told different stories and adopted distinct storytelling styles. But there has been a veritable explosion of news providers and distributors since the mid-1990s, initially capitalizing on the accessibility and distributive powers of the internet, and more recently taking advantage of increasingly ubiquitous hand-held communication devices, resulting in what Natalie Fenton (2010) calls 'the expansion of the locus of news production'. This new media ecology includes social networking sites as both research resources (e.g., Facebook,

MySpace, Ning, Wikileaks) and circulation sites (e.g., Twitter, YouTube). Although the bulk of the hard work, and most of the best journalism, still is produced by mainstream news organizations in so-called legacy media formats, many believe the future of journalism will be digital and will include many more independent journalists.

The traditional news media were among the first to jump on the internet bandwagon in the mid-1990s, and they continue to evolve their online presence and attract significant audiences, even if they have been slow to invest resources in their digital operations (see Box 10.6). But the ease of use and affordability of desktop computing and digital audiovisual recording equipment, the accessibility of the internet, and the increasing media production skills of more and more people have combined to lower dramatically the barriers to entry to journalism, spawning thousands of new participants in the fields of news production, distribution, and commentary. Some, like *The Tyee* (http://Thetyee.ca), *Rabble* (http://rabble.ca), *The Dominion* (www.dominionpaper.ca), and *The Real News Network* (http://therealnews.com/t2/), seek to provide independent and original news reporting and commentary. Many other sites aggregate news from other providers—e.g., http://canadanewsdesk.com, http://national newswatch.com—or house the personal blogs of professional and amateur commentators on every topic under the sun (e.g., www.blogscanada.ca).

This transformation of the mediascape is still underway and no one can predict precisely where it

One new way of broadcasting news is the podcast.

Source: © Alex Segre/Alamy

❧ BOX 10.6   NEWS BY DESIGN

Two of Canada's most important national news organizations—the CBC and *The Globe and Mail*—have redesigned their news packages in recent years, prompted by both financial and technological pressures. These can be read as attempts to become more economically efficient—deploying editorial resources to all platforms—and to adapt to both the possibilities created by online platforms and the new ways audiences consume news.

The CBC is in the process of redefining itself from a radio and television broadcaster to a multi-platform media company. Results of a three-year restructuring project were unveiled in October 2009. Among the most obvious changes were the complete merging of CBC News's television, radio, and online platforms, the renaming of CBC Newsworld to the CBC News Network, the introduction of local, 90-minute, supper-time television newscasts, and an expanded seven-day schedule for the CBC's 10 p.m. TV newscast, *The National*. These changes came in the wake of an anticipated $171 million budget shortfall and the elimination of almost 800 CBC jobs earlier in the year (Quill, 2009). While the CBC for a long time has used radio and television reporters, and French and English reporters, interchangeably, especially on foreign stories, the 2009 restructuring takes a much larger step towards breaking down medium-specific distinctions, bringing all of the Corporation's resources to bear on its news division in a more systematic way. Increasingly, all CBC journalists will produce stories for all platforms.

The CBC's restructuring is also a recognition that audiences increasingly access CBC news programming online and expect to be able to interact with program producers. For example, the CBC News

Network program Connect with Mark Kelley adopts a news talk-show format with audience interactivity via Twitter, Facebook, MySpace, and Skype (www.cbc.ca/programguide/program/connect_with_mark_kelley).

The Globe and Mail launched its new look on 1 October 2010, reformatting both the newspaper and the website. The newspaper appears to have moved in the direction of a daily news magazine. Printed by new presses on higher-quality paper to enhance a greater use of colour photography, it has introduced regular, theme-specific feature stories and some new sections (e.g., its Folio centrespread in the front section; its Globe Style section devoted to fashion and design). With colour capability on every page, it appears designed primarily to please display advertisers, who can now produce advertisements with much greater visual impact. The newspaper also seems to be shifting its balance between breaking news—better handled on the website, which can be updated constantly—and feature stories, commentary, and analysis, producing greater complementarity between the newspaper and the website. The website—www.theglobeandmail.com—remains text-heavy, but over the years it has made increasing use of video (mostly from news services), still photography, and interactive features such as blogs and discussion forums.

Newspapers frequently undergo redesigns, so time will tell whether *The Globe*'s redesign represents a fundamental change to enhance news coverage or merely one of cosmetics to please advertisers. Nevertheless, it remains interesting to watch how printed newspapers respond and adapt to the online environment, and how news organizations employ the full capabilities of digital media.

will lead. But it has both encouraging and worrisome elements. In the populist literature, it is celebrated as a 'revolution', a new declaration of journalistic independence and a significant step towards the democratization of mediated communication. Dan Gillmor (2004: xxix) writes: 'The ability of anyone to make the news will give new voice to people who'd felt voiceless—and whose words we need to hear.' Jill Walker Rettberg (2008: 85) maintains that the internet 'changed one of the greatest obstacles to true freedom of the press by eliminating or

greatly reducing the cost of production and distribution.' Clay Shirky (2008: 55) describes new digital communications technologies as 'social tools', as media for group co-operation and action on local and global scales. 'Our social tools remove older obstacles to public expression, and thus remove the bottlenecks that characterized mass media.'

Journalism has always been enhanced by citizens' participation, whether through news tips, letters to the editor, or telephoned corrections. The only footage of the assassination of US President

John F. Kennedy in 1963 was filmed by a spectator, Abe Zapruder, with an 8-mm home movie camera, and the 1991 beating of Rodney King by Los Angeles police was caught by a passerby with a video camera. New digital technologies only extend our surveillance capabilities, and knowledge and awareness of current events have certainly benefited from citizens providing photographs, videos, and eyewitness accounts: e.g., the 9/11 terrorist attacks on New York City and Washington, DC; the Boxing Day 2004 earthquake and tsunami in Southeast Asia; the 2005 London bus bombings; Hurricane Katrina in New Orleans in 2005; the 2008 terrorist attack in Mumbai; the 2010 earthquake in Haiti; the popular uprisings in Egypt, Tunisia, and Syria in 2011; the catastrophic Japanese earthquake and tsunami of 11 March 2011. Blogging, whether by professionals or amateurs, has expanded the range of commentary on news topics, but also has increased exponentially the number of sources journalists can draw upon for expertise and the number of people checking news reports for factual errors (see Glaser, 2010; Rettberg, 2008; Silverman, 2007).

Even critical scholars concede that people are using these technologies to create openings for communication exchanges—including news, analysis, and commentary—beyond the commer-

The coverage of devastating disasters, such as the 2010 earthquake in Haiti, often benefits from the contributions of amateur citizen journalists.

Source: © istockphoto.com/Niko Guido

cial media marketplace, as well as to facilitate resistance and opposition to corporate media. Nick Dyer-Witheford (1999: 71–2), for example, reminds us that all technologies are shaped in a socio-economic context of contending and contradictory forces: those of commodification, which use the media to enhance profit, and those of democratization, which employ media work to enhance citizenship. Dyer-Witheford's autonomist Marxist analysis allows for the possibility of deconstructing and reconstructing technologies as part of movements of resistance and opposition to capital. As discussed above, one instance of this can be seen in the establishment of the http://ruefrontenac.com website by locked-out workers of *Le Journal de Montréal*.

The central point made by critical scholars, however, is that new media technologies do not have lives of their own. Rather, they are embedded in a context informed by history, politics, economics, and culture. As David Sholle (2002: 9) puts it: 'If we are really to assess the "newness" of digital technologies, we must look beyond these technical elements themselves to changes that connect them to changes in social relations, values, goals, and modes of thinking.' Natalie Fenton maintains that the most significant characteristics of new media technologies—speed, space, multiplicity, polycentrality, interaction, and participation—must be evaluated in terms of their actual application. Speed refers to the immediacy of digital technologies and space refers to their expanded geographical reach in a global network. But in actual newsroom application, speed can have a negative impact on journalism when reporters are required to file constantly to keep websites current, preventing them from further developing stories and verifying information. And in the context of smaller news staffs filing stories more frequently, this can confine reporters to their desks, reducing the number of journalists working outside the newsroom and thus shrinking the geographical reach of their reporting. Multiplicity and polycentrality refer to the increasing number of news providers and the many-to-many dissemination of information. But as studies indicate, this mostly results in the same stories told the same way on more news sites. Finally, Fenton argues, the benefits of interactivity and greater participation have been greatly exaggerated (Fenton, 2010: 559–64). She maintains that 'many of the positive claims for new media reside in a small set of extraordinary examples and rest largely on the *potential* of new media alone to re-invigorate democracy rather than a consideration of technology in an economic, cultural, and technological context' (ibid., 561).

No one can predict journalism's digitized future, but clearly we are witnessing a significant transformation in the ways journalism is produced and distributed (see Box 10.7). Whether this constitutes a revolution, i.e., the democratization of news production, remains to be seen.

⋮⋮ BOX 10.7 THE END OF NEWSPAPERS?

There has been lots of talk in recent years about the death of newspapers—at least in the physical form with which we are most familiar—due to the rise of the internet and online news. The reality, however, is much more complicated.

The World Association of Newspapers announced in August 2010 that there were more daily newspaper titles in the world—12,477—than ever before, an increase of 2,000 titles in just the past two years. While global circulation figures were down 1.7 per cent in 2009 (including free dailies) during an economic recession, circulation was up 7.7 per cent since 2004. Six of ten countries for which circulation figures were available reported either stable or increased circulation. The five largest newspaper markets in 2009 were India, China, Japan, the United States, and Germany. The countries hit hardest by the decline in circulation were the 'mature' newspaper markets of Europe and North America; circulation dropped 10.6 per cent in North America in 2009, most of this in the US. Advertising revenues globally fell 17 per cent in 2009 and television surpassed newspapers as the world's largest advertising medium, accounting for 39 per cent of all advertising expenditures. Newspapers were next with a 24 per cent share, down from 40 per cent in 2007, prior to the recession (WAN, 2008). Online advertising accounted for 12 per cent (65 per cent of which was earned by Google alone) (WAN, 2010).

In Canada, there were 96 paid-circulation daily newspapers in 2009 as well as 18 free dailies. No dailies folded, but the Montreal papers *La Presse* and *The Gazette* cancelled their Sunday editions, the Brockville *Recorder and Times*, Chatham *Daily News*, and Pembroke *Daily Observer* (all in Ontario) reduced their publishing week to five days, while the Portage la Prairie (Manitoba) *Daily Graphic* reduced its week to four days and *The Reminder* of Flin Flon, Manitoba, reduced its week to three days. Two Ontario dailies—the *Cobourg Star* and the Port Hope *Evening Guide*—were collapsed into one new daily, the *Northumberland Today*. Average daily paid circulation among Canadian newspapers dropped 4.1 per cent, suffering most of that loss in Ontario, the largest daily newspaper market. Circulation in Quebec was stable, with the Montreal market showing a slight increase of 0.3 per cent. Advertising revenues declined 11 per cent in 2009, compared to 29 per cent in the US (Canadian Newspaper Association, 2009).

James Compton (2010: 592) argues that the impact of the internet on the newspaper industry must be understood within the context of a restructuring commercial news industry. This restructuring, which has been going since at least the 1970s, long before the emergence of online news sites, has resulted in the further concentration of newspaper ownership, cross-media ownership, declines in the sizes of newsroom staffs and declines in certain areas of news coverage, such as international news (ibid., 592–3).

Compton reminds us that newspapers were among the first to become online news providers, in the face of rising production and distribution costs and increased competition, initially from television and subsequently from all the other news providers entering cyberspace (ibid., 594). Citing a 2007 report by *Editor and Publisher*, Compton notes that, if website readership is included in circulation statistics, all newspapers show increased circulation (ibid., 596).

⫶ BOX 10.8 CANADIANS DON'T WANT TO PAY FOR ONLINE NEWS

The widespread and free provision of online news and commentary has been a serious challenge for commercial news organizations, which typically pay for the costs of their original news production through a combination of subscription fees and advertising. These 'legacy' media are responsible for the most significant and most popular online news sites, but their attempts to charge subscription fees for their electronic editions have largely failed, and they do not attract the levels of advertising their printed editions command. Some newspapers, like *The Times* of London, the *Wall Street Journal*, *The New York Times*, and Montreal's *Le Devoir*, continue to charge visitors to their sites for access to at least some portions of their news packages.

The Canadian Media Research Consortium reported in a March 2011 survey that most Canadians reject the idea of paying for online news. The study noted that 92 per cent of survey respondents said they would seek another free site if their favourite news sites started charging for content. Eighty-one per cent said they would not pay to read their favourite online news site (Canadian Media Research Consortium, 2011).

These attitudes may change, of course, particularly if more and more of the quality and specialty news organizations retreat behind pay walls and comparable information cannot be found free of charge. After all, Canadians quickly got used to paying for drinking water when they were sold on the idea that bottled water was superior in purity and taste to freely available tap water.

SUMMARY

Journalists are content producers and storytellers, not unlike the storytellers in other mass media. But news is constructed or produced within a specific context, and it is informed by professional ideals, the nature of its textual forms, the socio-cultural particularities of the diverse communities that journalism serves, the restrictions of Canada's legal system, the economic imperatives of (primarily) commercial news production, and the emergence of new technologies.

As a form of storytelling, journalism is based on real people and real events. But rather than mirroring reality, as is often suggested, the news media instead frame reality, selecting particular events, particular people, and particular aspects of a story as newsworthy, while excluding many others. News texts unavoidably attribute meaning to events, which is a significant matter when we depend on the media for so much of our knowledge of the world.

Journalism shares some of the characteristics of other forms of storytelling but is distinguished by the following features: its guiding ideals of truth-seeking, independence, and objectivity; the ethical and legal rights and obligations of the practice in a free press environment; and the institutional context of news production. Freedom of the press, one of the linchpins of news reporting, does not mean that journalists are free to report whatever they choose. Such constraints as privacy and libel keep news producers in line with accepted notions of integrity.

Similarly, most news production is conducted by media organizations that need to sell audiences to advertisers. Ownership in the news industry has become increasingly concentrated and most of our main news providers are now part of converged conglomerates that treat journalism as a product like any other. This is the principal concern facing journalism in Canada today.

The most exciting development in news production is the emergence of alternative media seeking to democratize communication. This ongoing experiment is creating new openings in the mediascape and forcing traditional media organizations to adapt by investing in new platforms and new ways of presenting stories to audiences. The question is whether these new media forms will allow journalists to produce original stories, or whether they will remain primarily distributors of, and commentators on, reporting produced by the mainstream.

KEY TERMS

access to information, p. 279
broadsheets, p. 276
contempt of court, p. 290
corporate concentration, p. 289
defamation, p. 291

framing, p. 278
freedom of the press, p. 279
gatekeeping, p. 276
libel, p. 290
libel chill, p. 291

objectivity, p. 280
operational control, p. 293
representation, p. 282
syndicated, p. 297
tabloids, p. 276

RELATED WEBSITES

Canadian Association of Journalists: www.caj.ca
The CAJ is a national organization of journalists, which both advocates on behalf of Canadian journalists and promotes excellence in journalism. The site contains news pertaining to journalism as well as a calendar of upcoming talks and meetings across the country.

Canadian Journalism Foundation: www.cjf-fjc.ca
The mission of this non-profit foundation is to promote and reward excellence in journalism. It contains news of interest to journalists as well as a calendar of events and programs it sponsors across Canada.

Canadian Journalism Project: http://j-source.ca/; http://projetj.ca/
A joint initiative by journalism educators across Canada, this comprehensive site brings together a wealth of news, commentary, and reference information about journalism and journalism education in Canada.

Media Magazine: **www.caj.ca/?p=391**
Published twice a year by the Canadian Association of Journalists, the magazine contains news and feature articles pertaining to the practice of journalism in Canada.

Fédération professionnelle des journalistes du Québec www.fpjq.org/
This association of Quebec journalists publishes a very good French-language magazine, *Le 30*, and holds a conference each fall addressing the practice of journalism and the theoretical issues facing the news industry.

FURTHER READINGS

Gillmor, Dan. 2004. *We the Media: Grassroots Journalism by the People, for the People.* Sebastopol, CA: O'Reilly Media. This book provides a celebratory discussion of how new forms of citizen journalism are serving communities in ways the mainstream media are not.

Kovach, Bill, and Tom Rosenstiel. 2001. *The Elements of Journalism: What Newspeople Should Know and the Public Should Expect.* New York: Crown Publishers. This well-written and concise book diagnoses several fundamental problems with journalism in the US today, but the problems it addresses and the solutions it proposes are largely applicable to the Canadian context as well.

Skinner, David. 2010. 'Minding the growing gaps: Alternative media in Canada', in Leslie Regan Shade, ed., *Mediascapes: New Patterns in Canadian Communication*, 3rd edn. Toronto: Nelson, 221–36. This is a current discussion of media reform and alternative media movements in Canada.

Silverstone, Roger. 2007. *Media and Morality: On the Rise of the Mediapolis.* Cambridge: Polity Press. This thought-provoking study posits the media as a contemporary social space in which we come to moral judgments about sameness and difference.

Stuart, Allan, ed. 2010. *The Routledge Companion to News and Journalism.* London and New York: Routledge. This comprehensive treatment of journalism covers a broad range of topics in both classic texts and new studies.

STUDY QUESTIONS

1. How and in what ways are news stories highly constructed?
2. What are some of the implications of this process of construction?
3. What does it mean to say that news stories frame, rather than mirror, reality?
4. What challenges do journalists confront in trying to produce truthful, fact-based news stories?
5. What is the critical realist approach to objectivity?
6. How do journalists produce meaning through the language they use to describe an event?
7. Why do we describe journalism as a socio-cultural institution? What does this mean?
8. Why does it matter who journalists are, in terms of their age, sex, race, ethnicity, education level, etc.?
9. Freedom of the press in Canada is not an absolute right. Why are there legal limits on this constitutional guarantee?
10. To what extent do corporate owners exercise control over the news produced by their organizations? How do they assert control?
11. Some people argue that new media represent a communications revolution. To what extent are we seeing a democratization of mass communication? What are the limits to the revolutionary potential of new media?

PART IV

An Evolving Communications World

CHAPTER 11

Globalization

The local is increasingly lived under the shadow of the global.

— STEPHEN COLEMAN AND KAREN ROSS, 2010

OPENING QUESTIONS

- What is globalization?
- How does globalization affect the ways we communicate?
- In what ways can the media be perceived as agents of globalization?
- How does globalization shape the international flows of communication goods and services?
- How does globalization affect our sense of community, our sense of place?

Learning Objectives

- To understand what globalization is and how it affects mass communication in Canada.
- To recognize the role of the media as specific agents of globalization.
- To review the theories of media imperialism, media dependency, and world systems.
- To learn about the extent to which communication exchanges—within countries and between countries—are uneven, and what this implies.
- To review international communications debates, from the New World Information and Communication Order to the World Summit on the Information Society.
- To consider what globalization means for how we think about community, place, and identity.

Introduction

Consistent with the title and purpose of this book, we have been talking primarily about communicative practices, policies, and structures within Canada. If we have emphasized that these practices, policies, and structures are in many ways particular to the Canadian social, cultural, political, and economic environment, it should be clear that they are in no way confined to Canada. In an era of globalization, national communication systems are merely subsystems within a much larger and increasingly integrated global communication system, influenced and shaped by extra-national social, political, and economic currents, as well as by the everyday practices of media users, whether they are downloading music or video, accessing social networking sites, or reading news from abroad. In fact, we could say that the development of new information technologies has been very much part of the global reorganization of the capitalist economy since the mid-1970s. This chapter examines globalization in broad terms and considers what globalization means for how each of us lives and communicates.

References to the term **globalization** abound; it has become a label for the period in which we live and it is easy to lose sight of its history. Our political leaders mention globalization frequently in their speeches and the term has become a cliché in the business community. But what does it mean? We define 'globalization' as the set of processes by which social, political, and economic relations extend further than ever before, with greater frequency, immediacy, and facility. More specifically, 'globalization' refers to the increased **mobility** of people, capital, commodities, information, and images associated with the post-industrial stage of capitalism; with the development of increasingly rapid and far-ranging communication and transportation technologies; and with people's improved (though far from universal) access to these technologies. Simply put, globalization means we are more closely connected to the rest of the world than ever before in history, even if these connections have significant gaps and are not shared equally by all Canadians, let alone by all citizens of the world.

Globalization affects each one of us, even if it does so in different ways. The central questions are how globalization changes the world in which we live and how it affects our patterns of communication within it.

The activities and institutions we have described under the heading of 'mass communication in Canada' are not, and never have been, exclusively Canadian. In television, radio, magazines, and on the web, foreign, particularly American, media abound in Canada. Similarly, Canadians' communicative practices—letters, telephone calls, emails, magazines, newspapers, books, music recordings, television programming, films, web surfing—have always been tied into international circulation. Federal and provincial cultural policy always has been informed both by universal covenants—e.g., freedom of expression, the sharing of the radio broadcast spectrum—and by the policies of neighbouring legal and political jurisdictions. Canadian media institutions were established and have continued to evolve in the context of other national media (particularly those of the United States). What distinguishes the current epoch is that the reach and speed of the mass media have increased so dramatically that borders, which in the past partially shielded one nation's mass media from those of other nations, have become increasingly porous. Distance is less an impediment to communication, and the distinctions between 'here' and 'there' are increasingly fuzzy. Globalization has altered our **media geography**, shifting dramatically the parameters of the world in which we live and in which we engage in communicative activities.

Many are tempted to look at technological innovation as the principal, if not sole, determinant of this global integration; but if **technology** has played an undeniably significant role in enabling global communications, so, too, have communication law and cultural policy, trade liberalization, and changing social and cultural conditions.

Defining Terms

While 'globalization' often refers to the world's increased economic interdependence—formalized by the World Trade Organization (WTO),

Source: © The Canadian Press/Jeff McIntosh

Canadian actor and director Paul Gross talks to his cast on the set of *Passchendaele*, based on the Canadian military's role in the 1917 Battle of Passchendaele.

the North American Free Trade Agreement (NAFTA), the European Union (EU), etc.—the term refers equally to economic, political, social, cultural, and environmental interdependence. In economic terms, for example, globalization means that many of us work for companies with operations in a number of countries around the world. The specific job we do may be part of a production process organized as a transnational assembly line, co-ordinated from a distant head office, and the product or service we offer likely is destined for export markets. Thomas Friedman (2005: 414–38) cites the example of Dell Computers, whose just-in-time production process includes designers, parts suppliers, and assembly stations in six countries. Those countries, their business leaders, and especially their workers compete with other governments, investors, and workers from all over the world to attract and/or maintain local economic activity.

In the political arena, globalization means that governments are increasingly implicated in events that occur well beyond their own borders. Whether the misfortune is famine, disease, war, or natural disaster, political leaders feel increasingly compelled to aid countries many of us can-not easily locate on a map. The January 2010 earthquake in Haiti, for example, obliged governments from Canada, the United States, France, and Venezuela to send equipment, food, soldiers, and financial aid to Haiti. The earthquake, which killed an estimated 250,000 and injured at least as many others, hit particularly close to home in Canada; 82,000 people of Haitian descent live in Canada (90 per cent of them in Quebec), including Canada's Governor General at the time, Michaëlle Jean, writer Dany Laferrière, singer Luck Mervil, and NHL hockey player Georges Laraque. The magnitude of the response, especially in Quebec, made it seem like the earthquake had hit a part of Canada.

Source: © The Canadian Press/Larry MacDougal

Haitian-Canadian Georges Laraque played in the NHL from 1996–2010.

In the social sphere, globalization means that friendships and family ties extend around the world and that our neighbours come from half a dozen different countries, speak different languages, wear different clothes and worship within different religions. When we shop, we buy clothes made in China, wine made in Chile, and furniture made in Sweden. When we go out to eat, we can readily choose among Chinese, Japanese, Thai, French, Italian, Lebanese, or Indian foods. This means that we are increasingly implicated in world affairs, and not merely through our shopping and buying habits. Diseases, too, travel globally and quickly. SARS (severe acute respiratory syndrome) was declared a global health threat by the World Health Organization within six weeks of its first diagnosis in 2003. It killed 800 people around the world. Yet, '[in] Canada, on average, 500–1,500 deaths every year are due to influenza alone. Annual incidence rates in Canada range from 10 to 20 per cent each year and can be considerably higher in epidemics' (www.

health.gov.on.ca/english/providers/program/pubhealth/flu/flu_07/flubul_mn.html). During the 2010 World Cup in South Africa, the English, Brazilian, and Italian teams were followed as closely in Toronto, Montreal, and Vancouver as they were in London, Rio de Janeiro, and Rome.

In the cultural sphere, globalization means that some Hollywood movies are as popular in Tokyo and Madrid as they are in Los Angeles. It also means that we come into contact with more and more cultures through such activities as vacation travel and foreign-language acquisition. Newsstands and bookstores, at least in urban centres, offer newspapers, magazines, and books from around the world in several languages; shops specialize in international recorded music and in movies from various parts of the world. The internet connects us to online radio stations and podcasts from places we've never been. What we consider to be Canadian art and cultural performance are increasingly infused by an array of international influences. Indeed, many of Canada's leading writers and performers have their roots in the Philippines, the Caribbean, Egypt, India, and Sri Lanka.

In the environmental sphere, we are increasingly aware that how we use natural resources—air, water, land, minerals, trees, fish—in one corner of the world has significant implications for the rest of the planet. Debates over the Kyoto Accord and the subsequent Copenhagen Protocol, international agreements addressing climate change, symbolize both the difficulty and importance of collective struggles to come to terms with how we are degrading the global environment. The April 2010 eruption of the Iceland volcano Eyjafjallaökull produced an ash cloud that shut down airports in 20 European countries for six days, and grounded an estimated 10 million travellers worldwide. Similarly, in March 2011, when a massive earthquake and subsequent tsunami in northeast Japan caused problems and fears of meltdowns at Japanese nuclear plants, other countries re-examined their own commitments to nuclear energy and safety, and explosions at the Fukushima Daiichi power plant created concerns about fallout in western North America.

Source: © Icerock/Dreamstime.com

The Iceland volcano Eyjafjallaökull ash cloud is another example of the way nature can override the technologies we have come to depend on. As the planet responds to the cumulative effect of these technologies, it is not clear that the technologists can keep the planet habitable for humans.

Source: © CP Photo/Calgary Herald—Mikael Kjellstrom

Today, immigrants come to Canada from all over the world seeking better jobs, education, and opportunities.

The term 'globalization' can be misleading, however, because it suggests that all significant social relations now occur on a global scale. Clearly, this is not so. Local, provincial, regional, and national levels are still extremely important in our lives. What the term more properly refers to is an intensified relationship between social activity on local and global scales (Massey and Jess, 1995: 226). Once predominantly local, face-to-face, and immediate, social interactions now commonly stretch beyond the borders of our local community so that 'less and less of these relations are contained within the place itself' (Massey, 1992: 6–7). While we still talk to our neighbours when we meet them on the street, we also communicate regularly with friends, relatives, and associates—by phone, by email, through social networking sites—at the other end of the country and on the other side of the world. Globalization has altered dramatically the nature of human mobility as our travels—whether for business or pleasure—carry us farther and farther afield, expanding the bounds within which most of us live.

Many of the features of globalization are not new. International migration is not new, nor is the mobility of investment capital or the global circulation of cultural products. What is new about globalization is its intensity: the expanded reach, facility, and immediacy of contemporary social interactions. The migration of people, whether regional, intranational, or international, whether voluntary or forced, has become a more common experience, and many of those who migrate return frequently to their countries of origin. Russell King (1995: 7) notes: 'Nowadays, in the western world, only a minority of people are born, live their entire lives and die in the same rural community or urban neighbourhood.' There is a greater circulation today of people seeking to improve their lives, whether they are refugees fleeing intolerable conditions, youths seeking educational and employment opportunities away from home, or what King calls 'executive nomads' conducting business in markets around the globe.

Investment capital, too, has become increasingly mobile as companies seek business opportunities wherever they can be found and flee from regions deemed uncompetitive or hostile to free enterprise. Regions of the world are seen primarily

>> BOX 11.1   CANADA'S CHANGING FACE

It should be clear by now that serving Canada, with its vast geography and its scattered population, is one of the greatest challenges facing media organizations, whether their content is music, news, or dramatic entertainment. But that task is even more formidable in an era of globalization when the Canadian population is more diverse than at any time in its history. The 2006 census conducted by Statistics Canada reported a Canadian population of 33.3 million people who claimed more than 200 ethnic origins. Diversity, of course, consists of much more than ethnicity; difference can be based on skin colour, mother tongue, religious belief, sexual orientation, as well as on age, sex, education, and income levels.

Canada's visible minority population grew 27 percent between 2001 and 2006, explained primarily by increased immigration from Asia, Africa, the Caribbean, Central and South America, and the Middle East (Statistics Canada, 2009: 155). Visible minorities account for 15 per cent of Canada's overall population. These populations are concentrated in Canada's major cities; for example, visible minorities account for 43 per cent of Toronto's population, 42 per cent of Vancouver's, and 16.4 per cent of Montreal's (ibid., 162–4). By 2017, visible minorities are projected to be in the majority in Toronto, and by 2031 Statistics Canada estimates that visible minorities will make up 59 and 63 per cent of the Vancouver and Toronto populations, respectively (Statistics Canada, 2010).

Immigrants account for almost one-fifth of Canada's overall population: 45.7 per cent in Toronto, 39.6 per cent in Vancouver, 24.4 per cent in Hamilton, and 20.6 per cent in Montreal (Statistics Canada, 2009: 158–9).

Canadians speak more than 200 languages. While English (58 per cent) and French (22 per cent) remain the majority languages, another 20 per cent of Canadians are allophones, reporting as their mother tongue a language other than English or French, although 98 per cent of Canadians can speak one or both official languages. The Chinese languages (Cantonese, Mandarin) form the third-largest language group in Canada, followed by Italian, German, Punjabi, Spanish, Arabic, Tagalog, and Portuguese. One in four residents of Toronto and Vancouver is allophone (ibid., 283–4).

Canada's changing demographic profile is of great significance for media organizations, especially when media managers try to imagine, and ultimately serve, their target audiences. How do they account for such differences of background, language, religion, culture, belief, and life experience? This is a matter of great concern because, as Henry et al. (2000: 296) note, the media 'are major transmitters of society's cultural standards, myths, values, roles, and images.' Because racial minority communities tend to be marginalized in mainstream society at large, 'many white people rely almost entirely on media for their information about minorities and the issues that concern their communities.' This applies to all media forms because they all represent or depict Canadian society through advertising, music, art, video games, films, news reports, blogs, and television dramas and sitcoms.

One response to increasing diversity has been the establishment of media dedicated to serving these distinct communities. According to the Media Awareness Network (2010), there are 250 ethnic newspapers in Canada (including seven dailies publishing in languages other than English or French), and a growing number of television and radio stations with programming devoted to minority populations. These media include television stations devoted to Canada's Aboriginal population—the nationally broadcast Aboriginal Peoples Television Network—and newspapers devoted to the gay and lesbian population (e.g., Pink Triangle Press, Xtra).

A second response—albeit much slower—has been the conscious attempt by mainstream media organizations to diversify their staffs, to normalize the depiction of Canadian society as multicultural, multiracial, multifaith, etc.

Diversity, however it is defined, is a particularly important issue for Canadians because the communications media have been assigned such a central role in creating a sense of national community, a theme that permeates federal cultural policy. The media are a principal source of images of our country, our fellow Canadians, and our place in the larger world, and the media therefore play a central role in our understanding of who we are as a society.

as markets—sales markets, resource markets, and labour markets—and corporate executives demonstrate less and less loyalty to their traditional places of business. American automakers, for instance, do not need to confine their operations to the Detroit area if cars and trucks can be made more cheaply with comparable quality standards in Canada or Mexico. Similarly, if Hollywood producers find the labour costs of the California film unions prohibitive, they can seek lower labour costs in Canada or Australia. The 3D blockbuster, *Avatar*, for example, was shot in both Los Angeles and Wellington, New Zealand. Some newspapers are following suit. California's *Pasadena Now* hired reporters based in India to cover Pasadena city council meetings as they were broadcast online, and the *Orange County Register* contracted Mindworks Global Media of New Delhi for story editing and page layout. Companies and their business activities are less rooted to their 'home' bases, seeking greater productivity and improved access to international markets wherever these advantages can be found. *New York Times* columnist Thomas L. Friedman celebrates this in his bestseller, *The World Is Flat* (2005: 8). He perceives globalization as the levelling of the 'global competitive playing field', arguing that 'what the flattening of the world means is that we are now connecting all the knowledge centers on the planet together into a single global network, which—if politics and terrorism do not get in the way—could usher in an amazing era of prosperity and innovation.'

Nowhere has capital been more successful at penetrating world markets than in the cultural sphere. Morley and Robins (1995: 1–11) argue that two key aspects of the new capital dynamics of globalization are, first, technological and market shifts leading to the emergence of 'global image industries', and second, the development of local audiovisual production and distribution networks. They refer to a 'new media order' in which the overriding logic of the new media corporations is to get their product to the largest possible number of consumers. The internet and new mobile, hand-held technologies have expanded the range, the speed, and the possibilities of media distribution networks considerably, by reducing distribution costs, opening up markets wherever people have access to wired or wireless networks, and lowering the barriers to entry for new media producers.

Media images also serve as a reminder of how far our social interactions stretch, the extent to which those relations are technologically mediated, and the implications of such mediation.

The screen metaphor also applies to globalization, the processes of which screen out large segments of the population. This is a point easily ignored by those of us with easy, cheap, around-the-clock access to communication technologies. We sometimes assume that *everyone* enjoys these advantages. Globalization's impact, in fact, is decidedly uneven, dividing people along class lines, in

BOX 11.2 INDIGENOUS BROADCASTING

The World Indigenous Television Broadcasters Network was established in 2008 'to retain and grow indigenous languages and cultures' by providing an international forum, support, and program exchange network for indigenous cultural producers who often work in minority languages and serve minority populations in their home jurisdictions. Canada's Aboriginal Peoples' Television Network was a founding member, joining broadcasters from Australia, Hawaii, Ireland, New Zealand, Norway, Scotland, South Africa, and Taiwan.

BOX 11.3 THE SCREEN AS METAPHOR

The screen is a powerful metaphor for our times: it symbolizes how we exist in the world, our contradictory condition of engagement and disengagement. Increasingly, we confront moral issues through the screen, and the screen confronts us with increasing numbers of moral dilemmas. At the same time, however, it screens us from those dilemmas. It is through the screen that we disavow or deny our human implication in moral realities.

Source: David Morley and Kevin Robins (1995: 141).

particular. While relatively wealthy, educated urban dwellers have considerable access to the fruits of globalization, those with less mobility, particularly in terms of declining employment opportunities and falling wages, are unable to pay the price— whether of tropical vacations, of expensive imports, or of new media access.

Not all of us are in a position to reap the benefits of global interconnectivity because we don't all enjoy the same degree of mobility. In fact, many Canadians have been hit hard by the new-found mobility of investment capital—when, for instance, sawmills are closed in British Columbia and automotive manufacturers leave Quebec and Ontario because their owners can simply shut down, pack up, and move in search of more hospitable investment climates. In such instances, those who control global capital are the only true 'global citizens'. As Zygmunt Bauman (1998: 2) states: 'Globalization divides as much as it unites; it divides as it unites—the causes of division being identical with those which promote the uniformity of the globe.' Corporations are increasingly free from the spatial constraints of nation-states. Their mobility creates a disconnect between their economic power and any sense of community obligation, whether local, regional, or national (ibid., 8–9). Thus some people, such as the major shareholders of transnational corporations, are full participants in, and major beneficiaries of, globalization processes, while a great many others are excluded from the benefits. Indeed, if many people are implicated at all, it is as victims of the economic instability that globalization has created, not as beneficiaries of the wealth that it has created.

Mass Media as Agents of Globalization

Sophisticated and accessible transportation and communication technologies have enabled globalization. As we saw in Chapter 2, transportation and communication networks have the ability to 'bind space,' to bring people and places closer together. They enable people to maintain close contact in spite of their geographical separation. Airline connections between major cities enable

business leaders and politicians to fly to a meeting in another city and to return home in time for dinner. Frequent email or text messaging connects friends and colleagues in remote locations, minimizing the implications of their actual separation.

In business, organizations need no longer be based on **Fordism**, in which assembly-line operations take place in a single, all-encompassing factory. The particular activities involved in the assembly of a product can now be dispersed globally to take advantage of cheap labour, ready supplies of resources, and/or lax regulatory environments. Or, the production process can be moved closer to markets to minimize distribution costs. Through telephone contact, email, text messaging, and video conferencing, managers can maintain two-way communication with remote operations, disseminating instructions to sub-managers and receiving from them regular progress reports.

Since the end of World War II, increasing mobility has created a new layer of international governance to co-ordinate the increasing number of integrated spheres of activity. Initially this meant the creation of the United Nations in 1945, which deals with military, economic, health, education, and cultural affairs between states. Today the list of international governing agencies includes the North Atlantic Treaty Organization (NATO), the World Trade Organization (WTO), the Association of Southeast Asian Nations (ASEAN), Asia-Pacific Economic Cooperation (APEC), the African Union, the Group of Eight (G8), the Latin American Integration Association (LAIA), the European Union (EU), and many others.

The flip side of this international co-operation is international interference in cases where states' interests conflict. Globalization means that national governments no longer enjoy uncontested **sovereignty** within their own borders. This has significant policy implications when issues such as Canadian content regulations, proposed quotas for theatrical film screens, subsidization of cultural production, enforcement of online hate speech laws, or enforcement of copyright laws are raised. Countries can choose to ignore international law— something of which China has been accused with respect to international copyright agreements—or they can exert their political and economic might to derail legislation—as the United States does with any country's attempt to protect its domestic film industry from Hollywood's dominance of commercial theatre screens.

The mass media play four important roles in the globalization process. First, they are the *media of encounter*, putting us in touch with one another via mail, telephone, email, fax, etc. Second, they are the *media of governance*, enabling the centralized administration of vast spaces and dispersed places, whether by governments, businesses, or non-profit organizations. Third, they *situate us within the world*, offering us a regular picture of where we are, who we are, and how we are connected to other people and places in the world. Fourth, they constitute a *globalized business in and of themselves*, conducting trade in information and entertainment products. Taken together, these roles alter fundamentally the geographical parameters within which we live our lives.

While face-to-face interaction remains integral to social relations in even the most globalized of environments—on the street, in the park, at work, at school—**proximity** no longer constricts our social interactions. Communications technologies like the cellular telephone and personal computer bind social spaces and enable people to maintain contact across distance. This is particularly so as these technologies have become more sophisticated, more accessible in terms of cost, ease of use, and availability, and as these media have entered the private sphere of the home. The high speed of technologically mediated conversations approximates face-to-face communication. As the promoters of the digital age delight in telling us (e.g., Negroponte, 1995), such media enable us to conduct social relations over great distances, and their increasing sophistication minimizes—though does not eliminate entirely—the obstacles inherent to physical separation. Often, of course, these media complement face-to-face interactions. There are perhaps no better examples of this than the social networking sites like Facebook, MySpace, and LinkedIn, which enable friends, relatives, acquaintances, and colleagues to keep in touch across distance and over time.

At the same time, as Innis points out, communication media enable the centralized governance of a political community on the scale of the modern nation-state and the centralized administration of a transnational corporation that spans the globe. Both national forms of governance and global forms of capitalism require efficient means of communication to establish a coherent agenda, to disseminate instructions and information, to monitor the activities of remote departments, and to receive reports from local managers or governors in the field. This relationship is one of power, in which an authoritative body exercises control over social space and social order (see Drache, 1995: xlv–xlvi), but it is also increasingly a two-way relationship in which citizens or workers can use the same media to react or respond to these attempts at control. If a country as large and diverse as Canada is difficult to govern, its governance would be virtually impossible without modern communication and transportation technologies.

In decreasing the importance of physical distance, the scale on which governments and organizations function today can also, paradoxically, isolate nearby regions and peoples, if they are not deemed integral to the networks of governance or of commerce: if they don't have a population base large enough to constitute either an important constituency with key votes or a viable market (see Castells, 1999, 2001). Such considerations frequently come into play when commercial airlines cut service to some cities and towns because those routes are not economically viable. In 2008, for example, Air Canada announced it was cancelling routes between Hamilton and Montreal, Hamilton and Ottawa, and Calgary and Prince George, BC, due to fuel price increases; the traffic on these routes did not compensate for the airline's increased cost of service. This, in effect, increased the distances between these cities because travellers of these routes were forced to choose between much slower bus, train, or automobile travel, or not travelling at all.

The mass media also provide us with a sense of place. They offer us depictions of who we are, where we live, how we are connected to one another, and how we differ from other peoples and places. These depictions contain value judgments, sometimes explicitly expressed, but more often inferred. Media scholar Roger Silverstone describes media work as 'boundary work'. The media draw 'macro' boundaries of national and linguistic cultures, but they also draw 'micro' boundaries, 'work which involves the continuous inscriptions of difference in any and every media text and discourse'. This is 'their primary cultural role: the endless, endless, endless, playing with difference and sameness' (Silverstone, 2007: 19). Advertisements, for example, often seek to portray 'typical' Canadians engaged in 'normal' Canadian activities, offering us a definition of what 'typical' and 'normal' Canadian-ness is and suggesting what we look and act like. Think of the portrayal of the family provided by Canadian Tire commercials, the picture of Canadian males provided by Molson Canadian beer ads, or the gender roles assigned to men and women in commercials for any number of household cleaning products.

Finally, the media have become a central constituent of globalization in what is called the 'information age' or the '**network society**'. This means, first, that the cultural industries are conducting a greater proportion of global trade by serving as the conduits for the exchange of information and entertainment commodities, including trade in hardware, such as computers, television sets, and sound systems, and in cultural products, such as books, magazines, CDs and DVDs, and music and video downloads. Instead of trading these goods and services regionally or nationally, they are increasingly traded on an international or global scale; the world is their market. Second, information and ideas are becoming increasingly important to an economy that now depends on innovation in all industrial sectors. Ideas that can lead to new product development, greater productivity, and the expansion of markets have become essential to maintaining growth in a capitalist economy. Corporate management guru Peter Drucker (1993: 8) maintains that the 'basic economic resource' in today's economy is no longer investment capital, or natural resources, or

labour, but knowledge. 'Value is now created by "productivity" and "innovation", both applications of knowledge to work.'

The economic role that the mass media play has considerable implications for how we define communication as 'commodity' or as 'cultural form' (Chapter 9, Boxes 9.1 and 9.3), for who gets to speak (on both the individual and the collective levels), and for what kinds of messages become privileged. As Edward Herman and Robert McChesney (1997: 9) state:

> We regard the primary effect of the globalization process . . . to be the implantation of the commercial model of communication, its extension to broadcasting and the 'new media', and its gradual intensification under the force of competition and bottom-line pressures. The commercial model has its own internal logic and, being privately owned and relying on advertiser support, tends to erode the public sphere and to create a 'culture of entertainment' that is incompatible with a democratic order. Media outputs are commodified and designed to serve market ends, not citizenship needs.

By making information an exploitable resource, the democratic ideal of free speech and freely circulating information has been transformed (at least in many sectors) into the media proprietors' freedom to exploit world markets with that speech and with that information. This transformation has created the network that benefits the global entertainment and information industries.

This problem is offset somewhat by the emergence of individuals and public-service organizations seeking to employ the same communication technologies for quite different purposes—perhaps to combat economic globalization or militarism, to support environmental or human rights measures, or simply to create their own cultural products. The question, Dave Sholle (2002: 3) points out, is whether new media technologies 'will be an agent of freedom or an instrument of control'. Lawrence Lessig (2008: 29–33) notes that the twentieth century was the first time in history that popular culture had become professionalized, creating a stark separation between artists and audiences, what he refers to as a 'read-only culture'. Digital technologies have produced a more participatory 'RW culture' in which people have the ability to create their own art or music or film, whether it is completely original or based on an artifact of popular culture (e.g., **mash-ups**, sampling, remixes, compilations, etc.). YouTube, for instance, features countless examples of such homemade videos. Consumers of media become producers as well, or what are sometimes called 'prosumers'.

In a more political vein, the same technologies enable the emergence of alternative media organizations; they are alternative in the sense that they present a non-commercial media model that emphasizes 'the promotion of public dialogue, the exchange of ideas, and the promotion of social action' (Skinner, 2010: 222). Such media include newspapers (*Georgia Straight* in Vancouver, *The Coast* in Halifax, *Le Mouton Noir* in Rimouski, Quebec), magazines (*This Magazine*, *Canadian Dimension*, *Briarpatch*), radio (Radio Centre-Ville in Montreal, Vancouver Co-operative Radio), television (iChannel, Working TV), and, of course, the internet (Rabble.ca, TheTyee.ca, StraightGoods.ca). These are examples of what Nick Dyer-Witheford (1999: 64) describes as autonomous Marxism, a movement employing the same media tools as corporations do, but to subvert or oppose capitalism, whether by workers or by activists. 'What makes their perspective peculiarly notable is that it grasps the new forms of knowledge and communication not only as instruments of capitalist domination, but also as potential resources of anticapitalist struggle.' These media, in other words, allow for a range of applications, from the corporate pursuit of profit to struggles for social change.

Global Information Trade

Like other aspects of globalization, the cultural sphere is witnessing the expansion and intensification of a trend that already has a substantial history. This history reveals that international cultural exchanges have always been uneven, with a few sources of communication serving many destinations. This asymmetry intensified dramatically in the second half of the twentieth century as large media companies exploited their increased capacity to reach far-flung markets, treating the world as 'a single global market with local subdivisions'. Herman and McChesney (1997: 41) write:

> The rapidity of their global expansion is explained in part by equally rapid reduction or elimination of many of the traditional institutional and legal barriers to cross-border transactions. They have also been facilitated by technological changes such as the growth of satellite broadcasting, videocassette recorders, fiber optic cable and phone systems. Also critically important has been the rapid growth of cross-border advertising, trade and investment, and thus the demand for media and other communication services.

Terhi Rantanen (1997) points out that a handful of European news agencies—Havas, Reuters, Wolff—began to dominate global news coverage in the mid-1800s and the development of the telegraph and submarine telegraph cables in the mid-nineteenth century meant that, for the first time, information could reliably travel faster than people. As Herman and McChesney (1997: 12) note in this regard:

> From the beginning, global news services have been oriented to the needs and interests of the wealthy nations which provide their revenues. These news agencies were, in effect, the global media until well into the twentieth century, and even after the dawn of broadcasting their importance for global journalism was unsurpassed. Indeed, it was their near monopoly control over international news that stimulated much of the resistance to the existing global media regime by Third World nations in the 1970s.

Herman and McChesney (ibid., 13–14) describe the film industry as 'the first media industry to serve a truly global market'. By 1914, barely 20 years after cinema was invented, the US had captured 85 per cent of the world film audience, and by 1925 American films accounted for 90 per cent of film revenues in Great Britain, Canada, Australia, New Zealand, and Argentina, and over 70 per cent of revenues in France, Brazil, and the Scandinavian countries.

Such developments have been criticized as instances of media imperialism—the exploitation of global media markets to build political, economic, and ideological empires of influence and control. If what used to be called media imperialism is now usually described as media globalization, concerns nevertheless remain that the mass communication sphere has come to be dominated by 50 of the world's largest media companies, the majority of them based in Western Europe and North America (McChesney, 1998: 13). The resources of these large, global media companies—e.g., General Electric, AT&T/Liberty Media, Disney, Time Warner, Sony, News Corp., Viacom, Seagram, and Bertelsmann—give them tremendous advantages over smaller, independent producers in terms of their ability to hire skilled professionals (including stars), the aesthetic quality of their productions, the power of their corporate brands, their access to distribution networks, and their ability to advertise and promote their products worldwide (see McChesney, 2003).

The point is that the interdependence inherent in globalization is rarely symmetrical. The decidedly uneven flow of information and entertainment products creates a situation in which a few countries, and relatively few companies, produce and profit from the vast majority of media content, leaving most of the world, to a great extent, voiceless. The United States, for example, is the world leader in the production and dissemination of cultural products; according to Datamonitor (2009), the market value of the global media industry was US$754.5 billion in 2009, and the Americas (comprising Argentina, Brazil, Canada, Chile, Colombia, Mexico, Venezuela, and the US) accounted for 42 per cent of this economic activity. Since the 1940s the US has adopted an aggressive posture in promoting the uninhibited flow of information and entertainment

products worldwide. As shown in Table 11.1, Hollywood films dominate box offices around the world. Any issue of *Weekly Variety* indicates that theatre screens throughout the world have become a global market for the same Hollywood films we see in North America, although in some countries, such as France and Japan, audiences support indigenous films. Table 11.2, on the other hand, shows that the international popular music scene is somewhat more diverse. Statistics compiled by the UNESCO Institute for Statistics (2005) for 2002 indicate the UK as the world's largest producer of cultural goods (with the US in second place), but with the US as by far the largest consumer of cultural goods (with the UK in second place). The US was the largest exporter of books (17.7 per cent of the world market), newspapers, and periodicals (20 per cent), other printed matter (18.6 per cent), and sound recordings (16.6 per cent). The UK was the leading exporter of visual arts (27.7 per cent) and China led the world in audiovisual media exports (31.6 per cent), a category that includes photographs, films, and video games. Canada, with a population one-tenth the size of the United States, was the world's leading importer of newspapers and periodicals (13.8 per cent of the market), the world's third-largest importer of books (8.7 per cent), the fifth-largest importer of sound recordings (6.0 per cent), and the sixth-largest importer of audiovisual media (5.2 per cent).

Public broadcasting systems, which operate on a public-service model, are under siege in Canada and around the world. Even the venerable BBC, which has come to symbolize the best of public broadcasting, has adopted commercial strategies in some aspects of its operation. The BBC launched its BBC World Service Television as a global commercial venture in 1991, seeking 'to capitalize upon the BBC brand name, considered to be the second most famous in the world after that of Coca-Cola'. In 1996, the BBC established joint ventures with two American corporations to create commercial TV channels for world markets. Herman and McChesney (1997: 46–7) write: 'It is clear that the BBC has decided that its survival depends more upon locating a niche in the global media market than

TABLE 11.1 Top Three Box-Office Films, Selected Countries, July 2010

COUNTRY	TITLE	COUNTRY OF ORIGIN
Germany	*Twilight Saga: Eclipse*	USA
	Shrek Forever After	USA
	Marmaduke	USA
France	*Toy Story 3*	USA
	Twilight Saga: Eclipse	USA
	Shrek Forever After	USA
Italy	*Chronicles of Narnia: Prince Caspian*	UK/USA
	Meet Dave	USA
	The Dark Knight	USA/UK
Sweden	*Mamma Mia!*	UK/USA/Germany
	The Dark Knight	USA/UK
	Star Wars: The Clone Wars	USA
Australia	*Knight and Day*	USA
	Toy Story 3	USA
	Twilight Saga: Eclipse	USA
Brazil	*Shrek Forever After*	USA
	Twilight Saga: Eclipse	USA
	Knight and Day	USA
UK	*Inception*	USA/UK
	Shrek Forever After	USA
	Twilight Saga: Eclipse	USA
Russia	*The Sorceror's Apprentice*	USA
	The Last Airbender	USA
	Despicable Me	USA

Sources: Information courtesy of The Internet Movie Database (http://www.imdb.com)

in generating political support for public service broadcasting.' BBC Worldwide is the commercial arm of the BBC, generating profits of £145 million in 2009–10 through its channels, content production, digital media, sales and distribution, magazines, and licensing (BBC Worldwide, 2010).

What has emerged is a tiered global media market dominated by US-based companies, which can capitalize on the competitive advantage of having 'by far the largest and most lucrative indigenous market to use as a testing ground and to yield economies of scale' (Herman and McChesney, 1997: 52). In the 1980s and 1990s, for example, Canada became an important site of Hollywood film and television production, as American film companies took advantage of the lower Canadian dollar and comparable technical expertise north of the border (see Elmer and Gasher, 2005; Gasher, 2002; Pendakur, 1998). The Hollywood animation industry has similarly taken advantage of the cheap yet stable labour markets of India, South Korea, Australia, Taiwan, and the Philippines for the time-consuming and labour-intensive execution of animation projects originally conceived in Los Angeles (Breen, 2005; Lent, 1998).

The large, transnational media companies are most interested in the world's most affluent audiences, which advertisers want to reach and because these audiences have the money to spend on advertised products and services. This means,

TABLE 11.2 Top Five Music Singles, Selected Countries, July 2010

COUNTRY	TITLE AND ARTISTS	COUNTRY OF ORIGIN
Germany	'Waka Waka'/Shakira and Freshlyground	Colombia/South Africa
	'Helele'/Velile and Safri Duo	SouthAfrica/Denmark
	'Wavin' Flag'/K'Naan	Canada
	'Alejandro'/Lady Gaga	USA
	'Schland O Schland'/Uwe Lena	Germany
UK	'We No Speak Americano'/Yolanda Be Cool and DCUP	Australia
	'Love the Way You Lie'/Eminem	USA
	'Airplanes'/B.o.B	USA
	'California Gurls'/Katy Perry	USA
	'Pack Up'/Eliza Doolittle	UK
Italy	'Waka Waka'/Shakira and Freshlyground	Colombia/South Africa
	'Alejandro'/Lady Gaga	USA
	'California Gurls'/Katy Perry	USA
	'We No Speak Americano'/Yolanda Be Cool and DCUP	Australia
	'Mondo'/Cremonini Cesare	Italy
Spain	'Wavin' Flag'/K'Naan	Colombia
	'Waka Waka'/Shakira and Freshlyground	Columbia/South Africa
	'Sick of Love'/Robert Ramirez	Spain
	'Replay'/Iyaz	British Virgin Islands
	'Break Your Heart'/Taio Cruz	UK
Australia	'Love the Way You Lie'/Eminem	USA
	'I Like It'/Enrique Iglesias	Spain
	'California Gurls'/Katy Perry	USA
	'If I Had You'/Adam Lambert	USA
	'Airplanes'/B.o.B	USA

Source: Music Charts and Box Office Ratings, 28 July 2010, at: www.allcharts.org.

for example, that the poorest half of India's billion people are irrelevant to the global media market and all of sub-Saharan Africa has been written off. '[Sub-Saharan Africa] does not even appear in most discussions of global media in the business press.' Specifically, the global media are most interested in markets in North America, Latin America, Europe, and Asia. China, with a population of 1.3 billion, is the 'largest jewel in the Asian media crown' (Herman and McChesney, 1997: 64–8).

That said, the global media market does see some two-way traffic. The Globo and Televisa television networks in Brazil, for example, have succeeded in capturing a respectable share of Brazil's domestic market, and their telenovela productions are major exports. Globo owns an Italian television station, has an ownership interest in an American network specializing in Latin American programming, and has joint ventures with AT&T, News Corp., and TCI. Canada, too, has begun to tap export markets in both the film and television industries, and it has quickly become the world's third-largest video games producer, behind Japan and the US (Boswell, 2010). In addition, a

Source: © istockphoto.com/Nikos

Broadcasting House is the BBC's headquarters in London, England.

Source: © Bell Media

CTV's hit sitcom *Corner Gas* was picked up by US station WGN America in 2006.

renaissance in Canadian feature-film production since the mid-1980s means that directors like David Cronenberg (*Crash*, *ExistenZ*, *A History of Violence*), Atom Egoyan (*Ararat, The Sweet Hereafter, Where the Truth Lies, Chloe*), Deepa Mehta (*Fire, Earth, Water*), Denys Arcand (*Love and Human Remains, The Barbarian Invasions*), François Girard (*Thirty-Two Short Films about Glenn Gould, The Red Violin*), Denis Villeneuve (*Maelstrom, Polytechnique*), and Jean-François Pouliot (*La Grande Séduction*) have made names for themselves in international film markets. And Canada has become one of the world's leading exporters of television programming (MacDonald, 2007). Among the Canadian television programs sold to US broadcasters are: *Being Erica, Corner Gas, DaVinci's Inquest, Degrassi: The Next Generation, Flashpoint,* and *Intelligence.*

All of this commercial activity, of course, both opens up and limits the circulation of communications goods. What the technology on the one hand enables is access to a greater variety of both commercial and independently produced cultural products and services. Chris Anderson (2006), the editor-in-chief of *Wired* magazine, talks about the long-tail phenomenon, which allows companies to increase their inventory of books, films, and music as the costs of storage decrease; iTunes, for example, can afford to offer older, more obscure, or less popular music because the costs of storing that music for the handful of customers who might want to download it is minimal. Unlike your local music store, which has only so much room on its display racks and therefore can't carry the same range of CDs, iTunes' storage capacity is virtually limitless.

That said, it is still all about markets. The corporate structuring of the media privileges the production and distribution of the most commercial products and services. We recall the comment from cultural theorist Raymond Williams (1989: 88), who underlined the commercial constraints on freedom of expression under capitalism, 'where you can say that at times freedom in our kind of society amounts to the freedom to say anything you wish, provided you can say it profitably'. The corporate structuring of communication also grants media companies the power to inhibit, even prohibit, the production and circulation of products or services with limited appeal, or products that are critical or threatening in some way (Box 11.4).

BOX 11.4   THE APPLE UNIVERSE

The much-lauded Apple Inc. provides an example of a corporation that, while introducing a range of innovative computer products and services (e.g., iTunes, iPhone, iPad, Genius Bars), has also constructed an enclosed Apple universe, the kind of walled garden that the internet was supposed to eradicate. Apple will sell you the iPad, but it also runs the only stores that sell the software for it. As was explained in *Newsweek*: 'Instead of making a one-time sale, each iPad sold becomes a recurring revenue stream for Apple' (Lyons, 2010: 49). The iPad runs its own microprocessor that means it will only run Apple's Safari web browser, and it won't run videos created in Adobe Flash software. This forces iPad users to buy their videos from iTunes, and those videos will run only on Apple devices. Other companies are following this same path; Kindle e-book users have to buy their books through Amazon, and Microsoft has its own Zune Marketplace for downloads to its Zune music player (ibid., 49–50). If Apple's walled garden keeps customers in, it can also keep undesirables out. Apple rejected a proposed iPhone application called NewsToons from Pulitzer Prize–winning editorial cartoonist Mark Fiore, because his cartoons ridiculed public figures. Apple's policy is to refuse all content deemed, by the company, to be obscene, pornographic, or defamatory (Trudel, 2010). Thereby, Apple's market power grants it a censoring power as well.

Theories of International Communication Flows

The predominant explanation for international communication flows has been **World Systems Theory,** as articulated by Immanuel Wallerstein (1974, 2007). Even though humans have engaged in trade for thousands of years (see Bernstein, 2008), Wallerstein argues that a European, capitalist 'world economy' emerged in the late fifteenth and early sixteenth centuries. This extra-national economy involved long-distance trade that forged links between Europe and parts of Africa, Asia, and what came to be known as the West Indies and North and South America (Wallerstein, 1974: 15–20). World systems theory focuses on the relationship between nation states—the world system—rather than nation-states themselves, and demarcated three zones in the world economy: the core states, characterized by industrialization and the rise of a merchant class; the periphery, comprised of state economies based on resource extraction; and a semi-periphery, made up of in-between states whose economies shared some characteristics of both the core and periphery (ibid., 100–27). Wallerstein suggests that 'the size of a world-economy is a function of the state of technology, and in particular of the possibilities of transport and communication

within its bounds. Since this is a constantly changing phenomenon, not always for the better, the boundaries of a world-economy are ever fluid' (ibid., 349). He proposes that capitalism requires a world system (2007: 24) because its participants seek constantly to expand markets and to exploit the most favourable labour markets, regulatory regimes and infrastructure, access to resources, and access to investment capital and government support.

The world system's asymmetry, particularly with regard to trade in cultural materials, drew the attention of communication scholars in the post–World War II period and led to the development of two closely related theories: media imperialism and cultural dependency. Oliver Boyd-Barrett (1977: 117–18) used the term **media imperialism** to characterize the unidirectional nature of international media flows from a small number of source countries. More formally, he defined 'media imperialism' as 'the process whereby the ownership, structure, distribution or content of the media in any one country are singly or together subject to substantial external pressures from the media interests of any other country or countries without proportionate reciprocation of influence by the country so affected.' Media imperialism research grew out of a larger struggle for decolonization in the aftermath of World War II (Mosco, 1996: 75–6).

Cultural dependency is a less deterministic means of characterizing cultural trade imbalances than is media imperialism. Whereas 'imperialism' implies 'the act of territorial annexation for the purpose of formal political control', Boyd-Barrett (1996: 174–84) maintains that 'cultural dependency' suggests 'de facto control' and refers to 'a complex of processes' to which the mass media contribute 'to an as yet unspecified extent'.

While both approaches contributed a great deal to documenting international communication flows and drew attention to an obvious problem, neither theory offered a sufficiently complex explanation of the power dynamics behind international cultural trade, nor did they provide satisfactory descriptions of the impact of such asymmetrical exchanges. The media imperialism thesis tends to be too crudely applied, assuming too neat a relationship between the all-powerful source countries and their helpless colonies.'

Ted Magder (1993) qualifies the media imperialism thesis by underlining four points: the imperial centre is rarely omnipotent; the target nation is rarely defenseless; certain actors within the target nation may stand to benefit from media imperialism; and the effects of media imperialism are often unintended and unpredictable. According to Magder, 'It is not enough to document the internationalization of culture in its various forms; rather, the limits, conflicts, and contradictions of media imperialism must also be evaluated' (ibid., xx).

While slightly more nuanced, the cultural dependency thesis shared a number of the shortcomings of the media imperialism thesis. Like media imperialism, Vincent Mosco (1996: 125–6) argues, the concept of cultural dependency created homogeneous portraits of both the source and the target countries. It concentrated almost exclusively on the role of external forces and overlooked 'the contribution made by local forces and relations of production, including the indigenous class structure'. Cultural dependency also portrayed transnational capitalism as rendering the target state powerless. Like media imperialism, cultural dependency did not adequately account for how audiences in the target countries used or interpreted media messages that originate elsewhere.

Nonetheless, the clear asymmetry of globalization remains an important issue for researchers who study cultural policy and the political economy of communication from a range of perspectives. Current research seeks to account for the heterogeneity of national cultures, the specificity of particular industries and corporate practices, and varying reception practices—how cultural products are actually used by audiences, including the extent to which people become active producers themselves through citizen journalism, mash-ups, sampling, and home-made videos (see Lessig, 2008).

As an alternative to Wallerstein's world systems view, Manuel Castells has proposed another way of looking at the contemporary world that places communication technologies at the centre of global economic—and by extension, social and political—interactions. Castells describes a 'network society' that, as its name suggests, depicts a networked, or interconnected, world, which is less inter*national* than inter-*nodal*, placing major global cities, rather than nations, at the centre of its analysis.

Castells argues that the internet has allowed people to forge a new kind of sociability—'networked individualism' (Castells, 2001: 127–9)—and a new global geography—'a space of flows' (ibid., 207–8). This interconnected world, then, has considerable implications for the inclusion and exclusion of people and places from the network of global **information flows**. Internet use, he notes, is highly concentrated within a network of 'metropolitan nodes' (ibid., 228), which become the new dominant hubs of economics, politics, and culture. According to Castells, 'The Internet networks provide global, free communication that becomes essential for everything. But the infrastructure of the networks can be owned, access to them can be controlled, and their uses can be biased, if not monopolized, by commercial, ideological, and political interests' (ibid., 277). For this reason, Castells places a new onus on democratic governments to ensure political representation, participatory democracy, consensus-building, and effective public policy (ibid., 278–9).

Saskia Sassen (1998: xxv) sees in this network society 'a new economic geography of centrality' in which certain global cities concentrate economic and political power and become 'command centers in a global economy'. If Sassen agrees with Castells that this new geography is produced by the internet's most prominent and active users (ibid., xxvii), Sassen is concerned with the conflict that necessarily ensues between 'placebounded-ness'—those peoples, activities, and institutions bound to a specific place, often in support of the network infrastructure—and 'virtualization'—those peoples, activities, and institutions capable of exploiting Castells's virtual space of information flows (ibid., 201–2).

The political economist Vincent Mosco describes the process of overcoming the constraints of space and time as **spatialization**, and he attributes to communication a principal role as an enabling mechanism. He cautions that the global commercial economy does not annihilate space, but transforms it 'by restructuring the spatial relationships among people, goods, and messages. In the process of restructuring, capitalism transforms itself' (Mosco, 2009: 157) by becoming increasingly mobile and, following Castells, by clustering together certain communicative activities in 'agglomeration' zones (ibid., 169). One of the oldest and clearest examples of such spatial agglomeration is Hollywood, which clusters together companies and workers devoted to film and television production, from the writers, actors, and directors to the specialists in editing, lighting, set design and construction, lighting, and costume design.

Clearly, what has emerged in the context of globalization is a new media ecology. James Carey has argued that the internet 'should be understood as the first instance of a global communication system', displacing a national system that came into existence in the late nineteenth century with the development of, initially, telegraphy and railroad transportation, and later national magazines, newspapers, radio and television (Carey, 1998: 28). He suggests that we are witnessing the emergence of a 'new media ecology, which transforms the structural relations among older media such [as] print and broadcast and integrates them to a new center around the defining technologies of computer and satellite' (ibid., 34).

Source: © Ryan Koopmans/Alamy

The sets of major Hollywood blockbusters are becoming common sights in Vancouver and Toronto. These cities are often referred to as 'Hollywood North' because of their popularity with the American film industry.

Carey underscores the point here that this new media ecology requires a cultural level to complement its global infrastructure, an imagining and an articulation of community on a global scale, enabled, but not automatically produced, by communications or transportation technologies alone.

All this is not to say that national (or provincial or municipal) boundaries are obsolete. On the contrary, in some ways they have never been more important, as they are necessary to ensure access and opportunities for all Canadians in this shifting environment. However, the main point is that the social conditions in which we live are changing and that technologies and processes of communication are at the heart of these changes.

New World Information and Communication Order

Cees Hamelink (1994: 23–8) observes that two features of international communication emerged in the last half of the twentieth century: the expansion of the global communication system and tensions in the system across both east–west and north–south axes. East–west tensions—i.e., Cold War tensions between the Communist bloc led by the Soviet Union and the Western democracies led by the United States—were most prominent in the 1950s and 1960s. North–south tensions—i.e., tensions between affluent, industrialized nations of the northern hemisphere and the post-colonial Third World countries of the southern hemisphere—arose in the 1970s as the Third World took advantage of its new-found voice in the General Assembly of the United Nations, and they remain pertinent today. A number of UN initiatives led to a proposed New World Information and Communications Order (NWICO), which sought compromise between the American advocacy of the **free flow of information** and the Third World desire for a balanced flow.

The US push for the free-flow doctrine began during World War II when the American newspaper industry campaigned for the freedom of news-gathering; in June 1944, the American Society of Newspaper Editors (ASNE) adopted resolutions demanding 'unrestricted communications for news throughout the world'. The UN held a conference on freedom of information in Geneva in 1948.

At this stage, the free-flow doctrine met its stiffest opposition from the Soviet Union, which insisted on the regulation of information flows and complained that the Americans' freedom of information position endorsed, in fact, the freedom of a few commercial communication monopolies. Nevertheless, the free-flow doctrine was largely endorsed by the UN, and Article 19 of the 1948 Universal Declaration on Human Rights states: 'Everyone has the right to freedom of opinion and expression; this right includes freedom to hold opinions without interference and to seek, receive and impart information and ideas through any media regardless of frontiers' (ibid., 152–5).

The issue of communication flows was revisited at the behest of Third World countries in the 1970s, when it became clear that the free-flow doctrine was a recipe for Western cultural **hegemony** as the Soviets had anticipated. Starting in the mid-1960s, satellites became a key element in the emerging global media system. Because they offered a means to set up a national telecommunications system without a massive investment in land lines and equipment, countries were quick to see their

The global spread of information is easier than it has ever been. Today, information from anywhere in the world can enter your home in many different ways.

advantage. But satellites also presented possible problems for developing countries. As Herman and McChesney (1997) note, the development and launching of **geostationary** and **geosynchronous** communication satellites in the 1960s and 1970s 'fanned the flames of concern about global media.'

> Satellites held out the promise of making it possible for Third World nations to leapfrog out of their quagmire into a radically more advanced media system, but at the same time satellites posed the threat of transnational commercial broadcasters eventually controlling global communication, bypassing any domestic authority with broadcasts directly to Third World homes. (Ibid., 23)

The major global institutions dealing with communication issues at the time—the UN, the UN Educational, Scientific and Cultural Organization (UNESCO), and the International Telecommunication Union (ITU)—all included majorities of Third World countries and sympathetic Communist states. The impetus for a renewed debate on international communication came from the 90-member Movement of the Non-Aligned Nations (NAN).

The international debate at that time focused on three points, as it still does to some extent. First, historically, communication services together with evolved information technologies have allowed dominant

⫶ BOX 11.5   THE DECLINING INVESTMENT IN INTERNATIONAL NEWS

International news coverage is an important source of information about the world we live in. In a period of globalization, when the people, places, and institutions that constitute our world are more closely connected than ever before, and when polls indicate a strong public appetite for foreign news coverage (Canadian Media Research Consortium, 2009), news organizations are decreasing their investment in international coverage. The principal reason is cost-cutting; the maintenance of foreign news bureaus is expensive, costing an estimated $200,000 to $300,000 per correspondent annually, and news organizations are opting to buy their international news from wire services like Associated Press, Reuters, and Agence France Presse rather than to produce it themselves. Because these news agencies serve clients all over the world, they deliver a homogenized form of reporting that perceives issues through the lens of their home countries (the US, the UK, and France, respectively) and ignores the specific needs of Canadian readers (Bielsa, 2008; Brown, 2009: 30).

Most Canadian newspapers do not have any foreign correspondents. They rely exclusively on wire services and only occasionally send one of their own reporters to cover a particularly dramatic story. Most metropolitan dailies devote more of their travel budgets to sports coverage than to foreign coverage.

Those Canadian news organizations that do maintain foreign bureaus are cutting back. When CanWest acquired the Southam newspapers, Southam News had 11 foreign bureaus; CanWest News Service (renamed Postmedia News) has five (in Shanghai, Paris, Washington, New York, and Jerusalem). In the 1980s, the CBC had 28 foreign bureaus, and now maintains half that number (in London, Paris, Washington, New York, the United Nations, Jerusalem, Moscow, Beirut, Beijing, Shanghai, Los Angeles, Kandahar, Nairobi, and Bangkok). CTV has cut back from nine to four (in Washington, London, New Delhi, and Los Angeles).

The Globe and Mail and La Presse are the exceptions in increasing their foreign presence and are distinguishing themselves as serious newspapers. The Globe now has eight bureaus (in London, Beijing, Rome, Jerusalem, Johannesburg, New Delhi, New York, and Washington), while La Presse has three (in London, Paris, and Washington) where previously it had none. These bureaus, however, often consist of a single reporter responsible for a huge geographical area and a great range of topics.

A study of the international news coverage of Canada's three self-described 'national' newspapers —The Globe and Mail, National Post, and Le Devoir— revealed that one-quarter of their stories were filed from abroad, but there were important qualifiers: the United States accounted for 40 per cent of all international coverage, 25 per cent of international coverage concerned professional sport, and most international coverage came from five countries (the US, the UK, France, Iraq, and Germany). These newspapers portrayed a highly circumscribed world, with the entire continents of Africa and South America largely absent. Eighty per cent of the international coverage in The Globe and Mail came from wire services, as did 89 per cent in Le Devoir. Only 6 per cent of National Post stories had foreign placelines (see Gasher, 2007).

⫶ BOX 11.6   AL JAZEERA ENGLISH

The world's first English-language global news network based in Doha, Qatar, came to Canada in 2010 and represents a significant step in the internationalization of Canadian television news. After having received regulatory approval as a digital cable channel from the CRTC in November 2009, Al Jazeera English reached agreement with the Canadian distributors BCE, Rogers Communications, and Videotron to be offered to their cable and satellite television subscribers as of May 2010. Previously, Al Jazeera English was available only via the internet (Krashinsky, 2010c).

Al Jazeera English was founded in 2006 as a sister network to the Qatar-based Al Jazeera Arabic. It is seen in 200 million households in more than 100 countries. Its managing director is Tony Burman, a Canadian and the former editor-in-chief and executive director of the CBC. Al Jazeera English is headquartered in Doha, Qatar, and has broadcast centres in Doha, Kuala Lumpur, London, and Washington. It plans to open a Canadian news bureau in Toronto (Al Jazeera English, 2010).

states to exploit their political and economic power. Through historical patterns and enabling technology, such as communication satellites, these dominant states have assumed a presence in the cultures and ideologies of less dominant states. That presence, whether it comes from being the principal source of foreign news or from beaming satellite signals into another country, is strongly felt by developing nations, just as it is in Canada.

Second, the economies of scale in information production and distribution threaten to reinforce this dominance. It takes considerable capital and infrastructure to engage in the mass production, circulation, and promotion of cultural products, which is why so many countries, for example, struggle to establish viable film industries. And any attempt to counteract a worsening situation must avoid feeding into the hands of repressive governments that would curtail freedom of expression and information circulation.

Third, a few transnational corporations have mobilized technology as a vehicle for the exploitation of markets rather than as a means of serving the cultural, social, and political needs of nations. In other words, the large corporations have seized the opportunity to develop and use communication technologies, but they have employed those technologies primarily to exploit the value of audiences to advertisers rather than to provide information, education, and entertainment to these audiences for their own benefit or for the benefit of the larger cultural whole.

Pressure from the Third World compelled the UN to broaden the concept of free flow to include 'the free and balanced flow of information'. International debate over the design of a New World Information and Communication Order coalesced around the final report of the 16-member International Commission for the Study of Communication Problems (the MacBride Commission), established by UNESCO in December 1977 (UNESCO, 1980).

The MacBride Commission (ibid., 253–68) advocated 'free, open and balanced communications' and concluded that 'the utmost importance should be given to eliminating imbalances and disparities in communication and its structures, and particularly in information flows. Developing countries need to reduce their dependence, and claim a new, more just and more equitable order in the field of communication.' The Commission's conclusions were based on 'the firm conviction that communication is a basic individual right, as well as a collective one required by all communities and nations. Freedom of information—and, more specifically the right to seek, receive and impart information—is a fundamental human right; indeed, a prerequisite for many others.'

Recognizing that leaving the development of communication systems solely to market forces serves to block access to them for particular groups of people and ideas, the MacBride Commission pointed to an essential conflict between the commercialization and the democratization of communication. Consequently, the Commission clearly favoured a movement for democratization, which would include respect for national sovereignty in areas of cultural policy and recognition that the 'educational and informational use of communication should be given equal priority with entertainment.' The report stated: 'Every country should develop its communication patterns in accordance with its own conditions, needs and traditions, thus strengthening its integrity, independence and self-reliance.'

The MacBride Report also criticized the striking disparities between the technological capacities of different nations, and described the right to communicate as fundamental to democracy: 'Communication needs in a democratic society should be met by the extension of specific rights, such as the right to be informed, the right to inform, the right to privacy, the right to participate in public communication—all elements of a new concept, the right to communicate.'

From NWICO to the Present

The MacBride Report proved to be a better manifesto on the democratization of communication than a blueprint for restructuring international communication exchanges. Even though UNESCO adopted its key principles—eliminating global media imbalances and having communication serve national development goals—the NWICO was poorly received in the West 'because it gave governments, and not markets, ultimate authority over the nature of a society's media' (Herman and McChesney, 1997: 24–6). In fact, the Western countries, led by the United States under Ronald Reagan and the United Kingdom under Margaret Thatcher, chose in the 1980s the more aggressive path of pursuing liberalized global trade. 'In the 1980s a wave of global "liberalization" gathered momentum, in which state enterprises were privatized, private businesses were deregulated, and government welfare initiatives were cut back.' The US and UK pulled out of UNESCO in 1985 in protest against the policy direction it was taking. Even Canada, which was one of the affluent industrialized nations identified by the MacBride Commission as being dominated by cultural imports, began to pursue the neo-liberal agenda of free trade and budget cutbacks in the 1980s under the successive Progressive Conservative governments of Brian Mulroney. Very little changed in Canadian government policy after Jean Chrétien's Liberals assumed power in 1993, and little has changed under the Stephen Harper Conservatives. Such issues as deficit reduction and freer trade continue to dominate the political agenda and the ministers of industry, international trade, and finance enjoy as much influence over cultural policy as the minister with the culture portfolio, if not even more (see Gasher, 1995).

International bodies like the World Trade Organization (originally, the General Agreement on Tariffs and Trade) have become more important to the major cultural producers than the United Nations, and the rules of the game for international communications have been written in such treaties as the North American Free Trade Agreement (NAFTA) and the Treaty on European Union. Herman and McChesney (1997: 30–1) write: 'The political design of all these regional and global trade agreements has been to remove decision-making powers from local and national legislatures in favor of impersonal market forces and/or supranational bureaucracies remote from popular control.' NAFTA, for example, 'requires that government agencies operate on a strictly commercial basis, and it

explicitly removes the possibility that governments can take on any new functions.'

The New World Information and Communication Order, in other words, was almost immediately supplanted by what Herman and McChesney (ibid., 35) call the 'new global corporate ideology'. As the communications media have become increasingly implicated in the global economy, media policy is governed more and more by international financial and trade regimes such as the International Monetary Fund and the WTO.

Nonetheless, as Mosco (2009: 178) puts it, the struggle continues to be to 'build a more democratic process grounded in genuinely global governance'. The International Telecommunications Union (ITU) launched the World Summit on the Information Society (WSIS, 2010), which took the form of international conferences bringing together scholars, civil society groups, governments, and policy experts in Geneva in 2003 and Tunis in 2005. The Geneva conference laid out a 67-point declaration of principles and an action plan, and the Tunis conference addressed the financial implementation of the action plan.

The Geneva declaration privileges an understanding of information as a resource for the promotion of freedom, equality, peace, and democracy, rather than simply as a consumer product, and its main target was the 'digital divide' between those peoples, organizations, and nations in the world with the ready access and the skills to take full advantage of communications technologies and those who lack that access and those skills (see Box 11.7). The Geneva declaration expressed the desire to create an information society 'where everyone can create, access, utilize and share information and knowledge, enabling individuals, communities and peoples to achieve their full potential in promoting their sustainable development and improving their quality of life.' Among its specific principles were: freedom of opinion and expression; greater access to technology; greater access to information and better information and knowledge sharing; and the need to address media imbalances due to 'infrastructure, technical resources and the development of human skills'.

⁑ BOX 11.7   THE DIGITAL DIVIDE

The digital divide refers to the gap between the information-rich and the information-poor, and can be measured on both an international scale—between the regions and countries of the world—and on a national scale—between populations based on where they live, their access to digital networks, and demographic characteristics such as household income, education level, age, and sex. The existence of this divide is a clear reminder that not everyone, even in our own communities, enjoys the same access to digital communication technologies. Given the importance of information in modern society, and the importance of access to computer networks, the digital divide represents a measure of inequality that can have a serious impact on quality of life.

Jan A.G.M. van Dijk (2005: 15) captures the significance of the digital divide and at the same time explains why, as a negative feedback loop, it persists and worsens:

1. Categorical inequalities in society produce an unequal distribution of resources.
2. An unequal distribution of resources causes unequal access to digital technologies.
3. Unequal access to digital technologies also depends on the characteristics of these technologies.
4. Unequal access to digital technologies brings about unequal participation in society.
5. Unequal participation in society reinforces categorical inequalities and unequal distribution of resources.

At stake here is full participation in, or exclusion from, contemporary society. The digital divide also provides a measure of the economic health of nations and peoples.

A study by the International Telecommunications Union in 2008 concluded that, globally, the gap between those with access to online technologies and those without is widening, as is the gap between countries on the same continents (Wakefield, 2010). Iceland was the world's most connected country—90.6 per cent of its population had internet access—followed by Sweden (87.8 per cent), the Netherlands (86.5 per cent), Denmark (83.9 per cent), and Finland (82.6 per cent). Canada enjoys a connection rate of 80 per cent.

While about three-quarters of people in the United States, South Korea, and the United Kingdom had internet access, fewer than 10 per cent in South Africa, fewer than 25 per cent in China, and only about one-third in Russia and Brazil were connected. The least-connected countries in the world were Myanmar (0.2 per cent), Bangladesh (0.3 per cent), Ethiopia (0.4 per cent), Congo (0.5 per cent), and Cambodia (0.5 per cent). The study noted that these figures can vary dramatically among populations within the same country. In the US, for example, fewer than 10 per cent of Native Americans have internet access.

Canadians are among the best-connected people in the world, but clear and persistent distinctions in internet usage remain, depending on income and educational levels, age, and community size. The Canadian Internet Use Survey conducted by Statistics Canada in 2009 found that, overall, 80 per cent of Canadians aged 16 and over used the internet for personal reasons in 2009, up from 73 per cent in 2007. This ranged from a low of 69 per cent in Newfoundland and Labrador to a high of 85 per cent in both Alberta and British Columbia (Statistics Canada, 2010).

The most persistent divide between internet users pertains to community size. Of Canadians living in communities of 10,000 people or more, 83 per cent used the internet for personal reasons, compared to 73 per cent in communities with populations under 10,000. The reason for this is that small communities are often poorly served by telecommunications providers as their economies of scale don't provide very good rates of return compared to larger communities. Income, education, and age are also important factors. Ninety-four per cent of Canadians living in households with annual income of $85,000 used the internet, compared to just 56 per cent in households with less than $30,000 in annual income. Eighty-nine per cent of those with at least some post-secondary education used the internet, compared to 66 per cent of those with no post-secondary education. And 98 per cent of Canadians aged 16 to 24 used the internet, compared to 66 per cent of those 45 and older.

Changing Notions of Place

A number of scholars have attributed to the communications media a significant role in how we imagine, define, understand, and experience place. The philosopher Charles Taylor (2005: 23) refers to this as the 'social imaginary', which he defines as 'the ways people imagine their social existence, how they fit together with others, how things go on between them and their fellows, the expectations that are normally met, and the deeper normative notions and images that underlie these expectations'. The widespread commercialization of cultural production, communication, and information exchange and the extent to which we rely on these media for our communicative activities raise a number of questions about the relationship between communication and culture. The perpetual flows of people, capital, goods, services, and images that characterize globalization carry significant implications for how we experience and imagine place, how we define community, and how we constitute identity. Doreen Massey (1991: 24) asks: 'How, in the face of all this movement and intermixing, can we retain any sense of a local place and its particularity?' Globalization has intensified struggles over the meaning of place. This is particularly the case in countries like Canada, whose citizens tend to be more familiar with cultural imports than with the ideas and expressions of their own artists and intellectuals. This struggle also owes something to Canada's policy of multiculturalism (see Box 11.8). If the literary critic Northrop Frye famously framed the Canadian identity question as 'Where is here?', we can follow that question with one that is intimately related: 'Who are we?'

Benedict Anderson defined the nation as 'an imagined political community' and depicted eighteenth-century newspapers and novels as implicated in the projects of nation-building and nationalism. The nation, he wrote, 'is *imagined* because the members of even the smallest nation will never know most of their fellow-members, meet them, or even hear of them, yet in the minds of each lives the image of their communion' (Anderson, 1983: 15). He described the novel and the newspaper as new forms of imagining, which provided the technical means to produce in people a sense of 'nation-ness'.

Philosopher Charles Taylor of McGill University, Montreal.

Source: © Jorge Uzon/Corbis.

If novels created a 'sociological landscape' through the depiction of simultaneous events tying together a population of imagined characters (ibid., 35–6), newspapers presented news stories whose sharing of the news cycle—their 'calendrical coincidence'—and whose juxtaposition on the newspaper page created connections among them (ibid., 37–8). The short shelf life of the newspaper—its 'obsolescence'—in turn created 'an extraordinary mass ceremony: the almost precisely simultaneous consumption ("imagining") of the newspaper-as-fiction' (ibid., 39).

John Hartley (1992, 1996), too, maintains that publics are created by institutions and discourses, arguing that 'the media are simultaneously creative and participatory. They create a picture of the public, but it goes live, as it were, only when people participate in its creation, not least by turning themselves into the audience' (1992: 4). Audiences, thereby, are 'discursive productions' (1996: 67). But Hartley points out that media can exclude as well as include, creating divisions between those who belong and those who don't belong. Communities,

⁘ BOX 11.8   REASONABLE ACCOMMODATION

The diverse makeup of Canada's population is often celebrated, but at other times it can be perceived as a source of conflict with, even a threat to, what we believe to be the Canadian way of life, our customs, norms, and values. This diversity raises the age-old, but always complex, identity question: Who are we as a people? And it can evoke a range of emotional responses, sometimes xenophobic or bigoted, but at other times serious and legitimate. These issues tend to get played out in the news media in sensational and simplistic ways, rendering difference a problem to be solved.

The question of 'reasonable accommodation' has been raised most noticeably in Quebec. Given the province's own concerns about its status within Canada as an identifiably distinct society, Quebec has long been uneasy about the Canadian Multiculturalism Act (1988), particularly what multiculturalism means for the status of Quebec's francophone population (Karim, 2009: 704). The aim of Quebec to be recognized as constituting a nation or a people conflicts with Canada's multiculturalism policy.

A number of specific controversies in 2006 and 2007 prompted the Quebec government to establish the Consultation Commission on Accommodation Practices Related to Cultural Differences (known as the Bouchard-Taylor Commission). The controversies included: a 2006 Supreme Court of Canada decision defending the right of a Sikh student from Quebec to wear a kirpan to school; a decision by a Montreal YMCA to frost its windows at the request of a neighbouring synagogue whose members objected to the sight of women exercising; a decision by Canada's chief electoral officer to permit Muslim women to wear a niqab or burka while voting; a *Journal de Montréal* poll in which 59 per cent of Quebecers considered themselves racist; and the 2007 decision by the Quebec town of Hérouxville (population 1,300) to adopt a 'code of living' that banned, among other things, the stoning of women and female circumcision.

The Bouchard-Taylor Commission was mandated to review accommodation practices in Quebec, analyze the issues, conduct extensive consultations with citizens, and provide recommendations to the Quebec government to 'ensure that accommodation practices conform to Quebec's values as a pluralistic, democratic, egalitarian society' (Bouchard-Taylor Commission, 2008: 17). Hearings were conducted throughout the province in the fall of 2007 and the commissioners, the sociologist Gérard Bouchard, and the philosopher Charles Taylor produced a report with 37 recommendations in May 2008. Central to their report was the concept of 'interculturalism', which posits a majority population (white, francophone Quebecers) and various minorities, and the need for two-way accommodation between the majority and the minorities. This is a rather different construct from Canadian 'multiculturalism', which does not presume a majority that must accommodate and be accommodated to. After all, Canada today is a pluralistic society and is so ethnically and culturally diverse that identifying a meaningful 'majority' in ethnocultural terms would not be possible.

that is, are largely defined by their distinction from other communities and by specific membership criteria. Newspapers, for example, speak to a particular audience of readers, so that 'news includes stories on a daily basis which enable everyone to recognize a larger unity or community than their own immediate contacts, and to identify with the news outlet as "our" storyteller' (1992: 207). The news, Hartley argues, is organized around strategies of inclusion and exclusion from *our* community, creating domains of We-dom and They-dom, dividing people into 'us' and 'them'. The boundaries of We-dom and They-dom are not coterminous with any formal political boundaries, but can be drawn from any number of bases: not only

citizenship, but gender, race, class, ethnicity, etc. (ibid., 207). News media, then, not only help to define and constitute communities, but in doing so draw boundary lines which divide communities into domains of 'us' and 'them'.

As noted above, the various flows we associate with globalization are not new. What globalization has done, however, has been both to increase the traffic—human, material, electronic, etc.—across some borders and to reconfigure others. Thus, for example, the Canada–US Free Trade Agreement was an attempt to facilitate trade across the border dividing the two countries. Although the legal boundary remains, the meaning of the border has changed, at least as far as trade relations are concerned. The signing in December 2001 of the Smart Border Declaration between Canada and the US, whereby the latest communications technology will be used to create a more secure shared border in the wake of the 9/11 attacks on New York and Washington, DC, means that the very term 'border' has taken on a rather changed and less Canadian-determined meaning for the foreseeable future. This applies to cultural exchanges as well; it has become more difficult for Canada to preserve some space within its own market for indigenous cultural products. Technologies like satellite television ignore terrestrial boundaries altogether; satellite TV is confined instead by satellite 'footprints', which mark the limits of a satellite's technological reach.

The heightened permeability of borders has been met, among some, by the desire for a more rooted, or more secure, sense of place. Gillian Rose (1995: 88–116) notes that place has been a privileged component of identity formation. 'Identity is how we make sense of ourselves, and geographers, anthropologists and sociologists, among others, have argued that the meanings given to a place may be so strong that they become a central part of the identity of people experiencing them.' Places, and the experiences we associate with places, both as individuals and as members of a group, inform memory and our sense of belonging. This sense of belonging is critical to understanding the relationship between identity and a particular locale. 'One way in which identity is connected to a particular place is by a feeling that you belong to that place.' We might, therefore, detect a very different sense of belonging between native residents of a place and migrants. Migrants such as refugees and exiles, who have not moved of their own free will, may feel little sense of belonging to their new place of residence.

Culture is another means by which identities of place are constructed and sustained. Stuart Hall (1995: 177–86) argues that we tend to imagine cultures as 'placed' in two ways. First, we associate place with a specific location where social relationships have developed over time. Second, place 'establishes symbolic boundaries around a culture, marking off those who belong from those who do not.'

Physical settlement, continuity of occupation, the long-lasting effects on ways of life arising from the shaping influence of location and physical environment, coupled with the idea that these cultural influences have been exercised amongst a population which is settled and deeply interrelated through marriage and kinship relations, are meanings which we closely associate with the idea of culture and which provide powerful ways of conceptualizing what 'culture' is, how it works, and how it is transmitted and preserved.

At the same time, Hall explains, 'There is a strong tendency to "landscape" cultural identities, to give them an imagined place or "home", whose characteristics echo or mirror the characteristics of the identity in question.'

The widespread migration of peoples so prevalent in our time—close to 20 per cent of Canada's population in 2006 were immigrants (Statistics Canada, 2009: 158)—brings together people with very different roots, histories, traditions, and values. In some instances these differences are embraced. But at other times they can be perceived as threatening to our sense of community, of place, of culture, of identity. Again, much of our engagement with our community takes place through the media, and our understandings of Canadian histories, traditions, and values not only come from news reports but from music, film, television, and printed sources (e.g., books, magazines).

If one impact of globalization has been to call into question the notion of 'place' as the basis for identity and/or culture, **postmodernism** and improved networks of transportation and communication facilitate the imagination of communities based on gender, race, ethnicity, sexual orientation, social class, etc. Proximity, in other words, is not a necessary element of identity formation. If culture and identity are not confined to a particular place, it follows that any one place is not confined to a single culture or identity—hence the Quebec conundrum of interculturalism and of its being a 'distinct society'. This issue of identity formation has precipitated localized struggles over immigration and language, as well as over urban development, architecture, and foreign investment. Mike Featherstone (1996: 66) remarks that 'cultural differences once maintained between places now exist within them.' For example: 'The unwillingness of migrants to passively inculcate the dominant cultural mythology of the nation or locality raises issues of multiculturalism and the fragmentation of identity.' Massey (1995: 48) argues: 'The way in which we define "places", and the particular character of individual places, can be important in issues varying from battles over development and construction to questions of which social groups have rights to live where.'

The conventional container of identity and culture that has come under greatest challenge from the re-imagining of community prompted by globalization has been the **nation-state**. Questions of citizenship and questions of identity have been increasingly dissociated (Morley and Robins, 1995: 19). The emergence of trade blocs in Europe, Asia, and North America and the prevalence of both international and subnational cultural networks have undermined the primacy of the nation-state in contemporary imaginings of community, identity, and culture.

We should not overreact to these changes, however. We still have democratically elected national, provincial, and municipal governments, which continue to pass laws and pursue policies that form the basic framework within which media organizations operate in Canada. These laws and policies are responses to pressures from both the global economy and local cultures. As we discussed in Chapters 7 and 8, laws like the Broadcasting, Telecommunications, and Income Tax Acts, the funding programs of Telefilm Canada and the Canada Council, and cultural institutions like the Canadian Broadcasting Corporation remain pre-eminent in structuring cultural production in Canada. No media industry is untouched by them. Globalization alters the context in which mass communication takes place, but local conditions of cultural production remain both pertinent and key to the ways in which it is undertaken.

SUMMARY

This chapter began with an extended definition of globalization and showed how it is not simply an economic phenomenon, but an intensification of social relations across time and space that touches every aspect of our lives, from how we shop to what we see on our television and computer screens. We then outlined four roles the communication media play in the globalization process: as media of encounter; as media of governance; as media situating us within the world; and as a globalized business in and of themselves. We subsequently reviewed the predominant theories to explain international communication flows and their implications, beginning with Immanuel Wallerstein's world systems theory, touching briefly on media imperialism and cultural dependency, and concluding with Manuel Castells's notion of the 'network society' and Vincent Mosco's discussion of 'spatialization'.

On this conceptual groundwork, we traced the history of international communication exchanges, concentrating particularly on the period from the 1940s to the present. We discussed the doctrine of 'free flow' promoted by the United States and then explained the rise, and subsequent downfall, of the New World Information and Communication Order, whose proponents sought to alleviate communication imbalances between national communities in the 1970s and to promote the 'right to communicate' as a fundamental human right. Instead, the 1980s and 1990s were characterized by further trade liberalization and the reinforcement of the commercial view of communication as commodity exchange. We summarized briefly the 2003 and 2005 conferences of the World Summit on the Information Society as the latest co-ordinated effort to democratize communication on a global scale.

The chapter concluded with a discussion of the impact of globalization on how we think about 'place', 'community', and 'identity', given the importance of communication and cultural exchange to our sense of belonging, and expanded on Castells's ideas about the new forms of sociability and the new global geography that characterize our time.

KEY TERMS

cultural dependency, p. 322
Fordism, p. 313
free flow of information, p. 324
globalization, p. 307
geostationary, p. 324
geosynchronous, p. 324
hegemony, p. 324

information flow, p. 322
mash-up, p. 316
media geography, p. 307
media imperialism, p. 321
mobility, p. 307
nation-state, p. 332
network society, p. 315

postmodernism, p. 331
proximity, p. 314
sovereignty, p. 313
spatialization, p. 323
technology, p. 307
world systems theory, p. 321

RELATED WEBSITES

European Union: www.europa.eu
The official site of the European Union includes an institutional overview, regular news dispatches, and official report.

International Telecommunications Satellite Organization (INTELSAT): www.itso.int
INTELSAT provides global communications services with a 'fleet' of 20 geosynchronous satellites.

International Telecommunications Union (ITU): www.itu.int
The ITU is an international organization through which governments and private corporations co-ordinate telecommunications networks and services.

UNESCO: www.unesco.org
The principal objective of the United Nations Educational, Scientific and Cultural Organization is to contribute to global peace and security by promoting international collaboration through education, science, culture, and communication.

World Summit on the Information Society (WSIS): www.itu.int/wsis/index.html
Taking the form of two international conferences, the WSIS is a co-ordinated effort to democratize the institutions of mass communication and to eradicate communicative inequalities between peoples and nation-states.

World Trade Organization (WTO): www.wto.org
The WTO governs trade between nations and seeks to promote trade liberalization throughout the world.

❯ FURTHER READINGS

Bauman, Zygmunt. 1998. *Globalization: The Human Consequences.* New York: Columbia University Press. This book looks at globalization from a critical and human perspective, considering its political, social, and economic implications on people's daily lives.

Castells, Manuel. 2001. *The Internet Galaxy: Reflections on the Internet, Business, and Society.* Oxford: Oxford University Press. Written by one of the foremost contemporary theorists on international communications networks, this book examines the internet from a number of perspectives, including its history and how it impacts the way people work, consume media, and interact socially.

Held, David, and Anthony McGrew, eds. 2003. *The Global Transformations Reader: An Introduction to the Globalization Debate.* Cambridge: Polity Press. This is a comprehensive reader with concise chapters from leading scholars covering every aspect of globalization, from its economics to its political, social, and cultural implications.

Herman, Edward S., and Robert W. McChesney. 1997. *The Global Media: The New Missionaries of Global Capitalism.* London: Cassell. The authors present a critical assessment of the rise of concentrated and converged media conglomerates, supported by documentation on which companies owned which media during the mid-1990s.

Morley, David, and Kevin Robins. 1995. *Spaces of Identity: Global Media, Electronic Landscapes and Cultural Boundaries.* London: Routledge. This is a provocative look at how the globalization of communication has undermined and altered conventional notions of national and cultural belonging. The ideas proposed in this book remain current.

Raboy, Marc, and Jeremey Shtern, eds. 2010. *Media Divides: Communication Rights and the Right to Communicate in Canada.* Vancouver: University of British Columbia Press. This book contains a number of important essays that follow up on the recommendations of the MacBride Commission and the WSIS in the Canadian context.

Taylor, Charles. 2005. *Modern Social Imaginaries.* Durham, NC: Duke University Press. Taylor provides an accessible philosophical study of the way we imagine our world and constitute identity in a period of significant political, economic, and social upheaval, a period of 'multiple modernities'.

UNESCO. 1980. *Many Voices, One World: Report by the International Commission for the Study of Communication Problem*s (MacBride Commission). Paris: UNESCO. The controversial MacBride Report was critical of the free-flow doctrine promoted by the US and proposed measures to ensure more equitable and balanced communication flows between nations.

Wallerstein, Immanuel. 2007. *World-Systems Analysis: An Introduction.* Durham, NC: Duke University Press. This up-to-date introduction to world systems theory describes the emergence of an extra-national economy involving long-distance trade links between Europe and parts of Africa, Asia, and what came to be known as the West Indies and North and South America.

⫸ STUDY QUESTIONS

1. Globalization is often used to mean economic globalization. Besides economics, what other globalizing forces impact the communications sphere?

2. In what ways are the mass media agents of globalization?

3. Is media globalization the same as media imperialism? Why or why not?

4. What is the argument in support of the free flow of communication? What is the basis for criticism of this position?

5. What was the MacBride Commission's position on international communication flows?

6. What is the World Summit on the Information Society?

7. What is world systems theory?

8. What does Manuel Castells mean by 'a space of flows'?

9. How is globalization liberating? How is it confining?

CHAPTER 12

Communication in a Digital Age

Where is the knowledge we have lost in information?

— T.S. ELIOT

- What is the difference between traditional and contemporary perspectives on mass communication?

- What does it mean to approach the study of media and communication from a critical perspective? Can globalization be seen as a wholly positive or negative force?

- What is the role of public policy in the media and communication industries?

- What are some of the problems of thinking of media and communication in simply economic terms?

- What does the case of Maher Arar tell us about the possible role and importance of the media in today's media environment?

Learning Objectives

- To appreciate the complex forces behind globalization.
- To discover some of the difficulties of approaching media and communication from a solely economic perspective.
- To understand the long-tail phenomenon and its application to communication studies.
- To develop an appreciation for the role of media in today's social, political, and economic environment.

Introduction

Communication media pervade practically all facets of our lives. They encompass traditional media—film, books, magazines, television and radio broadcasting, newspapers, telecommunications—as well as an increasing range of new electronic information and communications technologies. With computers, e-book readers, iPads, internet-based media, cellphones, and other emerging technologies, communications media are shifting how we understand our world and our place within it.

We began our study of the media and communication by considering the shifting nature of communication technology, reflecting on how media and communication systems are central to the functioning and operation of society, and examining how they orient our understanding of the world and our actions within it. We considered the broad history of media, and the ways they have been implicated in political, economic, and social development. We looked at a wide range of media theories, considered the different perspectives they provide on the broad processes of communication—particularly encoding and decoding—and weighed the different accents they put on the importance of structure and agency. We also examined the formal institutions of communication and the influence that professional values have on their operation, and considered the role of larger social forces, such as politics and economics, in shaping the development and character of these activities.

As we have seen, the influence exerted by these media ranges across all dimensions of society: politics, economics, education, culture, the family, and individual lives. The media also have an enormous impact on our world view and our frame of reference on events. But, as we have seen, media are incomplete and imperfect tools for understanding our world. To study the dynamics of media, as we have been doing in this book, is to attempt to understand the dynamics of representation and the ways in which it informs our understandings of the world.

This final chapter summarizes the various ideas and perspectives on media and communication

that we have examined, and points the way to future study and directions of growth and development of the field.

From Mass Distribution of Symbolic Products to Mass Communication

Media are central to how we understand culture and society and share in them. In this context, we have approached the study of media and communications from a *critical perspective*. That is, we have been considering how media are implicated in our knowledge and understanding of the world.

Our discussion of oral, literate, and electronic forms of communication introduced how media of communication can influence social form and structure. For instance, our discussion of oral communication illustrated that media shape the production and transmission of knowledge. An examination of written or literate communication shows how media can shrink social distance and shift relations of political power. Digital electronic communication does all this and more. It can have both binding and fragmenting effects as barriers to constructing relationships across space collapse. While many digital divides continue to cause inequalities both at home and internationally, the electronic media overall contribute to shrinking social, political, economic, and geographic distances. Who will reap the majority of the benefits from these changes remains to be seen.

But as we have seen, technology is not the sole defining feature of media systems. While specific types of media might have particular propensities, media systems are the product of a much broader set of political, economic, social, and cultural forces. Broadly speaking, in the context of Western societies, contemporary media reflect cultural forms and social practices engendered by the shift from feudal to industrial society, and the migrations and divisions of labour that characterized that shift. Moreover, in a large industrial nation such as Canada, the media are complexly woven into the social and cultural fabric. The unique characteristics of Canada, such as its large land mass, a small population spread primarily in a long thin line along the border with the US, its regionalism, two official languages, and multiculturalism, have all laid their stamp on the structure and character of the Canadian media.

Rising from these circumstances, media both orient and animate social life. On one hand, they reflect the larger set of social and cultural values that frame our lives. On the other hand, we come to know our society—its institutions, organizations, relationships—and the ideas, values, beliefs, and art forms that comprise our culture largely through media and our engagement with them. Set in this context, some of the questions we have considered are: Does it matter who owns the media? How does advertising influence what we see in the media? What role do the media play in the economy? In globalization? In the construction of our tastes and desires and personal identity? Does it matter if Canadian media are dominated by foreign, mainly American, media products? Are television sitcoms, shows promoting celebrities, and other seemingly innocuous programs simply 'entertainment', or do they play other roles in our lives? In other words, whose or what interests do media serve, and what role do they play in creating and maintaining social relationships, particularly relations of wealth and power?

In considering these questions we have seen that communications technology is currently a key site of social change and struggle, as a range of social interests fight for position in the shifting social landscape. Some might shy away from words like 'social struggle'. Neo-liberal critics might prefer 'new, open, more competitive markets' or, as those of a more idealist bent might put it, a 'new chance for democracy'. But a social struggle it is. Because they are embedded in a larger set of social and political circumstances, changes in our media systems signal much broader social change. In the current environment, we are not merely throwing out a bunch of old machines and bringing in some new, sleek, quieter, more effective ones. Rather, we are setting in motion the revision and reformation of the jobs associated with those machines. We are encouraging the reorganization and perhaps the

re-establishment of associated organizations and institutions. We are opening up for reconsideration the foundations of public **policy** governing those activities and institutions. And we are recasting the dimensions of the economy, the location of labour, and the role of the consumer. In some ways, we also are recasting notions of citizenship.

Practices and institutions of mass communication are currently being undermined by the fragmentation of media markets and the rise of a sophisticated, publicly accessible transmission system—the internet. For example, internet television, radio, and podcasting can circumvent the state and commercial apparatus controlling mass broadcasting. Independent recording labels and bands who sell their music via the internet have been able to get around the control of the recording industry giants—the Sonys, the EMIs, the Universals, the Warners. Consider, as well, open-source software, which is a concerted effort on the part of digital labourers to undermine the centralized production

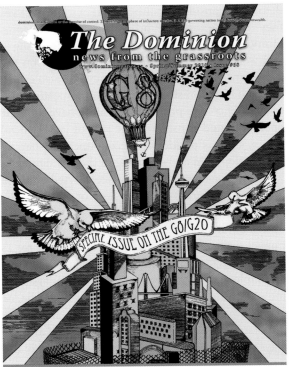

A cover of an issue of *The Dominion* from spring/summer 2010.

⠿ BOX 12.1   THE DOMINION

One of the most innovative online media organizations in Canada is the Dominion News Co-operative. Arising out of efforts to establish an alternative national newspaper, *The Dominion* newspaper has been published monthly in both print and online editions since May 2003 by a network of independent journalists across Canada. The Co-operative is federally incorporated and has three types of members—readers, journalists, and editors—each with their own interest and role in the organization. In an effort to promote a more hoizontal relationship between readers and the news organization, reader members are invited to participate in decision-making in terms of both developing story ideas and administrative issues. Journalist members are the main story contributors, and the editors do the administrative work for the organization. While some of the published material is contributed by volunteers, the Co-operative pays contributors wherever possible, in both cash and exchange. The or-ganizational goal is to set up local media co-operatives across the country that produce news at both the local and national levels. At present there are local media co-operatives in Halifax, Toronto, and Vancouver, and more are said to be on the way. Each of these organizations has its own website for local news as well. Despite the ongoing struggle of raising money and developing resources, the Co-operative has been steadily growing for over seven years.

and market domination by a handful of companies such as Microsoft. At the same time, news production, once generally the purview of large media corporations, is being taken up by bloggers, citizen journalists, and a host of small and financially tenuous news producers. Similarly, services like Facebook and Twitter offer an increasing range of new forms of social interaction. These are but a few examples in the growing range of interactive communications.

The foundations of this change from mass distribution of centrally produced media products to mass communication by and through an expanding range of people and institutions can be understood by recalling the definitions introduced in Chapter 2:

- Mass communication is the centralized production and dissemination of mass information and entertainment.
- Mass communication is also the decentralized production and wide accessibility of information and entertainment by means of public access to the internet.
- Mass communication is the interactive exchange of information (or messages or intelligence) to a number of recipients.

As we have seen, the latter two meanings of the term 'mass communication' are relatively new. The processes they describe are not new: decentralized, widespread production of content describes early newspapers and small literary magazines; widespread person-to-person communication by means of the postal system is very old; and the telegraph and telephone have been with us since 1846 and 1876, respectively. What is new in the case of widespread production of cultural products is vastly increased ease of access and interaction. The greater variation of media text, sound, and image, together with the capacity for immediate transmission, storage, and manipulation, greatly extends the capabilities of traditional media. The social challenge new media present is how they might be put to work in the broader **public interest** rather than the interest of large private corporations.

Communication and Democracy

Developments in communication media may interact with the fundamentals of democracy, particularly in terms of how ownership and control of media may enable or constrain the range of ideas and perspectives found in those media.

The history of this interaction can be traced back at least to the printing press in the mid-fifteenth century, which at first was controlled by the state or governing elite. But as the potential of communications technology for undermining and shifting the bases for political power became apparent, struggles over its control ensued. First, in the case of religion, Protestants such as Martin Luther sought to undermine the social control held by the Catholic Church in Europe in the sixteenth century. Later, governments sought to control the press and the flow of ideas that might stem from it. And in the twentieth century, the corporate control of media became a central question of concern. Should media organizations be free to use their potential power to advance their biases in favour of business, certain political parties, and certain policies, such as free commercial speech? Or should they act in a more constrained fashion, as self-aware institutions with a privileged position in society and, consequently, a responsibility to act for the social good of all, for a larger public interest? These questions exemplify how communication interacts with notions of democracy.

We saw in Chapter 3 that the social responsibility thesis, particularly in Canada, has provided a backdrop against which media performance in this regard might be measured—at least until the late twentieth century—not only in the press but also in the founding of broadcasting and specifically through the creation of a national public broadcasting service. Even more than the press, broadcasting was seen as a potential harbinger of greater social coherence, public expression, and responsibility in the media, offering enlightenment to individuals and encouraging the pursuit of democratic ideals. Drawing on Canada's tradition of government or public enterprise, the CBC gave the state the chance to finance a medium of communication on behalf of the people and the nation itself that would counterbalance the commercial media, which are often financed 80 per cent or more through advertising by the business sector.

At the international level, the efforts of UNESCO—beginning in the 1970s and carrying through to the 2000s—to extend the ideals of public communication through a new world order were founded on a similar idea of social responsibility. Dubbed 'fair flows of information' rather than 'free flows' (where the strongest in the market were free to dominate), the New World Information and Communications Order was championed by UNESCO in the 1980s as the possible impact and potential of new communications technology was becoming apparent. In large part, however, these efforts were squelched by the US and the UK when they pulled their support for UNESCO. The desire of these two countries to maintain their predominance as exporters of information, entertainment, and ideology to the world overrode any sense either had of social justice or of the value of celebrating diversity on a worldwide scale. Canadian policy, on the whole, was to a degree set against this kind of imperialism and, with the help of favourable government policy, we built up cultural industries capable of carrying Canadian creative content to Canadians in the face of the dominance of US media products in Canadian markets. More recently, given the ongoing advantages enjoyed by foreign, mainly American, media producers, pressures to re-regulate Canadian media in favour of more open markets are raising questions as to the continued ability of Canadian perspectives to maintain their place in Canadian media.

In the digital age, because of the opportunities new media present for expanding public participation in formerly cloistered venues of decision-making, the question is perhaps how quickly and extensively large corporations will move to consolidate their predominance and hence their control of changing media and media markets. This is already happening in terms of concentration of ownership of traditional media; the vertical integration of content producers, such as television networks and newspapers, with the telecommunications companies that provide access to the internet; and corporate consolidation and control of web-based media organizations such as Google, FaceBook, YouTube, and NetFlix. In the face of this ongoing consolidation, media policy becomes a particularly

FIGURE 12.1   YouTube Uploaders Related to Each of the Leaders in the Ontario 2007 Provincial Election

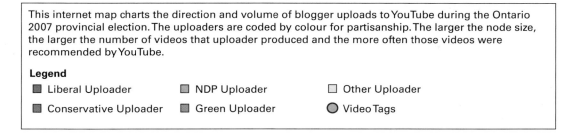

This internet map charts the direction and volume of blogger uploads to YouTube during the Ontario 2007 provincial election. The uploaders are coded by colour for partisanship. The larger the node size, the larger the number of videos that uploader produced and the more often those videos were recommended by YouTube.

Legend

- ■ Liberal Uploader
- ■ Conservative Uploader
- ■ NDP Uploader
- ■ Green Uploader
- □ Other Uploader
- ⬤ Video Tags

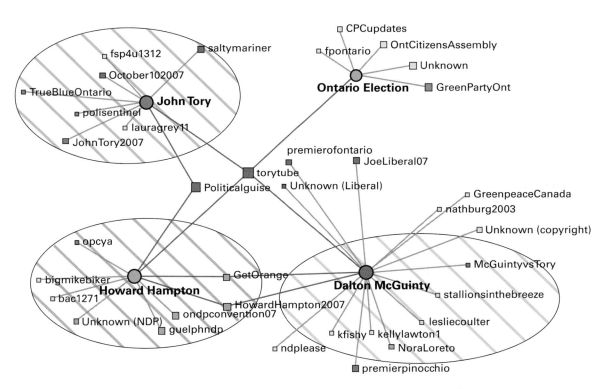

Source: Zachary Devereaux, Nexalogy Environics with data from the Ryerson Infoscape Centre for the Study of Social Media.

important vehicle for ensuring public participation and representation in both the development of new media and, perhaps more importantly, issues of governance in general. Meanwhile, as Figure 12.1 illustrates, new media such as YouTube are providing a whole new ground over which battles for votes are fought.

Content and Audiences

When we study communication, especially content, we are generally studying practices or processes of representation, that is, the act of putting ideas into words, paintings, sculpture, film, plays, television programs, or any other medium of communication. In this context, communication, or the making of meaning, is an active process that requires specific engagement at the levels of both encoding and decoding.

In the study of communication, the importance of a statement is not limited to whether it predicts events, can be refuted by others, or generates other interesting hypotheses—all standards used in science. What is interesting is how an act of communication re-presents or re-constructs something, and what gives a particular representation its force or its ability to persuade. Whatever makes a particular novel, painting, or film more popular or revered than another, or even a novel more powerful than a film, cannot be satisfactorily discussed by reference to the relative truth of each communication. Such media and individual works are discussed by communication scholars in terms of their rhetorical force or in terms of the nature or style of their representation.

Communication researchers use a range of analytical perspectives to wrestle content into some meaningful framework so that they might better understand how it is generated and how it frames our understanding of the world. Each theoretical perspective provides a particular point of view on understanding content. And different perspectives can be deployed as the situation demands. However, from a critical theoretical perspective, our task is not to understand variables affecting communication in an effort to attain seemingly perfect communication, as a mathematical model might lead us towards. Indeed, as we have seen, such an ideal is impossible, as everybody approaches the act of communication with different histories and assumptions. Rather, our task is to understand the social processes involved in the creation and transmission of meaning.

In approaching this task, we can focus, for example, on the agency of the individual producers: on the life and intent of the author and the dynamics involved in the publication of some sort of media text. Working from another direction, we can consider the ways in which larger social structures and processes impose limits and pressures on the media and media messages. For instance, like structuralists and semioticians, we can consider how both the organizational dimensions of a story and the signifiers deployed refer back to a larger set of social circumstances and ideas, how the sign system is itself part of a larger set of social processes and circumstances, or, following the lead of the post-structuralists, we can delve into the particularities of the meaning system that has been created by audience members in the act of interpretation.

Similarly, political economy offers insight into how politics and economics give form to media content. From this perspective, we can examine the production of content in terms of the interests of the producers and those paying for production, as well as the impact on content of government regulation, professional codes and values, and, especially, the profit motive. This perspective provides an account of why certain kinds of content are produced and disseminated and other kinds are not.

At quite a different level again, organizational analysis provides insight into how the characteristics of specific organizations—such as whether an organization is mandate-driven or profit-oriented—impinge on media content. We can also gain an understanding of content through analyzing the characteristics of particular media forms, such as news stories, ads, soap operas, documentaries, and music videos: how ads are constructed to draw us in; how news presentation privileges the news anchor or one of the protagonists in a story; how investigative television can present a convincing veracity where there may be none at all; and how soap operas captivate audience members in their presentations of fictional characters. Each of these perspectives contributes to the richness of our understanding of both referents (signifieds) and the symbols (signifiers) used to represent them.

With the overall understanding these various perspectives make possible, we can then extend our understanding of the nature and roles of the media in society. We can understand, for example, how the media are separate from, yet intrinsic to, society. We can appreciate the role they play in incorporating content from subcultures, making it part of the culture as a whole, or how they can reject as legitimate perfectly normal styles of living that are a part of any culture. We can also gain a sense of how autonomous the media are in their capacity to create their own realities, what their inherent shortcomings are, and, by extension, why we might need mechanisms that help ensure they cannot entrap us in a world of their own construction.

But the encoding or construction of media messages is only one side of the equation. Decoding, or how they are received, is another. Thus, we have also considered how audience members engage with the media—what they take from the media and how.

The first principle in understanding content–audience interaction is recognizing that it is an active process. Even when distracted, audience members are meaning-generating entities. That is, they filter information and entertainment through their own histories and understandings of the world, through established opinions and knowledge, and through situational variables—fatigue, their assessment of the presentation, other pressing concerns of the day, their anticipation of certain events, their position in the workforce, and so on. Similarly, the media are active generators of meaning insofar as they create programs targeted at certain audiences, with certain intensities, designed to engage audience members in a certain fashion.

Early studies of audiences perceived them as relatively passive, and the media as having direct effects on human behaviour and attitudes. While evidence for the idea that media have direct effects on people is controversial at best, the idea that they serve some sort of agenda-setting function, or that they work to cultivate particular conceptions or attitudes, has gained some credibility among media researchers. From this perspective, media don't so much tell people 'what to think' as they do 'what to think about.' Another perspective drawn from early effects research that we considered was uses and gratifications research, which analyzes the uses to which audience members put media content and the satisfaction and reward audience members feel they derive from media content.

Working from a different starting point, we also considered theories that focus on the ways that the media position audiences to reproduce dominant social ideas and values. For instance, Marxist perspectives on media illustrate how they often serve to promote the ideas and values associated with capitalism, while the Frankfurt School's examination of the industrialization of the production of information and entertainment illustrates how economics structures cultural form in general.

In the face of these critiques, researchers of British cultural studies strove to better understand the complexity of the dynamics between media and audiences. Working with youth subcultures and social movements, their emphasis was on audience members as active agents and the different ways different groups of people engaged with media content. Working from yet another direction, feminist research illustrates how media and practices of communication contribute to social inequalities in terms of sex and gender.

Industry-based research approaches audiences from another direction, as commodities to be sold to advertisers. Such a perspective emphasizes quite different variables. At a first level, the number of people in the audience is of central importance. Then come their age, education, gender, income level, location, and so forth, followed by a consideration of how these elements are indicative of certain characteristics such as specific attitudes, consumption patterns of particular products, and the time they spend listening, reading, and/or watching. Such information is valuable for the business of buying, selling, renting, and accessing audiences. It is also valuable in understanding general patterns in society.

How the media choose to engage audiences and how audiences engage the media are diverse, and the resulting interaction creates many social issues. The various starting points and perspectives we use to gain insight into what audiences make of content reflect that diversity. In simple terms, media content, such as hate speech, may serve as an igniting spark for anti-social behaviour—a good reason for us to be concerned about content generation and how media might contribute to anti-social behaviour. But media content may also inspire lifelong ambition, grand humanitarian gestures, respect for individual freedom, social plurality, cultural values, and the building of community. This positive spark is even more important to understand.

As interactive public communication systems become more common in society, it is increasingly important to understand how media systems and content frame and animate social life.

The Social Dimensions of Media and Communication

Having acquired some understanding of the character and history of media, as well as some of the key perspectives on their content and interaction with audiences, we can turn to some of the larger social dimensions of media and communications (1) policy, or, more comprehensively speaking, law and policy; (2) ownership and control of communication institutions; (3) the role and actions of professionals; and (4) information and communication technology and globalization.

Policy

Policy creates a framework for how these factors play themselves out. It provides a set of rules and regulations governing the way information and media products are created and consumed. For instance, copyright legislation works to develop markets for media products and other forms of intellectual property. Privacy legislation works to protect the rights of individuals (see Box 12.2). Advertising regulations frame the kinds of claims advertisers can make and the kinds of products they may advertise. Libel laws structure the way journalists and news organizations operate. And income tax policies encourage advertisers to spend their ad dollars with Canadian media outlets and ensure Canadian ownership of newspapers.

At a more basic level, policy also creates opportunities for Canadian media producers. As we have seen, the market is itself a form of regulation, and left to its own devices favours some interests over others. For instance, because of the economies of scale involved, it is simply much cheaper for broadcasters to buy foreign programming than it is to produce their own. Thus, particularly in English Canada, without Canadian-content regulations there would be even more US programming on television than there is now. Similarly, as we have seen, prior to the enactment of content regulations for radio in the 1970s, less than 5 per cent of the music

❖ BOX 12.2 PRIVACY: KEEPING OUR PRIVATE LIVES PRIVATE

As our lives become increasingly mediated by electronic technologies, information regarding our activities is being monitored and stored in massive databases. Every time you visit a medical facility, fill out an application, use a credit or debit card, give out your social insurance number, or even sit down at a computer work station, the chances are that information about that activity is being monitored and recorded. These records reveal much about ourselves and are often used by organizations to exact economic and political control over our lives.

Sometimes breaches in privacy can take on particularly sinister tones. Take, for instance, the case of Sean Bruyea, a Gulf War veteran and leading advocate for wounded veterans and their families. A story in the Toronto Star on 18 November 2010 reported that Bruyea launched a lawsuit against the government of Canada after learning that sensitive medical documents were accessed and passed around 'by hundreds of federal bureaucrats, including policy-makers', in an effort to discredit him and his lobbying efforts. The story detailed how 'Bruyea alleged bureaucrats wanted to use his medical records, particularly psychiatric reports, to "falsely portray me and my advocacy to help other veterans as merely a manifestation of an unstable mind."' Canada's privacy commissioner, Jennifer Stoddart, had 'ruled that Bruyea's case was "alarming" and the treatment of his personal information was "entirely inappropriate."' The lawsuit resulted in a settlement and apology from Veterans Affairs Minister Jean-Pierre Blackburn (Cheadle, 2010).

At a time when our every on-line move can be monitored and information about us is almost always stored electronically, keeping our private lives private requires particular vigilance.

played on radio stations was Canadian. This was not because Canadians did not make good music. Rather, because of the marketing and publicity spilling over from American markets into Canada, as well as other factors, it was simply more lucrative for Canadian radio owners to use American music. By the same token, there is not the same market in the US for Canadian cultural materials as there is in Canada for American products. Again, this is not because Canadian products are somehow of inferior quality but the result of simple economics. American producers create more than enough product to supply demand in their home market and—due to economies of scale—it is cheaper to use that product than purchase Canadian works. These economics necessitate some form of regulation if Canadian media products are going to find 'space on the shelves' in their home markets. The situation is somewhat different in Quebec, where a range of cultural factors allow homegrown products to compete with their foreign counterparts.

In short, public policy shapes the ground—particularly the economic ground—on which media products are created and, in turn, influences the character of those products and the ways they represent the world.

Ownership

Ownership has been a long-standing concern in Canadian media policy as forms of **ownership** and the interests of owners are seen to have significant effects on the content and character of media. In the face of cheap US media products, for decades Canadian ownership and content regulations have been used to create an economics of Canadian production and to prevent Canadian media companies and markets from becoming simple extensions of their American cousins. In the broadcasting, cable, and telecommunications industries, legislation imposes limits on foreign ownership. In the newspaper industry, tax policy ensures that newspapers stay in Canadian hands.

At the same time, however, as we saw in Chapter 7, a number of public inquiries have voiced concern about how the economic forces underlying private ownership lead to escalating concentration of ownership and a narrowing range of voices and perspectives in the media. Consequently, in Canada issues of ownership have been framed by various government regulations that, on one hand, have tried to keep the ownership of Canadian media in Canadian hands, and, on the other, have wrestled with the drawbacks and supposed benefits of large, privately owned media companies. As a result, no media industry in Canada is governed exclusively by **free-market** economics; the industries are governed by a panoply of regulations and, in some cases, reflect a complex mixture of public and private enterprise.

The central difference between public and private forms of ownership pertains to the mandate or purposes that guide their operations. In contradistinction to privately owned media that foreground the profit motive, public and community media are mandated to serve broad social purposes. For instance, as laid out in the 1991 Broadcasting Act, Section 3.1(l), the CBC is to 'provide radio and television services incorporating a wide range of programming that informs, enlightens and entertains'. Just as the Corporation did in the development of television, in the face of shifting technologies today the CBC has moved to develop a range of web-based services. Chief among these are an increasing number of television programs that can be downloaded from its website (www.cbc.ca) and CBC Radio 3, an internet-based radio service devoted to youth and new and emerging Canadian music. In November 2010, CBC Radio 3 had over 108,000 tracks by more than 24,000 artists archived on its website.

Community media also are expected to fulfill social goals. For instance, while the mandate of community television stations is not enunciated in legislation, in its 2010 Community Television Policy the CRTC specifies that 'the role of the community (television) channel should be primarily of a public service nature, facilitating self-expression through free and open access by members of the community' (CRTC, 2010a). Similarly, but set at the organizational level, the Statement of Principles of the National Campus and Community Radio Association/Association Nationale des Radios

Étudiantes et Communautaires (NCRA/ANREC), which represents 40 campus and community stations across the country, notes 'that mainstream media fails to recognize or in many instances reinforces social and economic inequities that oppress women and minority groups of our society' and commits members to 'providing alternative radio to an audience that is recognized as being diverse in ethnicity, culture, gender, sexual orientation, age, and physical and mental ability' (NCRA, 1987).

Still, private ownership is the dominant ownership form within the media system and, in the face of ongoing pressure to tie the expansion of Canadian media to the profit motive, to what degree a larger set of public purposes might be maintained within the system is in question.

One of the central features of Canadian media policy has been to protect the revenues of Canadian media producers in order to ensure that they are profitable enough to invest in production. Yet, as we have seen, particularly in the broadcasting sector, it has always been a struggle to get the big private corporations to invest in quality Canadian programs, and changes in technology are working to narrow the range of private corporations at work within the Canadian media system.

With the digitization of information, communication systems that were once capable of carrying only one type of message can now carry a range of signals. Telephone, cable, and satellite systems all can be used to transmit television, telephone, and computer data. Webcasting is poised to supplant traditional television and radio broadcasting, and maybe traditional newspaper and periodical delivery as well. And information-based products, like news and advertising, once destined for one medium, are now tailored for use across a range of media. Spurred by this technological convergence, companies in what were once separate industries, like newspapers and television or cable television and telecommunication, are vying to break into each others' markets and fuelling corporate convergence—in other words, concentration of ownership.

With companies trying to capture cost savings by forging new economies of scale and scope, recent trends towards concentration of ownership have raised particular concerns. Some of the important 'synergies'—as the efficiencies gleaned from consolidation are sometimes called—sought by these corporations are: reduced labour requirements; cross-promotion of media products; larger and more flexible advertising markets; the 'repurposing' of content created for use in one medium for use in another; the integration of executive and administrative functions; and vastly increased barriers to entry for would-be competitors. Consequently, concentration is seen as narrowing the range of perspectives and distinct voices available in the media, while new editorial policies and sanctions evolving through these changes are raising fears for editorial independence.

Professionalism

Professionalism governs communications and cultural production in its own way. Cultural producers are not, strictly speaking, 'professionals' in the same manner that lawyers and doctors are. Law and medicine require accredited formal training, permission to practise from recognized licensing bodies, and are subject to their own specialized regulatory authorities. But cultural producers nonetheless derive a sense of professionalism from their specialized skills, their practice-specific codes of ethics, recognized sets of qualitative conventions, and, above all, the conviction that their work is an essential contribution to culture in the fullest sense of the term. Like other kinds of professionals, cultural producers owe some allegiance to their employer or their client and they remain subject to laws particular to the communications field, such as those pertaining to libel, copyright, privacy, and access to information. But their professionalism means that cultural producers are especially responsible to uphold and advance the recognized standards of their practice and to earn the respect of their peers.

Cultural producers' sense of professionalism is tied very closely to the Enlightenment ideals of freedom of speech, freedom of expression, and freedom of the press, of questioning and challenging received wisdom and other forms of authority. They promote the notion that mass communication, in all its manifestations, renders society democratic. While we might attribute these ideals most readily to journalists, all cultural producers can make the claim that their communicative activities serve the cultural, political, social, and/or economic goals of society.

This sense of professionalism, though, is being eroded. Employers are increasingly treating cultural producers simply as workers like any others—replaceable parts in the assembly line of production, subject to layoffs and buyouts, relegated to contract work, compelled to emphasize quantitative efficiencies over qualitative merits. Newsrooms are shrinking across all platforms, television dramas share prime time with so-called reality formats, radio DJs are replaced by computerized music programming, and freelance magazine writers work for the same rates they were paid 30 years ago. The government policies that promote cultural production in Canada, as we described in Chapters 7 and 8, do little to protect cultural producers within their own industries. In addition, a veritable army of amateurs has entered the field to compete with the pros. More and more people have ready access to sophisticated communications technologies and software applications with which to make their own cultural statements—photographs, videos, texts, music—and they have easy access to distribution networks through the internet. Sites like YouTube render everyone a cultural producer, further undermining the professional status of those who seek to make their living in the cultural industries.

This helps to explain why those making their living from cultural production resent amateur

Source: Scott Greene, Channel Babel, oil on canvas, 1998. Courtesy of the artist and Catherine Clark Gallery, San Francisco, Calif., USA

Communication pervades our lives and communication media pervade modern society. The power of both the worldwide transmission of messages and the transformation that digital communication offers is the foundation for the remaking/reordering of society.

production and seek to defend their status. In a similar vein, labour organizations work at the negotiating table to maintain strict boundaries between in-house and contract work, professional associations continue to grant awards for qualitative achievements, and post-secondary film, television, journalism, photography, and creative writing programs insist on professional standards and ethical protocols.

Information and Communications Technology and Globalization

Technology does not exist in a vacuum or as a social force on its own. While different theoretical perspectives on technology afford both its developers and adopters differing levels of agency, technology is the product of a complex set of political, economic, and social forces that work to shape and configure its development. In this context, policy also helps to set the context for technology. Whether in terms of government aid for research and development, licensing that allows organizations to offer particular technological services (e.g., cellphones and cable or satellite TV), tax incentives that encourage individuals or organizations to adopt particular technologies, or ownership policies, policy can play a number of important roles in technological development. In communication, policy issues such as who can use what technology for what purpose, who can control that technology, and how that control can be exploited are critical.

Because technology encompasses machines, techniques, and social institutions, it has a substantial impact on the structure and functioning of society—not as a positive agent but, like

⁂ BOX 12.3 KONDRATIEV WAVES: TRACKING TECHNOLOGICAL CHANGE

Nikolai Kondratiev hypothesized that economies expand and contract with the introduction of new technologies. According to this theory the waves or cycles last approximately 50 years and there have been five such waves since about 1800, based on: (1) steam power; (2) the railway; (3) electrical and chemical engineering; (4) petrochemicals and automobiles; and (5) the current cycle, information technology, with its basis on the microchip and digitization.

FIGURE 12.2 Kondratiev Wave

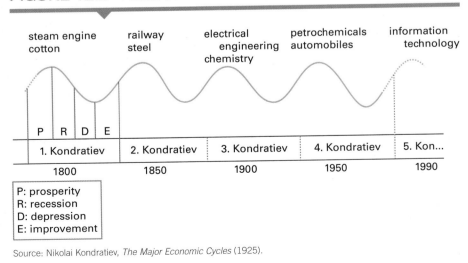

P: prosperity
R: recession
D: depression
E: improvement

Source: Nikolai Kondratiev, *The Major Economic Cycles* (1925).

communication itself, as a transformative agent, an agent of change that may bring both negative and positive consequences. And while we often think of information and communications technology (ICT) in terms of content, such as film, video, television, or music, one of the most dramatic changes it might be implicated in is a shift in the locus of control: the greater the ability to communicate, the further the control system can be from the phenomenon being controlled. As the history of communication illustrates, communication developments have often led to increased centralization of control. Whether in terms of the centralization of political control, as in the case of the railway and communications technology enabling early Canadian governments to exert east–west control over the northern territory of North America; or in the case of the centralization of economic control, as today's transnational corporations harness information technology to co-ordinate supply and demand in global markets (media markets and others), ICT is often a key vehicle for dealing with problems of spatialization.

ICTs are not the first set of technologies that have been seen as reshaping society (see Box 12.4). But the social changes arising from the widespread implementation of ICTs are far-reaching, and they are central to the industrial restructuring taking place both at home and abroad.

While the global economy is not a new development, and there has been strong global trade for over 500 years, since the mid-1970s, economic recession and the lure of cheap labour have fuelled international trade agreements and the investment of manufacturing capital in places like Southeast Asia, China, northern Mexico, and the American Sunbelt. To meet this competition, companies remaining in traditional industrial centres restructured, reducing staff and adopting labour-saving technologies.

Through facilitating the movement of capital and goods, ICTs have been important in facilitating this shift in labour processes. ICT provides a vital link between the newly industrialized countries where these goods are now produced and the markets in old industrialized

centres, such as North America and Western Europe, where they are consumed. ICT also has been central to the reorganization of industry in these old industrial centres, where it has been used to centralize control over operations, amalgamate responsibilities and functions, and more closely monitor and co-ordinate employees as companies have restructured to confront new global competitors.

As the information economy has taken form, ever-growing types of information commodities have been created, both in terms of products and services. For instance, changes in copyright legislation provide legal sanctions against the unauthorized copying of computer software, video and sound recordings, television programs, and other forms of data, and these changes have been instrumental in developing and expanding multi-million dollar markets for these products. Similarly, sanctions against photocopying for other than personal use and royalties on public photocopiers and blank tapes have created new revenue streams for creators. Twenty-five years ago, professors often copied readings and other course materials and handed them out to students for the cost of the copying. Today such behaviour might be subject to heavy fines or even imprisonment. The television universe available via cable, satellite, and the internet also has expanded dramatically, as has the cost. Video games have become big business. Education, a necessarily information-based activity, has become increasingly commercialized and responsible to market forces. The internet has given rise to an expanding range of new web-based businesses and services, and access to the internet itself has become an increasingly costly service. With a whole new set of mobile telecommunications and internet-based services and products soon to hit the market, the information economy is proceeding apace.

Issues and Policy Trends

Amid the shifting field of communication, various new issues are rising and old concerns are taking new form. Besides issues of ownership and foreign

❖ BOX 12.4   TWO CRITICAL OWNERSHIP ISSUES

As this book goes to press, two central ownership issues are on the public policy agenda. One deals with concentration of ownership, the other with foreign ownership.

In light of escalating concentration of ownership between broadcast distribution undertakings and broadcast producers, the CRTC has voiced concern regarding the possible impacts of vertical integration on the range and distribution of television programming within the system.

In February 2010, Shaw Communications, one of the country's largest cable and telecommunications providers, announced that it was buying CanWest Global, Canada's second-largest private television network. Then, in September of that year, Bell Canada, the country's largest telephone company and satellite broadcaster, announced it was buying CTV, the country's largest private television network. These deals give Shaw and Bell control over some of the largest producers and distributors of television programming in the country and raise the spectre that they might use their ownership of distribution networks to favour their own TV channels, making it difficult for their competitors to reach audiences.

In response to this concern, the CRTC announced that it would hold a hearing in May 2011 to investigate possible problems in this regard (CRTC, 2010b). How this issue plays out could have important implications for the range of programming available in the system in the future.

Increasing foreign ownership of Canadian media is also a developing issue. The Conservative government and its allies argue that increasing foreign ownership in the telecommunications sector will increase investment in the industry and result in lower mobile telephone prices and better services. Critics, however, point out a number of problems with this plan. First, given the growing cross-media ownership between telecommunications and broadcasting companies, allowing foreign ownership of telecommunications will inevitably lead to foreign ownership of broadcasting and a decline in investment in Canadian media production. Second, they argue that there is no incentive for foreign companies to invest in providing services in areas that present little return, such as in rural communities and the Far North—the areas most in need of investment to bridge digital divides. And third, there is concern that regulators are less able to exert control over foreign-owned companies than over their domestic counterparts. How this issue plays out could affect Canadian control over the long-term development of both the telecommunications and broadcasting fields.

control (Box 12.4), the CRTC is faced with trying to improve the coherence of the regulatory framework as convergence accelerates, and there are discussions around merging the Broadcasting and Telecommunications Acts. A concern here is what might happen to the cultural objectives of broadcasting should such a merger take place. Protecting access to the internet is also an ongoing concern, and net neutrality, throttling, and the possibility of metered billing for internet usage are other ongoing issues with the CRTC. To contend with ongoing ownership consolidation and rapid technological change, the CRTC is also asking Parliament for greater powers, particularly in terms of being able to issue fines to companies that do not comply with regulations. While the Commission has the power

to suspend an intransigent company's licence, it is loath to do so as such action might cause serious problems for the customers of those companies if they were unexpectedly shut down. Consequently, the CRTC is looking for more flexible means of discipline.

At a larger level, the federal government is also wrestling with developing a digital policy (see Box 12.5) and new copyright legislation. Updating the Copyright Act has proven particularly vexing in terms of balancing the rights of large corporate producers, performers, consumers, small producers, and educators. How many electronic copies should someone purchasing a song, film, book, or some other kind of information product be allowed to make? Who should he/she be allowed to share copies with? If someone is producing a song or video, to what degree, if any, might they incorporate elements of a previous work? To what degree might a video or some other kind of work be used in class or for some other educational purpose without having to pay a copyright fee? To what degree might images and quotes from other works be used in textbooks such as this one? The role of government is to try to balance competing interests, but these are not easy questions to address in regulation. After all, each of the stakeholders has a different perspective and a different interest.

At another level, **digital divides** at the local, regional, national, and global levels threaten to split the information society into a world of 'haves' and 'have-nots'. Without computers and high-speed access to the internet, or the knowledge of how to use these technologies effectively, many people are excluded from the political, economic, and social

benefits enabled by these technologies. As acquiring information increasingly hinges on the ability to pay for it, it is difficult for schools, universities, and public libraries to keep up with the rising cost. Consequently, the quality of education and general availability of information are being reduced and those people and organizations that cannot pay for it are in danger of being deprived of these crucial communications resources.

There are also many places on earth outside of the wired world and, thereby, outside the reach of information technology. In Canada, rural areas with small populations such as the prairies and the North don't present the economies of scale to make it profitable for large corporations to invest in communications infrastructure and supplying services. Hence, such areas sometimes are left outside of the digital world. Similarly, in many areas of the global South, people simply cannot

---

⋗ BOX 12.5   TOWARDS A CANADIAN DIGITAL POLICY?

Since the early 1970s, the federal government has been commissioning studies and reports focused on creating policy to spur the development of the 'information society' (Information Highway Advisory Council, 1997). One of the most recent efforts in this regard is the 2010 Standing Senate Committee on Transportation and Communication's Plan for a Digital Canada. Among the Committee's recommendations are:

- Canada should present a strategy for an inclusive digital society.
- Canada, in conjunction with the presentation of a strategy for an inclusive digital society, should appoint a Minister for Digital Policy.
- The government in its digital strategy should define universal as 100 per cent of its citizens.
- The government should use all the proceeds from spectrum auctions to provide high-speed internet (broadband) access for rural and remote areas.
- The Minister for Digital Policy and other federal ministers should work with their provincial counterparts to develop a comprehensive digital

literacy program that can become an integral part of the education system.
- The government should pursue open-access policies with respect to telecommunications infrastructure as a means of sustaining or improving competition in the telecommunications sector.
- The government should change the requirement for current spectrum licence-holders to spend 2 per cent of revenue on research and development and have the money redirected for the deployment of broadband to areas currently unserved.
- Industry Canada should promote wireless service in currently unserved or under-served areas.
- Industry Canada, in establishing policies to allocate and price spectrum, should consider pricing regimes in other countries, especially those in the United States.

The full report can be seen at: www.planpouruncanadanumerique.com/index.php?option=com_content&view=article&id=1&Itemid=10&lang=en.

Source: The Standing Committee on Transport and Communications (2010). *Plan for a Digital Canada, Senate of Canada.*

afford to buy into the communications transformation taking place.

Privacy, too, is of rising concern. As social life is increasingly mediated by ICT, information about our activities is being monitored and collected by numerous organizations and government agencies. The unauthorized use of this information threatens our privacy in a number of ways. In the workplace, ICT can be used to monitor email and telephone conversations, or to count keystrokes and attempt to measure the volume of work undertaken by employees. (Charles Frederick Taylor, the originator of scientific management in the workplace in the early twentieth century, would be pleased!) Insurance companies purchase health and accident records in an attempt to assess the potential risk of applicants, sometimes denying coverage on this basis. Law enforcement agencies are considering ways to use the information contained in databases to identify potential criminal suspects. And in the United States, there is ongoing debate between law enforcement agencies and public interest groups over the right of government agencies to monitor electronic conversations and data flow.

These concerns are compounded by the fact that both personal information and important social, legal, and economic information is often stored and processed outside of the country. Private corporations, governments, universities, libraries, and the legal and engineering professions all sometimes use data services and networks outside of Canada to process and store personal tax, credit, and medical data, as well as educational materials and information on natural resources and other matters of national import. Because this transborder data flow places the information outside of the reach of national laws and regulation, it raises a host of issues for both Canadian sovereignty and the economy, and leaves Canadians vulnerable to a host of potential problems including trade sanctions, bankruptcies, and theft.

Concern over these infringements on personal privacy centres on the issue of self-determination. As private corporations and governments increase their abilities to monitor and control individual action, personal freedom is reduced to a series of choices that are predetermined by forces outside of the individual's knowledge and control. However, as the 2010 debate over Statistics Canada's long-form census illustrates, comprehensive information about the population as a whole is also critical to intelligent social planning and efficient government (*The Globe and Mail*, 2010). Consequently, information collection and tracking is a double-edged sword.

Shifting Economic Currents

Is the unfettered market the best way to produce and consume social resources? As a society we don't seem to think so in terms of things like health care, education, and the environment. In fact, leaving such important social resources to a simple calculus of commercialism would necessarily lead to greater social inequity and environmental devastation as the market sorted between the services and activities that were the most profitable and those people that could afford to pay to access them. In other words, particularly in terms of education and health care, we would end up with fewer options, and fewer people being able to access them—in short, greater ignorance and illness. In terms of the environment, such a rationale would allow natural resources to be put to the purposes commanding the highest price, with little regard to the interests of the people or other flora and fauna that depend on the natural world for their survival. Global warming and the wholesale devastation of forests, fish, and other wildlife species are clear evidence of where this path leads.

By the same token, in the context of ICT and the media it encompasses, should our perspectives, knowledge, and understandings of the world be subject to a purely economic rationale? Historically, the Canadian public and policy-makers have answered with a resounding 'No.' For over a century, governments and others have recognized the need for regulation if Canadians are to enjoy fair and affordable access to communications services and media and cultural content that represents the breadth of Canadian perspectives. Common-carriage regulation in telecommunications, the founding of the CBC, ownership regulations, Canadian content regulations, production funds, and numerous other regulatory initiatives have been put into place to help ensure these purposes are met.

Yet over the last several decades a pattern has emerged of cutting back on various forms of media regulation in favour of regulation by market forces alone. Cuts to the CBC's budget, a gradual loosening of ownership regulations, including those governing foreign ownership and concentration, a winnowing of support for community and Aboriginal broadcasting, and the CRTC's reluctance to regulate the internet all exemplify this trend.

Although the internet is often touted as the solution to the traditional problems plaguing our media systems, left to simple market economics, the internet holds little promise for increasing the range of media products and perspectives available to us. In terms of film and television products, the internet does nothing to address the economic advantages conferred by economies of scale, and just as our television, movie, and computer screens are now dominated by American products, so, too, will they probably continue to be as the internet takes on a greater role in the distribution of such products. Although bloggers, citizen journalists, and a number of new web-based news sites seem to have increased the range of news available to us, quality news production requires a high degree of knowledge and skill on the part of the people producing it and, because of this expense, most internet news sites act as aggregators rather than producers of original news reports. Bloggers offer little more than opinions gleaned from professionally produced news. At the same time, and perhaps most importantly, cross-media companies that count newspapers, broadcast, and web-based media among their holdings have business strategies that hinge upon 're-purposing' media content generated for use in one medium for use in another. Consequently, whichever medium we turn to for news, the content is virtually the same.

Compounding these problems is the fact that, as commodities, information and cultural products have quite different economic characteristics than

other products such as soap, clothes, or cars. As Canadian lawyer Peter Grant and journalist Chris Wood point out in their book, *Blockbusters and Trade Wars* (2004), laws fundamental to economic thinking do not apply in the same way to information and cultural production. Rather, information and cultural products display a number of anomalies, or different economic characteristics from other types of commodities.

Anomaly 1: Cultural products such as TV programs, movies, and music are not consumed in the sense that they are not destroyed in our use of them. Your listening to music does not deprive the next person from listening to the same music on the same CD. The market for cultural products behaves differently from normal commodities markets.

Anomaly 2: The relationship between first-copy costs and run-on costs is far more dramatically different in cultural production than in the production of other commodities. For it to be the same, each single creation of a CD would require an artist to record anew. Similarly, for normal economic laws to hold, concerts-goers would each suck out a little of the sound so that with a maximum audience there would be no sound left over. For books, the implications of consumption would be that as each page was read (perhaps not by the first, but let's say by the fiftieth reader) the print would disappear and by the end, the book would collapse into dust. In short, while first-copy costs are enormous for cultural products, subsequent copy costs are often negligible—less than $1 for a CD; about 17 cents for a download—and in many cases the copy can be used again and again. Compare that dynamic to theatrical performances where the players must gather each night to put on the play. Or consider the creation of clothing where design costs are minimal and material and labour costs are fairly constant.

Anomaly 3: Consumption patterns of cultural products and services are also different. Certain cultural products—blockbusters—command a major share of the market while others don't come close to earning back their costs of creation. And reduced pricing is rarely successful in persuading a person to watch an unpopular movie, read a bad book, or listen to a dull, tedious piece of music.

Anomaly 4: Most often, hidden consumer subsidies in the form of advertising or grants (by governments or those with a vested interest) make cultural commodities 'free' (e.g., TV) or available at a much lower price than their cost of production (e.g., magazines, newspapers). Indeed, those with a vested interest can buy their way into cultural products—product placement in movies—so that the cultural consumer inadvertently consumes images that cause him or her to associate a product with a certain social dynamic—e.g., Apple laptops and powerful people.

Anomaly 5: There is a lack of predictability of appeal of cultural goods that is captured by Grant and Wood with the phrases 'Nobody knows' (whether a cultural product will succeed in the marketplace) and 'All hits are flukes.' With normal commodities, most supplies manage to capture some share of the market at some price.

The above anomalies in cultural product markets are significant. They call into question the appropriateness of applying standard economic theory to cultural products. Yet agencies such as the World Bank proceed apace. The World Bank regularly commissions textbooks from Britain and France for African countries that are the former colonies of those nations. (It might, alternatively, help build a publishing industry by restricting the eligibility of bidders to African countries or to firms within a single nation.) Such World Bank policies strengthen powerful entertainment- and information-exporting nations (and multinational companies) while jeopardizing the cultural integrity of less strong nations.

One other particularly important anomaly rests on the fact that information is not value-neutral. Economic analysis generally assumes that similar commodities are substitutable for one another. For instance, all things being equal, a stove from the United States is seen to be as good as one from Peru; or clothes made in China are as good as those made in Montreal. While there are a number of problems with this assumption, a key concern when applying this idea to media and information products is that the information such products contain is not value-neutral. As we have seen, Canadians often seem to know more about American politics, history, and culture than about their own. In this regard, media and information products reflect particular ideas and attitudes, and those ideas provide specific ways of approaching and thinking about the world. For instance, do imported educational materials incorporate Canadian values of diversity, tolerance, and common purpose, or are they underwritten by notions of competitive individualism that place the interests of the individual over the community at large? Do reports and studies authored elsewhere in the world and used by Canadian governments and industry to formulate policy and investment decisions take into account local and/or national environmental and community concerns or are they simply based on abstract global economics? As the lives of Canadians are spun in an ever-growing global web of dependencies, it is in our interest to consider carefully how media and information products are shaping our understanding of the world. The degree to which distinctive Canadian ideas and values are nurtured and carried into the future may, at least in part, hinge on the future of media regulation and its ability to keep those ideas circulating in our media.

The Long Tail

This is not to say that with the widespread application of ICT the economics of media production are not changing. One change in the way such products are thought of is the 'long tail' phenomenon, popularized by Chris Anderson, editor-in-chief of *Wired* magazine. Following a groundswell of interest in an article in *Wired* called 'The Long Tail', Anderson wrote a book with the same title. The book begins with a bow in the direction of blockbuster hits, which, as Anderson points out, are the foundation of massive media and entertainment industries. Hits rule, he says, and thus the factors that are fundamental to making hits also rule: centralized production, celebrities, massive production budgets, massive marketing campaigns, restricted distribution systems, and formulas that attract the main entertainment-consuming public. Everyone makes money when a hit comes along. An author such as J.K. Rowling makes a substantial amount of money with each new title in the Harry Potter series; and sharing in the economic windfall are her agent, her publishers around the world, the designers, the editors, the warehouse staff, the booksellers, the movie makers, the lawyers who draw up the movie rights, toy rights, and product rights, the actors, the theatres, in fact, everyone right down to the babysitter who fills in because the usual babysitter must see the latest movie.

So lucrative are hits that the entire industry is hooked on finding the next blockbuster. Potential sales channel and determine retail opportunities, whether space on a bookshelf, music store shelf, or magazine rack, screen time in a movie theatre, or a time slot or playlist on television or radio. To gain exposure, a product must fit an established category that sells. In books, such categories are mysteries, biography, romance, politics, self-help; on TV they are drama, reality TV, news, current events, game shows, and sports. Once comfortably slotted into a consumer category, the product must perform in comparison with established norms: it must sell at a certain pace from the opening days of its availability or else it vanishes unsold from the mainstream marketplace.

Cultural markets work in such a manner because the distribution and display system is both costly and highly competitive. Hits are the high flyers, but for the normal to slow sellers, it is a dog-eat-dog world; sales monitored week by week tell the tale of what products will survive and which will vanish. Moreover, the distribution/display system ends up being highly restrictive in the categories it is willing to display. For example, where the categories of music on display in a music store might be restricted to top 40, alternative, blues, classical, country, easy listening, electronic, folk, hip-hop, jazz, Latin, metal, pop/rock urban, and rhythm & blues, clearly this does not exhaust the world of music. Evidence comes from iTunes, where the 'electronic' category is subcategorized into ambient, breakbeat/breaks, dance, down tempo, drum 'n' bass, electronic cover songs, electronica, experimental, game soundtracks, garage, house, industrial electronic, techno, and trance. And even further, 'techno' is subcategorized into acid, Detroit, electro, gabby, happy hardcore, IDM, intelligent techno, and rave/old skool.

Anderson's point is that the distribution/display costs are much more forgiving in the online world. All one does is upload a piece of music with appropriate marketing enthusiasm and it can stay available at a very low cost, selling a few copies each year. This low-access cost accounts for the ability of US universities to make standard texts (e.g., Shakespeare's plays) or highly valued but relatively inaccessible archives publicly available at no charge.

Fine and dandy, you might think, but will anyone pay attention to material that does not benefit from vast promotion budgets? As it turns out, the answer is yes, and that is the 'Long Tail'. Figure 12.3 is taken from an online essay of Anderson's published under a Creative Commons licence (www.change this.com/manifesto/show/10.LongTail). It depicts a typical 'Long Tail' distribution and describes the different sales and different availability at Wal-Mart and Rhapsody: Wal-Mart carries 39,000 titles, Rhapsody well over 200,000. At the left-hand side of the graph are the hits and other bestsellers, with the vertical axis representing the number or frequency of sales. Moving to the right we see the pattern of sales for those titles that are not bestsellers. As the curve suggests, most surprisingly, a very high percentage of the products available are accessed by consumers. Similar data patterns are reported by Ecast, a digital jukebox company. At one point the company noted that 98 per cent of the 10,000 albums that were available sold at least one track every three months. In other words, when a

FIGURE 12.3   Anatomy of the Long Tail

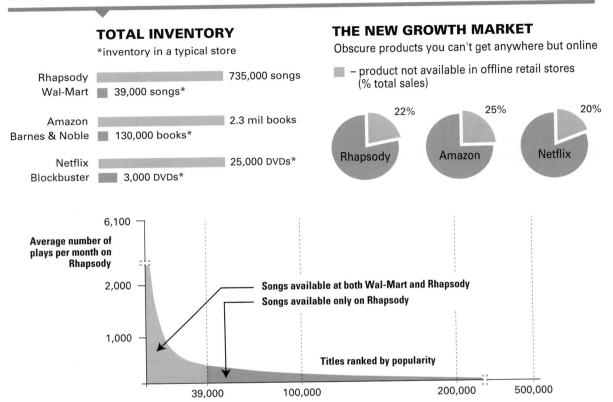

Online services carry far more inventory than traditional retailers. Rhapsody, for example, offers 19 times as many songs as Wal-Mart's stock of 39,000 tunes. The appetite for Rhapsody's more obscure tunes (charted in dark blue) makes up the so-called Long Tail. Meanwhile, even as consumers flock to mainstream books, music, and films (bottom), there is a real demand for niche fare found only online.

vendor has very low display/distribution costs, and item costs are low but access is easy, consumers choose widely rather than focusing their choices solely on hits. The same pattern is reported by Apple with its iTunes service.

Most heartening for a person who values diversity and variety, the pie graphs in Figure 12.3 indicate that the sales of music not carried by Wal-Mart and other major music stores are not trivial. They account for 20 per cent to 25 per cent of the profit for an online retailer such as Amazon. True, they may represent as much as 90 per cent of inventory, but when the cost of holding and managing the inventory is reduced to close to zero, as it can be with digital products and computerized control, there is a viable business. Anderson (2006: 19)

provides some figures for the music industry. He notes that allowing for healthy marketing and online delivery costs, as well as profit, music can be sold by the song for 79 cents where the customer gets to choose which individual song to purchase. Purchased on a CD through normal off-line retail channels, a packaged album of 12 tracks (with no choice) would cost $15.21 or $1.27 per song.

In this universe of expanded choice, low cost and easy access combine to produce exploratory behaviour. Such exploration by large numbers of people produces sales of all kinds of products. As Anderson says, these products can be of poor quality, but on the whole they are not. We need, he says, to begin to think about hits and niches, rather than hits and misses. We need to understand that the economics of online retailing allow for a fundamentally more inclusive and diverse set of choices than one governed by scarce and expensive retail display space. 'Scarcity (of inexpensive access and distribution) requires hits' (ibid., 8). What impact the Long Tail may have on the market for Canadian media products remains to be seen. In the meantime, however, it demonstrates that, even in a seemingly open market, market supply and market performance are not produced by simple consumer demand but rather by the structure of the system of production, distribution, and retailing. That system itself restricts supply and thus focuses demand. However, when provided with exposure, demand emerges for diverse cultural expression. Thus, as well as providing access to a wide range of cultural products in the name of cultural diversity, the economic rationale for making a wide range of such products available is made clear by the Long Tail of consumer demand.

Conclusion: The Media, the State, and Maher Arar— Lessons for Tomorrow?

One final matter of importance to understanding mass communication in twenty-first-century Canada needs to be considered. As many Canadians know, on 26 September 2002, just over a year after the 9/11 attacks on the Pentagon and the World Trade Center in New York, a Canadian software engineer, Maher Arar, was taken into custody by US authorities as he passed through—not trying to enter—the United States on his way to Montreal after a vacation in Tunisia. He was held incommunicado in the United States for 12 days and then shipped off to Syria where he was tortured for 10 months before finally being released. Upon his return to Canada, he found himself a further victim. As the Associate Chief Justice of Ontario, Dennis O'Connor, detailed in his Commission of Inquiry report:

> When Mr. Arar returned to Canada, his torment did not end, as some government officials took it upon themselves to leak information to the media, much of which was unfair to Mr. Arar and damaging to his reputation.

Over a period of time, Government of Canada officials intentionally released selected classified information about Mr. Arar or his case to the media. The first leak occurred in July 2003, even before Mr. Arar's return to Canada, and the leaks intensified in the period immediately following his return in October 2003.

There were at least eight media stories containing leaked information about Mr. Arar and/or the investigation that involved him. Typically, the leaked information was attributed to an unnamed government official, an official closely involved in the case, or some similar source. Some of the leaks sought to portray Mr. Arar as someone who had been involved in terrorist activities, mentioning, for example, that he had trained in Afghanistan. In one, he was described as a 'very bad guy'; in another, the source was reported to have said that the guy was 'not a virgin', adding that there was more there than met the eye.

. . .

The most notorious of the leaks occurred on November 8, 2003, when information from classified documents was published in the *Ottawa Citizen*, in a lengthy article by Juliet O'Neill that contained a large amount of previously confidential information.

The O'Neill article reported that security officials had leaked allegations against Mr. Arar in the weeks leading to his return to Canada 'in defence of their investigative work—against suggestions that the RCMP and the Canadian Security Intelligence Service had either bungled Mr. Arar's case or, worse, purposefully sent an innocent man to be tortured in Syria.' This rationale implies that officials believe leaking confidential information is justified if it suits the interests of investigators. According to this thinking, leakers get to be selective—picking and choosing what to leak to paint the picture that suits their interests.

There have been several investigations into the sources of the Arar leaks. To date, none of the sources have been identified. All witnesses at the Inquiry who were asked about them denied any knowledge. The sources of the leaks appear to be a complete mystery to everyone and the prospects of identifying those responsible seem uncertain at best. The only remaining investigation is the criminal investigation into the O'Neill leak, which is now two years old.

Leaking confidential information is a serious breach of trust. Obviously, it is important that all available steps be taken to prevent it.

Quite predictably, the leaks had a devastating effect on Mr. Arar's reputation and on him personally. The impact on an individual's reputation of being called a terrorist in the national media is severe. As I have stated elsewhere, labels, even unfair and inaccurate ones, have a tendency to stick. . . .

It seems likely that the smear of his reputation by the leakers has taken its toll. (Canada, 2006c: 46, 47)

The treatment of Arar is bad enough, but what the Commission of Inquiry has revealed is monumental in the history of Canada and the role of the media. The first two issues bear repeating—the official confinement of a Canadian citizen by the US government, his transportation to Syria, his confinement and torture, and the post-Inquiry refusal of the United States to recognize Arar's innocence comprise the first. Arar remains on the US no-fly list. The second is the behaviour of Canadian officials, not just those who leaked prejudicial information to the media but also those who supplied information to the United States in the first place and refused to fully acknowledge their role in Arar's arrest and confinement.

The tip of the iceberg of a third important issue can be grasped by the resignation of RCMP Commissioner Giuliano Zaccardelli, who admitted to a parliamentary committee that he knew of Arar's innocence within days of Arar's arrest. Not only is it stunning that this head of the RCMP

would keep that fact a secret for a year, but also it must surely implicate a complete chain of command within the RCMP, from the officers involved in the case right up to the Commissioner himself. No call has been made for a purge of all those involved. Nor has much attention been paid to the role of officials within the Department of Foreign Affairs and International Trade. In other words, even though we know that there was a concerted attempt on the part of a variety of police and government officials to create, and then hide, an injustice, Canadians and their government are content to let one man—Zaccardelli—shoulder the blame. This lack of a robust response in reaction to a gross injustice perpetrated on a completely innocent man is to be condemned. It indicates a willingness to live with the knowledge of institutional corruption in government and our police that has not been quite so apparent heretofore. This is saddening.

A fourth issue has been admirably brought forward by journalism instructor Andrew Mitrovica in an article in *The Walrus* magazine. It is the behaviour of the media in the Arar case and, of course, why this issue deserves attention in this book. As of the beginning of 2007, not a single journalist who received erroneous leaks from government officials has revealed his or her sources or apologized to Arar or the Canadian public. As Mitrovica (2006–7: 43) says, for those concerned with journalists revealing their sources, 'promises of anonymity are voided when sources are revealed to have lied.' Even those calling for the naming of the sources—Mitrovica credits Jeff Sallot of *The Globe and Mail* with having done so—have not explained their relationships with their sources so that the public can understand how they were given information by persons unknown to them.

The behaviour of members of Canada's media in the Arar affair brings forward several major concepts that we have discussed in this book. Most obviously, they include media responsibility and accountability. As Arar himself has noted, his strength to fight has been maintained by the support of many Canadians who have written to him and supported him in his struggle for justice.

The Canadian government in early 2007 issued a formal apology to Arar and his family, along with compensation of $10.5 million, only after lengthy negotiations between the two parties. Yet, where is the call, beyond Mitrovica's article and a few soft supportive journalistic voices, for the media to account and compensate both Arar and the Canadian public for their actions? Where is either some action or a call for accountability from those in the media who were duped, not just by leaks from the RCMP but also by government officials? What are the means by which Canada's media can be made to take responsibility for their actions? Is the symbiotic relationship between the news media and official sources so strong that the media dare not call the government and the RCMP to account? If so, then the media have undermined the basic trust the public places in them to ferret out, as best they can, the real truth rather than allowing themselves to be pawns in the manufacturing of 'truths' convenient to their sources. Will Arar himself have to sue members of the media to hold them accountable for their role? Why was the Commission of Inquiry given limited terms of reference, as opposed to a mandate to interview under oath all those in the RCMP and the federal bureaucracy, compelling them to give a complete account of their actions? And ultimately, what role do the news media have in democratic governance if they can be the pawns of news sources, this time government and the police, at other times large corporations or other powerful institutions in society?

If the Arar case indicts the Canadian news media in particular—whose reporters continue to cover terrorism allegations against Canadian citizens Omar Khadr, Abousan Abdelrazik, and Hassan Diab—it nonetheless asks us to consider the responsibility all media assume in the production and dissemination of knowledge about our world, and the responsibility we all share when we consume these texts. As we have underlined throughout this book, the communications media are in the business of producing meaning, and this includes group identifications or stereotypes. Those meanings can be reinforced through video games, films, popular music, magazines, advertising, and our own conversations. They can become the basis, even the rationale, for action: racism, sexism, homophobia, xenophobia. If, in other words, media portrayals repeatedly assign unfavourable characteristics to groups of people, then it becomes easier to accept that individuals belonging to those groups share those characteristics. We are encouraged to perceive them, not as individuals, but as representatives of their assigned group acting on their 'nature'.

But as we have also emphasized in these pages, the consumption of mass communication is a practice of active engagement by audiences, and thus conventional meanings—including stereotypes—can be criticized, debunked, and opposed. Media texts can be read critically; stereotypes can be identified and dismissed as such. The interactivity of new media technologies can be employed to debunk problematic assertions and portrayals, to propose other readings, to ask pertinent questions. Such critical engagement provides the basis for true democratic citizenship.

SUMMARY

This book has examined the nature of communication in contemporary Canadian society. This final chapter has echoed the major themes, issues, and ideas treated in the preceding chapters. We have also gone beyond the analysis provided in the preceding chapters and discussed some of the directions in which the development of media and communications technology appear to be headed and the issues that these developments raise. The chapter concludes by looking at the Maher Arar case, which raises several important and disturbing questions about the relationship between the media and the state in the twenty-first century.

KEY TERMS

digital divide, p. 350
free-market, p. 344
ICT, p. 347

the Long Tail, p. 353
ownership, p. 344
policy, p. 337

privacy, p. 350
public interest, p. 338
UNESCO p. 339

RELATED WEBSITES

Canadian Association of Community Television Users and Stations (CACTUS): http://cactus. independentmedia.ca
Canada's association of independent community television stations

Kondratiev waves: www.kondratieffwavecycle.com/ kondratieff-wave
A site devoted to discussion of the Kondratiev wave phenomenon.

National Campus and Community Radio Association: www.ncra.ca
One of Canada's largest alternative media organizations.

Report of the Standing Committee on Industry, Science and Technology: www.parl.gc.ca/HousePublications/ Publication.aspx?DocId=4618793&Language=&Mode= 1&Parl=40&Ses=3
Report on foreign ownership in the Canadian telecommunications industry.

STUDY QUESTIONS

1. Is the world being transformed by the internet, or will the internet soon be largely captured by business so that we will be back to where we started?

2. Are the media alone a solid foundation for democracy?

3. While the media industries look at audiences in one manner, scholars tend to view them in another. Are these two approaches reconcilable?

4. In your opinion, what does the future of mass communication and media look like?

5. What principal characteristics of cultural industries and markets make them different from other types of manufacturing and production?

Glossary

access to information Related to the concept of freedom of information, it refers to the principle that information collected by governments belongs to the Crown and citizens must appeal to governments for access to this information; this is the operating principle in Canada. In the US, 'freedom of information' is the more appropriate term because information collected by governments belongs to the people.

affiliate An independently owned radio or television station associated with either a private or public network of stations; a station not owned by the network.

agenda-setting The process by which priorities are established; it usually refers to elite actors or media owners and managers using their influence to shape society's priorities.

allocative control The kind of control over media operations exercised by people at the uppermost levels of management—publishers, station managers, chief executives, shareholders, directors—who assign resources of labour and capital to a media organization and determine the organization's overall mandate; it is control over the structural and philosophical context in which media content is produced.

Areopagitica An essay written by John Milton in 1644 to oppose press licensing in England, expressing faith in the power of truth to prevail through free inquiry and discussion; it remains a foundational document in the libertarian theory of the press and informs discussions of freedom of the press to this day.

bandwidth The frequency range within which signals are broadcast, typically measured in hertz; with respect to the internet, data transmission rates, the amount of data transferable over a given channel in a given amount of time.

barriers to entry An economic term that refers to the impediments one must overcome—e.g., raising investment capital, purchasing equipment or technology, finding a market niche, finding labour expertise—to enter into a new business enterprise.

Berne Convention The basis of international copyright law, which requires, among other things, that foreign authors be treated in the same way as domestic authors and that there be a minimum number of years of protection for a copyrighted work.

Birmingham School The media scholars at Birmingham University who developed the Marxist-derived, critical school of thought that became cultural studies.

bits Binary digits, that is, zeros or ones; the basis for the information-carrying capability of most computing systems. A byte is eight bits.

blogs, blogging Usually personal commentaries made public via the World Wide Web on topics of interest to the author or website owner; the word 'blog' is a contraction of 'web' and 'log', as in keeping a log or record of activities. Blogs customarily include text, images, and sound, often including material lifted from other sites, and can be opened for others to make comments as well. Blogging is the activity of creating a blog.

bourgeoisie In Marxist terms, the new land-owning class that emerged with the development of capitalism that generally controlled the means of production.

British cultural studies An approach to social analysis that began in the 1950s and was led by scholars Richard Hoggart, Raymond Williams, and Stuart Hall; it extended a Marxist class analysis to include race, gender, and other elements of cultural history, and asserted the legitimacy of popular culture forms as objects of study.

Broadcasting Act Federal legislation governing all forms of broadcasting in Canada.

broadsheets Full-sized newspapers (as opposed to half-sized tabloids) that tend to be targeted at middle-class or elite readers; this newspaper form generally has much more text and relatively fewer photos than the tabloid format typically displays.

Canadian content A legal definition of material that either has been developed by Canadians and/or contains Canadian information; in broadcasting, filmmaking, and publishing, Canadian content is defined by reference to a specific set of production criteria, rather than content per se, designed to encourage the production of Canadian cultural materials by Canadians.

Canadian Radio-television and Telecommunications Commission The federal agency that enforces the rules and regulations for broadcasters and telecommunications companies in Canada, as set out in the Telecommunications Act.

capital Funds invested, or available to be invested, for the express purpose of generating profits; not to be confused with money per se.

capitalism An economic system based on the private ownership of the means of production and the clear separation of capital—owners of the means of production engaged in the pursuit of profit—and labour—workers who satisfy their material needs (food, shelter, clothing) by exchanging their labour for a wage.

carriage A policy term designed to distinguish between the simple dissemination or transmission of communication (as in telephone service provided by telephone companies) and the production or selection of content; in regulation, this distinction is drawn in order to differentiate between carriage and content activities (e.g., distinguishing between the carriage and content-production or content-selection activities of a television network).

collective rights Rights accruing to groups of people or communities that are meant to privilege the collectivity over individuals; language laws in Quebec, for example, are designed to protect and promote the language of the French-speaking majority; Canadian content rules on radio and television are similarly meant to protect and promote the cultural expression of the Canadian community.

commercial media Media outlets organized to produce profits for their owners through the sale of content and/or advertising; regardless of what kind of content the outlet produces, a primary goal of a commercial institution is to produce regular profits. Their objectives and purpose are different from those of not-for-profit (e.g., the Aboriginal Peoples Television Network), community (e.g., community radio and television), and public (e.g., the CBC) media.

commodities Goods sold in the marketplace valued primarily for the earnings they can generate through market exchange.

common carriage Telecommunications services provided to all members of the public at equitable rates; a common carrier is in the business of providing carriage services rather than content.

communication The act of transmitting and exchanging information and meaning through any form of language; while communication typically refers to exchanges through verbal, written, and electronic forms of language, among other things, clothing, gesture, and architecture are also forms of communication.

communications policy Policy regime laid down by international regulatory bodies and national and regional governments to ensure that media serve not only their owners and content creators, but individual citizens and society as a whole.

compression The process of encoding information using as few *bits* as possible, thereby saving disk space and needed transmission *bandwidth*. The MP3 and zip file formats are compressed file formats. In certain cases compression results in a loss of *fidelity* (referred to as 'lossy compression').

concentration of ownership The consolidation of ownership of a number of media organizations by relatively few large corporations. There are a number of different types or forms of media concentration, such as horizontal or chain ownership, *vertical integration*, and cross-media ownership.

conglomerate A company that contains within it many companies carrying on a variety of businesses not necessarily related to one another: a media conglomerate does the majority of its business in the media; a general or non-media conglomerate has its foundation in non-media firms.

connotative Implicit, suggesting, implying; a connotation is an implied meaning; in communication theory, words and messages are said to have connotative as well as *denotative* (or explicit) meanings.

conservative A political stance oriented to preserving current conditions and power structures rather than adapting to, embracing, or instigating changed, often more egalitarian, conditions.

consortium A group, usually of institutions, gathered together for a common purpose such as marketing or lobbying policy-makers.

constructivism A point of view that argues that technology is constructed by members of society and shaped by social forces giving it both a technical and a social logic.

contempt of court A ruling by which a court of law determines that a person or an organization has disobeyed or contravened the authority of the court.

content analysis A quantitative research method that establishes units of analysis—specified ideas, phrases, sentences, column inches, placement, accompanying illustrations, categories of spokespersons quoted or cited—and counts them to try and analyze the meaning or perspective of a particular communication, such as a newspaper story or television news story.

contract carrier A company that provides *carriage* to a private client, usually a firm, to transmit or communicate signals, but does not offer the same service on equitable terms to others; the opposite of *common carriage*.

convergence Generally, bringing together once separate communication technologies such as telephone, broadcasting, computers, and sound and video recording into one technological platform such as the internet. The key to this technological convergence is the digitalization of media content such that it can be translated into a common format. Similarly, concentration of ownership is sometimes referred to as 'corporate convergence', as media companies combine the resources and content of two or more different media properties to realize cost savings in content production and cross-promotional opportunities.

copyright The exclusive right to reproduce a work requiring intellectual labour; this right belongs to the author and constitutes: (1) a property right, which may be assigned to others, and (2) a moral right, which may not be assigned but may be waived.

Copyright Act Legal framework governing the right to reproduce a published work.

corporate concentration An economic term used to describe a particular industry ownership pattern, whereby ownership of the participating companies is concentrated in only a few hands.

critical theory Generally, theoretical perspectives that focus on the ways in which wealth and power are unequally distributed in society.

cross-ownership Ownership of two or more different media in the same market—for instance, newspapers and radio stations.

Crown corporations Businesses owned by federal or provincial governments, but operating at arm's length from government as individual corporations.

cultivation analysis An examination of content for the way in which it may encourage or cultivate a positive attitude in the audience member towards a particular person or perspective.

cultural dependency A relationship in which one country comes to rely on the media products of stronger, exporting countries to satisfy the cultural and entertainment needs of its population.

cultural imperialism The ways in which one culture imposes ideas and values on another culture, with the effect of undermining the cultural values of the recipient; media and cultural products are a primary vehicle for such imposition.

cultural industries Groups of companies that employ large-scale, industrial methods to produce cultural products.

culturalist The perception of complex phenomena and institutions in terms of their cultural impact and cultural characteristics; such a view foregrounds and privileges the cultural aspect of issues.

cultural sovereignty The capacity of a state or group to govern cultural activity—i.e., form policy, establish laws and conventions—independent of interference from other governments or groups.

culture As Raymond Williams points out, generally 'one of the two or three most complicated words in the English language' (Williams, 1958: 87). In this book, it is used to indicate a 'particular way of life, whether of a people, a group, or humanity in general'. From this perspective culture includes 'knowledge, belief, art, morals, law,

custom, and any other capabilities acquired by man as a member of society' (Tylor in Thompson, 1990: 128).

database A collection of records or information stored in a computer in a systematic, structured way so that a computer program can consult it to answer queries.

data mining The compilation and analysis of data usually collected as part of a financial transaction and aimed at revealing patterns that are useful for a third party to know.

decoding Interpreting or meaning-making—for example, to interpret or make meaning from an advertisement, television program, or film, one must decode the signs and symbols used to construct those media texts.

defamation Injuring a person's good reputation by means of insults, or interference with the course of justice.

demographic (1) Used as an adjective, related to the statistical study of populations through the identification of characteristics of a given population (e.g., age, sex, education, income level); (2) used as a noun, it describes a specific group that may be identified through such analysis.

denotative Explicit, literal meaning of a communication; in communication theory, words and messages are said to have both denotative and *connotative* meanings.

deskilling The simplification of complex tasks into components that are readily mastered by workers, who often are working in conjunction with sophisticated machines.

determinism A point of view that sees technology as operating according to an inexorable logic that is inherent in the technology itself.

determinist illusion The notion of inevitability in the form and function of a particular piece of technology, as in, it was bound to develop in the way it did because it is such a perfect device for its current function.

digital A universal code that reduces sounds and images to a series of 0s and 1s; digitization allows the easy transfer of communications from one medium to another, enabling convergence.

digital divide The (increasing) difference in the development and use of information and communication technology between rich and poor countries and between the haves and have-nots within a specific society.

discourse In popular usage, all forms of text and talk; in communication studies, text and talk about a particular topic or field of activity.

disintermediation The elimination of those involved in between the creator and the final consumer, that is, the elimination of intermediaries such as publishers, libraries, record companies, film distributors.

dominant ideology The set of ideas most commonly used to explain events in a given society; conventional wisdom or conventional explanations of phenomena that are taken by most people as unchallenged assumptions.

economies of scale Efficiencies in costs that can be achieved via repetition of some aspects of the production and distribution processes—for example, the reduction of the per-unit cost of printing 10,000 copies of a book once the presses have been set up, as opposed to printing 1,000 copies.

economism The reduction of complex phenomena and institutions to their economic characteristics; such a view foregrounds and privileges economic values to the exclusion of political, cultural, or other social considerations.

effects The direct impacts of the media on human behaviour.

elite The few who are considered superior or more powerful in society or within a particular group in society.

encoding Placing meaning in a particular code, for instance, language, digital signals, song.

encryption The process of obscuring information to make it unreadable without special (decoding or decryption) knowledge.

Enlightenment An early eighteenth-century change in Western European world view distinguished by an intellectual approach based on a scientific and rational perspective on the world, a fundamental shift in world view that championed science over religion, justice over the abuse of power, and a social contract that specified individual rights and freedoms over the absolutist rule of kings and popes.

feminist research A perspective that is critical of the character of modern societies for the male domination of women (patriarchy) that has led to profound human inequalities and injustices.

fidelity In sound and electronic engineering, the signal-to-noise ratio, that is, the accuracy of electronic systems in reproducing the input signal—the higher the fidelity the lower is the noise in comparison to the signal.

file-sharing The practice of freely exchanging digital files through computer networks, most commonly referring to the exchange of music and video downloads through the internet.

Fordism The concentration of production on a single site modelled after Henry Ford's automobile assembly lines, whereby raw materials are turned into standardized finished products as part of a single, multi-faceted mass-production process.

formative research Research undertaken, usually by means of focus groups, to obtain reactions to television programs and films as they are being made.

fourth estate The media; refers to the role of the media in watching over the other powerful institutions in society.

frame/framing Both a noun and a verb drawing attention to the boundaries a picture, story, or other means of communication places on that to which it refers; these boundaries tend to limit the range of interpretation by audiences or privilege particular readings.

Frankfurt School A school of thought led by the German Jewish intellectuals Max Horkheimer, Theodor Adorno, and Herbert Marcuse, who argued, among other things, that cultural life in modern times has been profoundly changed by the detrimental impact of capitalist methods of mass production.

freedom of information The principle by which information collected by governments belongs to the people, rather than the state; this is the operating principle in the US.

freedom of speech The right of any individual to speak freely on matters of concern without fear of retribution; this freedom is not absolute, but subject to certain legal limits.

freedom of the press (1) The freedom of the press and other media to exercise the right to free speech, usually in the name of the public good; (2) the freedom of press and other media owners to pursue market interests unhindered by the state; this freedom is not absolute, but subject to certain legal limits.

free flow of information The doctrine that advocates the rights of producers to sell information to anyone anywhere, and, conversely, the right of any individual to choose to receive any information from any source.

free market (economy/theory) The general approach to commerce that posits that a free market is the most efficient way of creating and allocating social resources.

gatekeeping The control of access to media publication or broadcast that determines what gains access according to the identity or character of the media outlet.

geostationary An orbit situated directly over the equator in which objects (i.e., satellites) rotating around the earth remain in a fixed location relative to the earth.

geosynchronous An orbit twice the distance of geostationary orbit, which similarly allows for objects to remain in a fixed position relative to the earth.

globalization The processes by which social, political, and economic relations extend further than ever before, with greater frequency, immediacy, and facility.

global village A metaphor introduced by Marshall McLuhan that captures the sense in which the possibility of instantaneous communication brings societies closer together.

hegemony In simple terms, the social process through which the existing relations of social power are made to appear natural and legitimate.

horizontal integration The combination of a group of companies owned by the same company and operating in the same business but occupying different markets—also known as chain ownership; horizontal integration allows for economies of scale through the streamlining of common needs and business practices.

human agency The notion that human beings control their behaviour through purposive action; humans have subjectivity.

ICT Information and communication technology.

ideology A coherent set of social values, beliefs, meanings; in Marxist terms it is a critical concept that refers particularly to dominant or ruling-class values, beliefs, and meanings, what came to be called the dominant ideology.

individual rights Rights that accrue to the individual and that, in the first instance, favour the individual (usually over the community); individual rights include those dealing with free speech and privacy.

Industrial Revolution The application of growing scientific knowledge to production and industry that began to dominate in the late eighteenth century in Western Europe.

infant industries New (typically local) industries seeking to gain a foothold in a market already populated by established and dominant industries.

information flows Patterns of circulation of information commodities or products, for example, movies, magazines, television programs; a summary concept describing the imports and exports of goods, specifically information and entertainment products.

information society A society in which the production, distribution, and consumption of information takes on growing and significant political, economic, and social importance.

intellectual property The set of rights that accrue to an author by virtue of the work expended in the creation of a literary, dramatic, artistic, or musical work; the owned expressions of intellectual work derived from copyright law; intellectual property carries two sets of rights—moral rights and property rights.

interactivity As a descriptor of media, the inclusion of user-created content as part of what is presented to the audience. While it may be claimed that such devices as letters to the editor are an interactive element of newspapers and magazines, they are placed in separate sections from the content produced by the publication itself. Interactivity is strongest when the boundary between the content producers and the audience is least. To use a theatrical analogy, in strongly interactive media the boundary between the stage and audience vanishes.

invisible hand The notion proposed by Adam Smith that the marketplace generally works in the best interests of society by encouraging individuals to pursue their own self-interest and economic opportunity; refers to the self-regulation of a market economy.

libel (1) A published written statement that does damage to the good reputation of a person; in France and the US, libel can express true facts, while in the UK and derivative systems, truth is an absolute defence against an accusation of libel; (2) any false or insulting statement.

libel chill The threat, real or imagined, and under which authors and publishers live, that they will be accused of libel and need to expend considerable sums of money to defend themselves, especially when publishing controversial or critical material about powerful people and institutions; this threat often leads to self-censorship as a form of protection.

liberalism A political philosophy in which society is seen as composed of individuals (as opposed to social classes or definable communities) and that advocates the liberty of individuals as the primary social goal.

libertarian theory A political philosophy that views the sole purpose of the state as enforcing individuals' rights.

Long Tail, the Concept introduced by Chris Anderson whereby the distribution/display costs are much more forgiving in the online world. Because of very low costs for display and distribution, and because item costs are low but access is easy, consumers choose widely rather than focusing their choices solely on hits.

market externalities The costs and benefits of economic activity that are not accounted for by, i.e., are external to, the immediate economic transaction between buyer and seller.

market failure The inability of the free market to reflect the true value of (or provide) a good or service, for example, a work of art, which may be sold for a small sum during the life of the artist but for increasingly greater sums after the artist's lifetime.

Marxist analysis An approach to studying society that derives from the writings of Karl Marx, who emphasized class as a fundamental dividing element in society, separating and placing in conflict the interests of workers (the class that sells its labour for wages) from capitalists (the class that owns and controls the means of production).

mash-up Any kind of media product—website, song, video—that consists of content brought together from other sources.

mass audience A convenient shorthand term for the great numbers of people who constitute the 'mass entertainment' audience; rather than being conceived as homogeneous, vulnerable, and passive, the mass audience is better conceived as a great number of individuals of heterogeneous backgrounds who use the media for a great variety of purposes.

mass communication Historically, a term used to describe communication to a large undifferentiated group. More recently, the term is also used to describe communication between a large number of individuals.

mass media Newspapers, magazines, cinema, television, radio, advertising, some book publishing, the internet, and popular music.

means of production The mechanism or process by which we satisfy our material needs for food, clothing, and shelter, and thus ensure our survival.

media democratization A movement seeking to democratize media organizations through public or co-operative ownership, and by opening these organizations' decision-making processes to broad public participation.

media geography The physical space that any given media organization occupies and seeks to serve. For example, a national television network occupies and serves audiences and advertisers within a given country.

media imperialism The use of the media to build empires of influence and control.

medium Any vehicle that conveys information; plural: media.

mobility A characteristic that refers to the relative portability or transportability of people, cultural products, investment capital, organizations, etc.

models As in computer models, a pattern, plan, representation, or description designed to show the structure or workings of an object, system, or concept.

monopoly Exclusive control over the supply of a particular product for a specified market; a market in which consumers have a single source for a product or service.

monopoly capitalism A form of capitalism that encourages greater and greater concentration of ownership, resulting in monopolies and thus negating market competition.

moral rights The set of rights associated with intellectual property that are deemed to be the creator's by virtue of a work being created—they are most often associated with the integrity of the work; moral rights may be held or waived but not assigned to any other person; moral rights are distinct from *property rights* and not considered to be material.

multiplier effects Indirect economic activity that results from a particular industry—for example, movie theatres generate economic activity for popcorn sellers, parking lots, gas stations, and restaurants.

narrowcasting Used in contrast to broadcasting to describe radio and television services targeted at a small or niche audience.

nation-state A sovereign political unit that exercises political control over a territory and is composed of people who identify themselves as part of the nation, often sharing linguistic, historical, and ethnic heritage.

net neutrality Internet service providers (ISPs) treating all content and applications equally, without degrading or prioritizing service based on their source, ownership, or destination.

network Generally, a group of individuals or organizations that share and/or distribute information (e.g., a social network, computer network); a group of television or radio stations that share programming so that distribution is extended to a broader area. Network stations are usually, but not necessarily, owned by the same company.

network neutrality A characteristic of communication systems that refers to the network's capacity for transferring data without regard to the form or nature of data being transferred.

network society Taken from the work of Manuel Castells, a description of contemporary society as bound together less by physical location than by globalized social, communication, and economic networks.

new media Technologies, practices, and institutions designed to encourage public participation in information creation, production, and exchange (i.e., communication) on a mass scale by means of either increased access to production facilities (decentralized production) or through *interactivity*. They are usually, but not always, digital media.

objectivity The relatively impartial or unbiased perception of reality. A controversial but nonetheless core value of journalism that seeks to separate opinion from fact.

open-source software The production and development of software that allows users and others to see source code and thereby make adjustments to it to suit their needs.

operational control The kind of control over media organizations exercised by editors and producers who are responsible for day-to-day production decisions; these managers determine how best to employ the labour and capital resources assigned to them by upper management, who exercise *allocative control*.

packets The sending of blocks of data such as symbols, characters, or numbers using variable time intervals separating the transmission of the blocks in discrete recognizable sequences, each with addressing and error-checking information attached.

people meter Electronic device that allows audience members to record their media consumption habits.

piracy Theft of intellectual property—often of works by persons in one country by persons based in another country that does not recognize the laws of the first country.

policy The set of rules, laws, and practices that govern the operation of communication sectors.

political economy The study of the ways in which politics and economics enable and constrain the allocation, production, distribution, and consumption of social resources.

postmodernism A contemporary philosophical perspective that questions whether there can be any objective truth and views reality as a largely ever-shifting social construct.

primary definers Terms used to define the important elements of a news story; also used to designate those people who are first to assert a meaning to news events; primary definitions tend to be difficult to change.

privacy The right to protect certain aspects of personal life from media discussions; such rights do not exist in Britain in any formal way and are weak in the United States.

private ownership Ownership by individuals or corporations, including of publicly traded companies, as opposed to *public ownership*.

privatization The transfer of publicly owned enterprises into the hands of private individuals or corporations.

probes As used by Marshall McLuhan, probes were new, original, seemingly profound ideas that may or may not have much foundation; by calling his pronouncements probes, McLuhan was indicating that such ideas were works in progress.

product placement The insertion of identifiable commercial products into the content of entertainment or information media for the purpose of promoting awareness of them.

property rights The rights pertaining to the ownership of property; intellectual property rights pertain to the ownership and material benefit one may gain from *intellectual property*.

proximity The degree of closeness, which can refer to physical, cultural, or emotional closeness.

public interest The investment that a national group or other polity has in preserving or developing the best of its values and ideals.

public ownership Ownership by arm's-length government agencies, e.g., the CBC, or by groups of individuals, e.g., co-operatives, which members of the public can join for a token membership fee. Public ownership contrasts to commercial or *private ownership* of commercial companies, some of which are publicly traded and therefore called, in business circles, public companies.

public service An orientation, usually of public-sector, volunteer, or co-operative institutions and associations, that places the interests of society above the interests of individuals or specific groups.

public sphere A place or space where people can meet to discuss and debate issues and ideas of common concern.

reach The percentage of audience members who tune into a broadcast program at least once during a specified time period.

reception analysis A research method that investigates how and in what context audiences consume media products.

Renaissance A cultural movement between the fourteenth and seventeenth centuries in Western Europe that highlighted a return to classical forms of learning and knowledge.

representation The production or construction of ideas or images in a communicative form; the depiction through language of an idea, event, person, institution.

rhetoric A persuasive form of communication; a research method in which communications are studied as examples of persuasive speech.

right to communicate The expansion of the notions of freedom of expression, *freedom of speech*, and *freedom of the press* to include the right to be informed, the right to inform, the right to *privacy*, and the right to participate in public communication.

Royal Commissions High-level inquiries established by government to investigate problems and recommend solutions.

royalty payments A percentage of receipts received by copyright owners from those who trade in intellectual property.

satellite footprints The terrestrial areas covered by specific satellite signals.

semiotics The study of signs and sign systems and the ways in which they create meaning.

share The percentage of the average audience that tunes into a program or channel over any specified time period.

sign (1) A physical form (a word, gesture, even an object like a rose) used in communication to refer to something

GLOSSARY

else (an object, a feeling) and recognized as such; (2) the totality of associations, thoughts, understandings, or meaning brought about by the use of symbols in reference to an object, person, phenomenon, or idea.

signified The mental concept of what is referred to—for instance, an object as we think of it when we hear a word (image of table when we hear the word 'table').

signifier The physical form of the *sign*, for instance, symbols such as words.

silos In a converged, multi-platform media environment, specific media platforms—e.g., radio, television, newspapers, magazines—that are not converged.

socially contingent A point of view that emphasizes that technology arises and takes a particular form reflecting the dynamics of the society in which it emerges.

social responsibility theory The notion that the media have a responsibility to make a positive contribution to society and that they occupy a privileged position of which they should be aware.

society A general term for the larger set of institutions and relationships that contextualize the ways in which a relatively large group of people live.

socio-technical ensemble A term coined by Wiebe Bijker to describe a technical apparatus to reflect the fact that built into all commonly used technology are both social dynamics and technical feasibility (and history).

sovereignty The quality of independence, typically referring to the ability of nations to self-govern.

space bias An idea advanced by Harold Innis, which notes the tendency of certain communication systems and societies to privilege the extension of ideas over space or distance as opposed to time or history.

spatialization The process of overcoming the constraints of space and time, typically applied to organizations such as media companies.

spectrum allocation The process by which governments assign radio and television frequencies to over-the-air broadcasting stations.

structuralism A method and theory that emphasizes how the formal elements of a linguistic or social system limit or determine the agency of the individuals that use that system.

substantivism A point of view that sees technology as operating according to its own inexorable logic, and that this logic is at the expense of human concerns and hence humanity.

summative research Research that measures the effectiveness of a program after its completion.

symbol A sign that bears no direct resemblance to what it signifies, such as words. Thus, symbolic production is the systematic communication of ideas and images through language.

syndicated Material sold by an organization for simultaneous publication or transmission in a variety of places—for instance, a newspaper column or comic strip in various papers or a TV sitcom on different networks.

tabloids Half-size newspapers convenient for reading in limited space that often provide 'bare-bones stories'; tabloids often engage in yellow journalism, that is, the prying into the private and personal lives of the rich and famous in order to uncover scandal.

technological convergence The capacity of a variety of seemingly different technological devices to perform the same task.

technological determinism The notion that technology is an autonomous and powerful driving force in structuring society or elements of society.

technological imperative The notion that technological developments provide form and direction to social development.

technology From the Greek 'techne', meaning art, craft, or skill. From this perspective technology is considered to be more than simply tools, gadgets, or devices. Rather, it is devices or machines *plus* a knowledge or understanding of their use or operation, that is, an understanding of how they fit into a larger set of social circumstances or way of life.

technology transfer The transfer of a particular technology from one society to another.

Telecommunications Act The legal statute passed by Parliament governing 'the emission, transmission or reception of intelligence by any wire, cable, radio, optical or other electromagnetic system, or by any similar technical system'.

time bias An idea advanced by Harold Innis, which notes the tendency of certain communication systems and societies to privilege the extension of ideas over time or history as opposed to space or distance.

Toronto School Marshall McLuhan and Harold Innis lived and worked in Toronto—as such, the Toronto School is said to be composed of scholars who based their research on the ideas of McLuhan and Innis.

UNESCO The United Nations Education, Scientific and Cultural Organization, a specialized agency of the United Nations.

Universal Declaration of Human Rights Global declaration of basic rights adopted by United Nations General

Assembly in 1948, Article 19 of which is specific to freedom of opinion and expression.

Unix A computer operating system (trademarked UNIX) originally developed in the early 1970s by a group of AT&T employees at Bell Labs and made available to government and academic institutions, thereby becoming—in practice at least—an open system available for widespread and free use. Linux and Mac OS X are operating systems derived from Unix.

uses and gratification research A theory of media focusing on how audience members use the media—for instance, for information, for entertainment, for conversation—and what satisfaction they derive from media.

vertical integration A group of companies linked by common ownership that exist in a supply–demand relation to one another, such as a sound recording company and a radio network.

viewing time The time spent viewing expressed over the course of a day, week, or longer period of time.

virtual reality Computer generated environments that can simulate places and situations in the real world.

Web 2.0 The extension of web applications though the addition of new communication and interaction options that replace static informational sites with social media applications that allow people to discuss, collaborate, or otherwise interact.

WIPO copyright treaty One of 23 international treaties administered by the United Nations agency, the World Intellectual Property Organization. WIPO was created in 1967 to encourage creative activity and to promote the protection of intellectual property throughout the world. As of 2007, 183 states were members of WIPO.

world systems theory Theory articulated by Immanuel Wallerstein that focuses on the relationship between nation-states in a global economic system. The theory categorized nations as core, peripheral, and semi-peripheral states depending on the role they play in the international economic system.

References

Aboriginal Peoples Television Network (APTN). 2010. 'About APTN'. At: <www.aptn.ca/corporate/about.php>. (4 Nov. 2010)

Adorno, T., and M. Horkheimer. 1972. *Dialectic of Enlightenment*. New York: Herder and Herder.

——— and ———. 1977 [1947]. 'The culture industry', in J. Curran, M. Gurevitch, and J. Woollacott, eds, *Mass Communication and Society*. London: Edward Arnold.

Advertising Standards Canada. 2010. 'Broadcasting Code for Advertising to Children'. At: <www.adstadards.com>. (4 Nov. 2010)

Alasuutari, Pertti, ed. 1999. *Rethinking the Media Audience*. Thousand Oaks, Calif.: Sage.

Al Jazeera English. 2010. 'About us'. At: <english.aljazeera.net>. (28 July 2010)

Allan, Stuart, ed. 2010. *The Routledge Companion to News and Journalism*. London and New York: Routledge.

American Gaming Association. 2010. 'Industry information: Fact sheets: Industry issues'. At: <www.americangaming.org/Industry/factsheets/issues_detail.cfv?id=17>. (9 Aug. 2010)

Anderson, Benedict. 1983. *Imagined Communities: Reflections on the Origin and Spread of Nationalism*. London: Verso.

Anderson, Chris. 2006. *The Long Tail: Why the Future of Business Is Selling Less of More*. New York: Hyperion.

———. 2009. *Free: The Future of a Radical Price*. New York: Hyperion.

Anderson, Robert, Richard Gruneau, and Paul Heyer, eds. 1996. *TVTV: The Television Revolution, The Debate*. Vancouver: Canadian Journal of Communication.

Ang, Ien. 1985. *Watching Dallas*. London: Methuen.

———. 1991. *Desperately Seeking the Audience*. London: Routledge.

———. 1996. 'Dallas between reality and fiction', in Paul Cobley, ed., *The Communication Theory Reader*. London and New York: Routledge.

——— and Joke Hermes. 1991. 'Gender and/in media consumption', in Curran and Gurevitch (1991: 307–28).

Armstrong, Robert. 2010. *Broadcasting Policy in Canada*. Toronto: University of Toronto Press.

Association of Research Libraries. 2010. 'Copyright and intellectual property policies'. <www.arl.org/pp/ppcopyright/copyresources/copytimeline.shtml>. (25 Oct. 2010)

Babe, Robert E. 1979. *Canadian Broadcasting Structure, Performance and Regulation*. Ottawa: Economic Council of Canada.

———. 1988. 'Emergence and development of Canadian communication: Dispelling the myths', in R. Lorimer and D.C. Wilson, eds, *Communication Canada*. Toronto: Kagan and Woo.

———. 1990. *Telecommunications in Canada*. Toronto: University of Toronto Press.

Bagdikian, Ben H. 1990. *The Media Monopoly*. Boston: Beacon Press.

Baril, Hélène. 2003. 'Quebec engranger des profits de Star Académie', *La Presse*, 9 May, D1.

Barney, Darin. 2005. *Communication Technology*. Vancouver: University of British Columbia Press.

Barthes, Roland. 1968. *Elements of Semiology*, trans. A. Lavers and C. Smith. New York: Hill and Wang.

———. 1972. *Mythologies*. London: Jonathan Cape.

———. 1977a. *Image-Music-Text*. London: Fontana.

———. 1977b. 'The death of the author', in Barthes (1977a: 142–9).

Bashevkin, Sylvia. 1988. 'Does public opinion matter? The adoption of federal royal commission and task force recommendations on the national question, 1951–1987', *Canadian Public Administration* 31, 1 (Fall): 390–407.

Baudrillard, Jean. 1995. *Simulacra and Simulation*, trans. Sheila Glaser. Ann Arbor: University of Michigan Press.

Bauman, Zygmunt. 1998. *Globalization: The Human Consequences*. New York: Columbia University Press.

Baym, Nancy. 2000. *Tune In, Log On: Soaps, Fandom, and Online Community*. Thousand Oaks, Calif.: Sage.

BBC Worldwide. 2010. 'About us'. <www.bbcworldwide.com/aboutus.aspx>. (23 June 2010)

Beauvoir, Simone de. 1957 [1949]. *The Second Sex*, trans. and ed. H.M. Parshley. New York: Knopf.

Bennett, Tony. 1996. 'Media, "reality", signification', in Michael Gurevitch, Tony Bennett, James Curran, and Janet Woollacott, eds, *Culture, Society and the Media*. London and New York: Routledge, 287–308.

——— and Janet Woollacott. 1987. *Bond and Beyond: The Political Career of a Popular Hero*. New York: Methuen.

Bergen, Bob. 2002. *Exposing the Boss: A Study in Canadian Journalism Ethics*. Calgary: Sheldon Chumir Foundation. At: <www.chumirethicsfoundation.calgary._ab.ca/downloads/mediafellows/bergenbob/bergenbobindex.html>.

Berger, Peter, and Thomas Luckmann. 1966. *Social Construction of Reality: A Treatise on the Sociology of Knowledge*. New York: Doubleday.

Bernstein, William J. 2008. *A Splendid Exchange: How Trade Shaped the World*. New York: Grove Press.

Best, Steven, and Douglas Kellner. 1997. *The Postmodern Turn*. New York: Guilford Press.

Bielsa, Esperança. 2008. 'The pivotal role of news agencies in the context of globalization: A historical approach', *Global Networks* 8, 3: 347–66.

Bijker, Wiebe. 1993. 'Do not despair: There is life after constructivism', *Science, Technology & Human Values* 18: 113–38.

Bird, Roger, ed. 1988. *Documents of Canadian Broadcasting*. Ottawa: Carleton University Press.

Black, Edwin. 2001. *IBM and the Holocaust: The Strategic Alliance between Nazi Germany and America's Most Powerful Corporation*. New York: Crown Books.

Blumler, Jay, and Elihu Katz, eds. 1974. *The Uses of Mass Communications: Current Perspectives on Gratifications Research*. Beverly Hills, Calif.: Sage.

Bouchard-Taylor Commission. 2008. *Building the Future: A Time for Reconciliation*. At: <www. accommodements.qc.ca/ documentation/rapports/rapport-final-integral-en.pdf>. (25 July 2010)

Bowker, G., and S.L. Star. 1999. *Sorting Things Out: Classification and Its Consequences*. Cambridge, Mass.: MIT Press.

Boyd-Barrett, Oliver. 1977. 'Media imperialism: Towards an international framework for the analysis of media systems', in James Curran, Michael Gurevitch, and Janet Woollacott, eds, *Mass Communication and Society*. London: Edward Arnold.

———. 1996. 'Cultural dependency and the mass media', in Michael Gurevitch, Tony Bennett, James Curran, and Janet Woollacott, eds, *Culture, Society and the Media*. London and New York: Routledge.

Bradley, Dale. 2010. 'Balance or betrayal: Copyright reform and the right to culture in the digital age', in *Shade* (2010: 356–71).

Breen, Marcus. 2005. 'Off-shore pot o' gold: The political economy of the Australian film industry', in Greg Elmer and Mike Gasher, eds, *Contracting Out Hollywood: Runaway Productions and Foreign Location Shooting*. Lanham, Md: Rowman & Littlefield, 69–91.

Brethour, Patrick. 2002. 'Media convergence strategy praised', *Globe and Mail*, 25 Apr., B2.

Bright, David. 2002. 'The West wants in: Regionalism, class and *Labour/ Le Travail*, 1976–2002', *Labour/ Le Travail* no. 50 (Fall). At: <www. historycooperative.org/journals/ llt/50/bright.html>. (24 Oct. 2010)

British Broadcasting Corporation (BBC). 1987. *Handbook on Audience Research*. London: BBC.

Brown, Kimberley. 2009. 'Do foreign correspondents matter?', *Media* 14, 1.

Bryce, J. 1987. 'Family time and TV use', in T. Lindlof, ed., *Natural Audiences*. Norwood, NJ: Ablex, 121–38.

Buckler, Grant. 2009. 'Putting limits on who can view online video: How it works and why it's done', CBC News, 8 June. At: <www.cbc.ca/technology/ story/2009/02/04/f-tech-goblocking.html#ixzz13IRvzlJ2>. (9 Oct. 2010)

Buckley, Peter, ed. 1993. *Canadian Press Stylebook: A Guide for Writers and Editors*. Toronto: Canadian Press.

Burkell, Jacquelyn. 2010. 'What is "new media" anyway?', in *Shade* (2010).

Butalia, Urvashi. 1994. 'The issues at stake: An Indian perspective on copyright', in Philip G. Altbach, ed., *Copyright and Development: Inequality in the Information Age*. Chestnut Hill, Md: Bellagio Publishing Network.

Canada. 1929a. Order-in-Council 2108. *Canada Gazette*, 19 Jan., 2306.

———. 1929b. *Report of the Royal Commission on Radio Broadcasting* (Aird Commission). Ottawa: F.A. Acland.

———. 1951. *Report of the Royal Commission on National Development in the Arts, Letters and Sciences, 1949–1951* (Massey Commission). Ottawa: Edmond Cloutier.

———. 1957. *Report of the Royal Commission on Broadcasting* (Fowler Commission). Ottawa: Edmond Cloutier.

———. 1968a. Department of Industry, Trade and Commerce. *Report on Book Publishing* (Ernst and Ernst). Ottawa: Department of Industry, Trade and Commerce.

———. 1968b. Minister of Industry. *White Paper on a Domestic Satellite Communications System for Canada*. Ottawa: Queen's Printer.

———. 1969. *Report of the Task Force on Government Information*. Ottawa: Supply and Services.

———. 1971. *Mass Media, vol. 1, The Uncertain Mirror: Report of the Special Senate Committee on the Mass Media* (Davey Committee). Ottawa: Information Canada.

———. 1977a. Department of the Secretary of State. *The Publishing Industry in Canada*. Ottawa: Ministry of Supply and Services.

———. 1977b. Department of the Secretary of State. *The Film Industry in Canada*. Ottawa: Minister of Supply and Services.

———. 1978a. Department of the Secretary of State. *English Educational Publishing in Canada*. Hull, Que.: Minister of Supply and Services.

———. 1978b. Department of the Secretary of State. *French Educational Publishing in Canada*. Hull, Que.: Minister of Supply and Services.

———. 1980. Canadian Study of Parliament Group. *Seminar on Press and Parliament: Adversaries or Accomplices?* Ottawa: Queen's Printer.

———. 1981. *Report of the Royal Commission on Newspapers* (Kent Commission). Ottawa: Minister of Supply and Services.

———. 1982a. *Report of the Federal Cultural Policy Review Committee*. Ottawa: Minister of Supply and Services Canada.

———. 1982b. Federal Cultural Policy Review Committee. *Summary of Briefs and Hearings*. Ottawa: Minister of Supply and Services Canada.

———. 1984. *The National Film and Video Policy*. Ottawa: Minister of Supply and Services.

———. 1985. Canadian Multiculturalism Act. R.S. 1983 c. 24. At: <www.pch.gc.ca/multi/html/act.html>.

———. 1985. *Report of the Film Industry Task Force*. Ottawa: Minister of Supply and Services.

———. 1986. Minister of Communications. *Report of the Task Force on Broadcasting Policy* (Caplan-Sauvageau Task Force). Ottawa: Minister of Supply and Services.

———. 1987. Department of Communications. *Vital Links: Canadian Cultural Industries*. Ottawa: Minister of Supply and Services.

———. 1988. *Canadian Voices: Canadian Choices—A New Broadcasting Policy for Canada*. Ottawa: Supply and Services Canada.

———. 1991. Broadcasting Act. At: <www.crtc.gc.ca/_ENG/LEGAL/BROAD_E.HTM>.

———. 1993. Telecommunications Act. At: <www.crtc.gc.ca/ENG/LEGAL/TELECOME.HTM>.

———. 1996a. *Information Highway Advisory Council Report*. At: <strategis.ic.gc.ca/SSG/ih01015e.html>.

———. 1996b. Mandate Review Committee: CBC, NFB, Telefilm. *Making Our Voices Heard*. Ottawa: Minister of Supply and Services.

———. 1999. *Report of the Feature Film Advisory Committee*. Ottawa: Ministry of Canadian Heritage.

———. 2000. *From Script to Screen*. Ottawa: Department of Canadian Heritage.

———. 2002. *Canadian Content in the 21st Century: A Discussion Paper about Canadian Content in Film and Television Productions*. Ottawa: Department of Canadian Heritage, Mar.

———. 2003. *Our Cultural Sovereignty: The Second Century of Canadian Broadcasting*. Report of the Standing Committee on Canadian Heritage, June. Ottawa: Communication Canada Publishing. At: <www.parl.gc.ca/InfoComDoc/37/2/HERI/Studies/Reports/herirp02-e.htm>.

———. 2006a. *Final Report on the Canadian News Media*, vol. 1. Standing Senate Committee on Transport and Communications. Ottawa: Senate Committees Directorate, June.

———. 2006b. *Final Report of the Telecommunications Policy Review Panel*. Ottawa: Industry Canada.

———. 2006c. *Report of the Events Relating to Maher Arar: Analysis and Recommendations*. Commission of Inquiry into the Actions of Canadian Officials in Relation to Maher Arar. Ottawa: Government of Canada. Reproduced with the permission of the Minister of Public Works and Government Services Canada, 2011.

———. 2008. Department of Canadian Heritage. 'Canadian culture online strategic statement', 19 Nov. At: <www.pch.gc.ca/pgm/pcce-ccop/sttmnt-eng.cfm>. (11 Nov. 2010)

———. 2010a. Department of Canadian Heritage. 'The Canadian music industry: 2008 economic profile'. At: <www.pch.gc.ca/pgm/fmusc-cmusf/pubs/prfl_08/index-eng.cfm>. (1 Nov. 2010)

———. 2010b. Department of Canadian Heritage. 'Investing in the future of Canadian books: Review of the revised foreign investment policy in book publishing and distributing', July. At: <www.pch.gc.ca/eng/1276620365197/1278337615182>. (1 Nov. 2010)

———. 2010c. Department of Canadian Heritage. 'Canada Book Fund'. At: <www.pch.gc.ca/eng/1268182505843/1268255450528>. (1 Nov. 2010)

———. 2010d. Department of Canadian Heritage. 'Canada Periodical Fund'. At: <www.pch.gc.ca/eng/1268240166828>. (10 Nov. 2010)

———. 2010e. Digital Economy Consultation. At: <www.digitaleconomy.gc.ca>. (9 Aug. 2010)

Canada Post. 2009. *Annual Report*. At: <www.canadapost.ca>. (10 Nov. 2010)

Canadian Broadcasting Corporation (CBC). 1977. *The Press and the Prime Minister: A Story of Unrequited Love*. TV documentary directed and produced by George Robertson. Toronto: CBC.

———. 1999a. *CBC Annual Report, 1998–99*. Ottawa: CBC.

———. 1999b. 'It's Time to Talk About the CBC . . . Your Voice Matters', press release, 9 Apr.

——— 2003. 'Response to Broadcasting Notice 2003–54', 1 Dec. At: <www.cbc.radio-canada.ca/submissions/crtc/2003/BPN_CRTC_2003-54_CBCSRC281103_e.pdf>.

———. 2009. *CBC/Radio-Canada Annual Report*. Toronto: CBC/Radio Canada. At: <www.cbc.radio-canada.ca/annualre ports/2008-2009/index.shtml>.

Canadian Film and Television Production Association (CFTPA). 2009. *Profile 2009: An Economic Report on the Canadian Film and Television Production Industry*. At: <www.cftpa.ca>. (1 Nov. 2010)

Canadian Media Directors' Council. 2010. *Media Digest 09/10*. Toronto: Marketing Magazine.

Canadian Media Research Consortium. 2009. *The State of the Media in Canada: A Work in Progress*. At: <www.cmrcccrm.ca/documents/SOM_Canada_0702.pdf>. (13 July 2010)

———. 2011. 'Canadian consumers unwilling to pay for news online', 29 Mar. At: <www.mediaresearch.ca>. (30 Mar. 2011)

Canadian Newspaper Association. 2009. 'Daily newspaper paid circulation data'. At: <www.cna-acj.ca/en/daily-newspaper-paid-circulation-data>. (18 Oct. 2010)

Canadian Press (CP). 1993. 'Ontario's A-G orders probe into news coverage in case of serial-rape suspect', *Vancouver Sun*, 1 Mar., A7.

———. 1999. 'CRTC cuts CKVL's license over complaints about host', *Montreal Gazette*, 1 May, C5.

Canadian Radio-television and Telecommunications Commission. 1999. 'The means may be changing but the goals remain constant', speech by Wayne Charman to the 1999 Broadcasting and Program Distribution Summit, 25 Feb. At: <www.crtc.gc.ca/_ENG/NEWS/SPEECHES/1999/S990225.htm>.

———. 2000. 'CRTC approves new digital pay and specialty television services—more choice for consumers', press release, 24 Nov. At: <www.crtc.gc.ca/ENG/NEWS/_RELEASES/2000/R001124-2.htm>.

———. 2001. 'CRTC renews CTV and Global's licences—more quality programming and services', press release, 2 Aug. At: <www.crtc.gc.ca/ENG/NEWS/_RELEASES/2001/R010802.htm>.

———. 2009a. CRTC Monitoring Report 2009. At: <www.crtc.gc.ca/eng/publications/reports/policymonitoring/2009/cmr.htm>. (25 July 2010)

———. 2009b. Speech, 8 June. At: <www.crtc.gc.ca/eng/com200/2009/s090608.htm>. (10 Nov. 2010)

———. 2010a. Broadcasting Regulatory Policy CRTC 2010–622. At: <www.crtc.gc.ca/eng/archive/2010/2010-622.htm>.

———. 2010b. Broadcasting Notice of Consultation CRTC 2010–783. At: <www.crtc.gc.ca/eng/archive/2010/2010-783.htm>. (19 Nov. 2010)

———. 2010c. *Navigating Convergence: Charting Canadian Communications Change and Regulatory Implications*. Ottawa. At <www.crtc.gc.ca/eng/publications/reports/rp1002.htm> (13 Oct. 2011)

———. 2010d. *Communications Monitoring Report 2010*, July. At: <www.crtc.gc.ca>. (27 Oct. 2010)

———. 2011. 'CRTC forum: Shaping regulatory approaches for the future'. Ottawa, Mar. At: <www.crtc.gc.ca/eng/publications/reports/rp110324.htm>. (15 Apr. 2011)

Canadian Wireless Telecommunications Association (CWTA). 2010. 'Wireless communications: A strong signal for a stronger canada', July. At: <www.cwta.ca>. (8 Nov. 2010)

Carey, James W. 1989. 'Technology and ideology: The case of the telegraph', in Carey, *Communication and Culture: Essays on Media and Society*. Boston: Unwin and Hyman.

———. 1998. 'The Internet and the end of the national communication system: Uncertain predictions of an uncertain future', *Journalism and Mass Communication Quarterly* 75, 1: 28–34.

Castells, Manuel. 1996. *The Rise of the Network Society*. New York: Blackwell.

———. 1999. *End of Millennium*. Oxford: Blackwell.

———. 2001. *The Internet Galaxy: Reflections on the Internet, Business, and Society*. Oxford: Oxford University Press.

CBC News. 2008. 'Ex-hacker "Mafiaboy" tells all in memoir', 11 Oct. At: <www.cbc.ca>. (18 Nov. 2010)

———. 2009. 'Moore restructuring Canada Music Fund', 31 July. At: <www.cbc.ca>. (4 Nov. 2010)

Centre for Contemporary Cultural Studies. 1982. *The Empire Fights Back: Racism in Britain in the 1970s*. London: Hutchinson.

Chapman, Glen. 2010. 'YouTube serving up to two billion videos daily', Agence France-Presse, 16 May. At: <www.google.com/hostednews/afp/article/ALeqM-5jK4sI9GfUTCKAkVGhDzp-J1ACZm9Q>. (13 Aug. 2010)

Charland, Maurice. 1986. 'Technological nationalism', *Canadian Journal of Political and Social Theory* 10, 1: 196–220.

Cheadle, Bruce. 2010. 'Veterans advocate Sean Bruyea settles privacy suit with Ottawa', *Toronto Star*, 18 Nov. At: <www.thestar.com/article/892818--veterans-advocate-sean-bruyea-settles-privacy-suit-with-ottawa>.

Cherry, Paul. 1998. '"A bad day," photographers say', *Montreal Gazette*, 11 Apr., A4.

Cocking, Clive. 1980. *Following the Leaders: A Media Watcher's Diary of Campaign '79*. Toronto: Doubleday.

Coleman, Stephen, and Karen Ross. 2010. *The Media and the Public: 'Them' and 'Us' in Media Discourse*. Chichester, UK: Wiley-Blackwell.

Collett, Peter, and R. Lamb. 1986. *Watching Families Watching TV*. Report to the Independent Broadcasting Authority. London.

Collins, Richard. 1992. *Satellite Television in Western Europe*, rev. edn. London: John Libbey Acamedia Research Monograph 1.

Commission on Freedom of the Press. 1947. *A Free and Responsible Press*. Chicago: University of Chicago Press.

Compton, James. 2010. 'Newspapers, labour and the flux of economic uncertainty', in Allan (2010).

comScore. 2010. 'Canada: Digital year in review 2010', Mar. At: <www.comscore.com/Press_Events/Presentations_Whitepapers/2011/2010_Canada_Digital_Year_in_Review>. (25 Mar. 2011)

Coulter, Natalie. 2010. 'Selling youth: Youth media and the marketplace', in *Shade* (2010: 149–64).

Cox, Kirwan. 1980. 'Hollywood's empire in Canada', in Pierre Véronneau and Piers Handling, eds, *Self-Portrait: Essays on the Canadian and Quebec Cinemas*. Ottawa: Canadian Film Institute.

Crawford, Michael G. 1990. *The Journalist's Legal Guide*, 2nd edn. Toronto: Carswell.

Croteau, David, and William Hoynes. 2003. *Media/Society*, 3rd edn. Thousand Oaks, Calif.: Pine Forge.

CTV. 2010. CTV Inc. 'Properties'. At: <www.ctv.ca/properties/>. (3 Aug. 2010)

Curran, James. 1990. 'The new revisionism in mass communication research: A reappraisal', *European Journal of Communication* 5, 2–3: 135–64.

Curtis, Liz. 1984. *Ireland, the Propaganda War: The Media and* the 'Battle for Hearts and Minds'. London: Pluto Press.

Dale, Stephen. 1996. *McLuhan's Children: The Greenpeace Message and the Media*. Toronto: Between the Lines.

Darnton, Robert. 1982. *The Literary Underground of the Old Regime*. Cambridge, Mass.: Harvard University Press.

Datamonitor. 2009. *Global Media: Industry Profile*. At: <www.datamonitor.com>. (15 July 2010)

Day, Richard J.F. 2005. *Gramsci Is Dead: Anarchist Currents in the New Social Movements*. Toronto: Between the Lines.

DeFleur, Melvin L., and Sandra Ball-Rokeach. 1989. *Theories of Mass Communication*, 5th edn. New York: Longman.

De Kerkhove, Derrick. 1995. *The Skin of Culture*. Toronto: Somerville Press.

de la Haye, Yves. 1980. *Marx and Engels on the Means of Communication (The Movement of Commodities, People, Information and Capital)*. New York: International General.

Demers, David. 1999. 'Corporate newspaper bashing: Is it justified?', *Newspaper Research Journal* 20, 1: 83–97.

Derrida, Jacques. 1981. *Positions*. London: Althone.

Desbarats, Peter. 1990. *Guide to Canadian News Media*. Toronto: Harcourt Brace.

Dizard, Wilson P. 1985. *The Coming Information Age: An Overview of Technology, Economics and Politics*. New York: Longman.

Drache, Daniel. 1995. 'Celebrating Innis: The man, the legacy and our future', in Drache, ed., *Staples, Markets and Cultural Change: Selected Essays*. Montreal and Kingston: McGill-Queen's University Press.

Drezner, Daniel, and Henry Farrell. 2004. 'The power and politics of blogs', paper presented at the annual meeting of the American Political Science Association. At: <www.utsc.utoronto.ca//farrel/blogpaperfinal.pdf>.

Drucker, Peter F. 1993. *Post-Capitalist Society*. New York: HarperCollins.

Dubinsky, Lon. 1996. 'Periodical publishing', in Michael Dorland, ed., *The Cultural Industries in Canada: Problems, Policies and Prospects*. Toronto: James Lorimer.

Dubrowski, Wojtek. 2008. 'Quebecor's Sun Media to cut 600 jobs', *Ottawa Citizen*, 16 Dec., 3.

Durham Peters, John. 1999. *Speaking into the Air: A History of the Idea of Communication*. Chicago: University of Chicago Press.

Dutrisac, Robert. 2002. 'Concentration de la presse—Québec demandera à l'industrie de s'autoréglementer', *Le Devoir*, 6 Sept., A3.

Dyer-Witheford, Nick. 1999. *Cyber-Marx: Cycles and Circuits of Struggle in High Technology Capitalism*. Champaign: University of Illinois Press.

Eagleton, Terry. 1991. *Ideology: An Introduction*. London: Verso.

Eaman, Ross Allan. 1994. *Channels of Influence: CBC Audience Research and the Canadian Public*. Toronto: University of Toronto Press.

Eco, Umberto. 1982. 'Narrative structure in Fleming', in B. Waites et al., eds, *Popular Culture Past and Present*. Milton Keynes, UK: Open University Press.

———. 'The multiplication of the media', in Eco, Travels in Hyper-reality. New York: Harcourt Brace Jovanovich, 148–69.

Ėdinova. 2008. *The Diffusion and Distribution of French-Language Books in Canada*, Aug. Montreal: Ėdinova.

Edwardson, Ryan. 2008. *Canadian Content: Culture and the Quest for Nationhood*. Toronto: University of Toronto Press.

Eisenstein, Elizabeth. 1979. *The Printing Press as an Agent of Change*, 2 vols. New York: Cambridge University Press.

———. 1983. *The Printing Revolution in Early Modern Europe*. Cam-bridge: Cambridge University Press.

El Akkad, Omar. 2011. 'Canadians' Internet usage nearly double the worldwide average', *Globe and Mail*, 9 Mar. At: <www.theglobeandmail.com/news/technology/canadians-internet-usage-nearly-double-the-worldwide-average/article1934508/>. (9 Mar. 2011)

——— and Jacquie McNish. 2010. 'A regulatory nightmare: Facebook and its goal of a less private Web', *Globe and Mail*, 18 Nov., A16.

Ellul, Jacques. 1964. *The Technological Society*. New York: Knopf.

Elmer, Greg, and Mike Gasher, eds. 2005. *Contracting Out Hollywood: Runaway Productions and Foreign Location Shooting*. Lanham, Md: Rowman & Littlefield.

Ericson, Richard V., Patricia M. Baranek, and Janet B.L. Chan. 1989. *Negotiating Control: A Study of News Sources*. Toronto: University of Toronto Press.

Eslin, Martin. 1980. 'The exploding stage', CBC-Radio, *Ideas* (Oct.).

Everett-Green, Robert. 2010. 'COC uses cash infusion despite selling out every show', *Globe and Mail*, 27 Oct., R4.

Featherstone, Mike. 1996. 'Localism, globalism, and cultural identity', in Rob Wilson and Wimal Dissanayake, eds, *Global/Local: Cultural Production and the Transnational Imaginary*. Durham, NC: Duke University Press.

Fédération professionelle des journalistes du Québec. 2010. 'La FPJQ appuie la tenue d'une commission parlementaire sur le conflit au *Journal de Montréal*', 11 Oct. At: <www.fpjq.org/>. (18 Oct. 2010)

Feenberg, Andrew. 1999. *Questioning Technology*. New York: Routledge.

Felczak, Michael. 2006. 'Online publishing, technical representation, and the politics of code: The case of CJC-Online', unpublished paper.

Fenton, Natalie. 2010. 'News in the ditigal age', in Allan (2010: 557–67).

Fessenden, Helen. 1974. *Fessenden: Builder of Tomorrows*. New York: Arno Press.

Filion, Michel. 1996. 'Radio', in Michael Dorland, ed., *The Cultural Industries in Canada: Problems, Policies and Prospects*. Toronto: James Lorimer.

Fiske, John. 1987. *Television Culture*. London: Routledge.

———. 1989a. *Reading the Popular*. Boston: Unwin Hyman.

———. 1989b. *Understanding Popular Culture*. Boston: Unwin Hyman.

———. 1989c. 'Moments of television: Neither the text nor the audience', in Ellen Seiter et al., eds, *Remote Control*. London: Routledge.

Fletcher, Fred. 1981. *The Newspaper and Public Affairs*, vol. 7, Research Publications for the Royal Commission on Newspapers. Ottawa: Supply and Services.

Foot, Richard. 1999. 'Court orders magazine to stop writing about abortion', *National Post*, 3 May, A4.

Fornas, J., U. Lindberg, and O. Sernhede. 1988. *Under Rocken*. Stockholm: Symposium.

Foucault, Michel. 1980. *The History of Sexuality*, trans. Robert Hurley. New York: Vintage Books.

———. 1988. *Madness and Civilization: A History of Insanity in the Age of Reason*, trans. Richard Howard. New York: Vintage Books.

———. 1995. *Discipline and Punish: The Birth of the Prison*, trans. Alan Sheridan. New York: Vintage Books.

Franklin, Sarah, C. Lury, and J. Stacey. 1992. 'Feminism and cultural studies', in Paddy Scannell et al., eds, *Culture and Power*. London: Sage.

Friedan, Betty. 1963. *The Feminine Mystique*. New York: Norton.

Friedman, Thomas L. 2005. *The World Is Flat: A Brief History of the Twenty-First Century*. New York: Farrar, Straus & Giroux.

Friend, David. 2010. 'Sun papers publisher to cut 600 jobs across Canada', Saint John *Telegraph-Journal*, 17 Dec., B5.

Frith, Simon. 1988. 'The industrialization of popular music', in James Lull, ed., *Popular Music and Communication*. Newbury Park, Calif.: Sage, 53–77.

Gans, Herbert. 1979. *Deciding What's News: A Study of CBS Evening News, NBC Nightly News, Newsweek, and Time*. New York: Pantheon Books.

Garfinkel, Harold. 1984. *Studies in Ethnomethodology*. Cambridge: Polity Press.

Gasher, Mike. 1988. 'Free trade and the Canadian film industry', *Canadian Dimension* (Nov.): 31–4.

———. 1992. 'The myth of meritocracy: Ignoring the political economy of the Canadian film industry', *Canadian Journal of Communication* 17, 2: 371–8.

———. 1995. 'Culture lag: The liberal record', *Point of View* 26 (Winter): 22–4.

———. 1997. 'From sacred cows to white elephants: Cultural policy under siege', *Canadian Issues* 19: 13-29.

———. 1998. 'Invoking public support for public broadcasting: The Aird Commission revisited', *Canadian Journal of Communication* 23: 189–216.

———. 2002. *Hollywood North: The Feature Film Industry in British Columbia*. Vancouver: University of British Columbia Press.

———. 2007. 'The view from here: A news-flow study of the on-line editions of Canada's national newspapers', *Journalism Studies* 8, 2: 299–319.

———. 2010. 'From the business of journalism to journalism as business: 1990 to the present', in Paul Benedetti, Kim Kierans, and Tim Currie, eds, *The New Journalist*. Toronto: Emond Montgomery, 63–76.

Geddes, John. 2010. 'Voice of fire: Are we over this yet?', *Macleans.ca*, 21 Jan. At: <www2.macleans.ca/2010/01/21/are-we-over-this-yet/>. (3 Aug. 2010)

Geist, Michael. 2006. 'Libel case key for Internet free speech', *Toronto Star*, 31 July, D3.

Gendreau, Bianca. 2000. 'Moving the mail', in Francine Brousseau, ed., *Special Delivery: Canada's Postal Heritage*. Fredericton, NB, and Hull, Que.: Goose Lane Editions and Canadian Museum of Civilization, 125–39.

Geraghty, Christine. 1991. *Women and Soap Opera: A Study of Prime-Time Soaps*. Cambridge: Polity Press.

Gerbner, George. 1969. 'Towards "cultural indicators": The analysis of mass-mediated public message systems', *AV Communication Review* 17, 2: 137–48.

———. 1977. *Trends in Network Drama and Viewer Conceptions of Social Reality, 1967–76*. Philadelphia: Annenburg School of Communications, University of Pennsylvania.

Giddens, Anthony. 1984. *The Constitution of Society: An Outline of a Theory of Structuration*. Berkeley: University of California Press.

Gilder, George F. 1991. 'Into the telecosm', Harvard Business Review (Mar.–Apr.): 150–61.

Gillmor, Don. 2004. *We the Media: Grassroots Journalism by the People, for the People*. Sebastopol, Calif.: O'Reilly.

Gingras, Anne-Marie. 2006. *Médias et démocratie: le grand malentendu*. Québec: Presses de l'Université du Québec.

Glaser, Mark. 2010. 'Citizen journalism: Widening world views, extending democracy', in Allan (2010: 578–90).

Glasgow Media Group. 1976. *Bad News*. Boston: Routledge & Kegan Paul.

Globe and Mail. 2002. 'When violating rights becomes the routine', 19 Aug., A12.

———. 2010. 'Canada's long form census debate', 21 July. At: <www.theglobeandmail.com/news/politics/canadas-long-form-census-debate/article1647591>. (25 Nov. 2010)

Globerman, Steven. 1983. *Cultural Regulation in Canada*. Montreal: Institute for Research on Public Policy.

Goffman, Erving. 1959. *The Presentation of Self in Everyday Life*. Harmondsworth, UK: Penguin.

Goody, J.R. 1977. *The Domestication of the Savage Mind*. Cambridge: Cambridge University Press.

Grant, George. 1969. *Technology and Empire*. Toronto: Anansi.

Grant, Peter S., and Chris Wood. 2004. *Blockbusters and Trade Wars: Popular Culture in a Globalized World*. Vancouver: Douglas & McIntyre.

Gratton, Michel. 1987. *'So, What Are the Boys Saying?' An Inside Look at Brian Mulroney in Power*. Toronto: McGraw-Hill Ryerson.

Gray, Ann. 1999. 'Audience and reception research in retrospect: The trouble with audiences', in *Alasuutari* (1999: 22–37).

Grossberg, Lawrence, Ellen Wartella, D. Charles Whitney, and J. Macgregor Wise. 2006. *MediaMaking: Mass Media in Popular Culture*, 2nd edn. Thousand Oaks, Calif.: Sage.

Gunster, Shane. 2004. *Capitalizing on Culture*. Toronto: University of Toronto Press.

Habermas, Jürgen. 1989. *The Structural Transformation of the Public Sphere: An Inquiry into a Category of Bourgeois Society*. Cambridge: Polity Press.

———. 1996. 'The public sphere', in Paul Marris and Sue Thornham, eds, *Media Studies: A Reader*. Edinburgh: Edinburgh University Press, 55–9.

Hackett, Robert A., and Richard Gruneau. 2000. *The Missing News: Filters and Blindspots in Canada's Press*. Ottawa and Aurora, Ont.: Canadian Centre for Policy Alternatives and Garamond Press.

——— and Yuezhi Zhao. 1998. *Sustaining Democracy? Journalism and the Politics of Objectivity*. Toronto: Garamond Press.

Hall, Edward T. 1980. *The Silent Language*. Westport, Conn.: Greenwood Press.

Hall, Stuart. 1980. 'Encoding/decoding', in Hall et al. (1980).

———. 1993. 'Encoding/decoding', in Simon During, ed., *The Cultural Studies Reader*. London: Routledge.

———. 1995. 'New cultures for old', in Massey and Jess (1995).

———. 1997. 'The work of representation', in Hall, ed., *Representation: Cultural Representations and Signifying Practices*. London: Sage.

——— et al. 1978. *Policing the Crisis: Mugging, the State and Law and Order*. London: Macmillan.

———, Dorothy Hobson, Andrew Love, and Paul Willis, eds. 1980. *Culture, Media, Language: Working Papers in Cultural Studies*. London: Hutchinson.

Hamelink, Cees J. 1994. *The Politics of World Communication*. London: Sage.

———. 1995. 'Information imbalance across the globe', in Ali Monhmmedi, ed., *Questioning the Media: A Critical Introduction*. Thousand Oaks, Calif.: Sage, 293–307.

Handfield, Catherine. 2010. 'Journal de Montréal: Les syndiqués rejettent l'offre patronale', 12 Oct. At: <lapresseaffaires.cyberpresse.ca>. (18 Oct. 2010)

Hanitzsch, Thomas. 2007. 'Deconstructing journalism culture: Toward a universal theory', *Communication Theory* 17: 367–85.

Hardin, Herschel. 1974. *A Nation Unaware*. Vancouver: Douglas & McIntyre.

Hartley, John. 1987. 'Invisible fictions', *Textual Practice* 1, 2: 121–38.

———. 1992. *The Politics of Pictures: The Creation of the Public in the Age of Popular Media*. London and New York: Routledge.

———. 1996. *Popular Reality: Journalism, Modernity, Popular Culture*. London: Arnold.

Havelock, Eric. 1976. *Origins of Western Literacy*. Toronto: OISE Press.

Hayes, David. 1992. *Power and Influence: The Globe and Mail and the News Revolution*. Toronto: Key Porter.

Hebdige, Dick. 1979. *Subculture: The Meaning of Style*. London: Methuen.

Heflet, Miguel. 2009. 'YouTube eases the way to more revenue', NYT.com, 6 Oct. At: <www.nytimes.com/2009/10/07/technology/internet/07youtube.html>. (4 Aug. 2010)

Heilbroner, Robert L. 1980. *The Worldly Philosophers: The Lives, Times, and Ideas of the Great Economic Thinkers*. New York: Simon & Schuster.

Henry, Frances, and Carol Tator. 2000. *Racist Discourse in Canada's English Print Media*. Toronto: Canadian Race Relations Foundation, Mar.

———, ———, Winston Mattis, and Tim Rees. 2000. *The Colour of Democracy: Racism in Canadian Society*. Toronto: Harcourt Brace.

Herman, Edward S., and Noam Chomsky. 2002. *Manufacturing Consent: The Political Economy of the Mass Media*. New York: Pantheon Books.

——— and Robert W. McChesney. 1997. *The Global Media: The New Missionaries of Global Capitalism*. Washington: Cassell.

Hermes, Joke. 2006. 'Feminism and the politics of method', in Mimi White and James Schwoch, eds, *Questions of Method in Cultural Studies*. Oxford: Blackwell, 154–74.

Hester, Al. 1974. 'International news agencies', in Alan Wells, ed., *Mass Communications: A World View*. Palo Alto, Calif.: Mayfield Publishing.

Hickling Arthurs Low Corp. 2009. *Canada's Entertainment Software Industry: The Opportunities and Challenges of a Growing Industry*, 25 Mar. At: <www.theesa.ca/facts-and-research/research.php>. (12 Nov. 2010)

Hobson, D. 1980. 'Housewives and the mass media', in Hall et al. (1980).

———. 1982. *Crossroads: The Drama of Soap Opera*. London: Methuen.

Hogg, Chris. 2006. 'Taiwan breeds green-glowing pigs', *BBC News*, 12 Jan. At: <news.bbc.co.uk/2/hi/asia-pacific/4605202.stm>.

Hoggart, Richard. 1992 [1957]. *The Uses of Literacy*. New Brunswick, NJ: Transaction.

Industry Canada. 2009. 'Canadian ICT sector profile', Aug. At: <www.ic.gc.ca/eic/site/ict-tic.nsf/eng/h_it07229.html>. (12 Nov. 2010)

Infopresse. 2010. 'Télévision', in *Médias: Guide annuel des médias*. Montreal: Éditions Infopresse, 42.

Information Highway Advisory Council. 1997. *Preparing Canada for a Digital World: Final Report*. Ottawa: Industry Canada.

Innis, Harold. 1950. *Empire and Communications*. Toronto: Oxford University Press.

———. 1951. *The Bias of Communication*. Toronto: University of Toronto Press.

International Women's Media Foundation. 2011. *Global Report on the Status of Women in the News Media*. Washington: International Women's Media Foundation.

Ives, Nat. 2010. 'Mounting web woes pummel newspapers', *Advertising Age* 81, 26: 6.

Iype, Mark. 2010. 'CP news service to privatize', *Vancouver Sun*, 5 July, B2.

Jay, Martin. 1974. *The Dialectical Imagination*. London: Routledge.

Jeffrey, Liss. 1994. 'Rethinking audiences for cultural industries: Implications for Canadian research', *Canadian Journal of Communication* 19, 3–4: 495–522.

Jenkins, Henry. 1992. *Textual Poachers: Television Fans and Participatory Culture*. New York: Routledge.

———. 2006. *Convergence Culture: Where Old and New Media Collide*. New York: New York University Press.

Jensen, Klaus Bruhn. 1990. 'The politics of polysemy: Television news, everyday consciousness and political action', *Media, Culture and Society* 12, 1: 57–77.

Jhally, Sut. 1997. *Advertising and the End of the World*. Media Education Foundation (video).

Jiwani, Yasmin. 2010. 'Rac(e)ing the nation: Media and minorities', in Shade (2010: 271–86).

Johnston, Russell. 2010. 'Advertising in Canada', in Shade (2010: 104–20).

Karim, Karim H. 2009. 'Commentary: Pundits, pachyderms, and pluralism: The never-ending debate on multiculturalism', *Canadian Journal of Communication* 34: 701–10.

Katz, Elihu, and Paul Lazarsfeld. 1955. *Personal Influence: The Part Played by People in the Flow of Mass Communications*. New York: Free Press.

Kehaulani Goo, Sara. 2006. 'Ready for its close-up', *Washington Post*, 7 Oct. At: <www.washingtonpost.com/wpdyn/content/article/2006/10/06/AR2006100600660.html>. (4 Aug. 2010)

Khakoo, Salza. 2006. 'Colour TV', *Ryerson Review of Journalism* (Spring). At: <www.rrj.ca/issue/2006/spring/624/>.

King, Russell. 1995. 'Migrations, globalization and place', in Massey and Jess (1995).

Kovach, Bill, and Tom Rosenstiel. 2001. *The Elements of Journalism: What Newspeople Should Know and the Public Should Expect*. New York: Crown.

Krashinsky, Susan. 2010a. 'CRTC favours broadcasters in TV shakeup', *Globe and Mail*, 23 Mar., A1.

———. 2010b. 'Cineplex to unveil movie download service', *Globe and Mail*, 18 Nov., B10.

———. 2010c. 'Al Jazeera English to launch in Canada', *Globe and Mail*, 5 May, B8.

Krippendorf, Klaus. 2004. *Content Analysis: An Introduction to Its Methodology*. Thousand Oaks, Calif.: Sage.

Kristeva, Julia. 1969. 'Le mot, le dialogue et le roman', in *Sèmiòtikè: Recherches pour une sémanalyse*. Paris: Editions du Seuil.

Ladurantaye, Steve. 2010. 'Bell ushers in new era with CTV deal', *Globe and Mail*, 11 Sept., 1, 18.

LaGuardia, Robert. 1977. *From Ma Perkins to Mary Hartman: The Illustrated History of Soap Opera*. New York: Ballantine Books.

Larrain, Jorge. 1979. *The Concept of Ideology*. London: Hutchinson.

———. 1983. *Marxism and Ideology*. London: Macmillan.

Law, J., and M. Callon. 1988. 'Engineering and sociology in a military aircraft project: A network analysis of technological change', *Social Problems* 35, 3: 285.

Learmonth, Michael. 2010. 'Can YouTube rake in Google-size revenue?', *Advertising Age* 81, 5: 1–19.

Leblanc, Jean-André. 1990. 'Pour s'arranger avec les gars des vues, l'industrie du cinéma et de la video au Canada 1982–1984', in Gaëtan Tremblay, ed., *Les Industries de la Culture et de la Communication au Québec et au Canada*. Sillery, Que.: Presses de l'Université du Québec.

Lee, Richard E. 2003. *The Life and Times of Cultural Studies*. Durham, NC: Duke University Press.

Leiss, William, Stephen Kline, and Sut Jhally. 1990. *Social Communication in Advertising: Persons, Products and Images of Well-Being*, 2nd edn. Scarborough, Ont.: Nelson Canada.

———, ———, ———, and Jaqueline Botterill. 2005. *Social Communication in Advertising*, 3rd edn. New York: Routledge.

Lent, John A. 1998. 'The animation industry and its offshore factories', in Gerald Sussman and John A. Lent, eds, *Global Productions: Labor in the Making of the 'Information Society'*. Cresskill, NJ: Hampton Press.

Lessig, Lawrence. 2001. *The Future of Ideas: The Fate of the Commons in a Connected World*. New York: Random House.

———. 2008. *Remix: Making Art and Commerce Thrive in the Hybrid Economy*. New York: Penguin.

Lévi-Strauss, Claude. 1969. *The Raw and the Cooked*. London: Jonathan Cape.

Litt, Paul. 1992. *The Muses, the Masses, and the Massey Commission*. Toronto: University of Toronto Press.

Lord, A.B. 1964. *The Singer of Tales*. Cambridge, Mass.: Harvard University Press.

Lorimer, Rowland. 2002. 'Mass communication: Some redefinitional notes', *Canadian Journal of Communication* 27, 1: 63–72.

Lumpkin, John J. 2003. 'US officials examine the quality of information war planners had before invasion', 22 May. At: <www.sfgate.com/cgi-bin/article._cgi?f=/news/archive/2003/05/22/national1251EDT0637.DTL>.

Lynch, Jake, and Annabel McGoldrick. 2005. *Peace Journalism*. Stroud, UK: Hawthorn Press.

Lyons, Daniel. 2010. 'Think really different', *Newsweek*, 5 Apr., 47–51.

MacCharles, Tonda. 2010. 'No right to shield sources, court rules', *Toronto Star*, 8 May, 4.

McChesney, Robert W. 1997. *Corporate Media and the Threat to Democracy*. New York: Seven Stories Press.

———. 1998. 'The political economy of global communication', in Robert W. McChesney, Ellen Meiksins Wood, and John Bellamy Foster, eds, *Capitalism and the Information Age: The Political Economy of the Global Communication Revolution*. New York: Monthly Review Press.

———. 2003. 'The new global media', in David Held and Anthony McGrew, eds, *The Global Transformations Reader: An Introduction to the Globalization Debate*. Cambridge: Polity Press, 260–8.

MacDonald, Gayle. 2007. 'Wanted: Cancon everywhere', *Globe and Mail*, 24 Nov., R13.

McGuigan, Jim. 1992. *Cultural Populism*. London: Routledge.

McKercher, Catherine. 2002. *Newsworkers Unite: Labor, Convergence,* and North American Newspapers. Lanham, Md: Rowman & Littlefield.

McLuhan, Marshall. 1962. *The Gutenberg Galaxy: The Making of Typographic Man*. Toronto: University of Toronto Press.

———. 1964. *Understanding Media: The Extensions of Man*. Toronto: McGraw-Hill.

McQuail, Denis. 2000. *McQuail's Mass Communication Theory*, 4th edn. Thousand Oaks, Calif.: Sage.

Magder, Ted. 1985. 'A featureless film policy: Culture and the Canadian state', *Studies in Political Economy* 16: 81–109.

———. 1993. *Canada's Hollywood: The Canadian State and Feature Films*. Toronto: University of Toronto Press.

Mah, Bill. 2010. 'Netflix launches in Canada', *Calgary Herald*, 23 Sept., C1.

Malik, S. 1989. 'Television and rural India', *Media, Culture and Society* 11, 4: 459–84.

Marcuse, Herbert. 1963 [1954]. *Reason and Revolution: Hegel and the Rise of Social Theory*. New York: Humanities Press.

———. 1964. *One-Dimensional Man: Studies in the Ideology of Advanced Industrial Society*. Boston: Beacon Press.

Marshall, P. David. 2004. *New Media Cultures*. New York: Arnold.

Martin, Robert, and Stuart Adam. 1991. *A Source-book of Canadian Media Law*. Ottawa: Carleton University Press.

Marvin, Carolyn. 1988. *When Old Technologies Were New: Thinking About Electric Communication in the Late Nineteenth Century*. New York: Oxford University Press.

Massey, Doreen. 1991. 'A global sense of place', *Marxism Today* (June): 24–9.

———. 1992. 'A place called home?', *New Formations* 17: 3–15.

———. 1995. 'The conceptualization of place', in *Massey and Jess* (1995).

——— and Pat Jess, eds. 1995. *A Place in the World? Cultures and Globalization*. New York: Oxford University Press.

——— and ———. 1995. 'Places and cultures in an uneven world', in Massey and Jess (1995).

Masthead. 2010. 'Canadian Periodical Fund: Winners and losers', 21 Jan. At: <www.mastheadonline.com/news/>. (11 Nov. 2010)

Mayeda, Andrew, and David Akin. 2008. 'PM slams Quebec arts community; Protests over cuts fail to "resonate with ordinary people"', *National Post*, 24 Sept., A4.

Media Awareness Network. 2010. 'Ethnic media in Canada'. At: <www.media-awareness.ca>. (26 July 2010)

Mediacaster Magazine. 2011. 'TV or not TV?', 25 Mar. At: <www.mediacastermagazine.com/issues/story.aspx?aid=1000405845>. (25 Mar. 2011)

Media Education Foundation. 2002. *Killing Us Softly III* (video). Northampton., Mass.

Mencher, Melvin. 2000. *News Reporting and Writing*, 8th edn. New York: McGraw-Hill.

Meyers, Marian. 1997. 'News of battering', in Dan Berkowitz, ed., *Social Meanings of News: A Text-Reader*. Thousand Oaks, Calif.: Sage.

Meyrowitz, Joshua. 1985. *No Sense of Place*. New York: Oxford University Press.

Mezei, Jean-François. 2009. 'An analysis of telecom decision CRTC 2008–108'. At: <www.vaxination.ca/crtc/2008_108_analysis1.pdf>. (30 Mar. 2009)

Milberry, Kate. Forthcoming. 'Freeing the net: Online mobilizations in defense of democracy', in Kirsten Kozolanka, Patricia Mazepa, and David Skinner, eds, *Alternative Media in Canada*. Vancouver: University of British Columbia Press.

Miller, John. 1998. *Yesterday's News: Why Canada's Daily Newspapers Are Failing Us*. Halifax: Fernwood.

———— and Caron Court. 2004. 'Who's telling the news? Race and gender representation in Canada's daily newsrooms'. At: <www.diversitywatch.ryerson.ca/home_miller_2004report.htm>.

Miller, Toby. 2010. 'Why do so many First World academics think cultural imperialism is old hat when so many other people don't?', lecture, Canadian Communication Association, Montreal, 2 June.

Mills, Sara. 2004. *Discourse*. New York: Routledge.

Mitchell, D. 1988. 'Culture as political discourse in Canada', in Rowland Lorimer and D.C. Wilson, eds, *Communication Canada*. Toronto: Kagan and Woo.

Mitrovica, Andrew. 2006–7. 'Hear no evil, write no lies', *The Walrus* 3, 10: 37–43.

Modleski, Tania. 1984. *Loving with a Vengeance: Mass-Produced Fantasies for Women*. London: Methuen.

Moll, Marita, and Leslie Regan Shade, eds. 2004. *Seeking Convergence in Policy and Practice*. Ottawa: Canadian Centre for Policy Alternatives.

Morley David. 1980. *The 'Nationwide' Audience: Structure and Decoding*. British Film Institute Television Monographs, 11. London: BFI.

————. 1986. *Family Television: Cultural Power and Domestic Leisure*. London: Comedia.

———— and Kevin Robins. 1995. *Spaces of Identity: Global Media, Electronic Landscapes and Cultural Boundaries*. London: Routledge.

Morris, Peter. 1978. *Embattled Shadows: A History of Canadian Cinema, 1895–1939*. Montreal and Kingston: McGill-Queen's University Press.

Mosco, Vincent. 1996. *The Political Economy of Communication: Rethinking and Renewal*. London: Sage.

————. 1998. 'Militant particularism: Beta testing a new society'. At: <www.mip.at/attachments/362>. (31 May 2011)

————. 2009. *The Political Economy of Communication*, 2nd edn. Los Angeles: Sage.

Mulvey, Laura. 1975. 'Visual pleasure and narrative cinema', *Screen* 16, 3: 6–18.

Murdock, Graham. 1990. 'Large corporations and the control of the communications industries', in Michael Gurevitch, Tony Bennett, James Curran, and Jane Woollacott, eds, *Culture, Society and the Media*. Toronto: Methuen.

Murphy, Rex. 2010. 'A government gone viral', *National Post*, 19 Mar., A16

Murray, Catherine. 2010. 'Audience-making: Issues in Canadian audience studies', in *Shade* (2010: 83-103).

Murray, Laura. 2005. 'Bill 60 and copyright in Canada: Opportunities lost and found', *Canadian Journal of Communication* 30, 4: 649–54.

Nash, Knowlton. 1994. *The Microphone Wars: A History of Triumph and Betrayal at the CBC*. Toronto: McClelland & Stewart.

National Campus and Community Radio Association (NCRA). 1987. 'The NCRA statement of principles'. At: <www.ncra.ca/business/NCRAStatement.html>. (29 July 2004)

Negroponte, Nicholas. 1995. *Being Digital*. New York: Knopf.

Nesbitt-Larking, Paul. 2001. *Politics and the Media: Canadian Perspectives*. Peterborough, Ont.: Broadview Press.

NewMedia TrendWatch. 2010. Canada, June. At: <www.newmediatrendwatch.com/markets-by-country/11-long-haul/45-canada>. (11 Nov. 2010)

Nielsen, Greg. 2009. 'Framing dialogue on immigration in the *New York Times*', *Aether: Journal of Media Geography* 4: 22–42. At: <130.166.124.2/~aether/volume_04.html>.

O'Brian, Amy. 2006. 'Will this man save the music biz? Vancouver's Terry McBride, who manages a

clutch of superstars, found success by learning to ignore his critics', *Vancouver Sun*, 9 Sept., F3.

Olson, David R., ed. 1980. *The Social Foundations of Language and Thought*. New York: Norton.

Ong, Walter. 1982. *Orality and Literacy: The Technologizing of the Word*. London: Methuen.

Ontario Media Development Corporation. 2008. *A Strategic Study of the Magazine Industry in Ontario*, 30 Sept. At: <www.omdc.on.ca>. (10 Nov. 2010)

————. 2010. *Industry Profile: Book Publishing*. At: <www.omdc.on.ca>. (1 Nov. 2010)

Ó Siochrú, Seán. 2010. 'Implementing communication rights', in Raboy and Shtern (2010).

Osler, Andrew M. 1993. *News: The Evolution of Journalism in Canada*. Toronto: Copp Clark Pitman.

Osnos, Peter. 2009. 'What's a fair share in the age of Google?', *Columbia Journalism Review* 48, 2: 25–8.

O'Sullivan, T., J. Hartley, D. Saunders, and J. Fiske. 1983. *Key Concepts in Communication*. Toronto: Methuen.

Pagé, Gilles-Philippe. 2004. 'Greenpeace's campaign strategies', *Peace Magazine* (July–Sept.): 13.

Paterson, Chris A. 2001. 'Media imperialism revisited: The global public sphere and the news agency agenda', in Stig Hjarvard, ed., *News in a Globalized Society*. Göteborg: Nordicom.

————. 2005. 'News agency dominance in international news on the Internet', in Skinner et al. (2005: 145–63).

Payzant, Geoffrey. 1984. *Glenn Gould: Music and Mind*. Toronto: Key Porter.

Peers, Frank. 1969. *The Politics of Canadian Broadcasting, 1920–1951*. Toronto: University of Toronto Press.

————. 1979. *The Public Eye*. Toronto: University of Toronto Press.

Pegg, Mark. 1983. *Broadcasting and Society 1918–1939*. London: Croom Helm.

Pendakur, Manjunath. 1990. *Canadian Dreams and American Control: The Political Economy of the Canadian Film Industry*. Toronto: Garamond Press.

———. 1998. 'Hollywood North: Film and TV production in Canada', in Gerald Sussman and John A. Lent, eds, *Global Productions: Labor in the Making of the 'Information Society'*. Cresskill, NJ: Hampton Press.

Pew Research Center, Project for Excellence in Journalism. 2010. *How News Happens: A Study of the News Ecosystem of One American City*, 11 Jan. At: <www.journalism.org/analysis_report/how_news_happens>. (6 Oct. 2010)

Picard, Robert G. 1989. *Media Economics: Concepts and Issues*. Newbury Park, Calif.: Sage.

pipa/Knowledge Network. 2003. 'Study finds widespread misperceptions on Iraq highly related to support for war'. At: <www.pipa.org/OnlineReports/Iraq/IraqMedia_Oct03/IraqMedia_Oct03_pr.pdf>.

Plato. 1973. *Phaedrus*, trans. Walter Hamilton. Toronto: Penguin.

Press, Andrea L. 2000. 'Recent developments in feminist communication theory', in James Curran and Michael Gurevitch, eds, *Mass Media and Society*. New York: Oxford University Press, 2–43.

——— and Sonia Livingstone. 2006. 'Taking audience research into the age of new media: Old problems and new challenges', in Mimi White, James Schwoch, and Dilip Goanker, eds, *Cultural Studies and Methodological Issues*. London: Blackwell, 175–200.

Print Measurement Bureau (PMB). 1998. *PMB 98 Readership Volume*. Toronto: PMB.

———. 2006. *PMB 98 Readership Volume*. Toronto: PMB.

———. 2009. *PMB 2009 Readership Volume*. Toronto: PMB.

———. n.d. 'Introducing PMB'. At: <www.pmb.ca>.

Pritchard, David, and Florian Sauvageau. 1999. *Les journalistes canadiens: Un portrait de fin de siècle*. Québec: Les Presses de l'Université Laval.

Propp, Vladimir. 1970. *Morphology of the Folktale*. Austin: University of Texas Press.

Quebecor. 2010. 'Quebecor at a glance'. At: <www.quebecor.com>. (3 Aug. 2010)

Quill, Greg. 2009. 'CBC revamps news flagships', *Toronto Star*, 22 Oct., A24.

Raboy, Marc. 1990. *Missed Opportunities: The Story of Canada's Broadcasting Policy*. Montreal and Kingston: McGill-Queen's University Press.

———. 1995a. *Accès inégal: les canaux d'influence en radiodiffusion*. Sainte-Foy, Que.: Presses de l'Université du Québec.

———. 1995b. 'The role of public consultation in shaping the Canadian broadcasting system', *Canadian Journal of Political Science* 28, 3: 455–77.

——— and Jeremy Shtern, eds. 2010. *Media Divides: Communication Rights and the Right to Communicate in Canada*. Vancouver: University of British Columbia Press.

Radway, Janice. 1984. *Reading the Romance: Women, Patriarchy and Popular Literature*. Chapel Hill: University of North Carolina Press.

Rantanen, Terhi. 1997. 'The globalization of electronic news in the 19th century', *Media, Culture and Society* 19, 4: 605–20.

Resnick, Philip. 2000. *The Politics of Resentment: British Columbia Regionalism and Canadian Unity*. Vancouver: University of British Columbia Press.

Rettberg, Jill Walker. 2008. *Blogging*. Cambridge: Polity Press.

Rever, Judi. 1995. 'France faces off with Rambo', *Globe and Mail*, 4 Feb., C3.

Reynolds, Bill. 2002. 'Why your local radio station sounds like this (white bread)', *Globe and Mail*, 3 Aug., R1, R5.

Rheingold, Howard. 2003. *Smart Mobs: The Next Social Revolution*. Cambridge, Mass.: Perseus.

———. 2008. 'Mobile media and political action', in James E. Katz, ed., *Handbook of Mobile Communication Studies*. New York: Springer, 225–39.

Rice-Barker, Leo. 1996. 'Victor victorious', *Playback*, 6 May, 1, 5, 14.

Richer, Jules. 1999. 'La presse québécoise en plein marasme: Chantal Hébert sonne l'alarme', *Le 30* 23, 3 (Mar.): 11–13.

Rideout, Vanda, and Andrew Reddick. 2001. 'Multimedia policy for Canada and the United States: Industrial development as public interest', in Vincent Mosco and Dan Schiller, eds, *Continental Order? Integrating North America for Cybercapitalism*. Lanham, Md: Rowman & Littlefield.

Rose, Gillian. 1995. 'Place and identity: A sense of place', in Massey and Jess (1995).

Rose, Jonathan, and Simon Kiss. 2006. 'Boundaries blurred: The mass media and politics in a hyper media age', in Paul Attallah and Leslie Regan Shade, eds, *Mediascapes: New Pattterns in Canadian Communication*, 2nd edn. Toronto: Thomson Nelson, 332–45.

Rosenberg, Ross. 2010. 'Sexual addictions: An introduction'. At: <www.rosenbergtherapist.com>. (9 Aug. 2010)

Rosengren, K.E., and S. Windahl. 1989. *Media Matters: TV Use in Childhood and Adolescence*. Norwood, NJ: Ablex.

Roth, Lorna. 1996. 'Cultural and racial diversity in Canadian broadcast journalism', in Valerie Alia, Brian Brennan, and Barry Hoffmaster, eds, *Deadlines and Diversity: Journalism Ethics in a Changing World*. Halifax: Fernwood.

———. 1998. 'The delicate acts of "colour balancing": Multiculturalism and Canadian television broadcasting policies and practices', *Canadian Journal of Communication* 23: 487–505.

———. 2005. *Something New in the Air: The Story of First Peoples Television Broadcasting in Canada*. Montreal and Kingston: McGill-Queen's University Press.

Rotstein, Abraham. 1988. 'The use and misuse of economics in cultural policy', in Rowland Lorimer and D.C. Wilson, eds, *Communication Canada: Issues in Broadcasting and New Technologies*. Toronto: Kagan and Woo.

Ruddock, Andy. 2007. *Investigating Audiences*. London: Sage.

Ruggles, Myles. 2005. *Automating Interaction: Formal and Informal Knowledge in the Digital Network Economy*. Cresskill, NJ: Hampton Press.

Rutherford, Donald. 1992. *Dictionary of Economics*. London: Routledge.

Rutherford, Paul. 1990. *When Television Was Young: Primetime Canada*. Toronto: University of Toronto Press.

Sassen, Saskia. 1998. *Globalization and Its Discontents*. New York: New Press.

Saussure, Ferdinand de. 1974. *Course in General Linguistics*. London: Fontana.

Scannell, Paddy. 1988. 'Radio times: The temporal arrangements of broadcasting in the modern world', in P. Drummond and R. Paterson, eds, *Television and Its Audiences: International Research Perspectives*. London: BFI.

——— and D. Cardiff. 1991. *A Social History of Broadcasting*, vol. 1, *Serving the Nation 1922–1939*. Oxford: Blackwell.

Schlesinger, Philip. 1978. *Putting 'Reality' Together: BBC News*. London: Constable.

———. 1983. *Televising 'Terrorism': Political Violence in Popular Culture*. London: Comedia.

Schudson, Michael. 1978. *Discovering the News: A Social History of American Newspapers*. New York: Basic Books.

Schulman, Mark. 1990. 'Control mechanisms inside the media', in John Downing, Ali Mohammadi, and Annebelle Sreberny-Mohammadi, eds, *Questioning the Media: A Critical Introduction*. Newbury Park, Calif.: Sage.

Schulman, Norma. 1993. 'Conditions of their own making: An intellectual history of the Centre for Contemporary Cultural Studies at the University of Birmingham', *Canadian Journal of Communication* 18, 1: 51–74.

Schumacher, E.F. 1973. *Small Is Beautiful: Economics As If People Mattered*. New York: Harper & Row.

Seiter, Ellen, Hans Borchers, Gabrielle Kreutzner, and Eva-Maria Warth. 1989. *Remote Control: Television, Audiences, and Cultural Power*. London: Routledge.

Shade, Leslie Regan. 2005. 'Aspergate: Concentration, convergence, and censorship in Canadian media', in Skinner et al. (2005: 101–16).

———, ed. 2010. *Mediascapes: New Patterns in Canadian Communication*, 3rd edn. Toronto: Nelson Education.

Shannon, Claude E., and Warren Weaver. 1949. *The Mathematical Theory of Communication*. Urbana: University of Illinois Press.

Shea, Albert A. 1952. *Culture in Canada: A Study of the Findings of the Royal Commission on National Development in the Arts, Letters and Sciences (1949–1951)*. Toronto: Core.

Shirky, Clay. 2008. *Here Comes Everybody: The Power of Organizing without Organizations*. New York: Penguin Press.

Sholle, David. 2002. 'Disorganizing the "new technology"', in Greg Elmer, ed., *Critical Perspectives on the Internet*. Lanham, Md: Rowman & Littlefield, 3–26.

Signorielli, Nancy, and Michael Morgan, eds 1990. *Cultivation Analysis*. Beverly Hills, Calif.: Sage.

Silverman, Craig. 2007. *Regret the Error: How Media Mistakes Pollute the Press and Imperil Free Speech*. New York: Sterling.

Silverman, Kaja. 1983. *The Subject of Semiotics*. New York: Oxford University Press.

Silverstone, R. 1981. *The Message of Television: Myth and Narrative in Contemporary Culture*. London: Heinemann Educational Books.

———. 2007. *Media and Morality: On the Rise of the Mediapolis*. Cambridge: Polity Press.

Skinner, David. 2004. 'Reform or alternatives? Limits and pressures on changing the Canadian mediascape', *Democratic Communiqué* 19 (Spring): 13–36.

———. 2010. 'Minding the growing gaps: Alternative media in Canada', in Shade (2010: 221–36).

———, James Compton, and Mike Gasher, eds. 2005. *Converging Media, Diverging Politics: A Political Economy of News Media in the United States and Canada*. Lanham, Md: Lexington Books.

Smith, Adam. 1937 [1776]. *An Inquiry into the Nature and Causes of the Wealth of Nations*. New York: Modern Library.

Smythe, Dallas. 1977. 'Communications: Blindspot of Western Marxism', *Canadian Journal of Political and Social Theory* 1: 1–27.

———. 1981. 'Communications: Blindspot of economics', in William H. Melody, Liora R. Salter, and Paul Heyer, eds, *Culture, Communication and Dependency: The Tradition of H.A. Innis*. Norwood, NJ: Ablex.

———. 1994. *Counterclockwise: Perspectives on Communication*, ed. Thomas Guback. Boulder, Colo.: Westview Press.

Société de développement des entreprises culturelles (SODEC). 2010). 'Livres'. At: <www.sodec.gouv.qc.ca/fr/programme/route/livre>. (10 Nov. 2010)

Sontag, Susan. 1999. 'On photography', in David Crowley and Paul Heyer, eds, *Communication in History: Technology, Culture and Society*. Don Mills, Ont.: Longman, 174–7

Sotiron, Minko. 1997. *From Politics to Profit: The Commercialization of Daily Newspapers, 1890–1920*. Montreal and Kingston: McGill-Queen's University Press.

Standing Senate Committee on Transportation and Communication. 2010. *Plan for a Digital Canada*. At: <www.planpouruncanadanumerique.com/index.php?option=com_content&view=article&id=1&Itemid=10&lang=en>.

Stanford, Jim. 2008. *Economics for Everyone: A Short Guide to the Economics of Capitalism*. Black Point, NS: Fernwood.

Statistics Canada. 1997. *Recent Cultural Statistics (Highlights from Canada's Culture, Heritage and Identity: A Statistical Perspective)*. At: <www.pch.gc.ca/culture/library/statscan/stats_e.htm>.

———. 1998a. 'Focus on culture', *Quarterly Bulletin from the Culture Statistics Program* (Winter). Catalogue no. 87–004–XPB.

———. 1998b. 'Hitting a high note: Canadian recording artists in 1998', *Quarterly Bulletin from the Culture Statistics Program* 14, 2. At: <www.statcan.ca/english/ads/87-004-XPB/pdf/fcdart.pdf>.

———. 2001. *Overview: Access to and Use of Information Communication Technology*. Catalogue no. 56–505–XIE. Ottawa: Minister of Industry, Mar.

———. 2003. *Immigration and Visible Minorities*. At: <www12.statcan.ca/english/census01/products/highlight/Ethnicity/Index.cfm?Lang+E>.

———. 2005. 'More magazines, higher profit', 14 June. At: <www.statcan.ca/english/freepub/11-002-XIE/2005/06/16505/16505_02.htm>.

———. 2006. 'Canadian Internet use survey', *The Daily*, 15 Aug. At: <www.statcan.ca/Daily/English/060815/d060815b.htm>.

———. 2009. *Canada Year Book 2009*. Ottawa: Statistics Canada, pp. 155-166.

———. 2010. 'Canadian Internet Use Survey', 10 May. <www.statcan.gc.ca/daily-quotidien/100510/dq100510a-eng.htm>. (28 July 2010)

Steele, Emily. 2010. 'Google wins Omnicom as ally', *Wall Street Journal*, 15 July. At: <online.wsj.com/article/NA_WSJ_PUB:SB10001424052748704746804575367401477982456.html>. (12 Aug. 2010)

Steeves, Valerie. 2010. 'Privacy in a networked world', in *Shade* (2010: 341–55).

Storey, J. 1993. *Cultural Theory and Popular Culture*. London: Harvester Wheatsheaf.

Sutel, Seth. 2000. 'New media marries old', *Montreal Gazette*, 11 Jan., F1, F4.

Taylor, Charles. 2005. *Modern Social Imaginaries*. Durham, NC: Duke University Press.

Taylor, Lesley Ciarula. 2011. 'Canadian scientists crack code for tracing anonymous emails', *Toronto Star*, 8 Mar. At: <www.thestar.com/news/canada/article/950625--canadian-scientists-crack-code-for-tracing-anonymous-emails?bn=1>.

Thompson, Edward P. 1980 [1963]. *The Making of the English Working Class*. Harmondsworth, UK: Penguin.

Thompson, John B. 1990. *Ideology and Modern Culture: Critical Social Theory in the Era of Mass Communication*. Stanford, Calif.: Stanford University Press

———. 1995. *The Media and Modernity*. Stanford, Calif.: Stanford University Press.

———. 1999. 'The trade in news', in David Crowley and Paul Heyer, eds, *Communication in History: Technology, Culture and Society*. Don Mills, Ont.: Longman, 118–22.

Thomson Reuters. 2009. 'About us'. At: <www.thomsonreuters.com>. (15 Dec. 2009)

Thorne, Stephen. 2005. 'Court rejects radio station's case against CRTC', *St John's Telegram*, 4 Sept., A11.

Tiessen, Paul. 1993. 'From literary modernism to the Tantramar Marshes: Anticipating McLuhan in British and Canadian media theory and practice', *Canadian Journal of Communication* 18, 4: 451–68.

Trudel, Jonathan. 2010. 'Steve Jobs n'est pas le sauveur', *Trente* 34, 6 (juin): 5.

Tuchman, Gaye. 1978. *Making News: A Study in the Construction of Reality*. New York: Free Press.

Turkle, Sherry. 1995. *Life on the Screen: Identity in the Age of the Internet*. New York: Simon & Schuster.

Turner, Graeme. 1990. *British Cultural Studies: An Introduction*. London: Routledge.

Turner-Riggs Strategic Marketing Communications. 2007. *The Book Retail Sector in Canada*, Sept. Vancouver: Turner-Riggs Strategic Marketing Communications.

———. 2008. *Book Distribution in Canada's English-Language Market*, May. Vancouver: Turner-Riggs Strategic Marketing Communications.

UNESCO. 1980. *Many Voices, One World: Report by the International Commission for the Study of Communication Problems* (MacBride Commission). Paris: Unipub.

UNESCO Institute for Statistics. 2005. *International Flows of Selected Goods and Services, 1994–2003*. At: <www.uis.unesco.org/template/pdf/cscl/IntlFlows_EN.pdf>. (14 July 2010)

United Nations. 1948. *Universal Declaration of Human Rights*. At: <www.unhchr.ch/udhr/lang/eng.htm>.

Vaidhyanathan, Siva. 2001. *Copyrights and Copywrongs: The Rise of Intellectual Property and How it Threatens Creativity*. New York: New York University Press.

van Dijk, Jan A.G.M. 2005. *The Deepening Divide: Inequality in the Information Society*. Thousand Oaks, Calif.: Sage.

van Dijk, Teun A. 1985. *Handbook of Discourse Analysis*, 4 vols. London: Academic Press.

———. 1997. *Discourse as Structure and Process*. Thousand Oaks, Calif.: Sage.

van Ginneken, Jaap. 1998. *Understanding Global News: A Critical Introduction*. London: Sage.

Vipond, Mary. 1992. *Listening In: The First Decade of Canadian Broadcasting, 1922–1932*. Montreal and Kingston: McGill-Queen's University Press.

———. 2000. *The Mass Media in Canada*, 3rd edn. Toronto: James Lorimer.

Wakefield, Jane. 2010. 'World wakes up to digital divide', BBC News, 19 Mar. At: <news.bbc.co.uk/2/hi/technology/8568681.stm>. (2 Aug. 2010)

Wallerstein, Immanuel. 1974. *The Modern World-System: Capitalist Agriculture and the Origins of the European World-Economy in the Sixteenth Century*. New York: Academic Press.

———. 2007. *World-Systems Analysis: An Introduction*. Durham, NC: Duke University Press.

Warnica, Richard. 2005. 'Cultural diversity: Canada's UN victory', *The Tyee*, 28 Oct. At: <www.thetyee.ca/News/2005/10/28/CanadaUNVictory/>.

Waters, Richard. 2010. 'Exclusive: YouTube profits "coming this year"', *Financial Times* techblog, 22 Jan. At: <blogs.ft.com/techblog/2010/01/exclusive-youtube-profits-coming-this-year/>. (4 Aug. 2010)

Weir, Ernest Austin. 1965. *The Struggle for National Broadcasting in Canada*. Toronto: McClelland & Stewart.

Wikström, Patrik. 2009. *The Music Industry: Music in the Cloud*. Cambridge: Polity Press.

Wilkinson, Alec. 2006. 'The lobsterman: Solving a mystery off the Maine Coast', *New Yorker*, 31 July, 56–65.

Williams, Carol T. 1992. *It's Time for My Story: Soap Opera Sources, Structure and Response*. London: Praeger.

Williams, Raymond. 1958. *Culture and Society: 1780–1950*. New York: Columbia University Press.

———. 1974. *Television: Technology and Cultural Form*. London: Fontana.

———. 1976. *Key Words*. London: Fontana.

———. 1989. *Resources of Hope: Culture, Democracy, Socialism*, ed. Robin Gable. London: Verso.

Williamson, Judith. 1978. *Decoding Advertisements: Ideology and Meaning in Advertising*. London: Boyars.

Willis, Andrew, Susan Krashinsky, and Grant Robertson. 2010. 'New life for CanWest papers, but debt remains', *Globe and Mail*, 12 May, B1.

Willis, John. 2000. 'The colonial era: Bringing the post to North America', in Francine Brousseau, ed., *Special Delivery: Canada's Postal Heritage*. Fredericton, NB, and Hull, Que.: Goose Lane Editions and Canadian Museum of Civilization, 35–46.

Willis, Paul. 1977. *Learning to Labor*. New York: Columbia University Press.

Wilson, Kevin G. 2002. 'The rise and fall of Teleglobe', *Montreal Gazette*, 18 May, B5.

Winner, Langdon. 1977. *Autonomous Technology: Technics-out-of-Control as a Theme in Political Thought*. Cambridge, Mass.: MIT Press.

Winseck, Dwayne. 1998. *Reconvergence*. Cresskill, NJ: Hampton Press.

Withers, Edward, and Robert S. Brown. 1995. 'The broadcast audience: A sociological perspective', in Benjamin D. Singer, ed., *Communications in Canadian Society*. Toronto: Nelson, 89–121.

Wober, J. Mallory, and Barrie Gunter. 1986. 'Television audience research at Britain's Independent Broadcasting Authority, 1974–1984', *Journal of Broadcasting and Electronic Media* 30, 1: 15–31.

Women's Studies Group. 1978. *Women Take Issue: Aspects of Women's Subordination*. Birmingham: Centre for Cultural Studies.

Wood, Ellen Meiksins. 2002. *The Origin of Capitalism: A Longer View*. London: Verso.

Woodcock, George. 1985. *Strange Bedfellows: The State and the Arts in Canada*. Vancouver: Douglas & McIntyre.

World Association of Newspapers (WAN). 2008. 'World press trends: Newspapers are a growth business', 2 June. At: <www.wan-press.org/article17377.html>. (18 Oct. 2010)

———. 2010. 'World press trends: Advertising revenues to increase, circulation relatively stable', 4 Aug. At: <www.wan-press.org/article18612.html?var_recherche=2009+circulation>. (18 Oct. 2010)

World Summit on the Information Society (WSIS). 2010. At: <www.itu.int/wsis/index.html>. (23 June 2010)

York, Geoffrey. 2002. 'Great Firewall of China stifles dissent on the net', *Globe and Mail*, 5 Oct., A14.

Ze, David Wei. 1995. 'Printing as an agent of social stability during the Sung dynasty', Ph.D. dissertation, Simon Fraser University.

Zelizer, Barbie. 2010. 'Journalists as interpretive communities, revisited', in Allan (2010: 181–90).

Index